Restoring a reputation

Michael Wheeler finds this old-style life of a Victorian good value

"Nolo Episcopari": A Life of C. J. Vaughan
Trevor Park
St Bega Publications £14*
(978-0-9508325-4-8)
Church Times Bookshop £12.60

THE "lives and letters" of notable Victorian clerics often ran to three or four stout volumes in the 19th century. These are mines of information for the modern student of ecclesiastical history. They shed light on not only their main characters, but also the complex web of friendships and rivalries that make up "the Victorian Church". No publisher would touch such works today: too unfashionable, too long, and too expensive to produce.

Canon Trevor Park has circumvented the problem by publishing his life (and letters) of Charles John Vaughan himself. Running to almost 450 pages, this splendid request. Widely regarded as one of the finest preachers of the age, he was also famous for his innovative methods of ordination training: of several hundred "doves", as Vaughan's pupils were known, 18 became bishops, and two became archbishops. Benson, Davidson, Westcott, and Jowett all regarded him as one of the wisest and noblest clergymen in the C of E. Yet he turned down several episcopal appointments, possibly including Canterbury. Why?

Phyllis Grosskurth thought she knew in 1964, when she revealed that the the father of one of his pupils, J. A. Symonds, had accused Vaughan, then the youthful headmaster of Harrow, of sexual misconduct with a pupil. Like Mark Wagland in an article of 2008, Park argues strongly that Vaughan was innocent: a "besmirched reputation" is restored. Vaughan had "romantic friendships" with pupils past and present, but there is no solid evidence of misconduct. His subsequent refusal to accept preferment, Parks argues, was more to do with the nature of his vocation than a threat of exposure from an outraged Harrow parent.

Vaughan was the son of the Vicar Glittering prizes and a fellowship awaited him at Trinity College, Cambridge, and he became Vicar of St Martin's in 1841.

By 1845, he was running Harrow. In 1850, he married A. P. Stanley's sister, Catherine. Like the Stanleys, the Vaughans had no children. Having fulfilled what he claimed was his settled plan to retire after 15 years, as Arnold had hoped to do at Rugby, Vaughan returned to Leicester before serving with distinction as Vicar of Doncaster, Master of the Temple, and, in plurality with the Temple, Dean of Llandaff. His appointment as Deputy Clerk of the Closet kept him in touch with an appreciative Queen.

Would he have been a great bishop or even archbishop? Park believes that his avoidance of controversy and silence on such matters as ritual practice suggest not. Did he behave inappropriately with any of the boys? Park believes not. As in so many such cases, past and present, it might be safest to say, "Not proven."

Dr Wheeler is a Visiting Professor at the University of Southampton and a former Lay Canon of Winchester.

*Available from St Bega Publica-

What some of C. J. Vaughan's contemporaries said about him:

"No living man has laid the Church of England under greater obligations."
"The Dean's has been the most serviceable life in the Church in my time."
Edward White Benson, Archbishop of Canterbury

"A worker in the foremost rank of living Englishmen."
"Time after time when perplexities were rife, I kept wondering what Vaughan's shrewd and big-hearted Christian counsel would have been on particular problems."
Randall Davidson, Bishop of Winchester and subsequently Archbishop of Canterbury

"No Sunday is to me complete without reading a sermon of Dr Vaughan's."
Brooke Foss Westcott, Bishop of Durham

"He was the wisest man I ever knew."
Dr Benjamin Jowett, Master of Balliol College Oxford

"I can say, without reserve, that at no time in my entire life have I been so conscious of living in a directly Christian atmosphere, with Christian ideals of duty habitually set up for reverence, as during the happy years when Vaughan presided at Harrow."
Dr Montagu Butler, a pupil at Harrow under Vaughan and then his successor as Head Master, and who later became Master of Trinity College Cambridge

"Nolo Episcopari"

A life of
Charles John Vaughan
1816 - 1897

Trevor Park

St Bega
Publications

For my grandchildren:
Benjamin,
Thomas
& Bertrand

Michela,
Hannah,
Josephine,
Abigail
Maria
& Elizabeth

and for my great-grandsons:
Logan,
& Heath

ISBN 978-0-9508325-4-8

Printed and bound in Great Britain by
Berforts, Stevenage, Herts, SG1 2BH

A chalk drawing of Charles Vaughan
as the young Headmaster of Harrow
by George Richmond R.A.
courtesy of the Keeper & Governors of Harrow School

Contents

Acknowledgements

I started researching Vaughan's life and work over twenty years ago on a visit to Leicester as a guest preacher at the Cathedral where their archivist provided me with my first picture of this exceptional 19th century divine. Unfortunately, other commitments constantly got in the way of my research with the result that it was a slow and unsatisfactory 'on and off' process, mostly 'off' until I retired. So it has been a long haul to bring it to completion.

Given the dearth of private papers, I have had to rely very largely on the words of some of his contemporaries: former pupils from Harrow days and students who read with him whilst preparing for ordination, and on reports in local newspapers. The staff of numerous university and college libraries, municipal local history departments, county record offices and the curators of manuscript collections have been of great help in this respect, and I gladly express my deep gratitude to them and to the following for permission to quote material in their archives:

The Warden and Fellows of All Souls College Oxford for Vaughan's letters to his uncle Sir Charles Vaughan, and to Dr Norma Aubertin-Potter, the Codrington Librarian;

Bodleian Libraries, University of Oxford, for some Halford and Vaughan letters;

Borthwick Institute at York University for York's archiepiscopal archives;

Bristol University Library's Special Collections for A.J. Symonds's letters;

The British Library and especially their MSS collections for Vaughan's letters to Lord Althorp, W.E. Gladstone, his publisher Macmillan and to Bishop Christopher Wordsworth;

The Syndics of Cambridge University Library for Vaughan's letters to the Rev. Sedley Taylor;

Cheshire Record Office for many of the Stanley family papers;

Derbyshire Record Office for the Pares family papers;

Doncaster Library's Local History Department and Doncaster archives;

The Chapter of Durham Cathedral for Vaughan's letters to Bishop Lightfoot deposited in their Library;

Gloucester Record Office which holds the papers of Thomas Sotheron-Estcourt, a Governor of Harrow School;

Harrow Library's Local History Department;

The Governors of Harrow School for papers relating to Vaughan's time as Headmaster, and to their former archivist, Ms Rita Boswell;

The Trustees of Lambeth Palace Library and the Collections Librarian, Dr Naomi Percival, for Vaughan's letters to Archbishops Longley, Tait, Benson and Davidson;

The Record Office for Leicestershire, Leicester and Rutland for Vaughan and Halford family papers;

The Dean and Chapter of Llandaff Cathedral for Vaughan's letters to Canon W. J. M. Coombs in their archives;

The London Library where Symonds's manuscript *Memoirs* is deposited;

Macmillan Publishing Company's archivist Alysoun Sanders;

National Library of Scotland for Charles and Catherine Vaughan's many letters to Sir Charles Dalrymple and for Sir Charles's personal journals;

National Library of Wales for Alfred Thomas's papers and some of A.P. Stanley's;

Rugby Library's Local History department;

Surrey History Centre;

The Master and Fellows of Trinity College Cambridge for the Blakesley letters, and to Jonathan Smith for information on Vaughan's residence there as an undergraduate;

The archivists of Lincoln's Inn, the Inner and Middle Temple (Jo Hutchings, Celia Pilkington and Lesley Whitelaw) and the Master of the Temple, Canon Robin Griffith-Jones;

The *Welsh Journal of Religious History* for permission to quote from two articles about Vaughan;

Quotations from *The Oxford Diaries of A.H. Clough* ed. by Anthony Kenny (1990) are made by permission of Oxford University Press.

Quotations from David Newsome's books: *Godliness and Good Learning* and *On the Edge of Paradise: A.C. Benson Diarist* are made by permission of his literary executor.

Quotations from *Cambridge in the 1830s* are made by permission of Boydell & Brewer, and the editors: Jonathan Smith and Christopher Stray.

Help of a quite different kind came from an unexpected source: the Bank of England. Its website has an inflation calculator for the period 1750-2012, which I have used on occasion to indicate the purchasing power in today's terms of stipends, scholarships and salaries paid in the 19th century. The stipend of £460 a year, for example, which Vaughan received on appointment to Doncaster in 1860 does not sound much, especially as he had to pay two of his curates from it, but it equated to £47,365 in 2012 – much more than any incumbent earns now.

I am very grateful to the Governors of Harrow School for permitting me to use two portraits of Vaughan in their possession done by George Richmond RA, also to Peter Bell of Edinburgh, antiquarian bookseller and copyright holder of the picture of Vaughan originally published in *Men of Mark* in 1882.

I am especially grateful to the Rt Revd Dr Geoffrey Rowell, Emeritus Fellow of Keble College Oxford, for reading my draft manuscript. His expert knowledge of the Church of England in the 19th century ensured that there are no historical howlers in the text, and his praise for the ms's 'meticulous scholarship' was most welcome. Dr Anthony Reeve of St Bees kindly read the chapter on Vaughan's schooldays at Rugby; his doctoral thesis on *Aspects of the Life of Dr Thomas Arnold in the Light of Unpublished Correspondence* threw new light on life at Rugby in the 1830s. Many thanks also go to two good friends, Dorothy Warbrick and Lois Howard, who read the manuscript critically and made some helpful suggestions for improving it. Any errors or oversights are entirely of my own making.

Introduction

Charles Smyth writing in 1940 on the *Art of Preaching* praised C.J. Vaughan's sermons for their 'great technical merit' and added 'Justice has not yet been done to Vaughan as one of the really important figures in the history of the Church of England in the 19th century.' Seventy years on, that remains true despite the attention that a former Bishop of Leicester, R.R. Williams, gave to him in 1960 in an edited version of some extracts from Vaughan's writings. This volume is an attempt to meet the need.

Vaughan in his will 'desired' that no *Life* of him should be written and requested that all his personal correspondence should be destroyed after his death [1897], which has made any would-be biographer's task immensely difficult. This may have been out of genuine humility for he said that the only memorial he desired already existed in the hundreds of men whom he had helped prepare for ordination. Seven years later, however, Vaughan's request was disregarded when F.D. How devoted a biographical chapter to him in his book *Six Great Schoolmasters*. It is perhaps worth noting that Vaughan was not alone as a great Victorian in not having a standard two volume *Life & Letters* published after his death. One of his teachers at Rugby, James Prince Lee, who went on to become Headmaster of the King Edward School in Birmingham (where he had Benson, Westcott and Lightfoot among his devoted pupils) and then on to Manchester as its first Bishop, also had no *Life* written. Like Vaughan, he was reckoned to be one of the greatest headmasters of his day but unlike Vaughan, he made the mistake of accepting a bishopric for he was never happy at Manchester.

An alternative and more sinister reason was alleged in 1964, namely fear. Fear that the real reason for his having resigned the headship of Harrow in 1859 and his subsequent refusal of repeated offers of a bishopric would become known. The truth came out - if indeed it is the whole truth and that is by no means certain - when Phyllis Grosskurth claimed in her biography of John Addington Symonds that Vaughan had been pressurized by Symonds's father into resigning. According to the Symonds/Grosskurth narrative, this was due to a homosexual relationship he was alleged to have had with Alfred Pretor, who was reputed to have been one of his favourite pupils. The boy had confided in his friend Symonds Jr. who, a year later, told his father. Symonds's story, told in his private *Memoirs* written thirty years after the events, is, on a first reading, a plausible one. However, when it is examined more closely there are good grounds for doubting its veracity and consequently Vaughan's besmirched reputation should be restored. Even Grosskurth acknowledged that there are problems with Symonds's account, noting that 'this particular section contains more erasures and changes than any other part of the manuscript.' She also considered it 'strange' that Symonds claimed to have retained during his lifetime correspondence between his father and Vaughan, which would have been invaluable evidence in substantiating his case, but wanted it destroyed at his death.

Other correspondence, which Grosskurth had not read, includes letters written by Catherine Vaughan after her husband's death. In one she told a close friend, who had been taught at Harrow by her husband, that he had made the will, which contained the request that no *Life* should be written, at a time when he was deeply depressed. An understandable state in a man who had been so active and involved in so much for so many years but then incapacitated and bed-bound for much of the last three and a half years of his life. He was a long time a-dying. She also told him that her husband had made a new will shortly before he died in which there was no such prohibition. She and others wanted, at the very least, a collection of his letters to be published with an Introduction written by Dr Montagu Butler, another of his favourite former pupils who had succeeded him as Head. Letters that she believed would be a priceless blessing to many.

Columnists and literary critics made much of Grosskurth's revelation of what appeared to be a Victorian scandal cover-up and Vaughan's reputation was smeared. But the fact is that there is no hard evidence to support Symonds's story whilst there is much to challenge its truth. In fairness, Vaughan's record should be allowed to stand, and it is an impressive one particularly as a trainer of clergy: 'Vaughan's doves' among whom were eighteen future bishops, including Archbishop Randall Davidson. Likewise he deserves to be honoured as one of the most popular expository preachers of the Victorian era. That he revived the fortunes of Harrow School is indisputable where he is still regarded as one of their greatest Headmasters. He remains an important figure in the life of the 19th century Church and merits proper recognition which is long overdue.

Those who knew him well made mention of his prolific correspondence. I estimate from their observations that he wrote some 300,000 letters in his lifetime - possibly many more - yet (apart from a collection of some ninety business letters sent to his publisher

Macmillan and now deposited in the British Library) less than three hundred of them are extant or exist in the memoirs of some of his friends. He reveals himself in his personal letters as a wise counsellor, an encourager and a deeply affectionate friend who loved to "chat" in this way with the many former pupils, students and colleagues who admired and loved him and who had chosen to remain in touch with him. What these few surviving letters do not contain is any serious theological or social commentary on the issues and events of the day but what we do still have is the very large body of his published works. There are over one hundred and thirty of them which give voice to his priorities as a scholarly Evangelical in preaching and in ministry.

Having put behind him, for whatever reasons, offers of high office in the Church of England, the ordinary parochial ministry became for him the most important expression of mission and ministry to the nation, and during his years in Doncaster, he proved to be an exemplary parish priest. One of his contemporaries who knew him well, Archbishop Benson, said of him in 1894 "No living man has laid the Church of England under greater obligations." That testimony alone suggests that Vaughan was a man whose life's work is worth recording even though, in the absence of any diaries or extant personal papers apart from a small number of letters, it is almost impossible to know the man himself.

Harrow honoured him in 1945 at a centenary celebration of his appointment as Head at which one of his last 'doves', Dean White, was the guest preacher. Bishop R.R. Williams of Leicester revived interest in Vaughan in 1953 by a paper published in the *Church Quarterly Review*, and seven years later by editing a selection of Vaughan's sermons: *The Word of Life*. Canon H.G.G. Herklots, the Vicar of St George's Doncaster, initiated an annual 'Vaughan Memorial Lecture' in 1953. This was always delivered by some eminent educationalist or cleric in Doncaster Grammar School which he had helped re-found in 1862. The last of them was given in 1964 by Herklots himself.

He has been the subject of two academic theses at Sheffield University: by D.D.W. Mowbray in 1958 *C.J. Vaughan (1816-1897) Biblical Expositor. A Study in Comparison with J.B. Lightfoot, B.F. Westcott and F.J.A. Hort together with other English Contemporaries* and by M.D.W. Poole in 1966 who researched *The Educational Work of the Very Rev C.J. Vaughan*. Harrow's most recent historian, Christopher Tyerman, writing in 1999, devoted a long and generally positive chapter to his Headmastership. Most recently, Mark Wagland has argued the case against the reliability of Symonds's *Memoirs* in an article, entitled *A*

Matter of Justice: a re-evaluation of John Addington Symonds's allegations against C.J. Vaughan, published in the *Welsh Journal of Religious History* in 2008. None of the last four writers, however, drew on the large deposit of Vaughan letters in the National Library of Scotland, which throw new light on this remarkable man and his wife and on the Pretor/Symonds affair. John Witheridge in his biography of Dean Stanley, *Excellent Dr Stanley* published in 2013, wrote several pages about Vaughan's resignation but simply repeated the Symonds/Grosskurth account uncritically.

I first encountered Vaughan's name when I was doing doctoral research into the professional training of Anglican clergy in the first half of the 19th century. I happened to note that he was numbered among the first subscribers to the establishment of a Missionary College at St Augustine's Canterbury to train Clergy for the Colonies and that he had attended the college's dedication in 1848. Later, I discovered that he did not really favour theological colleges and in 1861 had developed his own method of helping men prepare themselves for Ordination. It made me want to find out more about him. The more I learnt, the more I found myself being drawn to him and impressed by what he had achieved in his life, and so this book gradually came into being.

The Vaughans of Leicester (1)

James Vaughan MD 1740 - 1813

m 1765

Esther Smalley 1740 - 1791 (granddaughter of the Revd Sir Richard Halford)

|

1   James Vaughan 1765 - 1788 who matriculated at Balliol 1783.

2   Sir Henry Vaughan MD 1766 - 1844 (who took the name of **Halford** in 1809) Royal Physician, President of the Royal College of Physicians.
m 1796 the Hon. Elizabeth Barbara St John 1762-1833. [Had issue]:
Sir Henry Halford 1797-1868 m 1824 Barbara Vaughan (d of Sir John)

3   Rt Hon Sir John Vaughan DCL 1768 - 1839 Judge, Privy Councillor.
m in 1803
(i) the Hon. Augusta Beauchamp St John who died 1813 daughter of the 12th Baron St John of Bletso. [Had issue]; and
m in 1833
(ii) Louisa, Dowager Baroness of St John of Bletso. [Had issue]

4   Very Revd Peter Vaughan DD 1769 - 1825
Warden of Merton College Oxford and Dean of Chester.

5   Almeria Selina Vaughan 1771 - 1837
m
Revd David Hughes DD Principal of Jesus College Oxford.

6   William Welby Vaughan 1772 - c 1803
The black sheep of the family who died on Jamaica.

7   Sir Charles Richard Vaughan 1774 - 1849
Diplomat & Fellow of All Souls College Oxford.

8   **Revd Edward Thomas Vaughan 1776-1829**
Vicar of St Martin's Leicester and Rector of Foston
m in 1804
(i) Elizabeth Anne Hill 1792 - 1808 [Had issue];
m in 1812
(ii) **Agnes Pares 1786-1878** [Had issue] She was the mother of Charles John Vaughan.

9   Wyamarus Nathan Vaughan 1777 [died in childhood?]

The Vaughans of Leicester (2)

Revd Edward Thomas Vaughan 1776 - 1829

m 1804　　　　　　　　　　　m 1812

(1) Elizabeth Anne Hill　　　(2) Agnes Pares

1792 - 1808　　　　　　　　1786 - 1878

| |

1 Anne Barbara Vaughan m 1830 Revd Valentine Green　|
2 Mary Esther Vaughan m 1834 Revd W.H. Thompson　|
3 Hester Vaughan m 1834 Robert Green　　　　　　|

　　　　　　　　4 Canon Edward Thomas Vaughan 1813 - 1900
　　　　　　　　　m 1839 Mary Rose [Had issue]
　　　　　　　　5 Lucy Agnes Vaughan 1815 -
　　　　　　　　6 Very Revd Charles John Vaughan DD 1816 - 97
　　　　　　　　m 1850 Catherine Stanley 1822 - 1899
　　　　　　　　7 Elizabeth Emma Vaughan 1817 -
　　　　　　　　8 Revd Edwyn Henry Vaughan 1819 -1868
　　　　　　　　　m 1849 Henriette Caroline McCausland [Had issue]
　　　　　　　　9 General Sir John Luther Vaughan 1820 - 1911
　　　　　　　　　m 1845 Mary Anne Bishop
　　　　　　　　10 Geoffrey Edgar Vaughan 1821 - 1829
　　　　　　　　11 Canon David James Vaughan DD 1825 - 1905
　　　　　　　　　m 1859 Margaret Greg
　　　　　　　　12 Ellen Mary Vaughan 1826 -
　　　　　　　　13 Sarah Dorothea Vaughan 1827 - 1885
　　　　　　　　　m 1849 Revd John Simpkinson 1817 - 1894 [Had issue]
　　　　　　　　14 Agnes Constance Vaughan 1827 -

Descendants of Edward Thomas Vaughan Sr. by his first wife:
1 Anne Barbara Green had issue – two sons, Valentine Green & Thomas Hill
　 Green, who were both educated at Harrow under Vaughan. Thomas later
　 became Professor of Moral Philosophy at Oxford.
2 Mary Esther had a son, Edward Vaughan Thompson, who was at Harrow
　 under Vaughan. He later became a solicitor and acted as Charles and Catherine
　 Vaughan's executor.

Descendant of Edward Thomas Vaughan Jr. 1813 - 1900
1 Professor Charles Edwyn Vaughan 1854 - 1922

Descendant of Edwyn Vaughan 1819 - 1868
1 Ileen Vaughan m Professor Sir Stuart Jones

Descendants of Sarah Dorothea Vaughan 1827 - 18..
1 Francis Vaughan Simpkinson 1851 - 1873
2 Revd Henry Walrond Simpkinson 1853 - 1934
3 Revd Edwyn Vaughan Simpkinson 1869 - 1952

Some other later Vaughans

Descendants of Sir John Vaughan 1768-1839 by his wife, Augusta 1782-1813

1 Augusta Vaughan 1805 - 80

2 Revd John James Vaughan 1806-81 m Mary Crew 1795 - 1872

3 Barbara Vaughan 1806 - 69 m Sir Henry Halford 1797 - 1868
          |
          Sir Henry St John Halford 1828 - 97 & Elizabeth Bagshawe [No issue]

4 Hester Vaughan 1807 - 1847 m Francis Hawkins MD (brother of the Provost
                                      of Oriel College Oxford)
          |
          They had 3 sons: Francis Vaughan Hawkins, Charles Halford Hawkins
          & Henry Beauchamp Hawkins who were all educated at Harrow

5 Professor Henry Halford Vaughan 1811 - 1885 m Adeline Jackson
          |
          a.William Wyamar Vaughan 1865 - 1938 m Margaret Symonds
                          | 1869 - 1925
          They had 2 sons [William & Jack?]
          and Dame Janet Maria Vaughan DBE 1899 - 1993 m David Gourlay
          |
          They had 2 daughters Mary & Priscilla

          b.Millicent Vaughan 1866 - 1961 m Sir Vere Isham, 11th Bt.
          |
          Sir Giles Isham, 12th Bt. 1903 - 76 [No issue]

          c.HHV had 3 other daughters : Augusta, Margaret & Emma

Descendants of Sir John Vaughan 1768 - 1839 by his wife, Louisa 1785 - 1860

6 Emily Vaughan 1824 - 98 m Sir Charles Isham, 10th Bt 1819 - 1903
          |
          a.Sir Vere Isham 1862 - 1941 m Millicent Vaughan 1866 - 1961

7 Revd Charles Lyndhurst Vaughan 1828 - 1895 m Jane Coote
          |
          a.Francis Philip Vaughan 1870 -

The Stanleys of Alderley

Sir John Owen Stanley 1735 - 1807 m Margaret Owen 1742 - 1816

John Thomas, 1st Baron Stanley of Alderley
1766 - 1850
m
Maria Josepha Holroyd, (d of 1st Earl of Sheffield)
1771 - 1863

1 Rianette 1797 - 1882
2 Lucy 1798 - 1869
3 Louisa 1799 - 1877
4 Isabella 1801 - 1839
5 Edward 2nd Baron Stanley
  1802 - 1869
m
Henrietta Maria Dillon 1808 - 1896
 (d of the 13th Viscount Dillon)
6 William twin with Edward 1802 - 1884
7 Harriet 1804 - 1888
8 Matilda 1806 – 1850
9 Alfred 1808 - 1811
10 Emmeline 1810 - 1906
11 Elfrida 1813 – 1817

Edward, Bishop of Norwich
1779 - 1849
m
Kitty Leycester
1792 - 1862

1 Owen 1811 - 1850
2 Mary 1812 - 1879
3 **Arthur Penrhyn 1815-81**
   (at Rugby with Vaughan)
   Dean of Westminster
   m
Lady Augusta Bruce 1822 -76
4 Charles Edward 1819-49
5 **Catherine 1821 - 1899**
   m
   Charles Vaughan 1816-97

This line of the Stanleys
died out with Catherine.

The family of Edward 2nd Baron Stanley of Alderley

1 Henry 3rd Baron Stanley 1827 - 1903
2 Alice 1828 - 1910
3 Blanche 1829 - 1921
4 Maud 1832 - 1915
5 John 1837 - 1878 A pupil under Vaughan at Harrow
6 Lyulph 4th Baron Stanley 1839 - 1929
7 Kate 1842 - 1874
8 Algernon 1843 - 1928 RC Bishop of Emmaus (*in partibus*)
   who was a pupil under Vaughan at Harrow
9 Rosalind 1844 - 1921

His Childhood in Leicester and a Father's Influence

Thou art here but the guest of a day. Not time but eternity is thy duration not earth but heaven thy dwelling place.

E.T. Vaughan *The Christian Mourner*: A Sermon preached on 19 November 1817, the day appointed for the Funeral of HRH Princess Charlotte of Wales.

Charles John Vaughan was born on 6 August 1816 in Leicester where his father was the Vicar of St Martin's which was the town's civic church. Today it is the Anglican cathedral. The Vaughans of Leicester were at that time a well-connected and upwardly mobile professional family, some of whose members had married into the local landed gentry. Their sons and grandsons would be numbered among what Noel Annan has called the 'Intellectual Aristocracy' of the 19th century.

He was the second son of the Revd Edward Thomas Vaughan and Agnes Pares who was the daughter of a prominent local banker and stocking manufacturer. Edward was a forceful Calvinist Evangelical with pronounced politically conservative views who had been appointed in 1802 at the age of 26 by the Lord Chancellor to the livings of St Martin's and All Saints. Ten years later he was also appointed by the same patron Rector of Foston, a tiny hamlet of just 28 souls with a Norman church and a Tudor rectory, six miles south of Leicester and worth an additional £240 a year [= £14,455 in 2012]. He still held St Martin's and Foston in plurality when he died 27 years later. In those years Edward had married twice, fathered fourteen children, played a prominent (and at times contentious) part in civic life and published more than a dozen books and pamphlets, mostly sermons.

In an age when family influence and patronage were important for any man wanting to advance and succeed in the world, C.J. was born with a goodly inheritance and he would grow up with the example of his successful uncles and his devout father to inspire him. His grandfather, James Vaughan MD who had trained at Edinburgh University, had been a prominent physician and one of the founders of the Leicester Infirmary in 1771. His memorial in Wistow Church describes him as 'descended from a respectable family in Herefordshire and practiced physic (*sic*) in Leicester about 40 years, with that felicity and success, which a quick perception, a sound judgment and a perfect knowledge of the resources of his art were calculated to command.' He had married Esther Smalley, the daughter of Alderman John Smalley and granddaughter of the Revd Sir Richard Halford of Wistow Hall. C.J. never knew his grandfather who had died four years before he was born but he would surely have heard stories of his formidable forebear who had been so ambitious for his sons.

James was remembered as a strict disciplinarian who was reported to have told his sons that he had rather follow them to their graves than that they should fail to achieve distinction in their respective callings! He impressed upon them that they would inherit nothing on his death for he was using all he could spare to give each of them a good education.[1] It certainly paid off. Five of them, but not all, became men of considerable distinction. James, the first son, died aged just 22; the second, Henry, became Physician to four monarchs – George III, George IV, William IV and Queen Victoria – and became President of the Royal College of Physicians. In 1800 he was created a baronet and in 1809 inherited the Wistow estate and changed his name to Halford; his marriage to the Hon. Elizabeth St John brought him wealth as she had inherited sugar plantations on Grenada. The third son became Sir John Vaughan DCL, a Privy Counsellor, and Attorney General and Solicitor General to Queen Charlotte; he, too, married into the St John family. Peter, born in 1769, had an almost unbroken career at Merton College Oxford, which he entered at the age of 17 and became its Warden in 1810. He continued to hold his university office with the Deanery of Chester from 1820 and the college living of Northenden until his death in 1825. Charles Richard, born in 1774, was knighted in 1833 for his diplomatic service to the nation as Minister Plenipotentiary to the United States of America; he was also a Fellow of All Souls Oxford from 1801 - 40. The youngest surviving son was C.J.'s father, born in November 1776, whose appointment to livings in the Lord Chancellor's gift was presumably obtained with the patronage of his influential older siblings. There was, however, a black sheep in this successful fraternity: William Welby, who had an illicit affair with the young widow of his older brother James. This led to an action being brought against him for 'crim con' and his being fined heavily. His siblings paid up and his lawyer-brother, John, quickly found him a post in Jamaica where he died unlamented by the family in about 1803, but not before they had bailed him out a second time guaranteeing to pay his debts incurred in a lawsuit in 1801. The compiler of a 'family-tree' of the Vaughans and Halfords now kept in Leicester Records Office chose to omit William and James. The latter's widow too seems to have been shunned. Sir Charles wrote in some surprise to Sir Henry Halford in 1844 that he had recently learnt that she was still alive.[2]

The brothers had all been educated at Rugby School which, in time, C.J. and his younger brothers would also attend. The school was situated twenty miles south of Leicester, and Henry became a trustee of the school in 1825. James progressed to Balliol, Henry to Christ Church, John to Queen's and Charles and Peter to Merton. Edward, the odd one out in this Oxonian sequence, was admitted a pensioner at Trinity College Cambridge in June 1791. He was appointed a scholar in 1794, graduated BA in '96 being 15th Senior Optime of that year, and MA in '99. In 1798 he was elected a Fellow of Trinity. He considered following a legal career and was admitted to Lincoln's Inn in January 1801 but soon afterwards he chose to be ordained and returned to his home parish as its new incumbent.

Edward married Elizabeth Anne Hill, daughter of David Thomas Hill of Aylesbury on 13 March 1804. They had three daughters, Anne Barbara, Mary Esther and Hester. His wife died giving birth to Hester. By Edward's own account they had a happy relationship despite having to live with some financial difficulties to begin with. This was presumably because St Martin's was a poorly endowed living worth just £140 p.a. [= £11,557].

> For a little while we felt the pressure of a straightened income; and I am the more inclined to mention this, because she met our little difficulties with remarkable patience, submission and discretion. She was most minute and judicious in avoiding every unnecessary expense; and contrived to mix great liberality and an honest independence of spirit, with real frugality . . . She had a strong sense of value of time, and was very methodical in the distribution of it. She had a time for devotional exercises; a time for house-affairs; a time for needlework; a time for visits. We did not usually see much company. This arose chiefly from necessity. My own numerous engagements, and frequently the state of her health, rendered much visiting impracticable to us. [3]

The memorial tablet which Edward placed for her in the sanctuary of the church reflects the Evangelical faith which they both shared. Even in death the Gospel had to be proclaimed:

In mournful and most affectionate remembrance
of the late
Elizabeth Anne Vaughan
wife of Edward Thomas Vaughan

Vicar of this Parish:
who died in child-bed
January 16th 1808 aged 26 years.
Reader
Let this early grave remind you
to lose no time in preparing for death.
Let the salvation of Jesus Christ be
the one object of your desire and pursuit.
Seek it with all diligence; but seek it
as the free gift of God.
Seek it in self-abhorrence; but in the
constant and lively exercise of
repentance, faith, hope, love, meekness,
and every Christian grace.
So shall you resemble the beloved person
whose earthly remains lie here.
'If we believe that Jesus died and rose again,
even so them also which sleep in Jesus
will God bring with him'
1 Thessalonians iv. 14

Four years later Edward married again. His new bride was Agnes Pares, third daughter of Thomas Pares of The Newarke, Leicester and of Hopwell Hall in the County of Derby, who was the founder of Pares Bank in the town. Her brother, also called Thomas, was the MP for Leicester 1818-26 and later High Sheriff of Derbyshire; politically he was a reform-minded Whig (the very opposite of Edward Vaughan) and had the distinction of being the first candidate ever to beat the Tory Corporation's nominated candidate. Edward and she went on to have six sons and five daughters. Family finances were now on a sounder footing as Edward's stipend had doubled the year he married Agnes thanks to his appointment to Foston. And they and their family had the additional pleasure of having the Pares' country seat of Hopton Hall just a few miles away which they could visit easily.

Edward chose to educate his children himself as long as he lived and by the standards of the time he was well qualified to do this. His eldest son, Edward, was educated entirely at home before being admitted a pensioner at Christ's College Cambridge in 1830 where he achieved honours, became a university prizeman and a Fellow of his college. Like many Evangelicals of that time the father had no faith in public schools, largely because they gave so little attention to the formation of Christian character and because they were seen as places where boys learned vice. His first wife, Elizabeth, had often stressed their first priority to their children: "My dear, we must train them up for God." A view that he warmly endorsed but boys also needed to be educated in the Classics. The foundations of C.J.'s classical knowledge had already been well laid by the time his father died. On his seventh birthday, at his own request, he had been taught the Greek alphabet and in the following six years he learned from his father's accomplished scholarship. A family memory of the boy claims that he showed remarkable quickness from the first. 'He would scamper through his own lessons and then lay his big head in his arms and sleep in comfort, while his slower, and perhaps more industrious companions were still labouring with theirs.'[4] This is one of the few anecdotes we have from his childhood but it is one that has a hint of the academic honours he would later win.

Fortunately, three letters written by C.J. to his uncle Charles have survived. This particular uncle must have been a fascinating figure to his young nephews and nieces as he had led an exciting life and travelled more extensively than anyone they knew. After first graduating at Oxford and then studying medicine at Edinburgh and London, he had won a Radcliffe Travelling Fellowship in 1800. His travels took him to Constantinople, Syria, Persia and then Russia via the Caspian Sea and the Volga, ending up in St Petersburg before returning to England in 1806. In 1808 he was in Spain in a private capacity where he was entrusted with dispatches to Sir John Moore at Salamanca relating to the Battle of Tudela. In 1809 he published his *Narrative of the Siege of Saragossa* which went through five editions and in that same year his diplomatic career took off when he was appointed Private Secretary to the Secretary of State for Foreign Affairs. Diplomatic postings followed quickly in Spain, France and Switzerland before being appointed Envoy-Extraordinary and Minister-Plenipotentiary to the United States of America in 1825. It is from this year that C.J.'s three letters date:

My dear Uncle
I am very much obliged to you for the book though I have not seen it yet. When shall you go to America? I was very much amused to hear the account you gave us of your travels into Persia and now we shall be very much pleased to look at the track you have marked for us on the map. Mama tells me that you desired I might have a new Greek Grammar. I hope you will come back from America in two years. When I have a new Greek Grammar I shall put the old one by and keep it for your sake. I shall be very glad to see you again. I wish you could write to me.
I am your very affectionate nephew Charles Vaughan [5]

The next indicates what a close knit family the Vaughans were and what a bright and happy place the nursery in St Martin's Vicarage was. It also shows how well and hospitably the members of the extended Vaughan family related to one another:

> My dear Uncle,
> I hope you are quite well. Edward and I are doing with Papa Lucian's Dialogue of the Cock and the Cobler in the morning, and Virgil in the afternoon. Papa hears us on Dr Bell's system. I am reading in the evening with Sister Mary and Sister Hester Dr Clarke's travels in Russia. We had a trial for Murder the other evening, in which Edward was Judge, and I was Uncle Sergeant, Counsel for the Prosecution. We went to Hopwell [their maternal grandfather's country residence] a few days ago. It is a very pretty place, and there are a great many very fine pictures there. On our way back, we dined with a Mrs Wright, a lady who formerly resided in America. Aunt Halford dined here last Saturday; and I believe she expects to be obliged to go back to London very soon, as Uncle Halford cannot come to her. Uncle Halford has hardly been at Wistow at all this summer.
> Aunt Hughes has got a very nice house in a new building at Leicester, called the Crescent. She has just begun to inhabit it. She was staying with us for some weeks, till her house was ready for her. She seems very well, and walks about a great deal without being tired. Edward sends his very best love to you.
> I am Your affectionate Nephew, Charles John Vaughan [6]

The third indicates what an extraordinarily bright nine year old C.J. was – his juvenile interest in the Law was presumably due to the influence of another favourite uncle, John, whose legal career was blossoming in London. The book he bought was widely considered to be the best general history of English law:

> My dear Uncle,
> I am very glad to hear that you are safe at America and I hope that you will come back as safely. I have bought Judge Blackstone's Commentaries on the Laws of England. Edward and I pretend that we are Counsellors, and we have Pretend Trials. I went to London a little while ago. I am generally the Counsel for the Crown and Edward for the Prisoner when we have Trials. When I was in London, I saw St Paul's Cathedral, both the Houses of Parliament, and Westminster Hall and Abbey. We are going to try a High Treason, this very night. I shall be very much obliged to you for a letter when you have any time to spare.
> I am Your affectionate Nephew Charles John Vaughan
> Thursday, 10th of November, 1825 [7]

There is a story from this time told about him by his older brother and passed on to his son Charles Edwyn, that C.J. sewed homemade robes and made a wig and 'loved to condemn his trembling brothers and sisters "to be hanged by the neck until they died".' [8]

A letter from Sir Charles to his brother Sir Henry, dated 27 February 1826, describes life in America but also contains a personal comment about two of their siblings. Referring to Peter, the Warden of Merton College and Dean of Chester who had died recently, he wrote: 'I consider that some of the best ability in the family was divided between himself and Edward and I consider that in both it has not produced fruit.' [9]

We turn now to the social environment in which the boy grew up and then to a more detailed consideration of his father's pastoral and teaching ministry as this would prove to be such an inspiration for him. So, what was the town like in which C.J. formed his earliest impressions of society and of the Church's place in its life? Leicester was at this time an important centre for the hosiery industry and one in steady expansion as the parliamentary censuses show: 1801 – 16,953 inhabitants; 1811 – 23,146; 1821 – 30,877; 1831 – 40,517. The population of the parish of St Martin's, however, in the town centre did not change much: in 1801 it was 3,167; 1811 – 3,254; 1821 – 3,200 and 1831 – 3.034. The parish of Foston, likewise, had a static population: 1801 – 24; 1811 – 28; 1821 – 24; 1831 – 32.

At the turn of the century there were some 70 hosiers in Leicester who employed 3,000 or more stocking frames in the town and in the surrounding villages. These frames were scattered about the district in small shops and in the houses of the workmen, so the industry at this stage was primarily domestic. In the three decades that C.J.'s father was Vicar that number doubled but these were turbulent years. Wages in the hosiery industry were pitifully low and large numbers of half-famished workers were reduced to abject poverty. In 1811 many of the framework knitters resolved to organise themselves along with workers in neighbouring counties with a view to improving their wages. They were also violently opposed to the use of improved machinery, especially the 'wide machines' on which several pairs of stockings could be woven simultaneously, as these were regarded as being injurious to their own manual labour. Secret meetings were held at night and much destruction of machinery took place. In March 1812 an act of parliament was passed making the breaking of a stocking frame punishable by death, and in the same month seven Luddites, as they were called, were sentenced at Nottingham to transportation. In the year C.J. was born, many more were tried at Leicester and afterwards executed, six at a time, on the drop in front of the Leicester County House of Correction.

In 1819 workers in Leicester and the neighbourhood formed a 'Frame-work Knitters Society' or Union, in which those who were in employment contributed to the support of the unemployed. At this time the wages of the knitters had dwindled to an average of five shillings a week after deducting frame rents, i.e. just £13 a year [= £965 today]. Some hosiers were sympathetic to their workers and supported them in their attempts to help themselves. Other landowners and leading citizens tried to alleviate the workers' plight by introducing an Allotment System, thereby enabling hundreds of workers to rent garden allotments where they could grow food for their families.

There were many other mills and factories for spinning and doubling worsted yarn, lambs' wool, sewing cotton and much else, several lace manufacturers, two extensive iron foundries and two large coach and harness manufacturers. There were also many of the crafts and trades necessary to the life of a well-ordered town – corn millers, brewers, and smiths of various kinds. Agriculture was also still important with no fewer than twelve fairs held annually for the sale of horses, cattle, sheep and cheese, and there were weekly markets on Wednesdays and Saturdays. Trade was greatly helped by the River Soar being navigable and connecting with the Leicester and Northamptonshire Union Canal. Most passenger traffic and much freight was still carried by stagecoach and by local carriers of whom there were very many. The railway did not come until 1832 when the Leicester-Swannington Railway was opened which was incorporated in the Midland Railway Company in 1846..

This growing industrial municipality had ancient roots going far back into pre-Roman times, and the Roman conquerors had made it a stipendiary town contributing a regular tax to the commander of the district. The Saxons gave it the name Leicestre, the fortress on what was then the River Leire. Its first royal charter was granted by King John in 1190. Soon afterwards, Simon de Montfort, Earl of Leicester, granted the burgesses a further charter which specified 'that no Jew or Jewess, in my time, or in the time of any of my heirs, to the end of the world, shall inhabit or remain in the town of Leicester.' Henry VII granted the Burgesses a new charter in 1487 relating to the management of the town's affairs. Elizabeth I granted the Corporation, for the first time, a common seal, and ordained that the governing body should consist of a mayor, two bailiffs, twenty-four aldermen and forty-eight common councilmen, the latter to act as assistants to the mayor and aldermen. The mayor, recorder, and the four aldermen who had last served the office of mayor were appointed to act as Justices of the Peace and to hold a Court of Quarter Sessions with jurisdiction over all cases not touching life and limb. Prior to the passing of the Parliamentary and Municipal Reform Acts of 1832 and 1835, the mayor, aldermen and councilmen were self-elected. Edward Vaughan served as Chaplain to this unreformed body which was solidly Tory and Anglican. That situation changed totally after 1835.

At the start of the century there were still many half-timbered lath and plaster houses but gradually these were being replaced by plainer but more comfortable and convenient stone dwellings. There were numerous fine buildings from the past, notably the Guildhall dating from the 14th century, the town's best medieval timber-framed structure, and situated near St Martin's Church. From 1821 the town was well lit thanks to the completion of a gas works that year. The water supply, however, was far less satisfactory and many inhabitants had to buy much of their supply from water carriers at a cost of a halfpenny for a full pail, and the only public fountain providing free water, called the Conduit, supplied with spring water, had been built in 1709 when the population of the town was only 6,500. A gazetteer described the town as 'pleasantly situated, and, although some parts of it are low and badly drained, the streets are generally wide, and the houses of the labouring classes are not crowded so closely together as at Nottingham and many other towns.'[10]

The town was divided into five ancient parishes. The largest and most central was St Martin's. The first recorded mention of its church was in 1086 when the old Saxon church was replaced by a Norman one. The parish was home to many of the professional men and merchants of the older and more established kind. The Borough Gaol was also in the parish. The assize sermons were preached in St Martin's and the Archdeacon held his courts here and the Bishop his confirmations. Here the mayor and aldermen went in procession in their scarlet gowns on the great occasions of the civic year. A sight sure to stir the imagination of any child watching them, especially if, as in the case of C.J. and his siblings, their father was in it and would shortly take central stage and address them all.

The church consisted of a spacious nave, chancel and three aisles, with a tower and a lofty crocketted spire (added in 1757), rising in the centre from four semi-circular arches, resting on massive Norman pillars. Much damage had been done to it after the Reformation and again during the Civil War. In Edward Vaughan's time the nave and two aisles were neatly pewed and seated about 1,800 worshippers. A comparatively recent addition had been an organ installed by public subscription in 1774 and first used 'at the anniversary meeting of the supporters of the Infirmary, when Lord Sandwich [First Lord of the Admiralty] was present and accompanied the band upon the kettle drums.'[11]

In addition to the 3,000 or so parishioners Vaughan had at St Martin's, he also had responsibility for All Saints which was in a populous district but he delegated the duties of this parish to a Curate. The value of All Saints had been augmented by grants from Queen Anne's Bounty in 1762 and 1802 and by a parliamentary grant in 1815 so that by the time Vaughan resigned that living in 1820, it was worth nearly as much as St Martin's.

In 1789 two Charity Schools had been built by subscription in Friar Lane in the parish of St Martin's. They had residences for the Master and Mistress and provided education for sixty boys and forty girls who were provided with uniforms in blue cloth – hence the name 'Blue Coat Schools'. Another charity known as Wyggeston Hospital stood near St Martin's church. It consisted of apartments for twelve men and sixteen women with the Master's house at one end and the chapel at the other. And there was a house for the Confrator (brother chaplain) who was required to read prayers in the chapel each evening for which he was paid a stipend of £100 p.a. [= £10,300]. Each of the alms people received a weekly allowance of four shillings with occasional additional allowances of money, coal, salt and oatmeal. This charity had been founded in 1513 by William Wyggeston, a wealthy merchant, who, dying childless, had bequeathed the bulk of his property to the charitable foundation. The Master had the right to appoint the alms people; his remuneration for these light duties was £300 p.a. and his house and garden, when he was non-resident, were let for a further £40 p.a. Two of Edward's sons were to benefit from this valuable clerical sinecure. It was the kind that Anthony Trollope would later pillory in his Barchester novels. There were a number of other small charities in the parish designed to ease the lot of the poorest, such as the one established by Thomas Topp in 1716 which produced £20 a year and was given in premiums with two boys, bound apprentice by the Vicar and Church Wardens, to trades in the town.

Nonconformity was strong in Leicester where Chapel seatings outnumbered those in the Established Church. Baptists were most numerous and had twelve large chapels. The Baptist cobbler William Carey, a pioneer of the modern missionary movement, had had his home here until he sailed to India in 1793. One notable Baptist preacher whose ministry at Harvey Lane Chapel was coterminous with that of Edward Vaughan at St Martin's was Robert Hall. His statue now stands in De Montfort Square. From 1826 the Baptists even had their own monthly periodical called the *Baptist Reporter*. The town was also home to the General Baptist College, an academy for educating and training young men for the ordained ministry, founded in 1798 by the Revd Dan Taylor.

The days when Evangelical clergy were figures of derision had largely passed in Leicester when Edward Vaughan returned home as Vicar of St Martin's. This was in no small measure due to the ministry of the Revd Thomas Robinson, who had served as Curate at St Martin's and Lecturer at All Saints from 1774-78, and then was appointed Incumbent of St Mary's by Lord Chancellor Thurlow. He founded the first Anglican charity school in the town, though not without opposition from those who feared it would be a nursery of young Evangelicals. He invited leading Evangelical friends to preach in St Mary's, among them Henry Venn and Charles Simeon. He worked willingly with Nonconformists to establish interdenominational Sunday Schools which catered for about six hundred children. He was prominent locally in the anti-slave trade campaign, the Bible Society and the Church Missionary Society, and he helped develop a Benevolent Society which benefited his parishioners through its system of visitors to the sick and poor in the parish. He helped save many young girls, mostly orphans, from a life of abuse or prostitution by opening a home for them (called the 'Female Asylum') where they could be cared for and trained for domestic service. When he died suddenly in 1813, an immense concourse of townsfolk gathered to pay their last respects at his funeral. Among them was Edward Vaughan, who two years later wrote a memoir of him and who now inherited Robinson's mantle as the leading Evangelical incumbent in Leicester.

However, when Vaughan introduced an evening lecture (in effect an informal service with Bible teaching) on Thursdays, the Vestry passed a motion in December 1806 saying that 'no expenses relating to or in any wise occasioned by the Lectures given by the Vicar' would be paid by the parish. That suggests many were still not enamoured of the new Evangelical spirit or saw the need for mid-week services.[12] The entry in the Vestry Minute book has 'Wednesday' amended to 'Thursday' which might indicate that the Wardens had never attended nor knew for sure on what night he held the meetings.

Eugene Stock, in his magisterial work *The History of the Church Missionary Society*, described him as one of the ablest of the Evangelical clergy whose 'work for the missionary cause at Leicester became a pattern to be pointed to for imitation.'[13] Vaughan regularly attended the annual meetings of CMS in London and preached the anniversary sermon in 1815. He was responsible for a welcome change in the way resolutions were framed at the AGM. Previously they had often referred to individuals with a lot of mutually congratulatory speeches on the part of the movers, now they were to refer solely to the events and circumstances of the year. He was assiduous in his support for CMS in the Leicester area and invited Josiah Pratt, the co-founder and first Secretary of CMS to stay with him. His support for missions ran wider still, preaching sermons in support of SPCK and SPG. His willingness to cooperate with dissenters in the work of the Gospel is evidenced by his joining with them in forming the Leicestershire Auxiliary Bible Society in 1810. But he was strongly opposed to non-denominational education, believing that religious instruction should be based on the beliefs and practices of the Established Church.

He furiously opposed a plan devised in February 1828 by members of the reform party to establish an Infants School Society on a non-denominational basis. He objected to children being taken from their parents' care at so early an age and 'declared that the canons of the Church forbade the children of Anglican parents to be educated by any persons who were not themselves churchmen.'[14] The following month, he was taken to task publicly in the pages of the *Leicester Journal* by G.B. Mitchell, the Vicar of All Saints, for meddling in the affairs of his parish, and accused of underhand dealings in having retained powers as Treasurer of All Saints School when he gave up the incumbency of that parish in 1820. Vaughan replied at length defending his right as a co-proprietor (he owned one eighth of the building) to question Mitchell's proposed alternative use of the building. The fact is he feared that the building might be used for non-denominational educational purposes.

In that same month the repeal of the Corporation and Test Acts was being considered by Parliament which would have allowed Roman Catholics and Nonconformists to be elected to public office. He and his Church Vestry opposed it and sent a petition to the Prime Minister and to Parliament which Sir Charles Hastings duly presented. The Archdeacon convened a meeting of the clergy of his archdeaconry which met in the Exchange Rooms in Leicester on Monday 10 March 1828 'to take into consideration the propriety of petitioning both Houses of Parliament against the concession of the R.C. Claims, the Repeal of the Corporation and Test Acts, and the Adoption of the Unitarian Marriage Bill.' The *Leicester Journal* reported on the 14th that the Archdeacon had been indisposed on the day of the meeting, so the numerous clergy present called Mr Vaughan to the chair. 'The Rev Gentleman proposed the several Petitions which were carried, and ordered to be presented to the Lords by the Lord Lieutenant of the County, and the Lord Bishop of the Diocese; and to the Commons, by the County members, and Sir Charles Hastings, Bt., one of the members for the Borough.' Their opposition had no influence or effect at Westminster. The following year, Dr Thomas Arnold, the recently appointed Head of Rugby School, who would become the educator of Vaughan's sons, wrote a pugnacious pamphlet entitled *The Christian Duty of Conceding Roman Catholic Claims*. His views and his style of expressing them angered many clergy. That was hardly surprising as he said that he regarded the clergy as narrow-minded, prejudiced and a 'stumbling block in the advancement of Christianity'! Had Edward Vaughan lived, he would certainly not have allowed his children to go to Rugby where they would have been in danger of being influenced by Arnold.

In later years C.J. remembered his father as having been a diligent pastor but the parish registers seem to challenge that view. In the first eleven years of his ministry, the baptismal registers do not indicate who the officiant was, so we have no way of knowing for sure how diligent he was in this respect. That information first appears in 1813. Of the 78 baptisms performed at St Martin's in that year, Vaughan officiated at just five, his Curate the Revd John Davies did 66, and the Revd Edward Morgan signed as the 'Officiating Minister' did the rest. The registers reveal that when he had an assistant curate, he left most of this work to him. In 1816, however, he did 66 of the 95 baptisms because his current Curate, John Ower, left in May and no one took his place immediately. One of those he baptized that year on 22 December was his son, Charles John, the subject of this memoir.

The Burial registers tell the same story. Entries are first signed by the officiant in 1813 – of the 71 funerals held that year, Vaughan ministered at just five and John Davies, his Curate, did most of the rest. In 1814 he did 13 of the 78 funerals leaving John Ower to do the others. He did better with weddings. His signature first appears on 1 July 1802 and he officiated at 17 of the 19 weddings that year – presumably because he was ministering on his own. The name of a Curate, the Revd John Anderson, first appears on 7 January 1803. In that year Vaughan did 21 of the 70 weddings, leaving Anderson to do the other 49. There was little to do at Foston. Between 1813 and 1830 there were just six weddings and Vaughan officiated at three of them; of the twelve adults involved five (two men and three women) were illiterate and simply made their mark in the register. He may well have been a diligent visitor in the homes of his parishioners but he did not share very much in what were significant milestones in their lives. There were exceptions, however, as the following story illustrates.

It seems that this very conservative churchman could be quite unconventional if pastoral need required it as this incident shows which was commented on approvingly years after his death by the *Baptist Reporter*. The article was headed 'The Font and the Tub' and purported to be a conversation between those two objects present at the baptism by total immersion in St Martin's church of one John Butler, druggist and resident in Wharf Street Leicester. The parish baptismal register for 1823 confirms that this did take place on 31 August when the candidate for baptism was aged 28. Vaughan baptised six others of varying ages that same day but presumably in the traditional way at the font. The man's request for baptism by total immersion caused Vaughan to read up on the theology of baptism and then to consult the Bishop of Lincoln during a visitation in Leicester. The Bishop advised that if the candidate wished it, he had better perform the ceremony even though its like had not taken place in St Martin's for two hundred years! C.J. would have been seven at the time and presumably in the great crowd present to witness this historic event. One wonders what impression it made on his young mind?

> Accordingly, last Sunday morning, to use the words of the Rev E.T. Vaughan, this "imposing ceremony" took place. Long before it began, the avenues leading to the font were crowded, and the church altogether had a fuller attendance than usual. At the conclusion of the Second Lesson, while the congregation was singing *Rock of ages cleft for me*, the Rev divine walked to the font attended by the candidate and his sureties, where was placed a large tub, made for the purpose, about seven feet in length and three in height, of an oblong shape, and containing about one hundred gallons of water. The minister having read the service for the public baptism of such as are of riper years, proceeded to immerse the candidate, who having taken off his coat, descended three steps which were placed at the end of the tub, got in the water, walked to the end, where the clergyman, assisted by his clerk, immersed this individual who had "renounced the devil and all his works."

Several prayers followed, appointed for the occasion, and the "imposing ceremony" terminated. The Rev. E.T. Vaughan, afterwards, preached an excellent sermon on the subject from Colossians 2. 11-12. [15]

How 'excellent' Vaughan's sermons were as a rule is open to question though two volumes of them were published along with several individual sermons. One of his curates who served with him for many years, the Revd T.B. Paget, described his former senior colleague as 'a nursing father in Christ, by whom he hath showed them how to search the Scriptures with accuracy, to compare spiritual things with spiritual, and to find grace and peace multiplied unto them in the knowledge or acknowledgement of the mystery of God and of our Lord Jesus Christ.' [16] Rather different is the judgement of another hearer who said of him that he 'preached mysticism and metaphysics in floods of eloquence lasting for nearly two hours.'[17] A parishioner wrote disapprovingly to the *Journal* in April 1824 complaining about his 'hideous ultra-Calvinistic doctrines.'

One sermon he preached on Sunday 23 November 1823 and subsequently published, *God the Doer of all Things*, was the culmination of six months preaching on predestination. For Vaughan, God's will was sovereign in all creation – 'the one source and spring of every event – thus ascribing what is properly called Freewill to God alone.' [18] In the preface he wrote, 'Style is what I neither profess, nor aim at; my only aim is to be *understood* and *remembered*.' [19] Clarity of expression, however, is what its 39 closely printed pages lack. It did provoke two printed responses from other clerics in Leicestershire, both of whom complained that he wasn't using his talents and position as the incumbent of the leading church in the county town to better effect. One of them reminisced disparagingly:

> I will state here a fact. Accident has led me (I think twice) to be in Leicester on a Sunday evening, when I have attended Mr Vaughan's Evening Service. In both cases, as I remember, certainly in one, the sermon from Mr Vaughan (I declare that I do not exaggerate when I say, that) I could not understand. Mr Vaughan, no doubt, will have his own way of accounting for this. But I cannot help thinking any discourse ill calculated for *general* edification, which any member of the Church of England possessed of ordinary faculties, could not comprehend. [20]

His other critic, the Revd John Owen, dismissed Vaughan's views out of hand: 'The Theology of this sermon is more erroneous, if possible, than its Philosophy. Not only is the reasoning incorrect, but its Divinity is most false and dangerous . . . though Scripture in abundance is quoted, but quoted illegitimately.' [21]

By his own admission Vaughan preached *extempore*, which is almost always a temptation to prolixity, and later wrote up what he remembered having said in the pulpit. One sermon preached before the Leicestershire District Committee of SPCK and SPG at their anniversary on 7 September 1827, *The Church's Expectation – A Sermon on the Second Advent of our Lord Jesus Christ*, runs to 154 printed pages! To his hearers it must have felt everlasting. I imagine some of his hearers wondering irreverently, would the sermon end before Christ returned in glory? In it he looked forward to the overthrow of Anti-Christ in East and West (meaning Muslims and the Papacy) and to the restoration of the Jews which would inaugurate the Millennium.

His politically conservative views voiced in a sermon at a Civic Service in 1826 and later published caused a storm which rumbled on for nearly a year in the columns of the *Leicester Chronicle*. In the sermon which he had entitled *Caesar and God* he stated that 'government is neither of the people nor for the people . . . supremacy in a single person is God's law, and there are no rights but such as he chooses to grant.' [22] Such trenchant views help explain why one of his successors at St Martin's wrote of him, 'I am quite certain that had you said to him, "Do you not sometimes fear that your sermons will upset people?" He would have unhesitatingly replied, "I hope so, sir. I hope so!"' [23] He certainly did not fight shy of controversy, attacking the town's Corporation in December 1827 for their 'internal disputes and for their failure to banish prostitutes from the streets and purify the houses of entertainment from lewd sports, riot, excess and profane words. "Must there be Theatres, Horse courses, and Masques?" he demanded.'[24] About this same time he published *A Letter to Thomas Burbidge, Esq Town Clerk of Leicester on the Divine Origin, Nature and End of Civil Government*.

When a neighbouring clergyman, the Revd James Beresford of Kibworth, used the occasion of a Bishop's visitation held in St Martin's, at which he had been invited to preach, to attack Calvinist clergy and doctrines, Vaughan took up the cudgels. He published a letter to Beresford entitled *The Calvinistic clergy defended and the doctrines of Calvin maintained*. The *Gentleman's Magazine* in its brief review whilst noting that he had 'undauntedly withdrawn the veil which had so long concealed the mysterious doctrines of Calvinism' was critical of Vaughan's tone: 'The letter begins with much courtesy; but the conclusion, with regret, we observe is too warm for the sober discussion of a grave Divine.' [25]

Vaughan used his own translation of the Bible in preference to the *Authorised Version*, for which he was criticised in the pages of *The British Critic*. He defended himself arguing that his primary concern was 'a zeal for truth' and was critical of the *King James Version*: 'Whilst I account our authorised version a fair transcript of the original, sufficiently accurate for general use, and beautiful in point of diction, I cannot allow that it is just to build any doctrine upon the authority of a mere version, especially if that version be, as ours confessedly is, an idiomatic one.' [26]

Being a competent classicist, he gave his children a solid grounding in Greek and Latin which he taught them each morning. It is not surprising, then, that his son C.J., in later life, paid so much attention himself to the study of the text of Scripture in its original tongues, became a prolific commentator on the New Testament and gave such a high priority to the ministry of teaching and preaching, and that he eventually took part in the task of producing the *Revised Version* of the NT. The father's early influence is manifestly evident in his son's later development. In a charity sermon preached by C.J. in St Paul's Cathedral at the 1851 Festival of the Sons of the Clergy, he referred to 'the indelible impression' that his father's devoted life had made on him as a young boy:

> The morning hours spent in the self-denying labours of parental education; noon and afternoon in the various toils of parochial visitation; evening till a late mid-night in the painful researches and deep meditation of a theology fruitful in power and in love and in a sound mind; interruptions, wearisome and exhausting, perpetually delaying business and destroying repose, yet, amidst all, the intellect ever occupied with truth, the heart ever communing with the unseen; life at length sacrificed, in the full vigour of manhood, to exertions unresting yet untiring – indeed, a labourer like this – there were such then, there are such now – a labourer like this is worthy of his hire. [27]

In April 1829, Vaughan had the distressing task of officiating at his youngest son's funeral. Geoffrey Edgar was just seven years old. Six months later, he too died aged 52. The death took place at Foston on Sunday 27 September and came totally unexpectedly. The previous month he had been more active than usual in taking the Occasional Offices. He took a wedding on the 6th, the funeral of a 32 year old on the 28th and baptised seven children (the oldest of whom was a 15 year old boy) on the 30th.

The *Leicester Journal* published an appreciative article, a kind of *apologia*, the following week about his teaching ministry but one that reflected what a contentious figure he had been:

> In this unwearied and conscientious course of duty, he encountered the judgement and criticism of public opinion, and was often brought into collision with the sentiments and feelings of other men. Qualified to exercise enlightened judgement on the most important subjects, and too independent in his spirit to be guided by the prejudices and predilections of a party, his writings occasionally drew forth expressions of an uneasiness from many quarters during the controversial contests of the day; but it must be remembered that the productions of his pen were the result of intense meditation on those features of divine truth, which few had, with equal power and patience of enquiry examined, & which, therefore, on their publication might be expected, more or less, to encounter the suspicions, prejudices, hesitation, or opposition of many, whether of contrary judgements, more limited researches, or indifference to every track of religious knowledge beyond that trodden by the multitude of professed believers. [28]

A letter of like sentiment written the day after his death was sent to the *Journal* by a gentleman signing it simply 'A Dissenter' but one who had, clearly, opposed most of Vaughan's political and doctrinal views:

> Rev E.T. Vaughan – The almost sudden death of this gentleman is now the theme of general conversation; and his virtues and defects will, no doubt, be canvassed and discussed – I hope with candour and with charity. His pretensions as a Scholar and gentleman were of the highest kind; & "not least though last", were his merits as a Christian. Differing with him on all political and many religious subjects, I yet admired his consistency in the one, and his fearless honesty in the other . . . His political opinions are too well known to need description. I differed from them all, as I believed them unfounded either on Scripture, reason, or sound policy. The warmth with which he embraced and maintained these opinions excited some hostility and ill-feeling towards him, and I certainly cannot plead guiltless on this head; but I can truly say,
>   "Thou art dead, Alonzo;
>   So is my enmity."
> With respect to his character as a Christian, considered apart from his peculiarities of doctrine, I rejoice in the belief, that, like his Divine Master's, his was a labour of love. Although frequently abstruse and metaphysical, yet the burden of his sermons was, "Christ, the gift of God."

The abstruse nature of his studies was the effect of an intense desire after a knowledge of "the Truth". He feared to be a "blind leader of the blind"; and I do believe, whatever might be his deviations, (and what mortal is wholly free from the influence of the world, and the deceitfulness of the heart) he desired to know naught among us "save Christ, and him crucified." – His prevailing wish was, "to vindicate the ways of God to man." . . .

I hope survivors, while they lament and avoid his errors, "will follow him so far as he followed Christ," – that they will imitate his earnestness, his zeal, his honesty and his charity . . .[29]

The *Leicester Chronicle* too mixed criticism with praise:

We were not among the admirers of Mr Vaughan's peculiar tenets, religious or political, but always felt disposed to give him credit for great zeal to do good in his own way; and believe, that none of his predecessors or contemporaries in the pastoral office, ever laboured more incessantly or with greater sincerity, to promote the temporal and spiritual welfare of the flock committed to his charge, than he did. [30]

The Gentleman's Magazine in its obituary of him classed him with 'the divines of the Evangelical school' and listed his publications. It reported 'Mr Vaughan's remains were, on the 3rd of October, conveyed for interment in his church of St Martin's preceded by twelve clergymen of the town and county, and attended by his widow and son (Edward), Sir Henry Halford, Miss E, Vaughan and others of the family. A public subscription has been opened for a monument to this much admired divine.' [31] The *Leicester Chronicle* reported that he had requested a funeral 'without pomp and ceremony' but 'several thousands thronged the church and churchyard on the Saturday evening when his remains were laid to rest in the family vault on the south side of the altar in St Martin's Church . . . Rev Mr Hill officiated, a relative of his first wife. Mr Nedham had recently completed a portrait of him in the pulpit.' [32]

His brother, Sir Henry Halford, composed the brief text on the memorial tablet erected in St Martin's 'by his affectionate parishioners':

> To record their attachment and gratitude to him
> for having taught them by his doctrine,
> and led them by his example
> the way to everlasting happiness
> through Jesus Christ.

Shortly after her husband's death, Agnes wrote to a friend confirming those words: 'I sorrow for myself, for my many fatherless children, for his congregation and for the church at large, but not as one without hope, we are not far asunder. He on that side the vail (*sic*), I on this.' [33] Sir Henry received a letter of complaint from one of his brother's admirers, a Mr Drummond who was a banker and zealous Irvingite, who felt that he had omitted to mention Vaughan's 'most eminent achievement': 'the peculiar line of your brother's divinity, in which he reduced to system and consistency, the loose declamations of Hooker, Charnock, Baxter and others, should, if possible, be noticed.' [34] Sir Henry chose to disregard it and kept the text of the memorial simple, short and conventional in its wording.

Fourteen years later a volume of his expository sermons was published, and they have been reprinted as recently as 2008. They had been taken down in shorthand at the time of their delivery by his friend, Mr Edward Bankart. It includes the sermons he preached on the morning and evening of the Sunday immediately prior to his sudden terminal illness, and were regarded by the editor as 'his dying testimony; a record of those principles, and of those views of the truth of God, which gave him in life so remarkable a measure of happiness, boldness and vigour, and in death so large a portion of the peace of God.' [35] His final sermon was on Matthew 12 v11-12, the parable of the marriage feast, and ended with these words: 'Study God in the only way in which He is to be known, - and that is his mystery in Christ. Think over what you have heard this night; let it lead you to an examination of his Word. Meditate upon his counsel so far as it has been discovered to you this night, and see whether that will not make your fruitful faith more fruitful.' [36]

The appeal was not lost on one devoted, young listener, his son Charles, who had recently celebrated his 13th birthday. In time he would come to share his father's view that there is no higher calling than the pastorate of souls and the faithful preaching of the gospel. But already now, these early formative years in Leicester had impressed upon him how important and influential the ministry of a faithful pastor and teacher could be for a town. The sight of so many thousands lining the streets and crowding the graveyard to show their respect for his dead father would have confirmed for him how much his father's visits to the homes of rich and poor alike had been appreciated. He had cared for and respected his people, whatever their station in life. The boy wanted to follow in his father's footsteps, and, educationally, that now meant going to Rugby and then, hopefully, on to Trinity College Cambridge, where he might emulate his father's academic achievements.

Agnes proved to be a strong and resourceful support for her children. She had a marriage settlement which now provided her as a widow with sufficient annual income to meet all the essential needs of her large household, and her father provided a house next to his bank situated near St Martin's. Her brother, Thomas Pares, told her that he could provide her with an additional £200 [= £18,600] whenever needed. She turned to him regularly for advice and help. Most of her surviving letters to him are undated but the contents give some clue to when they were written. This one probably dates from early 1830 when she was still trying to make suitable arrangements for her children's education:

> Foston   Thursday night
> It becomes necessary that I should arrange some place of instruction for my two dear younger Boys. The information I have obtained respecting Rugby leads me to give up all thought of it at present for dear Edwyn. I could not be comfortable to place him at so early an age in a situation in which, comparatively, he would be so much at his own disposal, neither do I think that from the tenderness of his disposition and his keen sense of right and wrong he would be happy in it. Two years hence, if he likes it, it may be as well adapted to his want as I have now every reason to be satisfied it is to dear Charles . . . [37]

She didn't know it but Arnold agreed with her about the unsuitability of sending boys under the age of 12 to his school because he feared the moral risk to which such young children might be exposed. She told her brother in the same letter that she was also concerned for her daughter Lucy's education in the Classics – 'having been brought as far as she has been in Latin and Greek to have her without assistance and that just at the age when Girls become sensible of the importance and worth of mental cultivation.' [38] She, accordingly, asked for his advice about a home tutor for the boys and Lucy.

Help and support were also forthcoming from the Vaughan fraternity. Her brother-in-law, Sir Henry Halford, provided her and the children with a rural retreat at Wistow Grange, a house he had built in 1820 near Wistow Hall. Sir Henry also used his influence to have her eldest son, Edward, awarded a Tancred Divinity Studentship during his years at Cambridge – the Tancred Charities, of which he as the President of the Royal College of Physicians was a governor, provided studentships in Divinity,

Physic and Law. It was also probably through his influence that the younger boys were sent to Rugby where he was a Trustee of the school.

In a letter to her brother written a few days after the first anniversary of her husband's death, she told him that Baron Vaughan [i.e. John Vaughan, successively King's Serjeant, Baron of the Exchequer, Justice of the Court of Common Pleas and Privy Councillor] was visiting her and that her father was there too. There is a hint of raw grief still being felt by her:

> I have just heard from my dear Charles who hopes to spend Wednesday week with me. I shall feel it a help to look to this pleasure when I have parted from my now dearest earthly treasure Edward. [Her eldest son was about to leave for Cambridge.] In prospect I am at moments overpowered but I doubt not the needed strength will be given to me when the moment of trial arrives. I have often cried in expecting that it should be communicated beforehand. I trust not so now.
> With truest love to your dear wife and yourself.
> Believe me, most affectionately yours   Agnes Vaughan [39]

Years later, Agnes showed that she too knew how to work the patronage system to the advantage of her sons. When Luther, who had chosen the army as a career, was about to be posted to India, she asked her brother Thomas (now the High Sheriff of Derbyshire) to write to a number of influential people and provided him with a list, which included the Commander in Chief and the Adjutant General! 'Perhaps Mary mentioned to you that we were anxious to get some influential introductions for Luther on his arrival in Calcutta. It is very important that he should be appointed to a good Regiment.' [40] She also asked him for '£300 [= £25,880] at least for Luther' so that he would be well provided for once he got there. The letters and money surely helped him at the start of his rise through the ranks, ending up a highly decorated general and knighted for his service to the Crown.

Agnes chose not to re-marry or to move away from Leicester where she was a person of some substance. She was to remain an important figure in the lives of all her children until her death there on 28 December 1878, aged 92. By then, her youngest surviving son, David, was Vicar of St Martin's and it was he who officiated at her funeral.

A Pupil at Rugby – the Master's Disciple

It must be your own choice and act, whether, indeed you wish this place to be 'unavoidably a seat or nursery of vice' or whether you wish to verify the words of our daily thanksgiving, that, by the benefit of our founders, 'you are here brought up to godliness and good learning.'
Thomas Arnold *Sermons* Vol. 2 p 122

C.J. was well equipped educationally when he arrived at Rugby School in January 1830 just three months after his father's death but he was still grieving. For a boy with no previous experience of school life it must have been a daunting prospect but here he was to form a deep attachment to the Headmaster, Dr Thomas Arnold, who would become for him an inspirational role model. And here he would also make two lifelong friendships.

The school had been founded in 1587 by a local benefactor and catered largely for the sons of gentlemen living in the Midlands. When C.J.'s father had been a pupil there, it had been ruled by an unusually violent Master, Dr Henry Ingles, nicknamed 'The Black Tiger', whose excessive beatings provoked a rebellion in 1797 which was only put down by further violence. He had been succeeded in 1806 by a gentler and more scholarly man, Dr John Wooll. In his long reign of 21 years as Headmaster, the Trustees had erected completely new school buildings in the neo-Tudor style and they later added a chapel. In 1825 an Assistant Master, the Revd C.A. Anstey, was appointed Chaplain with an additional stipend of £90 a year [= £7,120]. The number of pupils rose in Wooll's time to over 300 but had dropped to 136 by the end of his reign.

A new boy, Arthur Stanley, described his first impressions of the school in a letter home in February 1829 – 'an immense long building, towered and turreted of stone, and I don't think it all too new. At one end of it – joined to it, and just the same kind of building – was Dr Arnold's department, and on the other the chapel, close to it – small and pretty, but nothing very striking . . . The playground is a fine large field, with several fine trees.'[1]

Arnold had taken up the post of Headmaster in August 1828. One of his referees, Dr Edward Hawkins, the Provost of Oriel College Oxford, had predicted his appointment would change the face of education through all the public schools of England. That was to take time but in the end his prediction proved to be correct, and during Arnold's fourteen years at Rugby the school grew in reputation and pupil numbers rose to 375. One change he inaugurated as soon as was practicable was that boys should live under the supervision and pastoral care of an Assistant Master. Previously those not resident in School House under the immediate supervision of the Head had lived out in approved boarding houses run by landladies in the town. As these fell vacant, for whatever reason, a new house under the direct supervision of a master took its place. The first of these, opened in 1829, was named Anstey's after its Housemaster and stood on the Barby Road, which runs through land owned by the school.

C.J. was admitted to Mr Townsend's house which in 1830 was situated in the old market place in the centre of the town – "What a strange place!" was how he remembered it many years later. Strange indeed, for Rugby was a very small and insalubrious market town of about 2,500 residents whose streets at that time were neither flagged, lighted nor drained. There were cesspits and open ditches thick with filth in every direction. A start on drainage was first made in 1832 as a result of the coming of the dreaded cholera; gas lighting in the streets came seven years later. The school, at least, was surrounded by open land on three sides. Edward and Thomas Ryder, the eleven and fourteen year old sons of the Evangelical Bishop of Lichfield and Coventry, and Joseph and Thomas Burbidge, the thirteen and fourteen year old sons of a Leicestershire gentleman, were admitted at the same time to Townsend's. The Burbidge boys' father was Clerk to the Town Council in Leicester and would have known the Vaughan family.

Arthur Stanley, who was to become his most intimate friend, had spent his first term on that house just a year earlier before joining Anstey's, and he has left this description of it in a letter he wrote to his sister Mary a few days after his arrival at the school:

> We drove through the town, which is just behind the school, and stopped at Mr Townsend's. There we saw him and his wife. We went to look at the studies, some of which were ranged round a yard, and some upstairs; some were indeed small but some were a very tolerable size, with sofas, tables, bookcases, fitted up as nicely as could be . . . The dining room was a place with a large fire, and a table with benches, on the former of which was placed the dinner (which consisted of puddings and meat), and on the latter the boys – in number about seven – and two men-servants to wait upon us . . . Pudding first, and then the veal, and we certainly were not stinted in our allowance. Much laughter and joking passed among the boys,

and after dinner one or two of them spoke to me about where I was placed, &c . . . We had a good tea at half past five, when we were locked up from going into the streets. I sat the rest of the evening with a boy of about my own age whose name was Highton, from Leicestershire. He seemed to be clever, and had a very comfortable study, well stored with books – many English. My study was a small, comfortable room, with a table and two chairs; but as it was in the yard, and the boys might throw water and anything else in at the window, I thought it best to change to one upstairs. We had bread and cheese for supper. The bell rang for us at a quarter to ten, and at ten we were all in bed . . . In the morning I found it was a usual custom for new boys not to go to the first lesson, so I stayed at home . . . After breakfast, at a quarter to ten, I went with the other boys to the great schoolroom, where we sat construing the second lesson to one another till half past ten . . . We, then, of the fourth went into a smaller schoolroom, where Mr Bird, the master, in his college dress, made first one and then another get up and construe. I was very much confused, but I took two or three places, and found myself most deficient in grammar. At half past twelve we came out, and Arthur Pigot very kindly offered to walk with me; but as it was a wet drizzly day we soon parted. Dined at half past one . . . At a quarter past two to school again – third lesson – Ovid – the same manner as before . . . Fourthly, and lastly, Greek exercises, and we came home just as the locking up, and calling over, and tea began; and here I am in my study upstairs, with the FIRST DAY over. I think the only <u>misery</u> I have endured is that this night the boys have been smoking me with burnt paper through the cracks in the door. [2]

The 'misery' he was subjected to was in fact a common schoolboy practice at Rugby known as 'bogling'. He and his contemporaries were fortunately spared the more brutal initiation rites which earlier generations of Rugbeians had suffered before Dr Wooll's headship.

C.J.'s introduction to school life there was undoubtedly very similar. He, too, started in the Fourth Form after having been examined personally by Arnold in Homer and Virgil and been asked about his Latin verses. Already by Easter he had been promoted to the Fifth Form which relieved him of having to fag for older boys and gave him the privilege and responsibility of being a house prefect. It also brought him into close contact with Arthur Stanley who had just won the Fifth Form English Essay prize. Many years later, C.J. recalled his first sight of the boy in whose company he spent much of his time at Rugby:

The first time that I remember seeing our friend was on the Good Friday afternoon of that first half-year, when he came into chapel . . . his face turned by blushes from rose-colour to scarlet in the joy and pride of his first triumph, the prize for the Fifth Form English Essay (on "Sicily and its Revolutions") having been just adjudged to him. His face and look are as vividly before me as if it was a scene of yesterday – the black hair, cut close as always, the bright ingenuous child's face, the round jacket and twilled trousers, and the quick gliding movement, three steps to a man's one . . .

At Easter I was moved into the Fifth Form, and there we were together till a year and a quarter afterwards, when what was then a new invention, the Fifth Form examination for places, shook up the old fifty into all manner of strange reverses, and placed this young boy of fifteen at the head of the whole number for promotion into the Sixth at Midsummer 1831.

The Fifth Form, under "old Moor", was a really remarkable institution. He was an elderly man, to our eyes at least; and his rusty knee-breeches and worsted stockings, as well as a general slovenliness of apparel, added, no doubt, to his years. He was Vicar of Clifton, near Rugby, an excellent clergyman, with a voice, the melody of which is still in my ears as he read out to us from time to time some little English poem done in school by the youthful genius in which he took an evident pride and delight. He maintained a vigorous discipline over a somewhat difficult herd of fifty (for the most part) oldish boys, by various ingenious devices which lengthened the irksome school hours for the idle and abridged them for the good; and although the *idea* of the man was old-fashioned, his practice was thorough and sensible, and his love of modern history, and his keen enjoyment of poetry both ancient and modern, contributed something, I cannot but think, to the early interests and tastes of Stanley himself.

During our three years together in the Sixth Form under the daily teaching of Arnold himself, we grew by degrees into a very close and intimate friendship. Having neither of us any taste for games, our intercourse was chiefly in the form of long walks – indeed of walks long and short, for he had already that solemn sense of the *duty* of air and exercise which was characteristic of him to the end.

There were also endless talks in his study, some four feet square, at an upper corner of Anstey's boarding-house looking upon the Close, with its already considerable store of books, its metallic sofa, and its large copper kettle, generally hissing for the feeblest tea.

We discussed all things – politics and politicians, theology and theologians, notably (when their turn came) the Church Reform pamphlet of 1833 and the Thirlwall controversy of 1834. His own prize compositions, which I used to write out for him, furnished a fruitful subject. School politics, at times somewhat revolutionary, were treated as moral matters, with a little too much (it may be) of grown-up sternness. [3]

Their hero, Thomas Arnold, was clear about what he wanted the school to offer, namely a truly Christian education. In a letter to J.T. Coleridge, one of his closest friends from student days, he wrote: 'what we must look for here is 1st, religious and moral principle; 2ndly gentlemanly conduct, 3rdly intellectual ability.'[4] Priorities that he surely communicated to his praeposters [prefects] for he longed to share his own love of truth and goodness with them and the whole school. He hoped to achieve this great end by his own example and teaching, by the trust he placed in his assistant staff, and by his reform of the prefectorial system. His personal influence was seen notably in the chapel for whose ministry he persuaded the Trustees to appoint him Chaplain after Anstey had resigned the post. He applied at the same time to be allowed to introduce a continental disciplinary practice, namely solitary confinement for certain offences. This would have required special rooms to be built for the purpose but the Trustees refused to allow such a punishment to be tried in an English public school.[5] Both orders were passed by them on the same date: 25 October 1831.

In his letter of application for the Chaplaincy, he stressed its importance:

> Whoever is chaplain, I must ever feel myself as headmaster, the real and proper religious instructor of the boys. No one else can feel the same interest in them, and no one else (I am not speaking of myself personally, but merely by virtue of my situation) can speak to them with so much influence. In fact it seems to me the natural and fitting thing, and the great advantage of having a separate chapel for the school – that the Master of the boys should be officially as well as really their pastor, and that he should not devolve on another, however well qualified, one of his most peculiar and solemn duties.[6]

So began his practice of preaching to the assembled school each Sunday afternoon at four. C.J. wrote of his friend Stanley's devotion to Arnold the preacher 'No temptation of pleasure, no almost compulsion of illness, could make him an absentee from the joy and pride of his week.' As he mounted the steps of the pulpit, the two friends 'nudged each other with delight' in anticipation of what was to come. These boys were exceptional. For most schoolboys a sermon, even a relatively short one, was normally something to be endured rather than enjoyed, yet Stanley in his *Life* maintained that Arnold's sermons touched more than just the pious few:

> Even the most careless boys would sometimes, during the course of the week, refer almost involuntarily to the sermon of the past Sunday, as a

condemnation of what they were doing. Some, whilst they wonder how it was that so little practical effect was produced upon them at the time, yet retain the recollection, (to give the words of one who so describes himself,) that "I used to listen to them from first to last with a kind of awe, and over and over again could not join my friends at the Chapel door, but would walk home to be alone; and I remember the same effects being produced by them, more or less, on others, whom I should have thought as hard as stones, and on whom I think Arnold looked as some of the worst boys in the school." [7]

Thomas Hughes, author of *Tom Brown's Schooldays* and himself a pupil at Rugby from 1834-42, tried to analyse what it was about the Master which so caught and held the attention of the three hundred boys:

We couldn't enter into half that we heard; we hadn't the knowledge of our own hearts or the knowledge of one another; and little enough of the faith, hope, and love needed to that end. But we listened, as all boys in their better moods will listen . . . to a man who we felt to be, with all his heart and soul and strength, striving against whatever was mean and unmanly and unrighteous in our little world. It was not the cold clear voice of one giving advice and warning from serene heights to those who were struggling and sinning below, but the warm living voice of one who was fighting for us and by our sides, and calling on us to help him and ourselves and one another. And so, wearily and little by little, but surely and steadily on the whole, was brought home to the young boy, for the first time, the meaning of his life: that it was no fool's or sluggard's paradise into which he had wandered by chance, but a battle field ordained from of old, where there are no spectators, but the youngest must take his side, and the stakes are life and death. [8]

Written usually between the morning and afternoon services of the day with the ink barely dry on the last page, Arnold addressed his young charges in a direct and forceful style – in his own words 'in the language of common life and applied to the cases of modern life.' He returned again and again in his preaching to the twin themes of the evils and vices of public school life, and to the goodness that God wishes to see replace them in the lives of the boys. He had willing converts in boys such as Charles Vaughan, Arthur Stanley and Charles Lake. Here is an extract from one of his sermons to the boys which illustrates both his forthright style and its practical content:

But it may be asked, what is meant when public schools are called "the seats and nurseries of vice?" It is not difficult to find out in what sense a Christian writer must have used the expression. That is properly a nursery of vice, where a boy unlearns the pure and honest principles which he may have received at home, and gets, in their stead, others which are utterly low, and base, and mischievous, - where he loses his modesty, his respect for truth, and his affectionateness, and becomes coarse, and false, and unfeeling. That, too, is a nursery of vice, and most fearfully so, where vice is bold, and forward, and presuming; and goodness is timid and shy, and existing as if by sufferance, - where the good, instead of setting the tone of society, and branding with disgrace those who disregard it, are themselves exposed to reproach for their goodness, and shrink before the open avowal of evil principles, which the bad are striving to make the law of the community. That is a nursery of vice, where the restraints laid upon evil are considered as so much taken from liberty, and where, generally speaking, evil is more willingly screened and concealed, than detected and punished. [9]

Arnold saw it too as part of his vocation as Master and Chaplain to prepare the boys for Confirmation, though he shared this responsibility with other House Masters. Holy Communion was celebrated just four times a year and, at first, the only ones to attend were some of the Sixth Form, but Arnold encouraged and invited serious minded boys in all parts of the school to come. Stanley reckoned that occasionally 'a hundred and never less than seventy' out of the three hundred boys attended.

Sundays were thick with religious instruction of one kind or another – hardly a 'day of rest' but the boys were, at least, allowed an extra hour in bed in the morning. One of them described a typical Sunday:

At 8.30 in the morning we have prayers, and after that breakfast, after which I learn the gospel, or that and a psalm for first lecture which is at 10. At 11 I go to chapel, which lasts till about 12, when I walk till dinner (1) with G.P. After dinner I prepare 2nd lecture, which is 3 or 4 chapters of the Bible, till 3, when we go in to 2nd lecture: 2nd chapel at 4, after which I have tea, and from tea till ¼ to eight I have to myself. After prayers I prepare 1st lesson for next day out of the New Test. in Greek, which does not take me long, and I have from 9 till 10 for reading. [10]

For many a boy Sunday must have been a dreadfully dull day, but not so for all. Henry Watson Fox who was just a few weeks younger than C.J. wrote several letters from Rugby to his older brother and sister between 1833 and '36. They all reveal his intensely religious character; here is an extract from one, dated 7 April 1834, in which he shares with his sister Isabella his feelings about Sunday:

> I always find the Sunday too short for what I want to do on it. I therefore intend to make another day of the week like Sunday, and, except my lessons, read and think of nothing save God only . . . Last Sunday was a most beautiful day, and I took a walk by myself into the country, and never felt so happy before. I continued for more than an hour praising and praying to God, and thanking Him. I shall never neglect it again. I felt it as a preparation for heaven. [11]

This boy had even written his own 20 point *Subjects for Self-Examination* which dealt almost entirely with his devotional life rather than with any moral shortcomings – point 14 being the exception: 'Have I yielded to temptation?' After Rugby he went to Wadham College Oxford, was then ordained and went as a missionary to the Telugu people in South India, dying at the early age of 31. Clearly a pupil whose Christian character formed at home was further influenced by Arnold and by other members of his staff.

Previous to Arnold's coming, some of the staff had added to their salary as Assistant Masters by holding a small parochial charge locally as well. He insisted they made their work in school their chief concern. "No parochial ministry" he would say to them "can be more properly a cure of souls than yours." [12] For this reason too he wanted them to take responsibility for the boys' welfare outside the classroom and appointed them as resident House Masters and thereby increased their remuneration. He encouraged them to add to their knowledge and improve their skills as he himself did. Every three weeks he held a council at which all school matters were discussed and colleagues were free to express their opinions. With their aid his educational ideal might become a reality. Accordingly he took great care over appointments, which were subject to the consent of the Trustees. He was clear about what to look for in a man: 'What I want is a man who is a Christian and a gentleman – an active man, and one who has common sense and understands boys . . . I prefer activity of mind and an interest in his work to high scholarship, for the one can be acquired more easily than the other.' [13]

The first was Bonamy Price, a former pupil of his at Laleham. Price who had taken a double First at Worcester College Oxford joined him in 1830 and stayed at Rugby for 20 years before becoming Professor of Political Economy at Oxford. Three of his other assistants became Headmasters – James Prince Lee at King Edward's School, Birmingham, who later became Bishop of Manchester, G.E.L. Cotton at Marlborough, who became Bishop of Calcutta, and H. Hill at Warwick School. Lee was a Fellow of Trinity and considered the finest classical tutor in the college; he joined Arnold's staff in 1830 and stayed for eight years taking charge of the Fifth Form. Professor C.E. Vaughan, believed that his uncle, C.J., owed much to his dealings with Lee and Price. A letter written by C.J. in 1836 makes mention of these two in particular. His uncle, Sir Charles, had written to him asking for information about the school on behalf of a friend who was thinking of sending her son there but who had some concerns, particularly about the sleeping arrangements. C.J. answered:

> I think the expences of Rugby will be found to be, in practice, a hundred a year, <u>without</u> private Tutor, the expence of which is ten pounds a year more for a boy in the Upper School. I think this states the amount of actual expence at the highest ; and it is possible that rather less might be found sufficient. The Scholars live at different houses in the Town, which are now almost entirely <u>Masters'</u> houses – as the old boarding houses kept by private persons are discouraged by Dr Arnold, and fast dwindling away. The School House, over which D^r A himself presides, but which I don't think possesses any advantages over others, contains sixty Boys, and two other Houses forty each – the rest fewer. Every Boy has a separate bed, but not generally a separate room – in the School House one or two rooms contain fourteen beds – but they are singularly airy and clean. In the other Houses the number of beds in a room varies, perhaps from three to ten – six or five being about the average. But if I remember right, the two Wynn's were allowed a room by themselves at Mr Lee's House where perhaps you remember my going with you to call upon them. He is also a most excellent Private Tutor – and it strikes me that if Lady Webster were anxious to get a single room for her son, Mr Lee would be the person of all others <u>inclined</u> to accede to such a request. I do not know whether he could manage to do so but I am sure that he would, if he could. Mr Price is also an admirable Private Tutor – but his House being one of those which contains forty boys whereas Mr Lee's certainly does not accommodate more than twenty, might possibly make it in a Mother's sight less desirable. Both of them are very gentlemanly as well as learned and talented men. The School is full – upwards of three hundred are now there. Therefore application should be made early for admission, to Dr Arnold, even though it were not intended that he should go immediately.
>
> The hours at Rugby are early - School begins at 7 in the morning during the greater part of the year – at half past seven in the depths of winter – Dinner about one – School ends for the day at six – After dark the boys are not allowed to leave their respective Boarding Houses – Ten is bed time but anyone can go earlier – and many do. Sunday is well occupied – Two

Scripture Lessons, morning and afternoon – the full Morning Prayers in the Chapel; and the Prayers, with an excellent Sermon from Dr Arnold himself in the afternoon. Every Morning the School meets for short prayers in the great School, before work begins.

The Boys are divided into more than ten Classes – each attended to by a separate Master – Dr A. taking the 6th – the highest – himself. The Boys are placed on going there (after a little Examination in what they have before read) in the Form which their Tutor judges most adapted to their powers: and they are removed from time to time into higher Forms, as they get on in the work of their former one.

My paper is filled – but I shall be most glad to send you another sheet of information about Rugby if it is wanted. Meanwhile I hope this will be partly satisfactory. Thank you for your kind congratulations.

Ever believe me

Your affec^te Nephew Charles J. Vaughan [14]

The influence these new Assistant Masters had on boys was illustrated by Thomas Hughes in the conversation between his hero, Tom Brown, and his tutor after the last cricket match, when the latter explained how Arnold had effected change in the school and how he cared for him personally:

It was a new light to him to find that, besides teaching the sixth, and governing and guiding the whole School, editing classics and writing histories, the great headmaster had found time in those busy years to watch over the career even of him, Tom Brown, and his particular friends, and, no doubt, of fifty other boys at the same time, and all this without taking the least credit to himself, or seeming to know, or let anyone else know, that he ever thought particularly of any boy at all. [15]

Arnold depended even more on his praeposters, who were closest to the mass of pupils and could be effective role models for the younger boys. Other schools, like Rugby, had long had prefects who were expected to keep order, prevent bullying and punish those deemed to be behaving improperly: drinking spirits, frequenting pubs, smoking and the like. To this end they had the power to cane boys below the Fifth Form. Arnold's praeposters did all this but they were also given a nobler role. They were to be fellow workers with him in creating a Christian society, and so were to be attentive to the religious and moral health of the school. As one of them wrote: 'In effect the Sixth Form were to set the tone of the school.'[16] This could be a heavy burden on young shoulders as another of them reflected later – 'Every Sixth Form Rugbeian was bound under

50

Arnold's auspices to come of age in his teens, and to wield the sceptre placed by the great headmaster in his hands, with a solemn self-esteem too apt to degenerate for a season into priggish self-importance.'[17] His system was further flawed in another way. As Reeve has noted 'it was a sad but desirable necessity that praeposters should have brawn as well as brain.'[18] A diminutive sixth former, however intellectually able, who was not also a natural leader could cause the system to totter. A truth that Arnold did not really face up to: 'his implicit confidence in their ability to uphold discipline was frequently maintained in the face of evidence to the contrary.'[19]

One of C.J.'s school fellows recalled an incident in which that young praeposter exercised his powers. C.J. had come across a small boy disobeying an order of Arnold's which forbad angling in the nearby river. Having calmly asked him if he had enjoyed good sport, his eyes fixed on a willow with long and supple branches. "Will you please cut that stick and give it to me?" The culprit tremblingly complied. There then followed 'a dramatic object lesson on the sin of disobedience.'[20] Whether the same would have happened had the culprit been a big, strong fourth former is open to doubt.

Flogging of younger boys was retained by Arnold but was confined to moral offences 'such as lying, drinking and habitual idleness.' Lying to masters was regarded as a great moral offence in Arnold's eyes though a natural enough means of self-defence in a young boy's. To them he was a forbidding, disciplinarian who ruled by fear. The rod was still, in his eyes, a potent and proper means of enforcing obedience – obedience in learning school lessons and in conforming to the standard of behaviour he required of them. His hatred of lies, however, caused him at times to over-react. Even Stanley in his *Life* admitted that when Arnold paid one of his occasional visits to a younger class 'the chief impression was of extreme fear', though he could, conversely, be gentle and tender with the youngest boys, letting them sit on his lap as he questioned them. One day in 1832 when visiting Mr Bird's class to test the boys on some work he had been told they had prepared, he asked one of them, Thomas Gonne March, to construe a passage from Xenophon's *Anabasis*. The boy protested that this was not part of the work set. Arnold did not believe him and grew increasingly angry. He did not bother to check with the rest of the class who would have been fearful of answering him anyway. He sent a message to Bird asking him to confirm what work had been set, and he, mistakenly, put the boy in the wrong. Arnold double-checked with Bird alerting him that his answer would decide whether or not a pupil would be birched. Bird repeated his mistake, thus making the boy appear to be lying. Arnold was furious, calling him a liar, and gave him eighteen strokes of the birch in front of the class – an unusually severe flogging (Wooll had never given more than twelve strokes) particularly as the boy was young and sickly. He was off school sick for two days which Arnold regarded as malingering and punished him with extra work on his return. Later it transpired that the boy had told the truth and the Headmaster was in the wrong. He apologised both privately and publicly but such a display of violent anger had revealed an uglier side to Arnold's character.[21] Nor was this particular display of temper an isolated one as the nicknames 'Tiger Tom' and 'Black Tom', given him by the boys, possibly indicate, though the word 'Tiger' may have referred to his restless energy and 'Black' simply to his black hair and side whiskers.

The March affair was taken up by the Tory *Northampton Herald*, ever ready to depict Arnold as a sadistic tyrant unfit to be in charge of boys, which published an inaccurate account. He wrote to the Governors stating that he had used a 'worn-out' birch (i.e. a less painful instrument), hence the larger than usual number of strokes. Unpublished correspondence reveals that the boy's parents, far from wishing to withdraw him from the school, assured Arnold they were happy for him to continue to be under his care. [22]

One wonders what young admirers such as Stanley made of this at the time because it was in that very same year, 1832, that the three future Deans of Westminster, Llandaff and Durham: Stanley, Vaughan and Lake, became the 'Doctor's Disciples' and determined to further his aims in the school. They were not the first to do this. Fifteen year old Spencer Thornton entered the school the year Arnold arrived and was from the first a faithful Evangelical and evangelizing pupil who was confirmed the following year by Bishop Ryder. His biographer wrote of him, 'From this time he became a marked character in the school as a religious boy, visiting the poor in the town and neighbourhood of Rugby, distributing tracts, and labouring earnestly for the conversion of his school fellows.' [23] His parish visiting was done with Arnold's knowledge and blessing. In a letter home to his mother dated 4 November 1830, he told her 'It is now known by the boys that I give tracts, &c. They do not laugh at me as much as I expected.'[24] C.J. was among those he influenced – in 1850 when Thornton died, C.J. wrote to the mother of his old school-fellow:

One thing I remember – his habit of rising early to secure time for devotion before the first lesson began (and this was at seven); and I recollect his saying to me one day, how much he felt ashamed at seeing some poor tradesman already at his day's labour in his shop, before he had begun his morning worship. He said something about our caring so much less for our souls than a poor tradesman did for perishable goods.

His great object seemed to me to find out boys whose minds were capable of being led into good, either from early impressions, or from circumstances of affliction, &c at the time. But he was very *unobtrusive*, I think, also, in carrying out his object, and would not force advice on those who shrank from receiving it. [25]

Arnold wrote to his parents on the boy's leaving in 1832:

My obligations to your son are great, for he has done good to the school to an extent that cannot be calculated, and has left some behind him, I trust, who will follow his steps. It is far beyond all common congratulations to be blessed with such a son; and for myself, it will be a delight to me to see him, and to know him in his future progress through life. May we meet at last beyond it. [26]

If Thornton represents those whose childhood faith had been nurtured and whose Christian character was strengthened under Arnold, there were clearly others of a different mind who resisted him. Albert Pell (later MP for South Leicestershire) was admitted in the year Thornton left and he has recalled that the habits and practices of the school were extremely irregular when he arrived:

Smoking and drink were general. I remember a song (in which I joined) commencing with
        I'm a Rugby scholar and of a Rugby class,
        And by the wrinkles on my face have tippled many a glass,
and so on to other enormities. Some big boy would take me over to the Cock on the road to Dunchurch, and there, having spent our money on some abominable punch, we proceeded to a coaching inn at Dunchurch to await the arrival of the Manchester coaches . . .[27]

where he was then instructed to gibe at inoffensive drab-coated Quaker merchants as they left the coach! Drinking, bullying and such uncouth behaviour as Pell describes were never eradicated in the school despite Arnold's best efforts.

It seems that Agnes Vaughan was aware of this darker side to life at Rugby for she wrote to her brother in 1832 about the possibility of

Edwyn and Luther going to Rugby but feared the evils of the place. 'I look for evil in every situation. I find it at home. I know it is great at Rugby – the conviction drives me to my only refuge – confidence in God – to keep them in the midst of it, or if they fall into it to bring them out again in penitence and faith.' [28] She was also concerned about the cost though Thomas Pares had already told her not to worry as he would meet it.

As Thornton left for Cambridge, Vaughan, Stanley and Lake entered the Sixth and came under Arnold's immediate influence. George Rawlinson in a biographical essay on Lake has described its effect:

> The three boys formed a sort of triumvirate during the period in question, governing the school under their revered head, consorting almost exclusively with each other, and giving the tone to their entire body politic – a tone, it is almost needless to say, at once moral, religious and highly intellectual. On one occasion a contemplated rebellion, to which large numbers of boys had committed themselves, was stopped and averted mainly by the conjoint efforts of the three friends, who 'pointed out the folly of resistance, and brought the turbulent majority to reason and submission.' (Prothero's *Life of Stanley* Vol. 1 p.69) It is not too much to say that the lofty ideal of public school life first conceived by Arnold was fully shared in by his friends, and that it was greatly by their aid that he was enabled to bring the entire school into that excellent moral and intellectual condition which caused it to be held up for many years, in and after Arnold's time, as a model to other similar institutions. [29]

Rawlinson's claim that 'the entire school' lived by Arnold's ideal is surely an exaggeration as the memoirs of other old boys show all too clearly. G.G. Bradley (later Dean of Westminster) relates from his years there, 'By slow degrees a far higher tone of duty and morality on many essential points filtered slowly downwards into the mass of the school . . . indeed, the direct change of atmosphere worked by Arnold at Rugby at large was, I venture to think, rather moral than intellectual; certainly a too large proportion of Rugby boys in my own days looked on mental work of all kinds as an odious necessity, and characterized it by one expressive and contemptuous syllable.' [30] But to serious-minded boys such as this trio his power was awesome. In Lake's later judgement :

> On the whole, in the power of winning young spirits to love him and to love goodness for his sake, Arnold, as master of Rugby, can hardly be overrated. Nothing weak or inconsistent, no vanity or passion, ever marred the impression of his ability, his simple and manly earnestness, his high standard of duty, his devotion to what he felt was his appointed work.

54

> What wonder that many were formed upon his character and in a measure grew into it, looking on him with a mixed feeling of admiration and awe, as a father, teacher, friend, which no changes in after-years could alter! [31]

Another distinguished old boy, Alexander Arbuthnot who was the orphan son of an Irish bishop, had similar memories of his seven years under Arnold: 'the daily intercourse [i.e. during his two years in the Sixth form] with the great Headmaster made an impression upon me which no lapse of time has been able to efface. When I left Rugby as a boy of seventeen I had formed the opinion that Dr Arnold was the most high-minded man I had ever met.'[32]

Not all pupils remembered Arnold in this way, even ones who admired what he had achieved at Rugby and were proud of him. Frederick Mather who was a contemporary of Thomas Hughes at Rugby wrote in old age:

> I think anyone reading Stanley would gather that the boys at Rugby were ruled by love. This was not so – They were ruled by high respect and by fear. Arnold was to them Black Tom, as he was called. We shivered when he took the form. Hoping for 'Thank You' and dreading his 'Sit down.' He succeeded in making the boys study for themselves, reading books on the subject of their lessons. Leaving them free to make their own choice. His strong Radicalism made us Tories. [33]

Bonamy Price analysed Arnold's influence differently – 'Every pupil was made to feel that there was *a work for him to do* – that his happiness as well as his duty lay in doing that work well. Hence an indescribable zest was communicated to a young man's feelings about life; a strange joy came over him on discovering he had the means of being useful.' [34] Arnold's influence for good stayed with them after they left Rugby. An American who met many of them at Cambridge in the 1840s commented very favourably on the Master's influence: 'They were men of great weight and character; they seemed to have been really taught to think on ethical as well as purely intellectual subjects better than any set of young men I ever knew; they had better grounds for their belief, and always appeared to have looked into the reason of what they said and did, and to go back to first principles. Their veneration for Arnold's memory was unbounded. . .'[35]

If this trio, in particular, was moulded by Arnold, they also influenced one another enormously. Later in life, however, Lake realised that it had not all been gain in their friendship:

Certainly in most respects, no life could have been more happy than that which many of us spent at Rugby. But, especially to some who were naturally fond of games, it was rather prematurely intellectual. Thus nothing could be closer than the friendship of Stanley, Vaughan, and myself, but to me it was the loss of what had been my earliest friends, the cricket ground and football. These I gave up almost as a matter of course when I became an intimate friend of Stanley; and there were very few days when he, Charles Vaughan, and myself did not spend our spare hours in long walks and talks – a great mistake, and one which in after-life I have often bitterly regretted. [36]

Not so with Stanley and Vaughan, neither of whom had any liking for or enjoyed any prowess in the team games played at Rugby. Though they would have played football as every boy was required to do, for them the excitement and glory to be won in the annual football match between School House and the rest of the school, so colourfully described in *Tom Brown's Schooldays*, was a non-event. Their happiness and success lay in their mutual devotion to Arnold and in the string of prizes which they both won under his tuition. Their emotional energy was invested in the Arnoldian ideal they shared and in their relationship with each other. The closeness of their friendship is to be seen in the series of letters which Stanley began in June 1832 when he was 16 and Vaughan a year younger. Already then he recorded his debt to his friend who had taught him his first lesson in the difficult task of attaching himself 'deeply or long to anyone outside his own family.' [37] How much Vaughan meant to him is evident from letters he wrote to him shortly before leaving school – the sentiments expressed were undoubtedly reciprocated – but the letters also reveal that there had been areas of personal experience they had not ventured to share. Stanley wrote:

> If I have been any use to you, I am most thankful for it; will you believe me also when I thank you for all the good you have been to me? I hope you will not find that you have been leaning on a broken reed in trusting to me. Surely – I speak it out of the abundance of the simple truth – you must have seen over and over again, and the more, I should think, as compared with yourself, my extraordinary want of energy and real strength of character. For this I assure you I do look up to you most entirely . . . I have never ventured, very much as I have wished, to speak to you of your father. I should very much like to see the sermons you speak of – and now that I have lost my poor uncle who was a father to me in the few times I saw him, and would have been much more to me when I should have known him better. I feel that we have something in common. [38]

Later he wrote:

> Six Sundays more, and only six. Alas! Alas! I never in the days of my first coming wished so earnestly for the arrival of the holidays as I now dread it! Oh, may God grant you strength and health, that I may carry on to that last hour that association of almost perfect happiness which I have so often enjoyed here, and that as I trust we have begun, so may we end together in the service of Christ . . . Most sincerely must I thank God for his goodness in placing me here to live with Arnold. Yet I always feel that the happiness is a dangerous one, and that loving him and admiring him as I do to the very verge of all love and admiration that can be paid to man, I fear I have passed the limit, and made him my idol, and that in all I may be but serving God for man's sake . . . You too love him and admire him as much as he deserves – but not more, and not dangerously, and you can help me – I would hardly say to love him less – but to love God more. And now believe me, my dear Vaughan,
>
> Yours ever affectionately, A.P.S. [39]

C.J. had an outer circle of four younger friends too: John Simpkinson, who followed him to Cambridge in 1835 and who joined him later at Harrow as an Assistant Master; John Gell, who also joined him at Trinity in '35 and, on Arnold's recommendation, later became the first Principal of a secondary college in Tasmania; Thomas Burbidge, who became Master of Leamington College; and Arthur Hugh Clough, a very gifted boy, three years his junior, who warmly admired him. Simpkinson succeeded Stanley as Head of School House and Clough followed him. It was Clough who also inherited the mantle of the trio's moral leadership in the school after they had left for university and who frequently sent them news of what was happening at Rugby.

These boys enjoyed their years with Arnold not least because he himself so manifestly enjoyed teaching them and sought to create in them an appetite for learning. In Lake's words 'He inoculated us with his likings for his favourite books and characters, for Thucydides and Tacitus, for Alexander, and for some of the earlier Romans like Scipio, and history dislikes for Caesar and Augustus; and when we came to his modern history lectures, there were no characters which he taught us more to admire than some of the religious characters of the Middle Ages such as St Louis of France and Pope Innocent III.' [40] Arnold's joy in language is expressed in this extract from a letter which he wrote to Vaughan a year after he had left – 'I have begun the *Phaedo* of Plato with the Sixth, which will be a great delight to me. There is an actual pleasure in contemplating so perfect a management of so perfect an instrument as is exhibited in Plato's language, even if the matter were as worthless as the words of Italian music; whereas the sense is only less admirable in many places than the language.' [41] This love of the niceties and nuances of the Greek language he had successfully imparted to his former pupil.

He began each day with the Sixth Form in the same way – with a prayer of his own composition and one that reflected his own mind and attitude as a teacher as much as what he prayed would be their attitude as pupils. For him, both the work of a teacher and that of a pupil were a form of service to God and therefore to be done to the best of one's ability:

O Lord, Who by Thy holy Apostle, hast taught us to do all things in the name of the Lord Jesus and to Thy glory, give Thy blessing, we pray Thee, to this our daily work, that we may do it in faith, and heartily, as to the Lord and not unto men. All our powers of body and mind are Thine, and we would fain devote them to Thy service. Sanctify them and the work in which they are engaged; let us not be slothful, but fervent in spirit, and do Thou, O Lord, so bless our efforts that they may bring forth in us the fruits of true wisdom. Strengthen the faculties of our minds and dispose us to exert them, but let us always remember to exert them for Thy glory, and for the furtherance of Thy kingdom, and save us from all pride, and vanity, and reliance upon our own power or wisdom. Teach us to seek after truth and enable us to gain it; but grant that we may ever speak the truth in love: - that, while we know earthly things, we may know Thee, and be known by Thee, through and in Thy Son Jesus Christ. Give us this day Thy Holy Spirit, that we may be Thine in body and Spirit, in all our work and all our refreshments, through Jesus Christ, Thy Son, our Lord. Amen. [42]

We know the curriculum and timetable at Rugby during C.J.'s years there as Arnold himself contributed an article about them to the *Quarterly Journal of Education* in 1834. There was a total of 20 periods a week ranging in duration from one to two hours – 16 of them were used for Classics, Scripture and History, and the remaining four went to Mathematics and Modern Languages. Greek and Latin dominated the curriculum - a good deal of ancient history was studied in the original languages of the Greek and Roman authors, and part of the scripture teaching was on the Greek text of the New Testament. Arnold maintained that the task of translation into a style of English appropriate to the original was important in developing linguistic skills and fluency of expression in their own native tongue. Arbuthnot remembered this aspect of Arnold's method with great appreciation:

> Instead of being content with the prevailing practice of construing sentence by sentence from Greek or Latin into English, he accustomed the boys in the "Twenty" and the Sixth to read out paragraphs and sometimes pages from the classical authors into idiomatic English, thus making the lesson serve the double purpose of testing the pupil's acquaintance with the meaning of the classical passage, and of his ability to compose it in his own language. [43]

Above all, Arnold aimed to stimulate his pupils to acquire knowledge for themselves and he encouraged them to express their own views, so his method of teaching was largely by way of questioning. He preferred a boy to find out things for himself and to formulate his own opinion. 'I call that the best theme,' he wrote, 'which shows that a boy has read and thought for himself; that the next best, which shows that he has read several books, and digested what he has read; and that the worst, which shows that he has followed but one book, and followed that without reflection.' [44] Terence Copley, Arnold's most recent biographer, believes that what made him so different in the classroom from many of his contemporaries was his treatment of the classics as a means to an end: 'The classics were means of exploring history, poetry, philosophy, linguistics, ethics and aesthetics.' [45] An earlier writer commented similarly:

> The most important reforms in intellectual training that Arnold made were in the spirit in which he taught the classics. Though he clung to composition and mind-training through grammar, he concentrated, as had not been done for hundreds of years, on the content of the classics . . . He taught them for the moral ideas in them applicable to modern times. This meant that he encouraged comparisons with the present, and cared much more for idiomatic translations than he did for the dissection of construing . . . the classics thus served Arnold as instruments for moral teaching and mental stimulation, the two purposes that he had most at heart. [46]

Of course, not all pupils appreciated this or shared his love of the classics and many dreaded the regular examinations which determined their places in the school. Bradley relates how 'Three times a week the great majority of the school inked their fingers and bewildered their brains in composing what was called a "vulgus"; a certain number, from two to eight, of Latin verses on a given subject. Sturdy beggars, sometimes, like stalwart tramps, with a minatory importunity, met those who had a facility in such matters, and asked or demanded contributions in kind.'[47]

Arnold's way of teaching Scripture in the Sixth, which Stanley described in his *Life*, seems to have had a lasting influence on C.J. as elements of it re-appear in the style of his earliest sermons:

> In the Sixth Form, besides the lectures on Sunday, he introduced two lectures on the Old and the New Testament in the course of the week, so that a boy who remained there three years would often have read through a great part of the New Testament, much of the Old Testament, and especially of the Psalms in the Septuagint version, and also committed much of them to memory; whilst at times he would deliver lectures on the history of the early Church, or of the English Reformation. In these lessons on the Scriptures, he would insist much on the importance of familiarity with the very words of the sacred writers, and of the exact place where passages occurred; on a thorough acquaintance with the different parts of the story contained in the several Gospels, that they might be referred to at once; on the knowledge of the times when, and the person to whom, the Epistles were written . . . Whatever dogmatical instruction he gave was conveyed almost entirely in a practical or exegetical shape; and it was very rarely indeed that he made any allusion to existing parties or controversies within the Church of England.[48]

Stanley is making an important point here for Arnold's radical views (particularly about improving the living conditions of the poor and his attacks on the wealthy who exploited them) expressed in articles in the *Sheffield Courant* were not well received by parents or by the school's Trustees. The Head always insisted that he did not try to influence his pupils in such matters, though it was inevitable that older pupils would have been aware of his views.

To his Sixth Formers, Arnold chose to be a familiar guide and mentor rather than a dogmatic master, even allowing them a measure of informality in the classroom. His best pupils, it seems, received special treatment. Sir John Hoskyns who was a contemporary of C.J.'s at Rugby recorded how Arnold treated the trio in the Sixth:

> What struck me was the way in which Arnold referred to them in matters of criticism or points of history. "Stanley, what do you think about that?" "Vaughan, how would you construe that?" – folding his gown and leaning upon the table and looking towards them with such <u>respect</u>, shown in the very tones of his voice, and always getting a good answer. Then after their construes – very often in the most difficult bits of Aeschylus or Thucydides

– "Very good" – and not like the cold "that will do", or terrible "sit down, and come to me afterwards" – words which more than once made me quake.[49]

Thomas Hughes has given us the fullest picture of life there as seen through an average boy's eyes in his novel *Tom Brown's Schooldays*. Though his trio of heroes, Tom, Harry East and George Arthur were very different from Vaughan, Stanley and Lake, there is much in the story of those three fictional boys' friendship and experiences which reflects school life at the time of the real trio. Hughes tells too of the vices which Arnold so hated to see in that schoolboy community – the bullying and laziness, the dishonesty and use of crib sheets, the fear of standing up for what was right and giving a moral lead, and he even hints at unmentionable vices in the relationship of certain older boys who befriended younger ones – 'little pretty, white handed, curly headed boys' who learnt very bad ways from their older protectors.

To many of the boys Arnold was and remained throughout their school life a distant and forbidding figure (both Vaughan and Stanley had felt that at first). He exercised a searching discipline and, with a ruthless streak in him, was not averse to expelling boys or encouraging parents to withdraw sons who, in his judgement, were not suited to Rugby and who could be better helped elsewhere – a practice known as the 'super-annuation of unpromising subjects.' Reeve explains this term: 'It was a device by which he could remove those older boys who were not benefiting from the school or who were, or were likely to become, adverse influences upon their fellows. Such youths were often quietly removed at the end of a half year; no stigma was attached to them, to all intents they had simply been removed by their parents.'[50] 'Till a man learns that the first, second and third duty of a schoolmaster is to get rid of unpromising subjects, a great public school,' Arnold said, 'will never be what it might be and what it ought to be.'[51] His policy inevitably led to many private and public complaints about his treatment of individual boys. On one occasion, after his expulsion of a number of boys had provoked dissent among their fellow pupils, he stood his ground before the assembled school and told them – 'It is not necessary that this should be a school of three hundred, or one hundred, or of fifty boys; but it is necessary that it should be a school of Christian gentlemen.'[52] C.J. and his two close friends epitomised this. Of the three, Lake claimed to know Arnold best, Stanley was acknowledged to be his favourite – the 'hero pupil' (Vaughan's phrase) of the 'hero schoolmaster' (Lake's phrase), and Vaughan was arguably his most brilliant protégé who emulated his master when he in turn became the Headmaster of a great school. Lake summed up the lasting benefits that Arnold's character and influence conferred on the trio and on other boys like them:

> I should say, in two words, that he impressed upon us above everything the *blessing of high ideals* and of decided convictions. His ideal of Christianity, his ideal of Christ's Church, his ideals of great historical characters were all such as gave a noble view of life; and if they might be called exaggerated, they were at all events opposed to that pseudo-moderation which often means nothing more than looking after a man's own interests. The result was that, whether we consistently acted upon them or not, those of Arnold's pupils who knew him best were never afraid of expressing their convictions, and the only characters whom they admired in life were those who had distinct and manly convictions and carried them out. [53]

W.H.D. Rouse, the author of *A History of Rugby School,* who entered the school in the same year as C.J., wrote of Arnold's influence on the boys: 'His earnestness made them earnest, and his reverence made them reverent. He taught them to love all things that are lovely and of good report, to despise what is mean and base.' [54]

Arnold further strengthened his relationship with favourite pupils by inviting them to stay with him and his family at Fox How, a small estate between Rydal and Ambleside in the Lake District. He bought the land in 1832 and built a house on it. Vaughan stayed there with him for the first time in the summer of 1833. And Arnold continued to correspond with them long after they had left and to welcome them back to stay with him at Rugby and at Fox How. The trio responded to Arnold's teaching and friendship by bringing academic honour to the school. Stanley was the first to do this when he was placed first, above Eton's best, in the open examination for a Balliol scholarship which he won at the end of December 1833. Lake repeated this feat a year later. In the meantime C.J. was entered at Trinity Cambridge where his many academic successes were marked each time at Rugby with an extra half-holiday – this happened so often that the saying was coined 'a Vaughan half'.

Arnold had greatly increased the number of prizes and scholarships in the school as an incentive to hard work. C.J.'s first publication was his final prize-winning English essay at Rugby. It ran to just 17 pages and was entitled *What symptoms of decline are exhibited by the world, both physically and morally?* The young writer did not dissent from the view expressed in the title. It was published in Leicester where, since the death of her husband five years earlier, his widowed mother with all her children and step-children had been living in a large house belonging to her father situated close to St Martin's church.

C.J. was to have one last triumph before leaving for Cambridge. The final school examinations in 1834 were conducted on behalf of the universities by Dr George Moberly of Oxford (later Bishop of Salisbury) and by Dr Christopher Wordsworth of Cambridge (son of the Master of Trinity and a future Bishop of Lincoln). Stanley and he were bracketed first equal though the former's name, being the senior of the two in school, was announced first. Stanley wrote of this occasion: 'There is all that was necessary to gratify every individual feeling of vanity; all to make me happy for Vaughan, to whom I should not at all have grudged the first place; all to make me happy for the school.' [55] And he added generously that had it not been for C.J.'s long illness before the examination, he would have most probably been placed above him.

A decade later Lake gave in a testimonial his assessment of C.J. as a pupil at Rugby:

> When I knew him best, - which was very intimately while at School, - his character was unusually formed and manly; he always acted on the highest principles, and gave promise of that strength and earnestness which has always marked him since. His practical talents, his judgment and good sense, were considered by his friends to be unrivalled; and great energy, decision, and boldness in what he thought right, combined with high ability in other respects, and with an unusual power of persuasion, gave him the strongest influence over his schoolfellows . . . I would particularly allude to the *facility* with which he mastered everything that he undertook. His scholarship seemed almost to have come to him by nature . . . [56]

A year after leaving, Stanley wrote an article for *The Rugby Magazine* about the School as 'A little World' and in it describes the feelings of a school leaver – presumably autobiographical but probably true also of his two friends, Lake and Vaughan:

> It only remains to follow the denizen of school to his final departure. None, we believe, ever took his last leave without a touch of regret – without casting "one longing, lingering, look behind." But those who have entered into, and enjoyed deeply, the interests and the pursuits of the place – who have formed friendships, and gained incalculable benefit during their sojourn, - these must feel that to be present at the last lesson – to enter for the last time the walls of the chapel – to receive the last parting charge and blessing – to take our last farewell of those to whom we owe so much, and

those whom we love so dearly – to lose the last glimpse of the trees and towers which have been the scene of all our hopes, and joys and fears – that all this has surely much of the bitterness and much of the solemnity of death. [57]

One last aspect of the relationship between these two close friends needs to be addressed especially in the light of the later allegation that C.J. had an improper sexual relationship with a boy at Harrow – namely, how physically intimate was it? Stanley was, by all accounts, a very handsome and somewhat effeminate youth and in his first term he had to endure the nickname of 'Nancy' (C.J.'s was 'Monstrous Cute' which in schoolboy parlance meant 'very clever'). C.J. certainly never forgot the physical and emotional impression made on him at his first sight of Stanley. It is inconceivable that the gross sexual misconduct which existed in other public schools (expulsion for homosexual rape was not unknown) did not also take place at Rugby in their time there and the temptation to indulge must have existed for C.J. and his friends. However, contemporaries who knew them frequently commented on Stanley's purity of character and high moral ideals which would suggest that it is unlikely they were sexually intimate. If they were, it would have been a common enough occurrence in an all-male establishment and, for most boys, just a transient stage in growing up emotionally and physically. But there is no hint of this in Stanley's extant correspondence with C.J. from that period which is hardly surprising. There are, however, frequent expressions of warm mutual affection which were not uncommon then. If their relationship was sexually repressed, that was hardly surprising in an age when adults surrounded the subject of sex with a conspiracy of silence and adolescent boys were made to feel it was a shameful and nasty subject, certainly one that their hero, Arnold, would have included in his all-encompassing phrase 'the wickedness of young boys'. That was something C.J. was bound to resist however strongly he might have been tempted by the physical attractions of this friend whom he loved so dearly.

Stanley remained his closest friend, but Arnold was to be his lasting and most influential role model. Rugby's Head was the man who helped shape his character and whose example inspired the future Head of Harrow with particular priorities and practices. Among them I list the following eight:

Arnold engaged the loyalty of his Sixth Formers, making them see that they had a moral responsibility for the welfare of younger boys – in effect they were co-workers with him as he strove for the highest good of the school. He wrote 'The authority of the Sixth Form is essential to the good of the school . . . and is to be upheld through all obstacles from within or from without . . .'[58] A view that Vaughan shared as the Head at Harrow. And both men opened their homes regularly to prefects, inviting them to dine with them, in order to get to know them better and to win their trust and loyalty.

Classical studies were and should remain the basis of intellectual teaching and when they came under attack publicly, Arnold spoke in their defence: 'The study of languages seems to me as if it was given for the very purpose of forming the human mind in youth; and the Greek and Latin languages, in themselves so perfect . . . seem the very instruments, by which this is to be effected.'[59] As far as the school curriculum was concerned, he made no major innovations at Rugby and nor did Vaughan at Harrow.

'You come here,' he said, 'not to read but to learn how to read.'[60] Arnold saw his task as not so much the transmission of gobbets of information as that of showing boys *how* to gain knowledge. Stanley records that he taught by questioning, seldom giving information except as a kind of reward for an answer – he wanted them to work out for themselves the meaning of a passage in a classical or historical text. Vaughan did likewise, though providing a more detailed linguistic commentary on the passage.

The same held true in Scripture lessons. Arnold had a deep reverence for Scripture but he was no biblical fundamentalist. He consequently regarded it as important for his pupils to be able to search out the meaning of Bible passages and relate it to their own lives. He tried to equip them to be able to exercise their own judgement in the interpretation of the Scriptures. He wanted religion to be personal for them. So, when preparing boys for Confirmation, he endeavoured to enable them to say with conviction "Christ died for *me*", instead of the general phrase, "Christ died for us."[61] That personal conviction then had to be lived out. *Orthopraxis* was as essential as orthodox belief – a frequent theme in Vaughan's preaching.

The Chapel was the scene of his greatest personal influence on every boy in the school. There he laid bare in language the boys could not fail to understand the evils of school life and held up for them to see the highest ideals as revealed in Jesus Christ. He wanted to inculcate in them an abhorrence of sin and a love for Christ.[62] And Christian ideals should lead to a life of service. Again, this was a recurring theme in Vaughan's Harrow sermons.

Stanley relates that in addition to the private conversation that Arnold had with each boy when he was preparing them for Confirmation, he also used to 'devote an hour or more in the evening to seeing each of them [i.e. Sixth Formers] alone by turns, and talking on such topics as presented themselves leading them if possible to more serious subjects.'[63] A practice which Vaughan adopted at Harrow.

He encouraged visits by any former pupils who desired to continue the relationship with him and offered advice and support in his correspondence with them. He was also generous to those in need of financial help on going up to university, seeing it as a duty of his position to share his means in this way.[64] Vaughan followed his example.

There was one last and very distinct characteristic that Arnold passed on namely that of not giving his allegiance to any human party, sect, society or cause save that of 'all good men under their Divine Head.' Whilst others labelled him a radical and extremist, he was clear in his own self-judgement: 'There is not a man in England who is less a party man than I am, for . . . no party would own me.'[65] He wrote in a letter in 1833, 'May God grant to my sons if they live to manhood, an unshaken love of truth, and a firm resolution to follow it for themselves, with an intense abhorrence of all party ties save that one tie which binds them to the party of Christ against wickedness.' [66] Along with this broad, inclusive view of the Church went an unwavering loyalty to the Church of England. His oft quoted words, 'The Church as it now stands no human power can save' were a call to make it a more lively force for good and a challenge to extend its influence, and all to be done in the name and power of Christ.[67] This was a call and a challenge which Vaughan responded to in his own effective pastoral and preaching ministry.

There was, however, one aspect of Arnold's ministry and of his father's which he seems to have deliberately chosen not to copy despite his affection and admiration for both men. He knew that these two men who had meant so much to him as a boy were subjected to a great deal of public criticism and rough verbal opposition for their strong opinions. Arnold, for example, got a public roasting for his pamphlet on Church Reform and it scuppered his chances of ever becoming a bishop, though that did not deter him from continuing to write critically on matters of church and society. Unlike Arnold, C.J. decided to keep his political opinions to himself and to steer well clear of divisive issues in the life of the church.

Arnold possibly influenced Vaughan in one other crucial way at a critical juncture in his later career, namely his decision to resign after 15 years as a headmaster. Arnold had repeatedly indicated that this was his intention. By 1840 he had also come to the conclusion that, after Rugby, a life of peace and quiet spent at Fox How would be much more preferable to life as a bishop. In regard to a bishopric he wrote: 'I neither expect it, nor should I like it as it would so sadly interfere with Fox How.'[68] The last entry Arnold penned in his personal journal on the night before he died included these lines: 'And I thank God that as far as ambition is concerned it is I trust mortified fully: I have no desire other than to step back gradually from my present place in the world, and not to rise to a higher one.' [69] Were these words in Vaughan's mind when, after 15 years at Harrow, he resigned and found a peaceful haven only then to have to face the offer and temptation of a bishopric?

Honours at Trinity College Cambridge

What might not be hoped for, if all who have undertaken the sacred office of the ministry fulfilled their engagements in the way we have described? What if all prayed the prayers instead of reading them, and laboured out of the pulpit as well as in it? If there were such exertions in every parish . . . our churches will be crowded, our sacraments thronged, our hearers edified; good institutions will be set on foot; yea, and 'our wilderness world will rejoice and blossom as the rose.'
From Charles Simeon's sermon *The Excellence of the Liturgy*

The many prizes that C.J. had won at Rugby were a foretaste of greater things to come. He had four years of glittering success at the university, following in the footsteps of his older brother Edward, who graduated BA, 29th Wrangler and 7th Classic, the year C.J. arrived there. Trinity was the largest and best-endowed of all the colleges; roughly a quarter of all the undergraduates and Fellows in the university were members of it. More important for a potential high-flyer, it had some very able Tutors and Assistant Tutors, and the study of the Classics, in which C.J. would excel, was better taught there than in any other college and had a most important place in its examinations for Scholarships and Fellowships. Trinity was regarded as one of the more liberal colleges but like all the others it retained social stratification amongst its undergraduates. The Master, Dr Christopher Wordsworth, is said to have had an exaggerated sense of his own being and authority and lived on another plane altogether, rarely meeting with the Tutors and Fellows, let alone undergraduates. An attitude reflected in some Trinity men who looked condescendingly on the students in the smaller colleges and felt: 'They, too, are God's creatures.'

At the top of the undergraduate pile were the 'noblemen' and 'fellow-commoners' who numbered about ten per cent of the student body. They had traditionally enjoyed a number of privileges (such as dining at the Fellows' table in hall) though some of these privileges had been removed at Trinity where they had been required since 1753 to attend Chapel and lectures along with all the other students. They still wore distinctive gowns, however, publicizing their higher status and they paid for the honour – expenditure of £400-800 a year was the norm. Most students were admitted as 'pensioners'. These were usually the sons of beneficed clergymen or of other well-to-do professional men. C.J. was admitted as a pensioner. Their average annual expenditure at this time would have been between £150 and £250 a year [= £16,510-27,520], which is as much as most clergymen earned in a year. It was the Pares' family money which financed him and his brothers at the university, helped by the prizes and scholarships they won.

At the bottom of the social pile were the 'sizars', sons of poor clergymen and small farmers or even of tradesmen. Some of Cambridge's greatest scholars, such as Isaac Newton and Adam Sedgwick, had begun as sizars at Trinity. They paid much lower university and college fees and benefited from certain allowances and grants. In the recent past they had had to perform some menial tasks in college and at Trinity they still ate separately and after the other students had dined. They were not allowed to forget their comparative poverty but at least their meals were free and they often ate better as they received the leftovers from the Fellows' table.

The college buildings reflected privilege and power and could not have failed to impress even the noblest of undergraduates. The Great Gate pre-dated the College itself having been the main entrance to the earlier King's Hall and was erected between 1490 and 1535. On its outer side was a statue of Henry VIII, the founder of Trinity College. Passing through the gate, the student entered Great Court (the largest of any Oxbridge college) built in the latter part of Elizabeth I's reign when Thomas Nevile was Master. Isaac Newton had had his rooms here next to the Great Gate. The Chapel was begun by Mary Tudor and finished early in the reign of Elizabeth. The Master's Lodge was mostly built by Nevile and next to it was the college Dining Hall built about 1604, described by G.M. Trevelyan as 'one of the finest examples of a great Elizabethan Hall.' It has a magnificent hammer beamed ceiling, an ornately carved screen over the entrance, Elizabethan woodwork on the Minstrels' Gallery and a full length portrait of Henry VIII (a 16th century copy of the Holbein original) at the end of the dais. Beyond the Hall lay Nevile's Court also called The Cloisters, paid for by Nevile himself. Byron had lived as an undergraduate in this court. At the far side lay the College Library designed by Sir Christopher Wren and built in 1695. It is arguably the finest building in Trinity, both inside and out. More importantly it was one of the two best stocked libraries in the university.

Adjoining Nevile's Court was the College's newest addition when C.J. went up: New Court built to provide extra sets of rooms for the steadily rising number of undergraduates. It had been proposed by Christopher Wordsworth as soon as he was appointed Master in 1820 but he had to wait a couple of years before he could persuade the Seniority to go along with his plans and partly fund its construction (1823-25) in neo-Gothic style. One of its earliest occupants was Arthur Hallam, Tennyson's great friend who often visited him there. Wordsworth's main reason for providing this much needed extra accommodation was his desire to have as many undergraduates as possible inside College walls where their behaviour might be better controlled. College records note that C.J. took over the rooms F.4 in New Court from the Hon Philip Yorke Savile at the beginning of the Easter Term 1835 for which he paid a rent of £9.6s.8d. [= £1,000]. In the Michaelmas term of 1836 he moved into F5 for which the rent was £8.13.4d. and he retained these rooms until the end of '38. In 1839 he moved to rooms in Nevile's Court for which he paid £10; he left at the end of the Lent term 1840. Living in college, however, did not guarantee peace and quiet which a reading man needed for his studies, as he was to discover when he had a noisy neighbour.

The university and its constituent colleges were still unreformed when C.J. went up. Fellows were still required to be unmarried and with few exceptions to be ordained as well. Religious tests prevented Jews and Dissenters from graduating but not from studying or sitting examinations. The curriculum was extremely narrow and the academic standard required for a pass degree was abysmally low. The university dominated the life of this small country market town whose population numbered c 22,000 in 1834 and it still sought to exercise the kind of jurisdiction in it that it had had in the Middle Ages. The issue of university privilege came under attack in 1835 with the passing of the Municipal Corporation Act and the decision to establish a town police force in 1837 which raised the questions who would pay for it and what the relationship would be between proctors and policemen. Street brawls between Town and Gown still happened when both species of law-enforcers were needed.

Calls for reform had been made since the beginning of the century in many a university sermon and in pamphlets written by past and present members of the university. Some reforms had been made but much more still needed to be done. In 1821 when Wordsworth was Vice-Chancellor he had proposed that all candidates for the degree of BA, after having passed the Senate House examinations, which were primarily in Mathematics, should be obliged to take one in Classics and Theology, qualifying for honours if passed with distinction. His plan was rejected by the Senate. The following year, the new Vice-Chancellor, Dr French the Master of Jesus College, supported by Dr Kaye the Master of Christ's, succeeded in getting a variation of the Wordsworth proposals accepted. Candidates for a pass degree would now be examined on the first two days in the elements of Mathematics as had been the practice previously, on the third day in Locke's *Essay on the Human Understanding*, Paley's *Moral Philosophy* and his *Evidences of Christianity*, and on the fourth day they would be required to translate passages from the first six books of the *Iliad* and the *Aeneid*. A Classical Tripos was also established but only those who had first gained mathematical honours were permitted to sit for it, i.e. those classed as Wranglers, Senior Optimes and Junior Optimes. This much needed widening of studies came into effect in 1824 but it was not an alternative tripos to Mathematics, simply an addition for those who desired classical honours as well.

The Senate also approved another scheme proposed by Dr French, but only after having severely criticised it. This required all undergraduates to pass in their fifth term of residence an examination in one of the Gospels or the Acts of the Apostles in Greek and in a Latin author. This very elementary test which came to be known as the 'Previous Examination' or more vulgarly the 'Little Go' could not possibly promote either classical or theological studies but it found support even amongst its critics on the principle that 'half a loaf is better than no bread' and 'get the wedge once in, better things in due time will follow.' It was introduced in the Lent Term of 1824 for those who had started at the university in 1822. Alexander Gooden, a Trinity student, who sat the examination in March 1838 described it in a letter to his mother and commented: 'it is generally voted a *bore* and in fact serves merely to frighten the determinedly idle and to interrupt the studies of the reading men. It only lasts one day and has therefore the merit of conciseness at least.' [1]

Trinity had led the way in the university in being the first college to require all its undergraduates to sit annual examinations during their first three years of residence. It was one way of ensuring that all its men did a modicum of serious study and not just those hoping to achieve honours. Each May the freshmen were examined on the Classical authors who had been their lecture room subjects for that year and on 1st Year Mathematics. In C.J.'s first year they were the *Eumenides*, the first book of Thucydides, Cicero's *Oration pro Planco*, the first 6 books of Euclid, Arithmetic, Algebra and Trigonometry. The higher years were similarly examined. It all happened over a period of four days with two examinations being held each day from 9 a.m. to 1 p.m. and from 4 to 8 p.m. The venue was the dining hall – dinner was brought forward from 4 to 2 p.m. and at night supper was specially put on as well. C.J. came 2nd in the 1st Class in his Freshman's year scoring 1656 points. His friend Burbidge scored only 1015 and was placed in the 2nd Class. These College examinations had the added benefit that it prepared men for the more important Mathematical Tripos ones which were held in January, and for the Classical honours papers in February or March of a student's 11th term. Keen reading men, especially Foundation Scholars, often remained in residence in the long vacation to continue their studies privately. There was nothing to distract them during those weeks, no noisy sports-men or inebriated 'fast' men, no lectures, and they could read in peace on their own for as long as they liked each day and enjoy a couple of hours relaxation with like-minded students in the evenings.

Almost all formal instruction was given in the separate colleges by the Tutors and by the Lecturers whom they had appointed to assist them but this was of limited value to any man hoping for honours. Classes were often too large and were always composed of men of unequal talents and attainment. The lectures did not impress Alexander Gooden, a future Senior Classicist and Chancellor's Medallist: 'The lectures are poor – certainly not superior, and in some instances greatly inferior, to those I have been in the habit of listening to at the London University.' [2] When his Tutor, Thomas Thorp, informed the class that other more pressing duties compelled him to resign the guidance of his freshmen to other hands, Gooden wrote to his father: 'The loss of Mr T's instructions is not greatly lamented by his pupils.' [3] As Sheldon Rothblatt's study *The Revolution of the Dons* has shown, for those who wished to win academic honours their real mentors were the private tutors or coaches.[4]

These private tutors were able young graduates waiting for a Fellowship, or junior Fellows waiting for clerical preferment. They also included in their number some of the most able college lecturers who could earn far more as a coach than they did from their poorly paid official appointments. The regular fee for a private tutor was £14 a term if you went to him every day, or £7 if you went only alternate days. He normally saw five or six students a day, giving an hour to each, though a mathematical tutor might take several at the same time. Some coaches stayed up for the long vacation and charged £30 for a summer's tuition. Their reputation and potential income was naturally linked to the success their previous pupils had achieved. A Trinity man who wrote an account in 1827 of his years at the university claimed that 'Fellows of Colleges, and others, who are in more request, usually charge 20 pounds for the Term and 50 pounds for the long vacation. As some of these gentlemen receive a dozen pupils, their income thence arising must be about £1,320.'[5] [= £118,130] It was clearly a potentially lucrative business. Their task was to cram an undergraduate so that he won a high place in the examination lists; it was not to educate him morally and religiously *in loco parentis*. That, in theory, was the duty of his college Tutor. The trouble was that in a large college such as Trinity a Tutor might have a hundred or more students under him, so he could hardly be expected to discharge his various responsibilities to them all very well, however conscientious he might be.

It appears that Vaughan in his first term had either Charles Rann Kennedy (Senior Classic 1831) or George John Kennedy (Senior Classic 1834) as a coach – both were younger brothers of the more .famous Benjamin Hall Kennedy (Senior Classic and Chancellor's Medallist 1829) who was on the staff of Harrow at that time. C.J. mentioned in a letter to Lake written in November 1834 that he doubted if he would ever be 'anything like first-rate here. To be a term with Kennedy is a most effectual way of curing all one's ignorant vanity, of which I am afraid I had and have too much.' [6] It is likely that Vaughan then chose Richard Shilleto as his coach. He had graduated at Trinity as 2nd Classic in 1832 and was reckoned to be the greatest Greek scholar and the best classical coach of his generation in Cambridge. He did not, however, proceed to a Fellowship at Trinity as he married in January 1834 and, instead, made a living as a private tutor. He was an Assistant Master at Harrow 1843-44 and then returned to Cambridge. In mathematics, William Hopkins (7th Wrangler in 1827) was rated among the best; he was the first to make a permanent career of coaching.

For those not able to afford the fees of a private tutor, J.M.F. Wright (who was one of them) published a series of self-help aids in mathematics: *Self-Instruction in Pure Arithmetic* in 1829, and in the same year *Self-Examination in Euclid*. In 1830 he began a weekly journal *The Private Tutor and Cambridge Mathematical Repository* which provided examples of problems to be solved and gave detailed accounts of how examinations were conducted. In 1831 he published *Hints and Answers: being a Key to a Collection of Cambridge Mathematical Examination Papers; as Proposed at the Several Colleges*.

There were professors but professorial lectures were an uncommon and generally poorly attended phenomenon – the exception being those of Adam Sedgwick, Fellow of Trinity and Woodwardian Professor of Geology, who had made that science popular despite it not being a subject for examination. When Herbert Marsh was appointed Lady Margaret Professor of Divinity in 1807, he had marked it in a novel way by giving a course of public lectures in English and not in Latin. So unusual was this that the Divinity School could not hold the number of students wishing to attend and the lectures were delivered in Great St Mary's Church. Unfortunately Dr Marsh was not consistent in well-doing, lecturing only intermittently and not at all after he became Bishop of Peterborough in 1819, though he retained his professorship worth £1,000 p.a. until his death twenty years later. In the 32 years he held the chair, he delivered only 30 lectures. At least that was 30 more than Francis Barnes who held the Knightsbridge Professorship of Moral Theology or Casuistical Divinity from 1816-38 and never lectured once! It was left to William Whewell, Fellow and Tutor of Trinity College from 1818-39 and then Master 1841-66, to rescue this professorship from its torpor. John Kaye was appointed Regius Professor of Divinity in 1816 but waited five years before giving his first course of lectures. In the introductory one he apologised for lecturing but explained that as times had changed a course of lectures might be welcomed! He too lectured only intermittently and on becoming Bishop of Bristol in 1820 retained his chair at Cambridge, only giving it up when he was translated to the richer see of Lincoln in 1827.

The exception to this dismal roll of inactive academics was the holder of the Norrisian Professorship of Revealed Religion. The chair had been founded in 1780 and the holder was required to give 50 lectures a year in term time and no lecture was to count unless six students were present. For this he was paid £100 p.a., the most poorly paid of the Divinity chairs, though the holders of the chairs of Greek and Hebrew received even less - only £40 p.a. It was stipulated that in this course of lectures the Professor must read certain portions of Pearson's *Exposition of the Creed*; after this the general subject was to be 'Evidences of Christianity.' Bishops required all Cambridge ordinands to present a certificate of having attended 25 of these lectures. There was, however, no examination at the end to test whether those present had actually listened and learned anything, so the value of mandatory attendance was questionable.

In 1833 there was a renewed attack on the Divinity Professors and Lecturers. It came from a former Fellow of St John's College, the Revd F.R. Hall, in the form of a hard-hitting pamphlet: *A Letter respectfully addressed to the Heads of Houses and Senior Fellows in the University of Cambridge*. His particular concern was about the defective state of theological instruction, with reference to the candidates for Holy Orders, who formed a significant proportion of all the students at the university. About one third of all undergraduates were the sons of clergy and a similar proportion would go on to be ordained in the Church of England. Hall listed the various Divinity Professors in turn, publicizing their idleness. Thomas Turton, for example, who had been Regius Professor since 1827, and Dean of Peterborough since 1830, had yet to deliver his first lecture. The College Hebrew lectureships, he claimed, were sinecures and the College Divinity Lecturers only lectured on a Gospel or the Acts and on Paley's *Evidences*. Even the Norrisian Professor did not escape criticism who 'delivers yearly the same course of lectures, and, without any examination, gives a testimonial to every student or BA, who has attended twenty-five of them; though nothing is more notorious than that his lecture room is anything but a place of study, many indulging themselves in lounging upon the seats or reading the newspaper or a novel.' [7]

G.E. Corrie of St Catharine's College determined to make improvements when he was appointed to this chair in 1838. He began by giving additional private Divinity lectures to BAs of the university and to men of his own college. Five years later a new 'Voluntary Theological Examination' was introduced which Whewell, the Master of Trinity, succeeded in making virtually mandatory for Cambridge ordinands when he persuaded the bishops to make it a requirement for candidates for Holy Orders. The examination covered the Greek NT, certain assigned portions of the Early Fathers, Church History, the 39 Articles of Religion of the Church of England and its Liturgy. J.J. Blunt likewise contributed greatly when he was appointed Lady Margaret Professor of Divinity in 1839; his lecture notes on the work of a parish priest were published posthumously as *The Parish Priest. His Acquirements, Principal Obligations, and Duties.* It immediately became a best-seller. C.J. may well have been among their first post-graduate students.

A very different kind of reform was threatened in 1834 when the House of Commons passed a motion by a large majority (174:75) which would have allowed Dissenters to graduate at Oxford and Cambridge without having to subscribe to the 39 Articles of Religion of the Church of England. The motion was defeated, however, in the House of Lords by 187: 85. It provoked a flood of pamphlets. One of the many pamphleteers was Professor Thomas Turton, who argued that religious instruction would suffer if Dissenters holding unorthodox views were allowed to proceed to degrees. Connop Thirlwall, a Fellow and Assistant Tutor of

Trinity College, who favoured their admission demolished the Professor's arguments in his *Letter to the Rev Thomas Turton DD on the Admission of Dissenters to Academical Degrees*. In it he said things about college life which offended the Master and some of his colleagues: 'In the first place then I must observe – and I am almost ashamed of stating so evident and notorious a fact – that our colleges are not theological seminaries: that they are so far from being dedicated exclusively or principally to the study of theology, that among all the branches of learning cultivated in them there is none which occupies a smaller share of our time and attention.'[8] He then quoted from a series of addresses that the Master had given in the college chapel to those intending to be ordained. They formed a large minority: 413 of the 1239 men who matriculated at Trinity between 1831-40 were subsequently ordained – his advice to them had been to follow an appropriate course of *private reading in their leisure time* and he had recommended some theological works to them.

Turton had also made much of the role of College Tutors as religious educators of the students in their care. Again Thirlwall challenged this view: 'In whatever other point of view a college Tutor may be considered as standing in room of a parent, I am afraid that it would be a somewhat exaggerated idea of the intimacy of this relation, to suppose that he commonly thinks it a part of his duty, to inquire into the state of his pupil's religious feelings or habits, or that their private intercourse is one of the ordinary means by which religion is communicated to our students.'[9]

One of Thirlwall's colleagues at Trinity, William Whewell, disagreed with much of his criticisms but conceded 'with regard to the intercourse of the Tutor and his pupils, I am very ready to allow (with sorrow) that what has been done in the way of inculcating religious impressions falls very far short of that which is desirable, and which probably ought to have been attempted.'[10] The truth is Whewell was too occupied with his own studies to be bothered about undergraduates except when he had to discipline them.

Since 1822 there had been three 'sides' in the College, that is three Tutors each with a roughly similar number of undergraduates in their care. When C.J. arrived these were William Whewell (2nd Wrangler & 2nd Smith's Prize in 1816), George Peacock (2nd Wrangler & 2nd Smith's Prize in 1813) and Thomas Thorp (8th Wrangler 1819). Peacock had the largest side and was reputed not only to be a particularly caring tutor but also to have most of the 'clever men'. C.J. was fortunate to be one of Peacock's men. Thorp was not highly regarded and left much of his tuition to two more able assistants: Francis Martin (Bell and Craven Scholar, and 7th Wrangler in 1824) and the Master's elder son John Wordsworth who was reckoned to be the best scholar in the college – as an undergraduate he had won the Bell Scholarship and the Porson Prize. Whewell was assisted by Charles Perry (Senior Wrangler, 1st Smith's Prize & 7th Classic 1828, a missionary-minded Evangelical who became the first Bishop of Melbourne 1847-76) and by Joseph Blakesley (21st Wrangler, 3rd Classic and Chancellor's Medal 1831) who had replaced Thirlwall as an Assistant Tutor. John Moore Heath (27th Wrangler 1830) along with Christopher Wordsworth Jr. assisted Peacock. These men were the academic backbone of the college. One of their non-academic duties was to accept and sanction the bills that tradesmen submitted for individual students. In this way Tutors were able to keep a check on both parties – for overcharging on the one hand and extravagance on the other.

Thirlwall's criticisms went further than theological education and pastoral care. He also attacked the practice of compulsory attendance at chapel services – a practice common to all colleges. For an undergraduate to absent himself from a service without permission was a disciplinary offence. This was an issue dear to the heart of the Master of Trinity who, as a good Tory clergyman, was devoted to the Establishment in general and to the Established Church in particular. With the support of the Seniority in 1824 he had made it a requirement that 'every undergraduate, not having an *ægrotat* or *dormiat* [leave of absence from morning chapel] do attend morning chapel five times at the least in every week, or four at the least including Sunday; and the same number of times in the evening, under penalty that the week, in which anyone shall not have so attended, be not reckoned towards keeping the term of such undergraduate – unless that omission be repaired by extra attendance the week following.' [11] By the time C.J. entered college, the expectation was that students attended once a day and twice on Sundays, i.e. eight times a week. Wordsworth also exacted from his Tutors and Assistant Tutors the pledge that they too would attend chapel 'in the morning as much as may be, and on all evenings when you are not engaged by company at home or elsewhere.' [12] Thirlwall did not favour compelling students to attend: 'I greatly doubt whether the ordinary service of our college chapels, or our college lectures, can properly be numbered among the aids to religion which this place furnishes . . . If one half at least of our present daily congregation was replaced by an equal number of Dissenters, they would not have come with greater reluctance, nor pay less attention to the words of the service, nor be less edified, or more delighted at its close.' [13]

Wordsworth was deeply offended and dismissed Thirlwall from his post as Assistant Tutor despite 'urgent remonstrances' by Whewell on his behalf. Joseph Romilly, another senior Fellow of Trinity, also disapproved of Wordsworth's action, noting in his diary: 'Tuesday 27 May 1834 Today our Master was despotic enough and foolish enough to dismiss Thirlwall from his Tuition on account of the sentiments expressed in his pamphlet concerning the expediency of compulsory Chapel; he will repent so rash a step.' [14] Whewell was critical of his friend for giving publicity to his views whilst holding a college post, but Thirlwall refuted this charge arguing that his job as an Assistant Tutor did not have anything to do with discipline, and he regarded compulsory chapel attendance as essentially a matter of discipline: 'I conceived that my official duties were confined to giving literary instruction, and that whatever good I might do, by conversation and advice, to those with whom I stood in that relation, was left to my own discretion.' [15] Thirlwall was a serious loss to the College for he was an excellent Classics lecturer who had exercised a good influence on the men he taught. Three years later, Whewell, stoutly defended the rule of mandatory attendance at chapel in his book *On the Principles of English University Education*:

> I acknowledge, with regret, that a College chapel is not, in the sincerity and earnestness of its devotions, all that the friend of religion would wish it to be; but is the Parish Church? In both places there are the cold and careless; in both, the serious and pious. I trust that many a heartfelt prayer arises to heaven in the daily services of our Colleges; and that many, even of the thoughtless and callous, have their thoughts calmed and solemnized by its stillness and order. [16]

This was no empty pious hope as the letters and diaries of students testify. Charles Kingsley, famous later as a novelist, Christian Socialist and Regius Professor of Modern History at Cambridge, went up to Magdalene College in 1838 full of religious doubts. In a letter to his mother written in 1841 he told her: 'I am going to try what keeping every chapel will do to my mind. I am sure it ought to sober and quiet it. I now really feel the daily chapels a refreshment, instead of a useless and antiquated restraint, as I used to consider them.' [17]

Another of those who disagreed with Thirlwall's criticism of chapel worship was George Pearson, a former Fellow of St John's College, who kept a term in his old college early in 1834 in connection with his duties as Hulsean Christian Advocate. His college had at that time upward of 200 young men, who, he claimed, did not abuse the chapel services. 'I have not heard during that time a single disturbance; and with regard to the service in Chapel, which I have been consistently in the habit of attending, I never witnessed more decorum in any congregation whatever.' [18] This was nonetheless an issue which roused some feeling among the student body who in 1838 formed a Society for the Prevention of Cruelty to Undergraduates. It circulated weekly lists noting with ribald comments the poor attendance of Fellows at chapel!

C.J., like many other serious minded students, found spiritual support and sustenance outside the walls of his college chapel from the ministry at Holy Trinity Church whose incumbent was Charles Simeon, a Fellow of King's. Simeon had been exercising a special ministry since 1782 among the student body through his preaching and through the various 'Conversation Parties' which he hosted in his rooms. Abner Brown who attended them between 1827-30 recorded that these were of four kinds: 'Clerical Meetings, Sermon Classes, Undergraduates Friday Evening parties, and ordinary social parties.'[19] The meetings most generally known and attended, according to Brown, were the Friday tea-parties:

> Mr Simeon was accustomed, for a long course of years, to have every Friday what he called an open day, when all who chose went at six o'clock to take tea with him in his rooms at King's College, everyone asking what questions he would, and receiving an answer long or shorter as might be. Hence, a great variety of subjects came under review, subjects which could not be discussed in the pulpit. There was neither exposition as such, nor prayer, and the party lasted until the clock struck seven. The numbers varied with the state of the term, but not infrequently sixty or eighty were present . . . Occasionally the whole of an ordinary Friday party was occupied in remarks and hints which strictly belonged to sermon party subjects; for Simeon knew that the majority of the men who attended the larger never attended the smaller class of parties; and he often, therefore, spoke in the larger tea-party on points important for all who might possibly thereafter enter into Holy Orders, even if they did not wish to attend the sermon parties. [20]

Brown also attended the Sermon Parties which, he said, had assumed the form of colloquial lectures to a small invited circle of fifteen or twenty gownsmen, held at eight o'clock on every alternate Friday evening.

Whoever wished to attend waited on Mr Simeon, and at once received an invitation for that term, coupled with a request that he would attend regularly, and throughout the whole of the term, for each term had its own course of subjects. Towards the end of the allocated hour, Mr Simeon gave out a text, to be treated in some specific mode, and read on the next occasion; and each student who brought and read aloud his little written sketch received a few kind and pertinent criticisms on it, perhaps at times somewhat severe for young students, but always wound up with suggestions for a more effective and simple mode of handling the subject. The writer has found the lucid and pointed remarks which he heard at those sermon parties of the greatest practical utility in his own ministry. [21]

Simeon's ministry and that of his Curate, William Carus (Fellow and Dean of Trinity College 1832-50), who succeeded him in 1836 as Vicar of Holy Trinity cannot have failed to impress and influence C.J. A quarter of a century later he would begin his own special ministry to ordinands – men who would become known as 'Vaughan's Doves'. Simeon was a role model for him too by the calibre and content of his preaching. In the preface to his 21 volumes of *Horae Homileticae*, which contained 2,536 sermon outlines, he stated that the three-fold object of his preaching was 'to humble the sinner, to exalt the Saviour, and to promote holiness.' He eschewed church politics and church conflicts, choosing rather to be an exemplary parish priest and a faithful Biblical preacher – 'My endeavour' he wrote 'is to bring out of Scripture what is there and not to thrust in what I think might be there.' His influence on the student body and on many of the resident Fellows may be judged by the enormous turn-out for his funeral. One of those who was at it, Francis Close, wrote 'More than 1500 gownsmen attended to honour a man who had [once] been greatly despised. When his venerable remains were deposited in that glorious building [King's College Chapel], every bell of the College chapels tolled for him, and the Vice-Chancellor (Ainslie, Master of Pembroke) regretted that the great bell of St Mary's could not, as its use was confined to the Royal Family, or to a Vice-Chancellor dying in office.' [22]

Many of these young Evangelical undergraduates, including C.J., nurtured by Simeon and accordingly nicknamed 'Sims', shared in the ministry of the 'Jesus Lane Sunday School' in one of the poorest areas of the town. This had come into being in 1827 as a result of a discussion between a few Queens men on the sermon they had heard Simeon preach that morning. John Pollock tells what followed from that discussion in his book *A Cambridge Movement*:

Simeon must have stressed the need to prove faith by works, or had spoken of the pagan ignorance prevailing around Cambridge, for as they talked one of them, James Wright, remarked: 'It seems a pity that we could not spend part of our time in Sunday School teaching.'

They wondered if any parish would like their help. One said he had already asked all the town parsons and been turned down. Another suggested Barnwell, 'a sadly neglected place and near enough; why not try to do something there?' Barnwell was a straggling village on the Newmarket Road, still separated from the town by fields through which ran Jesus Lane. It was growing fast and had an unsavoury reputation ('heathenish and dissolute').[23]

With the help of some more students from other colleges, they went house-to-house visiting in the village to recruit children. They obtained the use of the Friends' Meeting House on Jesus Lane from its Quaker trustee and three weeks after the original discussion the Sunday School opened.

Some two hundred and twenty boys and girls had arrived. 'I shall not readily forget the shouting and uproar which saluted our ears on entering the building,' said one of the founders. He and his friends succeeded in quietening their 'unruly, boisterous, dirty and ragged' pupils and lessons began. The children were illiterate and the first task each Sunday morning was to teach a few letters; the teachers would then dictate a text of Scripture which the children wrote as best they could on their slates. Its meaning would be explained and the children repeat the text and be questioned on it. The first selected was from the third chapter of St John, and the sixteenth verse: 'God so loved the world that He gave His only begotten Son, that whosoever believeth in Him should not perish but have everlasting life.' In course of time all the great doctrines of the faith were taught in this simple way.

The founders of the Jesus Lane Sunday School lived to see it become an honoured and loved institution. After six years in Jesus Lane it moved round the corner to King Street . . . Prompt results were evident in the lives of some at least of the children . . . Whatever the effect on the children, the Sunday School influenced the lives of the teachers. It became a joint enter-prise in which dons, bachelors and undergraduates worked together, thus forging a valuable link between them for generation after generation. It was a training ground where men learned to prove their faith, to enjoy fellow-ship which could not become an end in itself, and to understand something of the lives of those less fortunate than themselves. [24]

The importance of this institution to evangelical freshmen is noted in the biographies of some of Vaughan's contemporaries. His old school friend, Spencer Thornton, became its superintendent during his time at Trinity, as well as being secretary of the Church Missionary Association, and making time to conduct prayer meetings in his rooms. He also continued his practice from Rugby days of distributing tracts and visiting the poor along with some fifty like-minded undergraduates. Another such student was T.G. Ragland who was to become famous as a missionary in India.

> Mr Ragland . . . became a regular teacher at the end of his first year; and thenceforward taught every Sunday, not excepting the Sunday in the week of the Senate House examination . . . About the same time [July 1838] he commenced the weekly distribution of tracts, in connection with the Cambridge Undergraduates' Tract Society; a society originally set on foot . . . for circulating tracts in the villages round Cambridge with the leave of the several parishes visited. [25]

Perowne tells too how much Ragland prized attending the evening lectures on the Greek Testament which James Scholefield, the Regius Professor of Greek, gave and of his habit of meeting every Saturday evening for private reading of the Scriptures and for prayer with a few men of his own year and college. Another like-minded contemporary was Harvey Goodwin, later to become Bishop of Carlisle. Goodwin's biographer H.D. Rawnsley describes how this young Sim's life was influenced at Cambridge:

> It is not many freshmen either who would have undertaken, as Goodwin did at the request of a friend, to collect subscriptions among his fellow undergraduates for the Mission for Christianizing the Jews. It is fewer men still who would have gone off a mile's walk, immediately after Chapel on a Sunday, to take a morning class in one of the Barnwell schools, and returned for a second class in the afternoon; yet this Goodwin did throughout his undergraduate career. It is true he had amongst his contemporaries men as serious minded as himself. At nine o'clock on Saturday evening some half a dozen of these friends used to meet for the purpose of an hour's Bible reading; and on Sunday evening Goodwin always went to Carus's room for his fatherly lecture with Scriptural exposition and devotional talk, which Mr Carus was so well qualified to give. [26]

Charles Astor Bristed, an American, who entered Trinity College in 1840, has left a detailed account of his impressions in his book *Five Years in an English University*. He was a very sympathetic observer of university life but critical of the state of morals and religion among the students, most particularly of their habitual hard drinking and sexual debauchery and this from men who would later be ordained. Despite the many examples of vice, he acknowledged:

> A young man who enters there and is disposed to find a truly "good set", can find one, or indeed have his choice among several sets of really virtuous and religious men. It was my comfort to know many right worthy of the name of Christians according to the highest standard that was ever lived up to; men of no particular clique or theological school, but holding various opinions and coming from various places and teachers; pupils of Arnold from Rugby; Evangelicals from King's London; other King's College London men of the Eclectic stamp, followers of Professor Maurice . . . [27]

The writer may well have had C.J. Vaughan, now a Fellow of his college, in mind when he referred to Arnold's former pupils.

A fairly full picture of life as a Cambridge undergraduate at that time can be gained from Bristed and from the letters of Alexander Gooden. The Tutors allocated the set of rooms a freshman would have and usually recommended a particular gyp [college servant] who would tend to his personal needs along with those of several other students. It was customary to take over the furniture of the former tenant and pay whatever the college upholsterer valued it at - £50 [= £5,500] was a typical price. The new tenant could add to it with pieces more suited to his personal tastes. His first purchases, however, would be new crockery and glasses which his gyp could organise. When he needed books, he didn't have far to walk as six booksellers were in Trinity Street close by the college. Local tradesmen were all too ready to provide credit, which led to some students accruing substantial debts even though all trades-men's bills were submitted through a man's Tutor.

The day began with a student being wakened about 6.30 by his gyp, who would have brought a pitcher of warm water to his room for him to wash in and who would have already lit a fire in his study. Chapel followed at 7 – his arrival being ticked off by a college servant – absentees could expect to face the Dean and receive due punishment possibly being confined to college for some days – or at worst, for persistent offenders, being sent down for a term. A light breakfast, usually just a buttered roll and coffee brought from the college buttery, was taken back in the student's rooms.

Lectures which normally lasted an hour were given in college between 9 and 12 noon. Freshmen were required to attend two every

83

day, one in Classics and the other in Mathematics. Second and third year men had a choice of three or four lectures but attended just one. In theory the rest of the day was meant to be spent in private study – Thornton records that he was in his rooms 'from eleven to two and am very seldom interrupted during that time. . . From two till four I walk, and if I have any unimportant visits to return, I do it then.' [28] Such was the practice of a reading man but for the majority who had set their sights no higher than a pass degree much of the day was spent in leisure pursuits which usually included some hard drinking in the evening. This occasionally resulted in vandalism and public disturbances – Joseph Romilly, the Registrar of the University, recorded such events in his diary of which the following extract gives their flavour:

> Tu 11 Feb 1834. An awful long Seniority [that is the eight senior Fellows who, together with the Master, ruled the college]: we expelled Hon G.A. Murray and Hunter for gambling (Murray won near £800 of Hunter, who confessed to Whewell): we confined to Gates and Walls Lord Cl Hamilton, Lord J Beresford, two Ponsonbys and eight more for a riot in the Court at 2 o'clock on Sunday morning after a Supper at Lord Claud Hamilton's: two lamps and part of the balustrade in Nevile's Court were pulled down, but by whom of the party unknown: three of the party, Conyngham, Herbert and Ponsonby (three Fellow Commoners) were very drunk and confined for a longer time than the rest. [29]

A month later he recorded that two more Trinity undergraduates had been expelled after being convicted in the Chancellor's Court of assaulting their landlady at three o'clock in the morning and holding a razor to her throat!

A light lunch was eaten before the afternoon's physical exercise. For reading men that was a long constitutional walk. 'The favourite route was the "Grantchester Grind" – out from the college along the Trumpington Road, then turning west past Trumpington Church, over the river past Grantchester mill and through the village back to Cambridge, taking the road or the river footpath.' [30] Bristed tells of eight mile hikes done in the couple of hours between 2 and 4 p.m., varied with jumping hedges, ditches and gates along the way. Longer walks of twelve to fifteen miles were frequently taken on Sundays or on the days following an examination. Most students walked with a friend and conversation with him was part of the attraction of the exercise. Bristed also mentions "pulling" on the river, cricket, football, fives and 'riding twelve miles without drawing bridle'. Rowing was a favourite activity. College rowing existed from the 1820s, Trinity's Boat Club being founded in 1825, and the first college race was in 1827 organized by Charles Merivale of St John's College. The sport became increasingly popular and competitive in the 1830s. Not a few of the rowing men were Sims – the original crew of what became Second Trinity were said to have been Sims to a man and the club dubbed 'the Hallelujah'. The first Inter-Varsity boat race was held at Henley in June 1829 which Oxford won; the next was not until 1836 when Cambridge had the winning boat. Cricket matches against Oxford also began about the same time – the first which was played at Lords was in 1827, held again in 1829 and 1836 and became an annual fixture from 1838. Some men kept a horse or hired one from one of the town's several livery stables and rode in the afternoon, but the university authorities forbad them riding to the races at Newmarket! Simeon encouraged men to play tennis and to fence. Christians had a duty, he told them, to exercise their bodies as well as their minds and spirits.

The main communal meal of the day for which all 400 or so resident members wore their academic gowns was served at 4 p.m. in the great hall at Trinity. The undergraduates' menu consisted of joints of beef and mutton or veal, served up in immense pewter chargers, and bowls of vegetables and jugs of beer set at short intervals on the long tables from which the men served themselves. Those who got a seat next to a joint had the first choice – arrive late and there might just be scraps left. Individual portions of soup, pastry and cheese were available, but had to be paid for. Not all undergraduates enjoyed this experience. Albert Pell, who went up in 1839 wrote: 'Now the food put before Pensioners in Trinity for dinner and the way in which it was served were abominable. It was inferior in quality and spoilt in cooking. We had three-pronged steel forks to eat with; before using them we passed the prongs through the table-cloth, and at once three black spots indicated the wounds on the cloth.' [31] He did not fail to notice how much better the Fellows fared. In addition to the Fellows' table, there were also separate tables for the Bachelors of Arts still in residence, who were regarded as being in statu pupillari until they became MAs, and another for the Foundation Scholars who received free commons as part of their award.

The hour or more between dinner and chapel was spent in relaxation – possibly a short walk in the college grounds or drinking a glass or two of port with a biscuit in a friend's room. Evening Chapel was at 6 to which all hastened who had missed the morning service. Bristed commented favourably on the men's deportment at this service: 'It must be owned that their conduct in chapel is very orderly and proper, considering the great opportunities afforded for subdued conversation by the way in which they are crowded together kneeling.' [32]

For a serious student who hoped to achieve academic honours, the hours that followed were important. Again Bristed tells how: 'After chapel the evening reading begins in earnest . . . not infrequently two or three meet in one another's rooms alternately to read some classical author or to talk problems together – a very sociable way of learning.' [33] Four hours of study was the norm for a reading man, interrupted only for some light refreshments at about 9. Men who chose to be out on the town in the evening were required to wear cap and gown so that they were readily recognizable by the proctors who patrolled the streets to keep order.

The evening might occasionally be spent in a larger forum for debate such as at the Union, founded in 1815, or simply reading the day's newspapers in its comfortable reading rooms. C.J. became an active member and stood for election as its President in 1838 but was defeated by a titled rowing man, Sir John Lighton. Bristed throws some light on why he lost:

> Whenever there was a contested election for the Presidency of the Union, it turned more on the personal popularity than on the actual services and reputation of the candidate, and generally came to be a contest between the reading and 'rowing' men. When it came to a hard fight the former usually succeeded; the same industry and ability that aided them in their studies, generally enabling them to succeed in their canvas. There was but one exception to this rule. When the rowing men were lucky enough to get hold of a title who would run for them, they were safe to win. There is no resisting John Bull's lord-worship. [34]

He then goes on to quote the case of Vaughan whom he described as 'altogether a gentleman of great abilities and merits' being beaten by 'a Johnian nonentity who had Sir before his name.' One of C.J.'s younger friends, William Butler (who would later found the Sisterhood of St Mary the Virgin at Wantage) actively canvassed support for him in his bid for the presidency and in the process nearly ended up having to fight a duel with a Johnian who had made offensive comments at the Union about Trinity men in general and Vaughan in particular. [35]

For the select few elected to it there was the 'Apostles Club', or to give it its original name, the Cambridge Conversazione Society. The founding members in 1820 were mostly from St John's. Some exceptional men from Trinity were soon invited to join, among them F.D.

Maurice in 1823 and John Sterling in 1825. In the following decade 80% of its members were Trinity men. In its early years it included some of the best: the future Poet Laureate Alfred Tennyson, Richard Chenevix Trench (later to become Archbishop of Dublin), Henry Alford (later Dean of Canterbury), and William Thompson (a future Master of Trinity College). Trench described the members as 'that gallant band of Platonic-Wordsworthian-Coleridgean-anti-Utilitarians.' [36] which clearly indicates who their heroes were. When C.J. went up in 1834, several of the resident Fellows of Trinity, including Blakesley and Heath, had been members and his brother Edward was elected an 'Apostle' in 1835. During his time at Cambridge a Trinity man was elected each year to this elite intellectual, secret club but C.J. was not among them. It met weekly on a Saturday evening in the rooms of the member whose turn it was to write an essay which was read and discussed. The theme might be literary, political, religious, whatever the host felt deserved examination and merited a sharing of views. Light refreshments were served which invariably included coffee and anchovies on toast. J.M. Kemble, a member from 1826-28, said of it:

> No society ever existed in which more freedom of thought was found, consistent with the most perfect affection between the members; or in which a more complete tolerance of the most opposite opinions prevailed . . . Its business was to make men study and think on all matters except Mathematics and Classics, *professionally* considered . . . To my *education* given in that Society, I feel that I owe every power that I possess, and the rescuing myself from a ridiculous state of prejudice and prepossessions with which I came armed to Cambridge. From the "Apostles" I, at least, first learned to think as a *free man*. [37]

Given the narrow academic curriculum in the university, such societies met a real educational need – they allowed men to be challenged intellectually by their peers, to think more widely, explore new ideas, and to escape the strait-jacket of Mathematics and Classics. C.J. too felt that need. In a letter dated 29 November 1834, just a couple of months after coming into residence, and written to his friend Lake to congratulate him on winning the Balliol scholarship at Oxford, he added this snippet of news:

> Perhaps you will be amused to hear that the night before last, at twelve o'clock, a thought struck me that we might have a very nice little *Rugby* Debating Society here among ourselves, and so expeditious were we in

setting it on foot that within twelve hours of my first mentioning it to Thompson we were an incorporated society, with president, vice-president, and laws and members. We held our first meeting in Burbidge's rooms last night, and had a nice stormy debate on private business. Mayor is president, Thompson vice-president, for the remainder of this term and next . ..[38]

Charles Mayor had matriculated Michaelmas 1833 and graduated BA 4th Classic 1837 – after Ordination he returned to Rugby as an Assistant Master. Archer Thompson had matriculated Michaelmas 1832 but did not graduate until 1839. Mention of these old Rugbeians shows that C.J. had already found a place among former schoolfellows in the college. A letter from his friend Arthur Clough, who was still at school, makes reference to the 'Rugby Set' at Cambridge.

One new friend he made who had entered Trinity two years before him was George Cotton. He had been educated at Westminster and like Vaughan was an academic high-flyer – he was elected a Scholar in 1833 and graduated as 8th Classic in '36 and became a Fellow in '38. Cotton was an Evangelical, a teacher at the Jesus Lane Sunday School and a member of various Christian associations among the undergraduates, but he distrusted and objected to much in the Evangelical system and had become an admirer of Arnold. Cotton's widow in the *Memoir* of her late husband, which she edited, mentioned C.J. several times and other Rugby men who welcomed a man who felt as they did about their old master. She says that 'Charles Vaughan above all, soon became well-nigh his chief friend . But no one was ever allowed to supersede or even rival the most cherished of all, W.J. Conybeare.' [39] It seems the three of them along with a few other friends found relaxation in a kind of quiz they had devised based on detailed knowledge of the *University Calendar*! Questions such as 'Who was 10th Wrangler in 1829?' or much knottier ones such as 'When would second Tripos Day fall in leap year, if Easter Day were on March 21st?' [40] Cotton used to make up fake Tripos lists for his own amusement awarding Smith's prizes for virtue and Chancellor's medals for sociability. On one occasion, as a prank, C.J. (or Conybeare, Mrs Cotton was unsure which) took the latest copy from Cotton's desk and pinned it on the wall at the foot of the staircase. He then told his friend what he had done who, mortified at the thought of who might see it and read it flew, shrieking with laughter, to the spot to tear it down. Too late! Another friend, not knowing it was a joke, had seen his own name on the list with a most unlikely award. [41] She claims that it was

Vaughan who first divined her husband's potential as a school master and was the cause of his going to Rugby. Arnold offered him a post as an Assistant Master and a boarding house where one of his pupils was John Conington who, if J.A. Symonds's private *Memoirs* are trustworthy, was later to have an indirect but crucial impact on Vaughan's career. Cotton went on to become Headmaster of Marlborough College in 1852 and Bishop of Calcutta in '58.

Mention of these friends, however, cannot hide the fact that like many another student, C.J. had felt lonely on coming up. He had left behind him his two dearest friends and the high position he had held as a leading pupil at Rugby – now he was just one more junior member of the university's most prestigious and aristocratic college. He expressed something of this sense of isolation when he wrote to Lake a month after coming into residence, begging him to join him at Cambridge rather than going to Oxford:

> I cannot tell you how thankful I should be if you were coming here. Is there the remotest chance of it? Do not say, 'I cannot do mathematics', because you know how very little I know about them, and yet I do not calculate on being quite plucked. It would be so pleasant. I have hardly one profitable acquaintance, except my brother, whom I certainly have far more opinion of than anyone I have seen yet. It sounds odd to say so, but to me there seems such a difference between his sensible and powerful mind and the clever little minds that are so common here. Give it one more thought. I think you would really like Cambridge better than Oxford . . . [42]

An article in *The Rugby Magazine* of July 1837 entitled 'School and College' tells of a conversation between two former pupils re-visiting their old school and comparing notes on life in Oxford and Cambridge. The Cambridge man felt school and college were essentially the same with no significant difference between lessons and lectures, callings over and markings in chapel, locking-up and locking-in, masters and tutors, schoolboys and gownsmen:

> From the first moment that I arrived at College, I was utterly unable to sympathize with the rapturous exclamations I heard round me in praise of the newly-attained Paradise, and the chorus of freshmen that dwelt incessantly on the charms and sweets of liberty. I found that within a week one of these enthusiastic believers in their own freedom had a heavy imposition for absence from lecture, another Proctorized for driving a gig up High Street, and a third rusticated for staying out of College all night: and as all these seemed to me very analogous to what we called at Rugby,

Punishments and Sending away, I was at a loss to conceive what symptoms of independence had so excited their admiration. For myself, in the mean time, the change was such as to be anything but gratifying to my feelings of self-importance and liberty. From a ruler in a commonwealth, I found myself a nobody in a disconnected society, unrecognised as a privileged member of a body, or only noticed to be laughed at as a freshman; constrained to be civil at the unprovoked conversation of my fellow novices . . . [43]

Stanley visited C.J. in Cambridge towards the end of his first term and stayed at Trinity in a room above C.J.'s. One of their topics of conversation was the recently proposed Rugby school periodical (following the example of Eton) to be edited by members of the Sixth. Stanley was initially opposed to it whereas C.J. favoured it, as did Arnold; both former pupils ended up contributing to the second issue in October 1835. Stanley wrote an article on 'School a little World' and Vaughan contributed a poem entitled 'The Eighth Day. To a Child on the Evening of the Day of Baptism.' Later, C.J. contributed a 'Hymn for the Dedication of a Church' which appeared in issue no 8 in October 1837.

Stanley was not impressed by the town but he loved the collegiate buildings: 'The change from the great sweep of High Street and Broad Street [in Oxford] to the wretched narrow, winding, collegeless streets of Cambridge, was at first quite overwhelming . . . I could hardly conceive it possible for a university to exist with any degree of grandeur in a place so vile!' [44] He said he wanted to blow up all the houses 'in these unsightly undignified streets!' But he pronounced Trinity 'somewhat finer than Christ Church, as being larger and more diversified . . . The view of the colleges from the gardens, through which flows the Cam, is finer than Ch. Ch. Meadows, and King's Chapel is not to be spoken of in the same breath as any of the Oxford chapels . . . being superior inside and outside beyond comparison.' [45] He rated the lectures at Cambridge as being much superior to those at Oxford but felt the manners of the undergraduates were 'more barbarous than with us' and that undergraduate society differed from that at Oxford – 'the inevitable result of the much greater numbers at Trinity, the ignorance in which each man lives of his neighbour, and the absence of any one predominating or "elect" company.' [46]

Stanley's uncle, Julius Hare, a former Fellow and Tutor at Trinity, was also visiting at the time and introduced him to Whewell ('his face . . . is the most good-humoured and good-natured that can be conceived') and to Thirlwall who was still in residence. Later at a party at Downing

College to which he was taken by his uncle he met 'the concentrated intellect of Cambridge' including his former examiner at Rugby, Christopher Wordsworth, and Blakesley who had replaced Thirlwall. 'Thirlwall was very silent and fell asleep over a book; Whewell talked a great deal . . . They seemed very happy all of them together and with much less restraint among them than I should think there was among men of the same standing at Oxford.' [47]

Whilst both men formed new friendships, theirs remained very special and lasting. He and Stanley corresponded regularly sharing all their news and their current concerns. Both men kept in touch with Arnold and returned to Rugby at regular intervals which was easy to do as there were regular coach services between the universities and Rugby: the 'Pig & Whistle' plied from Oxford and the 'University Drag' from Cambridge. They both stayed with the Arnolds in late December 1835 and Lake was there with them too in March '37. Arthur Clough, now Head of School House, wrote frequently to his old friends and often complained about the moral state of the school since they had left and all the 'evil most assuredly in the Upper part of the school'. C.J. wrote to encourage him and advised 'Example is the only medicine for a state like the present' and that 'there could be nothing worse now than a set of proselytising Pyms.' Clough shared this in October 1835 with his friend Gell at Cambridge and added 'I try to follow Vaughan's rule of going on one's own way firmly, and yet quietly.' [48]

C.J. became a Prizeman already in his Freshman's year as all those who were in the 1st Class in the college's annual examinations were entitled to a prize of books. In 1836 he began winning prize after prize whilst Stanley had failed at his first and second attempts to win the Ireland Prize (the highest distinction in Oxford for proficiency in Greek and Latin Scholarship), Arnold tried to ease the pressure which he rightly surmised Stanley was under. On 15 March 1836 Stanley communicated the news of his defeat to Vaughan who had just obtained the Craven Scholarship at Cambridge:

> You will be sorry to hear that your triumph has not been followed up . . . My greatest sorrow is the very great disappointment which I know it will be to you and all my friends. I was unduly hopeful myself, and therefore I am afraid you will all have been so. Arnold sent me a most kind and thoughtful message by Lake, begging me not to worry myself about having the responsibility of the school on my shoulders, as I had quite enough from my own anxiety without their unreasonable expectations. I have no doubt it has been ordered for the best. [49]

It is to Stanley's credit and a mark of his affection for C.J. that when he wrote home with the news of his own failure, he was glad to report his friend's success: 'It is also a good thing that Vaughan has got the University scholarship at Cambridge which is much more thought of there than the Ireland is here – so that though it would have been delightful for us both to be successful it is a great consolation that we have not both failed.' [50] Stanley finally won the Ireland Prize in 1837. In writing to thank C.J. for his congratulations, he disclosed just how much Arnold still meant to him:

> It has been a great pleasure to me – far more than I could have anticipated – for it was so long since I had gained any honour, or received any congratulations, that I had almost forgotten what it was. And it has been doubly (or rather, I should say, tenfold) delightful to be reminded in almost every letter that I have had on the subject that it is not my own fame only or chiefly which is advanced by my success, but the fame of Arnold, to whom I do most sincerely feel that I am indebted for my present happiness, and for whose sake it was always my chief aim and is now my chief joy, to gain the Ireland. [51]

He also won the Newdigate Prize for English Poetry with his poem 'Gypsies' and when the time came for him to declaim it in the Sheldonian Theatre, his friend Vaughan was there to hear him and to act as his 'prompter'.

By then C.J. had already been elected a Scholar of his college, won the Craven Scholarship (first awarded in 1649) and the more recently established Porson Prize (1816), all in 1836. At the beginning of the Easter Term 1836 along with about 70 other 2nd and 3rd year men, C.J. sat the examination for a Foundation Scholarship. This examination differed from the annual College ones in May in that the contestants went in not knowing what they would be examined in. It was more a test of their general knowledge, and of their classical scholarship in particular. There were seven papers, each lasting four hours spread over three and a half days: two translations, two in Latin composition, two in Mathematics and one with general questions in Classical history and philology. A week later the new Scholars were announced from the Chapel gate, among them was Charles John Vaughan. In addition to the pecuniary benefit it conferred, namely £30 a year [= £3,228], and the distinction it conveyed, it was a sign that here was a man with the ability to become a Fellow. He had also entered for an even stiffer test of his classical knowledge and abilities as a translator: the examination for a University Scholarship.

There were two examination papers each day from Monday to Friday and the final one on Saturday morning – each day's paper was set and marked by a different examiner. He was successful and was awarded the Craven Scholarship worth £50 a year [= £5,380]. His other prize that year was another mark of his particular academic strength – the Porson was for translation of Shakespeare into Greek iambics which also had to be accompanied by a literal Latin translation of the Greek. Charles Merivale who was a Fellow and Tutor of St John's when C.J. went up, commented in his autobiography on the importance of this prize:

> The institution of the Porson Prize for translation in Greek iambics had recently given definite direction to the study of the Greek language, as distinct from Greek literature, and this distinction became strongly marked in the character of Cambridge study throughout. Grammar and philology, as evinced in exact translation and composition, became definite objects of attention at Cambridge . . . Oxford professed to cultivate the spirit of ancient literature, Cambridge to acquire the most accurate appreciation of the ancient languages. [52]

This suited C.J.'s taste and mental abilities extremely well.

In June 1836 Christopher Wordsworth Jr., newly appointed Headmaster of Harrow, invited him to come and stay with him. Vaughan replied from his mother's home in Leicester:

> I was exceedingly pleased to read your letter, which I received yesterday. I have been long very near venturing to write to you, for I often feel the want of your kind advice at Cambridge. I wish indeed above all, that I could come and thank you in person for your very kind invitation to Harrow, which I should be delighted to accept immediately, but that I am intending to spend part of this Summer in the Lakes, and therefore am anxious to secure two or three weeks quietly at home before I go – but I quite hope before long to remind you of it, and come and see you in the midst of your new labours and honours. Thank you also for your congratulations on my getting the Porson. I am glad to say that this year I did not write for anything else, though I dare say, if I had, I should not have succeeded. I am going to read Classics hard this summer. I hope – probably at Grasmere, but I do not know exactly yet – Is there any chance of your visiting the Lakes this year? I have been spending a week at Dr Arnold's – He talks of you a great deal. [53]

The Trustees of Rugby School in recognition of his successes in 1836 gave him a gift of books each one inscribed in Arnold's own hand. The following year he won the Porson Prize again, the Browne Medal (in gold and valued at five guineas), prizes for the Greek Ode, for Latin and Greek Epigrams and the Member's Prize [i.e. given by the MP for the University] worth fifteen guineas to him for the best dissertation in Latin prose, besides carrying off the Trinity College 'First Declamation Prizes' both for English and Latin. All Trinity students were required to attempt at least one declamation during their time at university, as they were thought to promote the art of public speaking. Winning such prizes brought a man cash, silverware and books but equally important, his name was made known far and wide as the results were published in the London papers as well as in the papers of his home locality. It brought his name to the attention of potential patrons. And it added lustre to the reputation of the school that had first educated him – no wonder 'Vaughan halves' were celebrated at Rugby.

C.J., having won the College's first Declamation Prize, was required to compose and deliver an Oration in the College Chapel at the annual College Commemoration in December. He chose as his subject *The Difference between a Hearing and a Reading Age*. Stanley had suggested it to him in a letter in which he reported that his close friend at Oxford, W.G. Ward, had first suggested that he, Stanley, might take this theme for an article in the *Rugby Magazine*. Stanley offered his friend some hints for the essay which C.J. eventually read in Trinity Chapel and then had published. Here is a taste of this young man's style:

> We cannot restore the Hearing Age of the Church – the Age when creeds were hymns, - without restoring its Age of humiliation and persecution. Yet still the plain facts of the case call upon us to consider whether a Hearing Age like that of the Apostles could have had either the power or the inclination to scrutinize minutely the meaning of a word, or to extract a doctrine from the use of a tense; whether it must not have looked rather for lessons than for truths; whether it was not left for a Reading Age at once to systematize and to anathematise, at once to define and to exclude; while a Hearing Age required only that Christian principles should be exemplified in a Christian life, that we should be bound one to another under the same Master in the Unity of the same Spirit. [54]

Both friends achieved honours in 1838 being placed in the First Class in their respective universities. Vaughan, having first achieved a very respectable place in Mathematics as 10th Senior Optime after the five days of written tests, was thereby qualified to sit the Classical Tripos in the following month and to be a candidate for a Chancellor's Medal.

These were gold medals valued at fifteen guineas which were awarded to two commencing Bachelors of Arts who shewed themselves 'the greatest proficients in classical learning.' Stanley wrote to him from Alderley Park on 22 January 1838:

> Thank God - I see in the paper that you are safe as 10th Sen. Optime . . . I only hope you are well in body - & prepared for your coming hurdles – I was very anxious to hear as to tell the truth I had been rather alarmed – Peacock having said that he feared you would not be Sr. Opt. – I had meant to have written before to console you in your hour . . .[55]

C.J. cleared the 'hurdles' magnificently, becoming one of the two top classicists of his year, being bracketed Senior Classic, and equal, as Chancellor's Medallist with the 4th Lord Lyttelton. In his Greek papers he performed the unprecedented feat of not making a single mistake in the accents. Lyttelton's own account written to an old friend, Captain Abraham Hagley, tells the story from his perspective:

> My dear Abraham
> Many thanks for your very kind letter, congratulations and wishes. I take much shame to myself for not having written to one of my oldest friends after the Classical Tripos – but you must accept of the excuses common on such occasions of hurry and forgetfulness and unwillingness to write after the opportunity has gone by. I must now set you right as to the Medals, for the Newspapers did not fail to blunder as usual about it & indeed you to call me Senior Medallist whereas in fact Vaughan and I were again bracketed – you know we were bracketed in the 1st place of the Tripos, a thing never done before. In the Medal there were four Examiners, [?] Provost, Crick, Thorp, & Scholefield – they were two and two, and as they rather wanted to avoid bracketing they first tried a viva voce/short bit of Plato/ which utterly failed as to separating us, & then called in the Vice Chancellor who was for bracketing and ultimately they all came to that mind except old Provost who stuck out vehemently for me, chiefly I imagine, from his care for the Latin Composition, especially the verses in which I was first a good bit – So you see it was remarkably close & considering how well the two examinations confirm each other, that a double dead heat is a thing unprecedented and therefore memorable. I think nothing more satisfactory could have happened. Besides he is a great friend of mine. In the Medals, there was an original theme but no verses – but translation into Latin Hexameters – Elgiacs and Lyrics and I think I did quite up to my best & upon the which I leave Cambridge perfectly pleased – most delighted I am too that Eton is indeed most prosperous at Cambridge. [56]

Lyttelton later provided Vaughan with a generously worded reference when he applied for the Headship of Rugby which included these lines:

> It was my fortune to be placed on an equality with him at the final examinations at Cambridge in 1838. But I can say most unreservedly, that, as regards the consummate *taste* in the Greek and Latin language, especially in the former, as shown in composition therein – in the philosophical handling of ancient history – and in accuracy and extent of knowledge on Classical subjects, it never would have entered my thoughts that I could be put into competition with him. In the two former respects, I do not know many whom I should put on a level with him; in the first of them, I think, none. [57]

Bristed describes the scale of the feat these awards represented:

> Three things are requisite in the Tripos: first an accurate knowledge of Greek and Latin Syntax, and a corresponding dexterity in unravelling difficult constructions. Without this groundwork no man can be sure of a good place. Next, the aspirant must be skilled in Composition, must be able to write Latin and Greek Prose, Greek Iambics, and two or three kinds of Latin verse. Thirdly, he must have a very large vocabulary, so that he will seldom meet with a word which is not familiar to him. [58]

Unlike at Oxford where a candidate for the First Class selected his twelve authors on which to be examined, at Cambridge a man had to read as much and as widely as he could. The tests for a would-be medallist were even more demanding. Arnold was naturally delighted at the success of one of his favourite pupils:

> You have my most hearty congratulations on your success in the Examination, which I believe few will more rejoice than I do. I cannot regret your being bracketed with another man; for, judging by my own feelings about you, his friends would have been much grieved if he had been below you; and when two men do so well, there ought, according to my notions, to be neither a better nor a worse of them. Thank you so much in sending the Class paper, and for your Declamation, which I liked very much. How glad shall I be to see you when your Medal Examination is over, and when, the preparation for life being ended, you will begin to think of life, its actual self. May it be to us both, my dear Vaughan, that true life which begins and has no end in God. My wife and the children fully share in our joy on your account, and join in kindest remembrances. [59]

Sir Charles Vaughan was proud of his nephew's academic achievements and wrote in May 1838 asking for a complete list of his awards. C.J. replied:

I am greatly ashamed of my apparent delay in answering your very kind letter & sending you the Prize Essays. I delayed in order to get Copies made of the two College Declamations in Latin and English, for which I gained the two Prizes. The University Latin Essay I am sorry to say does not exist in a shape that could be sent to you. However I am afraid you will have more than you will care to read in those that I am able to send.

Your list of the prizes I have gained here, is very correct except in one or two points & as you so kindly wish to have it exactly I will just rewrite it in the order in which they were gained. 1. I was in the first class at the Trinity College Examination, 1835. 2. Craven University Scholarship 1836. 3. Trinity College Scholarship 1836. 4. Porson Prize 1836. 5. Porson Prize 1837. 6. Browne's Medal for Greek Ode 1837. 7. Browne's Medal for the best Greek & Latin Epigrams 1837. 8. Member's Prize for the best Latin Essay 1837. 9. First Prize for English Declamation in Trinity College. 10. First Prize for Latin Declamation in Trinity College. 11. First Prize for Reading in Chapel. 12. Senior Optime degree 1838. 13. Bracketted for the first place in the first Class of the Classical Tripos 1838. 14. Bracketted for the Chancellor's Gold Medals.

The Oration which you saw was not a separate Prize, but delivered in consequence of gaining the First Prize for the English Declamation on "Alcibiades and Mirabeau", which I now send.

I hope you will consider this list as much the statement of the facts you enquire about & not as an attempt to blazon my boyish achievements.

I have been spending some of my leisure making speeches at a great Debating Society here where (if you will believe it) I was the sole speaker, the other night, in behalf of the Revolution of 1688, the rest calling it a rebellion & an unjustifiable change. So much for the Toryism [of] the rising generation. We have had since then a debate which I opened in favour of the admission of Dissenters to the degree of B.A. in the Universities where I was in a decided minority of course. Lord Lyttleton's generous behaviour in our late contests has made us quite intimate. He is a very noble high minded man – He took his seat in the House of Lords a week ago, but he still pays frequent visits to Cambridge.

I am engaged in taking some private Classical Pupils here – I shall not sit for a Fellowship with the slightest chance of success till next year – though I hope to go in to the Examination, for form's sake, this October – They give the Fellowships, when there are so few as are now vacant, exclusively to the upper years.

With many thanks for your kind letter.

Ever believe me your very affectionate Nephew.   Chas J. Vaughan [60]

C.J. spent the summer at home in Leicester. It is a mark of the efficiency of the postal services at that time that Stanley addressed his letters to him there simply as 'C.J. Vaughan Esq., Leicester' and he received them. Stanley was denied his ambition of a Fellowship at Balliol and had to settle for one at University College to which he was elected in July 1838.

In October C.J. was back in residence as a Bachelor Scholar reading for the Trinity Fellowship examinations which were held each year in that month. Stanley visited him at this time – he himself being 'safe now in the cockboat of University.' [61] and wrote again in November to share the news that their mutual friend, Lake, had been elected to a Fellowship. For once C.J. was not ahead of his two friends. For Stanley, however, his own Fellowship was a settling for second-best – in another letter to C.J. written in November of that year he says 'Heavy clouds still hang over University [i.e. the college of that name] – intense light streams from Balliol.' [62]

Bachelors had to wait three and a half years before becoming a Master of Arts, which meant they had three opportunities to sit for a Fellowship. Being elected at the first attempt was not unknown but even senior classicists normally had to wait until their second attempt. C.J. succeeded in 1839 but not before his classical knowledge, in particular, had been put to a severe test once again along with his knowledge of Mathematics and Metaphysics. This time he was not the star candidate. Romilly made mention of the election in his diary entry dated Monday 30 September 'Tea at the Master's to elect 6 new Fellows . . . We elected 4 of the Upper Year viz Hemery, Conybeare, Humphry, Thacker, 1 of the Middle Vaughan (whose Uncle the Judge died a few years ago) and 1 of the Lower Year, Maitland the cleverest of the whole set. Maitland got far the most marks, next to him Conybeare.' [63]

The College Statutes provided for 60 Fellows who were required to be ordained within seven years of their graduating as Master of Arts. The appointment provided him with a good measure of financial independence as Fellows had free rooms and commons and a small share in the College's annual surplus of funds which varied considerably from year to year but was rarely less than £200 [= £17,570]. In addition, having been so successful academically he was now in demand as a private coach. A letter written to his cousin Halford in December 1838 from Rugby where he was staying with the Arnolds gives us some glimpses of his life at this time. He had recently been to London to enrol as a student of law at Lincoln's Inn:

I returned to hard work with my 11 Pupils (having found Whewell in the Mail as my sole companion from London) and then was seized by tooth-ache, which ended in having a tooth torn out, with many circumstances of aggravation – broken, & part left in, even after 4 successive extractions – altogether I have found no time for putting my parcel together for you – so I must defer giving you the papers till I come to London in January to keep next term at Lincoln's Inn, when I hope to remember to bring them – I can hardly suppose Sir H. to be dying of curiosity to see my VERSES . . . [64]

He proved to be an excellent coach. George Cotton stated in a testi-monial that two of C.J.'s private pupils were first in the Classical Tripos, and two gained University Scholarships.[65] One of his prize-winning pupils was Frederick Gell (who was awarded the Bell Scholarship in 1840 and gained a First in 1843, and later became Bishop of Madras), the younger brother of his friend John. Another was his friend, William Butler, who had tried to get him elected President of the Union. Years later Vaughan wrote a brief appreciation of him at the request of Butler's son, who was editing a biography of his father:

I can still see him as he was in the long vacation of 1837, the time of our closest intimacy, full of health and spirits, always brave and true, not yet developed into the devotion of his mature life, but already loved by good men like our common friend G.E.L. Cotton, and already with many "shades cast before" of what he was to be in due time . . . our life together was uneventful and our friendship without breach or jar. When we met forty or fifty years afterwards in Convocation, generally voting on opposite sides, the old alliance was still recognized both in speech and feeling on both sides. [66]

Stanley toyed with the idea of law – probably seeing it not so much as a profession but rather as a way into public life. He wrote to C.J. on 2 May 1838 from his father's house in London – 'I have been a good deal about Lincoln's Inn Fields and the Temple, and feel much reconciled to the life of a lawyer; so that if I should feel invincible obstacles to the Articles or Liturgy, I should not feel utterly incapable of taking another line of life, although it would certainly be still very much against the grain.' [67] He had looked forward to being ordained ever since he was a boy but now he struggled to reconcile himself to the damnatory clauses in the Athan-asian Creed. It was an issue he shared in his letters to C.J. and finally in interview with the Archdeacon of Oxford just two days before his ordination. To his relief he discovered that Archdeacon Clarke shared his views and in the end he was ordained Deacon by Dr Bagot, the Bishop of Oxford, in St Mary's Oxford on 22 December 1839 with, amongst others, Richard Church, afterwards Dean of St Paul's. Co-incidentally, Stanley's great hero, Thomas Arnold, had experienced similar turbulent doubts relating to the Athanasian Creed and to the doctrine of the Trinity at the time of his own ordination as Deacon and was nursed through the crisis by two of his Oxford friends, John Taylor Coleridge and John Keble.

Arnold had broached the subject of C.J.'s future in a letter dated 13 September 1837: 'I am anxious to know your final decision as to profession; but I do not like to attempt to influence you. Whatever be your choice, it does not much matter, if you follow steadily our great common profession, Christ's service.' [68] Vaughan's thoughts, like Stanley's, had turned to the Law as a possible profession. In September 1840 he took up residence in London where his mother assisted him financially in his London expenses. He occasionally returned to Trinity and his old school fellow, Albert Pell (who would later marry C.J.'s cousin Elizabeth Barbara Halford) recorded this memory of him from that time.:

> He [Vaughan] came up to keep Divinity terms. He had been reading for the Bar, but on the death of his uncle, Judge Vaughan [in September 1839], he left that pursuit in exchange for the Church. Unfortunately for him he was given rooms over mine in New Court, and as I was not a reading man, but an idle one with noisy companions carrying on our carousals through the night, with frequent convivial outburst in the day time, he was in great straits for opportunities for quiet study. At last I got a nice note sent down from above me: "MY DEAR PELL – If you will only tell me when you go to bed, if you ever do, I will avail myself of such periods for study and reading." [69]

C.J.'s nephew, Professor Charles Vaughan, in a biographical essay contributed to J.V. Morgan's *Welsh Political and Educational Leaders in the Victorian Era* claimed that the Law had always been his first choice as a career:

> Throughout his career as a schoolboy and undergraduate, he had looked forward to adopting the Law as his profession. The distinction of his uncle, John, had from the first turned his face in that direction, and even as a child, he had shown a preternaturally keen interest in the grim proceedings of the Assizes. Accordingly, on finishing his time at the University, he at once began to "eat his dinners" [i.e. at Lincoln's Inn], and at least once acted as Marshall to his uncle on Circuit. Considering the general cast of his mind, it is as certain as any such thing can be that he would have risen to

great eminence in that profession. But it was not to be. Conscientious scruples, in which the influence of Arnold, probably had some share, caused him to renounce all those prospects – by no means the last instance of the kind that we shall have to notice. [70]

Arnold did not support C.J.'s initial choice of the Law for in his judgement it was not a suitable profession for a Christian. When he changed his mind in favour of the Church, Arnold was delighted. He wrote to him on 4 November 1840:

> Your letter gave me such deep and lively pleasure, that I could scarcely restrain my joy within decent bounds; for to see any man whom I thoroughly value, delivered from the snare of the law as a profession, is with me a matter of the most earnest rejoicing . . . With respect to the other part of your question, while I should delight to see you in the ministry of the Church, I cannot quite think that the parochial ministry is so clearly to be preferred to the work of education. But in this men also have their calling, and I would not wish to tempt them from it. Nor would I have you think that I mix up any personal feelings at the possibility of persuading you to join us at Rugby, with my genuine thankfulness for your own sake and that of others, that, in so great a matter as the choice of a profession, you are disposed to turn from the evil to the good. [71]

Six days later Arnold repeated his encouragement to C.J. to consider joining him at Rugby: 'it would be my greatest delight to have you here as master; and that the field of good here opened, is, I think, not easily to be surpassed. If you decide on the parochial ministry, then I think that your calling would be to a large town rather than to a country village.' [72]

Ten weeks later on Sunday 10 January 1841, Vaughan was made Deacon by Stanley's father in Norwich Cathedral. He had offered himself for Ordination on the strength of his college Fellowship, just as his friend had done the previous year. The day after his ordination, C.J. gave up his membership of Lincoln's Inn – the Church rather than the Law would be his life. He remained in residence at Trinity Cambridge.

An invitation came out of the blue on 9 March from the Hon. and Revd H.D. Erskine, who had succeeded his father at St Martin's, to return to Leicester and take some services during a vacancy there. Erskine was an old-fashioned, non-resident pluralist who lived at the rectory in Swithland and left much of the duty in Leicester to a curate who lived in a house in St Martin's churchyard; in 1847 Erskine was made Dean of Ripon. C.J. was at that time in correspondence with the Rector of Denton

101

in Norfolk about serving a curacy there, albeit just for a couple of months, but he clearly preferred the prospect of returning to his home parish:

> Your most kind letter reached me this morning, and I need not say, interested me deeply. The idea of undertaking the duty at St. Martin's even for a few weeks (and I could not <u>dream</u> of it as more than a merely temporary thing, for I think it is very likely that I may feel myself obliged to return here for some time) is very formidable indeed to me, as you will at once believe - & what I never should have sought for myself – But the earnest wish you express that I should consider it as my duty to do so in the present emergency, weighs very strongly with me - & though I do indeed feel how totally unfit I am for such a post, yet I do not know that I could be satisfied to refuse to occupy it for a very short time, if nothing intervened to make it impossible.
>
> . . . I so feel that the only way in which I might for one moment think of coming to it, would be as a mere makeshift – And I must add that I am quite tied here, by my attendance on Divinity Lectures which the Bishop of Norwich requires of me, till the last of this month at the very earliest.
>
> You shall hear from me again, if all is well, very soon indeed – I fear I have hardly thanked you enough for all the kindness of your letter – but I am sure you will accept my most sincere thanks for it, and ever believe me,
> My dear Sir,
> Yours very faithfully & affectionately,   C.J. Vaughan [73]

He was not anticipating at this early stage becoming the Vicar of St Martin's but in September the Lord Chancellor appointed him to the living, now valued at £149 [= £13,090], and consequently he resigned his Fellowship. Normally a full year elapsed between a man's ordination first as a Deacon and then as a Priest. In his case the period was shorter because of his appointment as a beneficed incumbent. Bishop George Davys ordained him Priest in Peterborough Cathedral on Sunday 19 September.

Before leaving Cambridge, however, he had joined in the public debate about college statutes. Whilst still in residence as a junior Fellow in 1840, he co-authored with his friend, G.E.L. Cotton, writing under the pseudonym of 'Two Fellows' *An Earnest Appeal to the Master and Seniors of Trinity College Cambridge on the Revision of the Statutes*. Having experienced at first hand the futility of life as unemployed Fellows, they felt the post was an invitation to be idle as there was no incentive to engage in any serious research. There was no career structure for able young academics – in their words: 'if the whole society were now in residence, three fourths of the body would be unemployed, or busy only in private and for themselves.' [74] There was little to tempt a man of ability to stay on in Cambridge unless he had a real chance of becoming a College Tutor or of being appointed to one of the senior posts such as Bursar.

When the College Statutes were at last revised in 1844, Whewell, who was now Master, made certain that it was a very conservative revision (even to the extent that they were still written in Latin) which did not tackle any of the fundamental issues needing to be addressed. That was a task which Vaughan would return to in 1856 when, along with George Peacock, his friend and former Tutor at Trinity, who was now Dean of Ely, they were made members of the parliamentary commission appointed to look into revising the statutes of the university.

Return to Leicester

For how can we preach successfully, without an intimate and somewhat extensive knowledge of the human heart? How can we preach appropriately, without some insight into some at least of the souls before us? And where and how can this knowledge be gained, but by frequent and laborious intercourse with the people committed to our charge?
C.J. Vaughan *Sermons* p. 105.

Whilst it must have given him and his mother great satisfaction that he had returned home to have the cure of souls in the parish where his father had ministered before him, it was a formidable task he had taken on. He had the memory and example of his father to inspire him and subsequently of Arnold at Rugby and of Simeon and Carus at Holy Trinity Cambridge but he had had no professional training for what faced him now. Being a Senior Classicist and a Chancellor's Medallist was no preparation for the pastoral care of nearly three thousand souls, most of whom had no interest in or use for his classical or mathematical knowledge. Sitting through the mandatory 25 hours of listening to the Norrisian Professor reading Pearson's *On the Creed* was of little practical use – his time spent teaching in the Sunday Schools at Barnwell was worth far more. At least there, he had been engaged in trying to communicate with the children of ordinary working people. He had also gained a little experience there in visiting those whom he described in a letter to Arnold as 'the good poor' but he had had no opportunity of working as an Assistant Curate alongside and learning from a more experienced parish priest. He was plunged straight into the work of serving and leading a busy town-centre parish. Years later he described his ministerial unpreparedness as a 'leap into darkness'.

There was nothing unusual in this as it was still the norm in the Church of England in 1841. A theological college for Oxbridge graduates had opened in Chichester in 1839 headed by Charles Marriot, an Oxford man who was a friend of Pusey and Newman. A second one opened at Wells in 1840 whose Principal was J.H. Pinder, a former Warden of Codrington College in the West Indies, also known to be sympathetic to the Tractarians. Both of these institutions offered some instruction and direction in leading worship, preaching and the essentials of parish work and administration but only a handful of men seized the opportunity they presented. Vaughan was not among them. As an Evangelical whose views were influenced by Arnold, he was no friend of the Oxford Movement.

Coincidentally, in the same year that he was ordained, Charles Perry, another Fellow of Trinity College Cambridge, published an Open Letter to the Bishop of Lichfield on 'Clerical Education with an especial reference to the Universities.' He acknowledged that the universities were failing to prepare men for the ministry and proposed a post-graduate year for ordinands to be spent at the university studying theology. What he called 'the experimental' should be acquired 'by the use of such opportunities, as each individual may possess in his own private sphere . . . To accompany an active and judicious parochial clergyman in his private ministrations, when he may consider it discreet and fitting, - and to visit on his behalf, and under his direction, among his people, - to assist him in the superintendence of his schools, - to gather the lessons of his experience by communicating with him upon the various cases, which continually occur to his observation, - this will constitute the best experimental Clerical Education.'[1] Twenty years later C.J. would devise his own system of aiding men prepare for Ordination, having known and experienced himself what it is to come to the parochial ministry unprepared, and what he offered them was pretty close to Perry's proposal.

His appointment was only made possible by the dismissal of the Revd John Brown who held the two livings of St Martin's and St Mary's Leicester in plurality. The weekly *Leicester Chronicle* drew attention to this on Saturday 11 September 1841. A reader, sympathetic to Brown's cause, had written in asking why this particular clergyman was being deprived of one of his parishes when another local cleric was reputed to hold seven. Was it, he asked, because Brown was a supporter of the Liberal Party rather than the ruling Conservatives? The results of the municipal elections in November of that year showed a Liberal victory in every ward except St Martin's where two Tories topped the poll. There was a P.S. to the news item on the 11th. 'The "Medical agitating Dan O'Connell" of St Martin's [a possible reference to his uncle Sir Henry Halford or to his cousin of the same name] had better look to this also, and consider if a minister living in a town is not more fit to hold two contiguous parishes than a person holding two or three at a distance, whether a Conservative minister would have been as ready to give up the fees coming to him from certain pew rents' [a reference to Brown who had done this at St Mary's]. On 18 September, the paper reported 'We have authority to state, that the living is given to the Rev Charles Vaughan MA, Fellow of Trinity College Cambridge, and second son of the late Rev Edward Thomas Vaughan, Vicar of this parish.' It was later stated in the same paper that Brown's removal was 'on the ground that the population of the two parishes was too numerous for one clergyman' – the population of St Mary's parish at that time was 8,405 and St Martin's 2,866. It appears that some parishioners had proposed the separation of the two benefices, so maybe some of Vaughan's influential relatives had indeed been at work on his behalf.

At a meeting of the seat holders of St Mary's held later that month, Brown claimed that the Lord Chancellor and the Bishop of the Diocese wished him to retain St Martin's but 'So great had been the kindness he had experienced from the parishioners of St Mary's that he had preferred the latter living . . .' Brown did also apologize at that meeting for being 'unavoidably absent from his duties for some time, and expressed his hope that such a circumstance would not occur again.' [2] If this means that he had been an absentee incumbent, a not uncommon phenomenon earlier in the century, this too could have been used by the Vaughan supporters as an argument for separating the two parishes.

Leicester had grown and changed since he left it at the age of thirteen. It was now a town of nearly 51,000 people and was linked by rail to the capital. There had been much rebuilding of the older parts of the town and many of the lath and plaster houses had given place to what a gazetteer in 1846 described as 'plainer, but more comfortable and convenient dwellings, some of which have handsome fronts, especially in the principal streets where there are many elegant and well-stocked retail shops.' [3] Christ Church, a new church seating 1,200 worshippers, had been built by subscription in 1839 and two new private schools had been opened. The Collegiate School was an Anglican foundation with clergy appointed as the first Head and Second Master. The school building was described as 'an elegant edifice in the Tudor-Gothic style' built in 1836 with room for 300 pupils. C.J.'s elder brother Edward was appointed Second Master in 1836 and their younger brother David was amongst its first pupils before going on to Rugby. The second one, known as the Proprietary School, opened the following year 'in connection with the Dissenters'. Another private initiative was the building in 1838 of a 'General News Room and Library' which had 6,000 volumes but they were available only to shareholders who also had to pay an annual subscription for each facility. A Mechanics Institute with a much smaller library had opened in 1834.

The first democratically elected Town Council, which took office in 1835, had also been contributing to the building boom in its desire to provide better facilities for the growing population and for its markets and fairs. Under the Municipal Act 1835 the office of town councillor had become open to popular election by the ratepayers and by the freemen of the borough. The corporate body now consisted of a mayor, 14 aldermen and 42 councillors and was commonly known as the Town Council. The mayor and his predecessors retained the right to act as JPs but the Lord Chancellor now appointed a further 20 borough magistrates. The first election in November 1835 resulted in a vastly different council largely opposed to the old Corporation, most of whose officers they dismissed. From having been a Tory and Anglican monopoly, the Corporation/Town Council now became a Liberal and Nonconformist one. These were exciting political times at the local level. One of their immediate improvements to the life of the borough was to increase the size of the local police force considerably and to introduce a regular night watch. A consequence of this was that the number of burglaries, which had previously been high, dropped. In one respect, however, the town had changed little. There was still no piped water and people still depended on some 3,000 wells which supplied individual houses and groups of houses. A great many of them were contaminated through the seeping in of matter from cesspits and privies which must have contributed to the spread of infections and to the very high death rate that Leicester experienced in the 1840s.

There had been organisational change in the Church of England locally. In 1837 the Archdeaconry of Leicester had been transferred from the Diocese of Lincoln to the Diocese of Peterborough, and this came into effect two years later when there was a vacancy in the see. The Archdeacon's Court and visitations, however, continued to be held in St Martin's. The Archdeacon at this time was Thomas Kaye Bonney who carried out his visitations with thoroughness. He examined St Martin's on 22 June 1842 and recorded in his report that most of the fabric was 'good' or 'decent' but he made a number of criticisms: the inside walls of the church were dirty and needed cleaning, the carpet in the sanctuary was worn and should be replaced, some new communion linen was needed, four of the stoves were not in good order, some of the pews needed to be repaired and the pulpit steps needed to be altered as they were 'very inconvenient for the Preacher to ascend.' Outside, too, there was work to be done – the drains needed cleaning, rain was coming through the roof in some places where the lead was defective and he noted 'The tower and spire appear to be in good order, but a Crocket fell from the Spire last year.' [4] The faults listed by the Archdeacon were primarily the responsibility of the Churchwardens but it seems that the young, inexperienced incumbent had not been encouraging or chivvying them to do their duty – difficult enough to do at any time but even more so for him as they had been his seniors when he was just a boy.

The role of the parochial clergy had changed since the death of C.J.'s father. Their ties to the State were loosening and many more of them now had a clearer perception of the spiritual nature of their ministry. Fewer of them, for example, were willing to serve as magistrates. That function was now seen as being incompatible with their ministry as pastors. In Leicester not a single clergyman was a Borough Magistrate and only two of the twelve County Magistrates were clerics. Whereas previously most parish clergy had been closely involved in the administration of the old Poor Law, now many of them refused to be agents of the new and much harsher system introduced in 1834. They considered it to be unjust – the pauper was now confronted with the choice of either starving in his own home or entering the workhouse with its inevitable consequence – the break-up of his family.

The State too had stepped back in its relationship with the Established Church. By passing two Acts in 1836 dealing with Marriage and Birth Registration it removed certain civil administrative functions from the Church which provoked resentment and some friction. The parish clergy had previously been the *de facto* Registrars of Births – children brought to baptism had had their names registered legally. That latter function now passed to government appointed Registrars of Births, Deaths and Marriages and a feared consequence was that fewer babies would be brought to church for baptism. The parish priest now had to obtain a death certificate from the Registrar before officiating at a burial – failure to do so or to inform the Registrar within seven days of the burial carried the hefty penalty of a £10 fine [= £967]. The clergy remained Registrars for Marriage, though they had lost their monopoly on this as the Superintendent Registrars could now grant licences to Nonconformist ministers to solemnize marriages in their chapels or they could perform civil marriages themselves.

Another fundamental change was also in process in what had been a very important and personal aspect of an incumbent's relationship with poor parishioners. Previously in times of hardship, the poor had gone to the vicarage for aid – for food or money or help in getting medical attention. In this respect the Vicar was little different from local landowners who recognized and accepted that they had a certain responsibility for the welfare of villagers living and working on their land. Help now was more likely to come from one of the many new charitable organisations set up to meet such needs, and the Vicar was more likely to be involved *indirectly* as a leader and co-ordinator of it. And whereas previously his wife would have visited and taken food, medicines or whatever was deemed most needed by a family, this was now more likely to be done by a District Visitor. Any lively urban parish was expected to have such organisations and teams of lay assistants. From being a solo player, the parish priest was taking his first steps to becoming an effective team leader. Charles Bridges had written in *The Christian Ministry* in 1830: 'A minister cannot undertake everything . . . he must be the centre to a hundred hands and minds moving around him.'[5] Another writer in a book entitled *Parochial Ministrations* published in 1839 had praised the work and efficacy of District Visitors: 'In the largest parishes with the aid of a visiting society properly organised, a complete but not officious surveillance may be effected and by sections judiciously arranged, the most perfect order may be established, while the ministrations of the clergy, called in only when circumstances may require it, may be rendered far more efficient than it were otherwise possible in a large parish.'[6] C.J. had had opportunity to see this in practice at Holy Trinity Cambridge where Simeon had been among the first to introduce area visitors and use lay assistants in his parish.

St Martin's Leicester was not a very large parish. The 1841 census recorded it had only 538 inhabited dwellings and 2,889 parishioners (this figure included 23 persons in the Borough Gaol), so a programme of house-to-house visiting done by the priest himself over the course of the year was not out of the question. This kind of visiting was still highly regarded by Evangelicals and various pocket books were available in which the clergy could record and store all the information they had gleaned about the families they had visited – the *Clergyman's Private Register* (1838) provided four pages for each family! When an avowedly Evangelical theological college was founded at Birkenhead in 1846, all the students were required to do house-to-house visiting in the slums of Liverpool, across the Mersey, on two days a week as part of their training. There was manifestly a strong desire and will among the Evangelicals to take the Gospel of God's love into the homes of the poorest who were least likely to enter a church on a Sunday. C.J. gave pastoral visiting high priority in the sermon he preached to his clerical colleagues at the Archdeacon's visitation in 1842. In his opinion, clergy who did not visit their parishioners, in health as well as in sickness or on their death beds, and did not know their thoughts and needs were 'injuring the success of their preaching'.

Change had come, too, in the parish priest's work as an educationalist. Previously he might have acted as a private tutor to the sons of some of his wealthier parishioners, or even run a small school in his vicarage, now he was more likely to be raising funds for founding and financing new schools in his parish and then exercising some personal oversight of them. The National Society, founded in 1811, had been the most important agent in establishing, and part funding, new primary schools attached to the Church of England. They had raised money initially by public subscription but from 1833 Parliament made sub-stantial grants which enabled thousands more schools to be built. These still needed local support and supervision and the parish priest was a key figure in this work. The parish school, or schools (boys and girls were educated separately) were seen as useful agents of evangelism: places where children could be given a firm grounding in church principles and in their duties as obedient citizens. From the 1840s, however, any school in receipt of a government grant was subject to inspection by government officials.

C.J. preached a special sermon each Ascensiontide on behalf of the charity schools in his parish, urging his listeners to see the work being done in them as a spiritual priority and worthy of their financial support: 'We are this day called upon to make due provision for carrying on the great work of instructing the children of our poorer neighbours in such sound and wholesome learning as shall fit them for usefulness and comfort in future life, - but above all in the knowledge of those Holy Scriptures which are able to make them wise unto salvation through faith which is in Christ Jesus.' [7] The salaries of the Master of the Boys' School [£68.5s = £6,560] and the Mistress of the Girls' School [£35 = £3,350] were the chief annual expenditure, though clothing was also provided for the pupils. Most of the income came from individual donations – one guinea or half a guinea being the norm. Both Vaughan and his mother each gave a guinea a year.

A Committee meeting, which he chaired on 3 March 1842, resolved to send four men to the Boys' School which had 106 pupils and four ladies to the Girls which had 51. They reported back to the Committee that they had found the Boys School in a most satisfactory state. Not so the Girls. 'Although in the examination of the Girls they confined themselves to the simplest questions and these in lessons with which they were said to be most familiar, they found them for the most part unable to answer them, or to read even tolerably well; and that their examination on the whole decidedly proved their want of proper and efficient instruction.' [8] Mrs Peake, the Mistress, agreed to resign her position, but the Minutes of the AGM on 10 May record that the Governors 'desire to express to Mrs Peake that they have no charge to bring against her of any intentional neglect of her duties; that they sympathize deeply with her circumstances; and pledge themselves as individuals, to render her any assistance in their power in procuring a settled and comfortable situation.' [9] The post was duly advertised and testimonials were to be sent to the Vicar; Mrs Peake remained in post until the Committee appointed the wife of a schoolmaster at a special meeting on 26 July. The AGM also authorized the Committee to do whatever was necessary to 'increase the advantages of the girls in the Sunday School on the weekdays', to have the school cleaned and repaired, and to place it 'in union with the Archidiaconal Board of Education'. It was also resolved to give each child who was able to read, his or her own prayer book for use in church.

The impression given is that under Vaughan's leadership things would improve but there were problems with discipline as these two extracts from the School Committee Minute Book illustrate: [7 February 1843] 'Agreed – that John Mason be re-admitted to the School after such a punishment as shall be adequate to mark to the School the sense of the Committee of the criminality of his conduct.' [10] A special meeting of the School Committee chaired by Vaughan was convened on 20 March 1844:

> to consider the case of the boys Whittle and Denton, who having run away from the School on Monday 11th inst., had this morning openly refused to submit to chastisement from the Master
> This being not the 1st offence, it was
> Agreed – that Rule 37 must be enforced by the expulsion of the two boys.
> That, in order to restore the discipline of the school, which has been defied by the refusal of the boys to submit to punishment, - that punishment be carried out before they be expelled from the School.
> That the boy Lucas who has been guilty of like offence, also for the 2nd time, be also publicly flogged and expelled.
> That the boy Poole, who has been guilty of the like offence, but for the first time, be publicly flogged, but allowed to remain in the school. [11]

Both entries were penned and signed by the Vicar.

111

His own more direct and humane contact with children continued in church in the form of catechising, a task he regarded as important but not without its difficulty, as he confessed in an address given to fellow clergy in 1842:

> It is a duty, the right performance of which makes a larger demand upon our energy, skill, and patience, than perhaps any other. But, at the same time, it is a duty, the performance of which is, to a degree almost beyond any other, animating and encouraging. Not so much, it may be, at the moment of its performance; for then there may be much appearance of thoughtlessness and indifference in those to whom we speak; but most encouraging, when viewed in that light in which universal experience enables us to regard it, - as affording an almost certain hope, that, by God's blessing, some of those who receive instruction thus communicated will hereafter trace back to it their earliest, and never wholly forgotten, religious knowledge and impressions, *then* to bring forth fruit unto life eternal. [12]

Along with the catechising of the young went their preparation for Confirmation. Not all clergy provided this above a perfunctory preparation for the service itself which, given the huge number of children gathered together from many parishes, made it an impersonal occasion. As happened two months before Vaughan's arrival when the Bishop of Peterborough presided at a Confirmation in St Martin's at which 830 children from 14 parishes were presented to him. Vaughan wanted the youth of his parish to see it as an occasion when they truly presented themselves for ever to God 'as a living sacrifice, holy and acceptable unto Him'. So he chose to hold a short course in the weeks immediately prior to the Bishop's coming which included instruction about the Sacrament of Holy Communion, a means of grace they would then be able to enjoy.

What most people would have seen as being the parish priest's most important function remained, namely, leading public worship and preaching, and officiating at the *rites de passage* of his parishioners. In the past most of these functions had been performed on a Sunday. In the early decades of the 19th century the norm was still Morning Prayer and sermon at 10 a.m. followed by the Litany and Ante-Communion – something of a liturgical marathon for those attending. Evening Prayer with a sermon was at 3 p.m. – early enough to allow worshippers to return home in daylight even in winter. In the interval there would be the churching of women following childbirth, baptisms, weddings, funerals and catechising children in church. By the 1840s, especially in urban parishes, the so-called 'Occasional Offices' or 'Surplice Duties', such as weddings and funerals, had been moved to weekdays. Learning from the experience of Nonconformist chapels, Sunday evening services had begun to be held and at a time more convenient for domestic servants and other ordinary working class people. In a few parishes there were early morning services for the same class of people not free to come later. Likewise mid-week 'lectures', which were services by another name, were beginning to happen but they were not always held in church. They had a simpler and shorter format: a hymn, prayers, a reading from the Bible and an address. There was also something similar in the form of 'cottage lectures', which attracted people who would not normally have crossed the threshold of the parish church.

A *Guide to Leicester* published in 1843 noted that there were daily services at St Martin's at 9.15 and 3.30 in addition to the Sunday services at 10.30 and 6.30. It also reported that the average attendance on a Sunday was 1,500 and that 'One hundred and fifty children are taught on the Sabbath by two male and six female teachers.' It claimed that the parish had 'several auxiliary and benevolent associations' but gave no details. One of facts that the 1851 Religious Census would later reveal was that Church attendance in Leicester was much higher than the national average: 62% as compared to 49.7% nationally.[13]

Although he did not formally 'read himself in' as Vicar of the Parish until Sunday 10 October 1841, C.J. baptised his first child on 25 September and two more the day after. On the 26th he also took his first funeral: Elizabeth Hardy, a five month old baby girl. He buried three more children in the first week of October. By the end of the year he had baptised 19 children in all. In 1842 of the 59 children brought to church for Baptism, he officiated at 36, the others being done by Charles Mortlock, his assistant curate. In a few instances several children from the same family were baptised together: Richard (a draper by profession) and Ann Willey had three sons and two daughters, aged 11, 8, 5, 3 and eight months, baptised at the same service; a painter's four children, aged 8, 5, 3, and a new-born baby were baptised on 24 April 1842. Vaughan baptised whenever convenient and not just on Sundays – the 1842 register shows, for example, that he did six on Christmas Day, a further two on the 28th (Feast of the Holy Innocents) and one more on 29 December. In 1843 he baptised 28 of the 36 children brought to church, the last of them on Christmas Eve; in '44 he officiated at 22 of the 33 baptisms. The register entries seem to indicate that St Martin's was now more of an artisans' parish with fewer moneyed or professional people living there. The fathers' occupations listed are predominantly artisan and commercial: basket-maker, frame-worker, knitter, wheelwright, wool-comber, painter, printer, mechanic, tinplate worker, chimney sweep, baker, butcher, fishmonger, grocer, hairdresser, hatter, shoemaker, milkman, book-keeper, policeman, law clerk, hosier, surgeon, spirit merchant, as well as the occasional 'Gentleman'.

The same is reflected in the marriage registers. He officiated at his first wedding on 13 October 1841, John Bradley, a carpenter and the son of a carpenter, to Elizabeth Clitheroe, daughter of a labourer. There were four other weddings before the end of the year, two of them on Christmas Day, one groom is described as a blacksmith and the other three as labourers. He did duty at 15 of the 36 weddings in 1842, at six of the 16 in '43, and at 17 of the 32 in '44. A wide social spectrum is represented among them from labourer and railway clerk to wine merchant, druggist and gentleman. The last couple he married were William Lakin, a framework knitter, and Lydia Johnson, the daughter of another knitter on 25 November 1844.

There were many more funerals than baptisms: 76 in 1842, 78 in 1843, and 72 in 1844. C.J. did not officiate at all of them. He had assistance from his brother in January 1842 and a Curate, Charles Mortlock, from April of that year to the end of May 1843. Cosmo Gordon, who signed himself 'Curate of St Martin's', appears in the registers throughout June and July when C.J. was presumably away on holiday. Of all the funerals from 1842-44, he officiated at 45 in his first full year, 34 in his next and 51 in his final year – that is 130 of the 226. His last one being that of a 57 year old woman, Elizabeth Webster, on 20 December. What is clear from all the parish registers is that he was far more diligent in the performance of these particular parochial duties than his father had been. He made appropriate arrangements with local clergy when he himself was absent and did not have a Curate, licensed to St Martin's, to assist him. The higher number of funerals reflects the sad situation that Leicester had one of the highest mortality rates in the country. In the first report of the Health of Towns Commission in 1845, Leicester's rate of 30 per 1,000 was exceeded only by Bristol (31), Manchester (32) and Liverpool (35).[14]

In most parishes Holy Communion was still only celebrated four times a year: at the major festivals of Christmas, Easter and Whitsun and at some time in the autumn such as Michaelmas. Under the growing influence of the Oxford Movement, but also in some Evangelical parishes hostile to that movement, the frequency of celebrating this sacrament was increasing, and this was true of St Martin's. The Archdeacon's report in 1842 noted that Holy Communion was celebrated at St Martin's 16 times a year, i.e. once a month and at four great festivals.

The most high-profile events in any clergyman's weekly ministry were his Sunday sermons. Certainly more people saw and heard him and were open to being influenced by him when he was in the pulpit on a Sunday than on any other occasion in the week. Professor Blunt in his lecture at Cambridge 'On the Composition of Sermons', which C.J. possibly attended, stressed the primary importance of this ministry. More important, in his judgement, than 'going into the streets and lanes of the city' or in cottage visiting. He stressed too the need for thorough preparation which needed time if the sermon was not to be meagre and flimsy. For Blunt, classical scholarship was a great aid to reading and understanding the Scriptures and so being able to expound them – a view C.J. would certainly have shared. Unfortunately even the best classicists didn't always use their scholarship in the most helpful way. Richard Wilton, who went up to Cambridge in 1847, recorded in his diary an account of his first Sunday there: 'At 9.30 a.m. we had the full morning service in our chapel [St Catharine's College]. At two we went to Great St Mary's, the University Church, where the undergraduates are expected to attend, and heard Dr Christopher Wordsworth preach a sermon 75 minutes in length to prove that the Epistle to the Hebrews was written by St Paul. He proved his point most conclusively, but most of us would have been content with an argument 50 minutes shorter!' [15] After having attended the evening service in his college chapel that same day he then went to Holy Trinity to hear Carus preach 'a long sermon' in what he described as 'a delightful service'. The reason for this praise is possibly because, in his judgement, Carus had 'the most astonishing flow of language that rivets the attention of his hearers.'

His criticism of the length of some sermons was shared by his elders. Romilly's diary contains many such comments: 'Carus preached a good Sermon but dreadfully too long; it lasted an hour' and about a guest preacher in Carus's church 'He preached with great fluency, entirely *extempore*, but it was very hard and insufferably long, viz 70 minutes – we got sick to death of it.' And how the preacher performed when speaking on behalf of a charity could markedly affect how much was donated. One Sunday Romilly went to Barnwell to hear a sermon on behalf of the Female Refuge and wrote afterwards: 'I was delighted with his sermon and thought I had never heard any preacher who spoke of our Saviour in terms of such reverence . . . I had meant to give only five shillings but could not resist giving a Pound.'[16]

C.J. was to become a famous preacher but first he had to learn the art during his years in Leicester. It appears that he was not always successful in his efforts. Benjamin Jowett, a Balliol don and friend of Stanley's, having heard him deliver one of his early sermons, told him that he would preach very well if he would only take more trouble over his preparation! Two of his early sermons preached on special occasions, the one at the Archdeacon's Visitation in 1842 and the other a charity sermon on behalf of SPG in 1843 were subsequently printed. Three years later, he published, at the request of some parishioners, a volume of his sermons. It was in his own words 'a parting gift' to them and included 30 he had preached in St Martin's. Each one, eight to fifteen printed pages long, would have taken about 20 to 35 minutes to deliver – maybe having had to endure many an hour long sermon in Cambridge had taught him to be briefer.

In the preface Vaughan admits honestly that his sermons 'make no pretension to any great novelty or originality of thought'. They do, however, show a considerable knowledge of other passages which could be used to illustrate the text he was expounding. His language abounds in phrases and echoes of both the Bible and the Book of Common Prayer. The sermons are strictly exegetical with no allusions to contemporary events and affairs by way of illustration, but some of them are, nonetheless, personally engaging and at times very challenging in their tone and content. Others are turgid and heavy going. He normally provided a brief explanation of what the sermon's Biblical text meant in its original context, before going on to show at much greater length how it related to his hearers and their lives. He tried to make his listeners face up to the reality or unreality of their relationship with God. Many a worshipper would have left his church having been made to search his soul. Man's accountability before God and the prospect of the coming Judgement is a frequent theme. In his sermon on Christmas Day 1842, for example, rather than focussing on the miracle of the Incarnation he preached a stern warning on 'Discerning the Time' about the coming Day of Judgement. Apart from the opening sentence 'This is a day of universal rejoicing throughout the Christian world' there is no joy to be heard in his words to his hearers: 'My brethren, what to you is this Christmas season? What right have you to rejoice in a Saviour whom you have rejected and trodden under foot? Will you insult God by celebrating the anniversary of your Redeemer's birth with worldly and ungodly merriment, only adding sin to sin, turning that which should have been for your soul's welfare, into an occasion for falling?' [17]

C.J. at this early stage in his ministry seems to have been one of those Evangelicals who believed that the present generation was living in the 'end times' and that Jesus would soon return in glory to judge the living and the dead, so it was his duty to warn his parishioners. He did, however, in some sermons preach the good news of God's grace shown in Christ, and spoke of the gift of the Holy Spirit in a believer transforming his character. Every individual had daily choices to make and the end result of those choices could be sharing eternity with God or apart from Him. Faith had to be active in love. He has the added merit that he preached his own sermons which not all parochial clergy at that time could claim. Many of them, either from lack of time or lack of inclination to make the effort, chose to read other men's work, which is one reason why so many sermons were published – there was a market for them among the clergy as well as the laity.

The sermon he had preached at the Archdeacon's Visitation was a bravura performance from one of the youngest and least experienced clergy present. It gives a clear picture of how Vaughan saw the priorities of the ordained ministry. For him, preaching the Gospel was paramount. To do that effectively one needed not only good scholarship and much time spent in prayerful reflection on the text in its original language but also to know one's people, and that could only be gained by visiting them in their homes. Here is a small part of his argument which includes a tilt at the sacramentalism of the Tractarians:

> We hear that such is the incomparable grandeur of the Sacraments as instruments of grace, that nothing in which man is the speaker, even though God be its ordainer, can claim a place beside them without being chargeable with high presumption. And yet, is it not the experience of all who have for many years approved themselves as faithful ministers of Christ, that, while they could point out some, perhaps many, who traced up all their religious principles to instruction received in the parochial schools; while they could tell of much good done by laborious ministerial visitation from house to house, in the way of inducing many to frequent the house of God, of bringing home to an individual some lesson taught only vaguely to a congregation, of improving some providential circumstance to the awakening or comforting of those for whom it had been ordained; while they could show more than one instance in which sickness had led, under the blessing of God upon instruction given during its continuance, to a holy and consistent life, in one who, till then, had been careless or wavering; while all and each of these branches of ministerial labour had borne good

and abiding fruit; yet that, after all, preaching had been the one great means in God's hand of awakening the careless, guiding the ignorant, strengthening the weak, animating the despondent, and enlivening those who were ready to die. [18]

He began a practice in Leicester which was to become a major feature of his teaching ministry later in Doncaster, namely, preaching systematically on a single book of the NT – the sermons then formed the base text for a commentary. In the Preface to the 3rd and revised edition of his commentary on Romans (1870 edition) he told how it came to be written: 'My own special study of the Epistle to the Romans began in preparation for expository Sermons, delivered weekly during 1842 and the two following years in St Martin's Church at Leicester.'[19] Another fifteen years would pass before it appeared in print. When he wrote the Preface to the 1st edition, dated Sevenoaks August 6 1859, he dedicated the book 'To the Sixth Form Past and Present of Harrow School.'

By virtue of his office, he found himself having to chair a variety of bodies and committees. He chaired his first Vestry Meeting on Easter Tuesday 29 March 1842 at which the two Church Wardens for the ensuing year were elected. When the Vestry next met in April it was 'for making an Assessment and laying a Rate for the necessary relief of the Poor and for the other Purposes in the several Acts of Parliament mentioned relating to the Poor of the said Parish'[20] C.J. was conveniently absent on this occasion, and one of the Wardens chaired the meeting, which laid a Rate of one shilling in the pound for the Poor and two pence in the pound for 'the purpose of the Watching and Lighting Act.' He was there for the July meeting which, in addition to accepting and passing the Church Wardens' accounts for the previous year, had the unpopular task of laying a rate 'for and towards the repairs of the Church of the parish and for such other purpose as a Church rate is by law applicable to for the present year.'[21] A motion that the Rate be not granted was voted down by a majority of the ten men present and a rate of five pence in the pound was passed. Church Rates which were levied on Non-conformist citizens as well as adherents of the Church of England were not finally abolished until 1849. A Warden chaired other meetings later in the year at which a new Poor rate was levied. In 1843 C.J. chaired a potentially contentious one at which the Church rate was set at seven pence in the pound, but on this occasion it was passed without dissent. One item of expenditure each year was £30 [= £2,636] paid to the Vicar 'in lieu of a vicarage house'. He lived in a private residence on High Street not far from his mother's house on Highcross Street.

The town had become a centre for the Chartist movement and Thomas Cooper, one of the movement's leaders, resided there from 1838-42. Trade was seriously depressed and unemployment rose. By January 1842 it was estimated that 5,000 persons, ten times the capacity of the workhouse, were receiving poor relief. The unemployed and half-employed resorted to begging from door to door, and processions of the unemployed, several hundred strong, paraded through the town centre. Inevitably, the well-to-do feared what might happen to them and their property. In August there were strikes and more demonstrations. The magistrates swore in special constables, quartered yeomanry in the inns around the Market Place, and held in reserve the dragoons. Clashes began. The Riot Act was read to a crowd in the Market Place and on the 19th a "bloodless battle" was fought at Mowacre Hill outside the town and the strikers fled in all directions.[22] During all this public distress and disturbance, C.J. appears to have refrained from any public comment on or involvement in local politics and municipal affairs. There is no reference to these events in any of the sermons from 1842 which he chose to include in the volume he had printed.

The Minute Book of the Parish Officers does, however, reveal something of a caring attitude in the application of the moneys raised to benefit the poor in St Martin's parish – here are three examples from 1842:

June 13. Mr Adkins brought forward the case of William Brown who with his four children are now in the Poor House – Mr Adkins stated that Brown wished to come out of the House with his family on the officers allowing him a sufficient sum to redeem his Tools and furnish a House. Ordered that Mr Adkins be instructed to offer a sum not exceeding £5 for the above purpose.

July 11. Mr James Wragg of Hill St Leicester Butcher applied to have John William Sturgess bound an Apprentice to him and asked for a premium of £8 and a suit of clothes. Ordered that the boy should reside with his intended Master for one Month and that the case should be first considered after that time. [The meeting on the 8th August allowed the £8 and a further £1 for his clothes.]

September 19. William Parkinson a Parishioner with a wife and five children attended and applied for Assistance in going to Van Dieman's Land where he had a brother (as he states) in good circumstances. A letter was read from Messrs Stephenson Drapers giving Parkinson a good character and it was resolved that a sum of £5 with the concurrence of the Guardians should be allowed to Parkinson towards the expenses of the journey of himself, his wife and family. [23]

Up to this point C.J.'s life had closely mirrored that of his father: first Rugby, then Trinity College Cambridge where his father too had been a Senior Optime and a Fellow, both were entered at Lincoln's Inn, later withdrawing in favour of Ordination and the parochial ministry in Leicester. But in June 1842 Arnold died unexpectedly, and despite his young age, C.J. decided to apply for the post. Education, rather than parish ministry, attracted him. Several older and more experienced men, including Bonamy Price on the staff of Rugby, also applied. Several masters at Rugby (including Price) wrote testimonials for him, knowing that he would carry the school on in the spirit and principles of Arnold, and stated explicitly that they would be most happy to work under him.

In the event C.J. and A.C. Tait, a Fellow of Balliol who had the backing of Vaughan's friends, his fellow Oxonians Stanley, Lake and Clough, were the two front runners. Stanley had been the first to suggest to Tait that he apply but later he seems to have had second thoughts about his suitability, and according to Prothero, his biographer, 'endeavoured to procure Tait's withdrawal.'[24] At the Trustees' meeting to elect the new Head, Tait won by a single vote. He was a poorer classicist than Vaughan and proved to be a less effective teacher, but he was not without other gifts as his subsequent career shows. He went on to become Bishop of London and then Archbishop of Canterbury. A weakness in Vaughan's application lay in the fact that, had he been appointed, he would have had assistant masters under him who had been there when he was a pupil. He clearly felt a call to continue Arnold's work but it would have to be in a different school.

Stanley's support for Tait does not appear to have affected their friendship. He visited C.J. in Leicester after the appointment had been made and found him 'as kind and satisfied as possible.'[25] The following July, C.J. persuaded him to take a much-needed break from his work on the biography of Arnold and to travel to Paris with him for a week. Stanley wrote that seeing the splendour of Versailles was the highlight of that holiday for him.

Christopher Wordsworth's preferment from the Headship of Harrow to a Canonry at Westminster Abbey was made public in early October 1844. The Governors immediately began to receive letters from friends and acquaintances who were supporters of particular candidates. Thomas Sotheron-Estcourt, a wealthy landowner in the west country and himself a former pupil at Harrow, was an active governor at the time and retained such letters and testimonials in his private papers now deposited in the Gloucester Archives. Two of them illustrate how very differently supporters sought to influence the election. The first was written commending Charles Penrose at great length, who, like C.J., was a product of Arnold's Rugby and of Trinity College Cambridge, and who had also been a candidate in 1842 for the post of Head Master at his old school. The writer seems to have regarded the candidate's breeding as an essential qualification for the post!

> [he] is the son of a friend of mine in Lincolnshire of much literary eminence, author of a book on "Human Motives" and other works of deep thought, only too deep for this workday age, - and a grandson, on his mother's side, of Dr Cartwright, the inventor of the power loom. He is also the nephew of Dr Arnold and was educated by him at Rugby where he had every opportunity of appreciating his system, which he has shown himself well qualified to carry out – [Penrose was the Head of Grosvenor College, Bath] . . . He is in Orders, and is married to a very ladylike and amiable wife. Lastly, he is a <u>Gentleman</u>. His father is the nephew of the late Admiral Sir Charles Penrose, of a Cornish family; and his Mother was of a very old Nottinghamshire Family, and descended from a Sister (I believe) of Cranmer. . . [26]

The other came from a friend of Sotheron's from their time together at school who knew C.J. only by reputation; he identified in a brief letter the school's greatest current need and felt Vaughan was the best man in England equipped to meet it:

> Will you allow our common interest in Harrow to be my apology for writing to you on the subject of the Head Master.
> I hear that Mr Vaughan of Leicester is a Candidate. I am not acquainted with him, but I have often heard of him and from the character he bears I should think it difficult to find a man more likely to raise the School to what you & I recollect it. I feel much interest personally in the appointment of a Master who will improve Harrow., as I have 3 boys to send somewhere, & I do not feel satisfied with what I hear of Public Schools at the present day.
> The Education of the Poor has engaged much of the public attention. I hope that some portion of it will be directed to that of the higher classes which I have long thought still more defective. The appointment of a good Master at Harrow will do a good deal towards it.
> Pray pardon my mentioning this subject to you,
> & Believe me dear Sotheron Yours very faithfully, Harry Verney [27]

C.J. applied against the advice of some of his friends, such as his former Tutor, who felt he would be wasted on Harrow! There was a strong short list including three other highly placed scholars of Trinity College Cambridge: William Osborne who had been Senior Classic and 1st Chancellor's Medallist in 1836, Thomas Peile who had graduated as 18th Wrangler, 2nd Classic and 2nd Chancellor's Medallist in 1828, and Charles Penrose who won the Bell Scholarship in 1839 and graduated 2nd Classic that same year – he was also a Rowing Blue. All three men also had a potential advantage in that they had experience as Headmasters, Osborne at Macclesfield School, Peile at Repton and Penrose at a small school in Bath. The printed testimonials of all four men survive in Sotheron's papers. They even shared the same Cambridge referees attesting to the excellence of their classical scholarship. Penrose and Vaughan both had Bonamy Price among their referees. Price regarded Penrose as the next best scholar Rugby had produced in Arnold's time, second only to Stanley, but his preference seems to have been for Vaughan. He wrote: 'In his hands the fame of Harrow for scholarship would certainly be in safe keeping.'[28]

Several of his friends, including Stanley, Lake, Lord Lyttleton and George Cotton, bore testimony not just to the excellence of his scholarship but also to his character which so suited him to the work of a public school Headmaster. Cotton, who was at the time on Tait's staff at Rugby and would soon be a Head himself, wrote a particularly persuasive letter emphasizing that the Governors could expect Vaughan to bring to Harrow the kind of Christian influence that Arnold had had at Rugby:

> I have known the Rev. C.J. Vaughan for about ten years, and during the whole of that time he has been one of my most intimate friends.
> It is needless for me to speak of his scholarship, the excellence of which is evident from his brilliant University career. But he possesses other and higher recommendations for the office of Head Master.
> Of these the chief is, his deep sense of the importance of making a Public School a place of Christian Education: I know of no one more zealous, active, and conscientious, or more desirous to be in all things guided by religious principle.
> It is well known what great good Dr Arnold effected among the Rugby boys by his Sermons in the School Chapel. I think Mr Vaughan eminently qualified to obtain the same sort of influence by preaching. He is not only able and eloquent, but his Sermons are of that earnest and practical character which is most likely to benefit the young, and have at the same time

sufficient attractions of style and language to interest them and make them attentive.

Again, he is well fitted to carry on the details of school business, having a very clear and practical understanding. Educated at Rugby under Dr Arnold, and as the private pupil of Mr Price, he was familiar in his boyhood with excellent models of teaching, - and is not without experience himself, as two of his private pupils at Cambridge were first in the Classical Tripos, and two gained University Scholarships.

Dr Arnold's opinion of him was very high indeed, and he kept up the most affectionate intercourse with him to the end of his life. He was often a visitor at Dr Arnold's house at Rugby, and was in the habit of corresponding with him.

In conclusion, I sincerely believe that the Governors would do wisely in electing Mr Vaughan, as I have little doubt that the School would flourish under him, being a man of Christian feeling and principle, sound practical sense, first-rate scholarship, and great vigour and decision of character.[29]

His friend and former colleague at Cambridge, W.H. Thompson, now a Tutor at Trinity drew attention to other virtues which, he believed, qualified Vaughan for the post:

It strikes me, however, that there is one very remarkable feature in Mr Vaughan's character, which gives him an especial claim on the notice of any Board of Gentlemen entrusted with the responsibility of appointing a Head Master to a great Public School. This is the absence of any kind of fault that could possibly neutralize the natural influence of his great talents on the success of the School over which he might be appointed. Sweeping as this assertion may seem, I think that those who know Mr Vaughan would at once recognize its truth. He is a person of an eminently well-balanced constitution of mind: with great gentleness combining rare firmness: with high and inflexible principle, shrewd and strong common sense: with literary taste of unsurpassed purity and elegance, a decided aptitude for the duties of practical life. I may add that the high character he bears as a Clergyman is unsullied by the slightest particle of sectarian spirit: indeed I know that, in the Town where his present parochial duties are exercised, all parties are united in his praise. This alone is no mean testimony in favour of a Clergyman whose zeal is undoubted, discharging his functions in the midst of a large manufacturing Town where party and religious rancour naturally run high, seeming as it does to prove that Mr Vaughan's prudence and good sense are quite as remarkable as his energy and ability are admitted to be. [30]

Thompson could comment with some authority on Vaughan's ministry in

Leicester as he had been the first Head Master of the Collegiate School there with his friend, Edward Vaughan, as his Second Master - a school, incidentally, where C.J. took his older brother's place for a week in 1836 whilst Edward was away being ordained. And Thompson had married C.J.'s half-sister, Mary Esther, but he was not happy with life in a provincial day school and longed to be back in Cambridge. He asked Blakesley for advice who told him to bear it as one does the gout or a voyage to India 'by the help of considering that your state is not a permanent one.'[31]

C.J.'s letter of application shows that he was aware of the problems he would immediately face, if appointed. He began by stating why he had chosen the particular testimonials in his favour that he had as he could have sent others too. First among them was an extract from Arnold's letter offering him an Assistant Mastership at Rugby. He concluded the letter with another reference to Arnold:

> I trust I deeply feel the heavy responsibility attached to the appointment for which I am a Candidate. I cannot but foresee that, in addition to the ordinary anxieties and difficulties inseparable from such an office, the commencement of the new Head Mastership must be marked by some important alterations, both in the discipline, and in the general economy, of the School: the former making a large demand upon the wisdom, energy, and firmness of the Head Master, - while, in the adjustment of the latter, it will be his duty to place at the service of the Governors his best counsel and most zealous co-operation.
>
> It is my firm determination, if the choice of the Electors should fall upon me, to devote myself earnestly to the furtherance (by God's help) of the great work of Christian Education. And in offering myself, as I now do, for this purpose, to the Governors of Harrow School, I cannot forget that, however arduous the task set before me, I should always have one firm ground of encouragement and hope (the possession of which, I am well aware, must be my principal recommendation to their favourable notice) in my affectionate and most lively recollections of the example and instructions of Dr Arnold, whose teaching, - and not less his friendship, - I must ever regard as one of the greatest advantages and privileges that could possibly have been vouchsafed to me. [32]

His cousin at Wistow Hall, Sir Henry Halford, who had helped engineer his appointment to St Martin's supported him in this new step as this letter dated 12 December 1844 from C.J. implies:

> Many thanks for your kind letter, which I assure you I feel most grateful for.

A few days will, I suppose, decide my matter – and then you shall hear from me at once, in either event – I know no more than I did, about the probable result of the Harrow Election.

I congratulate you sincerely about Henry – and as to any little efforts of mine to procure him a Tutor, I can only say that they are gladly made, and have been repaid tenfold –

Ever believe me

Your grateful and affectionate   C. J. Vaughan [33]

He received the news he wanted a week later. The Harrow School Governors' Minute book has a terse record of their meeting chaired by the Earl of Aberdeen on 18 December: 'The Testimonials of several candidates were read and the Governors unanimously elected the Revd Charles John Vaughan MA, late Fellow of Trinity College Cambridge to be the Headmaster.'

C.J. had had three happy years in a parish for which he felt 'a peculiar closeness'. He recorded his gratitude for 'the singular kindness which I had experienced throughout the whole period of my abode in it.'[34] His final act in the parish was to baptise Sarah Marston, the daughter of a gardener.

He had, however, failed in one important respect. Thomas North noted in 1844 that the church's 'fabric was in a sadly decayed and decaying condition.' With the arrival of C.J.'s elder brother, Edward, the following year, 'St Martin's church entered upon a new era of its existence.' [35] Within two years plans were afoot to restore the chancel, the south and north chapels, and the roof of the south aisle. The work was carried out between 1846 and 1851. By then C.J. was already well on his way to becoming a restorer of a very different kind at Harrow.

Harrow – "A great Headmaster"

It is a great thing, my brethren, early in life to fight it out with the body; to settle the question once and for all, whether the body or the mind and soul shall be master.
C.J. Vaughan *Memorials of Harrow Sundays* p.187

Vaughan moved to the school on the Hill in January 1845 where term began on the 25th. At that time it still lay in an unspoilt rural setting. The houses of London were five miles away and separated from the school by fields and pasture land with just a few villas and country houses to be seen. Some of these were occupied by parents attracted by the opportunity of sending their sons on the 'foundation' as 'home-boarders', and thereby avoiding expensive fees. At that time Harrow was little more than a large village - the census of 1841 had recorded a population of just 1,359.

He knew that he faced huge problems but he was confident he could overcome them despite his youth and lack of experience. He was just twenty-eight and looked even younger – one local described him as 'a smooth-faced boy, with extremely gentle manners' [1] Richmond's pastel drawing of him fits well such a description. Queen Adelaide is said to have remarked "I did think he was one of his own boys." Francis Norman, a pupil he inherited from Wordsworth, later recalled:

> How young he looked – and was too – and smooth faced, but with a great reputation for scholarship, especially Greek, and with the atmosphere of Dr Arnold and Rugby, still enfolding him . . .
> We soon found that our new head was a schoolmaster, *natus*, as well as (very) *fit*! His manner was quiet, suave, self-possessed, but above all bland, yet a blandness behind which lay a large reserve of determination and action; and we were not long in discovering that the *suaviter in modo*, which was natural to him, could when necessary, be combined with an unmistakable exhibition of the *fortiter in re*. [2]

For him, to follow in the footsteps of his old Master was a vocation. The transformation Arnold had achieved at Rugby, he hoped to repeat at Harrow. His predecessor had left him an invaluable aid in the form of a 25 page hand-written notebook (with numerous crossings out and amendments) headed *Harrow School Head Master's Book* dated January 1845 and signed by Wordsworth. It listed what he needed to know about how school life had been organised hitherto. The book is remarkably

126

detailed concerning all manner of things – the Contents page lists in this order: Parish Church; School Chapel; Cathechizing; Confirmation; Holy Communion; Sermons; Authority of Visitor & Diocesan; Assistant Masters; School; Locking up; Lessons of VI Form; Other Forms; Boarding Houses; Monitors; Monitors week & Exercise; Excuse of Exercises; Examinations; Examinations at Scholarship Examiners; Prizes; Exercises for Speeches; Speeches; Punishments; Calendarium Harroviensis; and attention is drawn to 'Some miscellaneous rules and observations' which could be found 'towards the close of the book of Admissions'. Just how very detailed the guidance given was, can be seen from the following two extracts. The opening page about the Parish Church begins:

> The Boys attend the Parish Church on Sunday mornings, also on Ash Wednesday and the following Wednesdays in Lent. They are also confirmed in the Parish Church. (see further below, under article Confirmation.)
> The morning Service begins at eleven o'clock, the School bell begins to ring at ¼ before eleven and rings for eight minutes. The Head Master wears his Gown, Cassock, Bands and Cap, he goes up to Church so as to be there a few minutes before the Service commences: he takes care that the boys sit in their proper place according to their order in the School, the West Gallery being occupied by the Sixth and Fifth Forms; the North by the Shell and Fourth Form. He sees also that before they take their seats they kneel down for a short private prayer, and that they afterwards join in the responses and kneel at the proper times during the Service. The order of the boys is from the Head Master's seat towards the Under-Master's, i.e. from South to North, and in the North Gallery from West to East. The Head Master looks over the names of the Sixth Form, the assistant Masters those of their respective Forms. If any of the assistant Masters should on any occasion be prevented from attending Divine Service he gives previous notice to the Head Master. After the Service is over, the Head Master is the first to leave the Gallery, & is followed by the boys in their respective proper order. He remains under the Gallery till they have all left the Church. [3]

The section on punishments reads as follows:

> For grave moral offences the punishment inflicted on a Monitor of the School is Degradation: and for similar offences the punishment inflicted on the rest of the VI Form and on the V Form is Flogging.
> For less ~~flagrant~~ offences the VI and V Forms are <u>not</u> flogged the punishment generally is transcription of 300 lines or more according to circumstances for absence from a Bill &c. In the case of arrear of Exercise in his own class the Head Master ~~would find it an effective mode of punishment~~

~~to~~ takes the delinquent down with him from School to his own house and to detain him there till the exercise is done. Detention also by the Head Master, or by the Master to whose house, or class, the boy belongs is adopted for other parts of the School in case of arrear of punishment i.e. not done and shown up at the fixed time.

If a boy is late for Prayers in the morning in School or is not perfect in his lesson he has to translate the lesson in writing and this translation is always brought up in the School next following.

In proportion as religious discipline is maintained, and minor punishments applied, with private reproof and admonition, cases for degradation will be rare; and for expulsion still rarer. It is greatly to be desired that these two latter Punishments should be prevented by kindly communication with the Parents of the boy, and by a request for his removal. [4]

The final page is about Cricket and the expectation that masters should support it!

Here in the pages of this slim booklet is a record of the Harrow way of doing things which Vaughan needed not only to know but also to respect if he was to make changes which would meet with least opposition.

Within days of his appointment and before he had even arrived at the school he was already dealing with parents of prospective pupils. On 7 January 1845 he wrote from Trinity College of his hopes and plans to the father of one of them: 'The first of these is, that a material reduction is now to be made in the expenses of the School. The other, that the Head Master's Boarding House will, it is expected, shortly be rebuilt; and that, in the meantime, I propose, immediately after Easter, to make some arrangement by which a small number of Boarders may be placed under my own immediate care, to form the basis of that larger Establishment . . .'[5]

He recognized that his first priority had to be to raise public confidence in the school and thereby attract more fee-paying pupils and so be able to afford to appoint more teaching staff, some of whom would take the financial risk of investing in new boarding houses for the pupils. When Wordsworth resigned, the number of pupils had sunk to 69 of whom 14 were free scholars. There were just three small boarding houses run by the Revd Benjamin Drury at Druries, the Revd William Oxenham at Moreton's, and the Revd G.F. Harris at The Park. A fourth house, The Grove, reckoned to be the best Georgian building on the Hill, belonged to the Revd Thomas Henry Steel who had left in 1843 for a country living. It was temporarily under the Revd Richard Shilleto, an outstanding Greek scholar, but closed at the end of 1844 when he returned to Cambridge.

Robert Grimston, a lawyer and an active Old Boy who served on a small committee looking into the matter of providing a new boarding house for the Head, wrote to Estcourt on 8 February 1845 about the immediate positive impact that Vaughan's appointment was having:

> Mr Vaughan fully concurs with the view which you took with regard to the expenses at Harrow, and further he has acted upon it. At his own House the cost will be at least £40 per annum less than what it has been previously. The consequence of Mr Vaughan having received numerous applications to receive Boarders, he has hired a small house, pro tempore, which he will open after Easter with 13 new Boys. There were, I believe, fifteen new Boys this quarter, which shows at least that the Public have no objection to the reduction: I hear of quantities of Boys going to Harrow from all sides – and I do not wonder at it, for I believe Mr Vaughan to be the very best man in England to be at the Head of a Public School. We have received so many letters from Old Harrow men, willing to subscribe, but not knowing what sum to give, that we think it would be judicious to publish in the morning Papers of Thursday next, a list of those who have affixed sums to their names. [6]

The following month saw another piece of good news in the addition of 'Dr' to the new Head's title. On 5 March the Senate of Cambridge University conferred the degree of Doctor of Divinity on him by royal mandate.

In regard to raising public confidence in the school, Vaughan had a distinct advantage over his predecessor. He was known to be Wordsworth's equal as a classical scholar but more importantly he was known to have been one of Arnold's favourite pupils and likely to pursue his old master's policy of providing a distinctly Christian education and maintaining discipline. This appealed to Evangelical parents in particular, some of whom immediately began sending their sons. Twelve boys were admitted in January, by Easter a further 21 had come and by the end of his first year 73 new pupils had entered the school. Among them were Dudley Ryder, a future Lord Privy Seal and 3rd Earl of Harrowby, Thomas Charles Baring, who later joined his family's bank and became a benefactor of the school, and Edward Bulwer-Lytton, who became Viceroy of India. Their social standing was representative of many of the families who sent their sons to Harrow. Fathers who had themselves been educated at the school but had held back from sending their sons under the two previous heads now supported it again. Wealthy indust-rialists and entrepreneurs such as Isambard Kingdom Brunel (the creator and chief engineer of the Great Western Railway), George Hudson (known as the 'Railway King') and William Laird (the ship builder) now also wanted their sons to have the social advantages of a Harrow education. A year after his arrival, pupil numbers had risen to 138 and in January 1847 to 264 and so the increase continued. There were 438 when he left in 1859.

The Rugby grapevine noted his appointment and followed his progress closely during the first few months. Arthur Clough, now a Fellow of Oriel College Oxford, wrote to Burbidge on 31 December 1844:

> Well, you know of course that Vaughan is elected at Harrow. Price told me that he, Vaughan, wished Simpkinson to go and help him; and I do not doubt that he wrote to Simpkinson at once. At present with 90 boys and 500 per annum and furniture to be bought at a price at least equal to one year's salary, there will be no money to spare, I should suppose, and not much call for a new master, unless, a thing devoutly to be wished, one of the old ones should cut his stick.[7]

Three months later Clough brought his friend Gell up to date on Vaughan:

> Vaughan, I am told by Howson, whom I saw yesterday at Conybeare's, expects sixteen new boys to commence his own boarding house within the coming half-year. At Harrow they have *three* half-years. Howson says he writes in very good spirits; he finds his Masters willing and serviceable, and I hear that the boys like him, and that in general they all, both boys and Masters, look forward to do great things. Simpkinson . . . looks forward to joining Vaughan at Harrow. Vaughan will certainly have him there as soon as opportunity offers, and if the numbers increase as fast as it seems likely they will, that will not be long.[8]

A new house had been built in 1840 for the Headmaster, the previous one having burnt down two years earlier, and with the Governors' permission a new wing for boys, known as 'The Old Side', was added in 1845. This building was funded by donations from Old Harrovians as the Governors let it be known that it was not in their power to use School Funds to build a boarding house. Thirty-four of the new boys were entered on it in Vaughan's first year. He did not, however, prove to be a very successful Housemaster as his many other duties simply did not leave him enough time to be closely involved with the pupils residing on it. So he left the running of it very much to a housekeeper, and when, once a term, he inspected all their rooms, he sent his butler earlier in the day to alert them that the Head would be coming round in the evening.

Among the early boarders on his house was his young cousin, John Pares. John's brother, Thomas Henry, joined him on the house – Vaughan reported to the father that the boy had settled down quite quickly but noted that he was 'clearly not of a studious turn yet he does his work willingly – I hope more carefulness and close attention will follow.'[9] The father did not take the implied criticism amiss for he sent the Head (his nephew) the gift of a Stilton cheese four days later. Four other early arrivals on his house became particular favourites: John Hyde D'Arcy, who entered it in April 1845 and became Head of House in 1850 before winning a scholarship at Balliol where he died on 28 January 1852; Henry Mather Jackson, son of the MP for Birkenhead, who was another entrant in April '45; Edward Latham in June '45 and Henry Montagu Butler [the son of a former Headmaster] in November '46, who became Head of School and would succeed Vaughan as Headmaster. All four boys figure later in the story.

In 1846 Vaughan gave permission for two more assistant masters to take boarders: the Revd R. Middlemist, who extended the house known as Church Hill and Mr G.T. Warner, who turned two semi-detached villas into one house known as West Acres, which opened in 1847. The Grove re-opened in 1849 with Simpkinson as Housemaster who married the Head's sister, Sarah Dorothea, in St Martin's Leicester on 6 December that year, with Vaughan as the officiant.

Oxenham was the School's Second Master at the time of Vaughan's appointment and along with the Head he had the right to birch boys, which he did frequently. He was renowned among the boys for his swearing and his classroom was reputed to be a bear garden. Life on his House seems to have been little better. Augustus Hare, who boarded there from 1848-49, remembered it as a place where bullying, ceaseless fagging, beatings for bad service to fag masters, and blanket tossing were the norm.[10] The story is told of how the boys got the better of their Housemaster on one occasion:

> One night Mr Oxenham, being determined to catch the boys *flagrante delicto*, took off his boots and crept upstairs. The boys, however, had anticipated him, and had strewn the stairs with nails. The consequence was a "D—n, d—n, d—n," in crescendo as each stair was trod, and by the time he

reached the bedroom, the boys were apparently sleeping the sleep of youth and innocence. [11]

The boys occasionally got the better of him in the classroom too:

> Alas! Our form is under Mr. Oxenham. He has the power of flogging, and does flog very often for the least fault, for he really enjoys it. He is such an old man, very old, very sharp, very indolent, very preachy. Sometimes he falls asleep when we are in form, and the boys stick curlpapers through his hair, and he never finds out. [12]

His successor as Second Master was George Harris. Minchin records that he 'used to send before him his butler, a servant, if possible, more dignified than his master, whenever he paid a visit to the boys quarters in his house. He used even sometimes to have a bell rung to give all boys fair notice of his coming.'[13] His was not a happy House for a small boy to be on. Augustus Hare described

> the constant cruelty at "Harris's" where little boys were always made to come down and box in the evening for the delectation of the fifth form – of how little boys were constantly sent in the evening to Farrish's – halfway to the cricket ground, to bring back porter under their greatcoats, certain to be flogged by the Headmaster if they were caught, and to be "wapped" by the sixth form boys, if they did not go, and infinitely preferring the former . . . Indeed what with fagging and bullying, servility was as much inculcated at Harrow in those days as if it was likely to be a desirable acquirement in after life. [14]

Fortunately, not all masters were like Oxenham and Harris. One of Vaughan's undoubted achievements was his appointment of some very talented assistants. Almost all of them had high academic credentials – medallists, 1st Class graduates, College Fellows, and half of them were alumni of Trinity Cambridge. Of these the two most famous were the great N.T. scholar B.F. Westcott (who was a close friend of the Head's younger brother David), later to become Regius Professor of Divinity at Cambridge and then Bishop of Durham, who served as Vaughan's assistant with the Sixth Form, and F.W. Farrar, a future Dean of Canterbury, who wrote the best-selling children's book *Eric or Little by Little* whilst at Harrow. Farrar's particular contribution was the encouragement he gave outside school hours to those who shared his interest in science and literature. He also became a very popular preacher with the boys. Two of the others, S.A. Pears and E.D. Bradby, went on to become the Headmaster of Repton and the Master of Haileybury College respectively. One of his last appointments, made in 1859, was E.E. Bowen, another Prizeman, Scholar and then Fellow of Trinity and a Cambridge 'Apostle' who would stay at the school until his death in 1901 and who would write many of the most famous Harrow songs. Tyerman described him as possibly the most famous assistant master in the whole country and the archpriest of the adoration of games as a serious activity for adults and boys alike.

Westcott came on a temporary appointment in January 1852 pending the decision on a headship he had applied for in Jersey but such was his appreciation of the school he decided to stay when Vaughan offered him a permanent post. He told a friend who visited him there in July that Harrow was the best school in the world and he shared his delight in a letter to Lightfoot dated 11 September: 'My feelings with regard to Harrow remain still unchanged. I do not fancy that any school offers so good a field for training. I can enter into the system heartily, and with the utmost confidence in our head. Vaughan is almost too kind, and yet withal clear and very decided in his views.'[15]

Another member of staff whom he appointed in 1854 and long remembered for his loving, tender care of pupils was the Revd John Smith. George Russell described him as 'an Apostle to boys, if ever there was one, and the Guardian Angel of youthful innocence.'[16] John Addington Symonds (Rendall's 53-58) ascribed 'the only pure good' of his Harrow training to this man. Smith was an eccentric, if not slightly crazy, clergyman who frequently spoke to his pupils as though he had inside knowledge of the life of heaven! He made a point of having a personal interview with every new boy, warning them of the temptations of school life. He respected their privacy to the degree that when he went to check on the boys at night in Rendall's, where he occasionally assisted the Housemaster, he made a point of wearing hob-nailed boots so that they knew he was coming and would be safely tucked up in their own beds by the time he got there. For him, as he frequently reminded his young charges, cleanliness came next to godliness and he duly inspected their hands each morning. Another of his abiding concerns was making sure that every pupil learnt to swim, so he ran a 'swimming school' every summer in the school's pool, the Ducker. There he exhorted the fearful to dive from the highest board: 'See how all those wonderful fellows have gone head-first before you; jump laddie; feet first, if you can't the other way. There's no shrinking in heaven.'[17] The boys knew that he spent his free time doing good outside the school and respected him for it – on Tuesdays he visited in the gaols, on Thursdays he visited the sick and poor in the town, and on Saturdays he walked to Pinner to read to his mother and sister for whom he had made a home there. Occasionally he would take a boy with him, sharing his love of English poetry as they walked. Symonds greatly appreciated these walks with him not least for 'the stupendous amount of good English verse' he absorbed. Henry Trueman Wood who started his Harrow years in Smith's form in 1858 described him as the 'best loved of all the Harrow masters of his time.' But added 'He was not a fine scholar, and I take it he was not a particularly good teacher; but he was for small boys an ideal master, for he trained them to be honest, upright gentlemen, and he developed their character if he did little to educate their minds. His form adored him, while they recognized his eccentricities . . .'[18] A mark of his love for them all was that, unbeknown to them, he prayed for each boy in the school by name every week.

In sharp contrast to him was the Revd Robert Middlemist, who was remembered by some as 'a bully, a tyrant' and 'a terrible man.'[19] Wood remembered Ben Drury as being a genial person, popular alike with boys and masters. Edwyn Vaughan he judged not to be as strong a character or as good a scholar as his brother but said that he had good influence over the boys of his House, which was looked upon as the best in the school. About Westcott, he commented 'He was certainly better suited for a bishop than for a school-master.'[20]

It was inevitable that Vaughan would want to introduce Arnold's way of using the school monitors to further his own aims for the school but he wisely chose to go about it gradually, first winning the confidence of the existing Sixth Formers and honouring Harrow traditions. The ground for reform had already been prepared by Wordsworth and by the publication of Stanley's *Life* of Arnold in 1844. The head boy when he arrived was Charles Roundell, who later commented that 'the machinery, in fact, was there in working order. All that was wanted was the practical hand to set it going.'[21] And he named some of Wordsworth's monitors who were particularly helpful to Vaughan at the start of the school's moral reformation. 'This great reform, of unspeakable importance to Harrow School, was brought about thus simply and easily, and without – as far as I can recollect – any other contributing influence. It was also brought about at once.'[22] Other contemporaries suggest it took rather longer and one gave the credit for the change entirely to the Head – 'Dr Vaughan was a man of supreme tact, and felt his way, making friends first of all with the boys into whose hands he proposed to put so much power . . . I was in the Sixth Form, just passed into it, when Dr Vaughan came. His mode of procedure was to make friends with the Sixth Form, so that they might become a parliament for the control and well-being of the school. He, accordingly, invited us to dine with him, and was most agreeable.' [23]

It surely happened too because the new Head made it absolutely clear at the outset that he was determined to have things the way he wanted them even at the risk of pupil opposition and that he would stamp out the lawlessness and drunkenness that had previously prevailed. If he appeared to wear a velvet glove, there was to be no doubt that a mailed fist lay within. Montagu Butler said of him that the boys all knew they had a strong ruler who was not to be trifled with. He flogged boys publicly in an icily calm way. On one occasion, after ministering a particularly severe flogging he said gently to the boy, "Thank you, my dear boy, I will not trouble you any more today." More than one boy recalled in after years how he summoned the whole school minus the masters to the Speech Room to witness the flogging of Henry Dering. A note from Dering was intercepted by the boy's form master who passed it to Vaughan. The note was intended for a handsome Irish boy on another House who went by the nickname of Leila inviting him to share his bed between 4 and 5 that afternoon. Symonds described how the Head had the great assemblage of boys in the hollow of his hand: 'The stillness was phenomenal, and the impressions produced by the words addressed to the School in general and to the culprit in particular, cannot be exaggerated. Dr Vaughan had a way of pushing back his chair when the business was concluded, which seemed to say better than words that all was over.' [24] Dering was removed from the school and transferred to Winchester.

Charles Dalrymple (Middlemist's 53-58) saw a gentler side to him. He was born Charles Fergusson, 2nd son of Sir Charles Dalrymple Fergusson 5th Baronet, but assumed the surname Dalrymple at the age of ten on his father's death in 1849. It is possible that Vaughan became a surrogate father figure for him in his Harrow years and he became a lifelong friend of the Head's. He wrote: 'If he seemed formidable at first to boys from the quiet calmness of his manner, he won their confidence by his fairness, by his reliance on their word, by the gentleness of his glance.' [25] Lionel Tollemache (Mr Pears 50–56), who was no great fan of Vaughan's, admitted that they all owed much to him because of his discipline and because he trained them to be self-reliant and he made a point of trusting them as far as possible. He also cared about the boys as the following anecdote illustrates:

> In 1856, so the story goes, a new boy, Archie C__, arrived from the High-lands of Scotland in the middle of term to join the school. He was dressed in a kilt, and had never worn trousers! The Doctor had him locked up in his study until a tailor had made him a pair of the conventional leg coverings, and thereby saved him from much trouble and chaff. What made the Doctor's thoughtful act all the kinder was that he never allowed the story to leak out, and it was known only eventually through being told by some of the boy's relations in after years. [26]

John Spencer, Viscount Althorp, was another pupil who benefited from Vaughan's caring nature and personal ministry to him. The boy had entered the school at the age of 12 in June 1848 and enjoyed a good relationship with the Head who supported the teenager through two family bereavements: the death of his mother in 1851 and then of his older sister, Georgina, a year later. After the second one, the boy was minded to stay at home to support his father and not return to school. Vaughan wrote him a long letter of condolence and gently set out the pros and cons of the boy's proposed action – the most obvious argument in favour was the comfort he could be to his father. He then wrote:

> As to the other side, the thing that chiefly weighs with me, is the cherished hope, of which I have spoken to you, of your getting into the 6th Form at the end of this quarter. It is not, as you know, from a mere wish for your nominal advancement, still less, from any exalted idea of the advantages you would have from my more constant tuition; but I do estimate very highly the good you might do & I trust by God's blessing would do, to many many round you.
> Now the great fear is, that, though you would be able, I doubt not, to earn that step, it might not be quite so easy to give it you (if absent all the quarter), at Midsummer next. And this is a serious consideration, as I am sure you will feel – though I do not say that it is paramount or at once decisive . . . [27]

He went on to urge the boy to lay it all before his father and to be guided by him. He signed the letter as 'Your faithful and affectionate friend.' The boy returned and two years later went up to Trinity College Cambridge. It became a lifelong friendship – 18 letters from Vaughan to him survive – the younger man when he became 5th Earl Spencer frequently sought the older one's advice on clerical appointments in his gift.

Tollemache remembered his first meeting with Vaughan as a pleasant surprise, having arrived at Harrow with his head full of tales of how harsh school life could be:

> Imagine my relief when, on the morning after my arrival, I stood before Dr Vaughan. His benign face and gentle voice fairly took me aback. Could this angel in man's clothing be capable of the constant firmness and occasional severity which I had heard ascribed to him? My surprise, as I afterwards learnt, was shared by my companions. [28]

He also recalled appreciatively some of the civilizing reforms the Head had made in school life:

> At that time the principle of condoning a lie told by a boy to a master, in order to avoid incriminating himself, was not utterly exploded. It was Vaughan who at Harrow raised the moral standard in this respect. He also raised it by abolishing what were there called 'mills', that is to say, fights, which, like the famous one at Rugby described in *Tom Brown*, had taken place with the connivance of the masters on a plot of grass between the school buildings and the racquet courts, still known as the 'milling ground'. By these two innovations – the proscription of 'privileged lies' and of 'mills' – as well as by sundry other reforms, Vaughan rendered a great service to the school. [29]

One of his first reforms was to ban the Guy Fawkes Night celebrations, which in the past had been occasions for some wild, riotous behaviour but he offered in its place a dinner for the monitors. Fortunately for him, the number of boys present in the school who could remember what had happened in previous years was comparatively small, so this reform met with little opposition.

Wordsworth had already made some important changes in how the boys' corporate life was shaped – in 1838 he had the duties of fags put into writing and restricted what could be required of them in the Houses to making breakfast and running errands for the Sixth formers and out of the Houses to cricket fagging. He had also made the appointment of monitors a public occasion held in the Chapel which he had had built in 1839. Vaughan moved the ceremony to the Speech Room and made it a more solemn occasion. He raised the number of monitors to 15 and made it clear that the office of monitor was now one of duty not of privilege. They had responsibility for checking misbehaviour and for setting an example of what was right; they retained the power to flog boys – a practice that public opinion was turning against - and only the most serious cases of moral misdemeanour were reported to the Head. Despite these reforms, the fagging system remained open to abuse, both physical and sexual, and bullying remained a problem on some houses as noted earlier – even on the Head's as Herman Merivale recalled. He shared a bedroom with three scions of the nobility, one young lord and two honourables, 'and all three vied as to which could bully me the hardest.' [30] The danger of older boys corrupting younger ones was always present.

An important figure in any boy's life was the personal tutor he was given on admission to the school. The tutor was responsible for his pupil's general well-being and he sent a very brief monthly report to the boy's parents. He would supervise the younger boys' preparation and, if necessary, assist them with their translations. A good tutor (who could also be his form or house master) was probably the member of staff with the closest relationship with a pupil but not all tutors were as conscientious and caring as John Smith. Charles Dalrymple struck up a life-long friendship with his tutor and kept some of Westcott's reports on him. They illustrate how bare the detail was, e.g. 'Conduct in House - Good, Progress - Good, Place in Form of 40 - 1, Conduct - Good, Mathematics - Conduct & Progress v. good, Pupil Room - Works carefully.'

There was no official school uniform as such, though Vaughan did make one ruling that neckties should be plain black or white. A fairly conservative but contemporary form of dress was the norm – older boys wore a tailcoat and waistcoat of black broadcloth, trousers of cashmere, and a top hat of the type known as a beaver; younger boys wore a short coat.

More pupils meant greater earnings especially for housemasters. Those among them who didn't particularly like the Head, such as Oxenham, were none the less grateful to him for this. Oxenham made such a great profit from his house that he paid John Smith £300 p.a. [= £34,200] to take his teaching duties. Frederick Rendall, likewise, delegated all his private tuition to Smith. It also allowed Vaughan to raise the salaries of most of his Assistants from £60 p.a. to £150 – a few received even more. When he arrived there were only two assistant classics masters and one mathematics master in addition to the Second Master; by the time he left there were fourteen teaching classics and four mathematics.

More pupils also meant more parents who could be encouraged to help fund new building projects. The largest of these was the Chapel designed by Gilbert Scott and built in stages between 1854 and 1857 on the site of Wordsworth's smaller building. It had proved to be too small when pupil numbers passed the four hundred mark. The first stage, the chancel, was begun in August 1854 at a cost of £2,500 [= £234,700] and paid for by Vaughan himself; the north aisle was started shortly afterwards and was paid for by Assistant Masters and parents. A south aisle was added in 1856 in memory of the 22 Harrovians who had died in the Crimean War, and work on the nave and re-roofing started the following year thanks to the generosity of old boys and friends of the school. The new Chapel was consecrated on All Saints Day, 1 November 1857 by Dr Tait, who was now Bishop of London. Two months later a new organ was installed, mainly paid for from voluntary contributions made by members of the school. In the following months stained glass windows were added. Four of them in 1858 were paid for by the tradesmen and farmers of Harrow in testimony of their personal esteem for Vaughan.

An immediate consequence of the completion of the chapel was that the move away from the parish church begun by Wordsworth could now also be completed. Previously the boys had attended services in the parish church every Sunday morning and evening. One pupil who was at the school from 1841-46 described what it was like to worship in the parish church: 'The services at the church were purely formal. Mr Cunningham preached long sermons of the good old-fashioned evangelical type. They may have been very good, but we boys in our gallery at the west end could not hear a word that he said. Dr Wordsworth whiled away the time by reading his Bible in German, the rest of us as best we might.' [31] Later, Vaughan would use Cunningham's inaudibility as a reason for the boys ceasing to attend the parish church.

Wordsworth had argued successfully with the Governors that a school chapel would afford better opportunities for worship and religious instruction more suited for schoolboys, and he cited the experience of Winchester and Rugby in this matter. Initially, the Vicar, the Revd J.W. Cunningham, who was also a governor, had resisted the proposed change but eventually acceded when the Head agreed with him that the boys would continue to attend Holy Communion and Morning Prayer and the school chapel would be used only for Evensong on a Sunday. That arrangement ended for good in 1857. Symonds, in a letter home, reported the new time-table for Sunday worship was as follows:

We have the Sunday services altered now. As we do not any of us go to the

Church there is the Communion Service in Chapel before breakfast & the rest of the morning Service at 11. & at ¼ past 5 the evening Service. The reason for having the Communion before breakfast is that the Sacrament may be more frequently and conveniently administered.[32]

Like Arnold at Rugby, the school chapel was the centre of Vaughan's influence with the boys. It was here that he carefully prepared the boys for Confirmation. Their preparation lasted two months with a weekly lecture for which he provided them with a detailed summary and appropriate prayers. It was his practice to examine each candidate in private before they were presented to the Bishop for Confirmation.

A letter to a former pupil who had written in April 1857 asking for advice about suitable reading matter in preparation for his own forthcoming Confirmation as an adult candidate gives Vaughan's view of this rite. He recommended a *Manual for Christians after Confirmation* written by Dr Hawkins, the Provost of Oriel, and he sent him a copy of *Prayers for Public Schools* but added

> I am sorry to say that I have always found it difficult to meet with any book quite to my mind for the purpose of preparing for Confirmation: and to this account I am always anxious to give a few Lectures myself of a kind which I hope may meet the case. After all, the great hope is, that the occasion itself – the public declaration of a real desire and purpose to be a Christian indeed – may awaken in prospect more especially, those desires and efforts after God which He always blesses. [33]

In 1859 he published his own *Notes for Lectures on Confirmation* which became an instant best seller. By 1893 it had been revised twice and been reprinted 15 times, and was reprinted as late as 1924. Its tone is simple and practical and readily accessible to a schoolboy – here are two very brief extracts about prayer and Bible reading taken from the lecture on the 'Means of Grace':

> We ought every night to think over the past day; its blessings and opportunities, our use of each, our omissions of duty, our temper and spirit, language, acts, &c. It need not be a long process. With an honest purpose to know the truth, and a humble prayer for grace to do so, a few moments will do all . . . Love your Bible. Do not think of it as a burden, but as a pleasure. Treat it as you would a letter from a distant friend to whom you owe everything. Take pains to *understand* the Bible. This is a preliminary to *using* it. Hence the value of Scripture lessons. [34]

It was in the Chapel that he held them by his eloquence and earnestness Sunday after Sunday. The other members of staff who were ordained took it in turn to preach in the morning – the evening sermon was reserved for the Head. He took care to keep them short by Victorian standards and to relate the teaching of the Biblical text he had chosen to the lives of his young hearers. He always wrote his sermons out in full – he never preached *ex tempore*. His nephew explained why: 'He was convinced that the result was a less finished utterance, one less in accord with the mature thought of the speaker, less likely therefore to sink into the heart of the hearer and less worthy of the divine ministry which it was intended to fulfil.'[35] The sermons lack theological profundity and there are few references to the events of the times but there is always an earnest appeal to the boys to live by the highest and best that they know and to do it in the strength of God's indwelling Holy Spirit. Repentance and forgiveness, and an appeal to them to accept new life in Christ are repeated themes. Five volumes of these sermons plus a further 14 individual sermons preached on special occasions, often away from the School, were published in his Harrow years. One of those who heard him preach scores of times remembered them with gratitude:

> But only those who listened and worshipped in the chapel can realise the pathos and interest of Dr Vaughan's persuasive eloquence. The sermons were of almost uniform excellence, - the opening and the closing sermons of the school term being specially telling, - but there were occasions when such sermons as "A Nation watching for Tidings", in November 1854, in the dark days of the Crimean War, or "The Indian Sorrow, and its Lessons for the Young", preached at a school service in the parish church, just before the consecration of the new chapel, in October 1857, on the day of national humiliation for the Indian Mutiny, made the deepest impression, of which the lapse of forty years has not dimmed the recollection. [36]

A sermon such as *The Indian Sorrow* which was so memorable merits our reading a couple of extracts. It was preached on 7 October 1857, the Day of National Humiliation, and it illustrates how serious he could be and yet how engaging with young people. He urged them to pray that day for their country:

> That . . . she may have grace to review her past conduct towards the subject race, and to wipe off, nationally and individually, any reproaches which may have clung to it. That henceforth she may give all diligence to enforce upon her sons and her representatives in India such rules of

141

conduct and of government, as may set before heathen eyes examples not of evil but of good. That, while rigidly abstaining from all persecution of other Religions, *she may never be ashamed of her own*; may give all encouragement to its peaceful exercise, and to its propagation by methods of persuasion and by duly authorized men; refusing alike to use the arm of power for purposes of proselytism, and to make the possession of power an excuse for indifference to truth. [37]

He ended the sermon with a story which he acknowledged was probably already known by many of the boys but one worth re-telling as a moving example of 'a bold confession of Christ'. It was told with the clear intention of it inspiring and encouraging his young hearers to live courageous and faithful lives:

When the 6th Regiment mutinied and murdered their officers, an Ensign, only sixteen years of age, who was left for dead among the rest, escaped in the darkness to a neighbouring ravine. Here he found a stream, the waters of which sustained his life for four days and nights. Although desperately wounded, he contrived to raise himself into a tree for protection from wild beasts. On the fifth day he was discovered, and dragged by the mutineers before one of their leaders to have the little life left in him extinguished. There he found another person, a Christian catechist, formerly a Mahomedan, whom the mutineers were endeavouring to torment and terrify into a recantation. The firmness of the native was giving way as he knelt amid his persecutors, with no human sympathy to support him. The young officer, after anxiously watching him for a short time, cried out "Oh, my friend, come what may, do not deny the Lord Jesus!" Just at this moment, the alarm of a sudden attack caused the instant flight of the murderous fanatics. The Catechist's life was saved. He turned to bless the boy whose faith had strengthened his faltering spirit. But the young martyr had passed beyond all reach of human cruelty. He had entered into rest. [38]

Bishop Westcott spoke warmly of the admirable structure of his sermons, the beauty of his language and lucidity of his style but judged their power and influence to result from another of the Head's notable characteristics

The power of Dr Vaughan's sermons was not to be referred chiefly to perfection of form and expression, nor to breadth of view and soundness of judgement, but to something far more. *Dr Vaughan could make everyone to whom he spoke conscious of his real sympathy*. One master-thought, which found expression in innumerable ways, was the thought of personal fellowship with God, for which man was made, and without which no man can find peace. [39]

Westcott admired his chief and when asked by Vaughan for help readily assisted him with his commentary on Romans by providing a definitive Greek text. In a letter to Westcott dated 11 March 1858, Vaughan reveals not only his fairness in his dealings with his junior colleague but also his appreciation of his particular gifts: 'Having mentioned the subject, let me just so far set myself right with you as to say that the very least acknow-ledgement which I could possibly make to you of so great an obligation would be the half of any little profits that might result from a publication to which you would certainly have contributed more than half its value. To dream of anything else would be in the simplest sense to rob you of your actual property.' [40]

Sir George Trevelyan who became Head of the School in 1856 and won every school prize he contended for between '55 and '57 remem-bered Vaughan's sermons each Sunday evening as 'an event of the week, for great and small'.

> It is creditable to the fresh and unperverted judgement of boyhood to remember the blank dismay that fell upon the whole school when anybody except the Headmaster mounted the pulpit-stair. But apart from his public preaching, and his personal example, Doctor Vaughan's personal relations with his pupils had not specifically, or obtrusively, a religious complexion. There was nothing of the father-confessor, and nothing of the pedant or the dominie, in his intercourse with the leading Monitors, or with any Head of the School who was in a fair degree worthy of his regard and favour. Secure of his authority, he gave us an unbounded freedom of remark and reply, to an extent which sometimes bordered on presumption, but never on impertinence. [41]

Percy Thornton in a history of Harrow recorded that 'Several Harrovians have told the writer that Dr Vaughan's pulpit request to his pupils that, however weak their faith and infirm their purpose, they would, as a favour to him, *never* forget to bend the knee in prayer before retiring to sleep, *sank into their memories*, and was followed accordingly.' [42] Lionel Tollemache, who described himself as a 'Vaughan admirer', not a 'Vaughan lover' or 'Vaughan hater', to which categories, he said, 'nearly all Harrow men belonged' recorded this anecdote about how direct the Head's sermons could be:

Vaughan had a way of preaching such personal sermons as to make almost any exaggeration about them sound plausible. One such sermon, which I myself heard, lingers in my memory. To all appearance, it was distinctly pointed at an unnamed boy, who had gone to Harrow strongly imbued with the principles and sentiments of a pious home. The next term he retained his good resolutions, 'but with the unhappy addition of self-confidence'; and the result was that this same boy, who had but lately been shocked by even the slightest deviation from Christian charity, had himself become a persecutor and a bully. Some of Vaughan's friends tried to make out that he could not have possibly been preaching at a real boy; but the general impression was that his words would bear no other construction. An old Rugbeian, who was present, agreed in this opinion. He told me that he had heard strong sermons from Arnold, but never anything like that. [43]

Montagu Butler, a definite 'Vaughan lover', wrote:

I can say, without reserve, that at no time in my entire life have I been so conscious of living in a directly Christian atmosphere, with Christian ideals of duty habitually set up for reverence, as during the happy years when Vaughan presided over Harrow. The main cause was, no doubt, his impressive personality; his remarkable combination of deep devoutness with wit, penetration and delicate sympathy . . . but doubtless the spell of this personality was confirmed week by week by his admirable sermons, so keen in their insight, so tender in their touch, so winning in their expression, so rich in the fullness of Christ. [44]

Mention of his 'wit' deserves some illustration for it could at times be waspish and stinging as well as amusing and entertaining. To a self-important mother who asked Vaughan before she decided to enter her son at the school whether he was particular about his pupils' antecedents, he is said to have replied, 'Dear Madam, as long as your son behaves himself and his fees are paid no questions will be asked about his social antecedents.' [45] Of his relations with those with whom he had to deal he once remarked in later years that 'he had found the boys always fair, the Masters sometimes, the parents never, and as for widows, he confessed he had sometimes been tempted to reconsider his objections to suttee.' [46] His sense of humour could occasionally ease a situation as happened when a small boy named Dodds was sent to him for punishment. He asked him his name and as he proceeded to write it down asked him whether he spelt his name with one 'd' or two. The frightened boy replied "Please Sir, *with three*" which Vaughan thought was very funny and duly let him off with just a reprimand. He told this story to his head of house, Herman Merivale, and added "I could no more have punished that boy than flown. Nobody ever gave me such a lesson in spelling." [47] Merivale also remembers the Head telling him that he had 'a crowded pigeon hole which with a chuckle he labelled "Indignant Parents"' [48] Just how sharp his wit could be was remembered by Butler decades later when he preached in Llandaff Cathedral on the Sunday after Vaughan's funeral – 'At first – I speak from clear recollection - his bright wit and sense of the ludicrous were not always untinged with sarcasm. But he soon detected and conquered this temptation.' In 1857 he was elected a member of the Athenaeum under Rule II as a 'person of distinguished eminence' where his witty *bon-mots*, often about politicians, were relished and repeated in the club. He was also, inevitably as a public figure, the butt of his critics' humour – one of whom quipped that his two strengths were tact and Greek iambics! The club had been established in 1824 as an association of 'serious-minded men devoted to the life of the mind; not however in any way exclusive of the lighter side of life.' [49] His friend, Arthur Stanley, had become a member as early as 1838, the year that also saw Charles Darwin, Charles Dickens and Richard Monckton-Milnes elected.

The highest acknowledgement of his achievements at Harrow came quite early in his headmastership when on 16 November 1848 Queen Victoria and Prince Albert paid a visit. The Prince returned for Speech Day in June 1851 along with two Archbishops, five bishops and many notable public figures, among them Gladstone. Vaughan was to become something of a favourite with the Queen, who had appointed him a Chaplain-in-Ordinary in February 1851. The emolument was slight, just £30 a year, but the status it conferred on him was high.

He was developing a reputation as a popular preacher and speaker outside the school too. Among the many invitations which he accepted were the Festival of the Sons of the Clergy in 1851, special events at other great schools, guest preacher in St Paul's Cathedral and Westminster Abbey and annually at the Chapel Royal, St James's as a Chaplain to the Queen. Another important preaching engagement was the consecration of George Cotton, his friend from Cambridge days, as Bishop of Calcutta on Ascension Day 1858. Cotton's widow remembered it as 'a noble sermon'. Vaughan gave it the title *The Word, the Work and the Promise* and he spoke warmly about the blessing Cotton would be as 'a pastor to the young Englishmen living in Calcutta, to the families suffering bereavement or disease, to the clergy who would be gathered round him . . .' [50] Not all his speaking engagements, however, were as successful as this one. Symonds told his sister Charlotte about one such occasion:

> Dr Vaughan went up today to preach his sermon before the Queen. I wonder whether he feels nervous. He has not always been well received: indeed once at Exeter Hall he was lecturing on Passages from the Life of Cicero to or in behalf of the Young Men's Society & was hissed on account of the wearisome & heavy style of his discourse. He bore it & said that "He had come to read a Lecture & should do so." Such a funny small man he is! A little shorter than I am but with such a big head & enormous nose of a brazen colour, like an antique knocker, or the model of the well-known symbol of Mr V. Green's College [Brasenose College Oxford].[51]

There was one pulpit he particularly desired to occupy combined with a lecturing post at Cambridge and for which he put his name forward to the Vice-Chancellor in December 1852. He wrote to Whewell informing him that he had sent in his name, adding, 'I am too sensible of the responsibility of the office to be in the common sense of the word ambitious of obtaining it: but I confess that the renewal of my connection with the University would be particularly grateful to me now that I have so many of my former pupils engaged in its labours and interests.'[52] But he was unsuccessful – the Hulsean was not to be his. The lectures were usually delivered in Great St Mary's Church whose pulpit he would indeed later occupy year after year as one of the university's most popular Select Preachers.

Greater numbers of pupils meant more classrooms were needed. A new building consisting of six rooms was built on the north side of the Chapel in 1855 and came to be known as the New or Chapel Schools – the 'Old School' being the original school building founded by the will of John Lyon in 1572. The cost was met by donations from the Assistant Masters and parents. Plans were already being made by the time he resigned in 1859 for a new Speech Room, a gymnasium and a library and these were built by his successor. Extant letters show that Vaughan used Estcourt as a supportive Trustee in gaining the Governors' approval for all the building projects he initiated.

A business venture which Vaughan initiated in the interests of the boys was the School Bookshop. He invited Samuel Clarke, a Leicester bookseller, to open a shop in Harrow under the patronage of the School. Clarke took John Crossley (who had published Vaughan's sermons in Leicester) as a partner and together they became responsible not only for providing books for the boys but also for printing whatever was needed for all the School's special occasions such as Speech Day.

For a man who had little personal interest in sport of any kind, Vaughan did much to encourage the boys in their physical pursuits. One of his earliest improvements was much appreciated by them. A large pond known as the "New Duck Puddle" which the boys used was turned into a proper swimming pool between 1845 and 1851 – in time it became known as "Ducker". The sides of the pond were lined and a brick bottom put in place, changing sheds and a towel house were built, all of which Vaughan paid for himself. A cleaner water supply was provided for the swimming pool from an artesian well. Vaughan sought Estcourt's assistance in this matter in a letter dated 24 April 1849:

> The improvements . . . have received an unexpected hindrance. Lord Northwick refuses to allow a supply of water to be obtained from the well at the Sheepcote Farm by an increase of its depth, as had been proposed, and we are therefore reduced to the necessity of sinking a well for ourselves, according to a suggestion made by Lord Northwick himself, and in which therefore it will be easy to obtain his formal concurrence. But the sanction of the Governors also is obviously necessary, as Lord Northwick's tenants of the site of the Pond . . .[53]

Vaughan also wanted to build a hut or a small cottage for a 'watchman or keeper of the pond' and as he had already spent £700 [= £75,300] of his own money on the project, he desired a quick vote of approval by the Governors allowing him to dispense with the need and cost of employing an architect. In the same year six acres of land were leased to provide better facilities for cricket and football. In the following year, two rackets courts were built, known as the Shell and Fifth Form Courts – the cost being met in part by the Governors.

The organisation and management of games was very largely left in the hands of the boys. In 1853 the Philathletic Club was formed – membership being restricted to 30 VIth and V[th] formers. Rule 1 stated that 'the chief object of the Club shall be the encouragement and promotion of all manly Sports and Exercises, and every Member shall consider himself pledged to the attainment of this object by all lawful means in his power.' Rule 2 then defined the term: 'Under the head of "manly Sports and exercises" shall be included Cricket, Racquets, Football, Races, Jumping, Fencing, Gymnastics, Swimming, Skating, Quoits, or any other games which may meet with the approbation of the Club.'[54] There was plenty of time for games as there was no tuition on Tuesdays, and Thursdays and Saturdays were kept as half-days. Cricket flourished in his time thanks to two coaches whom he employed – from 1848 Harrow had a string of victories won at Lords over Eton which was a much larger school.

This apparent encouragement of 'manly sports and exercises' did not indicate that Vaughan was an early proponent of muscular Christianity, far from it. One of his Cambridge sermons in the 60s expresses clearly where he placed such activities:

> We do not join in that flattery of flesh and bone, that worship of muscle and sinew, that idolatry of strength and agility, which has been carried, we think, much too far in our Schools and Universities. We must be bold to speak of it, if we are Christians - nay, if we are rational beings – in terms more measured and less exalted. The highest height of bodily prowess is essentially lower than the humblest development of intellectual strength. And the loftiest flight of intellectual ambition never rises into the very lowest heaven of spiritual grace. These are gradations, not of man's making, but of God's ordaining. Soul first, then mind, last body. [55]

There were also other needs of a much more basic kind which had to be addressed. Sanitation in the school remained a problem until 1854 when water closets were at last installed. A Governors' Minute dated 3 February 1854 records:

> Mr Burton laid before the Governors the communications from the Harrow Local Board of Health on the state of the School privies. Upon which it was resolved that (having reference to those requirements arising from the great number of Scholars not on the Foundation now in the School) two of the privies should be closed and that self-acting Water-closet Apparatus should be supplied to the other three of them, and the Governors directed Mr Young to inform the Head Master they were of the opinion that half only of the expense of this work and of the future rates and other incidental expenses attending the conveniences should be defrayed out of the School Trust and that the other half should be borne by the School Charges. [56]

Vaughan objected to this additional cost being placed on the 'School Charges' [i.e. fees the Head levied on parents and which he administered]. Previously the boys had had to use waterless privies and ill-drained latrines. There were no bathrooms for the boys, just footbaths and sponging baths. The only lighting was by candles until a gas supply came to the village on 18 September 1855. And the school had no proper sanitorium until 1862. Throughout Vaughan's time, the care of sick pupils was left to House Masters and there was a local doctor whose service was available to them.

He did not make any ground-breaking alterations to the curriculum which remained little changed from that of his immediate predecessors. Classics still took up most of a pupil's time though Vaughan did introduce some authors not previously studied, notably Plato, Lucretius, Tacitus and Aristophanes. Translation of classical authors and the ability to compose verses in Latin took priority. Whilst most boys just accepted the fact that the school's curriculum was numbingly narrow, not all did. Augustus Hare wrote in his autobiography: 'I may truly say that I never learnt anything useful at Harrow, and had little chance of learning anything. Hours and hours were wasted daily on useless Latin verses with sickening monotony. A boy's school education at this time, except in the highest Forms, was hopelessly inane.' [57]

Science, history, and geography did not figure on the time table but there had been a mathematics teacher since 1819. However, to begin with, any boy wishing to learn from him had to pay an additional fee directly to him. Wordsworth gave mathematics a regular place in the curriculum, appointing J.W. Colenso, later Bishop of Natal, in 1837 to teach the subject and every pupil was now charged a guinea a term extra for his tuition but Colenso stayed only till 1842. Vaughan increased the number of teachers of mathematics, and from 1857 he made the study of French compulsory with German as an optional extra for those who were gifted linguistically though only two hours tuition a week was given to them. In 1851, recognizing how many Old Harrovians chose the Army as their career, he instituted an 'Army Class' whose pupils were given extra tuition in mathematics and in 'military science'. By 1857, the class had 45 pupils. Surprisingly, given that the natural sciences were not taught, Symonds told his sister in November 1855 that they were going to have an examination in Botany that Quarter and asked to have his microscope sent to him The exam was presumably based on their own private botanical studies whenever they went for long walks in the countryside.

Inevitably pupil opinion about the Head varied enormously. He was a man whom 'nobody ever saw in a hurry, seldom ruffled in temper; hedged in, in the eyes of youth, with a majesty befitting his position.' [58]

Another wrote:

Nothing could have been gentler than his manner; too gentle, it was thought by those who did not admire him. But it may safely be said that no boy was ever led to presume upon it; or that, if he did so once, he never repeated the attempt. For beneath the velvet glove there lay a hand of steel; and within the gentle lips there was a tongue which, on occasions, could cut like a razor. In his earlier days it is probable that he used his power of sarcasm too relentlessly; it was only by long self-discipline, and by unceasing watchfulness, that he brought them under control. From the first, however, he was alive to the dangers which beset this particular gift, and he said once, "I should be sorry to think that the boys were as much afraid of me as I was of Arnold." [59]

Others sensed that he was not genuine and the front they saw was not the real man. Symonds made this criticism in one of his weekly letters to his sister Charlotte but later retracted it.

Views about Vaughan as a teacher, judged from a pupil's standpoint, varied too. Kenelm Digby was in the Sixth Form from Easter 1852 to mid-summer '55 and later gave this critical account of his experience:

Vaughan himself was not a man of wide reading; we were taught little or no history; still less did he venture on anything approaching to philosophy; we were not so much as introduced to Plato [not the experience of Montagu Butler- see below]. The charm, I think, of his teaching was the perfect form and finish of his scholarship, the exactness of his verbal criticism, the spirit which he threw into the interpretation of the text of his favourite authors. Of these Greek dramatists took the first place. The authors we read most thoroughly and constantly were Sophocles and Aristophanes . . . He used to revel in the enjoyment of the fun of Aristo-phanes . . . We must have read a good deal of Homer and Thucydides, but I did not appreciate these books with Vaughan. [60]

Lionel Tollemache was another critic:

One consideration may serve to explain the death of originality among us. At school, we were sheltered from every whiff of Neology. Let me give an example. I left Harrow barely three years before the publication of *The Origin of the Species*; yet, during all the six years that I spent there, no doubt was ever whispered to me as to the accuracy of Archbishop Ussher's chronology. In my case, this expression of a 'cloistered and fugitive virtue' was not a success. Too sudden and violent was the change from Vaughan to Jowett . . . Dr Vaughan was an incomparable teacher within his own range, but that range, I repeat, was limited. Of modern history and literature we hardly knew anything . . . So, again, English literature was out of our beat, perhaps for the simple reason that it was out of Vaughan's own beat. Lake once told me that Vaughan, besides knowing nothing whatever of the Fathers, was not well up in English literature. This latter fact, if fact it was, is easily accounted for by the manifold and incongruous objects of attention – sermons, floggings, and parental 'visitations' – which make such cruel inroads into a headmaster's leisure. [61]

Montagu Butler, who venerated Vaughan in the way that the latter as a boy had esteemed Arnold, recalled his time spent in the Sixth in a very different light.

> While I was in the Sixth Form (January 1848-July 1851) we read the *Protagoras* and the very difficult *Phœdrus*. This was in form. Also I read with him and D'Arcy privately, after prayers in his study, the *Phœdo*. These were, perhaps, the happiest of all my hours with him. I should certainly add Thucydides and Plato to Sophocles and Aristophanes, in a decidedly lesser degree Æschylus and Demosthenes . . . I have known many of the finest classical scholars of the day – many with whom, in respect of mere learning, he would never have thought of comparing himself – but for the sheer scholar's instinct, the thinking and feeling in the great tongues of Greece and Rome, more especially the Greek, the exact perception of the force of words, whether separately or in their junction and their cadences, there are few, indeed, that could be placed by his side. [62]

Tollemache again:

> But Vaughan was admirable in his own line, not only as a teacher, but as a moral trainer. In both respects he is well known to have been a follower of Dr Arnold; so much so, indeed, that one is tempted to parody the Virgilian metaphor, and to say that he carried Rugby bodily into Harrow. Not, of course, that Vaughan was a facsimile of Arnold. My father used to say that Vaughan was 'much superior to Arnold, having far more common sense'; which was another way of saying that Arnold was vastly more original than Vaughan. But this deficiency of Vaughan may have helped him as a school-master. Indeed, I have quoted my father's praise of him as serving to show that, if he had encouraged free enquiry, he would have given a rude shock to the susceptibilities of parents, and perhaps to the fortunes of the school. But this caution of his was not the mere outcome of policy; it was part of his character. He told me that, though he had sometimes been brought into sympathetic contact with the religious difficulties of his friends, he himself had never to any serious extent suffered from such difficulties. On the whole we may conclude that Arnold was far more of a Broad Churchman, according to the standard of his time, than Vaughan was according to the standard of twenty years later. But, though Vaughan may in a manner be

described as merely Arnold writ small, he emulated his great master in impressing upon his pupils, both by precept and example, a conviction of the tremendous seriousness of life and what George Eliot called the self-scourging sense of duty.[63]

Whatever the shortcomings of the curriculum or of Vaughan as a teacher, the fact remains that the school did produce a stream of pupils under him who went on to achieve high academic success at Oxford and Cambridge. Among them were Charles Calverley (né Blayds) who entered the school in 1846. He won a Balliol scholarship and then the Chancellor's Prize for Latin hexameters at Oxford in 1851 before migrating to Cambridge where he won the Craven Scholarship and was placed 2nd Classic of his year in 1856 and became a Fellow of Christ's College; Francis Vaughan Hawkins won a string of prizes and medals at Trinity Cambridge in 1851-52 and was Senior Classic and 1st Chancellor's Medallist in 1854; Montagu Butler became a Scholar and Fellow of Trinity as well as being Senior Classic in 1855; in the same year Alfred Blomfield (son of the Bishop of London) gained a 1st at Balliol; Edmund Sergeant, Head of School in '54 achieved the same in '58 followed by Kenelm Digby who won a Balliol scholarship and graduated 1st Class in 1859 as did Herman Merivale; Lionel Tollemache was another Balliol Scholar who was awarded a 1st in 1860; Trevelyan, who had been Head of School 1856-57 became a Scholar of Trinity Cambridge in 1859 and was 2nd Classic in 1862; Symonds likewise gained a 1st at Balliol in 1862 and Alfred Pretor became a Scholar of Trinity Cambridge in 1861, graduated as 7th Classic in '64 and in '71 was elected a Fellow of St Catharine's College. Harrow under Vaughan became known for its highly accomplished classical scholars.

One may wonder what practical use such knowledge was for a man wanting to make his way in the world but as Minchin has observed 'Latin prose composition is so difficult that a boy who has mastered that can master anything.' [64] A view that Vaughan and many other educationalists would have most assuredly shared. There was, of course, a contrary view which the self-educated satirist and political pamphleteer William Cobbett expressed in his *Political Register*: 'I have always contended and have now proved that a knowledge of those languages is, generally speaking, of no use, and that as the acquiring of that knowledge costs much time and money it is generally speaking, *worse than useless*.'

When Vaughan took up office in 1845, there were few prizes awarded by way of encouraging classical scholarship. In 1820 Dr Butler had instituted annual prizes for Greek verse, Latin hexameters and Latin lyrics which were funded from the founder's estate, and in 1826 Sir Robert Peel founded an annual award of a gold medal for Latin prose. There was also the Beresford-Hope prize for Greek prose translation, first awarded in 1838. Vaughan instituted in his first year two prizes, one for an English essay and the other for an English poem. The following year the Gregory Memorial Medal for Latin prose translation was first awarded. Prizes for other subjects were also introduced: the Neeld Medal for Mathematics in 1852, and a friend from Cambridge days, Viscount Ebrington M.P., founded prizes for proficiency in French and German in 1854. That same year Mr Beriah Botfield FRS founded an annual gold medal for the promotion of the study of modern languages and literature – the choice of language was left to the discretion of the Head. Surprisingly, given that the subject was not included in the time-table, the Head instituted in 1856 prizes for proficiency in Natural Sciences, and the previous year he had awarded one for Military Science. Earl Spencer added to the list of scholarships open to Harrow boys who went on to university by an endowment of £1,000 [= £118,220] made on 31 December 1851. He stipulated that the qualifying examination for it, to be organized by the Headmaster, must include Mathematics. In September 1852 John Wallace Hozier became the first recipient of this award, tenable for three years.

Scholarship examinations were held over three days in July. Vaughan determined which books and authors were the appointed ones but he invited some other scholar to set the examination and have the papers printed for which an honorarium of £20 was paid. In July 1858 he invited Lightfoot, a Tutor at Trinity College Cambridge, to be the examiner and appointed Westcott to assist him in 'the looking over' of the papers. That year works by Livy, Virgil, Plato and Thucydides were set plus the Epistle to the Romans and part of Butler's *Analogy*, and 'composition of all kinds'.[65]

Later that same year he had dealings of a different kind, unconnected with Harrow, with Lightfoot whose support he enlisted. Vaughan had been appointed one of the Government's Commissioners to look into the workings of Cambridge University and he looked for support wherever he could obtain it. In April that year at a dinner party he had shared the confidential proposals of the Commission with Gladstone to whom he wrote next day:

I am quite sure it is needless – but I am anxious just to say that, as the

Cambridge Commissioners are desirous at this moment to keep their definite plans from becoming public, I should be greatly obliged by your regarding as confidential (as far as I am concerned) anything of that nature which I may have mentioned in conversation last night.

I was so glad to have the opportunity of asking your opinion upon some of the points at issue that I felt myself quite at liberty to talk to you as I should not have talked to a stranger.

Pray do not think of replying to this note. [66]

In November the Commission was planning to visit Cambridge to discuss their proposals with the college authorities. The Master of Trinity was not co-operating so Vaughan wrote a letter marked 'Private' to Lightfoot entreating him and another Fellow to write to the Commission:

> . . . I may say this much – that it has been, & is now more than ever, the one desire of the Commissioners to open wide their doors for the reception of every suggestion which may come from any quarter on the subject of the proposals which have been made to the College. It has been very unfortunate (may I say it to you?) that the Master of the College has assumed a tone so little favourable to friendly & free communication between the Commission & the Society. But even this, though it may add to the difficulty of the position, must not be allowed to defeat good and great objects. The Commission has proposed to him a conference next week with him & any of the Fellows who may be disposed to accompany him . . .
>
> The Master will incur a grave responsibility if he has withheld from the Fellows generally the knowledge of the invitation [?] or of the terms in which it was conveyed. [67]

The conference took place and Lightfoot attended. Vaughan wrote to thank him:

> I am very glad to hear that you thought the conference on Saturday tolerably satisfactory. I felt a wish that you could have given more of body & substance to your own views as a whole, but, after all, you pretty clearly indicated the direction of your wishes – enough perhaps to show us how far any meditated resolutions of ours would be likely to meet with your concurrence.
>
> May something come out of this chaos! [68]

*****

We turn now to the most important personal event of his years at Harrow. On 15 March 1850 Vaughan wrote to Estcourt to ask once again

154

for his help and mediation with the Governors. He announced his engagement to Catherine Stanley and his intention of getting married in the Easter holidays, and trusted that he would be permitted to retain his office of Head Master after the event 'without offence to the Statutes of John Lyon'. He had been told that 'the marriage of a Head Master was invariably followed by the addition of a week to the next vacation' and had announced the same to the school. He hadn't known that it also required the support of the Governors, so he apologized for acting precipitously.[69]

Catherine Stanley and Charles Vaughan had known each other since her brother Arthur's days at Rugby. They became engaged in February 1850 and on 2 April they married at St George's Hanover Square. The officiant was a family friend from Norwich days, the Revd C.M. Wode-house, Canon of Norwich Cathedral. He was 34 and Catherine was 28 years old, and by the standards of the time, she was a well-educated and much travelled young lady. An accomplished amateur artist, an extant sketch-book with watercolours she painted on her travels through Austria to the Danube in 1853 shows that she had a good eye for detail – particularly of women's clothing and bonnets! She was also a wealthy young woman in her own right – property and trust funds worth over £17,000 [= £1,938,000] were settled on her the day before she wed. She did not, however, enjoy good health and it was feared during one spell of grave illness at the Palace at Norwich in September 1841 that she would die. In the summer of 1845 she and her sister Mary had accompanied their brother Arthur and his friend Benjamin Jowett on a trip to Berlin.

In September of that same year, she and Mary travelled with their brother Charlie and his wife Eliza on the first leg of their journey to Van Dieman's Land, disembarking at Madeira where they spent the winter. The following April Arthur Stanley joined his sisters on their return journey travelling back through Spain and Portugal, calling at Cadiz, Seville, Ronda, Malaga and Granada. Jowett and Catherine developed a warm relationship – she once described him as 'the most charming friend and companion it was possible to have' and he, in turn, recorded having 'many a friendly battle on theological subjects' with her on his visits to Harrow.[70]

In August 1849, she left Norwich with her parents, and with Arthur and Mary for what would prove to be their last family holiday together in Scotland. The Bishop died at Brahan Castle near Dingwall on 5 September; his body was taken by boat from Invergordon to Yarmouth and transported to Norwich for interment in the Cathedral. The family had to vacate the Palace and Kitty Stanley and her daughters, Mary and Catherine, moved to 6 Grosvenor Crescent in London. Tragedy hit the family again soon afterwards. In December news came that Charlie had died suddenly at Hobart of gastro-enteritis and in March 1850 her brother Owen died of epilepsy on board his ship HMS Rattlesnake in Sydney Harbour – news of his death did not arrive in London until 4 July, three months after her wedding.

Shortly after their return to the Hill from their honeymoon, Catherine wrote a long letter to her cousin Louisa with whom she had a close relationship describing her new and happy life as the wife of the Head Master of Harrow. The impression she gives is that theirs was no marriage of convenience or lacking in love:

> Harrow. May 1 1850
> . . . You would indeed rejoice were you to see the quiet, peaceful nest I have dropped into . . . It would be too happy – but that our late warnings [her brother Charlie's sudden death] are ever reminding me that the happiness of a wife hangs upon one slender thread and that her rejoicing must be with trembling. It seems presumptuous to look for a long continuance of this present nest and happiness – and yet I feel that if it were now taken away from me tomorrow – I would be thankful for having known it – Alas – I thought I knew how to feel for poor Eliza [her recently bereaved sister-in-law] – but till now I never knew how a wife depends upon her husband – how she clings to him – and how entirely – if their marriage is a happy one, their two lives are blended into one - . . .
> There are many things I would talk to you about – but it must not be very long, - and I must bring you to this sunny nest upon the Hill, and try to make you see us!
> You ask about our Sundays – We go to <u>Church</u> AM and to <u>Chapel</u> PM. In the former place Mr Cunningham preaches – in the latter place – <u>my Husband</u> – and I wish you could see the deep attention with which every word he says is listened to – but it is not for me to tell you what his sermons are –
> I see little of him in the week – he is in School from half past 7 till 9, from 11 till 12 – from 3 till 4 – from 5 till 6 – and sometimes he has an Extra Class in the Evening for an Hour and when he is not in School – he is either the prey of boys who come with Compositions and Greek verses – or else devoted to getting his lessons ready for the next day – so that except from 2 till 3, when I <u>make</u> him take a walk, I rarely see him to speak to. Yet he likes me to be with him whilst he is busy – and I often sit curled up in the great leather armchair in his Study reading – whilst he stands at his desk writing his Sermon – or looking over his Examination papers.
> I write letters for him – and arrange his papers – and I hope to do a little more for him every day as I get more into the way of it – and I think I need

not tell you what a delight it is to receive him when he comes in tired and harassed, and I feel that one has the power of giving him rest and recreation – It is indeed a privilege! And I am daily wondering how it is that I have the Blessing of his Love – and <u>such</u> Love – so tender – so considerate - He is beloved by <u>everyone</u> from the Head Boy in the School down to the old woman who weeds in the garden . . . "There's not many that are so blessed as you, Ma'am" said the old housemaid the day after I came – and the Butler said to Sarah – "Mrs Vaughan is a happy lady to come <u>here</u>" – I am indeed – and every day as it closes, leaves me more impressed with the Blessing God has given me . . . [71]

That effusive laudatory comment by a servant, in fact, reflects the care and kindness Vaughan showed to his household staff. Two letters survive relating to one of them, a young man named George Fardell who had attended the Parish School in Leicester and been recommended by the Master there as 'one of the most deserving of all his scholars.' He worked in the Head's house at Harrow for two years and Vaughan had seen he was capable of better things, so he wrote to Lord Hardewicke asking him to use his influence to find a suitable post. He wrote: 'George Fardell is honest, steady, sober & industrious: a young man of quiet & inoffensive manners, and (I truly believe) of good religious principles. I can recommend him with much confidence as qualified for a situation requiring from its holder integrity and fidelity as well as punctuality and diligence.' [72] Three months later, thanks to Vaughan's testimonial, Farell was given a post in the London Post Office.

Catherine was now the head of a large domestic staff – a governess, housekeeper, lady's maid, cook, maidservant, six housemaids, a butler, a coachman and a footman.[73] She became a popular hostess with the boys who were frequently entertained in the Headmaster's home. Tollemache remembered those meals and the Head's way of ending them:

When the monitors dined with him, they naturally felt shy about fixing the moment of departure. Vaughan would catch the eye of the senior boy and look significantly at his watch. When the hint was taken, he squeezed the boy's hand and exclaimed in deprecatory accents: "Must you go?" Such diplomacy not even a Quaker would blame, but I cannot help feeling he sometimes carried it to a point that Polonius would have called 'indirection' and Mark Pattison 'economy of truth'. [74]

G.W.E. Russell tells an alternative version of this in his *Collections & Recollections* in the chapter he headed 'Flatterers & Bores' but, as usual with him, it is an unkinder account.

Catherine was not, however, starry eyed about everything in the school. In one undated letter to Louisa she discouraged her from visiting them that summer: 'I am only a little afraid that you would not like it this year so well as last – the Speeches are likely to be lamentably dull – the Prizes are stupid – and the Company not particularly brilliant . . .' [75] One wonders who the principal guests were that year.

Catherine's cousin, John Stanley, son of Lord Eddisbury who became 2nd Baron Stanley of Alderley, joined the Head's house in September 1850. She was very happy to have him there as he was a visible link to her earlier life at Alderley but he proved to be an undisciplined youth and caused them much heartache. The Stanley family correspondence shows how Lord and Lady Stanley blamed the Head for not knocking him into shape: 'Nov 27th/50. I think Dr Vaughan seems to give the boys too long impositions to write out, as it occupies their time and takes them from their usual studies. After all, the good old whipping is perhaps as good or better than anything for young boys.' [76] Vaughan, however, was not to be bullied by parents, even ones with noble titles. A year later, he wrote to John's father, alerting him that the boy might be expelled which did not go down well at Alderley. Lord Stanley wrote to share the news with his wife:

London Nov.20/51
My dearest love,
That Johnny is very troublesome and that he might likely commit some enormity for which he would have to be sent away is not improbable, but unless Dr Vaughan proposes to conduct his school upon the principles of the Quakers I hardly think he is making it the place of education and correction that it should be. If he abdicates the first function of a schoolmaster by getting rid of all those who want correction instead of improving & reforming them he may make an easy task of education & boast, like the Quakers, that there are no black sheep in the community. I, however, have heard of nothing that Johnny has done which wd be deserving of so severe a punishment as being sent away. I dare say he is not doing much good & it may be expedient to remove him, but Dr Vaughan is a prig & I should like to hear more of what he has to say before I do so. [77]

Two days later, whilst threatening to deprive his son of 'amusements which he might have had' over the Christmas holidays, he was still blaming Vaughan: 'Notwithstanding his faults, I still think Dr Vaughan an imbecile & if he continues to pursue such a cowardly system it will ruin the school.' [78] Johnny's behaviour did not improve and news of it was spreading. Lady Stanley wrote to her husband:

Alderley Dec. 4th
My dearest love,
Kate Vaughan wrote a most vexed letter to Alice [the Stanley's eldest daughter]. Johnny was flogged for secreting light & being up all night & also for jumping over the dining table when Dr Vaughan was there, which is considered a great breach of discipline. I am afraid he is *greatly* in the wrong and I hear the foulness of his language is as much complained of as his swearing. [79]

The boy added to his list of offences by swearing at shopkeepers in Harrow, a matter not regarded as much wrong by his father, who continued to blame Vaughan: 'To be sure impertinence to trades people is a small matter for a public school, & it seems to me that there is much pettiness & littleness about Harrow & its system. This minute inter-ference with the boys, & espionage, is but a low mode of proceeding, & these followers of Dr Arnold who clothe themselves in lion's skin look more like other animals than lions.' [80] Johnny was removed at the end of the term. He doesn't seem to have borne any ill will to the Head and Vaughan remained in touch with him after he went to India. In a letter home from Calcutta in July 1858 Johnny told them that Vaughan had sent him a sermon he had preached on Ascension Day [at Bishop Cotton's consecration] which he had liked very much and asked them to thank him for remembering him. Nor did it stop them sending another son, Algernon, in 1856 who apparently liked Vaughan greatly.

A more serious breach of school discipline occurred in November 1853 which became a matter of national interest and provoked the publication of private letters between aggrieved parents and the Head and the publication of an Open Letter from Vaughan to Palmerston, the Prime Minister, who was himself an old boy of the school. The letter explained and defended the rationale of the monitorial system and succeeded in reassuring many parents who might have been tempted to withdraw their sons from the school. The incident showed Vaughan in a determined mode and well able to defend himself and his way of running the school against his critics.

What had provoked the public debate was a monitor who savagely caned a fifth former for what was a minor act of disobedience on the football field but which was perceived as an affront to the former's dignity. The culprit, the Hon. Randolph Stewart, appealed to Vaughan

159

who advised him to submit to the monitor. The punishment which followed, known as a 'whopping', turned out to be excessive. He was given 31 strokes with an inch thick rod across his shoulders which necessitated medical attention afterwards. The doctor who attended him informed the Head of the boy's injuries. Vaughan immediately demoted the monitor. The victim naturally reported what had happened to his father, the Earl of Galloway, who protested to the Head that such savage physical punishment was permitted. The demoted monitor, in turn, sought support from his father, the Hon. Baron Platt. Platt Sr. defended his son's actions and requested his re-instatement, which Vaughan refused. A battle of wills began and spilled out publicly into print when Platt published the correspondence between himself and the Head. Vaughan's tone throughout was temperate but firm – he was not to be budged by an irate parent. His opening letter to Platt Sr., dated 26 November 1853, ends with these words:

> In the case of personal affront, I feel that your son should have been doubly careful to be moderate in the chastisement inflicted, and more particularly when he was acting as the representative of the Monitors generally. I do not blame him for the *act itself*; it was, I think, consistent with custom; but for an intemperate and cruel (however unintentionally so), manner of performing it. [81]

Vaughan also alluded to avoiding damage to the School's name but more so to Platt Jr.'s name. Inevitably the son presented the matter rather differently in his first letter to his father about it claiming that the Head had acknowledged to him that his reason for punishing him so severely was not because he thought the punishment was deserved but because he feared what people would say if he didn't. Two days later, Vaughan wrote again – 'I should extremely deplore his removal being connected in any way, in common opinion, with the recent occurrence – in which I have reason to know that his conduct was disapproved by his brother Monitors, the persons who would naturally be most anxious for the maintenance (by due means) of their joint authority.' [82] On 2 December he called an end to 'correspondence on this painful subject.' Palmerston became concerned and wrote to the Head. Vaughan's Open Letter to him, dated 14 December 1853, argued that boys could and should be trusted to exercise authority in a school. He refused to introduce the practice of some private schools of employing 'a body of Ushers; Masters of a lower order, whose business it shall be to follow Boys into their hours of recreation and rest, avowedly as spies, coercing freedom of speech and action, or reporting to their superior what such observation has gleaned.' [83] To Vaughan such a system would be 'ruinous to that which has been regarded as the great glory of an English Public School – its free development of character, its social expansiveness, in short its *liberty.*' [84] He then explained his practice:

> I have taught the Monitors to regard their authority as eminating indeed from mine, but yet . . . independent and free in its ordinary exercise. They are charged with the enforcement of an internal discipline, the object of which is the good order, the honourable conduct, the gentlemanlike tone, of the Houses and of the School. In these matters I desire that they should act for themselves; knowing well how doubly, how tenfold, valuable is that discipline which springs from within the body, in comparison with that which is imposed from above. It is only on the discovery of grave and moral offences, such as would be poisonous to the whole society, and such as they may reasonably be expected to regard as discreditable and disgraceful even more than they are illegal, that I expect them to communicate with me officially the faults of which they may take notice. [85]

It followed from this that the monitors must have some means of asserting their authority. He rejected the earlier practice of their setting written impositions (which masters often did) as this, 'if widely exercised, would come into collision with ordinary School duties'. He preferred a legalised exercise of physical chastisement. A monitor had the right to feel he could 'depend on the Master to stand by him, before the School and before the Public, so long as no wanton or tyrannical use of this power can be proved against him.' [86]

The problem was that this is exactly what had caused the public rumpus. An immediate response came in the form of a pamphlet written by 'Anti-Monitor' which advocated a strict limit on the number of strokes of the cane: 'Make it a stringent rule, that no single monitor be allowed to administer more than *five* blows for a petty offence, on his own responsibility; make it equally binding upon the whole monitorial body, when appealed to by any single monitor, that they never exceed *twelve* blows, in the gravest cases.' [87] It was, however, probably because of the adverse publicity the School had suffered rather than this particular pamphlet that Vaughan did in fact do what was suggested by Anti-Monitor. He limited a monitorial caning to ten strokes and pupils in the Upper Fifth were to be exempt from such canings. Platt left the school and later became a clergyman, Stewart stayed and went on to have a distinguished military career.

The matter dragged on in the press for several months. An editorial in the *Times* on 13 April 1854 took the view that discipline should be in the hands of masters not boys, and that fees in public schools were high enough for the employment of an adequate number of staff:

> The whole system proceeds on the supposition contrary even to proverbial experience, that they could never safely play the boy, a boy may be safely entrusted to play the master . . . We think the broad principle may be surely laid down that every boy at every school is entitled to receive such supervision as he requires at the hands of proper masters, without any delegation of such authority to boys like himself. [88]

Two days later, an old Rugbeian wrote to the paper to defend the monitorial system as practised by Arnold – 'They form a medium by which a higher and more manly sense of right and duty is kept alive in the school. They transmit insensibly (I say this without fear of contradiction) a healthy moral tone throughout the school, in a way which no code of law, no masters, no grown man ever could do.' [89] And so the debate rumbled on.

Even Gladstone (an old Etonian) contributed in a private letter which he wrote to Vaughan soon after the publication of the Head's *Open Letter*. Vaughan replied in his characteristically courteous and complimentary tone but he clearly stuck to the rightness of the Harrow system:

> I can assure you most truly that, as there is no one whose commendation could be more valuable to me than yours, so there is certainly no one, amongst the many persons who have expressed an opinion upon the subject [the monitorial system of honour at Harrow], whose insight into it has been more acute, or whose comprehension of its real difficulties has been more thorough.
>
> I have been struck by your remark upon the embarrassments brought into the Honour system by the <u>co-existence</u> in it of the two points in which it differs from the Eton constitution – viz. the use of the cane on the one hand, & the extension of monitorial power over the 5th Form on the other. Either of these <u>alone</u>, I understand you to say, might have involved little trouble: but the <u>union</u> of the two has introduced much perplexity.
>
> Whether even this perplexity must not be endured & struggled with, rather than that the monitors should be exposed to hindrances or insults from a body so numerous & so strong as the Fifth Form, & so likely to head resistance to monitorial authority even of the best kind – I may still doubt: but be assured that I shall ever retain a feeling of lively gratitude for the

kindness with which you have thrown your mind into this question, and an increased admiration for that wisdom & energy by which your whole public life is made so illustrious. [90]

One of the House Masters (probably Middlemist as a copy was kept in a collection of Dalrymple's school mementoes) sent a ten point printed letter to the parents of his boarders in April 1854 explaining and defending the monitorial system as practised at Harrow. Point 10 reads:

> In conclusion I will only add that if your Son, in the course of his School life, should want protection from wrong, he will find it in this system. If he is one whose natural temperament might lead him to oppress others, this same system will place an insensible but most effectual restraint upon him. But if unhappily he should ever commit an action calculated to cause public scandal and disgrace, he will then and not till then have reason to *fear* the power of the Monitors. [91]

The publicity over the Platt affair did not adversely affect the number of new entrants in May 1854 - in fact the reverse - though the total number of admissions for that year was down on the previous year's.

Vaughan returned to this issue in a sermon he preached at the tercentenary celebrations at Repton School. He gave it the title *The Vocation of a Public School*. He said 'I am not afraid to speak of that which, to many minds, is the blemish of the system; its graduated ranks, its internal discipline, its commission of authority (within strict limits and for lawful purposes) to the elder and abler over their younger or less capable or less diligent schoolfellows. It is this system of recognised subordination within the body . . . which makes the public school so excellent a discipline for life.' [92] In the same sermon he stated his own understanding of education at school level which echoed the views of Arnold which he had heard at Rugby:

> The real object of education, certainly of boyish education, is rather to form than to inform the mind; not so much to communicate what I may call pieces of knowledge, as to habituate to patience and accuracy and diligence in learning, with a view to the application of powers thus gained to future use, whatever be the particular calling or profession to which life is to be devoted . . . Our business is not so much how to teach as to show how to learn; and to this end habits of thoroughness and exactness are results far more important than any extent of present attainment in the way of sciences or of languages. The time for attainment is not yet. Our business is to sow; the harvest is afterwards. [93]

Another test of the Head's nerve was in winning the Governors' support for a change in the rules regarding 'foreign' parents, i.e. those who moved to Harrow simply in order to benefit by the provision in the founder's will of a free education for *local* boys. This had become something of a grievance among real locals, not that they wanted a classical education for their sons. An example of this was one Captain Trotter who had applied to have his sons admitted on the Foundation in September 1852. Vaughan wanted the Governors to refuse the request 'as he is not a bona fide resident of Harrow'. The Head claimed that the father proposed building a house in Harrow but not to reside in it himself – in effect creating 'a new Boarding House' for his sons.[94] On 9 April 1853 he wrote to Estcourt in preparation for tackling the Governors about a stricter admissions policy.

> Can you do me the favour of informing me whether the Governors of Harrow have ever entertained the question, or would be likely to do so, of requiring a 2 years previous residence in the Parish as a Condition of Admission to the Benefits of the Foundation? It is, as you are perhaps aware, the rule at Rugby, and it seems a very reasonable check upon the sudden inroads of persons for whom it can scarcely be said that the benefits of this Bequest was designed by the Founder – I can scarcely imagine that anyone would dispute the equity of such a rule. [95]

In May 1853 Vaughan wrote to the Governors requesting that they impose this condition. Initially they were hesitant as they doubted they had the power to require this but they did agree to give the matter further consideration. At their meeting in October they resolved to apply to the Court of Chancery for such power. In a letter to Estcourt thanking him for this, he expressed his concern about the growing population of Harrow and said the additions 'are created for the most part by <u>temporary</u> residents, who come here for the <u>purpose</u> of gaining education for their Sons.' [96] He also argued that the terms of the Founder's will which allocated the sum of £30 a year to the Master and £20 to an Usher was insufficient to provide free education for so many. In effect, the Head was being required to subsidize the cost of their education from the income he derived from the boarders.

It proved to be a much harder task getting the Governors' support for his solution to the locals' greater grievance. They wanted a more practical education for their sons. They had appealed to the Governors in 1849 to help provide it but without success. Two years later, Vaughan proposed a solution which the Governors also rejected, so without their blessing he established a 'Commercial School' at his own expense which proved to be a lasting success. In a letter to Estcourt, dated 20 April 1853, he set out the case for what he was doing.

> I am quite confident, as I before said, that, in doing something myself for the Education of the Middle Class in this place, I am relieving the Governors from a real and growing difficulty, while at the same time I can in no way compromise them by my individual proceedings.
> This letter you will kindly regard as the private and confidential expression of my mind to one who has always deserved to be treated by me not with distinct respect only but with zeal and [unhesitating?] confidence. [97]

Initially the school was held in an old barn and was known as the "English Form". Two masters were provided and Vaughan received a weekly report on each boy. He examined them himself from time to time and arranged for the main school's Mathematics and French teachers to be examiners too. Pupils were charged £5 a year for tuition but he insisted that their parents had to waive all rights to a free education at Harrow School which not all of them were happy about. Some of the tradesmen and farmers still felt that their sons should have some benefit from the John Lyon's trust funds.

The Governors denied any responsibility for this venture in 1854 but did not oppose the Head's initiative. By 1859 there were 20 scholars attending it. No wonder the locals paid for stained glass windows in the Chapel as a token of their gratitude to him. Better things were to follow years later when the Public Schools Commissioners ordered the Governors to build a new school in place of Vaughan's 'English Form', and in 1876 the newly named 'Lower School of John Lyon' came into being.

He and his wife shared in the life of the town and did what they could to promote a greater sense of unity between town and school. They entertained townspeople of all classes at their home and inaugurated an annual lecture in the School to which townspeople were invited. They were also invited to the rehearsals for Speech Day which became known as 'Town Speeches' – a practice he remembered from his time at Rugby. Catherine made her own contribution to the life of the local community by starting and managing an industrial home for girls, and by her generosity to the poor. In the opinion of F.D. How, the two of them 'tied the place together.' [98] A mark of this was that he accepted the position of first Chairman of the Harrow Local Board. When they left the Hill, the local tradesmen presented him with a clock and a letter expressing their gratitude 'for the many personal kindnesses' they had received from him and 'as a public recognition of the many and lasting benefits' he had conferred on Harrow during his 15 years residence among them. The letter ended: 'We would also express here as far as these feeble words of ours may do so, our lasting sense of the friendly sympathy, the ready help, the kind co-operation and Christian courtesy that has at all times characterized your intercourse with us, and on leaving Harrow we beg to assure you that you will carry with you our best wishes for the future happiness of yourself and Mrs Vaughan and our earnest hope that you may live long in the enjoyment of every blessing that this world can confer.' Fifty-six of them signed it.

*****

1859 began on a happy note with a gathering of the extended Vaughan families at the wedding of the Head's youngest brother, David, to Margaret Greg, at which he was the officiant. It was to be a year of change for him and Catherine too. On 16 September he informed the Governors of his intention to retire at Christmas:

> My Lords and Gentlemen
>
> At the close of this Term I shall have held the Office of Head Master of Harrow School for the full period of 15 years.
>
> I feel that the time will then have arrived, when retirement from a position of so much labour and responsibility will be desirable for myself, and, I am sure not injurious to the permanent prosperity of the School.
>
> I respectfully announce to you my intention to resign the Head Mastership at the End of this year.
>
> I would venture to add the expression of my hope that you will proceed to the Election of my Successor at as early a moment as may be consistent with [free?] competition and a deliberate choice.
>
> Any prolonged uncertainty on this important point must cause anxiety to the parents of the present Scholars and might lead to alteration in their plans which a prompt decision would probably obviate.
>
> I need not assure you that I shall retain in my retirement the same deep interest in the welfare of Harrow School which has always made this service a labour of love . . . [99]

He issued a short statement to parents the same day: 'I have resolved after much deliberation, to take that opportunity of relieving myself from the long pressure of those heavy duties and anxious responsibilities which are inseparable from such an office, even under the most favourable circumstances.' [100]

On the 19th he wrote a letter marked 'Private' to Esteron in which he expanded on his reasons for retiring:

> ... My Mastership here will reach the end of its fifteenth year next Christmas. And I have made up my mind, not without deep pain, but still with a full conviction of the propriety of the step, to retire from my present office at that time.
>
> The wear and tear of such a position is great! And I desire to find for myself some little repose for mind & body after a length of service which I think entitles me to claim it.
>
> To leave the School at its highest point of honour and prosperity has been my ambition. To have seen any symptom of diminution or decay in its well being, would have wounded me to the heart – and (which is more important) might have made the transfer of Harrow to my successor, whoever he may be, a matter of more risk than I trust it can now be.
>
> May your choice be wisely guided by Him whose Providence watches, I am sure, over such a work as this.
>
> Ever, dear Mr Esteron, most faithfully yours Chas J. Vaughan [101]

He also wrote on the same day to Charles Dalrymple to share the news. Catherine and he had been the guests of his mother, Lady Fergusson, at New Hailes on their way south after touring the Highlands just a few days before Vaughan announced his retirement. He had ended a Thank You letter, dated 10 September, to the young man whose loyal friendship would become so important to him: 'I cannot tell you how much I thank you for unbounded kindness & ever valued affection warmly returned. Ever your affectionate friend.' [102] His letter of the 19th reads:

> My dear Dalrymple
>
> I do not like you to learn from the paper first of all the announcement that I am thinking of closing my life here next Christmas. I shall then have reached my fifteenth year – a full term of service, which entitles me, I think, to claim a time of rest. I could not allude to such an idea till the School was assembled again, as it might possibly have led to some changes in the intentions of Parents which may now be averted by a new election [i.e. of a new HM] taking place before this term ends, & (as I trust) in favour of someone who will command the general confidence.
>
> You must have thought me, I fear, often very stupid & much pre-occupied during my visit to you. This will explain it; for I was then filled with the question which is now answered. I fear that once I replied not quite ingenuously to a question of yours as to why I asked your idea of Butler's fitness in such a place (or some such topic): but my notions were then too crude for explanation, & even to Mrs Vaughan I said nothing till a few days

ago. It has been a very serious time, I need not say - & the first announcement of it here has been <u>terrible</u>.

(I did just sound Currer when I was with him at the end of the Holidays as to what would be thought of such a step on my part.)

Do write to me soon: tell me that you are sorry, but that you do not condemn.

We talk of a quiet little house somewhere in the country. I have plenty to do, to prevent any risk of feeling lost in retirement, & we shall have just enough to live upon in a very humble but not squalid way.

Of course you will come to us here once more.

Ever dear Dalrymple

Your very affectionate friend Chas J. Vaughan

The kindness of everyone is almost overwhelming. [103]

His letter of resignation was greeted with dismay by the Governors. Lord Aberdeen wrote to Estcourt 'I cordially sympathize with you in lamenting Dr Vaughan's resignation of Harrow and feel that we shall have great difficulty in supplying his place; but as it is a matter of necessity, we must do our best.' [104]

Some saw his resignation as sudden and unexpected but Vaughan for his part insisted that he had always intended to do what Arnold had planned for himself, namely to resign at the end of 15 years as Head. In Arnold's case, however, death intervened in his 14th year at Rugby. Another likely factor was that there were early signs that numbers had peaked and were now beginning to drop: in 1857 there had been 143 new boys, in '58 148 but in '59 only 129. The trend is even clearer if we look at admissions in September each year: 57 (+ 7 In October) in 1857, 55 (+ 2 in November) in '58, and just 49 in '59. Had he announced his resignation only weeks earlier there would have been a real danger that even fewer new boys would have come in what was to be his last term. He chose to resign when the School was still riding high.

Compared to his predecessors, his resignation was certainly not sudden: George Butler announced his departure to a special conclave of Governors on 9 December 1828 and left at Easter 1829 – numbers had been falling which had caused the Governors to ask him to consider resigning in the interests of the school; Charles Longley, having been offered a choice of bishoprics by Lord Melbourne in February 1836, resigned on 14 March and Christopher Wordsworth was appointed on 31 March. The Governors tried to force Wordsworth out in June 1844 but without success. When the Prime Minister, Sir Robert Peel, who was an old Harrovian, came to their rescue and offered him a Canonry at Westminster Abbey, he resigned. That was on 21 October and Vaughan was appointed on 18 December. In contrast to that, Vaughan gave the Governors a full and long term's notice.

Catherine's account of events has also survived. She wrote to her cousin Louisa two days after the public announcement:

Harrow School Sept 18 1859

Dearest Louisa

Our wish is fulfilled and we are no longer "Schoolmasters!" As you will have seen I dare say in the paper before you get this. It has taken me quite by surprise, for although I knew he had a great desire for a life of greater quietness and peace I had not the least suspicion of his intention till he told me four days ago that he had made up his mind to hand in his resignation *this week*.

This is now done and the act irrevocable and I feel as if we had hurled a shell into the middle of the street – to explode and carry dismay and grief into every house – I know it will cause the greatest distress; but we always felt we would not stay here for life, and that we must leave it sooner or later – and he says it is best for the School to give it up while it is in the full tide of prosperity, and can command a good successor than to run the risk of delay and of some chance wind driving us against a sand bank –

Our design is to live in a little house not far from London – we think of Southboro. We shall not be rich – but I am sure we shall be happy – We shall have £600 a year and as our tastes are simple, and we have no offspring, I think we shall do very well. Work we shall always find to do wherever we are – and we shall enjoy a life of domestic happiness we have never known since we married.

We have three trying months before us – I dread the torrents of lamentation that will overwhelm us from every quarter. But we must not mind that, we must remain until Christmas.

It will be a dreadful [pain?] to him when his last Sunday comes. Indeed I think every day till we go will be a pain – But he felt he ought to so arrange it, as to give time for his transfer [and the election ?] so that all might be settled again before the next quarter begins . . . [105]

Nine days later she wrote to Louisa again, this time to ask for her help as the news had not been well received by her mother and her sister Mary.

My dearest Louisa

We are a little distressed at the view – not altogether approving – which Mama and Mary [appear?] to take of our Retirement –

Their letters are such a contrast to yours! Mary says "Mama is anxious to give a <u>favourable version</u> of it to the world."

169

We do not <u>want</u> a "favourable version of it" to be given to the world. We are not in the least ashamed of doing what Dr Arnold always intended to do – and as for the suddenness of it, I believe if he had contemplated it ever so long, he would not have announced it at a longer distance for everyone acquainted with Public <u>Schools</u> knows that anything like uncertainty or suspense with regard to the future is very injurious – keeping away many who have naturally come.

Poor man – I do think he may be allowed to judge for himself as to the propriety of his mode of proclaiming it – and also as to the length of time after which he may consider himself entitled to withdraw into a quieter sphere.

What I write for Dear Louisa is, to ask you to be so very kind as to beg Aunt Stanley, if she should be writing to Mama, to say something expressive of satisfaction.

Nothing influences her like this - & I know it would make all the difference . . . Eliza has written to us most kindly & so has Henrietta & it has been such a disappointment to get Mama's and Mary's – which you may suppose we had been looking forward to with greatest eagerness – I do not mean to say that they have written <u>un</u>kindly – only not very kindly – you know the difference. Perhaps your letters spoilt us & we expected all to be the same . . . [106]

Symonds, now at Oxford, noted the Head's resignation in a letter he wrote to Charlotte some time in September: 'Do you see by ye papers that Dr Vaughan has resigned ye Head Mastership of Harrow? It will be a great blow to ye School I fear, as well as a loss to some old Harrovians. I wonder whether he will hereby more easily get a Bishopric?' [107] There was apparently a general expectation that Vaughan would soon become a bishop; a view which he may have shared at the time.

Stanley was touring Northern Europe in August and September, so he was out of the country when the news broke. He wrote to his mother from Antwerp on 16 September and from Dover next day and to his sister-in-law Eliza from Harrow on the 21st, expressing his astonishment:

My dearest Eliza

First, as to the astounding news which greeted me on my arrival at St Leonard's! Mrs H at once showed me the paragraph which in an obscure corner of the Times, had escaped me altogether – You may suppose how it hastened my flight here yesterday. You have heard from Catherine the *how* and the *why* of the abdication – and so I need say no more. They are both perfectly satisfied and relieved though feeling the general grief of the place – On the whole it seems to me that the motives of the (HM) are understood and appreciated. All that I fear, is lest (what I see here and there), from the unusual and sudden notice of the event, people should imagine reasons which do not exist – *his* health, or *her* health – or something wrong in the School. – The fact is that, it was simply his own resolution, communicated to no one, and made at once, to [stop?] the evil of protracted [?], and at this time, because of there being no evil to occasion it, and of the close of the period of 15 years. I [?] hope that they will not have a *long* period of repose – a *short* one will be very well. [108]

He wrote to Eliza again the next day from Oxford:

You will have had my letter from Harrow. I don't think I have anything more to add. It is now supremely important to make the best of what is irrevocable, but I do not allow myself to dwell on anything beyond the fact that they are satisfied. I fear that there will be a good deal of trouble from the interminable conjectures of imaginary motives for such a sudden step. But as the real reason would have justified it sooner or later, in the eyes of everyone, perhaps they will justify it in the eyes of a large number now. [109]

We are given a sympathetic and positive reaction to the announcement of his resignation from Westcott, one of his colleagues and friends, who wrote on 24 September to his former pupil, Charles Dalrymple now at Cambridge: 'For Dr Vaughan's sake I am glad that he has made up his mind to leave Harrow . . . the only way to promotion such as I hope he may obtain before long. Had he stayed here I should have despaired of seeing him in the Church, now I hope that he may be placed there at once on the first vacancy.' [i.e. of a bishopric][110]

Life had to go on as normal for one more term though it must have been extremely difficult for the Head. He shared something of his feelings in a letter dated 8 October to Dalrymple who was due to visit them the following week and telling him 'how happy we always are to keep you as long as possible.'

We have both been very poor creatures this week, but hope to be all right before you come. I confess to finding it very sad work, this approaching departure. The Sundays are almost more than I can stand. We had a beautiful sermon from Mr Farrar on Founder's Day, last Thursday: it is to be printed.
I am extremely busy in School & next week the Camb. Comm[n] sets in again. How very much we shall have to talk of. The kindness of everyone here is more than I can tell you.
Our kindest regards – I had almost said, love – to the dear family at New Hailes. Tell Kitty how much her Hymnbook is prized [a gift from CD's sister

to Vaughan]: but the name must be written in it by her some day.
Ever dear Dalrymple Very affectionately yours   Chas J. Vaughan
You will have to select a Volume of Harrow Sermons for me while you are here! [111]

He was naturally concerned that his successor should be someone sympathetic to the Vaughan legacy. He would not be party to the appointment but he could offer confidential advice to his preferred candidate, Montagu Butler, whose candidature was strongly supported by several Cambridge 'Apostles' including Farrar who had been elected one the year before Butler. Vaughan felt that Farrar was being too eager in his support and cautioned Butler, 'your friends here – Farrar more particularly – would do well to hold back rather than to press forward. They may run the risk of provoking hostility.' [112]

On 1 November he wrote to Dalrymple about his approaching last Sunday at which he was expecting upwards of 110 guests and about the coming selection of the new Head. He mentioned two of the candidates, 'Barry & Riddell (of Balliol) seem to be formidable. I do not know whether you are acquainted with the latter, from Jamieson, or in any other way. But it is too soon as yet for me to take any side, even if I ever ought to do so. Meanwhile anything you can tell me of Butler, either as a preacher or in any other way, will be very valuable.' [113] He also gave him an update on *Memorials of Harrow Sundays* which Macmillan would be publishing.

On 17 November the Governors wrote to him to inform him that they had appointed Butler the previous day. The letter continues:

The Governors cannot approach the termination of their immediate connection with you without expressing in the most warm and cordial terms their regret at the loss which the School is about to suffer by your retirement from the Post of Headmaster.

They entertain a deep sense of the zeal, talent and ability by which you have conducted the School, and raised it with the efficient support of the other Masters and the respect and confidence of the boys to its present high position. They highly appreciate your munificent contributions towards the increasing requirements of the School in Buildings for Public Worship, and in provision for extended tuition, and they earnestly wish that you may enjoy the leisure which you have justly earned, with satisfaction of knowing that your period of administering the affairs of the School will always be regarded by the Governors, as well as by all who take an interest in the prosperity of Harrow, as one of bright and untarnished credit to the School.

We beg to subscribe ourselves with the highest sentiments of esteem.
Dear Sir
Your obedient Servants. [114]

The letter was signed by all the Governors. This minute is in stark contrast to the absence of any recorded thanks to Wordsworth on his resignation fifteen years earlier – an act they had pressurized him into taking.

Vaughan's emotions at the news of the appointment were immediately shared with Dalrymple:

My joy at the Election is what you know it would be – a sense of thankfulness (I hope) to God mixing with deep relief for the anxieties of the last few days (more particularly) when I saw that there was a real risk of another result. All is well: & many prayers, I am sure, have attended both the progress of the contest to its close . . . I confess to you, secretly, a little pain in finding myself really replaced.

It is a strange feeling, that of having a successor appointed – but let me think only what it would have been had any other than this one: that may well preclude all murmerings of heart. Indeed they are very superficial – only one pang at first. [115]

The Governors met with him for the last time on 1 December when he explained to them his motives for the formation of the 'English School' and offered suggestions to them about the management of the School in the future:

The English School
That he established this as a form of the School in order to meet a want of the superior tradesmen and to relieve the Foundation. That he paid the Master and Under-Master; that each Boy paid £5 per annum and the parents signed a Book declaring their readiness to abide by the Rules which were so arranged as to prevent these Boys from interfering with the higher School. That it had answered its purpose having quite extinguished all complaints on the part of the Parishioners which formerly used to break out. Dr Vaughan suggested that the Governors should adopt this School, and admit to it Boys as they did to the School Foundation, and that Mr Young should prepare a form of admission in that sense. "Upon which the Governors resolved accordingly." [116]

He also made recommendations relating to repairs needed to the Chapel and new buildings and gave them a list of current expenses (in addition to fees for Boarding) which all parents paid:

Public Tuition (i.e.)	
Master & Under-Master	15.0.0
School Charges	5.0.0
Private Tuition	15.0.0.
Mathematics	4.0.0.
Modern Languages	2.5.0.

£ 41.5.0 [117] [= £4,390]

Vaughan explained that he had raised the 'School Charges' from £2.12.6 on his appointment to £5 in order to provide an additional salary for Masters so as to render them 'more independent of profits upon Board and had been so applied.' He thought the charges were moderate and had heard of no complaints.

His last Sunday was 4 December. On its eve when he must have had so much else requiring his immediate attention he still made time to craft carefully a detailed letter to Tait, the Bishop of London, asking for his help and patronage in a family matter:

My eldest brother has just vacated the living of St Martin's in Leicester, which has been now held, almost in succession, by my Father, myself and him, though it is a Chancellor's living, and the appointment has been made in each case by a different Chancellor.

There is now a very strong wish on the part of the Parishioners, that my Brother David, of St Mark's Whitechapel, should succeed to it.

I think you are aware that a Hospital [i.e. almshouses] has been held with the living by my eldest Brother. This makes the Chancellor of the Duchy of Lancaster, Sir George Grey, a joint Patron with the Lord Chancellor of the preferment vacated by my Brother.

I have reason to believe that your Lordship's distinct recommendation of my Brother David to the Lord Chancellor for this living would be effectual. It would give me very real pleasure if you felt yourself able thus to interpose. You know my Brother's character, abilities and clerical qualifications, as well as his opinions; if you feel no reason to withhold so express a recommend-ation it would be very gratifying to us all, and more especially to my Mother, who still resides in Leicester and attends the Church where her husband lies buried.

If however you feel the slightest scruple in taking so decided a step in his behalf, I know how conscientious your feeling will be, and shall readily acquiesce in it.

Tomorrow is my farewell to the Chapel of Harrow School. It is a trying moment, and you will kindly forgive the faults of this letter. [118]

The letter is a model of tactful petitioning and penned at a moment when he knew Tait could hardly deny him his request. David was known to Tait personally as he had been a pupil in the Sixth Form at Rugby when Tait was appointed Head. He was duly appointed to St Martin's and went on to play a major role in the provision of adult education in Leicester. The Adult Education Department in the university today is named after him.

In what must have been for him an emotional sermon at Holy Communion the next morning, he took as his text *2 Timothy 3. 14* "But continue thou in the things which thou hast learned." And he chose to emphasize what, in his judgement, were the advantages they enjoyed as pupils at Harrow and five lessons the school had taught them, each of which he illustrated in words they could not fail to appreciate:

'1. First among these special lessons of a Public School, I will place *the value of time* . . .'

'2. The forming a right estimate of yourselves . . .'

'3. The necessity and the power of *adapting yourselves to a variety of persons and circumstances* . . .'

'4. *The meaning of a social as opposed to a selfish life* . . . that is the obligation to act for others and for the body, as well as for themselves . . .'

'5. The great lesson of *the consequences of actions* . . .' [119]

The evening service must have been an even more moving occasion. This was his farewell sermon. He took the three words 'Yet once more' from his text, Hebrews xii. 27 and began by applying them to himself:

To enter yet once more the well-known room where day by day for many years he has been the instructor and ruler; to use yet once more that form of prayer with which the day's work is begun, and then to turn yet once more to those familiar pages of some ancient author out of which he has taught with undiminished interest some five school-generations of intelligent and always docile pupils; to take his place yet once more, for purposes of mutual aid or kindly converse, at the head of a large body of beloved and honoured coadjutors, whose self-devoted toil and ready sympathy have been his constant support under a heavy burden of daily cares and duties; to do all these things with a distinct knowledge that the end is approaching, and at last to do each of them yet but once more, is no slight trial, it could not be wished that it should be a slight trial, to one who has a heart to feel, or is capable of appreciating the importance of the office which he is at last laying down. [120]

The sermon drew to a close almost on a tearful note:

> How am I to say those last words, *Finally, brethren, farewell*? I know not. I would fain postpone them; but until when? . . . How can I sever myself, even in imagination, from this place? What will it be when it has been done? Three months ago It seemed to be possible: the clearest and the most decisive judgement dictated it: but today it is hard to execute . . . [121]

His final request to them was to pray for the school: '. . . help, I say it again and again as my last words, by your prayers, to make this place all that a Christian school may be – diligent, truthful, pure, religious, the nurse of Christian men, the training-place of souls for heaven.' [122] After the service he stood on the steps of the chapel and shook hands with each boy as he left. An era in the school's history had ended.

Contemporary judgement on Vaughan's headmastership was largely very positive. *The Times* published a lengthy account on 7 December of a dinner held in the Freemasons' Tavern attended by about 250 Old Harrovians. Charles Currer was in the chair; he had entered the school during Wordsworth's headship and left under Vaughan's, so was well able to compare the two regimes – there was no doubt which he regarded the more favourably. The dinner was, he said, a 'public demonstration of respect, honour, and affection to one whom they felt they could never esteem over much.'

> Perhaps there were not more than half-a-dozen present who, like himself, belonged to that pre-Adamite period of Harrow history which was represented by the time before the headmastership of Dr Vaughan. The six years during which he was at Harrow from 1841 to 1846 formed a critical period in the history of the school, and in the history, he might add, of English public school education. They witnessed the whole process of transformation from the old to the new – from a state of government that had been humorously described as a moderate anarchy to that system of discipline and order under which Harrow now subsisted. When Dr Vaughan arrived at Harrow, in the beginning of 1845, the pupils were not more than 69 in number, and the whole place – school, masters, tradesmen, and all – was almost on the verge of bankruptcy. Nor was the moral aspect of the school any better. The reputation of the pupils was almost as bad as it could be, and he believed that Dr Vaughan, on his first visit to Harrow, was seriously recommended to expel the school *en masse*. [The Vicar of Harrow

had indeed recommended this to Vaughan.]   But that suggestion he rejected as soon as it was made. He determined to deal with the school as he found it. He resolved to trust to the pupils, and before long he found that they did not abuse his confidence. (Hear, hear.) No man, he was sure, would be more ready than Dr Vaughan to acknowledge that in the monitors of that day he found active and zealous co-operators in his great work of clearing that vast moral wilderness, which under his auspices, had since become as a smiling garden. The task was not an easy one, but it was accomplished in an incredibly short space of time, thanks to the combination of tact, judgement, and energy displayed by the Headmaster. (Cheers.) Dr Vaughan's success was a result of many causes. It was due, in the first place, to his admirable administrative power, his decision and promptness in the despatch of business, and to his large-hearted liberality. No man ever possessed to a greater degree the peculiar power of knowing his own mind, of driving at a definite point, of hitting the right nail on the head. (Cheers.) His patient attention to details was only equalled by the rapidity and independence of his judgement, although he was always ready to listen to the advice of others, and willing to modify, or at least reconsider, his own foregone conclusions. (Hear, hear.) But mere admin- istrative capacity would not have been enough for the great work which, at the commencement of his career at Harrow, he set before himself. He also possessed, in an eminent degree, the public school spirit. (Cheers.) Though himself one of the most distinguished of Dr Arnold's pupils, and though he might by the stroke of his pen have converted Harrow into a second Rugby, he determined from the first to sink or swim with the school of which he had been appointed Headmaster; he recognised its distinctive charac- teristics, and resolved, wisely and manfully resolved, that Harrow should be Harrow still, and not a medley half Rugby and half Harrow. (Cheers.) He had consequently won the entire confidence of the school, of five generations of pupils, who proudly claimed him as a genuine Harrow man. (Cheers.) Another striking feature in Dr Vaughan's administration was that he had combined with exquisite tact that strict discipline, that high moral tone, that manliness of thought, and that freedom of action which, together constituted the admirable type of the cultivated, liberal-minded English gentleman. (Cheers.) Harrow, unlike Eton, was peculiarly sensitive to the shifting and often contradictory decisions of public opinion. The menace of the withdrawal of an influential connexion – even a whisper of disaffection in a London drawing-room – was felt as a real calamity, and hence the success achieved by Dr Vaughan was the more remarkable and praise- worthy. (Hear, hear.) Thanks were likewise due to Dr Vaughan for the admirable staff of masters he had gathered around him – men of great ability, of high character, and of singular devotion to their work, men who knew how to carry out the system which he had established. (Cheers.) Nor upon such an occasion should they forget the noble use which Dr Vaughan had made of the emoluments of his office. He had never sought to make gain of Harrow; on the contrary, his left hand knew not the hundredth part of the noble acts of generosity which his right hand had unostentatiously done. (Cheers.) The name of Dr Vaughan, in short, was deeply engraven on the hearts of his grateful pupils, of some 1,800 Englishmen, no small or influential portion of the rising generation, who felt that they owed to him the formation of whatever was best and worthiest in their characters, of whatever was to give form and colour to the whole tenor of their future lives. (Cheers.) [123]

In his reply to the toast, Vaughan repeated that he had always intended to go after 15 years: 'The present was a marked, a peculiar, in one sense an unprecedented occasion. In ordinary cases the connexion between a headmaster and his school was broken by one of three causes – death, failing strength, ecclesiastical preferment. It had been his ambition to add a fourth, and to allow it to be said that one man at least had left the school where he had served during a considerable part of his working life, at the very summit of its prosperity.' [124] He went on to describe something of the pressures of a headmaster's position –

> It was a life at all times of great anxiety. To control something like 500 human wills, especially if they were young wills, subject to every gust of temper and passion, must always be a difficult, arduous, and anxious task. In such a life, indeed teaching was a relaxation. The hours he spent with his Sixth Form were the lightest he had known at Harrow . . . after 15 years of difficulties not small, and of occasional dangers not to be disregarded, [he] felt that he needed a period of repose, and he claimed it without fear of misconstruction. (Cheers.) It was his intention to have that period of repose, and he should not be robbed of it. It should not be a period of idleness or inaction, but a period of privacy, of comparative quiet, and he trusted of domestic though not of useless enjoyment. (Cheers.) [125]

The *Times* also reported that in the course of the evening it was announced that it was intended to establish a Vaughan Library at Harrow, for the use of about a hundred of the upper boys in the school. The cost was estimated at £4,000 [= £425,600], of which a half had already been subscribed – one of Vaughan's pupils had contributed £1,000. The cost in fact turned out to be much higher and a further meeting of masters and former pupils was held at Spencer House the following March to launch a formal appeal.

On 12 December he wrote to Dalrymple revealing his inner turbulent feelings:

I feel very strange today. We came over to Stanmore, Mr Glyn's House, yesterday to Dinner, & are spending our Sunday here [G.C. Glyn MP later 1st Baron Wolverton whose son would become one of Vaughan's curates in Doncaster]. It was absolutely impossible to remain in Harrow, with the sights and sounds of last Sunday so fresh upon me, yet all gone! I am tasting something of the bitterness of the change now! & yet I do not repent of it. I hope I shall become, if I might so express it, more of a Clergyman, less secular in my aims & thoughts, & ready for plainer & humbler work, & thankful to be permitted to do it, than ever before. I see now so many things that ought to be made different. You will think of me, & pray for me I hope now and then, in my present vacant life – for so it seems in prospect - & perhaps in a future busy one . . .

I am very sorry about the stupid letters in the Times, though I felt that Currer's speech was unwise in that point. It is a pity to give pain by such comparisons, & they are not wholly just. I do hope it will end now. Currer's letter was necessary, but I think also sufficient. One never knows. I was at my Commission each day last week: this week we must begin our preparations in earnest for departure: next week towards the end, I should hope that we may take possession at Southborough . . . wherever you are, I shall think of you. To have been without you last Sunday would have been a real loss to me. I think it made a strong impression – the whole scene I mean, upon many. I was myself in a maze the whole day. I could feel little and realize nothing . . . [126]

An important chapter in the school's life was ended but it would not be forgotten. The foundation stone of the Vaughan Library was laid by Lord Palmerston on Speech Day, 4 July 1861 and the work completed at a cost of £12,000 [= £1,209,600] in time for opening on Speech Day two years later. Old Harrovians then commissioned a portrait of him to be painted by George Richmond R.A. which was hung in the Library in 1868. He was to be commemorated in other ways too: by the reredos and brightly coloured stone inset panels at the East end of the school chapel, and on the North side of the chancel by his portrait in a marbled relief.

In 1945 the Headmaster, Ralph Westwood Moore, whom Tyerman has described as 'the Vaughan of the twentieth century', addressed the school on the centenary of his appointment. He began his address by referring to the portrait by Richmond:

It is the portrait of a young man in the prime of his life. What do you see in it? I see in it nobility, a quiet confidence and that happiest of gifts – the serenity of mind which proceeds not from complacency, but from sureness of faith. The eyes are calm and far-seeing: the mouth is sympathetic and firm. Here, if ever there was, is a man who saw life steadily and saw it whole; a man who will meet troubles with unfailing courage and with unfailing calm; a man whom no problems will dismay; a man whose human understanding will never fail; because his vision is unswerving and his faith in God and His purposes unbreakable. This was the greatest Head Master Harrow has ever had. [127]

An Allegation of gross Misconduct

I can say, without reserve, that at no time in my entire life have I been so conscious of living in a directly Christian atmosphere, with Christian ideals of duty habitually set up for reverence, as during the happy years when Vaughan presided over Harrow.
H.M. Butler *Ten Great & Good Men*

We come now to the affair which, according to Symonds's private *Memoirs* written in 1889, really ended Vaughan's career at Harrow. In a sentence: Symonds claimed that the Headmaster had had an improper sexual relationship with one of his friends, Alfred Pretor. The details of his account, in my judgement, are not to be trusted.

To begin with his opinions of Vaughan given in his weekly letters to his sister Charlotte written whilst he was a pupil at Harrow are at variance with the damaging things he wrote thirty and more years later. In Symonds's *Memoirs* Vaughan is 'a man for whom I felt no love, and who had shown me no special kindness.' [1] But that opinion is not the one he shared in his letters to Charlotte written at the time where there are frequent words of appreciation:

'I have just returned from Chapel where I heard Dr V preach. The sermon was excellent. He proved in a most conclusive & overpowering manner the Divinity of Christ.' (May 18 1856)

'I went to Dr V as I told you a few days ago. He seemed to like my composition. I have been getting on better with Mr Steel too . . . Yesterday he [Vaughan] laughed about my dislike to football when I was describing winter sports in verse & told me I ought to give a description of my study if I preferred that. I was very much pleased when he told me that "he always relied upon my investigating words & not using them until I knew their meanings."' (15 February '57)

'However he [Vaughan] was very kind & I have got to think him much more sincere than I used to. He is in great trouble just at present from the death of his sister [probably Mary Esther] although neither he nor his brother are yet in mourning.' (8 March '57)

'I had occasion to speak to Dr V today. I see more & more how kind he is for before I could say anything he exclaimed "Oh Symonds you look so unwell. I hope that you are taking care of yourself" & then made minute enquiries into the state of my health.' (14 March '57)

'It has been a tiring day. I have heard three sermons. The 1st was a Confirmation Lecture on the text "These things have I said unto you that in me ye might have peace: in the world ye shall have tribulation etc" It was

181

quite the best sermon of his I ever heard . . . The evening sermon was also from Dr V. on the words "in the Lord." It was one of what we call his "ponderous style" consisting of long winded sentences & arguments evolved by an immense number of involutions.' (17 May '57)

To his sister Maribella he wrote on 18 June '57 'I am just come back from dining with Dr V. I enjoyed it excessively: he was so kind and nice . . . I sat at dinner on Dr V's left hand & had long talk with him. He rather discomfited me by exclaiming as he carved me some beef "We all of us know how much Symonds wants beef & such things to fatten him. He has a great deal to bear." Why does everyone think I have so much to bear & am so weak?" . . . After dinner we walked with him in the garden . . .'

There is no dislike of the Head here. And in the very month that he would later claim Pretor had told him about his affair with the Head, he could still write to Charlotte: 'All as usual. Saw Dr Vaughan who spoke very kindly & asked me how I was etc.' (18 January '58). What is clear from his weekly correspondence is that he enjoyed Harrow far more than he was willing to admit to later in life, and that, as any pupil would, he appreciated it greatly whenever the Head showed a personal interest in him and his abilities. Equally, he was unhappy and critical when he felt he had somehow been dealt with unfairly as when Vaughan awarded a scholarship to a pupil whom he claimed the Head liked and favoured rather than to himself, or when he found almost all his friends were going on to Cambridge rather than to Oxford – 'It is all Dr. V's malign influence which is turned entirely in favour of Cambridge' (24 January '58)[2] This probably refers to Jamieson who at the time was thinking of dropping the idea of going to Balliol in favour of Trinity Cambridge. His other friends, Bosanquet, Dalrymple and Pretor, all went to Cambridge.

Before reading Symonds's account and allegations, consideration needs to be given first to some important, related issues. Several of Vaughan's former pupils have recorded that one of his strengths as a Head was the sympathy and care which he showed to the boys. It is also on record that he had close, affectionate and long lasting relationships with a good number of them, most notably Montagu Butler and Charles Dalrymple, and he was not afraid to give voice to his feelings for them, even to their parents. Edward Graham, the biographer of Butler in his Harrow days, recorded how the boy 'fell, immediately and literally, into love and hero-worship for his Headmaster, and *the affection was returned.'* [3] An adolescent crush, it would seem, on the boy's part, and acknowledged appreciatively by the Head. In August 1851, soon after he had left, Vaughan wrote to the boy's father to congratulate him on his son's academic success and included these expressions of his own affection:

> My love and esteem for him are, as I believe he has discovered, great indeed. You are happy in the possession of him, nor can I resign it without one of the severest pangs which I have ever felt in such a parting. He has been, for the last year, I may truly say, *everything* to me at Harrow. I do not know that I ever saw so happy a combination of ability and industry, firmness and courtesy, power of ruling and willingness to obey, as in him. You may imagine what it has been to me to have such qualities as these united in the Head of my House, and of the School. Where am I to look for the like again? . . . and give my very affectionate regards to him (*how* affectionate I hope I need not tell him). [4]

Vaughan seems to have found the parting with pupils to whom he was deeply attached very difficult. He wanted so much for them to keep in touch with him and to visit frequently. Was this, perhaps subconsciously, a result of his having been parted for ever at the age of thirteen from a much loved father? His wife was aware that he had such close and emotional relationships with particular boys and seems to have accepted it, even approved of it in some cases. She wrote, for example, to Butler just before he left school in the most affectionate terms.

> I can only say, "may you be hereafter all you have been here!" I really cannot say much to you, for I feel more than you would think at the prospect of losing you. It will be long indeed before we shall cease to miss your face; and to him who has taught you for so long, it is no trifling sorrow to part with you in one sense for ever . . . remember that you must count me and Dr Vaughan among your best and truest friends – and I think I need scarcely add that this house must ever be to you a second home. [5]

We need also to bear in mind that 'manly love' or romantic friendships were a recognised and honoured form of relationships between boys and young men at that time which feature in novels of the period. Horace Vachell's *The Hill*, based on Harrow where he was a pupil in the 1870s, is perhaps the most famous of its kind. The fictional relationships described in such novels had their parallels in real life. Charles Kingsley, for example, described Charles Mansfield, his closest friend at Cambridge, as his 'first love'. In a letter to his future wife he tried to explain this 'brotherly love' of one man for another, regarding it as an awesome and spiritual relationship. David Newsome, one of the finest

183

commentators on life in Victorian England, has stated: 'In the nineteenth century, the normality of both men and women forming highly emotional relationships with those of their own sex, of the same age or sometimes older or younger, as the case might be, was neither questioned as necessarily unwholesome nor felt to inhibit the same relationship with the opposite sex, leading to a perfectly happy marriage.' [6]

Nowadays, it is hard for us to dissociate in our thinking close male friendship from homosexuality (a word not yet coined in 1859), but that was not the case then when 'manly love' was regarded more as a brotherhood of a spiritual kind than of a physical one. For a more detailed and scholarly treatment of this emotional and spiritual tradition of 'manly love' in the 19th century, see Jeffrey Richards's essay *'Passing the love of women': manly love and Victorian society*, in *Manliness and Morality* edited by J.A. Mangan & J. Walvin (1987).

Newsome remarked in *Godliness and Good Learning* 'the word love was more frequently on their lips, used with real sincerity. The association between master and pupil seems to have often been very intimate, admitting of expressions of emotion on both sides' [7] and he cites several examples. Vaughan would have remembered only too clearly how passionately devoted Stanley had been to Arnold. He may well have longed to be the recipient himself of such affection, particularly from his most able pupils to whom he gave more time and personal attention, and it warmed his heart when they did.

Newsome, again, in *On the Edge of Paradise*, his study of the Eton House Master Arthur Benson a son of the Archbishop of Canterbury, reveals just how emotionally attached a master could become to a pupil but without ever being anything but scrupulously correct in his dealings with the boy. Benson described being a schoolmaster as a 'precarious trade' and wrote of the 'heart-hunger' which he experienced. Vaughan, I suspect, felt much of the same. Newsome comments:

> 'Heart-hunger' is a good word to express such a complex of emotions, embracing all the loneliness of the sensitive man set by nature or circumstances to guide and live among boys with whom he can never attain anything more than an ephemeral intimacy and from whom he is bound to stand professionally aloof. It is the very essence of 'bitter-sweet': to feel a love that can be agonisingly real – whether it be the paternal yearning for the son that never was or the romantic sublimation of some physical desire – but which can never be fulfilled. Age pays court to youth: but youth is too young to understand or to recognise the need of the other; and youth must move on while the other remains. [8]

184

Vaughan's young friend at Rugby, Arthur Clough, provides in the pages of his private diary rare, first-hand evidence and illustration of such romantic relationships, both as the object of a Tutor's affection when he was an undergraduate and then himself as the 'lover' of younger students. In the summer of 1841 after graduating at Oxford, he had acted as a private tutor on a four week long trip in the Lakes to 'Todo' Walrond, the head boy at Rugby, who was reading for the Balliol scholarship and the two became attached to each other. Clough wrote: 'I am now all along resting on the fancy of affection in Walrond whereas I have no reason to believe he cares for me, nor yet could be justified in expressing to him that I care for him. . . Wax, I fear, expansive to Walrond at tea; have recovered all my spirits after the walk, & lost I fear, my seriousness with the talk.*' [9] Later at Oxford their friendship blossomed – one entry reads 'Am now satisfied with the fancy of going to Walrond *' and the next day he notes 'Possessed wholly by Walrond.' [10] In stressful situations (such as a tutorial that was not going well) he would bring fond pictures of Todo to mind to help him get through it. There was another young man, whom he refers to cryptically in the diary as 'B...y' who also won his love. He describes him as 'refilling my as I seemed to see it, empty heart'.[11] Whilst still deeply attached to Walrond he also recorded '*last night I rested wholly in the belief & acceptance of B's love.' [12] There were other very close friends too, in particular his Mathematics Tutor at Balliol, W.G. Ward, and a fellow undergraduate, William Tylden, with both of whom he had stormy relationships and who made excessive demands on him emotionally and on his time. His diary notes by means of a large star * repeated occurrences of what he called his 'great sin' (something he had started committing in his Rugby days) which his biographer, Anthony Kenny, believes refers to the practice of solitary masturbation. He occasionally records the context in which he did it, such as 'lying in bed', 'after rowing', 'after too much exercise and perhaps too much wine', and even 'tho after a cold bath at ¼ to 11'. But there is nothing to suggest that he ever actually did it with any of the young men he loved, though the starred entries quoted above might suggest he had them in his imagination when he did it. Kenny who edited Clough's Oxford diaries comments:

> These relationships were clearly highly intense, and had a strong erotic element . . . But though in one sense Ward was clearly in love with Clough, and Clough with Walrond, it is unlikely that there was overtly sexual expression of affection between them. Anything of this kind would have

been seen by one of them – however they might differ over the finer details of Christian morality – as a heinous crime. Clough, who agonized so much over masturbation, would have been tormented with guilt by sodomy. [13]

Almost certainly, that would have been equally true of Vaughan, who, like Clough, had been brought up in a strict Evangelical home and whose moral outlook had been so much influenced by Thomas Arnold.

Trevelyan was another who enjoyed a long and affectionate relationship with his former Head and often stayed with him – he recalled 'the eagerness and frequency, and the almost filial affection with which we visited, and re-visited, our old Master Doctor Vaughan at Harrow.' [14] As late as 1880, he was still in touch with him, telling Dalrymple he had received 'a delightful letter' from him. Herman Merivale recalled 'loving and delightful' midnight walks with Vaughan, 'night after night'. It was possibly because of this that his parents removed him from the school, something he could never understand particularly as it was 'just when he was ripening under Vaughan.' [15]

> Dear Dr. Vaughan! My master; more my friend. It was a pain to him when I left Harrow just one year too soon . . . He hated my being taken away from him, for, as he often told me, he had not enough special time to devote to more than one or two, at the end, of those whom he believed to be his most promising scholars . . . But he made a friend of me. Night after night in my last Harrow summer, when the house was all abed, did he and I go out for night walks round Harrow Park, and about Harrow Hill. In all the loving and delightful converse, which keen and listening youth like mine can hold with mature and humorous wisdom such as his. Oh – but he was humorous – to those who knew, he of the Rugby manner as we called it, bred in the school of Arnold, with the velvet glove hiding the iron hand. [16]

Tyerman in his history of the school included extracts from correspondence between the Head and Edward Latham who was on his House from 1845-52 and head of it during his last year. The language of the letters is similar to that used about Butler. Vaughan described himself as his 'affectionate friend' and wrote with longing for the boy to visit him again after he had left for Cambridge. At the top of a letter to him dated 17 February 1853, Vaughan had written 'Burn this' which might suggest it contained some dreadful secret – in fact it simply reveals an emotional and vulnerable man who invested a lot of himself in his relationships and looked for and hoped for a similar return. He dared to be frank about his

186

feelings because he trusted Latham but naturally he would not wish all and sundry to know such personal details. He writes: 'I do not know whether you care for letters: I rather doubt it – at least for letters such as I should care for . . . I long to see you . . . I often wonder whether you have forgotten or changed towards me. But I do not know why I should suppose it – except that it seems improbable that anyone should remember me when I have been two or three months out of their sight.'[17] Tyerman noted, 'In November 1853, Vaughan suggested Latham might prefer to visit when they will be "entirely alone".' That phrase is open to a sinister interpretation but it could equally well mean no more than that they would be able to talk undisturbed till the early hours. On 16 January 1854, Vaughan wrote: "I always feel towards you so very much more than I can write – and I fear it makes my letters very absurd. But you are indulgent and kind – I do not fear you.' [18]

Similar sentiments are to be read in his many letters to Henry Mather Jackson written around the same time – Jackson had been on his House from April 1845 – '49. A large collection of his letters to Jackson dating from the time he left school right through to his death in March 1881 were deposited in the School archives by a descendent who clearly did not suspect there had ever been anything improper in the relationship; she wrote simply 'I think you will agree that these letters are full of charm. Great affection evidently existed between Dr Vaughan and his old pupil.' Here is an early one:

My dear Jackson,
Your kind remembrance of me on Saturday night gives me a plea for writing to you, which I have long wished to do, but (as usual) allowed myself to put it off. You do not forget the breaking down of all barriers between us, which was the consequence of our common sorrow and love in the Spring of this year. [John Hyde d'Arcy, a former head of Vaughan's House, had died on 28 January at Oxford where he was a scholar at Balliol. Jackson was at Trinity College Oxford at the time.] Did not you <u>promise</u> that we should henceforth be more to one another than we had been? That we would write, & meet again?
I do not say this to reproach you – or as if I were not myself more to blame by far than you if it has not quite been so. But I <u>do</u> want you to see me before long, & let us talk as we did once of our lost friend – whose life at a distance of several months, often moves me to tears, & fills me with bitter grief – though I know it is selfish, nor can I wish him back: at least so one says using the common phrase – but I fear I <u>do</u> wish him back. I long to hear him speak to me again, & to renew that affectionate converse which was so sweet at the time, & is still more so in the retrospect.

Write to me when you can, dear Jackson. I dare say you thought that what I said was mere words, & that I had forgotten all about you. Surely this note will at least show you that it is not so.

How I long to hear of Miller again [George Miller had entered Harrow in June 1846 and was a Scholar at Exeter College Oxford at the time of this letter] – has he quite forgotten me? I do not suppose any of you know how strong is the tie that binds me to you.

Ever my dear Jackson

Your affectionate friend   Charles J Vaughan   Harrow Dec 1. 1852

We go away on the 7th. But you <u>will</u> come to us in January? [19]

It is clear from this letter that Vaughan had affectionate relationships with several of his former pupils long after they had left the school and he was quite open about his feelings for them. Much of the extant correspondence with Jackson contains expressions of affection and his desire to see him again but it also has lots of common place items of news, e.g. about Jackson's successes at Trinity and about their various holiday plans - in one, dated 1 August 1853, Vaughan admits to hating travelling by train and how much he dreaded the journey to Germany as he knew no German. In the following summer he planned to meet up with him at Bowness in the Lake District where he (Vaughan) would be on holiday with his mother and sister. A letter from December 1857 says 'This morning I tried to write my sermon for Sunday while I was sitting here, but it is not a very good atmosphere for sermons – one is so interrupted by the incessant visits of monitors &c.' All perfectly normal and natural as between two friends. Likewise, his earliest correspond-dence with Charles Dalrymple, after he had moved on to Trinity Cambridge in October 1858, is full of school news that might be of interest to him: 'Burnett makes a very good and active Head & Pretor is getting on famously with his work . . . The Sunday services are very nice this Quarter, we now have Jackson's *Te Deum*, which they sing very well, and a good many new tunes for Hymns. I dare say you sometimes think of practising hour on Saturdays – 4.30P.M. . .' The letter ends, 'When you can write, you know how welcome your letter will be, and how truly I am Ever yours affectionately Chas J. Vaughan' A PS is added 'I have just lost my poor old Tutor and friend Dr Peacock the Dean of Ely.' [20]

Unlike Butler, d'Arcy, Dalrymple, Jackson, Latham, Merivale, Spencer and possibly many more, Symonds felt he was not numbered among the Head's favourites and it may/must have hurt. He was particularly angry in December 1857 when he felt that he should have been awarded a scholarship in modern languages which Vaughan had given, 'blindly through his affection', to another pupil, Henry Plowden. This boy was a monitor on Vaughan's House who went on to win a scholarship at Trinity College Cambridge and later had a distinguished legal career. Is it pure chance that Symonds in his later narrative dates the cause of Vaughan's resignation, namely his relationship with another favourite, to the following month? Mark Wagland in his article *A Matter of Justice* has argued that the real reason for Symonds's hostility to the Head was that he never won the many prizes or achieved the academic distinction at Harrow that he longed for, and was 'ready to lash out at the inattentive headmaster who had favoured his rivals.' [21]

Symonds's *Memoirs* reveal him as being obsessed at this time with sex, which both attracted him and yet disgusted him. He documents the sexual life on the boarding houses in a way that hardly any other Victorian's memoirs of school life do. The following brief extract gives the flavour of his account and his views:

> Every boy of good looks had a female name and was recognized either as a public prostitute or as some bigger fellow's 'bitch'. Bitch was the word in common usage to indicate a boy who yielded his person to a lover. The talk in the studies and dormitories was incredibly obscene. One could not avoid seeing acts of onanism, mutual masturbation and the sports of naked boys in bed together. There was no refinement, no sentiment, no passion; nothing but animal lust in these occurrences. They filled me with disgust and loathing. [22]

One of his few friends was Alfred Pretor. They had been confirmed together in June 1857 along with two Scots, Charles Dalrymple and Robert Jamieson, and two other friends, Randall Vickers and Gustavus Bosanquet. According to Symonds, in January 1858, shortly after his friend's 18th birthday, Pretor (who was on Mr Middlemist's House sent Symonds (who was on Rendall's) a note claiming that Vaughan had begun a love affair with him. Subsequently, having first sworn Symonds to secrecy, he showed him some passionate love letters written to him by the Head, which made mention of love scenes between the two of them played out on the sofa in the Head's study. No details, however, are recorded in Symonds's *Memoirs* of what was supposed to have happened between the two of them, which is very surprising given his readiness to describe explicitly in his private papers the sexual acts of others. Symonds said that he was appalled that the man who had prepared him for Confirmation and who regularly preached on holiness of life could be so morally weak and, as he supposed, a prisoner to the

189

very same lusts that he saw being satisfied by boys he despised. Given his own emerging sexual orientation, there was possibly (even probably) also a good measure of jealousy in his reaction to the knowledge that Vaughan preferred Pretor to him:

> Disgust, however, was mitigated by a dumb persistent sympathy. My own inclinations, the form which my erotic idealism had assumed, prevented me from utterly condemning Vaughan. I did indeed condemn Vaughan's taste; for I regarded Pretor as a physically and emotionally inferior being. But the love drama which I now watched daily, perusing the enthusiastic letters submitted to my curiosity by Pretor's vanity, roused a keen inquisitive interest in my mind. [23]

Symonds claimed that he respected the seal of secrecy but tried to persuade Pretor to break off the relationship, and that he considered confronting Vaughan and asking what the whole thing meant. He used to take essays and verses to Vaughan where they met in the Head's study, 'the scene of his clandestine pleasures'. He even wondered if Vaughan was making overtures to him:

> I remember once that, while we sat together reading Greek iambics, he began softly to stroke my right leg from the knee to the thigh. This insignificant caress, of which I should have thought nothing two months earlier, and which probably meant nothing, seemed then disagreeably suggestive. I never liked the man; he did not possess the intellectual qualities I admired. Now I began positively to dislike him. [24]

Whilst he could not be expected to share any of this in his weekly letters to Charlotte, it would have been natural enough for him at such a time to find other things to criticize the Head for – as he had done in the past. But there is absolutely nothing of the kind. In fact, the references to Vaughan in his letters to her in the early months of 1858 are generally favourable. This one is from a letter dated 15 March 1858:

> I went to Dr V. this morning at 11 & told him [about his father's decision re: leaving Harrow for Oxford]. He seemed pleased that I should go to Oxford & at the same time not sorry that I should miss the trouble of Trials. He sees no need for me to return to Harrow so that I shall come home on Friday week if all is well. When I was with him he gave me a volume of the Harrow Hymn Book nicely bound & wrote my name in it. He then asked me to call soon & walk with him while we saw the Eclipse. Accordingly I went at ¼ before 12. & we sallied forth into his kitchen garden & walked up &

down talking till after one. At first the sky was clouded. It got very obscure & dark until 1. when the sky brightened & we saw the sun very nearly annularly Eclipsed. All the fine things however about birds going to roost & the difficulty of reading small print were quite lost. I had a very nice chat about all sorts of things. [25]

Later in March he told his aunt about a new prize which Vaughan had announced. Symonds was fairly certain he would win it: 'I am quite charmed as it is an honourable prize, & the only marked record for an aggregate of steady exertion. One's good fortune seems always to come in the forms that are least expected.' [26]

About this same time, he read Plato's *Phœdrus* and then the *Symposium* which gave him an idealised understanding of love between men so different to what he had witnessed so often between boys in school. By now, he was more willing to admit to himself that his own sexuality was directed to other boys but it gave him, he wrote in his *Memoirs*, no fellow-feeling for the Head. He stayed on at Harrow until the end of the summer term before going up to Balliol.

There he came under the influence of Professor John Conington, who looked favourably on students enjoying intense emotional relationships with one another as long as they did not spill over into any kind of explicit sexual activity. He was an old boy of Rugby who had had an homoerotic poem published in *The Rugby Miscellany* in 1846 – he called it 'Your Schoolboy Friendships, what are they?' It includes these lines:

> When to dull eyes we weakest seem,
> We feel most truly human,
> Living in love's ecstatic dream,
> More dear than love of woman.
>
> 'Tis then our hearts within us burn,
> There in the loved one's presence,
> And in his features we discern
> All forms of loveliest pleasance;
>
> It cheers us midst our sternest toil
> To think *his* eyes regard us,
> Nor want we aught beyond their smile
> To welcome and to reward us. [27]

In the summer of 1859 Alfred Pretor ended his Harrow years by winning

191

the prizes for Greek Iambics, Latin Alcaics and Latin Hexameters, and the Peel Medal for the Latin Essay, and to crown it all on 7 July the Governors awarded him the Lyon Scholarship on the Head's recommendation following the open examination for it in the previous year. Was it the news of these prizes and the award which re-ignited an old jealousy in Symonds and triggered what he says then happened whilst on a reading party with Conington at Whitby that same summer?

In a letter written to his sister Charlotte from Balliol in July, he told her that 'Whitby will not begin till about the 25th.' [28] His first letter to her from there, dated simply 'Sunday' and presumably in early August, describes the town. Several more were sent to her that month, one of which includes the line 'will you also thank Papa for his letters.' [29] He was back in Bristol for a family wedding by the beginning of September. In his *Memoirs*, written 30 years later, he claimed that he made two 'solitary journeys' from Whitby to Bristol that summer to discuss the matter with his father, yet there is nothing in his letters from the time to suggest that this in fact happened. He was, however, in an anti-Harrow frame of mind as this extract from a letter written to his aunt, Mary Ann Sykes, indicates: 'There are a whole set of horrid Harrow people who I perpetually avoid. [T.H.] Green who is a cousin [he was in fact a nephew] of Vaughan's at Harrow and has met them there, has an equal abhorrence of them.' [30] His sister Charlotte later married his friend Green whose mother was Anne Barbara Vaughan, the Head's half-sister .

One day as Conington and he walked along the cliffs Symonds returned to the story of Vaughan's love affair with a boy at Harrow which he had first told him about earlier in the term. From Symonds's account it seems that Conington had not initially believed him but now he was advised to inform his father, an eminent medical man in Bristol. He duly showed him one of Pretor's letters. In his *Memoirs*, Symonds tried to justify his actions that summer:

> It was a singular position for a youth of eighteen. I had become the accuser of my old headmaster, a man for whom I felt no love, and who had shown me no special kindness, but who was after all the awe-inspiring ruler of the petty state of Harrow. My accusations rested solely upon the private testimony of an intimate friend, whose confidence I violated by the communication of his letter to a third party. To complicate matters, I felt a deeply rooted sympathy with Vaughan. If he had sinned, it had been by yielding to passions which already mastered me. But this fact instead of making me indulgent, determined me to tell the bitter truth . . . So I went through the business of exposure, painfully but steadily. It took as little to

convince my father as it had taken to convince Conington. The evidence was plain and irrefragable. [31]

According to the *Memoirs*, Dr Symonds immediately wrote to Vaughan offering to keep the matter confidential on condition he resigned at once and never accepted preferment in the Church. Vaughan is said to have travelled down to Clifton to meet with his accuser, and, having been shown Pretor's letter, he accepted the terms dictated to him. Symonds Jr. also claimed that Catherine Vaughan went to see his father a few days later and flung herself on her knees begging him to have mercy on her husband. She confessed that she knew of his weakness but said it had never interfered with his useful service to the school. The doctor was deeply moved by her plight but refused to change the conditions. Symonds Jr. also claimed that further negotiations were carried out on Vaughan's behalf by his brother-in-law, A.P. Stanley, the Professor of Ecclesiastical History at Oxford, and by Hugh Pearson, a devoted friend of Stanley's. No details are given about these 'negotiations' nor why someone such as Pearson, who was not even close to Vaughan, was now being involved in what was surely meant to be a totally confidential matter. Nor does he offer any explanation of how he came to be in possession of the letter to Pretor.

A large question mark, however, has to be placed against the accuracy, timescale and truth of this account because we know from Stanley's correspondence that he was touring Northern Europe that summer. Charles and Catherine Vaughan too were on holiday in Scotland and northern England in late August and early September. Wagland claims the Vaughans were in Switzerland in early August but does not quote his source.

The extant correspondence of key people simply does not support Symonds's account. There is, for example, no hint of fear of public shame in the two letters, quoted earlier, that Catherine wrote to her most intimate friend and cousin, Louisa, on 18 and 27 September. Nothing to suggest she had recently been through the traumatic experience of having to beg for mercy on her knees before Dr Symonds, and being rejected. Either she is lying or Symonds is.

If his account were true, then Symonds himself must have been gravely dissembling in the letter quoted earlier which he wrote to Charlotte in September: 'Do you see by ye papers that Dr Vaughan has resigned ye Head Mastership of Harrow? It will be a great blow to ye School I fear, as well as a loss to some old Harrovians. I wonder whether he will hereby more easily get a Bishopric?' [32] Earlier in that same letter he told her that he and his father had attended a performance of *Il Trovatore* the previous night. If, in fact, his father had met with the Head (and his wife subsequently) and given him an ultimatum, his son would have known that there was no possibility of Vaughan ever becoming a Bishop. To lie so blatantly to his favourite sister seems incomprehensible especially when there was no need for him to offer any comment at all. The letter suggests, rather, that he shared the general expectation of the time that Vaughan would become a bishop. It is also strange that he later told Charlotte he planned to visit Harrow in November though he did not make it as he accepted an invitation from the Vice-Chancellor to meet the Prince of Wales instead. Wagland reasonably comments: 'Vaughan was still headmaster at Harrow in November and, if the allegations are true, one could hardly think of a place where Symonds would less like to be, especially when he says in the *Memoirs* that he avoided Vaughan for the rest of his life.' [33]

Stanley's correspondence, too, quoted earlier, unless it is all part of an incredibly, carefully co-ordinated cover-up, puts a question mark against the account in Symonds's *Memoirs*. His letters on arriving back in England and hearing of his brother-in-law's resignation express astonishment. That is inconceivable if he had, in fact, been directly involved in negotiations on the Head's behalf with Dr Symonds.

According to Symonds's account, Pretor had also told Dalrymple and Jamieson, two of their other school friends, about the affair but was, nonetheless, very angry when he discovered Symonds's perfidy. Symonds claimed that none of these three ever spoke to him again. He said that he 'suffered deeply both in spirits and in health from the long exhausting correspondence with Pretor and Jamieson and Dalrymple, crossing and confusing the correspondence carried on by my father with Conington and Vaughan and Stanley. My brain and moral consciousness - the one worn with worrying thought, the other racked by casuistical doubts - never quite recovered from the weariness of those unprofitable weeks.' [34]

Whatever it was that Pretor had actually told Dalrymple earlier or what Symonds subsequently told others, it certainly did not alter Dalrymple's high regard and affection for his old Master. That much is abundantly clear from his letters to Vaughan at the time and more importantly from what he wrote in his private journals for 1858 and 1859 which still exist. We turn now to that first-hand evidence:

The journals do give some credence to elements in the Symonds narrative but not to the heart of the matter: Vaughan's forced resignation because of an improper sexual relationship with a pupil. Jamieson, Pretor, Symonds and he were clearly friends - that much is factual - exchanging letters in the New Year vacation of 1858 prior to returning to Harrow on Wednesday 13 January. He also wrote to the Head on 6 January. His diary entries usually start with an account of the day's weather and go on to list what he had done during the day, who he had received letters from or written to, and occasionally he adds comments on the page facing the dated entries. The following are some brief extracts from his diary for 1858 about Dr Vaughan and his friends, and entries which may have some bearing on Symonds's later allegations.

Wednesday 13/1: 'To Harrow by 7pm. Find things here much as usual.'
[Various entries show that his usual companions when out walking and talking were Jamieson and Symonds.]
Thursday 28/1: 'Pretor a little more amiable today after 3 days silence (these things ought not to be so).'
Saturday 30/1: 'Dressed and dined with Dr V. A very pleasant evening.'
Tuesday 2/2: 'Heard some startling things after which I pray my God may be untrue.'
Wednesday 3/2: 'Rather saddened by what I hinted at, at end of yesterday's diary.'
Thursday 4/2: 'I am more than ever uncomfortable with the forementioned matter.'
Monday 8/2 'Went to the Dr after 2. If I could get rid of disagreeable impression, it would have been perfect. As it was, we had tea and were on the whole happy.'
Wednesday 17/2: 'Rather plagued with thoughts about subjects formerly referred to.'
Saturday 20/2: 'I wd fain cultivate more <u>calm</u> & quiet temper, so as not to be affected by external things so much.'
Tuesday 23/2: 'Went to Dr V whom I sat with [?] for a long time. Delicious talk. How I do love him with my whole soul.'
Thursday 4/3: 'Had Symonds & Pretor to breakfast. Walked aft[ernoon] with Symonds & Jamieson to Sudby.'
Saturday 6/3: 'Whole School Day and a dose of indignation from the Dr after 3rd which nearly broke my heart. God knows I have sought to do my duty here.' [Saturday afternoons were usually free, so presumably the Head was dissatisfied with them all for some reason.]
Thursday 11/3: 'Called in to Dr's house, sat a bit in the drawing room then got asked by him to dinner. A very pleasant evening & I enjoyed it extremely. Several other fellows there.'

[During the Easter vacation he mentions writing letters to Jamieson and the Head].

Friday 7/5: 'Went at 3.20 to dear Dr V who was delightful but I had very brief visit with him.'

Saturday 8/5: 'Walked with S & Jamieson.'

Wednesday 19/5: 'Did hexameters. Went with Pretor to Mrs Wells. Rather oppressed today at unprofitable (life?) &c

Saturday 26/6: 'With S to cricket field . . . Chapel in evg – Dr V talked to me nicely.'

Monday 5/7: 'Walked in evg with S, very pleasant walk.'

Saturday 24/7: 'Dined at Dr Vaughan's, W. Munro etc'

Wednesday 27/7: 'Visited Cambridge for the first time.'

Monday 9/8: 'Got home [i.e. New Hailes] about 4. Dr and Mrs Vaughan came here to stay! Arriving at 5. How very delightful this is to me.'

Monday 16/8: 'We drove Dr and Mrs V to Edinburgh at 12.45. They went away to our great sorrow.'

Monday 23/8: 'Wrote to Dr V.'

Thursday 28/10: 'Wrote to Jamieson [at Oxford] & Pretor [at Harrow].' [35]

What may be deduced from the above? In early February he heard some very disturbing news but it is not clear from whom or about whom or what exactly it was. His relationships with Jamieson and Symonds seem to be normal but not entirely so with Pretor. His affection for Vaughan is unbounded. If the disturbing news did relate in some way to Vaughan (the entry on 8 February could be interpreted that way but not necessarily so), it clearly did not affect his view of the man: 'How I do love him with my whole soul', he wrote three weeks later, and he was delighted when the Vaughans stayed with his family for a week in August. There is no suggestion that some scandal is attached to the Headmaster, nor is there any mention of Pretor or of passionate love letters. And whatever it was that had so upset him in February seems to have soon passed over.

There are a few entries from early 1859 worth noting which show that Dalrymple, now at Cambridge, kept up contact with his old friends at Oxford and Harrow:

Friday 21/1: 'Very nice letter from Dr V.'

Tuesday 25/1: 'Dr Vaughan's Sermon at St Paul's on Sunday Evg very good, & is to be published. Jamieson & Symonds sent me a favourable Report of it.'

Wednesday 16/2: 'Wrote Dr V a right good letter.'

Tuesday 22/2: 'Unsatisfactory letter from Symonds wh made me feel sad nearly all day. Really I must not be so much affected by external things.'

Friday 4/3: 'Charming letter from Mrs Vaughan & wrote her. . . Letter from Dr V most kind.'

Tuesday 22/3: 'Letters from Mrs Vaughan & Pretor who will be glad to come to me on the 12 April (DV). . . I must try to go to Harrow on 2nd April but think it must be to [thank?]. Pretor's letter satisfactory, but that he mentions some gt [immorality?] which has caused great grief to Dr V. I can't wonder.' [This probably refers to another case of boy-sex in the school such as the Dering-O'Brien incident related in the previous chapter.]

Saturday 2/4: 'How it does rejoice me to be at Harrow again.'

[He was at Harrow again on Saturday 18 June and had tea with Mrs Vaughan.]

Thursday 23/6: 'Wrote Jamieson & Symonds.'

Saturday 9/7: 'Read letter from Pretor enclosed from Home.' [Dalrymple was away on military exercise with the local militia at the time.]

Saturday 16/7: 'Wrote Dr Vaughan.' [36]

The diary entries for August and September 1859 are much more detailed and throw some light on the Pretor/Symonds affair:

Saturday 6/8: 'Letters from Jamieson, Pretor & (latter?) telling me that the grievous things wh troubled me early in this year are not yet forgotten. Wrote at length to him, Symonds & Jamieson. S has suddenly been playing a dark game.'

Wednesday 10/8: 'Letters from Symonds & long one from Pretor also. This is a most painful & useless correspondence. Wrote to S who has a deal to answer for.'

Thursday 11/8: 'Long letter from Jamieson. Wrote him ditto & Robertson.'

Friday 12/8: 'Note from Pretor, enclosed horrid do from Symonds. Odious note from Symonds – His whole conduct at present is detestable.'

Saturday 13/8: 'Letters from Jamieson enclosing copy of his long letter to Symonds. Wrote Jamieson, Pretor & Symonds.'

Monday 22/8: 'Note from Dr V & letter from Jamieson who offers to come next month. Dr & Mrs V arrived by cab from Portobello at 6 for the second visit of a week. Walked both before and after dinner with him. How I would that all I have to fear here quite laid to rest & that letters I dread (?) cd be arrested.'

Tuesday 23/8: 'Walked about with Dr V & to Station. Note from Pretor but [aft ?] much anxiety as [writing?] last to him.'

Wednesday 24/8: 'Dr V very silent & as usual walked abt with him.'

Thursday 25/8: 'I walked with Dr V all abt.'

Friday 16/8: 'Dr V read the Preface to his "Romans" wh is most charming . . He and I went to Edinburgh by the 12.30 train.'

Saturday 27/8: 'Walked with Dr V. Mrs V did not appear till 1. He and I also after dinner when it was quite dark. So ends this week & nearly the visit of our dear & kind friends. May God keep & bless them.'

Monday 29/8: 'Walked with Dr V. We drove them into Edinburgh to meet 12.45 train to Aberdeen. Letter from S & long enclosure from Mr Conington, also [Stanhope?]. [Sg ?] to Mr C which I hope may do some good. Grieved to write so abt my dear friend who has this day left us. May His presence go with them where they go, who alone is the life of his people.'

Tuesday 6/9: 'Letters from Mr Conington.'

Monday 12/9: 'Very kind letter from Dr V. Wrote to Jamieson, Dr V. . . Such a kind letter from dear Dr V from Lampart Hall in Northamptonshire. They expect to be back at Harrow today.'

Thursday 15/9: letter from Pretor . . . I wrote Pretor.'

Monday 19/9: 'Wrote Mr Conington & I do hope the matter will now end. It is high time.'

Tuesday 20/9: 'Saw in Courant the announcement that Dr V resigns the headmastership of Harrow; very miserable all day abt this.'

Wednesday 21/9: 'Wrote Dr V as good a letter as I could . . . Got most kind letter from Dr V abt his retirement wh will be at Xmas. He wants [last? Dear Man?] & to retire when he will have completed his 15 years at H. I rejoice for him, grieve for H . . . Had a most kind note from Conington, thanking me for my acknowledgement of his last & giving a small statement &c.'

Thursday 22/9: 'letters from Jamieson, Pretor & Hone.'

Monday 26/9: 'Wrote to S & Pretor. Jamieson offers to come Friday & Saturday. Pretor's enclosure of a letter to Dr Symonds. Most absurd, & just like him!'

Sunday 9/10: reads Sermon of Dr V. 'Things Seen & Unseen.'

Thursday 13/10: 'Sat with dear Dr V after Ladies retired in his study & looked over sermons. Many old favourites will I hope be in [his last vol?]. Much pleasant conversation. May he prosper in [?] wheresoever he goes.'

Friday 14/10: 'Joined Dr V at the Athenaeum & so back to Harrow where we got at 7. Walked up the Hill. Lady Spencer here, & Hone, & Masson at dinner – a very pleasant party. Breakfasted about 9.30. Read Bp Stanley's Memoirs & chatted with Mrs V. To London with Dr V.'

Saturday 5/11: 'Meeting of Harrow men at T in Hudson's rooms. Butler, Currer &c spoke well on subject of the Vaughan testimonial. A library seems the best plan. I put down my name freely for £25.'

Wednesday 16/11: 'Pretor also came in.'

Sunday 4/12 : 'Dr V's text Hebrews XII 27 I trust the memory of this blessed Sunday will abide always with us & in the hearts of all those who shared in the Holy Feast and its (?) sacred service. Sunday spent in partying – with Mrs V to a party at Mme Massons.'

Tuesday 6/12: '& went to the Freemasons Tavern for the Harrow Dinner to dear Dr V. Saw countless old friends whom I had not seen for long. Dinner & Speeches very good, & had a very delightful moment or two with Dr V after.'[37]

This time it is clear (see 29/8 entry) that the unpleasant correspondence with Symonds does relate to Vaughan and that Dalrymple's sympathies lay with his old Head Master. Whatever the 'odious' things Symonds was saying about Vaughan, it seems that Dalrymple, and probably Jamieson and even Pretor too took Vaughan's part. It must have been so painful for this young man, having his dear friend and Mrs Vaughan staying at his ancestral home whilst this correspondence was going on, and be unable to talk with him about it. Despite the several references to letters to/from Conington and the many letters to/from Symonds and Pretor, there is nothing to suggest that Dalrymple was expecting Vaughan to resign as Head or linked the resignation, when it was announced, with Symonds's 'dark game'. It is also noteworthy that his correspondence with Conington seems to have been cordial. Months later he could not understand why Vaughan turned down the offer of a bishopric. Despite being so closely involved in the Pretor/Symonds affair, he did not link all these events at the time in the way that Symonds would claim thirty years later that they were. And most strikingly, he never lost his love and respect for Vaughan. There is, however, a single mention of Dr Symonds involvement when Dalrymple received at the end of September from Pretor a copy of an 'absurd' letter he had written to Symonds's father.

Dalrymple and the others probably cut Symonds off not just because of his betrayal of Pretor's confidence but also because he had totally mis-interpreted and later misrepresented as base, passionate lust what had been, at most, a romantic friendship. It is significant that no other pupil with whom Vaughan is known to have had a deep and mutually affectionate relationship ever intimated or accused him of improper behaviour towards them. In fact, quite the reverse – they clearly appreciated the warmth of his lifelong friendship with them. And most important, Pretor himself laid no charges against his old Head and main-tained a lasting friendship with him.

Vaughan wrote a glowing introductory letter on Pretor's behalf to the Revd. Richard Shilleto, the best classical coach in Cambridge, in May 1860. That is truly remarkable if Pretor had, as alleged by Symonds, been responsible in part for the Head's forced resignation. In the letter he described Pretor as 'an excellent pupil, diligent clever, and promising. He

199

distinguished himself highly at Harrow and possesses a recommendation sometimes, I fear, wanting in Harrow men – that of resolution and vigour for work.' [38] It sounds the kind of commendatory letter any caring Head would write for a diligent pupil whether or not the young man was a 'favourite'. But it is an extraordinary one if the pupil being commended had been the writer's *nemesis*.

One final observation: the likelihood of the Head writing any kind of letter (let alone a series of compromising ones which could open him later to blackmail or worse) to a Sixth Former whom he saw every day simply makes no sense. Almost all Vaughan's extant correspondence is with *former* pupils, i.e. the letters are dated *after* the boys had left Harrow. It is possible that Vaughan wrote to Pretor during the school holidays, and that such letters would have included expressions of warm affection if the young man was truly one of his favourites. And if such letters did exist and were shown to Symonds (though the latter left Harrow a year before Pretor), that could have re-ignited old feelings of jealousy. A jealousy then fuelled by his own sex-obsessed fantasies about what might have taken place between the Head and his friend. Wagland comments in this connection, 'The possibility of a letter couched in very passionate, romantic terms would not be surprising, but a letter containing erotic details is beyond belief for a man of Vaughan's intelligence and position.' [39]

Symonds's account, I am convinced, is not to be trusted. It is possible, and, in my judgement, far more likely that Vaughan was, at worst, simply guilty of writing letters expressing his deep affection to a young man to whom he was romantically attached. A case, it could be argued, of 'permanent adolescence', which, in the judgement of the historian Jeffrey Richards, was a not uncommon condition among public school and varsity educated men in the 19th century.[40] As to Symonds, it is not unknown for people to 'rewrite' their personal histories in order to try and make sense to themselves of their current psychological disposition. And in 1889 at the time he was writing his memoirs, he was exploring the topic of homosexuality with Havelock-Ellis and still trying hard to justify and make sense of his own sexuality, and more particularly of his earliest homoerotic relationships and observation of other adolescents engaging in same-sex activities.

John Roach in his article on Vaughan in the *Oxford Dictionary of National Biography* arrived at the same conclusion, noting that 'at the time of the alleged events he [Symonds] was in a highly excited mental state as he strove to come to terms with his own homosexuality. His credibility as a witness must be considered in relation to all these pressures. It seems impossible to go beyond a "not proven" verdict . . .' [41]

There is no hard evidence at all to corroborate Symonds's story – a sealed package reputed to contain the relevant correspondence between Dr Symonds and Vaughan was supposedly destroyed by Symonds Jr.'s literary executor. There is just the one mention in Dalrymple's diary of a letter sent by Pretor to the Doctor in late September. We simply cannot be sure of the nature and extent of his involvement. I find the tone and content of Vaughan's letters to Charles Dalrymple and the entries in the latter's diaries which do still exist, written during that final term and afterwards, indicate that there was no truth in Symonds's much later explanation of why Vaughan resigned when he did. But we shall probably never be absolutely sure.

Mark Wagland, who, having made a careful examination of all the evidence, is convinced that Vaughan was innocent of any improper behaviour, nonetheless accepts in his paper *A Matter of Justice* that Symonds's father did threaten Vaughan. He reckons that, even though the Head was innocent, 'he would have been faced with an incredibly difficult decision and there were sound reasons why withdrawal would be a sound course.' [42] He sees these as Vaughan's love for Harrow and his desire to protect the school's future which could have been adversely affected if there was even a whiff of a possible scandal, and secondly his desire to protect Arnold's good name and his educational legacy which could have been damaged if scandal was linked (however unjustly) to one of his favourite pupils. And as he was thinking anyway of retiring at the end of 15 years, he would have been reluctant to mount a vigorous defence against Dr Symonds. This is a plausible scenario but I doubt it, not least because the son's *Memoirs* which provide the only account of the father forcing the issue are so inaccurate and unreliable.

Co-incidentally, three years after Vaughan's resignation, when his 'accuser' was a newly elected probationer Fellow of Magdalen College Oxford, Symonds Jr. feared, but managed to avoid, exposure when C.G.H. Shorting, an undergraduate at Corpus who shared his sexual leanings but had fallen out with him, sent to the Fellows of Magdalen a copy of extracts from letters and poems that Symonds had written to him. Symonds was forced to face investigation by the College Council, which was humiliating.

Pretor, the supposed 'victim' of Vaughan's attention, spent his life at Cambridge where he was a Fellow of St Catherine's College from 1871. He is remembered there as a 'distinguished classic.' It seems he never forgot his old Head Master and presumably would have met him on the many occasions when Vaughan was a Select Preacher at the University. In 1897, the year of Vaughan's death, he dedicated his sole scholarly work to him, his *Letters of Cicero to Atticus*. In 1899 Pretor published a collection of semi-autobiographical stories entitled *Ronald and I. Scenes from Life*, one of which incidentally reflects his high regard for Vaughan as a preacher. His favourite story in the collection, he said, was 'On the Sands' about how his cousin Ronald was goaded into preaching a stunning impromptu sermon to a crowd on the beach. It transpired that the sermon was actually one of Vaughan's which the boy had had to analyse and learn as a Sunday activity at school. Pretor admitted in the Preface to the book that the incident which formed the groundwork of the narrative he owed to 'the happiness of a lifelong friendship with the late Dean Vaughan.' [43] Vaughan shared this view of their relationship for in one of his last letters to his publisher, Macmillan, written in May 1897 he described Pretor as an 'attached friend of mine.'

Pretor's obituary in *The Times* on 13 January 1908 states that his 'friendship with the then headmaster, Dr Vaughan, was close, and was maintained until the death of the latter, and, at the request of Dr Vaughan, Pretor undertook the duties of his literary executor.' This last detail is, I think, a mistake but possibly based on the fact that Pretor did edit and publish just after Vaughan's death one last collection of his old Master's sermons. In the Preface he paid a very warm tribute to his friend, whom he numbered 'among the foremost preachers of the century'. He clearly did not regard or remember his old Head as a sexual predator.

A brief Interlude at Southborough

I wish I could through you convey to Lord Palmerston the expression of my sense of his great kindness to me. I would ask you to oblige me by doing so, if you have the opportunity. I can never forget the obligation under which I lie to him.

C.J. Vaughan to Richard Monckton Milnes MP

They moved to Southborough near Tunbridge Wells to what Vaughan would later describe as a 'dear little house' which he had bought on leaving the school. He named it "Harrow Cottage" and described his new life there in a letter to Dalrymple dated 21 January 1860. By then he had already started his locum ministry at St Michael's Church in Chester Square Belgravia whose incumbent (an old friend of Vaughan's) was seriously ill:

> We go up every Saturday, till Monday, to Mrs Stanley's in Grosvenor Crescent. This makes us value extremely the intervening week of quiet here, and also gives me full occupation in preparing Sermons. I cannot but say that I like my present life extremely, just that combination of work and rest which is rarely to be found . . .
>
> Burnett [Head of School 1858-59] was our first <u>sleeping</u> Guest here: he came for two nights last week. Lang & Harrison [two recent members of his House] will, I think, do the same next week. We cannot profess to make our guests very happy here: for there is no one to see but our two selves, & very little to do. In the evening, when we are alone, I read aloud in the Drawing room, which is a really good and pleasant room, holding most of our Harrow Drawing room furniture and altogether most comfortable. The Study (in which we dine) is, to <u>my</u> mind, the very sweetest room I ever lived in: certainly very low, like a cabin, but so warm-looking, with a red paper, bookshelves in all the recesses, & two fire places, one at each end. It is properly two little rooms thrown together. I have put a bookshelf over one of the doors, as we did in the Drawing room at Harrow . . .
>
> Come and see us here some day, my dear Dalrymple. I think you might possibly just get through one or even two nights – not more, I am sure.
>
> Kindest remembrances, from both, to Lady Fergusson, your Sisters & Brother.
>
> Ever your affectionate friend Chas J. Vaughan [1]

Dalrymple recorded receipt of the letter two days later in his journal with the comment 'a very great pleasure to me.' [2]

Vaughan assisted at a great mission held in Reading from 26 February to 4 March led by Samuel Wilberforce, the Bishop of Oxford who preached the opening and concluding sermons. Wilberforce had invited a star studded team of bishops, academics and clergy to assist him.[3] He was also a guest preacher at Wells Cathedral.

Lord Palmerston, on the advice of the Earl of Shaftesbury [two of whose sons were at Harrow under Vaughan] whose influence on episcopal appointments was great with the Prime Minister, offered him a bishopric as soon as one was available and this became known in Harrow. Thornton recalled 'Mr Farrar granting a school [i.e. a free lesson] to his Form on the ground of the headmaster's elevation to a bishopric; but, alas! Before the glad hour arrived, Dr Vaughan's *nolo episcopari* was known, and the boys lost their leisure hour.'[4]

Dalrymple had noted the vacancy at Rochester and wrote in his diary on 17 February, 'Who will succeed him? Is a question I long to have answered, though one can't expect it yet.'[5] He was clearly hoping his old Head would be appointed. On the 23rd he noted, 'Have reason to think that dear Dr V is to be the new Bishop of Rochester. Wrote to congratulate him.'[6] His joy quickly turned to sad incomprehension. On the 29th he noted, 'Much distressed to see in the Times that dear Dr V has declined the Bishopric of Rochester. What next? & What can it mean?'[7] A lot of other people must have been equally puzzled. The *Morning Chronicle* had devoted a full column on Monday the 27th to a minibiography of Vaughan under the heading 'The Bishop Elect of Rochester' but by the next day the *Times* reported, 'We have authority to state that, after some hesitation, Dr Vaughan has finally declined the Bishopric of Rochester.'

The manner of his leaving Harrow and the offer of Rochester remained a topic of conversation for months in the family circle – Lady Stanley wrote to her mother-in-law Lady Maria Josepha on 2 March 1860 to put her right about the offer of the bishopric:

> My dear Lady Stanley,
> I am afraid you are in error respecting Dr Vaughan's acceptance – he had decidedly written to Ld Palmerston to *accept* the See of Rochester, he did so after two days consideration last Friday - & he wrote again Tuesday morning to Ld Palmerston to *decline* it – therefore, whatever blame is due to infirmity of purpose must rest with him. He has assigned no reason, but I do not imagine such a small matter as the position of the Palace weighed on his mind if he had felt equal to the duty. It is more, I believe, from a

morbid tenderness of conscience & want of moral courage to face all the difficulties of the position, which doubtless he would exaggerate.

Aunt Kitty [Catherine Vaughan's mother] has taken the event very well, full of tenderness for Catherine and determined to make the best of it. The Bishop of London naturally much annoyed as people do not like to be made fools of, he having taken much trouble about it; but some people are overwhelmed when responsibility comes near them. [8]

Westcott, in a letter to Dalrymple dated 3 March, made this insightful comment: 'to have refused the bishopric is far nobler than to have it; but to Dr Vaughan I can fancy that the sacrifice is immeasurably greater and he has been equal to making it.' [9]

Joseph Blakesley, the Dean of Lincoln and Vaughan's old lecturer at Trinity, wrote to congratulate him on his preferment to Rochester and received this letter in reply:

My dear Blakesley

The announcement of my ultimate refusal of the Bishopric and resolution to adhere to my publicly announced intention of securing a season of retirement will have perhaps excused in your eyes the long delay of my thanks for your kind congratulations on the appointment. The acceptance was too hasty, & longer reflection convinced me that it was better to carry out the plan proposed to myself in leaving Harrow. I am not so old but that the future may offer to me some career of usefulness, though not so brilliant a one in appearance as that which I have put aside. The disappointment and (in some cases) disapprobation of friends has been annoying and troublesome; but my judgement is now clear upon the subject, and the only thing really to be regretted is that it was not equally decided at first. Who the new Bishop is to be, is not so certain, apparently, as who he is not . . .

Ever truly yours   Charles J Vaughan [10]

Various strange and untrue stories circulated about why he had refused Rochester, one of which put the blame on Catherine for having converted and become a Catholic! Her sister, Mary, had converted four years earlier. Vaughan mentioned this one in a letter to Louisa written on 28 April. It was said that he had returned to Grosvenor Place after meeting the Prime Minister to tell her that he had accepted the bishopric only to be met by Catherine who fell at his feet and confessed.[11]

Dalrymple had probably heard some of these wild speculations for he commented in his diary on 16 March, 'How I long for something true about Dr V's refusal of Bishopric. I can't write to him of course. (yet?)' [12]

His mood had not been helped by a letter he had received the previous day from Symonds, 'Letters one from Symonds vexed me much & though I did not send it finally, wrote a strong reply. [The next line is crossed out and illegible and a section of the facing page where he had probably written some comments has been cut out.]' [13]

Why, indeed, first say "Yes" and then "No"? As regards the former, there was clearly a heavy burden of expectation on him to accept a bishopric when the offer came – not least, at a personal and family level, as he was married to a bishop's daughter. After just a few weeks of semi-retirement, that state no longer held the same attraction which it had had when he was inundated with all the tasks and duties of being a headmaster. The opportunity to become a leader again, albeit in a very different sphere to that of a school, would have naturally been inviting to a man of his ability and energy. Against it, was the decisive matter of whether this was what he was being called *by God* to become? He knew that he had a gift of engaging with and inspiring young men. It is possible that he was already considering how he might be able to provide opportunities for ministerial training to those with a real vocation to ordained ministry. This would allow him to continue in an educational role and to work with young men whose company he loved and who shared his view of life and ministry: i.e. life with a purpose and lived with a sense of accountability to God. Accepting a bishopric would make such a ministry less of a possibility. It could also be done without all the time-consuming work of administration which being a bishop would bring back into his life.

Many years later Professor C.E. Vaughan commented on this episode in his famous uncle's life:

> Those who know Dr Vaughan will be at no loss to understand his motives for this decision. It excited much surprise at the time. But there can be no doubt that, in the interests of his own Church and the whole community, as well as for his own sake, he judged aright. In a comparatively private position, he has been a far greater power for good than he could possibly have been in the ceaseless round of official ceremonies and business interviews, which engross so large a share of a Bishop's time. In a bishopric, his work as a preacher would have been seriously hampered; his work as a teacher would have been entirely closed. [14]

And writing with hindsight, he went on 'As it was, the most fruitful task of his life lay yet before him.' [15] Those words were written in 1894 when his uncle was still alive. A decade later in the biographical sketch he penned for Morgan's book *Welsh Politicians & Educators in the Victorian Era* he ventured a different interpretation of the events:

> It was a shock to the world at large, not least to those who stood closest to him, when, a day or two later, he withdrew his acceptance. All kinds of ridiculous explanations were offered for his conduct. As to his real motives, it is impossible to speak with certainty. Between him and the world it remained a closed subject to the end of his days. And if he ever opened himself to his private friends, it was under the seal of secrecy, a secrecy that has been inviolably preserved. Those who knew him best never concealed their opinion that, as in his earlier abandonment of the law, his action sprang from a rooted distrust of himself, a determination to tear up ambition by the roots. If this be the truth, nothing could prove more clearly the rare nobility of his nature, his readiness to sacrifice everything to scruples which most men would have put aside. [16]

Catherine shared her feelings at this time with Dalrymple in a letter, dated 30 March:

> It grieves me to think how great the disappointment we have caused to everyone who cares about us – But you will I know be quite sure that he only did what he felt to be right, and there we must leave it - & console ourselves with the thought that we may yet do some good service, though in a less exalted sphere; and some day, we shall think it of very little importance what position we hold in this world: quite as much <u>real</u> good may be done in an obscure station I am certain.
> Here we shall remain for the present, according to our original intention, & I suppose after a while, we shall seek some active parish work: in the meantime he is hard at work with the continuation of his Commentary [on *Romans*], & there will always be plenty to do, wherever we are – How glad – how delighted we shall be to see you here, whenever you can come – only it would be too dreadfully dull for you – There is not a creature to speak to, except us – the Cat - & the dog.
> Whenever you can, pray let us hear from you – your letters are charming – I am so glad to have been with your brother [Sir James Fergusson Bt.] & Lady Edith. I suppose the royal embrace was in consequence of her being the daughter of a Marquis. Dr Vaughan is going to preach to the Queen on Sunday. I suppose she felt a curiosity to see the man who had declined a Bishopric . . .
> Your sincere friend   Cath Vaughan [17]

The young man was grateful to hear from her. He noted on 2 April: 'Had a letter from Mrs Vaughan today which was a great satisfaction.' [18] He then recorded a personal disappointment, 'Sorry to find I was only 2nd Class in little Go.' For a conscientious reading man taking what was regarded by all as a fairly simple examination, that was a real disappointment and not the good news he would have been hoping to send to his old Tutor Westcott or to his old Head.

During the nine months gap between Harrow and Doncaster Vaughan was not idle. His first task was to get a collection of sermons ready for the press as *Memorials of Harrow Sundays*. It was reviewed favourably in the pages of *The Nonconformist* on 29 February: 'These discourses have qualities of highest excellence . . . They combine richly Scriptural exposition with vigorous practical remark, knowledge with sympathy, spiritual feeling with manly earnestness, suggestive thoughts with plain personal counsels.' The review also included some criticism - three of the thirty-eight sermons in the book were rated as 'commonplace' and more 'colour and illustration' would have been welcomed. They were published by Macmillan which was becoming his preferred option. It was a firm founded by two brothers, Daniel and Alexander Macmillan, from the Isle of Arran who set up in business in London in 1843 and opened a bookshop in Cambridge the following year. Vaughan developed a good and lasting working relationship with Alexander after the death of Daniel in 1857.

Another letter to Dalrymple, dated 30 May 1860, tells of his current activities. He reported that he had been invited to be a Select Preacher at Cambridge the following year and had accepted on condition he could preach in either November or May 'as we talk of going to Rome in the Winter, if we can do it safely.' [19] He had just finished for the Press 'a <u>very</u> poor little publication on the Revision of the Liturgy, in which <u>you</u> will recognize some old acquaintances'. He was also preparing the first volume of his St Michael's Chester Square sermons for publication and commented 'I do not know how you will like them. I think they will be rather dull for reading.' The letter goes on:

> I am likely to take that duty again for the month of July, & I have accepted (perhaps rather unwisely) the office of an Examiner for the coming Indian appointments – for which there will be an immense number of Candidates there being 80 appointments to fill up. I of course take the Classical papers, or rather one half of them; and there is to be a *Viva Voce* of each Candidate, taking 10 consecutive days (Sundays excepted) of 5 hours each. It sounds rather alarming, in July, & with Sunday duty also. But I thought it would be a good thing to have a little pressure of this kind for once in a way, & would brush up my Classics. [20]

The first course of his Chester Square sermons which he entitled *Epiphany, Lent & Easter* was published by Macmillan in June. He wrote apologetically in the preface:

> Most unexpectedly, and in some senses most unwillingly, I have been called to stand before you in another's room . . . In many respects the teaching of a temporary instructor must be most deficient. He cannot know, in detail, the cases and the circumstances of those to whom he is to minister. He must, to a great extent, draw his bow at a venture . . . (but) the human heart is not many, but one . . . (and) the Word of God suits all cases, and is the same in every place. [21]

He was back at Chester Square in July and preached a course of eight sermons which were added to the 2nd edition of the book in May 1861 which he dedicated to the congregation of St Michael's 'with affectionate respect.' The volume met with a tepid review in the *Morning Chronicle*: 'The sermons before us are excellent specimens of his earnest and thoughtful teaching; but, good as they are in themselves, it strikes us that they have been delivered on an erroneous understanding of the public taste. The worst of it is, that this very able writer is himself not insensible to the very fault for which he apologizes, and which we regret.' They took particular exception to his having used his own translation of the biblical texts rather than quoting the Authorized Version of the Bible which his hearers were accustomed to.

It was during this period that the storm broke over the publication of *Essays and Reviews*. One of the essayists was Fredrick Temple, the Headmaster of Rugby. Vaughan had played a minor part in securing Temple's appointment to Rugby as his cousin, Sir Henry Halford, had asked him to recommend a fit man to succeed Dr Goulburn in 1857, and he had nominated Temple, who was a Tutor at Balliol. He had also provided him with a testimonial in which he had confidently predicted 'an era of great distinction for Rugby' if he were elected Headmaster. [22] But now Temple was coming under some pressure to resign. Vaughan along with Stanley, Lightfoot and Westcott all felt this would be a national calamity if it were to happen and rose in his defence. Vaughan did not share Temple's critical stance to the Bible expressed in the essay but that did not prevent him recognizing the great work he was doing at Rugby and, as a recently retired headmaster himself who had been under fire publicly over the monitorial discipline affair, he would have felt a natural sympathy for Temple.

209

He had kept up his correspondence with a wide circle of friends and acquaintances, among them the Chancellor of the Exchequer W.E. Gladstone to whom he sent his latest book in July. The great man responded appreciatively and invited Vaughan to call. He replied:

> Your kind and encouraging words give me the utmost pleasure, & will strengthen my heart for any future service which I may be permitted to render to the beloved Church. I ventured to offer my little book to you, but it was in the sincere hope that you would think no acknowledgement of it necessary.
>
> I am in London only for this Sunday, & that only for a brief time: this month of July will end my engagement. It would give me the finest pleasure to accept your kind invitation on some Thursday morning when I am casually in Town, but I greatly fear it will hardly be before the close of the present season – in which case may I venture to consider the invitation as extending to another year? [23]

He received a reply by return confirming that the invitation was 'a standing one'. Another of his letters from this time proved to be a timely reminder to its recipient of his availability for service. On 16 May he wrote to congratulate Charles Longley on his appointment as Archbishop of York.

> I cannot refuse myself the pleasure of offering to your Lordship my hearty congratulations and assurance of my warm and affectionate interest, on the occasion of your translation to the Archbishopric of York – a position which the general voice, I well remember, had confidently assigned to you on its last vacancy 12 or 13 years ago.
>
> There can be but one feeling as to your pre-eminent claims upon this high position. Everyman of every party, I venture to believe, will rejoice together on the occasion of your being called to fill it. Believe, my dear Lord, that no one can rejoice with a more sincere gratification than I do in this great event.
>
> It adds much to my own pleasure, to remember how greatly that place in which you have always felt so lively an interest, Harrow, will feel itself honoured in your honour.
>
> This note will require no answer. Indeed I should not have written it had I not relied upon your Lordship treating it as the simple expression of warm feeling, amply repaid by the pleasure of believing that it will not be unacceptable. [24]

This was the same Longley, under whose gentle and ineffective rule the rot had set in at the school. That sorry chapter in his career had not, however, hindered his rise in the Church. Having been appointed after he left Harrow in 1836 to the new see of Ripon, a move to Durham followed in 1856 and to York in 1860. Co-incidentally, the living of Doncaster which was in his gift fell vacant at this time and he offered it to Vaughan.

To a lawyer friend who had written him a congratulatory letter on his approaching removal to Doncaster, he said that it was just what he desired but downplayed its value and importance – 'The living is, as you know, a very small one – under £300 a year, and I must have two Curates. But we shall be able to live very quietly, as at Southborough on what I have of my own, and it will be a pleasure to feel that one is not keeping others out of emoluments which they need more.' [25]

Upon his acceptance of the Archbishop's offer, a friend, Richard Monckton Milnes MP, afterwards 1st Baron Houghton, also nominated him to the post of Lecturer at Doncaster Parish Church which was in his gift. Vaughan wrote on 12 Sept 1860 to thank him and to tell about their impending move.

> Your kind welcome to my new home must not be left a day unacknow-ledged; though it reaches me in fact before we have broken up our inter-mediate home at Southborough. The thought of being near so kind and constant a friend as you have been to <u>both</u> of us, is not one of the smallest comforts associated with my new work . . . We hope to be established at Doncaster before the end of October. A delay in obtaining possession of the House is the only reason why I am not earlier in residence.
> Mrs Vaughan takes a very hopeful and cheerful view of the future home and its circumstances. I do trust that I shall not be disappointed in the hope of finding a place of useful labour, well suited to my wishes. The kindness with which my appointment has been received is most gratifying to us. [26]

He knew that he would need the help of curates and was naturally minded to employ former pupils who had taken Holy Orders, one of whom had approached him about a curacy. The applicant had been one of the earliest boys to join his House where he stayed for five years, so Vaughan should have known him well enough. Nonetheless he wrote to one of his old favourites in September for more information about him:

> My dear Jackson
> I am going to trouble you for the first time with a question about <u>Curates</u>. You know that I am going to be Vicar of Doncaster. It is a very unexpected but really pleasant prospect. The income is very small – under three hundred a year; and I must keep two Curates. But what I wanted to ask you about is this. I had a letter from John Watson, my old Harrow Pupil, asking

me to take him as my Curate. To say the truth, I sent him rather a discouraging answer – at least I fear it was so. I did not feel that I knew enough about him as a Clergyman, to be quite sure of his fitness for the office in question. Now would you tell me honestly what you think? I believe him to have been always good in character & conduct - & I think that he was religiously brought up. Have you any idea what sort of theology his is? Is he at all High Church, or how should you describe him? Is he a man of diligent habits? Again, as to his voice – is it powerful & good in reading? And once more, as to his manner – is he not rather gauche & awkward? I do not care about over refinement. I should rather dislike it, as you know: but he ought, in that position, to strike people as a gentleman, both in manner & feeling. These rough questions, asked of you in all confidence, will indicate the points about which I am chiefly anxious: & I know you will frankly tell me all you think on a matter of such vital importance to me. I suppose he has an independent income? Is his wife a nice person?

If you are able to write soon, it would be a great kindness. Address here.

There is one great inducement – that he is disengaged now, & could therefore, I conclude, come to me at once.

With kindest remembrances from both of us to both of you, & with ever cherished regard & affection from me, believe me ever your faithful friend.

Charles J. Vaughan [27]

Watson was not appointed as he received a far better offer: the living of Kemberton in Shropshire. The questions Vaughan had put to Jackson indicate some of his priorities in making such appointments – he wanted curates who were manifestly gentlemen, would be hard-working, had a good preaching voice, not High Church, and preferably with a private income which might then allow them to be employed for just a nominal stipend. It was not enough to be, as Watson was, a Harrow and Cambridge man. By early October he had another of his former pupils in mind as a Curate, who was currently assisting the Headmaster of Knutsford Grammar School. A replacement there would be needed if he were to be able to move to Doncaster so Vaughan wrote to Lightfoot to ask if he could help find someone, presumably an unemployed recent graduate, to take the Knutsford post.[28]

Milnes wrote again in early October inviting Catharine and him to stay with them later in the month, which Vaughan had to decline as by then he would be starting on his new work. He replied on 9 October and used the opportunity to send greetings to (and hopefully repair his relationship with) Lord Palmerston whose offer of a Bishopric he had first accepted and then declined:

I wish I could through you convey to Lord Palmerston the expression of my sense of his great kindness to me. I would ask you to oblige me by doing so, if you have the opportunity. I can never forget the obligation under which I lie to him.

We shall have your kind wishes and true sympathy in the commencement of new duties. It is a real pleasure to feel that we shall be near you. [29]

Had Vaughan known that Milnes was in the process of putting together the largest private collection of pornographic literature in the land, I doubt he would have been so glad to number him among his friends!

A week later, Catherine and he were on their way north. Family and friends may have privately regarded the living of Doncaster as a poor second-best to his being Bishop of Rochester or Head Master of Harrow but the post had its attractions. It had a magnificent new church which, like St Martin's in Leicester, was the civic church where important events in the life of the wider community were celebrated. He was known to and had the support of the Archbishop which would probably open up extra-parochial opportunities for ministry – as indeed it did. And – a very important consideration for Vaughan personally – it was just the kind of parish that his old master, Thomas Arnold, had once urged him to minister in and would certainly have approved of.

Doncaster – "Vaughan's Doves"

Out of all that is low and base and selfish and wicked – out of all that is dark and gloomy and desolate and solitary – out of all that is transitory and worldly and disappointing and temporal – into that which is bright and beautiful and satisfying and eternal – let the love of God lead us and guide us! So shall a new light rise upon our life, and a new impulse and spring be communicated to our being! Let us be God's, not in part, but wholly.

The Place of Love in the Gospel in Last Words at Doncaster p. 101

'I see by the papers today' Lord Stanley wrote to his wife on 10 August 1860, 'that the Archbishop of York has appointed Dr Vaughan to the Vicarage of Doncaster. This is a large but not a manufacturing town & the great sin is the Race Course.' [1] His Lordship had put his finger on the first controversial issue that Vaughan would have to address – what to do about the races? It had been the custom to ring the church bells on the day the St Leger was run. Vaughan did not approve of this but rather than provoke a confrontation he simply went away for the day and 'accidentally' took the keys to the bell tower with him! They were never rung again for a horse race. His Lordship was also right about the town. There was no heavy, dirty industry but the Great Northern Railway had had its engine building works there since 1853 and there were also a few mills along the River Don. It was essentially a prosperous market town with a population in 1861 of 16,406. Most of the workers were either employed by the Railway Company or as agricultural labourers. Vaughan's parish numbered just over 6,400 souls with a wide social mix including many of the town's shopkeepers and artisans.

The patron of the living, the Archbishop of York, issued the mandate for his induction as Incumbent of St George's on 15 August, appointed him Rural Dean on 1 September and two months later made him Chancellor of York Minster and Canon of Laughton. The latter two posts had by then been robbed of their former pecuniary emoluments by the reforms of the Ecclesiastical Commissioners. Further offers of preferment were made by the Prime Minister – the see of Worcester in 1861, Gloucester in '62 and Ely in '64 but his determination to remain a parish priest ensured that he refused.

The living of Doncaster was worth £460 a year [= £47,365] plus the vicarage, small beer compared to what he had earned at Harrow but more than enough along with his earnings as a writer plus their private income for the couple to live very comfortably. The census return of 1861 lists four female servants as being resident with them at the vicarage: a cook, a lady's maid, a housemaid and a parlour maid. And there were sure to have been some non-resident male servants too.

Vaughan's appointment was welcomed by the Editor of the *Doncaster Chronicle* as it was felt he might exercise 'great influence over the town and neighbourhood.' It was a view which had been expressed earlier in that paper on the death of the previous Vicar who had served the parish for 43 years: 'In a place like this the Vicar is the centre-figure of the little Commonwealth. He is the head of the hierarchy, and the chief in every secular movement for the public weal. The mayor is an annual dignitary, but the Vicar remains permanent and gains by his permanence a preponderating influence.' [2] It was common knowledge that their new vicar had refused a bishopric and this was noted with approval:

> We may also infer from his previous and magnanimous refusal of a bishopric, that income is not a subject which need engage his attention. He comes to us, moreover, laden with all the spoils and honours of classical learning, having been a University Scholar, having attained the highest classical honours in his degree at Cambridge in 1838, and having subsequently matured the acquirements of those years by directing and rendering pre-eminent the great public school of Harrow. Nor is he a scholar absorbed in books, but has extended his enquiries into the higher reaches of religious discussion, and is acknowledged to be one of the most original and eloquent of preachers, and an undoubted leader in the scholarly party of our Church. We use the word scholarly advisedly in order to distinguish the section in which Dr Vaughan must be classed from High Church and Low Church on the one side, and from the more doubtful body of Broad Church on the other. We are sure that Dr Vaughan will be welcomed on all these grounds and entrust that his incumbency will be prolonged for a lengthened period, and do honour to the town and district. It has been remarked that we have a magnificent Church and only want a great preacher to fill it. We trust that this wish is now accomplished, and that St George's Doncaster may again hold the pre-eminence and consideration which she enjoyed in ancient times. [3]

The ancient parish church dating from the late 12th century had been destroyed by fire in 1853 and a magnificent, new one designed by Sir George Gilbert Scott, Vaughan's favourite architect, had been con-secrated by Archbishop Thomas Musgrave on 14 October 1858. Pevsner has described it as 'the proudest and most-Cathedral like of Scott's

215

Parish Churches.' This was to be the scene of Vaughan's memorable nine-year long preaching and teaching ministry in the town.

His arrival was delayed by unfinished repairs to the large vicarage which the previous incumbent, Dr John Sharpe, had used in part as a school. When Catherine and he did finally arrive, they were greeted by the ringing of a peal of bells but he was suffering from such a bad head cold that it was feared he would be unable to preach on his first Sunday, 21 October. He did but not before the Mayor and town councillors had first entertained him to hot chocolate in the Mansion House after which they all processed to St George's where a very large congregation had gathered. The Curate, the Revd Thomas Tickell, read the prayers and Vaughan preached what was subsequently described as 'a beautiful sermon' on the text 1 John 4.7 'Beloved, let us love one another.' In the evening an even larger congregation attended and some were unable to get seats. A delegation led by the Mayor visited him next day to request that his first sermon be printed. So, a satisfying start had been made. The Council had already invited him to be their Chaplain and give them the benefit of his society and influence.

In his first week he met with those young people in the parish who were shortly to be confirmed together with candidates from two other parishes. On his second Sunday he read himself in at the morning service, i.e. he read aloud to the congregation the 39 Articles of Religion of the Church of England – a legal requirement at that time for all newly instituted incumbents. In the evening he preached to another over-flowing congregation on the sacrament of Holy Communion which the newly confirmed would be able to receive for the first time. The *Chronicle* commented 'and no doubt the fruits of his teaching will be found in an increased number of communicants.' A few days later, the Archbishop came to St George's and confirmed 360 candidates.

In what is one of Vaughan's longest and most relaxed, conversational letters, he told his young friend Charles Dalrymple about his first three weeks in office and he shared something of his hopes and plans:

My dear Dalrymple

It is Sunday night, within one minute to 11 P.M. And yet I feel much inclined for a few minutes of chat with you, such as a letter can afford. We shall have been here three weeks tomorrow: only 3 weeks: it seems much more. My 3rd Sunday is over. For the 1st time Mr Tickell (the Curate) preached this morning; I tonight, for the S.P.G. The Confirmation was on Friday. The Archbishop of York was with us the night before & we had just the 3 Incumbents (myself, by the way, being one of the three!) of Doncaster to meet him at Dinner: also Hone, & the said Mr Tickell. It was our first little party since we left Harrow: all did pretty well except a portentous pause after the fish – during which we looked studiously unconcerned, & talked with forced vivacity. (I am sure you cannot say that I do not mention trifles.) I had done what I could for the Candidates, after I came: but the time was sadly too short. I had one special Lecture in the Church, with the Litany at 8 P.M. on Thursday, which was extremely well attended by the congregation; and several private lectures in the Schoolroom. Still it was very unsatisfactory, especially as to the young women: I thought the Boys far more intelligent & promising. Last Sunday I read myself in – no slight labour in this great Church. In the morning I gave a little Address from the Pulpit as a preface to reading the Articles; which I then did interspersing a few words of comment here & there, & reading some of the more important ones with great emphasis, quite like a Sermon: the people seemed interested, & I felt it much myself. I was quite glad to have such an opportunity of bringing such important doctrines before them with authority. In the evening I preached a Sermon on the Communion, having given notice of the subject in my Lecture on the Thursday evening. The result has been a most interesting attendance this morning at the Sacrament; the Collection was all but 6 pounds [= £618 in 2012]: the last recorded having been just 12 shillings [= £62].

Everything is ripe for harvest: only may I be enabled to work in it diligently and faithfully! I look forward very much to having George Wood & Hone as my Curates after Christmas. I am forming so many little plans in the prospect of that time. How I shall delight to have you here (as I hope) on your way down to Scotland at the end of this Term: you will be able to stay then? I think you will be struck with the Sunday evening Service & Congregation. It is most inspirating (sic). The Church, when lighted and thronged, is most beautiful. And I expect that you will like the house too. In short, I feel that I have more blessings in my new position than I know how to be thankful for: (I think I already like it almost better than Harrow or is that a delusion?) . . .

Think of you having been actually at our Station! I say that we live there: for our House has all the sounds of the Station day & night, the screams & shrieks of the engines being as audible as if we were on the platform: and our house is visible also, under the Church on the north side, for a long way before you reach Doncaster from York, or after you leave Doncaster in going to York.

I feel that my position here is a very peculiar one, & well worth filling. It is a centre to a considerable tract of country, & all the Clergy come here for meetings, business, &c and are so glad of a leader (if I might so call myself: you know what I mean). I am Rural Dean to 44 Incumbencies round. In a few days I have to go to York to be installed as Chancellor of the Cathedral, to which office I was instituted by the Archbishop when he was here on

Friday. So you see I have a good many offices, though all honorary, so far as income is concerned. The living itself will not do more, I expect, than pay two Curates, & bear the charities that are requisite.

But I am again running into my own affairs. I have crowds of poor – yards and lanes running out of the streets at each side in every direction. I like them much.

Ever affectionately and faithfully yours

Chas J. Vaughan [4]

Later that month, he attracted great crowds including many working men. He had heard that an 'Infidel' using the cognomen of 'Iconoclast' had been lecturing in Doncaster on the question 'Who is Jesus Christ?' In response, he put out placards in the town stating that he would preach two sermons on the same question which he did on Sunday 18 November. It was reported that overwhelming congregations assembled on both occasions and consequently hundreds were unable to gain admission. The *Doncaster Gazette* wrote 'Dr Vaughan's description of Christ and his works upon earth were truly eloquent. His character was portrayed in most vivid language and with such earnestness as to absorb the attention of the overflowing congregations.'

Catherine wrote to her dear friend and cousin Louisa on 5 December to share her news. It is clear from the letter that she had every intention of being actively involved in parish life, exercising her own ministry to women and welcoming them into her home just as she had done at Harrow:

My dearest Louisa

. . . I have so many things to say! But so little time – I am out both morning and afternoon – and have so little spare time – I am going to have a Party of Poor Women every Wednesday evening at work in the long room upstairs – "an Industrial Meeting" we mean to call it – it consists of 12 already and I quite hope will soon increase to 30 or 40. Whilst they work, I shall read to them – they have met hitherto at the Ragged School.

The Vicar [i.e. her husband] wins golden opinions in the Yards where he gives his Cottage Lectures. "Sh – he's so mild and heavenly I could have stayed to hear him all night – that I could." [5]

In December, the senior curate, Thomas Tickell, a non-graduate who had trained at St Bees Theological College in Cumberland, left after six years in the parish to become Curate in charge of Colsterworth in Lincolnshire. On 2 December Vaughan was installed as Chancellor in York Minster and, according to the *Yorkshire Gazette*, 'delivered a most able and eloquent address.' He also preached at the Ordination held by the Archbishop at Bishopthorpe later that month on St Thomas's Day, and two of the newly ordained Deacons, Evelyn J. Hone and George Wood, joined him at St George's – both of whom had been pupils of his in the Sixth Form at Harrow. There was another curate already in post, the Revd Edward Cavendish Taylor MA, but he too left soon afterwards.

Severe winter weather hit the area in late December. On Christmas Day the temperature dropped to just one degree Fahrenheit, i.e. 31 degrees below freezing! Not surprisingly, the *Gazette* reported that 'the severe weather operated against a large attendance of worshippers.' More importantly it had put many people out of work as the river and the land were frozen solid. They were in desperate need of help – no work meant no wages for food. Vaughan was known to be a man good with words and generous to individuals in need, but now he needed to show he could be an effective leader and a man of action in the community. He convened a meeting at the Vicarage on Boxing Day attended by the Mayor and Aldermen 'with a view to the temporary relief of those poor inhabitants of the district attached to the Parish Church who are reduced to distress by the present severity of the weather.' Inevitably, a committee was formed and he let it be known that he was anxious to secure the assistance of his parishioners 'in this laudable work.'

The committee met on New Year's Eve. There was some disagree-- ment about how to ascertain the extent of the need and how to distribute help. A fund was opened which immediately raised £40 [= £4,120] – Vaughan headed the list of subscribers with a donation of £5 and the Mayor gave £3. It was agreed to provide a quart of soup to the value of 4d but to charge just one penny, and a loaf of bread to the same value at the same price. A proposal to supply coals was voted down. Finding containers large enough to make enough soup for hundreds of people was their first task – eventually facilities were provided at the Town Hall both for making the food and serving it. The Council gave £20 towards the costs - £12 for the Parish Church district and £8 for the district of Christ Church. Each wanted to be seen to be doing something for its own parishioners. Two thousand tickets were printed, each authorizing the bearer to receive one pint of soup.

On 21 January the *Gazette* reported that large quantities of meat of first rate quality had been purchased and on the following Tuesday applicants arrived to collect their soup. Vaughan and other members of his committee had first tasted the soup 'and found no fault with it, beyond its being slightly burnt.' A lot of people thought otherwise and expressed their discontent! On the following Friday a second serving was made – this time half a pound of bread was provided to a pint of soup and the charge was just half a penny. The *Gazette* reported that 657 pints of soup and 424 pounds of bread were distributed that day, and by the following Tuesday the third batch of soup was deemed to be excellent. On Friday 25th it reported that the fifth distribution had taken place at the Town Hall – this time 770 pints of soup and 440lbs of bread were supplied. 'The soup was of a most excellent quality, and none better could have been prepared for the purpose . . . made from 18 stones of beef and mutton and two of oatmeal, two pecks of potatoes and two of turnips, one peck of carrots and one of onions, three dozen celery etc.' This attention to detail was presumably a way of letting donors know how their money had been spent. Vaughan chaired a committee meeting at the end of January which decided to discontinue the distribution as the weather had improved markedly and people had been able to return to work. Accounts were produced which showed a surplus of income which was retained 'in case the frost returns.' The actual help provided was modest but given the quantities collected by the poor of Marshgate and Fishergate twice a week, it must have been a real help to very many hungry families. It had also allowed the parish's District Visitors to provide a useful social service by distributing tickets to the needy and by helping serve the food each Tuesday and Friday.

The timing was probably just coincidental but Vaughan was invited to be a Trustee of the Doncaster Charities on 28 December and appointed a Trustee of the Doncaster Savings Bank in January. Maybe his talents as a community leader in a time of need had been noted and appreciated. Catherine wrote to Dalrymple who had visited them on his way north before Christmas to give their latest news – she headed the letter 'Really not worth reading'. They had had lots of visitors including Professor Jowett and Dr Butler. The latter had preached a 'very interesting sermon' on the Sunday morning, she told him, but had been mistaken for the new curate! 'We have suffered most terribly ever since you were here from the cold. The thermometer 8° below zero on Christmas Eve – and in Nottingham 13 below zero. But we have far less snow than you have – the ground is covered but is not deep. There is some distress from the Rivers being "fast" but of course nothing compared to the destitution of other large Towns – and the younger part of the population console themselves by extensive sliding on the ice.'[6]

In a letter to Dalrymple, dated 26 April 1861, Vaughan told him of his plans for his first clergy chapter meeting due to take place a week later:

> On 2nd of May I have the first meeting of my Rural Deanery here. I think I told you I have 44 Churches – 60 Clergy in connexion with me in that office. We are to have the Communion at 11.30 then adjourn here for Discussion: a passage of Scripture 1st - & then the consideration of (an important practical evil in these parts) what are called "Statute Fairs", for the hiring of Farm Servants – at which great abominations are said to occur: after this, luncheon, then another Discussion, of a new Diocesan Society established by the Archbishop: then Coffee, & separate. I hope it will go off well but a good deal of responsibility will lie upon the Chairman. [7]

He told him too about two more new Curates who would be given a Title for Orders but, significantly, no salary. One of them was another former pupil, J. J. Trebeck who had left Oxenham's House in 1854 and was later at Christ Church Oxford. He wrote of him: 'He seems very good & devoted, and very vigorous & manly: most anxious to come.' [8] And he shared his first thoughts on the men who would come to be known as 'Vaughan's doves'.

> I think also of having a few good Harrow men, from time to time, to prepare themselves for Orders here; working under me in the Parish as a sort of District Visitors, & getting anything they could from me in the way of Greek Testament reading. I could not offer much time to them – nor, of course, would they reside with me: but I think some might like this better than going to a Theological College. They must of course be good men: I could do nothing in the way of reforming doubtful men. [9]

On 4 May the *Yorkshire Gazette* reported that he had been appointed Chaplain to the 1st West Regiment of Yorkshire Yeomanry Cavalry – a voluntary post not requiring much of his time and energy. On Trinity Sunday, he was in Cambridge where he preached a challenging sermon on choosing a career. As it was arguably the most important of all his university sermons and probably the most influential one of his entire preaching career, I have included the full text later in the book as Appendix 1. His text was *Acts* 22 v10 "What shall I do, Lord?" In it he urged upon his hearers the need of the Church of England for the most gifted among them to offer themselves for the ordained ministry. And he invited any student who was thinking of Ordination – 'men of blameless character, of steady purpose, of open mind, and of true devotion' to come and reside in his parish for a few months by way of preparation.

221

There they could see and assist in the practical work done by a parish priest and read with him for Ordination.

A few days later, Catherine wrote to thank Dalrymple for looking after her husband so well during his visit to Cambridge and said how much it had grieved her not to have heard his sermons. 'I think they must surely have made some impression' she wrote.[10] That proved to be a huge understatement.

Over the years, some of the most academically able men of Oxford as well as Cambridge accepted his invitation and thus was born the group of men who came to be known as 'Vaughan's doves'. This would become the most significant work of his entire ministry and his greatest contribution to the Church of England. The nickname 'dove' was reputedly given after a member of the Doncaster congregation asked "Who are these like doves?" when they processed in their white surplices from the vestry to their places in church. Catherine told Dalrymple in a letter dated 1 October 1863 that her husband was now followed up the aisle 'by no less than 11 surplices (counting the three Curates)' and what a striking effect the sight had on the congregation.

Fourteen years later Vaughan gave an account of how this work developed after his sermon:

> The first fruit of this appeal was reaped the same evening; and for the last fourteen years a large part of the time which could be spared from other duties has been devoted to the work . . . More than two hundred Clergymen, graduates of Oxford and Cambridge, now sprinkled all over parts of England, have received at Doncaster and in the Temple, the kind of training here indicated for their ministerial duties. To the active Parochial work which is made . . . has been added a careful study of the Greek Testament, especially of the Epistles; practice in the reading of the Lessons, the composition of Sermons, and the definite statement of Christian doctrines; advice, in the form of conversational Lectures, upon some of the special duties of the Ministry; a general direction of private reading with a view to the examination for Orders; and that sort of individual assistance in the selection of a Diocese and a Curacy which is perhaps not without its influence upon the comfort and efficiency of the subsequent Clerical life. No one can be so conscious as myself of the many deficiencies of the plan pursued: still I believe that it is an effort in the right direction, and I should be most unthankful if I did not earnestly acknowledge the reaction of happiness which it is sure to bring with it to the person who honestly and diligently seeks to carry it out. [11]

It may be because of this sermon and the immediate impact it had on the student body that his advice was sought by two undergraduates, J.F.B. Tinling of St John's and Alfred Maynard of Clare. They wanted to start a daily prayer meeting in the university 'to ask for the outpouring of the Holy Spirit on our university' but they had received no support at all, rather the reverse, from the two leading Evangelicals there whom they had approached. Maynard who came from a village near Doncaster where his father was the parish priest visited Vaughan during the vacation. Vaughan urged carefulness and caution but gave the two young men the encouragement they needed. Despite opposition, they started the prayer group on 24 November 1862 and a score of men attended the first meeting. It quickly became known as the D.P.M. (Daily Prayer Meeting) and was one of the forerunners of C.I.C.C.U. - the Cambridge Inter-Collegiate Christian Union – founded in March 1877.

Back in Doncaster after his visit to Cambridge as a Select Preacher, he was soon initiating a new piece of work. As a recently retired headmaster, he was naturally interested in the education of the older boys in his parish and more particularly in helping resuscitate the near-defunct Grammar School. The school had effectively shut in 1854 though it retained a headmaster and the odd pupil. Vaughan wrote to the Mayor in August 1861 suggesting a resolution of the problem which involved paying the Head a gratuity of £100 to resign and finding or building suitable new premises. He argued that it was essential that a town such as Doncaster had an effective, functioning grammar school. The Corporation responded positively to his proposals.

That same month he had the joy of officiating at the wedding in St Margaret's Westminster of Harrow's Headmaster, Montagu Butler, who married Isabella Elliot, the daughter of a former Chief Magistrate of Madras. His gift to them was a copy of his book *Church Prayers* which the couple used daily for their family devotions.

In October his friend, J.B. Lightfoot, was appointed Hulsean Professor at Cambridge and he wrote both to congratulate him and to suggest an issue deserving of his attention: 'May I venture to say how glad I shall be if a review of the possible departments of theological study should end in directing your thoughts towards the Interpretation of Scripture, as that which most urgently needs a sound and thorough treatment at the present time? Possibly I may overrate its comparative – but I am sure I do not overrate its positive importance.' [12] He had heard that Lightfoot was thinking of resigning the Tutorship he held at Trinity and, if so, requested that he would 'say a word of kindness in behalf of my young relation, Hodgson, to your successor.' [13]

In December he wrote to the Council again about the Grammar School, this time offering advice about the terms and conditions of the new Head's appointment. This included allowing him to take boarders and paying him a generous salary. He clearly envisaged that the Head would be in Holy Orders but it would be a condition of the post that he did not take on any parochial duties. He was also to be given a free hand in the appointment and dismissal of Assistant Masters and for the general running of the school.

It was proposed that the school would have two sides, a classical one which taught all 'subjects as are commonly taught in public schools' and an English one where the subjects would be such 'as are required for a sound commercial education.' His experience at Harrow clearly influenced these decisions. The *Gazette* commented on 6 December 1861 'The revival of this ancient institution will be carried into effect after the Christmas vacation . . . It is fortunate the town possesses so distinguished a scholar as the Rev. Dr Vaughan to assist in its resuscitation: for his experience and success at Harrow, and his knowledge and aptitude in these questions are the best assurance that the inhabitants will have the full benefit of a complete educational institution.'

Vaughan was given the task of chairing the selection committee. There were 52 applicants for the post. The successful candidate was the Revd William Gurney, a former scholar of Emmanuel College Cambridge, and a man who had already proved his competence as the Head of Stockport Grammar School for 13 years. The school re-opened under him, assisted by three other teachers, on 6 August 1862. Vaughan's active interest in the school continued as he visited it frequently and always took the Chair on Speech Days.

Catherine too was busy in her own way. In January 1862 after returning from a visit to her family at Alderley, she wrote to Louisa about her newest project and begged for a modest donation for it. 'I have been overwhelmed with business lately – endeavouring to establish a School for young women of which I send you a prospectus in the earnest hope that you and Rianetta will send me a shilling a piece towards it. Very soon we hope to be able to start it – but we still want a little more help – and I think without fear of reducing them to beggary, I may ask my friends for 1/- each.' [14] Her Girls' Home and School of Industry was opened at 9 Hall Cross Hill later that year. It was supported entirely by voluntary subscriptions for 'the religious and secular education of 28 orphaned, friendless and destitute girls aged 10 – 14 years of age.' [15] Later, the two of them set up a training school for girls wishing to go into domestic service. Catherine also aspired to be a writer. In May 1863 she told Louisa that she had 'two little works in the Press!' which were to be two 'Advanced Reading Books' for schools and that she had already published *Words from the Poets for use of Parochial Schools and Libraries*.

Catherine's mother died on 5 March 1862 and was buried at Alderley. Charles Dalrymple was among those who were informed immediately – a mark of the friendship which existed between the two families. Later in March Vaughan wrote again but this time in a fatherly vein to console the young man in his own troubles. He had been a conscientious student at Trinity, a reading man, but he had failed to do as well as he had hoped, achieving just a 3rd in the Classical Tripos:

> It vexed me to allow yesterday to end without writing to you – and the more so after reading your kind & really delightful letter.
>
> You wrote about the Tripos in so manly and right a spirit that I do indeed feel that Education has not been in vain for you, however in itself disappointing one of its outward results.
>
> Little will remain hereafter of the most brilliant place on a Tripos – though I do not undervalue such honour: but <u>much</u>, very much, will be left of such a character as your letter indicates. And you will always feel that you have shown <u>practically</u> your regard for Mr Westcott and for me, in a way which nothing else could have done. You have pursued your reading to its regular close, amidst outward circumstances which almost anyone would have accepted as sufficient excuse for turning aside from it.
>
> It may seem silly to say it - & quite unnecessary: but do, at the close of your Education, let me say, for once, how affectionate a feeling there must always be for you in my heart. Perhaps you may not dislike <u>my</u> reminding you of this now.
>
> As you go back, you will come to us? Mrs Vaughan will quite enjoy having you. She is pretty well & somewhat cheered by hearing (by telegraph) of her Brother's receipt of the sad, sad news of his Mother's illness & death all in one: it met him at Cairo, last Sunday, & the telegraph from General Bruce the next morning (which reached Miss Stanley the same evening at 7) said that, though overwhelmed, he was bearing it with firmness, & had "nobly resolved" to go on with the Prince to Palestine. We are thankful for the alleviation of our anxiety about him.
>
> The Queen has been very kind. Do come to us dear Dalrymple. [16]

In the summer he had a week's holiday at St Leonard's with his mother which left him feeling 'extremely well' but by 12 August, when he wrote to Dalrymple, he was already wishing he had stayed longer. That letter

225

reveals how much he was in demand as a guest preacher away from the parish:

> Engagements are thick upon one another: a Sermon in Ripon Cathedral on the 21st – then one at Leicester early in September – at Sheffield on the 3rd of September – at Harpenden in October & in between those last a grand opening of our Organ (with the Bishops of Lincoln, Oxford & Lichfield, & probably another to preach) on Sept 25, 26 & 28 . . .
>
> In November I preach 4 Sermons at Cambridge & the 5th Sunday at York in my turn. This, & the necessary holiday, of the four dear Curates, together with a few acts of charity in helping other Incumbents, will leave but little chance of a holiday for me: indeed there is at present a Guildhall meeting every Tuesday evening (for Exposition of Scripture) which I must take myself while it lasts. But why this long list? Do not think that I do not like my work: it is much otherwise. Only I feel that it is no use doing it by halves, & that I must throw myself into it, heart and soul, if it is to do any good. I have chiefly said this, to show you why I cannot entertain the hope of coming to New Hailes this Summer. How much I should enjoy it – more I think than ever. I trust you will come to us before long, tho' we have missed you in going home. We are just now rather less happy than usual, as Hone & Robertson are away. They are two whom I miss particularly. Long was to come towards the end of August, I think . . . [17]

In November 1862 he took the lead again, together with other local notables, in calling on the Mayor to convene a public meeting to consider the best means of affording the unemployed 'distressed cotton-workers in Lancashire and Cheshire assistance in their unprecedented calamity.' The meeting was duly held at which Vaughan moved the first motion which called for a national response to a national calamity – rich and poor, he said, must come forward to assist. A donation list was immediately started to which the Town Corporation subscribed £105 and the Mayor £25 – Vaughan gave £100 (equivalent to nearly a quarter of his annual stipend) and his wife £10. The poor also responded with the local railway workers contributing weekly from their pay.

In March 1864 he wrote to tell Dalrymple of a recent visit to his brother-in-law in London [Arthur Stanley] and his 'very dear Bride'. The evenings had all been spent 'with my favourite Cousin, Augusta Vaughan [Sir John's daughter], in Chester Place, Regents Park. How I wish you knew her!' [18] This was hardly an attempt at matchmaking as his cousin was 59 years old. Some years later, however, Catherine did try to tempt him with an heiress worth £2,000 or more a year by inviting him to meet her at a tea party she was going to host.

In 1864 Vaughan joined a campaign to provide new and larger buildings for the growing number of pupils at Doncaster Grammar School and in December 1865 he made an appeal to the public to support the building fund to which he donated £50 himself. William Henry Forman, a wealthy landowner and property speculator in the town, gave a two-acre site on Thorne Road and donated £1,000. The Corporation promised a further £2,000. Forman requested that the buildings be designed by Scott, the architect who had designed St George's. Forman was one of the Church's benefactors who had paid in full the cost of building the 'Lady Chapel' on the south side. In 1867 Vaughan was appointed to the committee which supervised the building work. The foundation stone was laid on 18 December 1867 and to mark the occasion the Mayor gave a luncheon at the Mansion House and included among his guests all the boys at the school. The new premises were opened on 2 April 1869 and later that year the Charity Commissioners made a Scheme which put a body of Trustees in charge. The Corporation made an annual grant of £250 in return for appointing ten Corporation Scholars who won their free places by means of a competitive examination.[19]

His interest in the welfare of the Grammar School did not slacken – he personally funded two prizes to be awarded annually, and in 1866 he encouraged the institution of six free 'choral scholarships' which would also benefit the parish church. At the time of his leaving Doncaster he pressed the Corporation to offer bursaries to pupils who went on to university. He wanted poor but academically able boys in the town to have the opportunities a university education could bring them. The revived Grammar School proved to be a great success and it was rated by the Endowed Schools Enquiry Commission in 1868 as one of the three best schools in the West Riding of Yorkshire.

He had also quickly turned his attention to the education of younger children, chairing his first meeting of the National School's Committee just eight days after his arrival in Doncaster. The parish had had a church school since 1816, founded in association with the National Society, but it was located some distance from St George's. The purpose of this foundation was 'to teach the children reading, writing and arithmetic; to accustom them to be orderly in their behaviour, to communicate moral and religious feelings, and to engraft on them right views of Christian doctrine and practice; and thus to influence the character and form of the rising generation.' [20] Although it was a C of E school, children were allowed to attend those places of worship to which their parents or

227

guardians were attached – in other words it served as a community school rather than as a place of nurture simply for young Anglicans.

School buildings were an important asset in any parish as they provided meeting rooms for other organisations and for social events in the parish as well as being available for Sunday schools. The existing building, however, needed replacement and this was raised in the local press just a month after his arrival. The *Gazette* reported on 2 November 1860 that the erection of new National Schools to be situated nearer to the Parish Church was being proposed. 'The Rev. Dr Vaughan feels, at the commencement of his career, that unless his schools are easy of access to the very persons whom they are intended to benefit, his usefulness will be contracted.' He raised the matter again publicly in July 1862 and the following year he bought up the lease on a piece of land close to St George's belonging to the Corporation and then urged them to give the freehold so that a new school could be built on it. He launched a public appeal for funds in January 1866 and himself made a very generous contribution to the building costs. A contemporary writer described it and how it came into being:

> The town is indebted to the disinterested exertions of our esteemed vicar, the Rev. C.J. Vaughan DD for the substitution of a noble and commodious structure, in place of the present somewhat inadequate and inconveniently situated schools. From the very commencement of Dr Vaughan's ministry in this borough he did not fail to notice this objectionable feature with regard to the National Schools, viz. their position at the corner of the parish, away from the Parish Church, and consequently, to some extent, from under that supervision which the clergy could necessarily devote to the schools were they situate nearer the Church, as is the case with the greater proportion of parochial schools in this country. The cost of the building, about £4,000, has been subscribed for, including the Vicar's donation of £1,000; the accommodation is for 500 children. The style of the schools may be said to be English Gothic of the 14th century, adapted to modern requirements. The walls are built of kiln brick, with best Ancaster stone dressings to doors, windows, &c. The schools for boys and girls form two wings of about 20 yards by 11 yards placed above the master's and mistress' houses, with an approach from the playground by stone staircases, which are situated in external towers; and under each staircase is provided a lavatory. Between, and connecting these wings, is the infant's (*sic*) school, on the ground floor – about ten yards square – and half the area above the forms respectively the classrooms for boys and girls. [21]

The foundation stone was laid on Tuesday 23 October 1866. Fifteen months later, on a bitterly cold Sunday morning in January 1868 the Archbishop of York came to open the school buildings. He kept his brief address fairly informal and homely which was delivered outside to the crowd standing in the cold. He directed his words first to the Sunday School teachers and then to the children. Having first made the point that children are capable of thinking and asking deep questions about life and death (and not just wondering what they would be given for their next meal), he then offered the teachers some advice expressed in simple, practical terms:

> My dear friends, try to get the child to open his mind to you. Try to put yourselves in its position, and think what it can understand; and further that there is no receipt but the one Love. The great secret of gospel success is love. Christ said "Suffer little children to come unto me." Christ wished his followers to be as little children; and we must not snub them or depress them by our fine, superior minds. We must be very careful if they put a question that might excite a smile, not to let them think that we laugh at them. That would stop the action of the child's mind . . .[22]

Although it had no attachment to St George's, Vaughan also supported the town's Ragged School, which provided a basic education for the poorest children who had no connection with any other school. In 1863 he was elected on to the school committee and immediately made his presence felt by organising weekly services for the children.

As has been noted earlier, one of the measures of how active and personally involved a priest is in the lives of his parishioners is the pastoral care (or lack of it) which he shows in what are known as the 'Occasional Offices': Baptisms, Weddings and Funerals. Some vicars delegated much of this ministry to their curates – not so, Vaughan. He had a string of curates during his years in the parish but always took a fair share in this pastoral work and he did not restrict his personal ministry simply to the wealthier members of his congregation. He was a man for all people. Of the 150 children brought to Baptism in 1861, he was the officiant for 56 of them, his two curates George Wood and Evelyn Hone did 48 and 46 respectively. By the following year he had five Curates but still officiated himself at 32 of the 213 Baptisms that year. Christmas was a particularly popular time for this – Vaughan baptised six children on his first Christmas Day in Doncaster: the offspring of a fireman, a tailor, a painter, a carriage fitter, a labourer and a waterman. He ministered Baptism to twice that number on 23 December 1863 – this time their parents were a potato dealer (2 children), a shoemaker (2), a

229

painter (2), a green grocer (2), a blacksmith, a tea dealer, a fishmonger and a second shoemaker. Two of his curates baptised 25 children on Christmas day 1864.

What we don't know is what preparation, if any, apart from a short homily at the actual service, was given to the parents and sponsors. He also tried to remedy what he perceived to be a shortcoming at these services, namely the absence of any proper sponsors. In an evening sermon (the second in a series which were later published as a commentary on *Philippians*) which he preached in October 1861 he raised this as an issue for the congregation. He had noticed that it was the custom in Doncaster for the parents to stand as the only baptismal sponsors or to have some casual bystander as the third one whose responsibility to the child ended with the service. What was needed was some Christian who would take responsibility with the parents for the Christian education of the child. So he challenged the congregation:

> Has it ever occurred to the Christian women of this congregation how great a benefit they might confer upon the children of the poor by becoming sponsors for them? If the District Visitors, for example, and if the Sunday School Teachers, and if a few others voluntarily offering themselves, would permit application to be made to them, one or another, on behalf of those who are about to be brought to the font of Baptism without any proper sponsors; if they would, in such cases, be present at the font, to join their prayer with those of the Minister and the parents, and to give life and meaning to the service as they might do by their very presence; and if they would regard any child for whom they had answered, as possessing a claim upon their notice, upon their kindness, and upon their interest in his Christian training; I am persuaded that a new bond of spiritual brotherhood would be formed and cemented among the various ranks of our parishioners . . . [23]

He took a lesser share of the weddings – the most was nine out of the 71 in 1865 though that number was shared with five curates, and in 1867 he did none.

St George's churchyard had long since ceased to be used as a burial ground. The town cemetery registers show that Vaughan took his share of burying infants as well as adults, and at great festivals too. The register entry on 24 December 1863, for example, states that he officiated at the burial of Mary Suzanna Kirk (37 years), and on Christmas Day at the burials of four infants, namely Richard Winter (15 months), Charlotte Moore (9 months), Alice Duke (1 yr. 10 months) and Henrietta

Brooker (3 weeks). Infant mortality below the age of one in Doncaster was very high, varying between 1 in 4 and 1 in 6 live births in the 1860s. Crowded courts, filthy drains, and foul water were the usual deadly contributing factors. 1866 was a particularly bad year as cholera swept through the town – of the 611 deaths registered that year, 166 of them were infants.

His nephew reckoned that his pastoral ministry during the epidemics was never forgotten by the townspeople: 'When a severe outbreak of cholera occurred in his earlier years, he completely won the heart of the town and neighbourhood by the bravery with which, in contempt of a general panic, he trudged from house to house, throughout the time of the epidemic, doing all that could be done to comfort the sick, the dying and the mourners.' [24] The cemetery records confirm that he did have direct contact with some of the bereaved families. On 27 September 1866, for example, he buried nine people including four children – among them was Margaret Marsh, a 28 year old widow and two of her sons: eight year old Frederick and two year old George. Seven of the nine had lived on the same street in the town.

There had been a dispensary 'for the relief of the sick poor in this town and neighbourhood' since 1792 funded in part by the Corporation but there was no proper hospital. In December 1863 Vaughan proposed that an infirmary be combined with the dispensary and that they be based in a new building designed for the purpose. He formed an Infirmary Committee to examine selected sites and to solicit financial support for the hospital which the town so badly needed. Two months later the Corporation made a grant of £500 to match a bequest and public support soon followed.[25] The proposed building was to 'comprise four principal wards containing 25 beds in all with suitable apartments for the Senior Surgeon, Dispensary and facilities for future additions.' [26] The foundation stone was laid on 13 July 1865 by the Mayor, Henry Moore, in the presence of the Archbishop of York, Vaughan, and all the aldermen, councillors and local magistrates. Finally on 1 May 1867 the new hospital-cum-dispensary was taken into use. By then the town had two physicians and 12 surgeons (three of them with the degree of M.D.). Later that year it received a modest boost to its funds from the publication of one of Vaughan's sermons. The Mayor that year was Henry Woodmansey who died suddenly on 1 October as a consequence of an accident. The following Sunday the Town Council attended St George's where Vaughan preached an appropriate sermon. Afterwards the Council unanimously resolved to ask for its publication at their expense with all profits going to the newly opened Infirmary.

The old dispensary building was immediately taken over by another charity close to Vaughan's heart: the 'Doncaster Girls' Home and School of Industry' which his wife, Catherine, had founded five years earlier. The stated purpose of this institution now was to 'receive orphan and other friendless or destitute girls, to save them from the evils of pauperism, to train them to earn their own living, and to meet the daily increasing demand for good working servants.'

One of those from whom Vaughan had solicited support for the infirmary was Lord Houghton though adding, with his usual smoothness, 'If, as I cannot but feel to be more probable, the demands made upon your generosity by others and nearer schemes of this, do not trouble yourself to reply to this note. I shall perfectly understand your silence.' [27] Six months later he had occasion to write a more personal kind of financial request to him but again done with his customary tact:

> Do you remember kindly nominating me to a Lectureship (or some special foundation) in the Parish Church of Doncaster when I came here in October 1860?
> I find in my Bankers Book (Messrs Cooke & Co Doncaster) a payment in your name of £4.15.10 on January 17 1861, a payment of £9.11.8 on May 6 1861, and a payment of £9.12.6 on November 11 1861.
> From the last date I find no similar entry. Will you at your leisure do me the favour of just looking at your Memoranda to see whether (as is so probable) I have made some careless oversight of later payments. [28]

As a piece of 'Local Intelligence' the *Gazette* had published in May 1863 a comprehensive list of the staff and the range of activities in St George's Parish. What it reveals is how well Vaughan had shaped and organized parish life since his arrival and how he was trying to reach out to the poor who were much less likely to cross the threshold of the church on a Sunday:

VICAR
C.J. Vaughan DD late Fellow of Trinity College Cambridge
CURATES:
J.G. Wood Theological Associate of King's College London
E.J. Hone BA late Scholar of Wadham College Oxford
J.J. Trebeck BA Christ's College Oxford
T.F. Morton BA Trinity College Cambridge
J.G. Gibbs BA Trinity College Cambridge

STUDENTS FOR HOLY ORDERS:
R. Long BA Trinity College Cambridge
C.H. Weekes BA Exeter College Oxford
R. Sainsbury BA Trinity College Cambridge
SCRIPTURE READER: Mr Sanderson
DISTRICT VISITORS
Twenty-five ladies, amongst whom the Parish Church District is accurately distributed for domestic visitations and delivery of tracts.
BIBLE CLASSES
Sunday at 2.30 Parish Room, Monday at 8p.m. Vicarage
MOTHERS MEETING
Tuesday at 7p.m. Vicarage
WINTER EVENING CLASSES
MEN
Guildhall Monday and Thursday in conjunction with Christ Church at 7.30p.m.
BOYS
National School Monday and Wednesday at 7.30p.m.
YOUNG WOMEN
Girls National School Monday and Wednesday 7.15p.m.
NATIONAL & SUNDAY SCHOOLS
Daily visited by the Clergy and Students
COTTAGE LECTURES
Two or three weekly at houses of the poor specially offered for the purpose of each occasion
CATHECHIZING OF THE YOUNG
Chancel of the Church. Sunday at 3p.m.
CONFIRMATION CLASSES
Four, weekly, during the months preceding a Confirmation.
VISITATION OF THE SICK AND POOR constantly carried on, for which purpose the Parish Church district is divided into four principal sections for each of which one of the Curates is responsible under the general oversight and with the assistance of the Vicar.
SERVICES AT THE PARISH CHURCH
Sundays at   11a.m.
             3.30p.m.
             6.30p.m.
Full service with sermon on each occasion.
Holy Communion at midday on the 1st Sunday of each month and at the great festivals; at the afternoon service on the 3rd Sunday in each month.
Holy Baptism administered in the public service on the last Sunday in each month and on weekdays after the daily prayers, when required.
Daily prayers throughout the week at 11a.m.

233

Special evening services with a lecture on the Friday before a Communion once a month also on Wednesday during Advent and Lent at 8p.m. During Passion Week every evening.

At Sandall our Sunday service and sermon at 3.15p.m. at present in Mr Lawson's granary until a schoolroom can be built and duly licensed for this purpose. [29]

Vaughan successfully negotiated with the Corporation to build a school room which would also serve as a chapel in the hamlet of Sandall but it was joined to the neighbouring parish of Kirk Sandall before the school could be built. Joseph Gibbs, one of his own curates, was appointed the curate in charge of this parish in 1864.

George Austen joined him as a 'dove' in 1863 prior to being ordained to the curacy of St Mary, Nottingham the following year – in time he became the first of his men to achieve ecclesiastical distinction as Chancellor of York Minister. Another of the 1863 intake, W.J. Lawrence, became Dean of St Albans. Austen reminisced about Vaughan at a meeting of the 'doves' in 1925 and in particular about him as a parish priest in Doncaster.

He took a full share in all the duties of a parish priest. He was almost always three times at church on Sundays, generally preaching twice. He attended daily Mattins and gave an unwritten address at one Evensong in the Forman Chapel. His deliberate and reverent reading of the Bible and the prayers was most impressive. There were numerous weekday meetings – a Bible Class (one treating of St John's Gospel to be specially remembered), a class for Sunday School teachers, one for district visitors monthly, one or more for Confirmation candidates as occasion required (once he started with 140). He visited the Grammar School daily; he was largely responsible for re-ordering the National Schools, and might be seen in the afternoon – stick in hand (as always afterwards) – starting to visit the sick, suffering and sorrowing . . . His correspondence was immense. He sometimes wrote thirty letters a day, every one of them in his own neat, legible handwriting, and when standing up at his desk . . .

Now when was all this work done? At all hours. A great deal after dinner, when he would disappear and lock his study door. Later on he returned to the drawing room for prayers. There was a charm in his manner difficult to describe. His influence was extraordinary. Servants would do anything for him. He treated everyone with unusual respect. [30]

We get another picture of how Vaughan was running his parish from the Visitation Return which he completed for the Archbishop in January

1865. In answer to Q. 2 which was about his residence in the parish in the previous year (275 days being the required minimum) he wrote: 'Yes. Much more.' Q.9 was about catechising children to which he answered: 'At 3 p.m. on a Sunday. A Book of Scripture (one of the Gospels, or the Acts) is taken in course, from 10 to 15 verses each time.' The Visitation Returns show that his neighbours at Christchurch and at St James in Doncaster catechised just once a month. After giving the number of communicants at all the major festivals (there were 194 on Easter Day 1864) and details of the frequency that Holy Communion was celebrated (Q.11), he was then required to report on 'the average number of your congregation'. His answer reads: 'At 11 a.m. on Sunday from 500 to 800 roughly. At 3.30 p.m. on Sunday from 150 to 200 roughly; on Sunday at 6 p.m. from 1000 to 1200 roughly. At daily morning prayers ['10 a.m. throughout the week'] from 15 to 30.' The Sunday figures show that a fair proportion of the population of his parish was attending church. He said his parishioners numbered about 7,000 and commented 'The morning congregation (S) is affected by the consequences of the late market on Saturday night (besides other more obvious reasons).' He returned to this in answer to Q.19 which was about impediments to the parochial ministry: 'It is obvious to mention (1) the Races: chiefly, I think, affecting the Church in this way, that consciences are uncertain about the right or wrong of them and their concomitants, and rendered uneasy and vacillating in religious duties in consequence. (2) I should suppose the late Saturday Market is an evil in many ways in its effect upon the observance of the Sunday. I have sometimes wished that it might be closed by authority at an earlier hour as is done (I believe) in Liverpool and doubtless elsewhere.' Lastly, his answers to Q.16 and Q.17 show how he was struggling to retain contact with young adults. The first one asked 'Are you able to retain your young people in your Sunday School after they have ceased to attend the Daily School?' His answer was: 'With great difficulty, none beyond 16 or 17 years of age.' The next one asked: 'Have you adopted any other mode of retaining them under instruction by Adult or Evening Schools? If so, with what success?' He answered: ' Evening Schools during the winter months for Men and Boys. Successful in 1861, diminishing since; now not more than from 25 to 40 Scholars, and very few of these men. There is also a Weekly Bible Class at the Vicarage: (1) for Men, 15 to 30 attend; (2) for Women, 20 – 30; (3) for Sunday School Teachers about 25.' The Vicar of Christchurch reported that he had closed his evening classes for men as the numbers attending were so small but added 'We have Adult evening schools open for the

<u>town</u>, managed by the Parish Church Clergy. I believe only moderately attended.' [31]

Catherine adds some further detail of their doings that year in a letter to Dalrymple written in October:

> Our holidays consisted of a week in Wales – a week in Cheshire – and a week in Norfolk. Now we are rooted fast again for the winter.
> We have a nice set of Readers – and all goes on well. Think of Dr Vaughan's Bible Class on Monday evening, having now risen to 70 or 80. Is not that encouraging? [32]

Another picture of his ministry is to be seen in the press reports of yet another of his innovations in the parish. This was an annual 'Tea Meeting', first held in the Guildhall a week before Christmas in 1862. These meetings which were akin to a modern day 'Annual Parochial Church Meeting' attracted some 600 parishioners! He used the occasion of the first one to share his views on the need for new school buildings in the parish – at this stage it was just the seed of an idea which would produce fruit three years later. He used this annual event to report on the ministry in the parish and to tell of what had been achieved in the past year – usually a tale of yet more modest growth supported by a mass of statistics. This brief extract from the *Gazette*'s account of the fifth such occasion (1866) gives the flavour of Vaughan's detailed reports:

> During the past year the sacrament [Holy Communion] had been administered on 35 occasions on 28 different days. There had been 2,589 acts of communion; last year 2,491 . . . in 1862 when the figures were first taken and laid before the congregation the figure was 1,612 . . . the average number of communicants for the present year was 86 . . . the average attendance at the evening service was 117 in 1864, 118 in '65, and this year 120 [these figures refer to those who stayed on after Evening Prayer for the Holy Communion].
> This year there had been ten collections for special objects; viz. The new National Schools, the church on Marshgate, two for the Infirmary, the York Diocesan Aid Society, the Church Pastoral Aid Society., the Missions to Seamen, the Society for the Propagation of the Gospel in Foreign Parts and the Church Missionary Society . . . the sums received for the above societies £323.2s.11½d. The average of the collections (i.e. for charity) was for 1861 £22, 1862 £23, 1863 £24, 1864 £25, 1865 £27.4s and for this year £30. 6s.8d. [33]

236

Their annual charitable giving that year [£323] equals in today's money about £33,000. He was also able to report greatly improved attendances at the men and boys' Monday evening classes which had risen from an average of 50 in the previous year to 91 in 1866, the top attendance had been 118 against 64 the previous year. Another of his initiatives enjoying success was the 'Penny Savings Bank' which he had set up three years previously. Deposits had grown from £84 in 1864 and £74 in '65 to £184 in '66, and the number of depositors had likewise grown from 98 to 107 and then to 163 that year. The following year deposits rose even higher to £301 [= £28,540]. In December 1867 the *Chronicle* commented approvingly on this scheme for helping the poorer townspeople – a savings bank 'to educate the working classes in the virtues of thrift.'

The report given at the Tea Meeting in 1867 referred to another change which Vaughan had introduced a couple of years earlier but not without some opposition. He had pressed the need for having a celebration of Holy Communion in the evening as this was a more convenient time for mothers and servants to attend. The change had proved to be a popular one and the average number of communicants had risen as a consequence – from 59 in 1862 to 109 in 1867. Vaughan has sometimes been accused of holding a low view of the sacrament but that flies in the face of his determination to increase the frequency of celebrations of Holy Communion and the frequency with which he preached on it. There had been 161 candidates for Confirmation that year, 90 girls and 71 boys – a larger proportion of boys than usual. A notable event had been the visit of the Archbishop of York on 29 March to license the school-chapel on Marshgate. Some information was also given about the work which the ladies did as District Visitors – one of their tasks was to encourage cleanliness as being next to godliness: 'going from house to house, and yard to yard, enforcing upon the poor the necessity of tidiness and cleanliness in their homes.' [34] Given the awful infant mortality rate, this was much needed advice.

The souvenir booklet published for the centenary of St Andrew's Marshgate pays tribute to the Vicar's role in its founding – his 'Marshgate venture is not so well known, and yet it was of a pioneering nature in the field of education which was typical of Dr Vaughan's whole ministry.'[35] The land was conveyed and building began on 11 January 1866. It was completed at a cost of £900 plus £150 for internal fittings and first used for worship on Sunday 13 January 1867 led by its first Curate-in-charge, the Revd Ernest Wigram. It consisted of a single well-proportioned room lighted by gas and heated by a hot-water system. It

237

was calculated to hold 250 children and 200 adults – during the week it served as an Infants' School and on Sundays as a church.

Together with the Revd H.F. Brock of Christchurch and the Revd John Campion of St James', Vaughan tried to make provision for adult education classes in the town, something which the Mechanics Institutes had done so successfully in many towns and cities but not very well in Doncaster. Vaughan's efforts in this area likewise met with little success. Alan Thrall has described one of their initiatives:

> Vaughan and Brock joined forces in 1861 in providing evening classes for workmen, a praiseworthy effort at supplying education for the industrial classes. Rooms were obtained for the purpose in French Gate and Cleveland Street and the management of each establishment placed in the hands of a committee. Membership numbers were restricted to 40 at French Gate and 20 at Cleveland Street. A subscription of 2d per week was charged and it was agreed that if any member's was not forthcoming for three consecutive weeks he would cease to be a member. There was to be no spirituous liquor, but smoking was allowed and coffee provided at a penny per cup. The venture unfortunately was short-lived and soon faded into history. [36]

As noted earlier, Vaughan's Visitation Return for the year 1864 records diminishing success since 1861 with the evening classes for young adults in the parish. Three years later, however, he reported that things had improved and that they now had about 100 men and boys attending the evening classes being held in the new Church school, and for which a fee of 1d per evening was charged. Separate classes were held for men and for the boys.

Vaughan is remembered as a great preacher and an educationalist but he also recognised and valued the important role that music can play in public worship and he did what he could to improve it. A new organ designed by Edmund Schulze was installed in 1862 thanks primarily to the zeal of Jeremiah Rogers who had been organist at St George's since 1835. He loved to play loud and long preludes which were not entirely to Vaughan's liking whose vestry adjoined the organ, but true to his nature he avoided confrontation with the long-established musician. He encouraged higher standards in the choir and invited York Minister's organist to assess the voices of the boys who were candidates for the choral scholarships at the Grammar School which had been instituted at his request.

Another of his initiatives was the Annual Festival of Parochial Choirs held in Doncaster. Parish choirs from all over the deanery came to St George's on Thursday 19 May 1864 for two great choral services. The Archbishop of York preached at the first in the morning which was followed by a civic luncheon for 150 guests. At 4 in the afternoon, the Bishop-designate of Peterborough, Dr Francis Jeune, was the preacher [one of Jeune's sons had been a pupil of his at Harrow]. Vaughan had suggested the festival to the clergy of his deanery twelve months earlier and it proved to be successful – 420 choristers took part and 58 clergy processed in their robes, including the Dean of York. He attracted a series of eminent churchmen as preachers in the years that followed – Walter Hook, the Dean of Chichester, was at the second one. Hook was no stranger to Yorkshire or to urban ministry having served as a very successful Vicar of Leeds for many years; at the luncheon he described Doncaster 'as a model parish in the kingdom' and one where 'a great Christian work was being carried out.' [37] Vaughan also actively supported the South Yorkshire Church Choral Union which had been established in 1863 and was the preacher at its second festival held in Penistone Church. And in 1865 he was back in his home town of Leicester as the guest preacher at the annual festival of the Church Choral Association there.

We turn now to his educational work of a different kind. His years in Doncaster saw the publication of more than a score of new books as well as revised editions of a few earlier ones. The following selection of extracts from his correspondence with Macmillan, his main publisher, shows him to have been an astute businessman as well as an able communicator. He was concerned about the presentation of the finished work and even offered suggestions obviously intended to make a book look as attractive as possible to potential buyers. He was concerned too about publicity and getting favourable reviews, and about his financial gain. As always with Vaughan, the tone of the letters is courteous but firm. This one is dated 28 July 1863.

Dear Mr Macmillan,
It was careless of me to miss the "Revelation" advertisement for I looked down the column in quest for it.
I shall be obliged if you will reprint the Harrow Memorials without my seeing the Proofs if you can find a very careful person to look them over. My experience shows that this is necessary even in reprinting.
We agreed, I think, to do away with the red edges this time and in other

aspects make this Volume a <u>little</u> different. Could even the paper be slightly thicker?

You will judge. Many many thanks for <u>all</u> things!

Ever truly yours. C.J. Vaughan

You will kindly send me any notice of the Revelation which may appear in periodicals? I have seen none as yet. If it <u>should</u> reach a 2nd Edⁿ I shall ask you for a rather thicker paper: I think it would improve it: but everyone thinks it a charmingly got up book. [38]

Vaughan's relationship with Alexander Macmillan was to prove highly profitable for both parties but he also used other publishers, among them John Murray and Alexander Strahan. Sometimes he experienced disappointment on that front as the following extract illustrates. He shared his feelings in a letter to Macmillan dated 5 September 1863:

> . . . I will confide to you <u>but not to be repeated</u> that I have thought it a little strange that I have been asked to take no part whatever in a new Family Bible just being started by Murray, under the patronage of the Speaker of the H. of Commons & the Abp of York – conducted by Mr Cook of Lincoln's Inn. I was consulted by the Speaker before even the Archbishop was applied to; & it seems to me a work for which my training somewhat qualifies me. This gives me almost additional reason for doing something of my own. I hear that Murray embarks £20,000 in this work; showing his confidence of a large sale. The "Aids of Faith" men, as they are popularly called, are to be the authors – the attempt being to produce a work <u>up to</u> the level of modern science, but not adopting its supposed sceptical deductions. (Please keep entirely to yourself my personal feeling). [39]

With an eye to his share of the profits, he wrote to Macmillan on 2 November 1863: 'I have sometimes thought of asking you whether you could <u>with safety</u> diminish at all the expence of advertising my works? I know it would be bad economy to carry this curtailment too far; but it is a heavy drawback to profits.' [40] But profits were not all that mattered to him for in the same letter he also asks that copies of his lectures on *Philippians* and on the *Revelation* be sent to Bishop Patteson as a gift from himself as the Bishop had written 'so warmly and strongly about my edition of the *Romans*, that I am induced to ask him to accept these also.' [41]

On 16 January 1864 he sent a receipt for the remittance Macmillan had sent him for sales in 1863. It amounted to £189.13s.8d [= 20,180] And he took the opportunity to give them his latest requests and instructions:

240

I enclose a Proof for Revision of proposed Advertisement. Be so kind as to let me see it again.

I should much like to see a copy of the 4th Edition of Harrow Memorials.

I highly approve of republishing "The Book & the Life" <u>with the former</u> University Sermons, as you propose.

How do "Words of the Gospels" sell? And is there any progress in the sale of "Philippians" & "Revelation"? [42]

In November 1868 he was Select Preacher at Cambridge and hoped to have the course of sermons he was delivering published immediately. By now he was an established author whose work sold well, and he felt able to ask for better terms:

I am preaching this month before the University, and I think it probable that I may wish to publish the four lectures – of which the general title is <u>The Foes of Faith</u> (or, <u>Four Foes of Faith</u>). (1. Unreality – 2. Indolence – 3. Irreverence – 4. Inconsistency.) I should, of course, prefer asking you to be the publisher. But I should not be inclined to publish them on the same terms as before.

And I therefore take the liberty of asking whether you would be inclined to undertake the little volume on the terms of paying me <u>one shilling for each copy sold</u> – the publishers bearing all risks and expenses?

This would give me £50 for every thousand sold. I should of course retain the copyright.

Pray do not [hesitate?] to tell me exactly what you think of this proposal – as I would not on any account burden you. I think I could find a publisher who would give me these terms – and I think also that you are aware that it is not in a merely <u>mercenary</u> spirit that I seek what appears to me to be a fair price for my publications. [43]

Macmillan responded positively by return of post and Vaughan then immediately made further suggestions:

Your kind and friendly response must not wait for its acknowledgement.

I trust that, in accepting my proposal, you are not forgetting that it is made in much ignorance, & might prove disadvantageous to yourself. If I do it, pray let it be done with due consideration of this question.

I fear that the Sermons, being but four, and not longer than those of the last Series will scarcely make more than a 3/6 Volume. But this will be in your hands if you undertake it.

I think that it may save time if the Sermons were set up first in [slips?] not in pages, so that I might add references or make any alterations in the first proof without disarranging the pages. You will think of this.

I have a line from you on Sunday or Monday <u>morning</u> at

Magdalene Lodge

Cambridge

I will leave the MS at the Pitt Press, or at your Cambridge premises, before I leave finally on that Day.

The title, I think, had better be simply "Foes of Faith" without either "The" or "Four".

"Wholesome Words can be reprinted, without my seeing the Proof, if you will kindly have them <u>well looked over by some one.</u>

<u>Your other generous proposal (respecting my former publications) is entirely your own.</u> I must beg you to do only what you feel to be just towards yourself, as well as thoughtful (it is indeed too much so) towards me. [44]

Two thousand five hundred copies were printed before the end of the year, and a further 2,000 of *Wholesome Words*. *Foes of Faith* also proved to be a successful venture and went to a reprint of a further 2,000 copies in 1873.

The text of almost all of Vaughan's books had first appeared in the form of sermons and lectures. Two groups deserve special note. The first was a kind of popular, yet scholarly, commentary on books of the N.T. The first volume to appear was in late 1859 on the Greek text of St Paul's Epistle to the Romans with his notes in English – clearly intended for educated gentlemen who had kept up their Greek from school and varsity days. Later two revised editions of it would appear. His *Lectures on the Revelation of St John* were first printed in 1863 and were reprinted in '75 with a new edition in '82. In a letter to a H.E. Hutton [a pupil at Harrow from 1844-47 and on the staff from '55 – '90] written very late at night on 8 February 1865 he gives us a glimpse into his busy life and of how his commentaries came to be written:

We have a famous set of laymen here just now, reading for Orders, ten in number – about half of them Harrow men . . . You must try to get to us at Easter, if it be possible: for there are, as you say, many things which cannot be written, and which yet I should be delighted to talk over . . .

You kindly ask about my Edition of the Epistles: yes, I am hard at work upon it at all times that I can command from other engagements. At present it is the Galatians: for I am now giving a Lecture in the Chancel of the Church (Thursday at 8p.m.) upon that Epistle, and trying to keep up my writing, with the place which I reach week by week in lecturing: at present I have not been able quite to do even this. I find two verses a day as much as I can accomplish for the [Press?]; and if I get 4 days in the week, I am fortunate. I am so glad that you like the beginning of the work. It is very laborious – far more so than it looks when finished. My chief desire is that when done, it should be right and exact and true. [45]

Lightfoot had just published a commentary on *Galatians* and Vaughan wrote a letter full of praise to him on 29 March about it: 'I have been reading with eager interest your Book on the Galatians: doubly interesting to me just now, when I am preparing my humble comment upon it for English Readers . . . how able . . . how candid and judicial – how clear and profound . . . how kindly is its tone.' [46] And he then went on to ask a few questions about details in it.

In December 1864 the first volume of *The Church of the first Days* was published; two more volumes appeared in '65. They contained 56 lectures that he had given in Doncaster on the Acts of the Apostles. These lectures still read well today. This one extract taken from the sermon headed 'A primitive Sunday' based on *Acts* 20.v7 re-lives St Paul's last night at Troy, and, incidentally, reveals Vaughan's own priorities in preaching:

> From towards evening, until a late midnight, St Paul was still speaking to them the words of eternal life. Well can we imagine, from his recorded sermons, and from Epistles still in our possession, what some of his topics were. How would he detail to them, first of all, the revelations which he had also received, concerning Christ crucified and Christ risen. How would he set before them one and but one object of trust; a Saviour dying for our sins, and raised again for our justification. How would he show them again and again, the lost state of man without Christ, and the completeness of him who possesses Christ. How would he expose to them the secret workings of their own sins, and the utter futility of all human efforts, apart from Christ and from grace, to conquer or eradicate them. How would he point them to the cross of Christ for pardon, and to the Spirit of Christ for renewal and life. And then how would he draw out before them the particulars of Christian duty; beginning with its work within, in habits of earnest and life-long prayer; and passing on to its work without, in a faithful discharge of every relation, and in the fulfilment of the all-embracing, the all-explaining, the royal law, of love to God and love to man. [47]

Nearly thirty years later, when a single volume edition of his lectures on *The Church of the First Days* was published, he paid Doncaster a warm compliment. In the preface he described the volume as 'one of several memorials of a nine years' Ministry in one of the kindest and most affectionate of the towns of northern England, and at the same time as a contribution, however humble and unworthy, to the intelligent and practical study of the treasures of Inspired Scripture.' [48]

The second group deserving note were collections of sermons which he had preached before the University of Cambridge. 1861 saw the first volume to be published. A second in 1862, *The Book and the Life*, sold well and went to a second edition together with other varsity sermons two years later. Montagu Butler commented on these in a letter he wrote on Christmas Day 1862 to F.J.A. Hort.

> If you have read his lectures on the Philippians, you will, I am sure, have been struck with his wonderful power of speaking to the <u>hearts</u> of a congregation. In this respect he seems to me quite unequalled among living preachers. All is graceful and simple, deeply earnest and devout. He seems resolved to win a victory, and that not for his own sake. I fancy I trace a marked spiritual progress in his sermons.
>
> In the Cambridge volume there are a few pages which I dislike; but when he gets off speculation, and is thinking simply of securing souls, he speaks as no man now speaks – I doubt whether you will agree in much of this. The defects in his mind, which I admit, will assume with you more serious proportions than they do with me. [49]

The letter's recipient would become one of the century's most able N.T. scholars but just then he was serving as a parish priest in rural Hertfordshire. He had had a scientific training and retained a lifelong interest in the natural sciences and was one of the very first churchmen to welcome Darwin's *Origin of Species*. He read it as soon as it was published and told Westcott he found it 'unanswerable'. This seminal scientific work, however, barely merits a passing mention in Vaughan's writings.

Whilst he made no detailed references in his sermons to the controversies created by its publication and by biblical criticism, he was, of course, aware of them but his faith does not seem to have been seriously challenged or threatened by them. It is clear from a sermon preached later in life that he did not take the Genesis account of creation literally and felt that the opening book of the Bible had nothing to do with scientific discoveries. He advised his hearers not to be alarmed by such discoveries for the Bible had not been given to teach science but to mould the heart of man into the likeness of its Divine author.

He rarely preached on other matters of public note. One exception, however, was the death of Prince Albert, the Prince Consort, in

December 1861. As a chaplain to the Queen, he would have met the Prince on numerous occasions, so the sermon was unusually personal but also quite outspoken about royalty. He knew too that the Prince was not universally popular and that older people could remember how badly the monarchs immediately before Victoria had behaved. He entitled the sermon *The Mourning of the Land, and the Mourning of its Families*. These extracts give the flavour of it:

> The family life of England owes much to the departed Prince – and the national life of England owes much to the departed Prince – and we believe that God's Providence, as well as our own irreparable feelings, bids us this day to treasure up some of the thoughts which are in our hearts concerning him, before we return back to our common tasks and toils in which we must no longer have him before us for our guiding example . . .
> Is it nothing to us that for more than one and twenty years it secured the happiness of the Queen; lightening the pressure of the cares of sovereignty and giving her that rarest blessing of a monarch – a serene, a tranquil, a holy and a restful home . . .
> Dreadful is it to have to tell the young that sin is one of the prerogatives of kings; that they must not imitate it because their rank is not exalted enough for its justification. And there have been times when this dreadful experience has been that of England. A quarter of a century passed in the opposite condition has almost made us forget to give thanks to God for the change. We, the younger half at least of this congregation, have grown up to regard the royal family as a pattern for our own. We no longer wonder at this: we accept it as of course . . .[50]

The sermon was printed at the request of the Mayor and Corporation of Doncaster. Three sermons that he had preached in April and May 1865 entitled *Life's Work and God's Discipline* were printed later that year. The four sermons he preached before the University in November 1866 appeared the following year as *The Wholesome Words of Jesus Christ* to be followed by *Foes of Faith*, the four sermons he delivered in November 1868. That he was repeatedly invited back to Cambridge as a Select Preacher (over 40 times) is a mark of the esteem in which he was held. Whenever he was the preacher great numbers of undergraduates as well as senior members of the University attended. His local paper in Doncaster picked up an item from the *Pall Mall Gazette* of 27 November 1866 which stated 'that the four sermons at Cambridge, by Dr Vaughan, the last of which was preached on Sunday, have attracted larger congregations than those of any preacher since Professor Kingsley delivered his famous discourses on "David".' And it noted that 'The number of ladies present has been something remarkable.'[51]

In one of his university sermons in 1862 he acknowledged that the Bible itself was the battleground of their generation and warned his hearers not to ignore the difficulties, but still to keep their heads amid the rattling storm of Criticism. For an expository preacher of the Gospel, such as himself, there were other priorities as this extract from a sermon in Doncaster illustrates:

> To refuse the Gospel is to refuse life and to choose death. To trifle or to procrastinate with the Gospel is to trifle or to procrastinate with the destinies of eternity. To put aside Christ is to choose sin: and *the wages of sin is death*. It is not with the refinements of modern criticism, and it is not with the intricacies of modern science, that we are concerned here. The question of faith or unbelief is, for us at all events, the question of godliness or sin. [52]

It was such priorities that he sought to impress upon the men who came to read with him at Doncaster. There are two memorial tablets in the chancel of Doncaster Parish Church naming 88 of those who came during his time there – hundreds more would follow in his years at the Temple in London and at the Deanery in Llandaff. Already by 1864 the early 'doves' had left their mark on the church as they paid for a stained glass window in the north wall of the nave commemorating Vaughan's work as a teacher. Not surprisingly the theme of the window is "Hold fast the form of sound words" (2 Timothy 1.13) and pictures some of the great teachers of the past. The wording of the memorial indicates how they saw this work: 'the grateful and loving gift of eighty-eight of those graduates of Oxford and Cambridge who here prepared themselves for Holy Orders under the guidance of the Reverend C.J. Vaughan D.D., Vicar of Doncaster.'

The words *'prepared themselves'* does, in fact, describe what happened. Vaughan did not try to cram them for passing the Bishop's examination – he guided their reading and suggested suitable books but left it to them to do what was necessary. They learnt from his example of scholarship, earnest Biblical preaching, piety and the pastoral care he showed for his parishioners, not least the children in the schools in his parish. Many of his 'doves' were later given high ecclesiastical preferment – 1868 was a vintage year. Its intake included eight future dignitaries, among them four who would become Bishops: G.C. Fisher (Suffragan Bishop of Ipswich), H.W. Yeatman-Biggs (Bishop of Southwark and then of Worcester and Coventry), C.H. Turner (Suffragan Bishop of Islington) and the Hon E.C. Glyn (Bishop of Peterborough). In all, 18 of his men became Bishops, four were appointed as Deans, and 13 as Archdeacons. They included men who served the Church overseas, notably E.A. Parry, Archbishop of the West Indies, and H.H. Montgomery as Bishop of Tasmania (more about him later).

Bullock in his *History of Training for the Ministry of the Church of England* touched, however, on a drawback to the form of preparation that Vaughan offered:

> Those who came under his influence found his teaching most helpful and inspiring. The drawback was that there was little, or no common life, as in a theological college. Each student lived in lodgings by himself, and did not see much of the others except at services and lectures. Vaughan's work with the ordination candidates was entirely personal; no one assisted him with it, and no one followed him after his death. [53]

F.D. How has drawn attention to one of Vaughan's notable strengths in this work of assisting men prepare for ordained ministry. In reading the Scriptures with them and giving them instruction in sermon preparation 'he avoided any interference with a man's special theological bent. He let each one's mind work as freely as possible, and thereby avoiding the narrowing of ideas or the turning out of men entirely of one pattern.' [54] It was said of him that he did not so much teach *what* to think as *how* to think. In effect, he wanted them to think for themselves. One of the first to come to him in Doncaster was George Marsham Argles, the son of a Dean and son-in-law of a Bishop, who had been educated at Harrow under him and then at Balliol. Argles served most of his ministry in York where he became one of its leading clergymen. There he paid Vaughan the compliment of copying his practice by helping men prepare for ordination. The Greek NT he used during the months he spent with Vaughan with all the notes he made on the text still survives in York Minister's archives. Part of its value is that it shows Vaughan's mind on the many books of the NT for which he did not write commentaries.

How quotes the testimony of one of the 'doves': 'He encouraged confidences in all matters of doubt or difficulty, and gave himself pre-eminently to the *spiritual* side of the ministerial work of those whom he trained. A beautiful example was always before them, and their various gifts were consecrated under the guidance of the keenest and most profound discernment of character, and with a compelling earnestness that nothing seemed able to withstand.' [55] Their attachment to him, which continued for decades after they had left him, suggests he had a great gift for friendship. Montagu Butler, who knew him as well as any man did, put it another way. He said in his funeral sermon: 'In these young men the childless man found his children, the old man found his sons. They were the renewal, and more than the renewal, of his Harrow youth, the wings as it were, of his active intellect, the support and comfort and romance of his age.'[56]

Bishop Yeatman-Biggs recalled his time spent with Vaughan:

> The freshness of the Doncaster life was amazing. Imagine some twenty men just down from the University . . . Think of them, for the first time in their lives, teaching in schools, visiting in districts, comparing experiences, and planning attacks on evil, yes, and dreaming future dreams, but yet all the while manly young English gentlemen to the very bone, and you can guess the tone of life at Doncaster. Then there was Dr Vaughan, somewhat the Head Master still, somewhat repressive, a little alarming by reason of a certain quiet academic precision of utterance and a still more quelling precision of listening, but yet entirely sympathetic, and so desirous of bringing out all that was truest and noblest in his men, that not the dullest of them could mistake his intention.
>
> And there was Mrs Vaughan, Stanley's sister, in whose presence commonplaceness found it hard to live, who loved the thoughts which young people love, and could express them in epigram and newness such as they delighted to hear, and yet who never ceased to be the standard of a good woman and a lady, who reverenced her husband. Amidst all this, the young graduates moved and learnt earnestness in such seductive fashion as has fallen to the lot of few . . .
>
> Vaughan liked his men to consider themselves his friends, there by their own will, "free as air," was his expression, but one may fancy that if there had been undue irregularity in the appointed work, there might have come a quiet reminder that freedom might mean freedom to go; yet it was part of the Vicar of Doncaster's remarkable power that no one dreamed of challenging such a reminder, all the more because there was not an ounce of pressure. All this was in itself a most valuable training for life, and men lived under a growing sense of responsibility, none were driven, save by their own consciences, stimulated by one whom in all ways they could respect . . .[57]

He did not accept all and sundry to read with him. He wanted only earnest and diligent men of good moral character. They usually came to him on the recommendation of others already known to him. Lightfoot, for example, recommended a man in January 1866 and Vaughan replied:

I cannot hesitate to express my willingness to receive here one of whom you speak so highly.

I have only just to say that I could not take anyone for less than 6 months of actual residence here.

You will kindly say to him that there are no payments whatsoever here, except what it costs a man to board and lodge himself.

If, when you have quite done with his letter, you are so kind as to let me have it again, it might be of use to me in forming an idea of the man – of course in strict confidence. You will judge. [58]

Vaughan corresponded with his men long after they had left him. A fine example of this is the extant collection of letters which he started writing to Sedley Taylor in September 1861, who had been one of the first to respond to his sermon. Vaughan seems to have developed a particular affection for this young man. Taylor had graduated 16th Wrangler in 1859. He was appointed to the curacy of St Michael's Handsworth, Birmingham in 1863 but gave up the following year to return to Trinity where he served as Junior Bursar 1866-69 and College Librarian 1870-71. The letters cover the period 1861-69.

In his answer to Taylor's initial letter of enquiry Vaughan was keen to dampen any exaggerated ideas that he might have about what was on offer in Doncaster:

You will provide yourself with lodgings in Doncaster, and be your own Master in all respects. I should hope to give you some little help in your reading as far as the Greek Testament is concerned – and such Advice as I am capable of with regard to your theological reading generally. I should propose to assign to you a district for visiting among the poor, and you would be very welcome in the Schools of the Parish as far as your time would permit. [59]

A fortnight later Vaughan wrote to congratulate him on his election as a Fellow of Trinity and offered him hospitality at the Vicarage for a few days while 'looking for an abode.' Taylor duly joined the small group of men preparing for ordination though he seems to have stayed only for a few months. By May 1862 Vaughan was advising him about possible curacies in London but warned him off one particular church whose congregation he described as 'frightfully touchy.' In a letter dated 15 May 1862, he recommended that he be ordained at Ely (presumably on the strength of his College Fellowship) and added 'you will then be able to look about you quietly afterwards. And as long as you can stay at

Doncaster you will know that your presence will be welcome and delightful to us all – and not least to your sincere and faithful friend Charles Vaughan.'[60]

The following month, he wrote to him on the eve of his ordination to the Diaconate: 'We all think much of you, and shall do so tomorrow. I trust that your mind has been at peace, during this week of special preparation – and that a very large and life-long blessing will rest upon your Ordination.'[61] He then went on to urge him to serve a curacy with Alfred Blomfield:

> Son of the late Bishop of London – a Fellow of All Souls – a Classical 1st Class at Oxford, and formerly Scholar of Balliol. He was at Harrow under me. He is a singularly clever man, and thoroughly good, I believe, also! A most agreeable companion, and full of genial kindness. I strongly advise your closing with his offer. I do not know a man so likely to suit you in all respects . . . [62]

He also offered to write to Blomfield about Taylor – possibly to alert him to the man's indifferent health and his preoccupation with living either with or near his mother. In the event Taylor rejected Vaughan's advice (something he did repeatedly in after years). The reason was two-fold: Blomfield had wanted him to be responsible for a district of 5,000 souls and he would have been too far away from his mother.

A brief note dated 2 May 1863 again indicates the closeness of their relationship: 'My dear Taylor, A single line to tell you what joy your letter gives us in the prospect of seeing you here on Monday. You have no idea how welcome you will be. Ever affectionately Charles Vaughan.'[63] He continued to be generous in his support and encouragement but ready to write critically when he felt it necessary.

By 1869 Taylor was having a crisis of conscience about clerical subscription; he declined to be ordained Priest and resigned his Fellowship at Trinity. He also absented himself from the reunion of 'doves' and curates in Doncaster that summer prior to Vaughan's departure from the parish. Vaughan still tried to keep the relationship alive and in July that year sought to support him in his decisions and added 'but I trust that in <u>London</u> you will let us feel that we are still your old and unchanged friends. Ever affectionately C.J. Vaughan'[64] In what appears to have been his last letter to Taylor, dated 12 October 1869, Vaughan again wrote supportively: 'But you have done what you felt to be right – and may God bless you' and begged him 'not to wander further than you can help from the faith in which you and I once worshipped together.' [65]

Some of the first men who came to read with him stayed on at his invitation as Curates. Apart from one who received £120 funded by the Ecclesiastical Commissioners, he had to pay them from his own income and the going rate was £100 p.a. paid in quarterly instalments. During his nine years in Doncaster Vaughan was assisted by 14 newly ordained curates in addition to the two whom he 'inherited' when he arrived. The Archbishop ordained candidates at Bishopthorpe where he resided and his registers record that the following men were licensed to serve in Vaughan's parish. Their licences usually state that they had to reside within the parish – non-residence, particularly by Incumbents, had been a major problem earlier in the century. Occasionally a licence notes that the candidate is replacing a previous curate. In three cases, Sainsbury, Smith and Glyn, Vaughan paid just a nominal stipend of five shillings. And in Trebeck's and Morton's case the clause concerning the stipend is crossed through. This is the full list of his assistant curates:

Evelyn Joseph Hone ordained Deacon 21.12. 1860, Priest '61
John George Wood ordained Deacon 16.1.61, Priest '62
James John Trebeck ordained Deacon 22.9.61, Priest '62
Thomas Fitzharding Morton ordained Deacon 22.12.61, Priest '62
Joseph Games Gibbs ordained Deacon 1.3.63, Priest '64
Robert Sainsbury ordained Deacon 2.12.63, Priest '64
Albert Smith ordained Deacon 31.7.64, Priest '65
Ernest Wigram ordained Deacon 11.6.65, Priest '66
Edward William Chapman ordained Deacon 24.12.65, Priest '66
Henry Charles Russell ordained Deacon 23.12.66, Priest '67
Francis Henry Walker ordained Deacon 16.6.67, Priest '68
Frederick Fox Lambert ordained Deacon 11.2.68, Priest '69
The Hon. Edward Carr Glyn ordained Deacon 27.9.68, Priest '69
The Hon. Francis Godolphin Pelham ordained Deacon 23.5.69, Priest '70 [66]

The Archbishop's registers include the candidate's references, the certificate showing in which churches his *Si Quis* had been read out (which gave parishioners the opportunity to register objections) and the formal agreement between Vaughan and the curate about residence and stipend and signed by both men. In the case of Russell, for example, who was a nephew of the Prime Minister, Lord John Russell, his first reference was signed by the Master of Trinity College Cambridge and the eight senior Fellows and the second by Vaughan and two other local incumbents who had known him personally for eighteen months and could vouch for his character and orthodox views. There is also the agreement he made with his future Vicar and penned by Vaughan himself. It reads as follows:

To the Most Reverend Father in God William by Divine Providence Lord Archbishop of York.

These are to certify your Grace that I Charles John Vaughan Vicar of Doncaster in the County of York and your Grace's Diocese of York do hereby nominate Henry Charles Russell, Bachelor of Law, of Trinity College in the University of Cambridge to perform the office of Curate in my Church of Doncaster aforesaid and do promise to allow him the yearly Stipend of one hundred pounds to be paid by equal quarterly payments. And I do hereby state to your Grace that the said Henry Charles Russell intends to reside in the said Parish in a House situated in Hall Gate in Doncaster distant from my Church not more than one quarter of a mile: that the said Henry Charles Russell does not intend to serve as Curate any other Parish, nor to officiate in any other Church or Chapel: and I do hereby promise and engage with your Grace and the said Henry Charles Russell that I will continue to employ the said Henry Charles Russell in the office of Curate in my said Church until he shall be otherwise provided of some other ecclesiastical preferment, unless for any fault by him committed he shall be lawfully removed from the same: and I hereby solemnly declare that I do not fraudulently write this certificate to entitle the said Henry Charles Russell to receive Holy Orders but with a real intention to employ him in my said Church according to what is here expressed.

Witness my hand this twenty ninth day of November in the year of our Lord 1866. Charles J Vaughan

We the before named Charles John Vaughan and Henry Charles Russell do declare to the said Lord Archbishop of York as follows; namely, I the said Charles John Vaughan do declare that I *bona Fide* intend to pay and I the said Henry Charles Russell do declare that I *bona Fide* intend to receive the whole actual stipend mentioned in the foregoing nomination and statement without any deduction or reservation whatever.

Witness our hands this twenty ninth day of November, 1866.

Charles J. Vaughan

H.C. Russell [67]

That legal agreement expresses one aspect of the relationship between an Incumbent and his Assistant Curate, that of employer and employee. Equally important was how they actually related to each other day by day as colleagues. Vaughan seems to have enjoyed good and friendly relationships with his junior colleagues (some of whom he had known as schoolboys). In a letter to Sedley Taylor written in March 1863 he mentions George Wood, for example, one of Taylor's contemporaries in Doncaster: 'Wood is far more vigorous, and his sermons more lively than before; he is a most admirable Curate. We are just trying to get the Union Chaplaincy for him on Mr Wilton's going to Worksop – where he has got a small living.' [68]

He gave his considered assessment of the Vicar: Curate relationship in a paper about ministerial training which he read many years later at a Church Congress.

> One closing word must be given to the subsequent training. We understand by this the office of the older ministry to the younger, to use the poor speech of the day, the voice of the incumbent to his curate. What shall I have to say of this? Let it be at once brotherly and fatherly; in other words, at once truthful and helpful. I counsel no foolish complimenting, at the cost of the congregations, as to an equal use of the pulpit or an alternate precedence in the administration of the Sacraments. This is unreal talk and unwise conduct. But I do advise that that each youngest curate should have his own charge, and know it. It may be the smallest and humblest of chapels or schoolrooms, it may be the poorest and most remote of hamlets and districts, and neither the one nor the other should be barred for a moment against the entrance of his chief; only let him feel, as hearts feel without words, that in his own department he is trusted, that no suspicious eye watches, and no jealous ear listens. Thus youthful ministers grow – thus the Church recreates itself. Yet above even trust I place help. A young minister feels himself a child in the face of souls. The last thing he desires is to be treated as if he were perfect and entire, wanting nothing. To be told to go and do his best, to be told that he must "use his own judgement", to be told that he "do this, that, and everything else perfectly well" – has been the moral paralysis of many a young deacon. For this kind of treatment he would gladly take in exchange any imperiousness of direction and any severity of reproof. This is coldness, this is indifference, this is selfishness in disguise. [69]

One of the many things his students and curates would have learned from him was the benefit to be gained from, as well as the need to give support to, the Church of England's many evangelistic, mission and aid agencies. Vaughan personally supported the overseas work of the evangelical Church Missionary Society, and the more high church Society for the Propagation of the Gospel, and of the 'home mission' organisation called the Church Pastoral Aid Society. He helped inaugurate a branch of the Church Teachers' Association in the town. He was elected

President of the Doncaster branch of the Missions to Seamen, chaired meetings of the Religious Tract Society and was a keen supporter of the local branch of the British and Foreign Bible Society. The Church's oldest mission agency, the Society for the Promotion of Christian Knowledge founded in 1698, and the more recent Society for Promoting Christianity among the Jews (1809) both included him among their supporters. He chaired meetings of the Young Men's Christian Association and supported its educational work. There seems to have been no end to his energy and well-doing! His talents were also used extra-parochially – he served as a member of the Durham University Commission set up in 1862 and in 1868 he sat on a Commission looking into scientific education in the army. For an educationalist with no apparent interest in science, that was an odd appointment!

In 1868 he was involved in setting up a free town library in the old Grammar School buildings – again using his influence with the Corporation to bring this about and later to fund it through the rates. He proposed Henry Charles Hammond as the first Librarian who was appointed at a salary of £75 p.a. In addition, he established his own parish library of about 400 books which were housed in St George's School.

Offers of preferment were made and rejected. Stanley wrote to Tait, the Bishop of London, at the request of his brother-in-law, on 13 November 1862 about one such offer:

> My dear Bishop
> On Monday last (the 10th) Vaughan received from Lord Palmerston the offer of the Bishopric of Gloucester, and declined it immediately, saying that he had two years ago determined on devoting himself to parochial life for some years, and that experience had confirmed that decision.
> He wishes you to know this – not that it may be talked about, but that, if it is talked about, you may know what has taken place. [70]

News of this offer did get out and Lake wrote to him about it. Vaughan replied on 21 November:

> I value your kind words about the bishopric. It grieves me to vex my friends by a seeming waywardness in such matters; they must do their best to believe that I would not act thus except from a strong sense of its being right for me; at present I am fully at work where I am, and desire no change either for greater dignity or greater usefulness. But *do* not imagine that I undervalue the other and higher office in either respect. [71]

According to Mowbray, Vaughan was also offered the Deanery of Westminster in 1862 and declined it 'largely because he did not feel at home in the social atmosphere into which such a position inevitably took him. But he was happy to go to the Temple where he was unfettered, where he would have the type of congregation that appealed to him, and where he could also carry on the work begun at Doncaster of training ordinands.' [72] He is probably correct in his judgement about the Temple but certainly not about Westminster as A.P. Stanley was offered the post by Palmerston on 8 November. His correspondence shows that he was already anticipating this in September. Whatever it was that Vaughan had declined (almost certainly the See of Gloucester and not the Deanery of Westminster), the *Chronicle* wrote approvingly on 13 November 1862:

> This remarkable instance of self-denial speaks for itself: it teaches a useful and salutary lesson – that the richest and most coveted prizes, and the greatest honours, do not always possess irresistible charm. Personally we rejoice at the decision of the worthy Vicar, and no one can have listened to the fervid eloquence, and observed the heartfelt interest Dr Vaughan manifests for the spiritual and temporal welfare of his flock, without admiring his singular disinterestedness. [73]

Years later the *Pall Mall Gazette* claimed he had also been offered the Bishopric of Ceylon in 1862.

In January 1864 Lake's mother died shortly after his father. Vaughan naturally wrote to express his sympathy and made mention of how kind she had been to him – presumably as a schoolboy and as a student. The theme of ecclesiastical preferment came up in the same letter,

> And, dear Lake, how can I thank you enough for your words of sympathy and confidence? I will indeed pray for you as I can, but my prayers are poor and sinful, and I am utterly unworthy to be ever anything more than I am in the Church of Christ.
>
> Do not think that I act from *whim or caprice* [i.e. in refusing the bishopric of Ely] in the course which I have taken, and to which I feel I must adhere. But I think that my mind is too well known to make it at all probable that I should again be compelled to express it.
>
> Cherish towards me the old kindness and believe that I feel towards you as ever. Your friendship is precious to me, and not the less because we have so seldom the opportunity of expressing it in actual intercourse.
>
> But there is surely a life of rest after this sinful turmoil, and there may we be together at last!

Ever your truly affectionate, Chas. J. Vaughan
I have not half said what I would of your great bereavement, but you *know* that I do not like to write a mere commonplace of sympathy. [74]

In March 1866 Whewell, the Master of Trinity College Cambridge, died. The *London Standard* reported on the 8th that rumours were already circulating about who would succeed him. Of the four names mentioned, Vaughan's was placed first. Lightfoot wrote to Vaughan to sound him out about his becoming a possible successor. He replied, marking his letter Private:

> Mr dear Dr Lightfoot
> I am deeply touched by your letter.
> I hope it is needless to tell you how strong an attachment I feel to our great College, or how noble a work I feel to lie before its new Master.
> But I also feel most distinctly that that great work is not for me.
> Years ago it might have been otherwise. But I could not now resume the responsibilities of an Educational life, on so large a scale, & with such interests involved.
> I hope & believe that no such offer will be made to me. It would cost me much to refuse it, & I would gladly be spared the pain (and in some quarters the reproach) of doing so.
> While you were writing to me, I was writing about you to others.
> May the decision, whatever it be, have a blessing upon it.
> Have the heartfelt gratitude of your obliged and faithful
> Chas J. Vaughan [75]

Catherine told Dalrymple in a letter dated 28 October 1867 about another offer of preferment that her husband had refused: 'Dr Vaughan has been offered the Deanery of Exeter – But he did not wish to leave Doncaster & I cannot say I much regret it.' [76] A year later, Tait took soundings to see if Vaughan would now accept a bishopric (Lichfield was vacant at the time) and was told firmly by Dudley Ryder, the Earl of Harrowby, that he 'decidedly objects to the idea of taking the Bishopric, that there is no use in proposing it. He strongly urges Lightfoot.' [77]

He also figured in matters of preferment in a different role. His advice was sought by patrons who wished to appoint good men to livings in their gift. In April 1869, for example, Lord Spencer wrote asking for his advice about a particular man whom he had in mind for such an appointment. Vaughan replied:

> Reginald Hibbert is as nice as possible. A little artistic, very musical, not (I trust and believe) ritualistic.
> He is, as you say, a man of good sense – much liked as a Clergyman – persuasive and impressive, I believe, in ministry.
> I do not think you could do better than take him. Blomfield no – Walrond no – both provided for – or, at all events busy in London. [78]

He was inevitably invited to be a guest preacher on behalf of a variety of charities and good causes but did not always accept. In March 1867, for example, he declined an invitation from Sir J.F. Pollock to preach at the anniversary of the Foundlings Hospital: 'I much regret to say that the state of my health and a multitude of home engagements compel me to decline for this year all invitations of this nature which are not rendered imperative by some claim of actual duty.' [79] He even declined invitations from influential old friends such as Lord Spencer who got a polite 'No' on at least two occasions. The last one for which he solicited financial support was on Sunday morning 11 July 1869. The object he needed their money for was the school-cum-chapel which he had established at Marshgate in the poorest part of the parish. The result of his brief appeal at the end of the sermon in the morning was not very good so he pressed the need more urgently and at greater length at the end of his sermon in the evening:

> I am commending to-day to your Christian bounty a School-Church, or a Church-School, erected some three years ago in a distant quarter of the Parish. It has answered all our hopes, as regards the number of its scholars. About a hundred children have been present Sunday by Sunday – scarcely fewer week-day by week-day – for instruction in the things of time and the things of eternity. At this moment, its Sunday service with the Holy Communion, is being celebrated amidst a population before unfavourably situated for attendance upon any public ordinances of the Church. Hitherto we have been enabled to support the School and the Church, without any subscription-list, by this one annual almsgiving. But the bounty of this evening must far exceed that of the morning, if this hope is to be realized once again. The utmost economy cannot bring the expenditure within thirty or five-and-thirty pounds a year, in addition to the weekly payments of the children. I beg you, with great earnestness, not to be wanting to us at this crisis. Let the pathetic charge of Jesus in both its parts - *Feed my sheep* - *Feed my lambs* - be audible and persuasive to your hearts tonight. [80]

So much for his many good works done publicly. What about his private, home life? In the absence of any extant diaries and family correspondence it is hard to imagine what life in the Vaughan household was like but this one anecdote provides a glimpse. The Hon. George Russell once stayed with the Vaughans at Doncaster when he was a schoolboy and he recorded this entertaining if not very flattering anecdote of life in the Vicarage as experienced by him in about 1868. The story does, however, show that the great man was not in fact as imperturbable as his public persona suggested and it tells how Catherine dealt with him:

> My only brother was one of his curates; the Vaughans asked my mother to stay with them at the Vicarage, in order that she might see her son, then newly ordained, at his work; and the visit falling in the Harrow holiday, they good-naturedly said she might bring me with her. Dr Vaughan was always exceedingly kind to boys, and one morning, on our way back from the daily service, he said to me – "Sir Grosvenor Le Draughte [not his real name] has proposed to break his journey here, on his return from Scotland. Do you know him? No? Well – observe Sir Grosvenor. He is well worthy of observation. He is exactly what the hymn-book calls 'a worldling'." The day advanced and no Sir Grosvenor appeared. The Doctor came into the drawing room repeatedly, asking if "that tiresome old gentleman had arrived," and Mrs Vaughan plied him with topics of consolation – "Perhaps he has missed his train. Perhaps there has been an accident. Perhaps he has been taken ill on the journey" – but the Doctor shook his head and refused to be comforted. After dinner, we sat in an awe-struck silence, while the Vaughans, knowing the hour at which the last train from Scotland came in, and the length of time which it took to drive from the station, listened with ears erect. Presently the wheels of a fly came rumbling up, and Dr Vaughan exclaiming, "Our worst anticipations are realized!" hurried to the front door. Then, welcoming the aged traveller with open arms, he said in his blandest tones – "Now, my dear Sir Grosvenor, I know you must be dreadfully tired. You shall go to bed at once." Sir Grosvenor, who longed to sit up till midnight, telling anecdotes and drinking brandy-and-water, feebly remonstrated; but the remorseless Doctor led his unwilling captive upstairs. It was a triumph of the *Suaviter in modo*, and gave me an impressive lesson on the welcome which awaits self-invited guests, even when they are celebrities. [81]

During his years in Doncaster, he had enjoyed a good working relationship with the Town Council and, as we have seen, they had frequently supported projects he had suggested to them and accepted his advice. He did not, however, always get his way with the councillors. On the last day of 1868 he wrote to the Mayor imploring him to use his influence with them to reject a motion soon to be brought before them that the grant towards the cost of the Races in September should be increased. The letter was reproduced a week later in the *Gazette*.

My dear Mr Mayor

I learn, on authority which I cannot question, that a proposal will be submitted tomorrow to the Town Council for the augmentation of the annual grant in aid of the races.

You will bear me witness that I have not been eager or fanatical in denouncing that great national gathering to which Doncaster owes a large part of its celebrity.

I have earnestly laboured to hope on, even against hope, that the abuse of the system might yet be proved to be separable from its use: and that so an amusement in which thousands doubtless participate without intention or consequence of evil might come to be regarded by Christian people with a less sweeping and indiscriminate reprobation.

But I cannot be blind, as a Christian and a clergyman, to the many social and moral evils which, as a matter of fact, attend the races, and of which the permanent inhabitants of this town are left to reap throughout the year the bitter fruits. And I must take leave to remonstrate, respectfully but firmly against the perpetual renewal of the attempt to lay a heavier and yet heavier burden upon the borough fund for the maintenance and encouragement of racing.

Into the legality of this application of our public resources it is not my office to enter. It may be questioned, I imagine, whether any justification can be found for such a largesse, so long as there lies upon the inhabitants of the borough any rate or impost of a public nature for the supply of water or light to our streets and homes. But of this I am persuaded, that he is the best friend to the permanent interests of Doncaster, who labours to turn the energy and intelligence of our people into those common channels of honest industry and lawful commerce, in which there is the least possible encouragement to indolent vice or reckless venture.

And I would entreat you, my dear Mr Mayor, to use your influence with the powerful and honourable body over which you so ably preside, against a proposition which, I am well assured, would find little support in the wishings (*sic*) and feelings of the majority of our independent and disinterested fellow townsmen.

He preached against it from the pulpit of St George's and spoke against it at the Mayor's Banquet in the Mansion House but to no avail and he had to endure some hurtful criticism for his intervention. The races were simply too important economically to the town. He was not alone, however, in his opposition – 'The Rev John Campion of St James' Church reported to the Archbishop that racing more than anything else impeded his work and the Vicar of Christ Church, the Rev H.F. Brock, wrote in 1868 that Doncaster races were the curse of the town.' [82] In the spring of 1869 Vaughan was still smarting under this public rejection of his advice and moral leadership, so the invitation and opportunity to move south came as a Godsend. It is possible - even likely - that he initiated the process of being nominated for the Mastership of the Temple. What we do know for sure is that he wrote to Gladstone on 1 May in terms which show that his brother-in-law, Stanley, had already spoken to the Prime Minister on his behalf.

> The Dean of Westminster has communicated to me the conversation that you were good enough to hold with him in reference to my appointment to the Mastership of the Temple.
> I desire to say that, after the fullest consideration of the circumstances which you desired me to take into account in entertaining the thought of that position, I am prepared thankfully to accept it, if it should be consistent with your sense of duty to nominate me to the vacant post.
> I am beginning to find the charge of this large Parish, and the ministry of this great Church, a somewhat heavy tax upon my strength after many years service of the Church here and at Harrow and I trust that I might do some good though humble work in the Mastership of the Temple if it should be in your power to confer upon me that honourable preferment. I have enough to live upon, and desire only some charge in which I may serve the Church and its Master during the remaining years of my active life. [83]

Three days later he wrote again, having already had a confirmatory reply from the Prime Minister.

> I deeply feel the kindness of your letter.
> I fear that my communication was quite premature but you have been good enough to forgive my impatience.
> It would be a satisfaction to me if the opportunity should arise for mentioning the subject to the Queen before Her Majesty's departure for Scotland. But this is in kind and wise hands; and in the meantime I will regard your letter as confidential and refrain from mentioning the subject to any of my friends until I have your express permission to do so.
> I will only add, yet once more, the expression of my sincere gratitude to you for the prospect of an opening which I cannot but regard with a peculiar interest.
> Believe me, my dear Sir, with the deepest respect,
> Your faithful and obliged Servant   Charles Vaughan

PS I ought perhaps to add that the Dean of Westminster and one other friend were aware beforehand of the possibility of the appointment. But I do not think that the knowledge of what has passed can possibly extend to more than three or four people. [84]

On 30 June 1869 Catherine wrote to her cousin Louisa to share the joyful news that they would soon be heading south:

I have now a little piece of news to give you which I think will gladden your hearts in the midst of your sadness. [Her sister Lucy and brother Edward had died that year.] It is that we are about to be restored to our friends and to leave Doncaster for ever!
This day has the Mastership of the Temple been offered – and thankfully accepted. Only £100 a year – and a house in the Temple but a position of unbounded influence – and a life of interest and leisure which is just the very thing he wants after all the hard years of the treadmill he has been going through. We shall live in the Temple – but keep Southborough for our suburban retreat – and a home for the dogs. I am so happy dear Louisa I do not know what to do. For grieved though I am to leave this place – still: the new life is delightful to think of. [85]

Two days later the *Doncaster Chronicle* published the text of a letter which Vaughan had written to the Mayor. In it he described his new post as 'an office of no emolument' but one that offered him 'the prospect of some usefulness, with God's blessing, for the later years of my life.' He added 'I have felt of late an increasing sense of the weight of the parochial charge which has here lain upon me; and although the parting will be bitter to me in the extreme, I do most earnestly hope that God will raise up the right man to follow me in the charge of my beloved Church and people.' The *Chronicle* bitterly lamented his leaving:

There is not a man, woman or child in this place, who will not feel, if indeed they have not already felt, they are about to lose a near and dear friend – one who in some way or other has made himself known to each one of them, making them somewhat happier, more contented, more prosperous, less of strangers to one another, more of friends and brothers, and fellow-workers. Not one who is old enough to understand can resist the depressing, dejected feeling which we confess is upon us as we write – a feeling which seems to say that we, as a community, are being deprived of our very centre and mainspring – are about to lose the most real and active presence, the best, highest, purist, and noblest influence that ever blest a community like us. It is a calamity for the town . . . [86]

If the tone of that article sounds gushingly exaggerated to our ears today, the fact is it does reflect the influential role that the incumbent of the parish church in an urban community could and in many cases did exercise in the Victorian age. This small northern town recognized that it had been privileged to be served by a priest of extraordinary talent and energy for the past nine years. It paid tribute to him in a variety of ways – one of the houses at the Grammar School was named Vaughan's, an avenue was named after him, and a large portrait of him was commissioned for the Mansion House in 1878. After his death in 1897 Old Boys of the School erected a tablet in the library 'As a token of their affection and regard in recognition of the invaluable services rendered by him in the restoration of this ancient Grammar School AD 1862'. It still hangs in what is now the Upper School Campus library of Hall Cross Academy. In addition, there were windows and memorial tablets in St George's church erected in his honour. The church also has a fine portrait of him. In more recent times, from 1953 to 1964, there was an annual Vaughan Memorial Lecture given by a noted scholar – the series ended, however, following the allegations made by Phyllis Grosskurth in her biography of Symonds.

He let it be known that he did not wish to receive any personal leaving gift from the parish but that did not stop well-wishers donating £435. 16s. 6d [= £43,930], which was almost equal to a year's stipend, to a Testimonial Fund. Vaughan deposited it in the hands of the Mayor, Aldermen and Burgesses and directed that the interest earned on it was to be used for Testimonial Prizes to be given to scholars at the Grammar School for such subjects as the trustees determined.

As he prepared for his own move to a new sphere of ministry, he was also trying to help his friends Westcott and Lightfoot. The former had been appointed to a Canonry at Peterborough Cathedral in January but was not happy as the job was not defined and he questioned what the proper functions of a cathedral were, and there was no house so he would be separated from his family when his turn as canon-in-residence came. He had shared all this with his old school and college friend Lightfoot who wrote to Vaughan about him. Vaughan replied on 22 July:

> I should indeed rejoice to see Westcott placed <u>anywhere</u> in a post of honour & usefulness, and I feel that he must be rescued <u>somehow</u> from his present scheme of self-destruction & family slaughter in the Stall at Peterborough!
>
> In these complicated political times, it is not everyone who can approach

Gladstone with an Ecclesiastical Candidate. If anything should suggest itself I will not lose sight of it. But I cannot do it <u>myself</u> for some obvious reasons.

I should think Moberley a very probable D of D [Dean of Durham]

You do not congratulate me, I perceive, on my change of work & home?

Promise to let me know from yourself, if <u>you</u> are offered Durham – before you say No. [87]

The Bishop of Peterborough offered Westcott the post of Archdeacon of Northampton in June 1870 but, on the advice of Lightfoot, he wisely declined it. Then largely through the active support of Lightfoot at Cambridge, he was elected the new Regius Professor of Divinity on All Saints Day 1870 and so entered on that 'post of honour & usefulness' that Vaughan had so desired for his old colleague.

One of the many who did write to congratulate Vaughan on his move south was Christopher Wordsworth, the Bishop of Lincoln. In his reply, dated 14 August, he gave some indication of his hopes for this new post:

It is so refreshing to hear from one who recognizes the position which I trust God has given me as a <u>work</u> at <u>all</u> – not as a <u>dereliction</u> of duty, a <u>shrinking</u> from work – and who therefore can bid me "God speed" with a real meaning in his words.

I hope to find it a very real, though not overwhelming work, and to combine with it, even in London, that which has become a second nature to me here – the training of young men for Holy Orders.

I trust that I shall be able to dispense with any supplementary preferment, and to give myself wholly, in a modest way, to this one thing.

The thought of your Lordship's sympathy is a very true encouragement to me. [88]

His nephew later singled out three reasons why the move south was such a welcome one: 'he was conscious that he would have the more strength and leisure left for what he was coming more and more to regard as the main work of his life, the preparation of young men for the ministry. He was also pardonably glad, and perhaps his wife, who had brilliant social gifts, was still more so, to be brought once more into connection with the stirring society of London.' [89] He also saw it as a return to a teaching ministry but now his teaching would be directed 'to a special end, and that it was more closely connected with the service of ministry.' [90]

The Archbishop offered the living (now valued at £650 according to the *Hull Packet*) to Dr Francis Pigou who visited the town prior to accept-

263

ing the appointment. The Vaughans did not give him much encouragement, rather the reverse!

On my arrival I was first introduced to Mrs Vaughan, who characteristically thus welcomed me. "I knew," she said, as I entered the drawing room, "that a distinguished visitor was coming." "Pray," I replied, "do not call me a *distinguished* visitor." "I cannot do otherwise," she replied, "because whenever we have a distinguished visitor coming, we always have one or two bad smells: one from a bone manure factory, the other from a tanyard. You must be *very* distinguished, because we have <u>both</u> bad smells today!" What could I say, as I stood in that drawing room, with those bad smells pervading the room? "Do you think," she proceeded to say, "of coming here? If you do, I pity you from the bottom of my heart. There will be days when you will certainly wish to <u>commit</u> <u>suicide</u>!" . . . Nor did I receive much more encouragement from Dr Vaughan. We sat up together far into the night discussing the matter. How well I remember Vaughan saying to me sadly, "If you come, it will probably be shortly after the races. I feel that the races undo all my work of nine years. There is something peculiarly paralysing to all spiritual work in a town that lives, like Doncaster, on races . . . [91]

Pigou went on to become Dean of Bristol and it is to his credit that in his memoirs he placed Vaughan's ministry in Doncaster way above his own saying he had raised the town 'to a level which it had not before his time, and has not had since.' [92]

One of several special services prior to his departure was held on Tuesday evening 24 August when a very large number of his former students and curates returned to St George's. They had come from almost every diocese in the country and Vaughan rightly described it as 'an unprecedented gathering'. The scores of clergy present were all robed in surplices and academic hoods. The civic authorities recognized its importance and had turned out in support as had many parishioners. The printed edition of his sermon lists the 114 clergy who had been invited. Vaughan was deeply moved by this public show of affection and appreciation. He had chosen as his text 1 Peter 5. v1 'The elders [i.e. priests] which are among you I exhort, who am also an elder' and his words were directed primarily at the large number of clergymen present whose priestly formation had been shaped in part by himself. Here is a taste of the wise advice on 'divine humanity' which he must have shared with them privately many times in the past and now offered again to his younger brothers in the Ministry there that evening:

The secret of all influence is, Be human. The moment that the Clergyman wraps himself in his dignity, parades his authority, tries to speak the tongue not of men but of Angels, thinks it gain to be thought (as his people are willing enough to think him) one of a different mould, far more pure, far more ethereal by nature than their own, that moment he loses all access, all true influence – if for no other reason, because he is then forgetting that Christ Himself, his Divine Master, when He came to redeem, *took not on Him the nature of Angels*, but was made in all points like unto His brethren, that He might bear their sorrows and carry their sicknesses.

One word of genuine kindness, of hearty compassionate sympathy, will be worth ten thousand expositions of your claim to reverence: it will open hearts otherwise barred against you, and, letting you in, will let in Christ after you; will prepare the way for your Gospel, and make men feel when you die that there has been an Evangelist and a Physician amongst them.

And as in your intercourse, so also in your preaching. Let it indeed assert strongly, far more strongly than in these days is usual, the direct revelation and inspiration of your Gospel. Claim for it the acceptance of your hearers as that superadded gift of God, above reason and conscience, above education and genius, whereby He has enlightened the darkness of nature and removed the veil spread over all nations. But, in the enforcement, in the application of this Divine Gospel, speak as a man to men; speak as one who knows the nature, the life, the heart, to which he has to offer it, and has learned, not from books but from men – in the cottage, in the hospital, yea, in the study too, and the chamber – what is that deep-seated disease, what is that vice and crooked bias of Nature and of the Fall, what is that heart-sickness too, and eager inward thirst, to which Christ his Lord came to minister, and has of his infinite mercy set him to minister in his absence, in His presence! [93]

He met with his men again early next morning for a celebration of Holy Communion and at 11 they all gathered in the 'Long Room' at the Vicar-age when he said 'a few words on some topics connected with Clerical work.' This first reunion provided a blue-print for others to come later.

Vaughan preached his last sermons at the morning and evening services on Sunday 5 September – there were 108 communicants at his last celebration of Holy Communion which followed the vastly better attended service of Morning Prayer. He had still one more duty to perform as Vicar. On Tuesday the 7th he officiated at the funeral of W.H. Forman, a generous benefactor of St George's and of the town. Catherine and he were at last free to leave for their private residence near Tunbridge Wells.

He wrote later that month to Alexander Macmillan to tell him that he was pushing on with the revision of *Revelation* Vol. 2 but also to explain why he had chosen another publisher for his last Doncaster sermons: 'Strahan have my Farewell Sermon in hand with those of the last two months, in a little Volume. I was anxious for extreme cheapness this time, and went to them partly on that account.' [94]

The staff and pupils of the Grammar School had penned an address to him on his departure. There are phrases and Biblical references in it which would have warmed his heart as a pastor and preacher:

> Reverend and Dear Sir – We, the masters and boys of the Doncaster Grammar School, many of whom have also long been your parishioners, wish to be allowed, in the brief language of genuine sorrow, to express our deep and most respectful regret, that our connection with you is now so soon to terminate. Words of commendation would ill become us, when addressing one of whom even a nation speaks – rather do we offer words of gratitude; and we further pray that you may, even in this life, by faith, enjoy the fruition of that benediction, for which is all our warfare – "Well done, good and faithful servant". Words of affectionate gratitude, however, are never out of place; and these shall form our simple offering for all the advantages we have enjoyed at your hands. The seed sown may not all have been seen to sprout by the eye of the sower; but if, as we believe, the Kingdom of Nature but ill illustrates in this respect the Kingdom of Grace, may we not hope, that much of that seed may yet meet with the dew of heaven and the warmth, which shall furnish the occasion, and so produce abundant fruit even after your departure?
>
> We will, therefore, hope that "at that day" you may experience a happy surprise in the abundance of the harvest of your own individual labours.
>
> For ourselves, we cannot but feel the deep responsibilities under which we lie, in having so long listened to your words.
>
> Receive, therefore, reverend and dear sir, this simple expression of our affection and of our sorrow for your departure among us; and allow us to remain still amongst the numbers of your sincere, grateful and respectful friends.

The address was signed by the Headmaster, three other members of staff and 126 boys.

Although he had declined any parting gift, the Mayor, C.W. Hatfield, was determined that something fitting should be crafted and presented at a later date. He was chiefly instrumental in having a testimonial inscribed on six pages of vellum and housed in a 'very handsome casket of polished oak, surmounted by the crest and monogram of Dr and Mrs Vaughan, richly carved and gilt. The illuminated portion, as a work of art, cannot be too highly spoken of. The style is that of the 12th century.' [95] Hatfield and the Town Clerk travelled to London to present it to them at the Master's House on Saturday 20 November.

The town was still not finished with honouring him. In September 1877 he returned to preach one Sunday at the morning and evening services. The *Morning Post* reported that he preached to 'enormous congregations . . . the mayor and corporation attending both services in State.' In the following August the mayor chaired a meeting at which the corporation unanimously agreed to commission a large portrait of Vaughan to hang in the Mansion House as a permanent reminder of his association with Doncaster. It was estimated that the cost would be between 400-500 guineas, of which 70 were immediately subscribed. Doncaster had truly valued his ministry and recognized his greatness.

Master of the Temple – a popular Preacher

We may depend upon it, that each self-denying, self-sacrificing, self-forgetting Parish Priest is doing more to deepen the foundations of the Church itself, where alone they can be securely laid – in the heart of the people – than the ablest, the foremost, the most eloquent champion of that Church in the chief place of public concourse.
From a sermon on *The Pastoral Office* preached in 1875.

Catherine's description of her husband's new post as one of 'unbounded influence' was no exaggeration arising from wifely pride. His new congregation included not just the leading barristers and judges in the capital but also many other influential city people who were attracted to the church by the beauty of the building, the quality of the worship, the excellent choir and, not least, the preaching. The Prince of Wales often attended as did Gladstone. It was certainly a fashionable church to be seen at.

Bayliss, writing in 1893, describes what was expected of the Master and what he received:

> The Master is expected to preach thirteen sermons in the year himself, and he is responsible for all the morning sermons, when the church is open, either by appointing an Assistant Preacher, or by securing the services of a Deputy; in either case remunerating the preacher from his own income.
> The Master has for his residence the Mansion or Lodge (free of rent) at the northeast corner of the Church, with the garden in front, east of the Church . . . When the present Master was appointed in 1869, the whole income of the office per annum was £25 from the Crown, £100 from the Inner Temple, and £70 from the Middle Temple. After some years the Middle Temple (unsolicited, without notice or remark) raised their annual payment from £70 to £100. A few years after the present Master became Dean of Llandaff, the two Societies (unsolicited) respectively doubled the payment of £100 each during his tenure of office. [1]

The Master's position in this 'royal peculiar', however, was a highly unusual one stemming from its history. A round church known as 'the Old Temple', had been built by the Knights Templars in Holborn about 1135 but they soon moved to the present site near the River Thames. Here they built a larger and more splendid church (the 'New Temple') which was dedicated in 1185 by Heraclius, the Patriarch of Jerusalem who was visiting England in the hope of gaining King Henry II's support for another Crusade. When the Templars were finally suppressed in 1312 at the Council of Vienne, the Pope directed that all Templar property should pass to the Knights Hospitallers but the Crown took possession of the church and the site before leasing it to the Hospitallers in 1332. Lawyers made their appearance in the neighbourhood soon afterwards and became their tenants. The origins of the two societies now known as the 'Inner Temple' and the 'Middle Temple' probably date from this period. The religious order of the Knights Hospitallers was dissolved by Henry VIII in 1540 and the two societies of lawyers then held the Temple on lease from the Crown. James I granted them a Charter in 1608 permitting the lawyers and students to reside and practise law at the Temple subject to paying an annual fee. The two societies were, in addition, required to pay an annual pension to the principal clergyman or 'Master Keeper or Rector of the Temple Church' and were made responsible for its upkeep and repair.[2] The Crown, however, retained the right to appoint the Master. In 1705 the two societies finally obtained the absolute freehold and it was agreed that responsibility for the church's upkeep was to be shared. Their duties were set out in a Deed of Partition dated 2 November 1732 - the Inner Temple was to be responsible for the southern half and the Middle Temple for the northern half, and members were to sit on their respective sides during services.

Over the centuries there had been many additions and alterations to the building but by the beginning of the 19th century extensive restoration work was needed and this was carried out in part in the 1820s and more was done in the early 1840s. There had also been developments in relation to the provision of music. There had been an organ from at least Elizabethan times but a new and greater one, built by Bernhardt Schmidt, was installed in 1688. A rudimentary choir consisting of just two ladies first performed in 1827 soon after Canon Christopher Benson had been appointed as Master. It later transpired that he was no lover of church music. When the church was due to be re-opened in 1842 after the restoration work had closed it for two and a half years, the Benchers decided it was an opportune time to introduce cathedral style services and have a surpliced choir. At that time there were only three such choirs in London – at St Paul's Cathedral, Westminster Abbey and the Chapel Royal.

The first fully choral service took place at the re-opening on Sunday

20 November 1842 with a choir of six boys and three men. The weekly *Church of England Magazine* marked the event with two articles (possibly written by Benson) in January 1843, the first about the building and its history, and the second a detailed account of the renovations. Benson, however, objected to the singing of everything – chanted psalms, the Litany, the Responses, the *Te Deum* and *Jubilate*. A short anthem might be admitted 'for the lovers of ecclesiastical Music', but he thought that none of this constituted worship and added that 'a choir there has never been, I believe, until now.'[3] He was, in effect, challenging the authority of the Benchers and implying that he, as Master, should determine the nature of the services in the Temple. He was tactfully disabused of this notion and by March 1843 there was a 'double choir' with six boy choristers and three men on each side. On 7 May 1844 the Benchers appointed a permanent committee 'to have the superintendence and regulation of the Choir of the Temple Church.'[4] This was the original 'Choir Committee' whose successors have ever since been responsible for ordering the affairs not only of the choir but also of all matters connected with the church. Benson did not like the new regime and resigned in May 1845. His successor, Dr Thomas Robinson, seems to have been happier as he stayed for 24 years.

This was the situation that Vaughan who had been used to deciding matters all his professional life was faced with. His Letters Patent from the Crown described him as 'Master and Keeper of our house and church of the New Temple' and directed that he should 'preside over, rule and govern the house and church aforesaid and the ministers of the same church whether clerks or laymen'. In reality, he was to be 'Master' only in name.

The layman he would have to work most closely with in leading worship was Edward John Hopkins, who was a brilliant organist. He had been appointed in May 1843 and a few months later was given charge of the young choristers and music, and finally in 1869 (the year of Vaughan's arrival as Master) the Benchers appointed him Director of the Choir with authority over the men as well, and increased his salary to £290 a year which was £95 more than the Master received. Hopkins led the musical life of the Temple with growing success for 55 years. Significantly, he was answerable solely to the Choir Committee and was not subject to the Master's direction. Fortunately he enjoyed an amicable and mutually respectful relationship with Vaughan.

There was also another cleric responsible for preaching at the afternoon services who was chosen and appointed by the Benchers - his official title was the 'Reader'. When the post fell vacant in 1865 the Benchers decided that they wanted a priest who could intone the choral parts of the service. Six candidates were short listed and Alfred Ainger was appointed and given a salary of £400 a year. 'Once having listened to his voice, the assembly elected him unanimously. His rare beauty of tone, low and vibrating – his manner of reading, vivid without being dramatic, impressive without the slightest striving for effect – were indeed unique, drawing many to the Temple for nearly forty years to come.'[5] He also proved to be an effective and popular preacher, and was appointed Master when Vaughan resigned in 1894, much to the latter's delight. Relations between the Master and Reader had not always been smooth. When Richard Hooker, arguably the greatest Master the Temple ever had, was in post between 1585-91 the theology he expounded at the morning services was constantly being challenged at the afternoon services by the Reader, Walter Travers, who was an extreme Calvinist – 'the pulpit spake pure Canterbury in the morning, and Geneva in the afternoon.'[6] Vaughan and Ainger (who was 21 years younger) quickly became good friends so there was no danger of personal jealousy or doctrinal competition between them. Ainger was a bachelor and became a frequent guest in the Vaughans' home.

His biographer wrote of the 'strong sympathy' which quickly grew up between them.

> Ainger admired his chief both as a man and as a preacher. His feeling was returned, and the two saw a good deal of each other. Every Sunday was spent with the Vaughans in the Master's House, which became a home to him 25 years before he himself went to live there. By that time it already held for him many memories of bygone intercourse, and so did the Vaughans' house at Llandaff, where he often spent summer holidays. For the Dean loved good talk and good literature, and anyone who promoted them. A third friend still keeps the impression of the two men standing absorbed in conversation, their lighted bed-candles in their hands, on the drawing room landing of the Temple. Some grease fell on the carpet from the Dean's slanting candle. 'How neat he spreads his wax,' was Ainger's immediate comment – to the great pleasure of Dean Vaughan, who was not above remembering Dr Watts and 'the little busy bee.'[7]

Tollemache in his *Old and Odd Memories* has an alternative version of this story which he locates in Llandaff and Ainger is the culprit. Vaughan had been sitting for his portrait and discussing Ainger with the artist who was their common friend:

271

Vaughan observed, He is terribly harum-scarum, absent-minded and scatter-brained, but such a dear, delightful fellow that one cannot be angry with him. He was staying with me at the deanery, and kept me up talking till the small hours. When I gave him his candle to show him to bed, he went on talking and dropping the wax all over the stair-carpet, and when I said, "My dear Ainger, do look what you are about," he only laughed and quoted Watts, "How neat she spreads her wax!" [8]

There had also been an assistant priest, the Revd G.F. Maclear, who had served as the previous Master's deputy when he was absent, but Vaughan made it clear from the outset that he would take all his official duties himself. That changed in time and Ainger frequently stood in for him when it was required.

His inaugural sermon was delivered on 7 November. He told them in clear and forcible words what they could expect from him as a traditionalist in matters of the Faith and what he would assume about them:

This is no common church – famous in its records, august in its impressions. Call it not the language of subserviency (*sic*), God forbid! If I dare to say in all literal simplicity, This is no common audience. You will find in all England, in all Europe, none exactly its like . . . Men have said to me in the prospect of this ministry, "You must be careful what you advance in that pulpit, Say nothing there which is not sound in logic, whatever it be in rhetoric. Assume nothing – prove your points – recollect your audience." My brethren, is there to be any misunderstanding then between us, between me and you, as to the basis, as to the foundation, on which I stand here? Is the Gospel to be, as between me and you, an open question? Am I bound every time I mention the Incarnation, the Resurrection, the Divinity of Christ, to prove each to you by some novel argument? Am I to come hither in a profane parody of St Paul on Mars Hill, to reason with you on premisses of nature if haply I may draw you towards a Faith and a Revelation not yet accepted? Honestly, earnestly do I say this to you, If that is what you wanted I am not the man. You should have sought some man of original thought, of profound learning, of dialectical subtlety, under whose master hand you might have been moulded into believing. These gifts are not mine. If you believe not the Gospel, I cannot hope to prove it to you. If I may not assume the Gospel, I descend from this pulpit immediately and for ever. [9]

He quickly made his mark with the Benchers and immediately won the approval of Gladstone who included his name in a letter, dated 3 January 1870, to Lord Chancellor Hatherley in which he listed a score of men whom he had marked as worthy of 'cathedral preferment' - Vaughan's name was second on the list.[10] A deanery lay ahead but for the present he was packing the pews of the Temple Church.

His first 'year' at the Temple ran from 7 November 1869 to Sunday 7 August '70 and twelve sermons from that period duly appeared in print as *Half-Hours in the Temple Church*. They are remarkable in that one, entitled 'Infallibility', makes explicit and highly critical reference to the First Vatican Council, and the last one which he called 'Neutrality' refers to the Franco-Prussian conflict [Britain had that summer declared itself neutral]. This was most unVaughan-like. To comment on current affairs was simply not his style or practice – especially not in a sermon.

His relations with the Benchers were occasionally ruffled as when in 1872 he pressed to have the Master's place in Hall recognized as being next to the Chair. A committee of the Middle Temple was set up to examine the question of the Master's precedence and duly submitted their report to the Benchers. It begins by setting out why the need for such a report had arisen:

> It appears from a correspondence between our Treasurer [i.e. of the Middle Temple], Sir Thomas Chambers, and the present Master of the Temple, in January 1872, that the latter claimed precedency, when invited as a guest on grand days, over all other guests, whatever their rank might be, and that he intimated that unless this claim was recognized he would decline to accept our invitation.
>
> In the course of a subsequent correspondence between the Master of the Temple and the Treasurer of the Inner Temple the claim is somewhat modified. The Master states in his letter dated 7th June 1872, "I believe, however, that the Master's place is next to the Treasurer even in the Inner Temple, *unless* there be guests of such importance as to remove him a few steps from the Chair."
>
> The Master, however, disclaimed any personal feeling or desire for precedency, and stated that he made the claim as of a right belonging to the Master, and as in duty bound to transmit the office to his successor unimpaired. [11]

They had looked at all the evidence including the patent of the Crown which was silent on the matter. Having considered the report, the Benchers resolved 'That the Master has not, in respect of his office, the right of any precedency when he dines in the Hall on the invitation of the Society.' His place at the table of the Bench was to be 'that to which he would be appointed by the rules of society generally'. A disappointing, if not a somewhat humiliating, result for Vaughan. He had been firmly put in his place.

A year later, he crossed them again. It was the practice not to have collections during services at the Temple, not even for charities. His predecessor's request to have one in 1856 in aid of those who had suffered in the Crimean War had been refused. Vaughan requested that a collection be taken for the Lord Mayor's Hospital Sunday Appeal – the Middle Temple agreed but the Inner Temple refused. He duly informed the Lord Mayor and somehow his letter appeared in *The Times*. After more correspondence with the Inner Temple, they agreed that a retiring collection could be taken at the door but no plate or bag was to be passed around the congregation during the service. Permission was also granted in 1874 and it then became an annual fixture.

Fortunately, they agreed to all his proposals over the years relating to the nature and frequency of services beginning with the introduction of a mid-week evening service in Advent 1870 and later for the same during Lent. New services were also held in the morning on Good Friday and on Ascension Day. His Lenten services attracted great crowds and some of the addresses were later published. They approved his request to have early morning celebrations of Holy Communion on those Sundays when there was none at the regular Morning Service. They also agreed to his holding early morning lectures during the week on the Greek Text of the New Testament and the Middle Temple offered the use of their lecture room for this purpose. A contemporary and appreciative paragraph about them prefaced a biographical article which appeared during his time at the Temple:

> Among the strange sights of London, there is none more characteristic than one of those early morning studies of the Greek Testament, held by the Master of the Temple during Term-time. Eight o'clock a.m., and a raw winter morning, are not conditions which will attract any but a very earnest student of Hellenistic Greek, or a very determined sight-seer indeed; but Dr Vaughan generally finds a fair gathering of students, not of sight-seers, when he enters the Temple library at that precocious hour. One by one the visitors drop their card as they come in and quickly pass to their seats, Testament in hand. It is an institution with some folks, who would as little think of missing it as the all-the-year-round bather would forego his accustomed dip in the Serpentine. The only parallel is a lecture at the Gresham Institution; but these lectures are in the evening, and – shall it be ungallantly said? – ladies are admissible to them, so that there is sure to be an audience, albeit sometimes but a small one. Only gentlemen attend Dr

Vaughan's Greek Testament lectures, yet there is always a gathering, and not generally a small one. Perhaps this power of getting together apparently unlikely people at times which are beyond question inconvenient and uncongenial (before the world is what Charles Lamb called comfortably warm) affords the truest index of the influence exercised by Dr Vaughan. [12]

The *Morning Post* usually provided some free publicity before each new course commenced, informing its readers that the 'readings' were 'open to any person interested in the study of the Greek Testament, whether members of the Temple or not.' Not surprisingly, when the 3rd edition of his commentary on the Greek text of Romans appeared in 1870 he changed the dedication to 'the younger members of the two learned and honourable societies of the Temple' some of whom were attending the early morning NT study group he led and who would very likely buy a copy.

He had been in touch with Alexander Macmillan about it at the end of December 1869 seeking some specialist help with the index:

> Can you find some careful person to prepare the "Index of Greek words" for my revision? I do not wish an unmeaning Index: but a good one will be invaluable, as forming almost a Lexicon of St Paul's Epistles, so far as the "Romans" represents his vocabulary - & it does so to a wonderful extent. Will you think this over? But I must see it after him, whoever he is.
>
> Next, can you suggest any thing about a notice or short Review of the book in the Guardian? I know a Mr Wilkins, Fellow of Merton, who writes reviews in that Paper — would there be any indelicacy in my asking him to do it?
>
> Will you kindly let me have a dozen copies of "Liturgy & Worship"? or even six copies?
>
> When shall I get some copies of the new Ed[n] of "Lectures on Revelation"? [13]

Preaching was his primary task and the first ten years of his ministry at the Temple proved to be the most prolific decade of his career in terms of volumes of sermons published. Compilation volumes included *Half Hours in the Temple Church* 1869, *Sundays in the Temple* '71, *Words of Hope from the Pulpit of the Temple Church* '74, *Earnest Words for Earnest Men* '75, and then there were volumes of his published 'lectures' given during the seasons of Lent and Advent of which the first was *Christ satisfying the Instincts of Humanity. Eight Lectures delivered in the Temple Church Lent 1870*. He wrote to Macmillan in March 1870 when he was just half way through his Lenten course to tell him he was

275

delivering them 'to an overflowing Church' and asking his advice about publishing them.

There were several volumes of his university sermons delivered mostly in Cambridge but with some preached in Oxford, among them *"My Son, give me thine Heart" Sermons preached before the Universities of Oxford & Cambridge 1876-78*. And many individual sermons preached on special occasions all over the country – in 1872, for example, at an Ordination at Rochester, at the re-opening of Rugby School Chapel and at St Olave's School York on its 301st anniversary. Two years later *The Solidity of True Religion; and other Sermons preached in London during the General Election and Mission Week February 1874* appeared following his involvement in the London Diocesan Mission. His work on NT books continued – a commentary on *Ephesians,* and H*eroes of Faith: Lectures on the 11th Chapter of the Epistle to the Hebrews* were both published in the 70s with more to come in the following decade. His 'best seller' (second only to his *Notes on Confirmation*) was a devotional book called *Family Prayers*, published by Alexander Strahan. It first appeared in late 1871 and sold 8,000 copies in its first year. It was reprinted again and again in the following three decades and must have been used in tens of thousands of homes at their daily devotional family gathering.

Macmillan did not accede to all his requests and suggestions. Vaughan wrote in October 1970 proposing 'a little work entitled *Notes of Lectures & Sketches of Sermons given to Students for Holy Orders*'. It later transpired that by 'little' he meant 200 pages and it would have been the substance of the addresses he gave to his 'doves' – the topics would have included Preaching, Visitation of the Sick, Visitation of the Whole, Clerical recreations, Treatment of Dissenters, Study of Scripture. But nothing came of it. There also seems to have been the occasional upset between them particularly as regards his royalties. He wrote in a more formal tone than was his custom, for example, in March 1876 about a loss-making collection of sermons which he had edited entitled *Solidity of True Religion*.

> Dear Sir,
> The deduction of the debt against *Solidity of True Religion* from the profits of my publications, seems to imply that this liability was a joint one between you and me. In all previous transactions with Publishers I have found it otherwise. They have taken the risk, whilst dividing the profits.
> You will oblige me by referring me to any special arrangement made

between yourselves and me when the publication of this work was undertaken, such as should justify the Deduction now made.

Your faithful Servt C.J. Vaughan [14]

In 1872 he wrote the preface to the English translation of a French book – not a theological work, nor a Bible commentary or a collection of sermons but a memoir of recent events: *Eight Months on Duty. The Diary of a Young Officer in Chanzy's Army.* Vaughan had met the young man and his mother, 'the Baroness de M', on holiday in Folkestone the previous year. He wrote warmly of the virtues, particularly duty, displayed by the young French officer and his friends 'suddenly called from their books and their homes into the sternest necessities of an uncongenial employment – those very virtues which we have sometimes arrogantly vaunted as the monopoly of Britain.' [15] Was this yet another example of Vaughan's romantic infatuations with young men?

The style of his sermons did not change markedly from the ones he preached in Harrow School Chapel or at Doncaster. There was the same earnest exhortation to live the Gospel in daily life. He showed them how to honour God in the little things of life and he continued to avoid controversy and divisive theological issues. As a writer in *Vanity Fair* put it in 1872: 'Dr Vaughan is not a keen partisan; he is not fond of snubbing and humiliating bishops; he can preach a sermon without treading on several Orthodox corns at once. But for all that he has done good work . . . He is a preacher of the most eloquent and persuasive order, gentle, earnest, scholarly, tolerant.' [16] And many years later a writer in *The Record* commented in a similar vein on his preaching ministry at the Temple: 'Dr Vaughan's sermons became widely popular, not from their learning and eloquence, and still less from their straining after effect, but solely from their unaffected earnestness, simplicity, and straight-forwardness, and their enforcement of the lessons inculcating faith, love, unselfishness and duty.' [17]

There was very little call on his time for officiating at the Occasional Offices. Baptisms were few and far between – one of his last ones was Shiam Sinha, son of the late Portap Sinha, Rajah of Typur in the North West Province of India. This young man had been born in June 1856 and was baptised on 25 July '89. The last one was Felix Charles Lovett, the infant son of two of his own domestic staff, born on 31 May 1892 and baptised on 5 July by Vaughan but the child died the following January. There were, however, Memorial Services which were important events in the life of that community. Bayliss gives this account of one:

> At the Temple Church, at three o'clock on January 20th 1892, the day of the Funeral of H.R.H. the Duke of Clarence + Avondale, there was a Special solemn Memorial Service; it was attended by a full congregation of Masters of the Bench, Barristers and Students of the Middle and Inner Temple, and others.
>
> The Middle Temple Staff, as is usual, the Duke having been a Bencher of the Middle Temple, was draped with black crape.
>
> The Master of the Temple, assisted by the Reader, impressively read the portion of the Burial Service. The Organist, Dr Hopkins, at the conclusion played the "Dead March" in "Saul", the congregation still standing. [18]

There was also notable work for him to assist with outside the Temple. On 22 June 1870 he was one of a group of scholars who met at Westminster Abbey at the invitation of the Dean, his brother-in-law. Their task was to produce a revised translation of the New Testament. The Convocation of Canterbury meeting on 6 May had appointed a Committee consisting of eminent Biblical scholars and leading churchmen 'with power to revise, for public use, the authorized version of 1611, and to associate with them representative Biblical scholars of other Christian denominations using that version.' The Committee divided itself into two Companies, one to work on the Old Testament, the other on the New. After celebrating Holy Communion together, they met for the first time in the Jerusalem Chamber which was to be their usual meeting place in the years to come. The chairman of the NT committee was C.J. Ellicott, Bishop of Gloucester & Bristol. It included the great Cambridge triumvirate of Lightfoot, Westcott and Hort as well as Kennedy, the Regius Professor of Greek. Coincidentally, earlier in 1870 before the committee first met, Vaughan had written to the Vice-Chancellor of Cambridge urging that his former colleague, Westcott, be appointed Regius Professor of Divinity. [19] The committee met for four successive days a month, apart from August and September. Their working practice was to bring their own personal suggestions on the portion of Scripture due to be translated – usually about 35 verses a day. Of the 407 meetings held Ellicott attended all but five of them; Vaughan attended 302. [20]

After ten years and five months of labour their task ended at 5 p.m. on 11 November 1880 (St Martin's Day) and the committee joined in a special Service of Thanksgiving in St Martin-in-the-Fields Church. Soon afterwards, Vaughan preached a course of Lenten sermons in the Temple Church on some of the texts in which the Revised Version differed from the Authorised. It seems that he was not entirely happy with the finished work but ready nonetheless to defend it from attack. In March 1882 he wrote to tell Macmillan that crowds were attending his Lenten lectures and offering them for publications under the title *Authorized or Revised?* and explaining why he hoped they would appear in print.

> You may say that I have published too many Sermons. Or you may say that the interest in the R.V. is dying out. I shall accept your judgement cheerfully. My <u>motive</u> is a spirit of indignation stirred within me by the really <u>brutal</u> treatment of the R.V. by Dean Burgon in the Quarterly, & by the hectoring tone of Mr Gladstone and Mr Murray in private on the same side. I should <u>like</u> to have my say about it, though not a red hot partisan, if you can see your way to it. But not otherwise. [21]

Macmillan had faith in the venture and printed 2,500 copies. Years later Vaughan had cause to feel displeased about an aspect of the publication of the *Revised Version.* He and the others were awarded honoraria of £100-£150 for their ten years' and in some cases twenty years' labour, 'It appears to me to be little short of disrespectful' given that the University publishers were expecting to receive £20,000 from the sale of the Revised Version. [22]

He continued to train men with a vocation to the Ordained Ministry and this very special and personal work won him much praise. One of those who admired him for it was Edward White Benson, the first Headmaster of Wellington College, who confided to his friend, Professor Lightfoot, in a letter dated December 1869 that he too would love to do such a noble work. 'And now I earnestly hope that I shall some way be allowed to lay down Wellington College, where I feel my work – in submission to God – to be complete . . . and to go away to some Cathedral to work in what is to my eyes *the* work of the Church for the training of her clergy, now that the Universities are surely making us *some* work to do, and which training for the Pastoral office has been so abundantly blessed in Vaughan's work.' [23] His wish was fulfilled three years later when Bishop Christopher Wordsworth invited him to become Chancellor of Lincoln Cathedral and to found a theological college there, the *Cancellarii Scholae*. Many years later, when Benson was Archbishop of Canterbury, he encouraged his youngest son, Hugh, to train under Vaughan and was deeply grateful for what the young man learnt from him. On the day he had the joy of ordaining Hugh, Benson noted in his diary: 'We are unspeakably indebted to Dean Vaughan's wise, searching επιείκεια [considerateness, forbearance] in training our Hugh. When you multiply such a debt as this by the number of men for whom he has done the same, I doubt whether the Church owes so much *to anyone* at all. What is greater than the formation of Ministers for the spreading of the Kingdom?'[24]

When he moved to London, the *Morning Post* immediately reported approvingly on the coming of his men too:

> The Rev Dr Vaughan, the new Master of the Temple, is about to confer a great benefit on the adjacent parish of St Clement Danes, many parts of which are as degraded as any district of London. The rev doctor has with him in the Temple, as he did at Doncaster, many young men who are reading for the ministry and in order that they may obtain an insight into parochial work, they are about to pay daily visits, two by two, to the lowest haunts of poverty and vice in and about Clare-market. Hitherto there has been a weekday evening service in the parish church but the Rev R.J. Simpson, who has within the last few weeks become the rector, has announced that henceforth there will be two weekday evening services, one on Wednesdays and one on Fridays, at which Mr Vaughan's students will read the lessons and otherwise assist.[25]

In the early 1870s he is said to have had as many as twenty men under his supervision at any one time. The increase in the number of students may, of course, be explained by the attraction of their being based in the capital rather than in a small northern town. Just how important this work was to be to the Church may be judged by the following brief accounts of three of the men who came to him soon after his arrival at the Temple.

His most famous 'dove' from this period came on the personal recommendation of Westcott who had been the young man's house-master at Harrow. Randall Davidson was his name, he was 23 and had just graduated from Oxford. Westcott wrote on his behalf in October 1871 but alerted Vaughan that he might not appear until the following year. Vaughan told him that he would require no testimonial 'of a man of whom you speak so highly'[26] and added a PS 'This is, I think, my 30th letter today. I preached at Rugby on Sunday in the new-old Chapel.'

Davidson was not physically strong and there was a question mark over his ability to sustain any demanding work. The plan was to see if his health would hold out for the proposed six months of study in London where he arrived on 16 April 1872 from a tour of Italy. He was assigned to visit in a poor and squalid neighbourhood north of the Strand under the supervision of the local curate, the Revd Brook Deedes, himself an old 'dove'. Davidson's biographer, G.K.A. Bell, noted how difficult this was for him: '[he] found real difficulty in the visiting of the district, owing partly to shyness, which hampered him again, he used to say, in his curacy days, and partly to the difficulty, which most young laymen would have found, in explaining his identity and mission to a suspicious occupant of a slum dwelling.' [27] But he did have the stomach to visit St George's Hospital 'to see operations performed as a bit of training for my nerves.' [28] After just three months he began to suffer headaches and exhaustion and the doctors prescribed more rest, open-air life and foreign travel, so he left for a tour of the Middle East with some close friends from Oxford days including Crauford Tait, the Archbishop's son.

Davidson has left these reflections on his time spent with Vaughan:

All this life was wholly unlike the routine of an ordinary theological college. Indeed Vaughan spoke with scant respect – though with marked reserve – about theological colleges, of which practically, as one must be honest, he knew very little. The teaching he gave us was personal, not according to any examination system . . . He gave us very little history, either primitive or later; scarcely anything philosophical; but he had an extraordinary power of bringing out from the text of Scripture things new and old; thoughts basic after all in the best theologies, and practical in their ceaseless referring of us back to the teachings of the Bible itself . . .

We wrote sermons for him every week, and he used to read out to the assembly one or more of these after he had carefully examined and annotated them all. I was not infrequently subjected to the rather trying ordeal of having one of my crude productions thus set forth in all the smoothness of Vaughan's manner of speech. But sometimes we were allowed to send, not an actual sermon, but just our carefully arranged notes for it, and he would then give us his own notes on the same subject. Besides all this he used to set us the task of writing on subjects like the Atonement, Forgiveness, or the like, and in these we could speak freely about our thoughts and beliefs without fear of jarring upon him. Nor would he at all object, unless it were with placid humour and wit, to our putting forth opinions of an ecclesiastical sort with which he had little or no sympathy. Of course, it was an extraordinary example of a man making his personality felt in his pupils . . . [29]

Later he added; 'Looking back at it now, I honestly think that it would have been difficult to find any other plan of preparation for Orders which would have suited me so well as Vaughan's arrangements did.' In the few weeks that they were together, a close friendship was formed that lasted until Vaughan's death. Davidson turned to the older man for advice when he had important decisions to make about his career. And Vaughan used his influence at a time when there was a vacancy on the Episcopal bench to press for Davidson's preferment to a bishopric of sufficient seniority to make him a member of the House of Lords at once.

Vaughan's first letter to him, written just a week after he had left, was in the same vein as the emotional letters written earlier to his favourites at Harrow:

> You would think me very weak if you knew how much my thoughts have been fixed upon a letter from you, ever since that dear parting in my Study, which I shall never forget. It is come now, and Oh I trust you will not let it be the only one to fill up what seems to be such a long interval till June 1873. It looks *worse*, I think, as you write it thus in *years* 'A.D.', than if you had described it by its real duration.
>
> I shall be used to it in time. And of course you know how many things and persons I have to occupy me – so that I ought not to make you think that I care too much about it. Only I had got to think of you as one who could feel as I felt and who *anticipated* half of my thoughts ere they were uttered.
>
> May God ever help you. If I *never* had you here again, still I should always think of you as my friend . . . [30]

And as with earlier favourites, he did not hesitate to let the man's father know of his feelings. Henry Davidson had written a letter of appreciation to Vaughan and asking for his daily prayers for his son during his travels abroad. Vaughan replied as follows:

> I must not lose another day in telling you how deeply I have been touched by your letter, and how earnestly I will endeavour to do, and do again and again, that which you asked of me in behalf of that dear Son. I do feel, more than with regard to common men, that his life is specially in the hands of God, and that there we must humbly seek to touch the spring of it. You know in some degree, though perhaps not fully, how deeply he endeared himself to me in that brief, too brief, stay with me in the Temple. To think that the feeling was in some sense reciprocal is a very precious thought to me. If it might be so, that we could be together again in the same dear relationship it would be a great joy to me. Meanwhile let us hope that in another and truer sense the tie is not broken, is not weakened, even now.
>
> From time to time I trust you will kindly let me hear of him – of his welfare, his health, his spirits, his hopes. I would not impose upon him the task of writing, but he knows how welcome will his already well-known hand be in my sight, if it ever can be good for him and easy to him to write to me. Meanwhile, you, my Dear Sir, have pointed out <u>one way</u> in which I may hope to be near him daily. [31]

Randall Davidson was ordained alongside his friend Crauford Tait in St Mark's Kennington on 1 March 1874 for service in the diocese of Canterbury, initially as Curate of Dartford in Kent, just 15 miles from London. Three years later he became a much valued Chaplain to the Archbishop, then at the age of 35 he was made Dean of Windsor - like Vaughan, he was one of the Queen's favourite clerics - before being appointed Bishop of Rochester in 1890. Three years later he was translated to Winchester, and finally to Canterbury. His last service to his old friend and mentor was to officiate at his funeral in Llandaff Cathedral.

The 'doves' were not all of a kind in terms of churchmanship or politics. Elliott-Binns in his *Religion in the Victorian Era* mentions Stewart Headlam (1847-1924) as being 'for a time a "dove", though not a very tame one.' [32] Headlam may have appeared to be an ideal candidate for Vaughan: schooled at Eton, where Crauford Tait had been his fag, and a graduate of Trinity College Cambridge, though a very lowly placed one in the Classical Tripos and a man of real faith with a commitment to love and serve people. The major influence on his life at Cambridge had been F.D. Maurice, the Professor of Moral Philosophy, who had been sacked from King's College London on the grounds of heterodoxy when he had challenged the traditional view that the unsaved suffered eternal torment after the Final Judgement. Headlam's biographer, F.G. Bettany, claimed that Maurice provided him with 'a hero to worship' and 'an anchorage for his faith.' His father did not approve of this zeal for Maurice and his views and sent him, after he had graduated, to read for a year with Herbert James, an Evangelical clergyman. He failed to change the young man's views. *Pater* Headlam then sent him as a last resort to Vaughan where he spent seven or eight months with him before proceeding immediately to ordination.

Headlam was already by now well on the way to becoming the staunch supporter of trade unions and the doughty champion of Labour which he proved to be all his ministry, a Christian Socialist in action as well as by conviction. At one of their daily study sessions, Vaughan who was normally tolerant of the personal opinions of his 'doves' grew impatient with his fervour for Maurice and told him he was tired of Maurice's 'jargon about righteousness and peace.' [33] The aspect of the training that Headlam most appreciated was the systematic visiting he had to do. St Clement Danes, a populous district adjacent to the Temple, was divided up into small districts with a 'dove' in charge of each and it was here he gained his first experience of meeting ordinary people in their homes. From now on, face to face encounters would always matter dearly to him.

Despite their differences, it was through Vaughan's influence that he gained his first two curacies, the first of these being with the Revd R.G. Maul, Vicar of St John's, Drury Lane. His lifelong love and support for members of the theatrical profession began here, though that was work regarded by most clergy as sinful. He had been ordained Deacon in 1870 and would normally have been priested a year later but the Bishop of London, John Jackson, objected to some of the socialist views he expressed in the sample sermons he submitted prior to ordination. The result was he had to wait a further year. In 1873 he moved to St Matthew's Bethnall Green whose Rector, Septimus Hansard, was a Broad Churchman and friend of Arthur Stanley and a man sympathetic to Headlam's views. It was here, however, that he delivered a lecture that was to blight his clerical career. It was on 'Theatres and Music-Halls'. In it, in addition to admitting that he frequented the theatre himself and took young people with him, he recommended that young women should be encouraged to attend performances at such places of entertainment. This was regarded as a scandalous view for a clergyman to be expressing in a public lecture. When a printed copy of it was sent to the Bishop of London, Headlam experienced episcopal anger for the first but not the last time. He refused to recant. It was not in his nature to compromise or admit that he might be wrong. Vaughan, too, complained of the lecture's 'levity, flippancy and bad taste.' [34] Three months later, he was dismissed from his curacy.

Bettany was critical of Vaughan's disapproval of his former student:

> It was while Headlam was smarting under Episcopal censure and needing the help of a friendly hand that his old tutor, Dr Vaughan, taking his "Lecture on Music Halls' as a text, tendered him a piece of extraordinary advice, or, if such words are too strong, anticipated a strange development on his pupil's part. After lecturing him on his "arrogant and contemptuous way of dealing with the convictions of older and more experienced brother ministers," Dr Vaughan declared:
> "Your continuance in the parish or in the diocese, except as a Dissenter, is evidently out of the question . . . No Church could possibly stand if its junior officers were at liberty thus to express themselves as to their superiors and commanders . . . I see no alternative but your leaving the diocese, and either establishing yourself as an independent minister in a chapel of your own, or else (after an interval spent in thoughtful reconsideration of your

position) seeking a title somewhere else after full explanation both with your future incumbent and your future bishop." [35]

Given that Headlam was in no way heterodox in his faith and regarded his priesthood as his most valued possession, this was a strange intervention and a sorry suggestion on Vaughan's part. Perhaps it was because the man had trained with him and he now feared that he himself might be tainted by association. Not surprisingly, Headlam later regarded himself as a disappointment to Vaughan. But if he was, he was not the only one – his biographer relates how an unnamed former contemporary 'dove' visited Headlam during his first curacy to share with him that he had abandoned a clerical career for medicine and that he no longer believed in the existence of God. 'His statement produced a stunning effect on Headlam. Vaughan's pupils had sometimes debated together airily as to what was the ideal form of Christianity, but this was something altogether strange and disturbing . . . [It] was as though he had been forced to look over the edge of an abyss.' [36]

Despite his clashes with his diocesan bishop and later with his successor, Frederick Temple, Headlam was not without episcopal support. Archbishops Tait, Benson and Davidson all befriended him at different times during his ministry and Davidson wrote him a touching letter of admiration and appreciation shortly before his death. He may have been a disappointment to Vaughan and to other traditionalist clergy but he was recognized by many as a great friend of the poor, the scourge of secularists, an educationalist devoted to the welfare of the children of London, and one of the leading Christian Socialists of his generation. He was one of Vaughan's greatest 'doves'. Just how different Headlam was to all the other 'doves' is shown by his support for Oscar Wilde for whom he bravely stood bail in 1895 and then fetched him to his own home from Pentonville Prison on 19 May 1897, the day he was released.

Another from this period who had a memorable ministry but of a very different kind was Henry Montgomery (1847-1932). He was a contemporary of Davidson at Harrow and of Headlam at Trinity Cambridge. He had had a stern Evangelical upbringing – in his own words 'I think I may say I was brought up on almost undiluted hell fire. On the whole such diet has done me immense good, for it has left behind in me an awful sense of the Holy Will of God.' [37] His wife, Maud, in a *Memoir* of her late husband which she based largely on his own as well as her recollections was fulsome in her praise for Vaughan.

In January 1870, Henry Montgomery prepared for holy orders under Dr Vaughan, Master of the Temple. It was an unique experience. In 1921 Henry preached the sermon and presided at the annual meeting of the "Doves," as Dr Vaughan's men were called. In this sermon he tried to place on record something of what they all owed to their great teacher. Dr Vaughan's teaching was confined almost exclusively to three or four fundamental doctrines, and these clustered around personal religion, our sinfulness, and our Saviour. Henry's childhood's convictions were deepened. "I believe," he writes in his sermon, "the best kind of churchman is likely to be one who began as an Evangelical and went on afterwards to the truths about the Church and the sacramental life." Another lesson all his men learnt from Dr Vaughan was to read the services reverently, to realise the possibility of finding in the Prayer Book all that was needed for the spiritual life . . . The tie between Dr Vaughan and his men was fashioned in the quiet morning hours, as he unfolded the riches of the sacred Word and taught them that the message of forgiveness was the miracle of the Christian Gospel. [38]

He served his first curacy at Hurstpierpoint where his fellow curate was E.A. Browne, a friend from Harrow and Cambridge days, who had also trained under Vaughan. Another fellow curate was James Hannington who would later be martyred in Uganda where he was sent as its first bishop. In 1876, on Vaughan's recommendation, he joined Dr Farrar who had just moved from being Headmaster of Marlborough to St Margaret's Westminster. This brought him the additional blessings of meeting and marrying one of Farrar's daughters and of becoming a close personal friend and secretary to Dean Arthur Stanley, next door at the Abbey. In 1879 he began his ten years ministry as Vicar of St Mark's Kennington where, with the help of some hardworking curates, he built up huge congregations.

In 1889 he was invited by Archbishop Benson, again on Vaughan's recommendation, to move to Tasmania as its fourth Bishop. Vaughan's hastily scribbled note to the Archbishop who had asked for his opinion reads as follows: 'My dear Lord Archbishop, I have but a moment but it is enough for the purpose – to say, Unqualified confidence in the person you mention, from a twenty years intimate knowledge. I need say no more – except to thank you for the wonderful kindness of your words. Your Grace's dutiful servant, C.J. Vaughan' [39]

His wife tells how he went to see his old mentor at the Temple: 'Of course Vaughan knew all about it, and had assented. They knelt together and prayed, and Vaughan quoted from the psalm "From the ends of the earth will I call upon thee; when my heart is in heaviness."' [40] Montgomery had an impressive and far-reaching ministry in Tasmania, often away from home for months as he visited isolated bush settlements, the islands where the half-castes lived, solitary mines and lonely lighthouses – wherever people were to be found. It was during these years that he became a champion for world mission. In June 1901 a telegram sent by the Archbishops in England summoned him back to become Secretary of the Society for the Propagation of the Gospel. This was to be his life's greatest work promoting and supporting Christian mission all over the world. He organised the Pan-Anglican Congress in 1908 and assisted Davidson at two Lambeth Conferences. The Archbishop of York said of him: 'I don't suppose that anyone in his generation did greater work for the Church than he did. The new attitude of the Church generally towards its worldwide work is very largely due to him'[41] He too must be numbered among Vaughan's greatest 'doves'. Unwittingly, he also did the nation and the world a great service in fathering a son who would grow up to become Britain's most famous soldier in World War II: General Bernard Montgomery, the victor at the battle of El Alamein in 1942, who was later promoted Field Marshal and Commander-in-Chief of British Land Forces during the invasion of Europe.

The variety of churchmanship among Vaughan's 'doves' represented by these three men is further emphasized by the testimony of the famous schoolmaster-missionary Tyndale-Biscoe of Kashmir. He took his BA in 1886 and then went to York to read Theology with the Revd E.A. Lane before being accepted by Vaughan. He wrote in his autobiography:

> I am always thankful that I went to Dr Vaughan to read for orders as every-one who had that privilege has been, for Dr Vaughan was a truly outstand-ing Christian gentleman who influenced every one of his pupils and left his mark on them for life. He thought far more of character than dogma. He expressed himself at one of his daily Greek Testament lectures in this way. "What pleases me at my Triennial meetings (when three hundred old pupils meet at an Oxford or Cambridge College) is to see their diverse clothing, some with soft hats and white ties, some with hard hat and stiff dog collar, some with hard hat with tassels and some in cassock and biretta. I don't care what you are, so long as you are Christian gentlemen. [42]

In Vaughan's opinion, parties in the Church distorted the truth and created mischief and schism among believers; he taught his 'doves' that truth 'as it is in Jesus' was not the exclusive possession of any party.

It was during Vaughan's time at the Temple that reunions of his 'doves' began to be held at roughly three yearly intervals. In preparation for the first of these which was held in Salisbury in 1875, he asked Lightfoot for help in providing a list of recommended reading for his men. In doing this, he was pioneering what is now a standard element in a newly ordained clergyman's ministry: P.O.T. = Post-Ordination Training:

> I continue to persecute you with letters: the subject of this one will be its best apology.
>
> I am anxious to define a little, for young Clergymen, who have been with me the sort of reading which might occupy such time as they can spare for reading, after the second Ordination [i.e. to the Priesthood], say for 5 years following. I have even thought of sending to my "Men" year by year just a short list of books for each particular year. I need not say that my men are seldom clever or superior, seldom German scholars, or men of letters in any sense: & the value of such an Idea for them would be diminished by over-shooting their powers, either in quantity or quality.
>
> It has occurred to me that, with your great knowledge & experience, you might be able (& would, I know, be willing) to give me material aid by putting down some 20 English books, whether translations or originals, such as a commonplace man might profitably make his own, thoroughly, in the course of some 4 or 5 years, making allowance for the great pre-occupations of a young Clergyman's life, both parochially & in Sermons.
>
> There is no hurry in the matter: & if you do not feel able to write about it, pray do not scruple to be silent.
>
> Books, published in Clark's Theological Library, are particularly easy of access for such a purpose. [43]

Lightfoot did as requested and sent the list to Vaughan whilst the first reunion was underway. Vaughan replied from Salisbury on 2 October: 'Your most kind letter could not possibly have come more opportunely, & I do most heartily thank you for it. I have had a meeting of more than 50 of my "Men" here for the last 3 days, and your kind intention of helping me had been much in my thoughts in connection with it - & yesterday my best hopes were realized. Many, many thanks – though in sad haste.' [44]

The list was appended to his *Addresses to Young Clergymen. Delivered at Salisbury* which were published later that year. And following the reunion, the first edition of their newsletter, *The Advent Record*, appeared. They then met at Beverley (1877), Charterhouse ('79), Corpus Christi College Cambridge ('82), Trinity and Wadham Colleges Oxford ('85), Pembroke & Peterhouse Colleges Cambridge ('88), and the last one during Vaughan's lifetime was at his old college, Trinity Cambridge ('93). The highlight of these occasions apart from meeting with their old mentor and friend were the addresses he preached to them. At the first reunion he preached a sermon on *The Pastoral Office* in which he challenged them to keep face-to-face pastoral engagement at the heart of their ministry even if they were at the head of a big team:

> I dread the hackneyed phrase – used sometimes as the highest recommendation of Parish or Curacy – "Such a man is a splendid organizer." It means too often that the chief minister, in experience as in office, is sitting at the council-board of planning and scheming, while the terrible struggle between Christ and Satan on the battlefield of some anguish-stricken or dying soul is directed (if at all) by the youngest deacon, or the most ignorant layman, or the feeblest woman, upon whom human chance or Christian compassion has devolved this most arduous, most responsible service. The Pastoral Office is a hand-to-hand, heart-to-heart, soul-to-soul ministration. In its highest exercises, at all events, it is an individual work, alike in the Minister and in the ministered unto. The individual must be first sought and found – then he in turn becomes a new centre of personal light and warmth to other individual lives and souls around him. [45]

Pastoral care could be shown in other ways too as when Vaughan took the initiative on 18 July 1882 to write to his former pupil Randall Davidson, now Chaplain to Archbishop Tait, about the Temple's organist:

> I want to ask you whether it would be at all possible, and consistent with rule, for Mr Hopkins, the Organist for nearly forty years of the Temple Church, and underlined as a Church Organist to obtain the honour of a degree of Doctor of Music from the kindness of the Archbishop. I do not know that he wishes or would accept it. But I felt that I might just put the question to you. There is, of course, not the slightest hurry in giving me an answer. I ask solely for myself. [46]

His reputation and standing at Lambeth was such that his request met with an immediate and positive response. Inevitably there were formalities and fees to be dealt with. Vaughan wrote again to Davidson on 2 August to give him an update:

> I am so greatly obliged to you for your reply about Mr Hopkins. I find the idea so warmly received by a leading Bencher of the Temple, Sir Thomas Chambers, the Recorder, that I have ventured to draw up a formal petition from myself to the Archbishop asking for the Degree. Sir Thomas Chambers assures me that he believes the two Temples will most gladly pay the requisite fee, so as to do honour to Mr Hopkins by relieving him from any

expense in the matter. There is no doubt that it will be a most popular act, and I should wish that my name as Master of the Temple may be connected with the application as recorded in the book of such Degrees. I hope I am not travelling too fast in my reading of your kind letter. [47]

Three days later he replied to Davidson's latest letter written on behalf of the Archbishop:

I deeply feel the kindness of the Archbishop in giving Mr Hopkins the degree of Doctor of Music without imposing the usual conditions. I would beg you to tell his Grace how much his kindness will be appreciated both by Mr Hopkins himself and throughout the two Temples.

I believe that the fees will certainly be paid by the Benchers. If not, I shall set on foot a subscription list, so that Mr Hopkins may receive his honour without being the poorer for it.

I am here for two Sermons tomorrow – then to Llandaff for a Chapter Meeting and <u>Welsh</u> Choir Festival. I then return to work here on the 15th. [48]

Hopkins recorded how the Master broke the news to him.

One Saturday afternoon, just as the weekly choir rehearsal was closing, Dean Vaughan entered the church and calling up to the organ loft said, "Mr Hopkins, if you can kindly spare me a few minutes I shall be glad to speak to you in the Vestry." He told me that both Societies had recommended him for the degree of Doctor of Music and that they would bear all expenses – he had been in touch with his friend, Dr Tait and had at once granted the diploma . . . [Hopkins expressed both surprise and pleasure as he had heard nothing about it.] The Dean smilingly said, "That is what I hoped might be the case. Then may I tell the benchers you consent?" "I shall, of course, be only too proud to do so." "Very well! Now I have a favour of a personal nature to ask, which is, that you will allow me to present you with your Doctor's gown and hood." [49]

Tait personally presented the diploma naming him a Doctor of Music and Vaughan vested him in the gown and hood of the degree. Maybe it is just a coincidence, but I like to think that the decision of the two Temples, made that same year, for each of them to increase Vaughan's stipend by £100 (in effect a 100% increase) was a mark not just of their affection and appreciation of his ministry in general but also as recognition of what he had just done for their Organist in particular.

Vaughan, as a former headmaster, naturally took an interest in the education of the choristers. A joint school for choristers of the Temple and of Lincoln's Inn Chapel had been established at 10 New Boswell Court in 1854 but Vaughan felt it had too few pupils to make it viable. Fortunately all the interested parties agreed with him and they presented a report on 1 February 1875 to the Council of the Inns:

> The present system of the Choirs School appears to us to be unsatisfactory. The great variety of ages and attainments which is unavoidable in a School of this nature, is doubtless in large part the cause of failure. We would suggest the propriety of either sending to some large Public School (such as the Stationers') at the cost of the Societies, or else allowing the Parents to send their Sons, to such Schools as they may select, with such assistance from the Societies as may be arranged by communication with the Parents. [50]

The choir school was subsequently closed and the boys were sent to the Stationers' Company's School which had been started in 1861. He was also concerned about the boys' welfare on Sundays as they had previously been left to fend for themselves between services. With the support of the Benchers he saw to it that they were provided with a cold lunch, and then with a pudding from his own kitchen. Henry Humm, the greatest treble soloist in Hopkins' day, remembered him as: 'a benign old gentleman who wore nice black gaiters, as befitted his shapely legs and ecclesiastical dignity. On rare occasions, we were invited to take a very uncomfortable tea at his house.' [51]

There were others who found tea-time at the Vaughans rather more to their taste, notably Catherine's brother Arthur, the Dean of Westminster. It was his custom at 3 p.m. either to go to Evensong in the Abbey or to drive or walk along the Embankment to see his sister where 'Five o'clock tea was his favourite meal.' [52] After his wife's death in March 1876, his visits became more frequent as he found solace in their home and company. She became a popular London hostess often attracting famous and literary figures to her afternoon or evening parties which could be crowded to suffocation. Several invitations to Charles Dalrymple survive written in her quirky style: 'Now – permit me to enclose this Card – in the fervent hope that you will put aside every other Engagement & let nothing prevent you from assisting us on the nervous occasion of our first <u>Forensic Tea</u>.' [53] 'Are you and your ladies to be had for an Afternoon Tea to (?) on a very <u>reduced scale</u> and consisting entirely of the dregs of society?' [54] 'Merely to say that a young lady who is heiress to £2000 a year (or perhaps 3) besides a charming estate in Surrey will be drinking Tea under the Pear Tree <u>next Monday</u> from 4 o'clock till 6 - & you <u>must</u> come and meet her.' [55] On another occasion she told him 'I invited 80 or

291

rather <u>100</u> intimate friends – on the supposition that 40 would appear. They <u>all</u> took it into their heads to come! & you may imagine the crowd & confusion.'[56]

Some unusual tales are told of her behaviour on such occasions which suggest she was not quite the perfect hostess. G.G. Coulton recalled one: 'Once, she noticed in a corner, Sir Willoughby Jones, an old friend, for he was a Norfolk squire and she daughter to the Bishop of Norwich. He looked bored: so she worked her way to him on behalf of a similarly silent lady in another corner who was "dying to meet him". When they had worked their way back, she introduced him to his own wife, recently married and therefore unfamiliar to Mrs Vaughan.'[57] Nineteen year old Florence Sitwell [a great niece of Catherine Tait, wife of the Archbishop] recorded in her journal on 30 March 1877 a visit to one of Catherine's tea parties and her impressions of the hostess:

> On Monday at Mrs Vaughan's tea-party. I felt very much excited for we were to make the acquaintance of Mrs Charles [a popular author] . . . We went in, up some small dark stairs which led right into the central apartment of the little chain of rooms where the parties are held. Such quaint old-fashioned rooms, opening out of each other. The tea-table was in the middle one, and in each there were groups of people, standing and sitting, talking. Dean Stanley was at one window talking to a friend. It is a wonderful face – it struck me very much last Monday. I should have so much liked to have heard their conversation, but could not, for the noise going on round.
> Mrs Vaughan is such a funny, fussy little woman . . . We were given some tea, and then sat down on a round sofa in the middle of one of the rooms. Mrs Vaughan introduced three or four people to Grace [her cousin] as "Miss Sitwell", telling each how anxious she was to meet Mrs Charles' acquaintance. Poor Grace did not know what to do, but at last managed to explain. [It appears that the hostess had mistakenly assumed she was Florence.] Mrs Vaughan introduced one middle-aged man to Mother, as he had once been curate to her son! He had indeed once been curate to some Albert Sitwell, who may possibly be a sixth cousin. One man was telling Mother that there were two men whom he had always loved, though he had never known them and those were – "Dr Vaughan and Dean Stanley", broke in Mrs Vaughan's voice from behind "because you know there are only two men in the world of whom you could say that." She was quite right.[58]

Florence Sitwell recorded another anecdote about life at the Vaughans:

292

There were some grand Brahmins staying in London not long ago, and Mrs Vaughan had it very much on her mind that Dr Vaughan ought to try and convert them. "But, my dear," said the Doctor, "it would be no such easy task, for these people are much cleverer at arguing than I am." However, nothing would satisfy his wife but that they should be asked in one evening for the Doctor to have a talk with them. They were to arrive at eight o'clock, but nine passed and still no one came. Mrs Vaughan got first fidgety, then anxious, then in despair made enquiries from the servant, if no one had come. No one had been "except some Christy minstrels an hour ago whom I sent away." . . . Poor Mrs Vaughan! Of course after that the proud Brahmins would not take the slightest notice of them. [59]

Another of her husband's 'doves' recalled how Catherine 'watered' the tea cups:

She was very well read, with a wonderful power of conversation, great wit and originality. She was very hospitable and kind to us, asking us in to meet her guests. She was afflicted with a nervous movement, a curious jerkiness which sent her napkin flying across the room three or four times at a meal. No one surely has poured out tea as she did. With a large tray in front of her, full of cups, she used the teapot as a watering can, passing it backwards and forwards above the cups, into which some drops of tea found their way, but most of it was on the tray, and all the while she was talking vigorously, engrossed in her conversation. She was an extra-ordinarily clever mimic, and it was not a little embarrassing as you saw the people whom she had so well taken off coming into the room. [60]

We get another glimpse into Catherine's life from a letter Vaughan wrote to Davidson in October 1878 accepting an invitation to the latter's wedding but adding that he couldn't answer for Catherine as she had taken 'her annual flight to Guernsey'. Further anecdotes were told shortly after her death by the Revd Joseph Leycester Lyne alias 'Father Ignatius' in a letter he sent to the *Western Mail*. Lyne was a distant relative of Catherine's. He was a self-styled Benedictine monk [in Deacon's Orders in the Church of England] who had founded a small community near Abergaveny in Wales. In addition to being an 'abbot' there he spent much time doing mission work in London and other large cities where he was a champion of orthodoxy and a severe critic of modernists such as Catherine's brother, the Dean of Westminster. He claimed that Catherine used to attend the services and meetings at which he was preaching or speaking when he was in London and that when he publicly attacked the Dean's theology, she heartily approved of his condemnation of her brother's views. She persuaded him to come to one of her crowded 'At Home' social events at which there would be some 'Parsees and Mahometans' and he agreed on condition he could either give a Bible reading or lead in prayer. He ended up doing the latter as he sought to get some the Christians who were having a loud theological argument to find common ground and pray together as an act of witness to the non-Christians present. Not what was expected to happen at polite social gatherings!

Among their many guests, they still welcomed visits from favourite Old Harrovians as well as from former 'doves'. Herman Merivale tells of one such visit:

> Our curious friendship lasted to the end. Many, oh many years afterwards, when I was married, I brought my wife to introduce to the doctor, at luncheon in his Temple home. "Mrs Merivale" he said to her as I was talking with his own delightful partner, a Stanley of the Stanleys worthy of him, "I want to show you something in my study." My wife was perhaps a little tearful when she told me of their talk. It was a picture of myself over his fireplace. "That was my favourite pupil, Mrs Merivale, through all my Harrow years." Have I some reason to be proud of that? At all events in all this world, no pupil ever had a more beloved and congenial master. What is the least talked of, may one day be best known. [61]

George Russell in his usual fault-finding way saw Vaughan in a very different light during these years. In a section on Deans in his *Collections & Recollections* he wrote: 'And there was Dr Vaughan, Dean of Llandaff, who concealed under the blandest of manners a remorseless sarcasm and a mordant wit, and who never returned from the comparative publicity of the Athenaeum to the domestic shades of the Temple without leaving behind him some pungent sentence which travelled from mouth to mouth, and spared neither age nor friendship nor affinity.' [62]

Given his position in the city and his fame as a public speaker, it was inevitable that he would be called upon to use his talents in a variety of ways. When the Lord Mayor, for example, formed an influential committee in February 1885 with a view to raising a fund to provide a national memorial to General Gordon, he invited the great and the good to serve on it. The committee was headed by the Prince of Wales and included such national figures as the Archbishop of Canterbury, Cardinal Manning, Gladstone and Vaughan. On Wednesday 13 July 1887, he was a last minute stand-in for Viscount Cross at the presentation of awards to students at Guy's Hospital Medical School. He was in demand at society weddings in such churches as St Margaret's Westminster (where he officiated in 1888 at Montagu Butler's second marriage) and at St George's, Hanover Square. And he was a frequent guest preacher in the Abbey.

Another side to Vaughan's daily ministry was his correspondence. Thirty or so letters a day, all written standing at his writing desk, was the norm. They were often in response to requests for help and advice and from old students looking for his support in their applications for a new post. Some were an exercise in the gentle use of patronage for the good of others, writing to those who had the power to make appointments, such as the one quoted earlier in reference to Montgomery. Sometimes it was to encourage and urge acceptance of an offer as in the case of Lightfoot, who in 1879 had been offered the See of Durham but felt himself ill equipped for the post and was thinking of refusing it. Vaughan spoke at length with him and then, fearing he had not been persuasive enough, wrote him a long letter early the next morning and sent it by hand for immediate delivery. As in so many of his letters, Vaughan underlined particular words which he would have stressed had he been speaking with him face to face:

> Twelve hours' pondering leaves me clearer than ever as to this great duty.
> Unsought – unwelcome – an office is thrust upon you. Responsible men, of various positions and characters, have fastened upon you as a man capable of filling it – nay, <u>marked out</u> to fill it.
> Some advisers say to you, Other work is more important. On such a principle, the Episcopal office is disparaged. <u>We</u> say, If the Church is worth keeping, worth saving, <u>no</u> work can be more urgent than that of being its Overseer . . .
> I will not go over all the anticipations which I breathed to you last night. The opportunities of <u>kindness</u> – the conviction of <u>sympathy</u> not talked but felt – the <u>confidence</u> of laymen and Clergymen in the knowledge, in the wisdom, in the sincerity, of the Chief Minister – the wholesome <u>counsels</u> for the rash and the young, for the one-sided & half-sighted, for the elders & rulers of the Church in <u>council</u> . . .
> My dear Friend! In this crisis of your life you will let me call you to – and you will let me express, in one closing word, the <u>intensity</u> of my conviction that a large part of the well-being of the Church is contained in your this day's decision. O let me not sleep one night more in doubt of it! In the Name of One whose strength is made perfect in weakness, hesitate not longer, but gird yourself for the difficult work – and <u>never, never</u> look back.
> Ever faithfully, Respectfully, Affectionately   Yours C.J. Vaughan

I write in bed – you will forgive all deficiencies. Of course you will find me any time. [63]

Not satisfied with that, he then wrote a second, equally pressing letter after having discussed it with Hort and with Lake (who was the Dean of Durham).[64] To their great relief, Lightfoot accepted the offer of preferment. Four years later Vaughan told him that he had hoped he would be translated to Canterbury on the death of Archbishop Tait, but the post was offered to Benson. He wrote to Lightfoot at the time:

> It has been no disappointment to yourself, but to me it has been a very great disappointment, not to have you placed – with your will or without it – in the great seat of Canterbury. You, I doubt not, will be able to rejoice in the appointment which has been made, with a knowledge and appreciation of which I have had no opportunities. It is a moment of deepest interest to the whole Church.
> Forgive my saying these few words quite from the heart. I had felt that in you we should have had that combination of learning with human dealing, of moderation without laxity, & of power in union with love, which would have best secured the continuation of our departed Chief's spirit with another generation . . .
> Not to answer this. [65]

Sometimes, he was not entirely sure that his advice was right as this one written in July 1882 shows. It was sent in response to a request for counsel from Davidson, who had been offered a residentiary canonry at Canterbury:

> I feel your kindness in asking my counsel. Surely it must ever be at your service, and a loving desire with it that it may help you.
> You know that I have felt strongly that your presence with the Archbishop is the best work you can offer to the Church, while he wants you – and long may that want continue! Anything that removed you from him, even if it were the Archbishopric of York, I would counsel you to put aside while he lives. But here is a thing which except for a comparatively small part of the year, need not separate you from him. It is only a multiplying of journeys – and those very much shorter than mine between Llandaff and the Temple – which will be involved for you in obeying each faintest call from him, while the fact of your having a separate position will give you more weight, with the world, and even with the Church, in serving him.
> It is not exactly what we should have thought of for you. There may even be a moment's challenging of your claim at quite so early an age. But already there are many who will justify it, from what they have seen and heard of

you, and the rest will feel that the Archbishop is responsible for the appointment, and knows what he is doing.

I have felt ever since I dissuaded Pelham from taking Croydon, that it is playing with edge tools to attempt to settle for oneself or for another, exactly what is the suitable thing: - on the whole there should be a good reason (I thought there <u>was</u> in that case) why a man should not allow the wisdom of those who are in authority and who must to a great extent represent to us the Providence which is above than to fix his work for him – even when at first sight it may not be the very thing that our own or another's idea would have chosen as the fittest.

Such are my thoughts on reading your letter and thinking of it for one hour. There is that in each man which forms an instinct of judging, and he does well to follow it even when friends counsel otherwise. I do not ask to override <u>that</u> – but, recognizing it as paramount, I venture notwithstanding to "give my advice" in the affirmative. [66]

Davidson refused the offer despite Vaughan's 'affirmative' advice. He was made Sub-Almoner to the Queen in August and a year later was appointed Dean of Windsor. On that occasion, Vaughan's letter of congratulations revealed how tender and sentimental he could be:

My thoughts, my sympathies, my poor prayers, will be yours. If it ever makes me for a moment proud to remember that you were once a Harrow boy, and once one of my little flock in the Temple, <u>you</u> at least will not despise me for it, knowing that I love you.

With all the fullness of my affection. I am ever your friend. [67]

Some of Vaughan's correspondence was naturally written to old friends simply by way of encouragement, appreciation or to show solidarity with them when they were going through hard times. The following brief selection written to F.W. Farrar, shows an attractive side to the man. The first is undated but was clearly written during their time together at Harrow in the late 1850s:

MY DEAR FARRAR: I must not insult you by compliments upon your sermon of yesterday: but neither can I leave you without the expression of the deep debt of gratitude which I feel *myself* to owe you for such a noble effort for the good of souls. I cannot doubt that it will be remembered by many, as it was listened to with profound attention by all.

The time will come, I hope, when you will publish that sermon with others. Perhaps a sermon published by itself does not possess the *permanence* of character which one would desire for it: but I am sure that, when the time comes for publishing a volume of *sermons*, you will not find them passed by. [68]

The next one is a letter of appreciation for what became a religious best-seller:

August 20, 1874

MY DEAR FARRAR: Just before I left London I had the pleasure of receiving your book [*The Life of Christ*] from yourself, and it is furnishing both Mrs Vaughan and me a profitable and interesting study during our season of rest. It is, indeed, a marvellous proof of your industry and power of abstraction, that you should have been able to create such a work in the *horœ subsecivœ* of such a laborious life as yours. Its success seems to be an accomplished fact within the first few weeks (I had almost said *days*), of its publication. May you receive on all sides the thanks and the applauses which you have so richly earned. Active and useful as your life has been hitherto – and never more so than in your present great sphere – I do not wish that education (in the narrower sense of that word) should engross the whole of it. I look forward to seeing you compelled, ere long, to give your mature and disciplined powers to the more *direct* (though not perhaps the more *real*) service of the Church in her highest ministries.

I have never thanked you as much as I ought and would, for your wonderful kindness to me in my illness. I never knew till then the *soothing* capacity of a telegram. [69]

Here is another acknowledging receipt of Farrar's latest book:

The Temple, May 3, 1879

MY DEAR FARRAR:

I have trespassed unduly on your long friendship by delaying thus long my expression of gratitude for the gift of your book [probably *The Life and Works of St Paul*]. Hitherto, I have not been able to read it continuously; I have dipped here and there into its contents, at points of special interest, finding always something to admire, if also (as must be the case where one has lived so long and so intimately with the subject), something also to hesitate or to pause upon.

You need not words of mine, dear Farrar, to assure you of the success of your great undertaking, both as a matter of public interest and of grateful and devout study. I know which of the two you will most value, - the heart-felt thanks of those whom you help, to enter with a fuller appreciation into those immortal writings, or the more superficial applause of people who admire eloquence and assent without judgement.

I shall have the book always near me. I shall use it, as I have used 'The Life of Christ,' whenever I want to be sure that I have not overlooked something vital in the interpretation or enforcement of the inspired Word.

May the highest and best of blessings be upon your work and upon the workman! Your attached old friend,   C.J. Vaughan [70]

He wrote an encouraging letter to Farrar on his move from Marlborough to Westminster in 1876 which made mention of the emotional wrench leaving the boys must have been for him, and he added these warm words of welcome: 'How happy it will make me to feel that in the great, and sometimes homeless, world of London you will find at the Temple a love and a sympathy at once *old* and *new*.' [71] And when, many years later, Farrar's son Cyril died in China, he sent him this short and tender message:

The Temple, February 8, 1891

MY DEAR OLD FRIEND:

I could not read unmoved the tidings of your great sorrow. The loss of a dear son seems to me (to whom it can only be an imagination) almost too hard a trial to be lived through. But you are borne up by a firmer faith than mine. The distance adds to the bitterness – depriving you of the sorrowful comfort of looking upon the dear face in death and laying the precious body in its last bed.

May God comfort you and the dear patient sufferer beside you – and dear Eric too, and the loving sisters. I hope and I hear, that your great effort of last Monday was got through before you actually knew of the departure from earth.

Always, in joy and sorrow,

Affectionately and gratefully yours,   C.J. Vaughan [72]

Two other letters of condolence give us cherished memories from his own earlier life. The first was written to Gladstone in 1876:

The death of my dear and noble-hearted friend Lord Lyttleton has touched me so deeply that I cannot rest till I have poured out something of my sorrow to you who knew and loved him as he deserved. I go back in my thoughts of him to the 2nd of March forty years ago, when he brought me the first news of a youthful success upon which he forgot every selfish feeling in congratulating me. The recollection of him as he was that day in the great Court at Trinity is as fresh in my heart at this distance of time as if his figure were before my eyes. And from that day to this I have not one memory of him which is not generous and brave and unselfish and pure. I saw him last on the 5th Sunday after Easter, but three Sundays ago, in the Temple Church, where he stayed for the Sacrament – and little did I think that he was already suffering in health and spirits, & that I should see him no more in this life.

But there is no one "sting" in the thought of that death, save what has been for ever healed and charmed away by the slipping off of that mortal body in which, like the Saviour whom he faithfully served, he was "straightened" till the great "Baptism" was "accomplished".

I know that you will forgive, & more than forgive, the utterance to you of my sorrowful sympathy, and of my earnest desire that the Comforter may be powerfully present in the hearts that will be mourning tomorrow beside his grave. [73]

The second was to Davidson on the death of his father:

I hear with true sorrow of the heavy distress which has suddenly fallen upon you. May you be comforted in the only real way by Him who alone can do it.

It carries back my thoughts some 10 or 11 years to the time when you were in like manner recalled from abroad by one of the same kind of sorrows which shake the very life.

Sixty years ago, when I was 13, I lost my father. The sorrow was life-long – I never lose the memory of that long and awful Sunday in the early morning of which he died, leaving his 14 children in the charge of a Mother, who survived him almost 50 years, and whose death is the other calamity of a long life.

Forgive my obtruding self upon you at this moment. It will at least show you that I can feel with you. [74]

Vaughan wrote three letters of consolation to Lord Althorp, first on the death of his mother in 1851 and a year later of his sister whilst the boy was still at Harrow, and then in December 1857 on the death of his father. On that occasion he wrote:

It is needless to tell you how many ties of respect and gratitude bind me to your Father's memory, or how sincerely I mourn his loss. Rather let me say, in brief words, how tenderly I feel for you in the keen sorrow which now has been sent upon you, as well as in the prospect of the heavy responsibilities which are so early crowding around you [i.e. on his assumption of the title of Earl Spencer]. I never can forget your earlier years under my roof at Harrow, nor cease to take the deepest interest in your joys and sorrows as a man. [75]

But there were also happier occasions which were marked with congratulatory letters such as his election in April 1857 as an MP. On that occasion he wrote: 'You enter Parliament under the happiest auspices: may you have all the success and all the enjoyment which this life can afford without endangering the next.' [76] Twelve years later, he wrote to congratulate him on his appointment as Lord Lieutenant of Ireland 'a position of vast influence and, at this crisis certainly, of enormous interest.' [77] A letter of a different kind to him shows Vaughan once again seeking to promote the career of his brother David. Lord Spencer had written asking his advice about appointing a particular man as the next Vicar of Battersea. He replied that he knew nothing of the man but suggesting in his place David, to whom the previous Lord Spencer had offered Brighton. He wrote warmly of David's success in ministering to working men, crowds of whom attended his Advent and Lent lectures in which 'he has dealt plainly on the difficulties of belief as well as on more directly practical topics . . . My Brother is a Liberal in every sense. He incurred Odium, I fancy, by his declared opinion in favour of the Dis-establishment of the Irish Church.' [78] David was duly offered the post but declined it. Vaughan wrote expressing his disappointment but acknow-ledged 'the purity and rectitude of his motives' and recommending Dr Pears, one of his former assistants at Harrow and now Headmaster of Repton. Vaughan had good reason to be grateful to the Earl, who provided a living in 1868 for his brother-in-law, John Simpkinson, when he left Harrow. The last surviving letter written by Vaughan to the Earl was again in answer to a request for advice about a clerical appointment, and ended on a very personal note: 'It gives me great pleasure to think that you heard me in the Chapel Royal chiefly because I love to remember the old days of all, and to believe that my voice still wakes an echo in your heart.' [79]

It seems that no letters to his brothers or sisters have survived but there is a handful to his cousin, Henry Halford Vaughan, son of the judge, Sir John. He wrote in 1848 to congratulate him on his appointment by Lord John Russell to the post of Professor of Modern History at Oxford (the first layman to hold this post): 'How can I express the pleasure this gives me? Accept my warmest congratulations on that which seems to be the very thing that would at this moment best suit you, & which is in itself so highly honourable & gratifying a position. May you have all health & happiness in filling it.' [80]

There are several letters to him from his Temple days including this affectionate one written in May 1874:

It was a touching pleasure to me to be permitted to see your face once more, & to renew those memories which, as I feebly tried to assure you, are ineffaceable to me, of your goodness to me when I was young, & when the Temple was already the centre for me of so many ambitions, which have since taken so different a turn, & which yet have landed my elder life, though in so unexpected a form, in this centre of legal energy and interest. My dear Halford! I shall always venture to feel that we love one another through absence & distance – may we be permitted to meet at last where there is no parting! Your ever affectionate C.J. Vaughan [81]

Vaughan was constantly busy and on the go. His letters to friends often tell where his recent preaching engagements had been or where forthcoming meetings would be. Inevitably with age he became worn down and had to retreat with Catherine to their home in Southborough to recuperate. Concern about his health had begun to figure in his letters already from 1873 as in this one written from there to Davidson:

I hope to begin, in my Study, in the Temple at 8 a.m. on Tuesday the 21st of October. Rather late you will say but I have not yet felt myself at all up to work and feel that I require a long rest still. I shall not preach in the Temple Church till November, but have made a few engagements (as usual) elsewhere for October.

I hope, my dear Davidson, that I shall be of <u>some</u> use in the way of work by that time. My head has been uncomfortable thus far: but I hope something from a new remedy which I am to try. [82]

Here is another in similar vein written to him from Southborough on 2 April 1875:

I am pretty well – though my last light days of Lent were additionally burdened by a very bad cold – through which, however, I struggled, even preaching in St Paul's on Good Friday evening – and now we are here for a few days between Sundays . . . I have to preach at Westminster Abbey next Sunday evening – the Dean being away in Scotland and deputing to me the first Sermon. [83]

To Gladstone who had written to invite him to call, he replied on 18 May 1876: 'Your kind letter finds me in the country recovering from an illness which has proved more lingering than I expected. This alone would prevent my accepting your kind invitation for the 8th of June – and indeed my Daily Service (which falls upon myself and begins at 10 o'clock) has stood in the way of my proposing myself as your guest according to your kind invitation in days gone by.' [84]

By 1879 his personal medical advisor was recommending that for his health's sake he must move out of London for part of the year. His mother died in January of that year but he was not present at her funeral in Leicester, presumably because he was too ill to travel. Soon afterwards, an invitation came to him from Alfred Ollivant, the Bishop of Llandaff which must have seemed to be a Providential solution, albeit one with a heavier workload attached. He was 63 when he accepted the Deanery of Llandaff, which he then held in plurality with the Temple but not before he had thoroughly checked that this arrangement would be legal. He wrote at great length to Gladstone about this:

> As it is to your kindness that I owe the office which I so deeply value and love, the Mastership of the Temple, it seems natural that I should not leave you to learn by common report any circumstance that may affect in any way its terms and exercise.
>
> The Bishop of Llandaff has surprised me (for he is almost a stranger to me) with the offer of his Deanery – to which, as you are aware, he, as one of the Welsh Bishops, is called to appoint.
>
> Before returning an answer to what various considerations of health and other circumstances inclined me to view as a not undesirable proposal I felt it to be necessary to ascertain what view would be taken by the Crown Lawyers of the compatibility of the Deanery with the Mastership. I do not feel that the time has yet come for relinquishing my situation in the Temple – although I do not deny that I should like to know that I could retire from it at any moment – without becoming of necessity a perfectly unoccupied man.
>
> After a careful examination of the Acts bearing upon the question, the Lawyers have come to the conclusion that the Mastership is not a "benefice" in the sense which alone would prevent it being held, under the present law, with a Deanery. The term "Rectory", occurring in the Patent of the Mastership, seems by the context, as well as by the known facts of the case to be interpreted simply into "government", in the sense in which it is familiar in connection with certain Headships at Oxford or with some of the Scotch Universities. In point of fact, as you know, I exercise and can exercise no one right of an Incumbent, nor do I receive any one of the payments which would be my right if the Mastership were, in the Ecclesiastical use of the word, a Rectory.
>
> All this being so, I have decided to accept the Bishop's offer, which will involve indeed the usual "residence" in a remote village – "city" but which will leave me longer time for residence in the Temple, than either the duties or the customs of the office appear to render necessary.

The income of the Mastership (after a recent small augmentation by the kindness of one of the two Societies) amounts but to £225 a year: the income of the Deanery will be £700. I earnestly hope to escape from any serious [imputations?] of <u>cupidity</u> in combining the two.

The opinions of the Crown Lawyers, I am told, is always regarded as <u>confidential</u>: but the [remit?] of their advice on the subject to the Prime Minister is that which I have stated, namely that the acceptance of the Deanery will not be treated as an avoidance of the Mastership.

That the Mastership is not a "benefice" should, I think, be sufficiently attested by the fact that my Predecessor for one year held both a Rectory & a Canonry with it – though the law against Pluralities was, I believe, already enacted.

Forgive me, my dear Mr Gladstone, for having appealed to your past kindness in apology for troubling you with this long statement. [85]

Llandaff had an additional attraction for him as it was not far from where Jackson, one of his Harrow favourites, lived with his family. He wrote to him from the Temple on 9 April 1879:

My dear old friend, You can imagine how much you have been in my thoughts since I first pondered the idea of being Dean of Llandaff. How <u>homelike</u> does it make my future abode, to feel that I shall have your beautiful house, your warm welcome within my near neighbourhood, at least during your visits there in the intervals of your busy and useful life in London.

I cannot tell you, as I would fain do, all that that visit to Llantilo had in it for your old Master, both of pleasure at the time, and of delightful memory ever since & for ever.

I hope the dear wife and children are all well. I have not <u>expressly</u> thanked you for your congratulations but they lie warm at my heart.

Ever affectionately yours C.J. Vaughan [86]

Sadly, the two friends were to be robbed by death of the pleasure of seeing each other again in Wales.

C.J. Vaughan

Men of Mark: a gallery of contemporary portraits

Thompson Cooper 1882

Dean of Llandaff – the Twilight Years

This new life, to be lived, must be entered upon. With no display and no proclamation and no signal of itself, beyond what men may chance to take knowledge of by its consequence in an improved temper and a sweetened disposition and a more charitable tone and a kindlier converse, the change is within . . . The man who lived once for himself lives now for others and for Another.
From a sermon, *The drifting Life, and its Opposite*, preached in Llandaff.

It may be an apocryphal story but it was retold by the Vicar of Llandaff and reported in the *Western Mail* that the thought "Here is the man for my vacant deanery" suddenly struck Bishop Ollivant as he was walking past the Temple. And this despite not knowing Vaughan personally, only by reputation. The two men did, however, have a good deal in common. Both were former Fellows of Trinity College Cambridge, where Ollivant had earlier won several of the high awards that Vaughan did a generation later. The Bishop was a Hebrew scholar and one of the Revisers of the OT, and he had been Vice-Principal of St David's College Lampeter from 1827-43 educating future clergymen. It is also told that when Vaughan received the Bishop's letter, he initially misunderstood it thinking he was being asked for advice about the appointment! Whatever the truth in these stories, the offer certainly came at an opportune time for Vaughan and he was glad to accept. The Benchers were happy too for him to continue as Master and to make use of a deputy when he was in residence at Llandaff. One price he had to pay for accepting the Deanery was that he had to resign as a Chaplain-in-Ordinary to the Queen. His recompense came three years later when she appointed him to the more prestigious post of Deputy Clerk to the Closet. She genuinely valued his personal ministry to and affection for her, and invited him regularly to preach in the chapel at Windsor Castle.

His appointment as Dean was welcomed by most in Wales, albeit with some surprise that such an eminent preacher would wish to come to such a poor and lowly deanery when he could have had his pick of dioceses in England as a bishop. There were some clergy, however, in north Wales who disapproved as they believed a Welsh-speaking native should have been given the post. The Deans of the four Welsh cathedrals were appointed by their particular diocesan Bishop, unlike in England where such appointments were made by the Crown. So they made their disapproval known publicly in an open letter to Ollivant. When Vaughan heard of it, he immediately offered to withdraw his acceptance but the Bishop begged him not to. He told the Bangor clergy that rather than reproaching him they should be thankful to him that 'by presenting his cathedral preferments to men of eminence, [he] endeavours to maintain what has hitherto been the proud distinction of his Church, and *to set before his clergy a standard at which they themselves should aim . . .'* [1] He felt the clergy of his diocese would benefit far more from Vaughan's example, learning and spirituality than they would from any command of the Welsh language that another man might have.[2]

In response to a letter of encouragement from his old school friend Dean Lake, he shared his manifest pleasure with the move to Llandaff:

> I was installed yesterday – a sweet little cathedral, lovely, reverent service, crowded congregation, and a welcome which I shall remember for ever.
>
> It is a strangely unexpected thing, but I am charmed with it. Just as you say, changes, alternations of work, *now*, and hereafter retirement and a peaceful grave. I do feel so grateful. To have, unsought, the very thing that seems to suit me is so pleasant that I dare to call it providential.
>
> It is the first thing that I ever *took* that I did not (virtually) ask for, and the first thing *offered* me that I have not *refused*. [3]

His working life was now to be lived in two very different worlds: in the heart of the nation's capital for about four months of the year and in his mini cathedral city, which in reality was just a large village, in south Wales for much of the rest of the year. Vacations would usually be spent at their private residence in Kent. Travelling between Llandaff and London 160 miles away would not be a problem for him as there had been direct rail connection between Cardiff (just two miles away) and the capital since 1850, and postal communications were excellent with three deliveries and collections a day. A gazetteer published in 1880 described Llandaff as standing 'on a gentle eminence, the houses are neat, and have an air of comfort, and there are several fine residences in the vicinity.' It was well on the way to becoming a desirable dormitory for successful Cardiff industrialists and merchants who built new houses there. One of the most splendid older properties was 'Llandaff Court', three storeys high and built between 1744 and 1751 for Admiral Thomas Mathew who chose, however, not to live in it. He declared that having lived so long at sea in a 'three-decker' he was not going to die in one! In 1850 the diocese acquired it for use as the Bishop's palace and it continued as such until 1958 when the Cathedral School moved into it. In 1861 two large houses, designed by Iwan Christian 'in the style of

307

country parsonages with steeply pitched green slate roofs and tall chimneys' were built on the Green facing the cathedral.[4] One was the new residence for the Dean (today it is the Bishop's residence) and the other the Canonry. Two other large mansions with extensive grounds nearby were Ely Court (also known as Insole Court) built for the coal magnate James Insole in 1873 and Rookwood built in 1866 for Colonel Sir Edward Stock Hill, the son of the founder of Hill's Dry Docks in Cardiff. Slater's Commercial Directory of 1880 listed over fifty individuals under the heading of 'Nobility, Gentry & Clergy' who resided in the village. Dean Stanley stayed with them in August 1879 and described Llandaff as 'Paradise'.

At the heart of the village was the cathedral, a Norman foundation dating from the early 12th century but which had fallen into a ruinous state by the beginning of the 19th. E.J. Newell, an historian of the diocese, dates the first impulse to its restoration to 1835 and 1836 when the Precentor Henry Douglas placed his dividends at the disposal of the Chapter for that purpose. Part of the money was used for refitting the Lady Chapel. In 1843, a further effort was made at the instigation of William Bruce Knight, the Chancellor, and afterwards the first Dean when that office was revived. The *Church of England Magazine* printed three rather lovely pictures of the roofless cathedral in its edition of 4 March 1843, and an article four weeks later was about the building: 'the west front we remark still beautiful in its ruins . . .' [5] The writer noted that previously the Bishop had also been the Dean but 'the new establishment will consist of a Bishop, Dean and four Canons.' [6] The Bishop at that earlier time was Dr Edward Copleston, formerly Provost of Oriel College Oxford, and also Dean of St Paul's who divided his time between Llandaff and London – as Vaughan was to do.

The work of restoration continued under Knight's successor, Dean Conybeare. On 16 April 1853 divine service was again held in the choir and nave which had been restored, and for the first time since 1691 the service was choral, a choir having been lent by the Dean and Chapter of Gloucester and the preacher was Samuel Wilberforce, the Bishop of Oxford. The next work was to rebuild the western part which lay in ruins. The restoration of the cathedral, undertaken from 1843 by John Prichard and his partner John Seddon, was completed on 19 April 1869 when the last stone was lowered onto the spire at a ceremony presided over by the Bishop. A great service was held on 13 July 1869 to celebrate the completion of the work.[7]

In 1876 the oversight of the Parish of Llandaff had been transferred from the Dean and Chapter to its own Vicar. The Bishop, without consulting the then Dean, appointed the Revd Richard Ferguson to the post. The Cathedral services as such at 11 a.m. and 3 p.m., now became separate from the 'parish services' held at 9.50 a.m. and 7 p.m. and a monthly celebration of HC at 8 a.m., though all were held in the same building. There had been regular choral services since 1861 and some provision for the choristers' education had been made in the parish's National School situated a mile away in Canton. A Minor Canon, the Revd E.A. Fishbourn, who had served previously in Ireland, had proposed setting up a proper cathedral choir school but the Chapter had not supported the idea.

It was Fishbourn as Succentor and with his knowledge of the form of service used in Cashel Cathedral in Ireland who devised the liturgy for Vaughan's installation by the Bishop in the morning of 1 April 1879. Ollivant was determined that compared to what had gone before, this was to be 'a very great function'. The *Cardiff Times* reported that it attracted one of the largest congregations seen within its walls for many years and noted:

> A respectful address, signed by a very large number of residents of Llandaff and the neighbourhood, has been sent to the Bishop of Llandaff expressing the deep satisfaction which those immediately around his Lordship feel in regard to the recent appointment, the pleasure it will give them to welcome the new Dean among them, and their profound conviction that in the introduction of so eminent a scholar and theologian into the Diocese, the Bishop had solely at heart the best interests of the Church, and that in such appointment his Lordship has exercised a wise and sound judgement. [8]

The *Western Mail* reported that he had stayed with the Bishop but returned to London the same evening after his installation and would not take up residence until the end of June. It noted he had taken the opportunity in the afternoon 'of making what is understood to be his first acquaintance with the place, his walks extending to the suburbs.'

He was in fact back much sooner because a few days later, the Bishop gave Vaughan the opportunity to address a large gathering of prominent local Church people gathered for the annual meeting of the Diocesan Church Extension Society. He was to become an active committee member and along with his wife generous donors to its funds. He was thus already embarked on a wider ministry than just to his cathedral congregation but first he had to make his mark in the cathedral and show that his reputation as a great preacher was well deserved.

In October 1879 the annual Church Congress met at Swansea, the first time it had been held in Wales and the Dean was one of three who read papers by way of introduction to a debate on the Ministry and more particularly training for it. The other two speakers were the Principals of Cuddesdon and Wycliffe Hall. Vaughan used the occasion to describe his own alternative to theological colleges. It is his fullest and most personal treatment of the subject:

> Forty years ago there was practically no place of clerical preparation for the graduate of the University. We must not exaggerate the evil. Men of intellect, men of genius, thought and read for themselves, and they escaped the dwarfing influences, if they also missed the elevating . . . It was not in the choice spirits of the Church that the destitution of special preparation showed itself. In the rank and file of the ministry it showed itself disastrously. The oversight of souls was a mere guesswork and haphazard. The entrance upon a parish was a mere leap into darkness. It is possible that even now a first-rate man does best to dispense with any regular intermediate training . . . It is a cheap as well as easy sarcasm which has defined a theological college as a machine for raising dullness into mediocrity . . .
>
> Admitting all the drawbacks of a theological college, the comparative prevalent professionalism of its tone, still it has an office, in those cases, at all events, not to be disparaged; and many men will owe it, not their ministerial future only, but "their very own souls besides." Another experiment has been tried. It sets up no rival to the theological college. It has a different scope, a different idea, and a different material. It deals with the case of graduates only, and of graduates whose college career has been satisfactory. It is inapplicable to men who require either discipline to make sure of their conduct, or tuition to make sure of their study. The students take care of themselves as to their lodgings and maintenance, and there is no "account of giving and receiving" between them and their chief. He, on his part, gives them free access to his parochial meetings, whether of school teachers, district visitors, communicants, or Bible-readers; assigns them districts among his poorer people, classes in his Sunday-school, places in his choir; reads with them daily in the Greek Testament, sets them texts for sermons, subjects for essays on doctrine; looks over, comments upon, suggests alternatives of idea, arrangement of, and treatment; counsels them as to their future ministrations in the Church Offices, and in the various departments of parochial visitation; advises and assists them in their negotiations for curacies, and seeks to turn them thus, and their endeavours, into channels which his larger experience has shown him to be

wise, right and true. When through change of position [a reference to his own situation as Master of the Temple and Dean of Llandaff] he has himself been without a parish, he has supplied through others this part of the work, keeping a general supervision over all, and seeking to maintain in everything that personal charge of influence which is the keynote of the whole system. [my emphasis] In the course of the last eighteen years some 200 men have passed through this course under one person. [9]

Vaughan went on to encourage others to do similar work, even if it was no more than taking a single young candidate of 'small means and modest attainments' into his own household and training him to be a minister. As an encouragement to do such work, he claimed, 'It needs no extraordinary gifts of scholarship, no remarkable store of knowledge: the devotional study of Scripture is always more than the exegetical: the pious influence of an experienced pastor is far more valuable for his purpose than any brilliancy of speech or any profundity of learning.' [10]

Back in Llandaff, his immediate and primary concern was the conduct of worship in the Cathedral. It had no tradition, such as he had known at the Temple Church, of magnificent choral worship and preaching of a high order likely to attract crowded congregations. All that was about to change. Vaughan asked which of the two Sunday services was most poorly attended and was told it was the afternoon service. He decided that was the one he would always preach at and the number of worshippers quickly rose. People came in their hundreds from Cardiff to hear him. In his early years he gave several series of Bible readings and expositions which attracted crowds including many Nonconformists. It was not unknown for Nonconformist ministers to attend worship in the cathedral in order to hear the Dean, such was his reputation as a sound preacher and teacher of the Faith.

When Vaughan arrived, improving the standard of choral music became his first priority. He listened carefully to his junior colleague's proposals but judged them not ambitious enough. He raised the matter at his first Chapter meeting in the autumn and gained approval for a boarding school for between 30 – 40 boys to be located in the old deanery on the Green. Vaughan chose the Revd C.E. Butler to be its first Head but this proved not to be one of his better appointments. The Dean had managed to get an annual salary of £150 [= £15,290] and a free house offered as remuneration to the Head. Ernest Owen replaced him three years later and the Cathedral School began to flourish under him. It was run on the lines of a traditional Preparatory Boarding School. At its first Speech Day on 26 July 1880, Vaughan declared that this was to be no mere musical school. The boys' wider education must come first and their musical training and singing duties in the cathedral second. The school became his 'pet child, my chief interest, next to my men.'[11]

W.R. Compton-Davies, writing in 1896, said that it was Vaughan who had paid for most of the cost of adapting the old deanery to the purpose of a school and for the new buildings and had been its guiding light.[12]

> The object Dr Vaughan had in view was the establishment of a school which should be a cathedral Choir School, but something more, as it was felt that there was room in the Diocese for a first class Preparatory School. Provision was therefore made for about 50 boarders who should be sons of gentlemen, from 8 to 14 years of age, and who would be prepared for scholarships and entrance at the Public Schools. Of these fifty boys a certain number are selected with a view to the requirements of the Cathedral Choir. Twenty Choral Scholarships, in value from 39 to 75 guineas, are attached to the School to be competed for by boys with good voices, and in order to prevent the general work of the choristers being interrupted by their choral duties it is arranged that they should attend one service only on weekdays, viz., at 6 p.m. . . .
> Since 1883 over 30 Scholarships and Exhibitions, besides other honours, have been gained at the Public Schools, direct from Llandaff . . . The Dean of Llandaff acts as Visitor, with the Dean and Chapter as Governors.[13]

Vaughan had endowed two of the choral scholarships and he left sufficient money in his will to fund them during the remaining years of Ernest Owen's headmastership as well as leaving the Head a personal gift of £1,000. He recognized that the large measure of success enjoyed by his 'pet child' was thanks to Owen's leadership. Although not directly involved in their management, he also supported the local National School, a specialist school for deaf and dumb children, and 'Howell's School' built in 1859, a Public School for girls funded by the bequest of Thomas Howell, a wealthy 16th century member of the Drapers' Company in the City of London. Half of the 60 boarders at Howell's were orphans who received free board, education and clothing. Inevitably, the Dean was asked to serve on a variety of educational governing bodies, among them the Glamorgan Education Board and the Cardiff School Board, and he was a regular guest speaker at school speech days.

As at the Temple Church he had very few Occasional Offices to officiate at and not much of a pastoral ministry. The Baptismal Register for 1880, for example, shows that of the 51 baptisms performed in the Cathedral that year most were done by the Vicar of Llandaff, the Revd

H.R. Buckley, a few by minor canons and none by the Dean. In the course of his 18 years as Dean, he baptised only eight children, officiated at just two weddings and three funerals – two of the latter were those of Bishop Ollivant in December 1882 and of his widow, Alicia, in July '86. But he did pick up again what had been his custom as the Vicar of Doncaster and that was to give support to local charities and to show an active concern for the health and well-being of local people. One of his first charity sermons preached in the cathedral was on behalf of a house of mercy in Llandaff for reclaimed prostitutes and three years later, together with John Scott Lidgett, a prominent Methodist, they founded a preventive home for girls caught up in prostitution in Cardiff.

Two years after his move to Llandaff, Arthur Stanley died. Catherine sat with him on his last day, Monday 18 July 1881 and 'at intervals repeated the simple hymns in which he delighted.' [14] Both Vaughan and Archbishop Tait came to the Deanery to pray for him. Stanley's dying wish, written down at the time by Canon Farrar, was that Vaughan should be the preacher at his funeral in the Abbey: 'I have been so very intimate with him. He has known me longest.' [15] Vaughan duly obliged and preached about his friend at Evensong in the Abbey on Sunday 24th. The day before he delivered the address he wrote to Davidson:

> I am much overwhelmed & most unequal to tomorrow. May God help me.
> I start for London in two hours.
> Mrs Vaughan has borne up beautifully, but is today in great pain with eyes and head. She did not intend to go up again.
> With love strong and true. [16]

In his address he went back to their time together as schoolboys at Rugby and his earliest impressions of the young Stanley and spoke of the enduring influence that Arnold had had on him. Stanley would have approved of that.

On the day of the funeral Catherine decided she could not face it and consequently her husband became the 'chief mourner.' Edward Parry, the Bishop of Dover, who had married into the Stanley family described the service as 'a touching and interesting spectacle but far too long. From the time our family procession left the Deanery, to head the longer general stream, until the final blessing it was a good hour and a half – mostly spent in slow walking or standing.' [17]

Catherine was deeply affected by the death of her last surviving sibling as this 'Thank You' letter written by Vaughan on 29 July to her cousin, the Hon William Stanley, reflects:

I feel myself much in your debt for your kind and beautiful letter of (alas) nine days ago. We have been passing through many days of exertion as well as sorrow and the multitude of our fellow-mourners has made itself felt in the innumerable letters of sympathy which pour in by every Post.

Dear Mr Stanley, you have always been so kind to me that a letter from you at this time comes with peculiar tenderness. We have indeed lost much, and life can never be the same to us. Many, I am sure, who did not live so closely in friendship with him as I did, are yet saying the same words.

Catherine has borne her great sorrow her real desolation – left, as she is, the very last of her family with characteristic firmness and courage – but I fear the very composure is symptomatic of the deeper suffering which lies under it.

We are in sweet quietness and beauty here – but the distance makes these repeated long journeys trying, and I am in great fear of having <u>again</u> to visit the Deanery where Lady Frances Baillie, after nursing him most tenderly, lies ill herself of the same terrible disease. May this [sword?] be averted by God's mercy – but we are very anxious.

Ever, Dear Mr Stanley, Sincerely and affectionately yours   C.J. Vaughan [18]

Dean Stanley had been a very wealthy man and left estate valued at £83,948 net - in today's terms over eight and a half million. Among his many bequests were gifts of £500 each (= £51,500) to his two sisters, Mary Stanley [who had in fact died in November 1879] and Catherine Vaughan, and to six of his old friends including Vaughan and Hugh Pearson. His sisters were to receive, in addition, the interest and dividends on his stocks and shares and it was to be 'for their separate use, independent of any marital control'. It made Catherine a very wealthy woman in her own right which would allow her to buy her own property when the time and need came for this.

It was believed by some that Vaughan was subsequently offered the Deanery of Westminster but declined it. He had discovered a new happiness and more than enough opportunities for useful service to satisfy him in his Welsh mini-city with its ancient cathedral. Liddell, the Dean of Christ Church Oxford was definitely offered the post but declined it, as did Montagu Butler, the Headmaster of Harrow, and in the end it went to Bradley, the Master of University College, a former pupil of Stanley's

He was to lose another dear friend, his old pupil Jackson, in 1881. He had written a warm congratulatory letter to him on 3 March:

I must not sleep till I have congratulated my dear old Pupil & Friend on the news which I read in the Evening Paper.

314

He is my first Harrow Judge – and it makes me <u>very</u> <u>proud</u> <u>and</u> <u>very</u> <u>old</u>. It is a magnificent office, & you are worthy of it.

I am glad to have been permitted to see your career from its very beginning till this crowning success.

I hope I shall be spared to watch your course yet a little further – always with happiness, always with sympathy, always with thankfulness.

Let Lady Jackson know that I am proud and happy <u>with</u> <u>her</u>.

Your affectionate old friend & once Master C.J. Vaughan [19]

Three months later, his friend was dead. His letter of condolence to Jackson's widow shows how deeply attached he had remained to a pupil from over thirty years earlier:

You may well believe that my thoughts are often with you in your sorrow and solitude, & that I find it very hard to reconcile myself to the removal from us (for I must place myself with you, though at a long distance behind, in the bereavement) of so dear and loving a heart as that of our dear friend. How everything lives in my memory! That happy stay with you – then Sunday – the drives and walks – his tender visits to me in my room, where I had a very bad cold – then the dear little family breakfasts – such a picture of love and duty!

What you say touches me very deeply – about my last note to him – written in such ignorance – in such joy at his new office – and then of his feeling about me.

Then I go back all those years to his own <u>marriage</u>. What a bright beginning of a true & constant wedlock – faithful even unto death.

Forgive me for all this – the subject is near my heart.

I should like to do what you so kindly suggest for me. I am (only) a little afraid of my <u>Latin</u> – so very rusty now. I know you will not mind my calling in Dr Butler, if I find it desirable. I think he also loved him, though I doubt if any one loved him so much as <u>I</u> (out of his own home, I mean).

Take a little care of yourself, dear Lady Jackson. You have something to live for – were it only to love those whom he loved.

Your sincere friend, C.J. Vaughan [20]

He had lost a dear friend whom he had hoped to see more of by moving to Llandaff but it had also brought him nearer his cousin Henry Halford Vaughan who had settled with his family at Upton Castle in Pembrokeshire in 1867. A letter to his cousin written in 1880 which is largely about an upcoming family funeral also implies that Catharine and he had become attached to their children. It includes an invitation to allow the dear children to come to us two or three days beforehand when you are taking them to London, so that you should pick them up in passing Cardiff and take them on, it would be a real pleasure to us to continue & increase our affectionate interest in them.

Not that the dear Parents would be very welcome if they could bring instead of sending them.

Forgive this scrawl. I have many letters to write and you will not complain of the incoherence of this. [21]

Halford and his wife had four daughters and one son, William Wyamar, who would later become Headmaster of Rugby, the post Vaughan had once hoped to have himself.

He won new friends among nationalists and Nonconformists by his warm support for the movement to have a proper university in Wales. This was something that the Bishops in Wales and the clergy generally had not given though the first request to the Government of the day for a "Commission to inquire into the present condition of Higher Education in the Principality" was drawn up by Bishop Ollivant and signed by the four Welsh Bishops in July 1877. [22] Sadly, Ollivant did not think the time was then ripe for a Welsh University and it was left to Nonconformist ministers and laymen to press for it. Vaughan had much valuable experience to offer to the committee in that he had sat on two important university commissions earlier in his life which had proposed substantial reforms at Cambridge and at Durham.

Together with the Town Clerk, Mr Lewis Williams, he was invited to argue the case for Cardiff as opposed to Swansea before those who would determine the location for the new university. The arbitrators were Lord Carlingford, Lord Bramwell and the Rt Hon A.J. Mundella (Vice-President of the Council on Education) who met at the Privy Council Office on 7 March 1883 and recorded their unanimous decision in favour of Cardiff. Vaughan's eloquence and good sense had helped win the day. Upon hearing the good news, Vaughan immediately wrote to Cardiff Town Council and his letter was read and minuted at their meeting on 12 March: 'I am most anxious that the kindest consideration should be shown to the naturally wounded feelings of Swansea. It must be our first care now to try and carry with us the sympathy and co-operation of South Wales, and particularly of the rival town, which has undergone what we must feel to be a trying mortification.'

What action, if any, was taken by the Mayor and Council in response to his wise advice was not recorded. The Royal Charter was granted by the Queen on 14 March. The committee had already secured by then a grant of £4,000 p.a. from the Treasury and by the end of the first Session (1883-84) it had received subscriptions amounting to £12,217. [23] The College was opened twelve months before the grant of the Charter was actually received. The first Principal was John Viriamu Jones, aged just 27 but already with experience as a Lecturer at London and Oxford and as Principal of Firth College, Sheffield. He enjoyed from the start the warm support and friendship of Lord Aberdare and of Dean Vaughan both of whom had been elected to the committee which formulated the scheme for administering the College. The latter frequently accompanied Jones when his presence could be of help as this letter describing the first of many meetings he and the Dean had with Cardiff Corporation shows:

August 19th – I entered Sheffield Station at 12.30 A.M. (*sic*), Cardiff Town Hall at 10 a.m. Meeting of the Council. At 11.30 we went to interview the Corporation Committee. They offered us rooms that will not suit: we replied to that effect and asked for £400 per annum, the interest of the promised sum of £10,000. They refused. We went to inspect the premises offered and afterwards to the Infirmary. All pleased with the Infirmary: probably on Monday we shall decide to take it.

The Dean was at the meeting and made a conciliatory speech to the Corporation Committee, but apparently did not convince them. I did not speak a word, not wishing to meddle with the matter. In the evening I dined at the Deanery. The Dean was extremely kind, and Mrs Vaughan. Perhaps you know she is Dean Stanley's sister.

I passed the morning looking over numerous applications [for positions on the teaching staff]. This afternoon I went to the Cathedral. The Dean preached. The text was on Elisha's protection by the invisible hosts seen by the young man when his eyes were opened. [24]

The Dean had been invited to address the South Wales National Eisteddfford which was meeting in Cardiff in that same month and he used the occasion to encourage local support for the fledgling college. In the same speech he put on record his claim to be descended from an ancient Welsh family, the Vychans of Kington in Radnorshire – in effect a Welshman, albeit not a Welsh-speaking one, come home after two centuries of exile in England.

The College was formally opened on 23 October 1883 – the day being kept as a public holiday in Cardiff and the surrounding district. Lord Aberdare, the first President of the College Council, gave the inaugural address and the Dean offered prayer and gave the blessing as they entered the refurbished Old Infirmary. One hundred and nine men

317

and 42 women were enrolled for the first Session which started the following day. The College was founded as a secular institution on the lines of University College London and some of its critics regarded it as an anti-Christian institution. This wasn't helped when one of the first members of staff to be appointed was discovered to be a member of the National Secular Society. For a while the Dean contemplated resigning from the Council but decided to retain his seat.

It was about this time that he was put on the spot in a different way. The story is told how at a dinner party in 1883 the Mayor of Cardiff tactlessly asked his host about his political opinions. The Dean looked down the table at his wife and asked "My dear, what are our politics at the present moment? I can't quite remember." She replied wittily and changed the subject leaving the Mayor rather puzzled but without loss of face by his *faux pas*.

Because the College was so poorly endowed, obtaining finance for each new department and for more staff was a constant challenge for the Principal and the Council in the early years. The need for a hall of residence for women students was successfully addressed in 1885 thanks in no small measure to the example and leadership of Lady Aberdare. Her daughter, the Hon. Isabel Bruce, generously offered to act as Principal. Catherine Vaughan warmly approved of her practical capacities. When the name of the Hall was under consideration, she wrote: 'Do you know we have had the audacity to Christian (*sic*) the Hall ourselves? The Dean said directly I asked him to think of a name, '*Aberdare Hall*', and Aberdare Hall it is to be. I quite think it is the best and most melodious name on the list of Ladies' Halls.'[25]

Vaughan attended Council meetings regularly and his views were listened to with respect by all members among whose number were several leading Nonconformists. In a letter to the Principal about the proposed Building Fund he commented that 'the voice of the charmer' would be needed to inspire generous subscriptions - a role which he himself frequently played. At the Council meeting in January 1893 he drew members' attention to the success of the College's students at the degree examinations of London University:

Eighteen present and two past students graduated at the London University in the past October – total 20. This was the greatest number of students sent to the University of London by any institution in the United Kingdom. Aberystwyth (which headed the list in 1890) stood next to Cardiff this year with 15 present and 4 past, and the Mason College, Birmingham, with 16.

And three years before three Cardiff students for the first time succeeded in the M.A. examination. [26]

Writing to the Principal in October 1895, Vaughan described the progress of the Institution as being 'in leaps and bounds' and added 'to you, more than to any other man, we owe it.' [27] Katharine Viriamu Jones in her biography of her husband was equally generous in her praise and gratitude for the support the Dean had given him and made these personal observations:

> Dean Vaughan received Viriamu Jones with the glad and tender confidence which a father gives to a favourite son, and his friendship deepened with each year . . . His election as President of the College was proposed by Mr Alfred Thomas (now Lord Pontypridd of Cardiff), a Nonconformist, seconded by Mr Lewis Williams, a member of the Wesleyan body, and supported by Bishop Hedley, who held the Roman Catholic See of Newport and Menevia. In 1888, he wrote to the Principal: 'You always think too much of me as a factor in the interests of the College, and you cannot indeed exaggerate my love for it.' This was his feeling to the end.
> Coming from his unceasing labours for the Church he served, there was about him an air of detachment as of one dwelling on serene mountain heights; but so great was his kindness for others and courtesy to all men weaker or less gifted than himself, that his presence brought a sense of well-being and strength to all – he touched the harshest differences with genial consideration and subtle humour, and before his influence the shadows of discord fled away. [28]

Some of Vaughan's letters to Alfred Thomas still survive in the National Library of Wales including this one about him succeeding the Marquis of Bute as President of the College which he wrote on 16 February 1894:

> Your unfailing goodness to me has surpassed itself in this crowning act of kindness.
> I was startled by the first intimation that such an honour was in store for me – chiefly due, I suspect, to your partial preference, of which I have received so many infallible proofs.
> I feel myself most unworthy of the position in which I find myself placed.
> But if everything else be wanting to me, there is just this to [be ..?] my qualifications – a strong attachment to the educational interests of the land of my ancestry & of my adoption.
> Gratefully yours,   C.J. Vaughan [29]

Vaughan enlisted Thomas's help a year later in a matter which shows his deep desire to be a unifying and conciliatory figure in Welsh public life:

> I have received a circular from Mountain Ash, proposing to make the enlargement of the Parish Church there a "national memorial" (or some such phrase) to Lord Aberdare.
>
> This is so evidently a preposterous proposal in this form that I am deeply anxious to see something else set promptly on foot to fill its place in a shape somewhat less utterly inadequate.
>
> Lord Aberdare's monument ought to be neither local nor in any sense sectarian. If he was a public benefactor, it is quite plain that anything which is to commemorate him ought neither to be buried in an obscure corner, nor yet made a party move.
>
> The latter consideration makes me hesitate to make it too exclusively connected even with the University College. We may regret it, but it is the fact that neither the Tories nor Churchmen have (as a rule) shown any interest in that Institution, and would not be likely to respond to a proposal to honour Lord Aberdare's memory by a benefaction to its funds.
>
> I was already full of these thoughts when I heard that they were occupying Mr G.J. Clarke's mind in what I fear may be his last illness. I should like to secure his ever ready bounty, before it is too late, in a tribute which he evidently desires to pay to the memory of Lord Aberdare.
>
> My own feeling is in favour of a Statue occupying a prominent place in Cardiff – if possible, in close proximity to University College, and yet not so tied to it as to make it less than a national monument from men of all sects and parties, recognizing his long years of patriotic service in the Principality & in the country at large.
>
> No one, dear Mr Thomas, could more powerfully take up the matter than yourself – so popular with us all, and so well able to take the lead in widening instead of narrowing the scope and sphere of the movement. Can you spare for it a few of your thoughts at this busy and exciting moment? [30]

A statue was eventually sculpted by Herbert Hampton and unveiled on 2 March 1899. It stands on King Edward VIII Avenue overlooking the main building of Cardiff University.

Vaughan was involved in one other major Welsh issue in addition to the foundation of the University. When a bill was being prepared which aimed to disestablish and disendow the Anglican Church in Wales, he took sides publicly for the first and only time on a major political issue. All but one Liberal candidate in Wales in the General Election of 1885 supported disestablishment; on the Conservative side Lord Salisbury pledged that his party would oppose it. A.J. Williams, a leading Welsh Liberal, predicted in his election manifesto a Liberal majority government and asserted: 'From this Liberal majority alone shall we obtain that religious equality which loyal Wales declares must no longer be denied to it. AS THE CHURCH OF ENGLAND IN WALES IS DISESTABLISHED AND DISENDOWED, its endowments will pass into the hands of bodies chosen by the people, to be applied with due regard to vested interests for the good of all.' [31] Vaughan, himself a Liberal, immediately took issue with the writer and argued in a letter to Williams that 'the Constitution knows no Church of Wales but as an integral part of the Church of England. To disestablish the Church of Wales Parliament must begin by creating it.' [32]

A disestablishment motion was introduced in the House of Commons in March 1886 and was supported by 229 members but fell short of being passed by twelve votes. Motions were again introduced in the House in 1891 and 1892. A.J. Williams now predicted, 'The state Church in Wales is doomed.' [33] He was wrong.

Alfred George Edwards, the Bishop of St Asaph and Archbishop of Wales, led the opposition and at the Church Congress held in Rhyl in 1891 he won the support of the Archbishop of Canterbury, who declared that England would not stand by and see the Welsh Church disinherited. The Bishop of Llandaff convened a public meeting in Cardiff on Tuesday April 4, 1893 on the subject of the Welsh Church Suspensory Bill. The Dean gave a rousing, inspirational and humorous address, interspersed with much applause, and subsequently reported by the *Western Mail*. In it he said that he would have liked to have seen on the platform 'a good gathering of honest hardworking Welshmen from our mines and from our hills and dales who would say to us, "I owe everything to the Church. I owe to it my education; I owe to it the education of my children; I owe to it my happy Sundays; I owe to it sympathy in my troubles; I am jealous for the Church with a godly jealousy."' In a letter to Sir Edward Hill dated 25 February 1893 he highlighted some of the absurdities of what supporters of reform were proposing:

And see the absurdity of the result (to take but one pair of instances). Oswestry (Salop) is to be disestablished because it happens to be in the Diocese of St Asaph, and Montgomery is to be left established because it happens to be in the Diocese of Hereford.
It is the greatest folly to say that boundaries are so clearly & so intelligibly defined as to make it a simple matter to say 'the four Welsh Dioceses'. There is a ragged edge, which must cause a vast amount of re-adjusting, or else a ludicrous incongruity. Bits of Wales still established (whatever that means) and bits of England disestablished (whatever that means), and poor

Monmouthshire shovelled into disestablishment for the crime of belonging (though an English county) to the Diocese of Llandaff. [34]

Sir Edward subsequently quoted Vaughan's letter in one that he wrote to the *Times* and published on 1 March.

Vaughan's opposition was also directed at the prospect of Wales no longer having a national church – he would have preferred to see the Baptists in such a role rather than none at all. He presented a petition to the House of Commons in which he stated in measured terms his opposition:

> That your petitioner views the isolation of the four dioceses of Wales from the rest of the Established Church as an arbitrary and capricious treatment – unfair in itself and insidious in its suggestion. That your petitioner is not insensible to the past shortcomings of the Church, alike in Wales and in England, in rising to the height of its holy mission. Nor, on the other hand, is he unthankful for the services of the various Nonconformist communities in the cause of faith and religion, in the Principality as elsewhere. But he is convinced that a voluntary system does not, and cannot, supply the national recognition of religion which is afforded by an Established Church, nor yet secure the right, guaranteed by an Establishment, of the poorest inhabitant of the towns and villages of England to the ministrations of the Gospel, in all circumstances of life, in times of sickness, and in the approach of death. That your petitioner entertains serious doubts whether the feeling of the religious (as distinguished from the political) Nonconformists in Wales is either unanimous or vehement in its antagonism to the Established Church, of which the founders of the chief denominations were attached members, in life and in death . . . [35]

The bill was re-introduced in the House in 1894 and 1895. It passed its second reading in the Commons on 1 April 1895, by a majority of 44. Twenty-eight of the 30 Welsh MPs supported the bill. Before it emerged from Committee Rosebery's government resigned, and it never came to its third Reading. The ensuing election turned mainly on the question of Welsh Disestablishment and the result was the Liberals suffered their most disastrous defeat since 1832. The Church was spared for a few more years.

As a cathedral dean Vaughan was automatically a member of the Convocation of Canterbury where he occasionally contributed to debates. Though showing no desire to be seen as an ecclesiastical politician, he was not afraid to state his view even if this meant being in a minority of one as happened in July 1883 when he opposed a motion

322

expressing support for the House of Lords' rejection of a bill which would have legalized marriage with a deceased wife's sister. In 1887 he took a prominent part in the debate on some proposed additions to the Prayer Book Catechism. He moved an amendment to send the report back to the Committee but it was voted down 57:11. This defeat didn't deter him from moving a series of amendments to the wording of the proposed additions, all of which failed to gain a majority when it came to a vote. His former Harrow assistant, F.W. Farrar, now Archdeacon of Westminster, frequently spoke in support of his old chief. But this was not so with Davidson. In a letter to him written during the meeting of Convocation in March 1889, Vaughan commented 'I listened to you with great delight in the Convocation, though I observe we do not always <u>vote</u> together.' In another letter written four days later, he voiced his views on the controversy raging at that time over ritual practices:

> When I read Mr McNeale's letter in the Guardian, I awoke to the fact – which you notice – namely, that his proposal does not stop with <u>toleration</u> of – or <u>acquiescence</u> – in forms & ceremonies not to our mutual taste, but goes on to accept and to adopt them if the Archbishop would sanction them (and I suppose by acquitting the Bp of L[incoln]).
> This is more than I can undertake to do. No power could make a chasuble to fit me.
> Meanwhile a visit from Mr [K...?] yesterday proposed my presiding at a Meeting of Moderates to discover how far they can go towards the two extremes, not only in matters of ritual but also in (the Bp of London's hobby) broad views of interpretation etc.
> Two hares running at once will not help the chase. So I think I shall retire into my shell, and not try to be a <u>Leader</u> . . .
> Tell me whenever you are offered things (will you?) from the Papacy downwards. You will perhaps guess my meaning when I say that the dear Bp of Ripon was here yesterday . . .[36]

Among his many interests, duties and activities, Vaughan's attachment to Harrow remained constant and he remained a favourite visitor there. When he attended Speech Day in 1877, the *Morning Post* reported that 'his presence was greeted with repeated rounds of cheering' by the boys. On 12 June 1883 he chaired a meeting of Old Harrovians in St James's Hall, Regent Street at which the Harrow Mission Association was born. Speakers included Dr Butler and Lord Shaftesbury, now aged 82. An Old Harrovian, William Laws, who was the senior Curate of St Mary Abbots Church Kensington, had already been appointed the first Priest-Missioner, and the masters and boys had guaranteed his stipend for the first seven years. It was hoped the Association would raise the funds needed to purchase a plot of land and build a mission room and church in what was in those days one of the poorest and most deprived areas of London (on Latimer Road in Notting Hill). They succeeded for the Mission building was opened on Trinity Sunday 1884. The church was consecrated by the Bishop of London four years later. Vaughan, Butler and Davidson were all present for the occasion. [37]

More importantly, his voluntary work in assisting men prepare for Ordination continued. During the years 1879-94, when he held the Mastership of the Temple and the Deanery of Llandaff in plurality, Vaughan took his 'doves' with him from place to place which meant they spent the winter in London and the summer in Wales. In London they were housed in chambers at the Temple and in Llandaff in lodgings in the village. He never liked the term 'doves' and never used it himself; to him they were simply "my men". Two of those who were with him during these years have left detailed and deeply appreciative accounts of their time spent with him. The first comes from the historian G.G. Coulton who coincidentally had been a fellow pupil of Owen's at Felsted and then his colleague at a small preparatory school in Malvern in 1881. Coulton came to Llandaff initially to inspect the Cathedral School and whilst there he asked Owen to intercede on his behalf with the Dean to let him join the current group of ordinands studying with him, and was duly accepted. Later he looked back on these months as an idyllic period in his life:

Our work was mainly Greek Testament, text and exposition, with a weekly sermon to write. Vaughan was a specialist in Greek scholarship as understood in his youth: he 'properly based *Oun*', and would not pass on until he had squeezed out every drop of sense or suggestion. This was, no doubt, too microscopic: but nothing could have been sounder in its own way. He did not tempt us to believe that we were scientific theologians in the scholastic sense. Vaughan, consciously or not, was following an even greater Dean, John Colet of St Paul's, who for the first time in English history lectured straightforwardly upon what St Paul had actually intended to convey to the readers of his own time, and not upon what hundreds of later commentators had deducted from Pauline texts. As to his sermon teaching, it was just perfect common-sense, of which one prime factor lies in the preacher's recognition of his own limitations . . .
While at Llandaff we had a certain amount of district-visiting assigned to us in the poorer parts of Cardiff. In my street was one peculiarly painful case: a drunken wife and children neglected, practically abandoned. Nothing I had seen in the poorest Norfolk cottages approached this sordid story. The

woman, they told me was niece to a Free Church Minister at Pontypridd, some twenty miles distant; so I went off by train to see him. His story was that the husband, a miner, had driven her to drink by his ill-treatment . . .
Ordinarily, we had our afternoon exercise as freely as at Cambridge: to me, indeed, it was a real Indian Summer. We were roughly, contemporaries, and mostly Cantabs, though I remember two Oxford men. The school boy spirit was far from dead . . . [38]

He was ordained Deacon on 21 December 1883 by Bishop Claughton of St Albans but in 1885 he decided, on grounds of the serious doubts he had about priesthood, to give up the Ministry and return to being a schoolmaster. He tells in his autobiography how 'Vaughan was distressed, as he had just reason to be; and he naturally tried to dissuade me, but with no violence of persuasion: that was not in his nature or in his system.' [39] Another Llandaff 'dove' ordained at that same service with Coulton was Henry Rogers who went to be Curate with the Dean's elder brother, Edward, who was now Vicar of Harpenden.

J.H. Greig who studied with him in 1888 and later became Bishop of Guildford also commented on Vaughan's devotion to the Greek Testament which, he said, the Dean knew by heart:

not verbally only but with full possession of the inner meaning and exact shade of every passage . . . expounding slowly, minutely, clearly, but always avoiding pedantry, and making his hearers conscious that this was no mere literary exercise, but something essentially spiritual. He was holding up to the light and minutely examining each word and construction, not because Hellenistic Greek is full of interesting problems, or St Paul a great thinker, but because here was the Word of God and the Mind of the Spirit . . . He was learned indeed, but his learning was subordinate to his belief that through the Scriptures God is still speaking directly to anyone who will humbly and reverently listen. [40]

A.C. Harman who read with him in 1892-93 was the other late 'dove' to leave an extensive account. In his eyes, Vaughan was a star preacher:

In his composition he was a master of English, and is described by one of the greatest preachers of that generation as the most remarkable he had ever heard, alike for thought, matter and style.
For the making of his sermon he would stand at a high desk, writing it all out. He took his MS. into the pulpit, but beyond turning over the page he never seemed to look at it. There was no impression of a read sermon, all

was so arresting, so personal, so earnest, spoken in a beautiful voice, clear as a silver bell. [41]

Coulton was equally impressed with him as a preacher and remembered, in particular, the last sermon he heard him preach in the cathedral. It was at an ordination shortly before Christmas:

> He was a most impressive preacher and reader. I have never heard his equal with the Pauline Epistles: he rendered them with the slow measured diction of a man who was recording his own personal convictions on some occasion no less vital than Baxter's
>
> > 'I preach'd, as never sure to preach again,
> > And as a dying man to dying men.'
>
> The thoughts seemed to come straight from the well, with no suggestion of a personal intermediary. I could not, if I would, get away from his words in Galatians, 'From henceforth let no man trouble me: for I bear in my body the marks of the Lord Jesus.' His sermons were much of the same character when delivered, though naturally much evaporated in print. They were scholarly, weighty, unadorned but nearly perfect in their union of plain Bible English with classical rhetoric in the best sense of that much-abused word. [42]

Harman, writing in the 1930s, looked back on his year spent with Vaughan in Llandaff and at the Temple as 'a delightful time' – for him the retrospect was 'like the opening of a door into another world'. He revered his old teacher and has left the longest and most detailed record of him in old age and of his methods as a mentor:

> His methods were as unlike those of a theological college as could be, and sometimes, perhaps after ordination, we may have found ourselves somewhat lacking in the training and teaching of a theological college; but, on the other hand, it was a priceless privilege and experience to be with a man so saintly, so wise, so great, whose influence and impression was so lasting.
>
> He had his own plan – "inapplicable to men who require either discipline to make sure of their conduct, or tuition to make sure of their reading" – a high standard, to which he generously gave us credit for living up to. He trusted us, and so far as we could we responded . . .
>
> He made no attempt to coach you for your exam. This was left to yourself, and taken for granted. His knowledge of us was remarkable. After the first fortnight he seemed to know you through and through. It was his personal influence which counted for so much, and in this was the secret of it all . . .

In his treatment of us there was nothing of the Don or the Divine. He was more the Good Companion, treating us as equals.

In his views he was no narrow ecclesiastic who wished all to be alike. There was nothing stereotyped in his handling of us, no mould in which we were cast, no label which could fairly be attached to us. He himself had a horror of labels, a dread of the one type, of anything artificial or mechanical. "Do be human," he would say . . .

Our week's programme was as follows: On Tuesday mornings we went to him for two hours to read the Greek Testament. He was a great authority on St Paul and the Epistles. He expected you to know, without reference, the contents of each chapter of the Acts as soon as St Paul arrives upon the scene. He gave us a wonderful insight into the Epistles, emphasizing the importance of the Greek particles, the value of the tenses, bringing out the meaning of nouns, adjectives, and verbs, with their special derivatives. It was all an illuminating experience, and we took down notes as best we could.

On Thursday evening we spent with him a devotional hour. On Saturdays we sent in a sermon on a text he had given us, and which he returned on the Tuesday with some criticism in the margin, incisive, but always kindly.

Once a fortnight he had us in by ourselves to tea in his study, when for half an hour he would talk in the most intimate, confidential way on events of the day, on people that he knew, and those in high position whether in the Church or State. This was one of his ways of trusting us, and no one to my knowledge was ever the worse for such talks . . .

As to curacies, he was most particular, sending us almost invariably for the first start to large industrial parishes under the charge of his own men whom he knew he could rely upon . . .

In his personal religion, and in his teaching, he had no place for sentiment or emotion. He would impress upon us the importance of building upon facts as incorporated in the creeds and in the life of the Incarnate Son of God. He would plead with us to draw from them such information as fired St Paul and as has accounted for the lives of the saints through the ages.

As a Churchman I would describe him as an Evangelical of the best type.

In appearance he was of middle height, very well made and proportioned. He had a very fine head, most kind smiling eyes, with a decided twinkle in them, and a pair of the most shapely calves for gaiters that you could wish to see. He lived a sedentary life, one of those men who never take exercise and rarely take a holiday. He was a most hard worker. After dinner, even when there were guests, he would disappear and lock his study door, returning later to the drawing-room for prayers. His correspondence occupied a great deal of his time, sometimes thirty letters a day, all written while standing at his desk. Servants would do anything for him . . .

He could be very caustic if he chose, and it was always said that he had to keep a great restraint upon himself in this matter. I only had one instance of this myself. At one of those half-hour afternoon teas in his study the conversation had turned on the Cathedral services, at which one of the dignitaries when in residence used to afflict us all sorely by his preaching, Vaughan included. In his quiet way he summed up these sermons in the most devastating of criticisms, "Rinsings, Harman, mere rinsings." This, however, was very unusual. He very rarely let himself go, for he was the most kind and gentle of men, always quick to look for and find the best in others. [43]

He also included two more anecdotes about Catherine:

In the drawing-room at Llandaff there were two large cabinets which contained her very interesting collection of London street toys, and which, when we happened to be there, we were called upon to show off to the guests after dinner. With all her wit, Mrs Vaughan never got the better of the Dean. If she tried to cross swords with him she always got the worst of the encounter. At a large luncheon party I well remember her speaking down the table and saying, "There! Charles takes no interest in antiquities or archaeology. Why if he was told that Pharaoh was walking on the pavement opposite he wouldn't go across the street to look at him." "No, my dear," came the answer back without hesitation. "But if it was Pharaoh's daughter I might."
With all her peculiarities, she was a serious-minded woman, with strong religious convictions. She used to write for S.P.C.K. and brought out a little work, *Rays of Sunlight for dark Days*, for the use of mourners and those in sorrow. [44]

The 'doves' gained their practical and pastoral experience in the parishes of Cardiff, Canton in particular. It had once been part of the cathedral parish of Llandaff but In 1855 Bishop Ollivant took the lead in providing it with its own parish church dedicated to St John the Divine. Building on the church continued until 1871 – the architects, coincidentally, being the same two men who had overseen the cathedral's restoration, Prichard and Seddon. The Revd Vincent Saulez, a non-graduate who had trained at St Bees Theological College in Cumberland between 1853 and 1855 was appointed the first Rector of Canton in 1863 and remained in post until his death in 1889 at the age of 55. Both the Dean and Catherine gave generously towards the cost of building a second church there in 1883. It was rumoured that each had given £1,000 [=£103,000] – and she laid the foundation stone. The church was dedicated to St Catherine (of Egypt not Llandaff). Canton was a natural choice as a training ground for Vaughan's men not just because of its proximity to

Llandaff (just a mile away) and its having been until very recently part of the cathedral parish but because of its social mix. It was a rapidly expanding parish (the population more than doubled in the 1880s and stood at 32,805 in 1891) thanks to the export of iron ore and coal from the mines of South Wales through the Cardiff docks built earlier that century. In 1875 it was incorporated into the borough of Cardiff whose total population had grown to nearly 129,000 by 1891. The suburb of Canton became the site of much new housing for various social classes and it was described in the 1880s as having a 'broad social mix mainly notable for its respectable artisan and lower middle class character.'[45] It also had some much poorer housing. It was a good parish in which prospective clergymen could gain some experience of parish visiting and assisting in a church school. There had been a National School on Leckwith Road since 1856 which was affectionately known as 'The Leckwith College' - one of whose alumni, William Goscombe John, the son of a wood carver, would become one of Wales's greatest sculptors. John was one of those pupils who sang in the cathedral choir.

In January 1893 he received an enquiry from F.F. Halsey, the M.P. for Hemel Hempstead, about the possibility of his son, Frederick (Eton & Magdalen College Oxford) becoming a 'pupil to prepare for Ordination' and requesting 'terms & other particulars.' It seems Vaughan was a bit miffed by the man's ignorance of his work and sent him a stiff reply by return:

> I do not "take Pupils" in the ordinary sense of that expression – nor have I any "terms" to send you.
> As a labour of love, I have for more than 30 past years allowed a few graduates of Oxford & Cambridge to reside near me for instruction in some parts of their future Clerical Duties and of their studies for Ordination. There are no payments whatever to me – they take lodgings (approved by me) & provide for themselves in them.
> I require a <u>private</u> letter of recommendation from the Head or Tutor of their College.
> You will kindly let me know whether this altered view of the case leaves you still desirous to communicate with me on behalf of your Son. [46]

Halsey did. Vaughan reiterated the need for a 'private letter' from the President of Magdalen and asked that the son should write himself 'as to his wishes and plans.' Freddy Halsey was to become one of his last friends. He wrote from Llandaff to the young man in March saying it would be 'very nice to see you when I am in London in June or July.

Meanwhile let our engagement stand for the Autumn, <u>here</u>. I am quite laid aside, and obliged to disperse my Men for the present.' [47] Ill health had been dogging him on and off for years and it would soon get much worse.

He had been sick in the summer of 1884 and again in early '85 and was off work for prolonged periods, convalescing at his home in South-borough or at Bath and other resorts. At least these periods away from the Temple and Llandaff gave him opportunity to keep up his reading. He wrote to Lightfoot in October 1885:

> I could not write to thank you, as I do with all my heart, for your wonderful kindness in sending me the valuable Volumes of your latest work for the Church, until I had just "tasted with my first lips" the produce of your labour.
> I am indeed not worthy of such a gift, which can but absorb me with the contrast of my own ignorance. But even humiliation is good for me, though it come too late to remould a life.
> May life and strength be still long spared to you, my dear Lord, for your great two-fold work – such is the heart's desire of
> Your faithful and grateful C.J. Vaughan [48]

Periods of ill-health continued to plague him. By early 1888 he was looking for an assistant to take some of his preaching duties at the Temple, and asked Davidson for help in finding a suitable person. He set out some of the requirements:

> It is rather a precarious audience. Anything affected, pretentious, or tricks-ical would not do. <u>Argumentative</u> preaching is not wanted, nor liked unless <u>admirable</u> . . . <u>Ryle</u> had occurred to me thinking that possibly 20 Sermons (or so) in the year might not be incompatible with his new Cambridge Professorship. The Salary, I believe, was £100 – paid by the Master who also, I <u>believe</u>, appoints without sanction or veto from the Benchers . . . I generally take 30 Sermons myself, even now. For all the years before I came here [Llandaff], it was about 50. [49]

In January 1890 he told Davidson, 'I am still a close prisoner coughing as if my heart would break many a time and oft. But I have let the men come back yesterday, & today I gave them a reading . . . Seven replace seven. Some very nice ones among them. One Sinclair, from Aberdeen, son of the new (but 16th) Earl of Caithness.' [50] In the same letter he had told Davidson that he had written to the Queen's Private Secretary on his behalf requesting that his former pupil be appointed to a senior episcopal post. He had heard that his letter had 'moved H.M. considerably'. [51] Illness prevented him taking part in Westcott's paying homage to the Queen on his appointment to Durham. On 22 May he gave an update on his health to Davidson: 'I ventured to the Communion yesterday in the Cathedral, but took no part in the Service. I was particularly well, & the day was beautiful. But a bad night has made this a rather trying day to me – and tomorrow being the quarterly Chapter brings guests to us – rather formidable after so long a seclusion.' [52]

In June a letter from Gladstone cheered him. He had sent the great man a copy of his commentary on the *Epistle to the Hebrews* which he had read. Gladstone loved *Hebrews* but challenged the Pauline authorship of the Letter. Vaughan replied:

> You place in a very striking light what is involved in disbelieving the completely Pauling authorship. I say "completely" Pauline because one can scarcely help seeing in it a breath of St Paul's inspiration.
> But I must not try to occupy another moment of your time in correspondence about so slight a matter as my Commentary upon the Epistle.
> It delights me to hear you speak as you do of the Epistle itself – of its superlative eloquence and immense logical force. I wish I thought that such an estimate was the common voice of the Church. Too often, I imagine, it is one of the less popular Books of Scripture with the exception perhaps of its eleventh Chapter.
> Your letter will be carefully treasured, as it is gratefully received, by your ever obliged Servant C.J. Vaughan [53]

Westcott, who was in London a month later shortly after his enthronement as Bishop of Durham, called on Vaughan at the Temple having heard that he had been taken ill again. 'I had a long talk with Mrs Vaughan – for two hours, I should think. Dr Vaughan was sleeping then, but I promised to go after the afternoon service on Sunday.' [54] He duly returned and recorded 'He was as kind and sympathetic as usual, and interested in the work of the North, which he curiously watches. He seemed to be weak, but the tea was forthcoming. "I think nothing," he added, "of a house in which tea is not laid on to every storey." So we talked a little, and then I hastened back to Lambeth, having originally promised to have tea there.' [55]

He continued to follow episcopal appointments always with Davidson in mind. In September he advised him to accept the offer of Rochester rather than Worcester should it come:

> I confess that the idea of the present R[ochester] going to Winchester had never crossed my mind. Affected, ill-bred, pretentious, as he is, yet one may rejoice in so good and effective a man [i.e. Davidson] entirely free from party, and from High Church superstitions being lighted upon by Lord {Liverpool?} for so high a place. [56]

Winters were becoming more difficult. In October 1890 he refused for the second time an invitation from Professor Powel, excusing himself with the words 'I am obliged at present to avoid evening engagements. My cough still clings to me, and I dread reviving the Bronchitis this winter. You will understand me & forgive.' [57] In November Davidson invited his old friend and mentor to preach at his consecration but Vaughan declined:

> What shall I say in reply to your deeply solemn and anxious proposal?
> I feel the kindness which breathes in it, and you know how delightful it would be to me to be thus in closest contact with you at this most eventful moment of your life. But – I shrink from the task, in the view of the increasing uncertainty of life and health at my present age [he was 73] and after the experience of last winter.
> Also I am inclined to like the thought of a Consecration Sermon being an opportunity (as it so often has been) of bringing forward a young man, himself perhaps destined soon to fill the same office.
> I think I shall do best to draw back from the kind and dear offer, which for me, from various causes, would involve more of strain, mental & spiritual, than perhaps for anyone else in the world.
> Dearest friend, you will feel with me in what I say, & not think me ungrateful.   Your loving friend C.J. Vaughan [58]

Ill health continued to plague him into the summer of the following year. He wrote to Mrs Davidson on 25 July 1891: 'I am still languid and feeble – at Brighton two weeks – next week Ramsgate – here for the Sunday only – the dear men dispersed. I hope to finish the Law Year by a Sermon on August 2 – After that a Long vacation and Llandaff.' [59]

By 1893 he was beginning to consider retirement, as was Dean Lake in Durham who had also been unwell. He wrote to him from Llandaff on 24 February of that year:

> MY DEAR LAKE, - I have been thinking of you in my illness and longing to write to you. Your letter was, therefore, a very real pleasure. It bids me hope that you are on the way to further life and work, without any need to think of resignation.

I have been a wonder to myself during the last two or three years – able to travel regularly to the Temple for alternate Sundays, and preaching here when I was not there. I have just now had a rather rough awakening in the shape of a severe illness, which I find it difficult to shake off. I began today to talk of giving up my various employments, but the doctor thinks this premature.

You will wonder what leads me to burden you with the last of my many publications. Accept it just as a token of the old affection, and do not trouble yourself to read it.

I am interested in a new Life of Keble by a Mr Lock. It is difficult for me – it would not be so for you – quite to throw myself into the spiritual agonies which cost the leading spirits of that movement so intense a life.

I think you may be hopeful (in your kindness) about my recovery this time; but 'seventy-seven next August' is a fact not to be forgotten . . .

Always affectionately yours,   C.J. VAUGHAN [60]

Another of his 'doves' during this late period of his life was Hugh Benson, youngest son of the Archbishop of Canterbury, who came to him in 1893. In Hugh's autobiographical *apologia* entitled *Confessions of a Convert*, written in 1913, he left a warmly appreciative account of his time spent with Vaughan, who by then was a frail septuagenarian. Given that by the time he wrote his account, he had converted to Rome and been re-ordained, his appreciation and gratitude is all the more striking. He regarded Vaughan as 'the most eminent Evangelical of his day':

> I read for Orders for a year and a half with Dean Vaughan at Llandaff. He was a unique and exceptional man, and it was owing no doubt to his extraordinary charm of personality and his high spirituality that my father, in spite of the divergence of his views from those of the Dean, decided to place me under his charge. I think that he was in some respects the most remarkable preacher I have ever heard. He wrote out his sermons with infinite pains, word for word, destroying, I believe, the entire manuscript and beginning it all over again if he were interrupted during his composition of it; and then delivering it word for word from his paper with scarcely a gesture except quick, slight glances and almost timid movements of his head. But the English was simply perfect, comparable, I think, only to that of Ruskin and Newman; his voice was as smooth and pointed and pliable as the blade of a rapier; and above all, he possessed that magnetic kind of personality that affected his educated hearers, at any rate, like a strain of music.
>
> He was a pronounced Evangelical in his views: I still possess somewhere a couple of sets of notes that I wrote for him, under his influence, on the sacraments of Baptism and the Lord's Supper, in which anything

approaching to sacramental doctrine is explicitly denied. Yet his faith was so radiantly strong, his love of the Person of our Lord so intense, that his pupils, I think, whatever their predispositions, were almost unconscious of the lack of other things. When we were under his spell it appeared as if no more could be necessary than the love and devotion of our master to God.

His wife too, a sister of Dean Stanley, was another great feature in our life. She was a strange old lady, resembling in face Queen Victoria, and one of the cleverest women I have ever met. She talked and wrote letters brilliantly and wittily, and it was a real delight to be in her company. When three of four of us were bidden to dinner at the Deanery, we used to compare our notes of invitation in order to triumph in her variety of expression. Each note was quite different from all the rest, yet each was vivid.

I remember the Dean's gentle pleasure when he discovered that, during a grave illness of his, his wife had, in despair of his recovery, actually engaged a house to retire to for her widowhood. He told us the facts in her presence, while she jerked her features about in humorous protest. "No, my dear", said the Dean at last, with his eyes twinkling like stars, "you see I am not dead yet, after all, and I am afraid you won't get to your new house just yet."

We led a very harmless life, reading Greek Testament with the Dean every morning, composing a sermon for him once a week, playing a great deal of football, and attending the cathedral services every day. It was one of the proudest days of my life when I was selected by a club to play half-back against Cardiff. But here, in spite of the Dean's strong Evangelicalism, commended though it was by his charming and spiritual personality, I began to have a glimmer of more Catholic views, and, for the first time in my life, began to prefer Communion before breakfast. [61]

That particular 'dove' turned his back on Anglican Orders. Some years earlier another 'dove' desiring them was denied them. Bishops did not automatically accept a candidate for Ordination simply because he was an Oxbridge graduate who had read with Vaughan. He wrote to Davidson whilst still Chaplain to Archbishop Tait: 'I am sorry about Donkin. He was a man of good disposition & of much humility, but sadly wanting in self-discipline & concentration of mind. I am glad that he did not put his brief connexion with me prominently forward. It would not have been ingenuous to do so.' [62]

At the beginning of 1894 he was involved in another episcopal appointment at the request of Bishop Selwyn, who was keen to see a particular candidate appointed as Bishop of Melanesia. He wrote to Archbishop Benson from Llandaff:

Bishop Selwyn desires me to say to your Grace that I know Cecil Wilson well, and count him worthy of the high call which has reached him to become Bishop of Melanesia.

He was with me here, in preparation for his first Ordination. And his whole life and spirit drew out my warmest admiration. So humble, so manly, so devout, so made for respect and for influence, one might almost have foreseen that he would fill a foremost part in the Church some day, though the actual crisis has come upon him & upon us all by surprise.

I feel sure that your Grace will find him one upon whom you can lay the consecrating hand with assurance. [63]

Catherine wrote to Sir Charles Dalrymple on 7 March 1894 to inform him that her husband had suffered a stroke.

The Paralytic Seizure of last night has extinguished our last ray of hope. The Dr says this morning "the vital powers are failing."

And we can only pray that it might be so since a protracted life could only mean a living death. He is conscious today but the use of his right hand is gone & he is so very, very feeble – that we can hardly make out what he says –

He does not know that there has been Paralysis. But the look which he turned upon me when I went in this morning, and the tears which for a moment overcame him told me that he knew – the long (Darkness?) was not far off. [64]

She wrote to him again the following day:

. . . We have everything we can have in the way of help & alleviation - & more than all – we are upbourne in the wings of the tenderest love that was ever shown to any mortal being – He has been wrapt & enshrouded in love from the first moment of his being laid aside – I never knew before what was the power of love – even this poor human love. [65]

Medical bulletins appeared in the London press and were reproduced later in provincial newspapers. The Queen sent a special messenger to obtain a firsthand account of his condition.

A week later, Catherine was able to report better news: 'He shows signs of real amendment – We dare not venture to hope that this ray of sunshine is more than a transient gleam but still we have it to cheer us for the moment. And to show you how much better he feels himself to be, he said to me just now "There is one person I should very much like to see – and that is Dalrymple."' [66]

On 2 April she had mixed news to give:

He is certainly a little stronger - & today is even sitting in his chair. But –
Alas, that I should have to say it. As his physical power appears to be
flowing in again, his mental power seems to be gradually decreasing –
This morning he did not know what <u>house</u> he was in – "What was its
name?" Where was the Drawing Room? And the Dining Room? And the
Study? And the Deanery – where were the rooms <u>there</u>?"
If as they tell me, this results from "Softening of the brain" we can indeed
only hide our eyes and weep.
It is like seeing a beautiful Temple – laid in ruins. [67]

We are given another touching account from the pen of the Temple
organist, Dr Hopkins, who wrote to tell his daughter of what had
happened.

The incident that occurred at the Temple on Sunday morning last – Easter
Sunday morning – was one that will never be effaced from my memory. On
reaching the church, a messenger informed me that the Master wished to
see me; therefore, I went at once to his house. On entering the sick
chamber, the dear good Dean, with a sweet affectionate smile on his
countenance, feebly raised his arms and received my hands in both of his.
My nerve utterly broke down and he, seeing that, hopefully said, "I <u>may</u> see
you again. Continue in the course you have been so long following: improve
you cannot." Then offering up a prayer to God on my behalf, he placed his
hands on my head and gave me his blessing. Those hands from which I had
for so many years been receiving the Holy Communion (I hope to my
unspeakable benefit), I convulsively seized and kissed many times and then
– the dear Master and I parted. [68]

Vaughan recovered enough to want to return to the Deanery but Dr
Vachell, his medical advisor in Llandaff, was fearful that he would not
survive the damp air on the long journey by train from London, so an
unusual alternative was devised. The Dean was shut in his carriage,
together with his doctor and a nurse, outside his London home. They
were driven to Paddington Station where the carriage with the three
passengers still inside was loaded onto a wagon. It was unloaded some
hours later in Cardiff, horses were attached and driven straight to the
Deanery where the doors were opened for the first time since leaving
the Temple. It worked and the Dean survived.

"Going down the hill steadily but with pauses"

In the prospect of death, a little nearer or further off, I wish to state explicitly that I have put my whole trust in the revelation of the Gospel as made in the Gospel of St John and in the Epistles of St John and St Paul. I believe in the forgiveness of sins as the foundation stone of the Gospel and commit myself humbly and hopefully to God in this faith for life, death, and eternity.

The opening lines of his last will and testament.

Vaughan was a long time-a-dying. He would have a slow but steady decline for the next three and a half years before letting go of life. His first step down, after arriving safely back in Llandaff, was to tender his resignation as Master of the Temple. He wrote to inform the Treasurer:

I am placing in the hands of the Prime Minister the resignation of the Mastership of the Temple on 1st July next on which day I shall have completed my 25th year of service in that interesting and honourable office.

With what constant affection I have endeavoured to serve the two learned and honourable societies, with what gratitude I have felt the many generous courtesies, and with what pain I take the step I now announce to you, I cannot trust myself to try to put into words – this ill written scrawl will best tell its own story.

I pray you, dear Mr Treasurer, to do what I cannot do, in the expression of my feelings to your brethren of the Bench of the Middle Temple.

Believe me, with respect and perpetual affection

Yours faithfully till death   C.J. Vaughan [1]

The Benchers later voted him a testimonial of £300 [= £33,000]. The Treasurer of the Inner Temple wrote to him conveying the deep sense of irreparable loss felt by the Benchers 'for there never was a Master of the Temple for whose noble character and distinguished merit the Benchers could entertain more sincere reverence and affection than they do for you.'[2] Vaughan wrote to Lord Cross seeking his advice for he was thinking of repeating what he had done on leaving Doncaster, namely to give the testimonial money away.

I shall hope to write a more formal letter of thanks to the Bench of each Society when I receive their generous gift. Meanwhile I address this line of acknowledgment to you, my dear Lord, for the sake of asking you (privately) whether my thought of offering the £300 as a Donation to the <u>Barristers'</u> <u>Benevolent</u> <u>Association</u> would or would not seem to you a respectful use to make of what I feel to be intended as a personal memorial to myself. A single line in answer to this question will set my mind at rest, and guide my course decisively. [3]

His old student, A.C. Harman, reckoned him to be second in rank only to Hooker as Master of the Temple. High praise indeed! The *Western Mail* commented:

> Dr Vaughan's record is not only a distinguished one, but it is also unique. Today he might have been Archbishop of Canterbury had he cared to accept a seat on the episcopal bench, but his refusal in 1860 of the Bishopric of Rochester, then a larger and more important diocese than it is today, while he accepted shortly afterwards the Vicarage of Doncaster, and nine years later the Mastership of the Temple, marked him out as a man singularly devoid of worldly ambition, and pre-eminently as a scholar exemplifying in himself the attributes associated with scholarship.[4]

Three days earlier Montagu Butler, now Master of Trinity, had written to comfort him:

> I long for weeks of warm sun that you may get out and bask. There is nothing ignoble in such a physical inertia after all these years of intense labour and strain, mental and spiritual. Earth will never be *too* dear to you. I read every day some parts at least of your sermons, and love to think how close the tie which binds us still continues. If it is not eternal, it will be my fault alone. [5]

In a letter written on 3 August he gave news of his progress:

> I am wonderfully restored to comfort and enjoyment – <u>not</u> to strength or to work. My day has but a fragment of its twelve hours – and I am idle in my use even of this. I have fallen to a Bath Chair – upon which I used to look down as the equipage of the "doleful creatures" dragged about at Brighton and elsewhere under the scornful gaze of insolent youth. "The blessedness of being little" has its charms – I feel them.
>
> My beloved students, ten of them, waited and watched for me, and welcomed me back to life and to companionship even when I could do nothing for them. As soon as it was possible I began a half-hour's reading with them twice or thrice a week and found it my best medicine, Now they are dispersed, and it depends upon my little holiday somewhere at the sea

how far I dare hope to be permitted to go towards a little quiet and obscure work in the few days or months which may be in reserve for me.

It is good for me to be laid low – I have loved my work for its own sake too much, too little for the sake of others – now I feel it. [6]

By the middle of the month he was well enough to travel to Cornwall to recuperate. He wrote to Lake from there on the 20th:

MY VERY DEAR OLD FRIEND, - Your endless kindnesses during my illness have gone to my heart, and I have long wished to tell you so with my own pen. But writing is still a little difficult, and not very good for me, so I have put it off till now, when the paper tells me that you are meditating the resignation of your important and beautiful office just when I was hoping that the reason for doing so was disappearing, and that I might have had the pleasure of seeing you retain it – at least while I lived.

The tie is a very strong one which binds us two together – a friendship of more than sixty years, and a thousand memories of the dead and living. It is delightful to me to have had so many infallible proofs of your affection for me being as strong as ever, now that opportunities of actual intercourse are so few.

I have never expressly thanked you for the honour [an honorary DD at Durham University] done to my brother David through your kindness. He will do no discredit to his new university, and I felt that he had scarcely been recognized before, as his work deserved [in the provision of Adult Education in Leicester], anywhere except in the actual scene of it, where he is a centre of force and attraction.

You will ask how I am going on after these six months of weakness and peril. I *did* think myself not quite so well lately; but my doctor declared he saw no sign of stagnation, and we are now at a place in Cornwall of singular beauty and comfort, near St Ives, from which I hope I may return not only refreshed in spirits, but strengthened for such a *modicum* of usefulness as may still be granted me. [7]

At the beginning of September, however, he suffered a setback in the form of jaundice – Catherine described it as being back 'in the trough of the Sea.' [8] She wrote to Dalrymple on the 9th:

He is much about the same as regards the Jaundice - & on Monday, he was distressing, feeble and exhausted – You could hardly hear him speak - & he looked aged and emaciated – but yesterday & today, he seems a little brighter & more like himself. At the best, it will be a long time before he emerges again out of the dull, invalid, inactive life. But if only the dreaded foe, Paralysis, can be kept in the distance, how thankful we shall be. [9]

Her prayers were answered and his remaining years were spent quietly at Llandaff, preaching about once a month but still training new 'doves'. That work went on until his death. The *Advent Record* shows that he had eight men with him in 1894, eight more in '95, and just one, Alan Dalby in '96. A coincidence maybe but a fitting one that his final man should be, like himself, a native of Leicestershire, a former pupil at Rugby and a graduate of Trinity College Cambridge. In his annual letter to his men written on 29 November 1895, he reported:

> Another year of quiet and restful work has been granted to me, and I turn back to you at the end of it to give in my account.
>
> The continuity of our 35 years special work has never really been broken, though my dangerous illness of last year suspended for some months its active prosecution. It was gradually resumed as strength came back to me, and for the last twelve months has been going on much as of old.
>
> I have received a touching proof of your loving kindness in the gift to me of a portrait of myself by Mr Ouless . . . I shall want to learn from you where you would like it to find its home when I and one other person are gone . . .[10]

In a letter to Davidson written earlier that month, he told of his sittings with the artist:

> Yesterday I ended my sittings for the picture. May the result be such as to satisfy the loving wishes of those who have given so self-sacrificing a proof of their regard for one who has nothing to repay them with but his unchanging love. I do not think the picture is yet quite finished – but what remains can be done without me. Mr Ouless is a delightful companion – I wish he could know how I appreciated the privilege of thrice twelve hours spent in converse with him . . . [11]

He then went on to ask his friend to use his influence on behalf of a relative, Bernard Pares, to obtain a post at the British Museum. He had been a pupil at Harrow for five years, then a scholar of Trinity College Cambridge where he graduated 2nd Class in the Classical Tripos. He then spent two years in France and Germany studying languages and History. His problem was that he needed someone to nominate him for examination 'and that he will be superannuated for this in little more than a year.' At the age of 78 Vaughan was still being assiduous in promoting the interests of those for whom he felt a special responsibility.

The *Guardian* carried an account on 18 December of the presentation to him of the painting subscribed for by his 'doves'. The idea of the portrait was first mooted at the reunion in Cambridge in 1893 but his illnesses delayed the sittings with the artist. Because of his ill-health, the presentation was made at his home by the Bishop of Winchester with just a few others in attendance. Davidson said that they all wanted people of future times to know what manner of man he was.

> When 35 years ago, you declined a position which would have made you now the senior English Bishop, it was in order to undertake an even larger work, a work the magnitude and character of which we who are gathered in this room can best appreciate though all England has by this time learned to know something of what it means. Has there, I wonder, been ever in the history of Christendom another who has in quite the same degree set his personal seal upon so vast a number of those who are called, in a national Church, to minister the Word and sacraments of God? I hardly think so. Or, to put it in another form, is there anything in England today which quite corresponds to the personal allegiance gladly owned towards you by more than 400 men so widely sundered not only in age and experience but in character, and even in opinion? Again, I think not. A work thus unique in its plan; unique in its magnitude and continuance; unique in the indescribable "tone" which belongs so peculiarly to it; unique above all in the strength of the personal link which we all understand and cherish – such a work, carried on unbroken for five and thirty years, places the worker in the foremost rank of living Englishmen, and it is for that reason that it would have been a disaster had this picture not been painted . . . a work which in its own special way is as great, perhaps, as any that the Church has seen. [12]

High praise, indeed, from a future Archbishop of Canterbury.

Cardiff Town Council at its meeting on 13 January 1896 resolved unanimously to place on record 'its unqualified admiration of the Christian character' of the Dean who had 'won the unanimous respect and esteem of the inhabitants of Cardiff', and deputed the Mayor, an Alderman and the Town Clerk to call on him with a special request. They wanted him to bequeath the 'magnificent painting of himself (by Mr Walter W. Ouless) recently presented to him' to the Town Council 'as a memorial of his long connection with the Borough, and continuous and disinterested labours for the social and educational welfare of its inhabitants.' Vaughan replied to the Town Clerk on the 21st declining a visit: 'I am scarcely equal to the strain upon health and spirits which would be involved in my waiting upon them in a place more convenient to themselves.' He also explained that he could not acquiesce immediately to their request without consulting with the donors, several of whom were Trinity men like himself and he knew that they were assuming their old college in Cambridge 'would be the home of the picture in the years to come when it could be mine no longer.' [13]

Even in old age, he was still contracting affectionate friendships with particular young men who were among his 'doves'. William Joseph Mundy Coombs who had graduated in 1891 at Cambridge and joined him in '94 was such a man. In a letter Catherine wrote to him years later she said, 'You were a favourite with everybody as I am sure you well know.' [14] A collection of 14 letters written by Vaughan or by Catherine to him has been deposited in the Cathedral archives. The first of them is a welcoming letter written in November 1893 which shows him trying to be helpful as ever:

> I rejoice also that you purpose to go in for the Cambridge Preliminary at Easter. It will give definiteness to your reading before you know your future Diocese.
>
> I can scarcely advise you about <u>books</u> for the purpose of that Examination. I do believe none are prescribed, and almost any one who has passed the Examination would be better able than I am to tell you which are the most usual. But pray tell me if you have no one to consult, and I will try to get advice from someone likely to know.
>
> May our time together be as helpful as I am sure it will be pleasant.
>
> Ever truly yours   C.J. Vaughan '
>
> You will like some advice by and bye about lodgings here from me. [15]

By the end of 1894 when he wrote to him on the eve of his Ordination to the Diaconate, the ending had become 'Yours affectionately' and later it would become 'Your attached and affectionate C. J. Vaughan'. The affection and attachment was clearly mutual. They corresponded regularly and in the final stages, Catherine was writing on his behalf.

On 1 November 1895 he wrote to Coombs:

> Your kind and loving letter is already almost four days old – forgive me! It brings many an affectionate thought of you into my heart. I remain very well – a wonder to others and to myself.
>
> We are now 8 in number – I might say 9 – but the one who arrived on the 30th is already attacked by Asthma (to which he is terribly liable) and I am inclined to advise his not staying in poor little Llandaff through its many winter risks and liabilities.
>
> We are going on steadily and (to me) delightfully. We ended this morning 2 Cor iii. I preach now and then - last month on the 13th and 27th.

I like to hear of you as busy, because I know that means two good things – useful and happy.

I fear I must end – for the letters of the day are not quite ended.

I heard from your Bishop last night, and wrote to him today. He says nothing of illness, but I heard of it from others. Always tell me what you see or hear of him.

Your attached and affectionate   C.J. Vaughan [16]

Coombs lived to become a Canon of York and in his old age was the source of a number of anecdotes which he shared with D.D.W. Mowbray about Vaughan, e.g. the story about Bishop Ollivant's letter offering him the post of Dean, and another about Vaughan's encounter with one of H.M. Inspector of Taxes in Cardiff who wanted to know what profit he made from his 'theological college'. That had amused Vaughan greatly because, as Coombs noted, 'his work was entirely a labour of love – we paid nothing except our maintenance in lodgings.' [17] Coombs gave this vignette of the elderly Dean: 'His appearance was so striking, his voice so beautiful, and his reading of the Scriptures, notably St Paul's Epistles, such as I have never heard equalled.' [18]

Another late favourite was R.L. White who was made Deacon at the same service in Durham at which Coombs was ordained Priest. Vaughan took pride that some of his men went north. In December 1895 he wrote to him 'the usual Exodus southwards has not quite left us unrepresented under the great Bishop [Westcott] – for such indeed he is.' [19] His nephew Edwyn Simpkinson was also in the diocese at Bishop Wearmouth.

White's granddaughter made available to D.D.W. Mowbray in 1957 some of Vaughan's letters to him which show that even when approaching the age of eighty, he was still initiating close and affectionate relationships with young men who held a particular attraction for him. The tone and language is similar to that used in letters written forty years earlier to Harrow favourites. In a letter to White dated 30 March 1895 (that is fairly soon after he had joined Vaughan in Llandaff), he wrote 'Dear White, Just one line – to tell you how welcome was your report of yourself this morning . . . Must it be only 'sincerely' between thee and me? No – 'very affectionately' am I yours C.J. Vaughan' [20] In August he shared with him information about the dealings of the Cathedral Chapter:

I have made a poor return for your letter, but I have been greatly worried (to use the feminine word) by the Minor Canonry competition, and was almost ill with it.

343

That is now settled. We had three selected candidates to interview us in Chapter on Tuesday, and elected the Rev. Ellis Gregory Roberts, a 2nd in 'Mods' and 'Greats' at Oxford, a 'bi-linguist' (which Archdeacon Bruce says means 'one who has forgotten his Welsh and never learned English'); a very small man, less than the Bishop . . . but one who impressed us all by his intelligence, decision and good countenance . . .
Ever your affectionate C.J. Vaughan [21]

On the eve of White's ordination in December he wrote to him:

My very dear White
Just one line – to say over again how earnestly my thoughts follow you, first through the long wearisome journey, then through the three days intervening, on to the day of days when you enter upon the new life. May the day be hopeful and helpful, and the life to which it admits you interesting, full and satisfying.
I shall never forget you while I live. Yes, be still (as you say) 'one of us'.
Think of us – pray for us – come back here whenever you can, and let our life be one, still and for ever.
May God ever help you and keep you.
Your loving friend C.J. Vaughan [22]

Perhaps the student closest to his heart in these closing years was Freddy Halsey. His letters to the young man written between the time of his ordination to the Diaconate in December 1894 and his appointment as one of Archbishop Benson's Chaplains in 1896 contain many expressions of tender affection as well as providing some glimpses into his life at this time. The first is dated 20 December 1894:

My heart is very full of you these days. I hope you are happy, trustfull (*sic*) and hopeful – able to rest upon the strength that cannot fail you . . .
I grieve that your friend is not with you at first: but I trust he soon will be, & it will be like having you both while I have him. [Halsey's friend Tapsfield was still studying with Vaughan.]
May God ever bless you. My love to Mr Lambert [Halsey's Vicar] – I know how kind he will be to you. [23]

Four days later he wrote to Halsey's father:

I deeply feel your words of kind, too kind, feeling for what I have tried to do for your dearly loved Son. For indeed it has been a labour of love all the time. He has endeared himself to me most deeply.

I see in him so much of real and unpretending and thorough goodness – so steady a <u>growth</u>, both in knowledge, gift and grace – so sure a promise of the <u>work</u> of a Christian minister; - not to mention <u>minor</u> things such as good sense, right judgement, calm temper, and beautiful manner – all of which, when consecrated by true piety, are invaluable in our Church Pastors.

May the blessing of God be upon him all his life! And may you, my dear Sir, and his Mother, live to be proud of him and thankful for him.

If he is with you, tell him that <u>I</u> <u>preached</u> <u>yesterday</u> after ten months of silence. I wish he could know how much I love him.

Gratefully and faithfully yours C.J. Vaughan [24]

Knowing it would give the old man great pleasure, Halsey sent him a photograph of himself in May 1895. Vaughan replied immediately and predictably:

I cannot wait one day before I thank you for the <u>beautiful</u> photograph of a face so dear to me. It could not possibly have been more lifelike and it rouses in me a great longing to see you again. Let it not be long before you tell me you are coming to <u>stay</u> with us.

This is a Sunday evening – half past six –the heavy bell just ringing for the Vicar's Service. I administered the Sacrament this morning, but did not go to church again in the afternoon. I have been rather the worse for my week in London over the picture [sitting for the Ouless portrait] – it seems ungrateful to say so. Next time I must confine myself <u>entirely</u> to that one thing, & hide myself from everybody.

It is rather sad being in London houseless & homeless after having had so nice & dear a dwelling there for a quarter of a century. But who can complain with Llandaff still left to him? . . .

My heart is very full of you with this photograph to talk to me.

It is no use trying to tell you how I thank you.

Mr Lambert seems to be very happy with you both. [Tapsfield was also a Curate in the same parish]

Again and again Your loving friend C.J. Vaughan [25]

In September he gave him news of life at the Deanery.

You know something of the joy which a letter from you gives me – only just less than seeing you. It is a comfort to feel that you <u>know</u> what I feel for you.

We are at work again since the 9th – five old men, & two new – with one or two more to come shortly.

Only one Oxford man among them all. We have finished St John's Epistles (a "select" subject) and are now taking the 2nd to Timothy, before setting to 2 Corinthians.

I am very well – preaching last Sunday, & reading daily my Lesson in the Cathedral. Mr Downing is gone, & next week we expect the new M.C. [minor canon] – a very small man, the very reverse (in every way) of his predecessor.

The Triennial Musical Festival is going on, and the Cathedral is a desert – while it lasts. Archdeacon Bruce writes: "While [Skrimshere?] fiddles, the Cathedral burns." . . .

Give my love to Tapsfield – it was a great pleasure to see him – always so kind & so responsive.

Come when you can – you hold out a hope for the late Autumn. Meanwhile that beautiful photograph must represent you . . . [26]

He wrote again in early December 1895 with Halsey's Ordination as a priest soon to take place

Your letter delights me by its tidings of the Examination, but most of all by itself. You know how I always cared for you, & to know that you think of me is precious to my very heart.

May every blessing attend your second Ordination. I hear of you from your Vicar, & from Tapsfield, & I feel that my estimate of you is realizing itself in every way.

I shall indeed look forward to a visit from you, just when it best suits you. If it is after the Men return here, there are those among them whom I shall like you to know & who will like to know you – specially one.

I am very busy with the Advent Record. It is difficult to get such a number of names, & places of work, quite accurately up to date. Wonderful that I am still here to do it.

The photograph is always before me – I never saw quite so good a one.

And with loving remembrance. Always yours C.J. Vaughan [27]

On 27 December he wrote to both father and son.

How can I thank you as I ought for your most kind letter?

To serve your Son must ever be my delight. He wound himself round my heart.

He was too modest to tell me about his Examination. I thank you for giving me the pleasure of knowing it. May his new office be a happy one to him, as I am sure it will be an education in the best of schools for a life (as I cannot but expect) of great trust and usefulness. [28]

To Halsey Jr. he wrote:

You who know my great love for you can understand the deep joy with which your beautiful letter received this morning fills me. It was followed by one from your Father for which I am most grateful. There is something so delightful to me in having had so unexpected an opportunity of testifying what I think of you and feel for you as the Archbishop's application gave me.

I can almost envy him the having you always with him as his devoted helper in work & home.

May it be to you, dearest son, a happy & eventful time, qualifying you for high trust hereafter when I shall be no longer here to love & bless you in them!

It is sweet to hear (you were too modest to tell me) of the Examination you have just passed for Priest's Orders.

I must not now hope to see you quite so soon as next month – for I know how closely you will be tied in your new sphere of duty. But you will now and then give me a thought in your heavy duties and will perhaps now realize my love for you more than you could do when I had you opposite to me in the Lecture Room here.

May God be with you as your very present help in all things. [29]

The last letter in the Halsey collection is dated 4 March 1896:

Of course I have been full of the thought of you, but I had such an impression of the heavy burden of work that was upon you in your early days at Lambeth that I spared you even the reading of a letter and I feared that perhaps your promised visit would have to be postponed. It is a great joy to think of seeing your dear face again.

I was inclined to be jealous of M[r] Owen [his friend, the HM of the Cathedral School], who always seems to be my 'supplanter' in the matter of visits from my Men. But on reflexion I see that it may be more cheerful for you to be there than here – and I well know that you will let us have you very often at the Deanery. I think you have seen how I love to have you with me . . .

I was laid up for a fortnight with a very severe cold but it never got quite to the dignity of bronchitis, & yesterday I began work again with my Men, though I have not yet been out.

I am quite in good spirits, and enjoying my resumption of work.

Always, dear Halsey, Your loving friend C.J. Vaughan [30]

In February 1896 Alfred Thomas wrote to Vaughan about the expectation laid upon the College's President that he should give an address. The Dean replied immediately in the plainest terms refusing to give one:

I have made no secret of the precarious state of my health or of the medical prohibitions and limitations under which I live or of the necessity laid upon me to decline all demands of an exciting or exhausting nature. The very idea of an Address, still more of an Oration, is out of the question for me – and if (in your kindness) you propose to suspend it over me for six months, I can but say that it were better for me to fix it absolutely for tomorrow.

But I gather from your letter that this contribution of a Presidential Address is regarded in some (perhaps in many) quarters as a sine quâ non on the part of the holder of the President's office.

If this is so, I shall at once carry into effect what I have always regarded as the right and proper thing to be done by a person situated as I am – namely, to resign the Office at the earliest moment compatible with the convenience of the authorities of the College. I shall not cease to feel all the interest I have ever felt in the Welfare of the Institution or to remember with gratitude that I was once elected its President. [31]

Vaughan resigned and was succeeded by Lord Tredegar. It gave him great pleasure that his work on behalf of the university had been noted by the Prince of Wales who wrote to him. In June 1896 he told Davidson about this, 'What a kind remonstrance I received from the Prince of Wales on his hearing that I was resigning the Presidentship of the University College of South Wales, and how kindly he directed a second letter to be written today that he thoroughly understood my having replied that the step was irrevocable, & for such and such reasons.' In the same letter he declined an invitation to stay with the Davidsons: 'My visits are over & done – but not my loving thoughts which often find their rest where you are.' [32]

One of his last 'doves', who was with him from January 1895 to June '96, was G.L. Gosling, later to become a Canon of St Albans and another source of anecdotal evidence for Mowbray's doctoral thesis in 1958. He went to serve his title in the large urban parish of Halesowen in the Diocese of Worcester. He noted that Vaughan preferred his men to begin their ministry in such parishes and to learn their ministerial skills from clergy who had read with him. In the case of Halesowen, there had been three rectors who were 'doves' and Gosling reckoned he was the 30th 'dove' to serve as an assistant curate there.

Vaughan wrote to Ralph White on 23 April 1896 and was feeling strong enough to have him visit –

Just one line, dear Ralph, to say Welcome, most welcome, at all times and particularly on the 7th to the 11th of May.

Did you, could you, doubt it? This is a busy day – getting up my Colossians and looking over the seven paraphrases of Titus for tomorrow, besides several letters. So you shall have only the assurance of my loving welcome, and the old signature.

Your loving friend. C.J. VAUGHAN [33]

A month later he was ill again. Catherine wrote to Coombs on 24 May to tell him this and reported 'Some internal obstruction – and then followed by Congestion of the Lungs and for two days our anxiety was great – But he seems to be getting over it. And Dr Vachell expresses himself as satisfied with the progress made.' [34] By June Vaughan was describing his condition as 'going down the hill steadily, but with pauses.' The last such pause which allowed him to preach in his cathedral was 21 June. By August he was so weak that Catherine had to act as his secretary. On the 5th she wrote to Alfred Thomas:

I wish I could give you a more cheering report of him. But his strength is so ill "maintained", that his Doctor says it is not possible for him to speak with any certainty as to the issue of this illness. "I hope" – he told me yesterday – "that he may pull through but I cannot speak with any confidence."

Tomorrow he will be 80 – and under the circumstances, he knew that the time of our earthly companionship must be short. Every day that he has left to us is as an especial gift – and blessing – calling for our sincerest gratitude . . . [35]

In addition to her letter, Vaughan sent a telegram the same day to him at the House of Commons which read ' Touching and deeply felt letter. Still too ill to write but not too ill to feel. Dean Llandaff.' [36]

By 9 October Catherine was fearing the worst. 'Again the clouds are gathering,' she wrote to Dalrymple. 'Dr Vachell says "he is in a very critical state".' [37] But a week later she was more optimistic: 'The elements have spent their fury & the Sun has come out once more. Contrary to all expectations, he is better.' [38] On 2 November she sent a brief message to Dalrymple: 'One Word - & one only. He is – I can hardly bear to say the word – but he is "sinking".' [39]

Despite his worsening condition, his 'Men' were never far from his thoughts. On 12 November he wrote to Davidson to tell him he had been working on what would be his last letter to them via the pages of the *Advent Record*:

The last day or two have been occupied with the sad task of drawing up my

349

last Advent Record. It has cost me some nights of anxious thought. But it has not injured me really – and I did long to do this last little word myself.

You can imagine with what mingled feelings I have done it. Deep humiliation, I trust, has been the predominant thought. But I will not try to express this sorrowful aspect of the long past – it lies too deep.

Glyn [a former 'dove' and curate in Doncaster], most kindly, came to see us for a few hours. You can imagine the pleasure of seeing him not only as Bishop, but the Bishop of my own old home, & dear Sister & Brother, & all the familiar villages of my father's neighbourhood in the county – such as Foston (his own Parish of four houses where he died) . . .

Dearest Bishop, pray for me when you receive the last Advent Record, that the great Atonement may reach even to me. [40]

He added a PS: 'A rather good day permits me to scrawl these few lines.' A fortnight later Davidson travelled to Llandaff to see him. Vaughan scribbled a Thank You note to be given to Davidson before his departure:

8a.m. Monday Nov 29 1896

I must send my love to the dearest Bishop before he ends his kindest, most welcome visit to us. I thank & bless him for it. It has not been in vain. A night of quiet dozing has run its course into calm and trusting. The Incarnation, the Life, the Table, the Garden and the Cross, bore our sins – it is enough. 'Lord, I believe . . .'

Your 'holy kiss' represented to me that of the 450. God be with you in your journey today – in your life and in your life's end. [41]

In December his last edition of the *Advent Record* was sent out. His letter reads:

This is no doubt my last 'Advent Record'. My work is ended. Life may be prolonged a few weeks, or even months; but it is limited by sure causes, and I would not have it otherwise. My desire would be to feel myself lying on the brink of the dark river; or rather, perhaps, standing in it to the waist or to the ankles, speaking still to many faithful friends who seem resolved not to leave me till the little boat comes, with room but for one, to carry me across into the dim darkness where there is but one known Person, yet sufficient if known.

Is the truth which I have been teaching all these years substantial and supporting now? Never before were the two (almost contiguous) clauses of the Church Confession so vivid in their significance as now, in the near prospect of the great change, 'The burden of them is intolerable', and 'For the sake of Thy Son, our Lord Jesus Christ, forgive us all that is past'.

I would pray you, my dear ones, from whom I am soon to be severed, to make very sure of the great revelation of the forgiveness of sins, early (or, if not early, then late), that you may be able to make it the keynote of your ministry as a thing not heard of, but known, and the stay of your own souls as a thing not to be groped after then, but simply clung to 'when the towers fall'. It is a revelation which none could have made but He who had seen it in heaven: nevertheless, it is the very power of God for salvation to every-one who believes it.

That I loved you to the end needs not to be said. These few calm words, will carry that message, perhaps after, more probably before, I close my eyes upon a world of opportunity and wonder. [42]

In fact his health improved and he was well enough by January 1897 to have a visit from Alfred Thomas along with his two sons who were pupils at Harrow. In a note to him he wrote 'I am wonderfully better, though not likely to regain a full measure of health.' [43] Catherine's letter to Coombs written on 4 January was similarly upbeat: 'The beloved Dean is surprising. So far better is he – that he has been out once for a short drive and he has even been to the Cathedral – on New Year's Day – for the [Canons'] Service. He is again in his Study – and I do not despair of your seeing him yet many times . . .' [44]

He was well enough in February to write a pamphlet about the financial needs of the Cathedral, have it printed and distributed to all the members of the congregation. A copy was sent to Dalrymple who kept it with his personal papers. It appears they were having difficulty paying the stipends of all the staff, including the Dean and the four Residentiary Canons; and is evidence of a very early version of 'planned giving', an aspect of almost every parish's life nowadays. In it he wrote:

Two years ago we introduced what is known as the weekly offertory, but with results somewhat disappointing when compared with other Churches of less capacity and less dignity . . .

Is it too much to hope that the Congregation will help us, by a steady increase in its weekly offerings, in this effort to place the several respon-sibilities of this ancient and beautiful Cathedral upon a more satisfactory footing in the one point of a sufficiency of means, and so of obviating what appears to be the only alternative, a permanent diminution of our own (certainly not exorbitant) salaries as fixed by Act of Parliament in 1840 and 1843? [45]

Though frail in body, he retained his mental faculties and was still able to read and to write letters in a legible hand. And he was still in regular

351

correspondence with Macmillan. The first letter to him in 1897 is dated 6 January and, still couched in gracious terms, put a proposal to them:

> I have been looking at the annual report of my publishing account.
> I cannot but feel it a record of failure, for which no one is to blame, but which leads one to ask oneself whether any good can yet be done with the relics of the labours of long days gone by.
> I am going to give you the suggestion of "my head upon my bed" the last night or two.
> I should like to make a large <u>distribution</u> of these shoals of unsaleable volumes, in the form of <u>gifts</u> (say 100 in number) to various Institutions such as Theological Colleges, University Colleges, Free Libraries, &c – in the United Kingdom & America. Each gift to consist of 12 8vo volumes, with the addition of 4 <u>smaller</u> publications to be included in each parcel, viz. The Prayers of Jesus Christ, Restful Thoughts in Restless Days, Last Words in the Temple Church, & Lectures on Confirmation.
> I do not think that such distributions would materially injure either Author or (but here I speak ignorantly) Publishers. Might it not rather serve as an advertisement?
> And I confess to you that I should like to do my little part towards bearing my testimony to what I feel to be Evangelical truth against Sacerdotalism and Semi-Romanism which is becoming rapidly <u>the</u> religion of the Church of England.
> The cost of carriage to the various destinations must of course be my affair. I do not know that it would come to a very large sum.
> I have told you my project. I do not forget that it must wait for your consent. For I could not afford to think of it but as involving the generosity of the Publishers as well as the Author's fancy. If the whole idea strikes you as preposterous, kindly say so, and we will dismiss it as the dream of a sick man. [46]

The answer came by return of post informing him of costs unforeseen by him. He replied next day:

> I fear that I had dreamed of a supply from <u>bound</u> stores, which I now see to be illusory. The charge for binding (or boarding) will so much increase the cost of the proposed gifts that I fear I must largely reduce the scale of my projected distribution.
> Thanking you for your acquiescence in what I fear may have struck you as an unusual request. [47]

By the 18th he had made the decision not to proceed as the proposed 100 benefactions, he said, would be quite beyond his means. Given the size of his estate, that was not true. 'I will return to my usual more modest method, and when I see what my late gift to the <u>Aberdare</u> Theological College cost me, I shall be able perhaps to afford a few more gifts of the same kind without trespassing upon you.' [48]

He penned one last brief letter to his dear "Society of Friends" on 29 March 1897:

My very dear sons & brothers.

This long, protracted but merciful illness, with its perpetual oscillations between better and worse, makes me long for some communication with you before an 'Advent' which I may not live to see . . .

At all events it will tell you that I am thinking of you, and anxious that your ministry, begun well, should also end well; that no sense of dullness or weariness should be allowed to drop your hand from the plough, but that all should be pressing forward to the glad "Well done."

I cannot tell you how I myself am – so frequent are the changes – one Sunday in the Cathedral, & the next weak in bed.

We are in the hands of God. Enough for us. 'Though He slay me, yet will I trust Him.'

Your devoted Friend   C.J. Vaughan

Multitudes of kind & beautiful letters lie unanswered, alas, alas! The pen no longer flies, it lingers, it loiters, it procrastinates. Forgive, forgive. [49]

He wrote what was probably his last letter to Lake at the end of May 1897 as his old friend had heard an exaggerated report of his condition:

I cannot say that I think the end is *very* near, but I get thinner and feebler, and find my bed my desired haven, though I am up, and indeed down, for some hours most days.

Weariness and drowsiness and abhorrence of food are my chief conscious witnesses to the decay of the 'humiliating' body; they are, I think, infallible.

My happiest half hour is the earliest when I try, on my bed, to enter into the chamber of the soul, and pray to my Father which is in secret; I hope, and sometimes feel, as though He hears me.

I still read the paper, or skim it, and the life of some great man. I hope it is not wrong to 'love the world I leave.'

The post is going; but this will not reach you till Monday. Your beautiful letters will be dear to me till the end. – Your loving friend. [50]

In May he also wrote to George Macmillan with another proposal but one about which he seems to have had mixed feelings:

I hope that this will find you at work again after your serious illness.

A Harrow Pupil & attached friend of mine is anxious to be allowed to publish as a second Volume of my <u>University Sermons</u> some (or all) of those which I <u>omitted</u> in the 8vo volume in 1888.

I said in reply (1) that you were jointly interested in my publications, & must of course be consulted – (2) that few of my works had now any sale to speak of, & that I could not suppose that you would encourage the publication of one which consisted of Sermons already slighted and omitted by myself.

But my poor friend is kind enough to be 'sadly disappointed' & cannot rest without an appeal to you.

He has drawn up a pathetic [here meaning 'moving'] little Preface, and has written me still more pathetic letters which I think I must ask you to glance at before you answer him finally.

I am really too ill for business, but there are some things which one <u>must</u> do for oneself while it is possible.

With kind remembrance of a long past. [51]

The anonymous preface-writer and editor of this collection of sermons was Alfred Pretor. Letters between George Macmillan and him about the proposed volume are included in the Macmillan letter books deposited in the British Library. The financial agreement was on a 'half-profit basis' and at Vaughan's 'special request [is] being made with you, not with himself or his representatives.' The Dean had also requested that the volume should not appear until after his death. They offered to send Pretor copies of volumes of Vaughan's sermons 'to pick some out at no charge.' [52] The Dean had already requested Macmillan in February 1896 to send gift copies of his *Helpful Thoughts in Restless Times* and *Last Words in the Temple Church* to Pretor at his home, Belfield House near Weybridge. Presumably these had been requested by his former pupil. Sadly their private correspondence exists no longer.

He robed himself and occupied his stall in the cathedral for the last time on Jubilee Sunday at the end of June 'in honour of that Gracious Lady who has been so good to me.' [53] A week later he sent his last greeting to Old Harrovians via Montagu Butler, who read the letter to those who gathered for a reunion on 7 July:

Once again – surely for the last time – I send my greetings to my own old Harrow, gathered in diminished numbers, but with the old Harrow heart, at their Triennial Anniversary. You may not have the opportunity, but, if you have, tell them I was not *half* kind enough to them when I was their master. It is wonderful how the very words of those days come back in sleepless nights or meditative early hours, now. What would I not give to unsay, or to ask forgiveness for one little half-sentence in the Speech Room to one still living! These things are scarcely fit subjects for a Triennial Dinner. The Harrow of 1845-1859 would not know me now – an old man, full of regrets and sorrows for many things, but most of all for this – that he is laden with a gratitude which he does not deserve, and with love which he can now repay only by idly loving back. [54]

What was surely an unprecedented international episcopal public greeting appeared in the *Guardian* on 18 August. It would reappear later that year as the frontispiece in his last publication before the anonymous Preface to a final selection of his sermons. It was signed by some of the Bishops who had been attending the Lambeth Conference and now were visiting Wells.

The Palace, Wells, Somerset,   August 3rd, 1897

'Dear Dr Vaughan – In the least formal manner that is possible, we who have met at this time in a country so near to your own, and on a day so near to your birthday, wish to take this opportunity of assuring you of our heartfelt appreciation of the great services you have done for our beloved Church, of the high standard of life and of pastoral care which you have set and have taught, and of our deep thankfulness to our God that He has thus enabled you to be of blessing to countless numbers throughout the world. We pray God to comfort and sustain you in your sufferings, and to grant you in peace an entrance into that life of eternal service to the hope of which you have lifted so many hearts.

W. Cantuar.	John Truron.
G.W. Bath and Well.	Alfred Barry (Bishop).
Edward R. Calcutta.	G. F. Stepney (Bishop designate).
M. London.	Joh. Norvic.
Randall Winton.	G. Worthington (Bp of Nebraska, U.S.A.).
Wm. Sz. Sydney.	Waite H. Falkland Islands.
W. T. T. Brisbane.	S. Morley (Bishop of Tinnevelly and Madura).
J. J. S. Worcester.	G. Mott Williams (Bp of Marquette, U.S.A.)
R. F. L. Hullen.	E. C. Petriburg.
J. Hereford.	John N. Quirk.
George Henry Guildford.	T. D. Bernard.
H. Frank Colchester.	Alex. Colvin Ainslie.
H. H. Tasmania.	T. W. Jex-Blake.

William D. Walker (Bp of Western New York). Hilton Bothamley. David Robertson. [55]

That private and public expression of thankfulness for his life and ministry must have warmed his heart. A letter at the same time from his brother Edward, however, unsettled him and caused him to write a tetchy letter to his publisher:

> I was startled by receiving the enclosed paragraph in a long letter from my eldest brother, whom you remember as Rector of Harpenden till this year.
> I could not help feeling surprise & some annoyance when I heard of what I feared might interfere with the sale of my almost only remunerative publication and your share in the copyright. It was the last thing my brother would wish to do. But I think the <u>title</u> of this book should be changed.
> And I think his idea of making it a <u>gift</u> to the S.P.C.K. tells just the wrong way, as enabling them to sell it for almost nothing.
> You will see by my writing that I am increasingly ill, and utterly unfit for business.
> But I know you will kindly forgive me for troubling you "yet once more".
> I will do what you think right in the matter.
> My brother has retired to St Martin's Lodge, Worthing.
> Will you kindly (if necessary) communicate with him there? And, if it be possible, spare me further communication?
> Ever gratefully yours, C.J. Vaughan [56]

His brother's book was published later that year by SPCK with the title *The Fatherly Hand. Being the substance of instruction given to the candidates for Confirmation in a country parish*.

His last letter to Macmillan is simply dated 'Monday morning' and almost certainly written in August:

> One line – from my bed – to ask your kind attention to my new little book –
> I cannot learn that any of the Presentation Copies have yet been received – though the publication was promised me <u>a fortnight ago.</u>
> It is a small matter – but you will forgive the fidgeting of a man laid aside – I slept better last night & am in less pain this morning. [57]

He added a PS requesting that one of his presentation copies should be sent to The Rev Professor Salmon DD at Trinity College Dublin with a slip inside saying "<u>With Dr Vaughan's special acknowledgement of help derived from Dr Salmon's Sermons</u>".

Soon afterwards he weakened further and became entirely dependent on others. During the last few weeks of his life he was unable to read or write but was happy to listen to Catherine or others read to him. He retained his interest in current affairs and had the daily papers read to him. They also read at his request Stanley's *Life of Dr Arnold* and the biographies of the missionary Henry Martyn and of Bishop Patteson which were his favourites after the Bible and the Harrow School hymn-book.

Catherine gave voice to her own deep faith in life beyond the grave when she wrote to Dean Lake on 5 September about her dying husband:

> What a true and faithful friend you are! Your letter was most *reposeful* and beautiful. We feel so exactly what you do as to the 'wonderful thing life is,' and the 'awful idea of the Being,' in whose Presence we shall so soon find ourselves, and the nature of the world to come – such great realities as the end draws near. What should we do but for the direct assurance that His name is love, and that He has promised to us the forgiveness of sins, and that when this impenetrable veil is uplifted there will be a 'glad surprise.'
>
> That end is drawing very near. He is quite confined to his bed, and is almost too feeble to speak . . . When this earthly life does cease, we must only give thanks that he has been allowed at last to enter 'within the gates into the City.' How can Dr Jowett dare to say we shall not meet our loved ones hereafter, when we have the express assurances to the contrary? I cannot think our *chief* happiness in that world beyond the grave is to consist in meeting again with those we have loved here; but that we shall meet them, and that it will form one of our many unspeakable joys, who can deny?
>
> We should so like to see you once again, but it is to be no longer thought of . . . May you have a less lingering journey through the dark valley than has been given to him. We are sorry to hear of your infirm health, which I am afraid is leading you in that direction.
>
> What centuries it seems since we met at Royat! How many are gone since then of that gay circle who sat together on that terrace!
>
> Yours most truly and sincerely, Cath. Vaughan. [58]

Within weeks of Vaughan's death, Lake too had died.

Ralph White (the last of his men to become a dignitary as Dean of Maritzburg) visited him just a few days before he died. White was the Guest Preacher at Evensong in Harrow School Chapel on Vaughan's Commemoration on 21 January 1945 and he told the boys about that visit:

> In the course of conversation, he referred to our Lord's words in the 14th chapter of St John: 'In my Father's house are many mansions: if it were not so, I would have told you; for I go to prepare a place for you.' He pointed out how faithful our Lord was in foretelling trials and troubles and sufferings to His Apostles: they knew He could be absolutely trusted and therefore when He spoke of the many mansions and the rest that remaineth, they knew it would come to pass for His own. Dr Vaughan did not mince matters in declaring what he knew to be truth, but all his

teaching was based on the Foundation apart from which no man can lay, even Jesus Christ. [59]

The Queen had asked to be kept informed of his progress and she received regular medical bulletins from Dr Vachell. Archdeacon Bruce attended him daily. On Thursday 14 October he was bright and cheerful but he had a premonition that the end was very near and repeatedly asked his doctor if he could say how long it would be. He had a troubled night and it was clear by Friday morning that he was sinking fast. Archdeacon Bruce was sent for from Newport and arrived late morning but by then he was in a semi-conscious state. His wife, a sister and niece, together with Nurse Forrest and all the servants were gathered there with him as he had requested. He died peacefully at five past six in the evening. When the news of his death reached the Queen, she wrote personally to Catherine and her representative at the funeral, Major the Hon. Charles Harbord, brought a wreath of white chrysanthemums with a card from her. The Prince of Wales too sent a personal greeting expressing his sadness to Catherine. Charles Dalrymple received the news direct from Catherine: 'He is <u>gone</u> at 6 after a day of perfect unconsciousness & a most peaceful, tranquil end.' [60] She wrote at greater length to Davidson:

> You will have seen that the end has come – that the blow so long impending has fallen at last.
> He became unconscious at 11 this morning. We watched with him till 6 aft. When he breathed his last – so tranquilly that it was only when the Nurse said: "He is quite gone now." – that we could believe he had really left us.
> I can only now give thanks - & I think of him as he <u>is</u> - & wonder with a hopeless, hopeless wonder – what he has <u>awakened</u> to.
> But this we shall never know till we have joined him. There was really no <u>shadow</u> of pain upon his countenance – nor any indication of suffering. [61]

Ernest Owen, the Cathedral School's Headmaster, also wrote to him and included these re-assuring lines: 'Nothing could have been happier – Mrs Vaughan, his sister, his niece, the faithful Hammond and Miranda & Nurse Forest were all around him – it was just the peaceful end he had always longed for.' [62]

Vaughan had chosen the burial site himself in a shady spot within sight of the bedroom windows of the Deanery. On the day, the inside of the grave was lined with moss and a crown of white chrysanthemums had been placed where his head would lie to represent the crown of glory. Despite the family's request that no flowers be sent, there were many wreaths which were laid near the grave among them a pretty one sent by the laundresses of the Temple who had once been in Catherine's Bible Class there.

The *Church Times* published an account of the service written by one of the many churchmen who had travelled from London to be present:

> As we drove up from the station all Cardiff seemed to be trudging the same way; out from the town and across the green which leads to the village city of Llandaff was a long line of black wending its way to the cathedral, and what a sight was there! The church stood up with its two unequal towers in glorious autumnal light surrounded by a wealth of tinted trees, and presently there wended through a vast and orderly crowd, a procession headed by the Chapter and followed by the Master of Trinity, the Bishops of Llandaff, Winchester, Bath and Wells, Peterborough, Southwark and Southampton. Then came the coffin carried on a bier and covered with a simple purple pall; there was no display of flowers or ornaments, only a single wreath was carried, and that bore the inscription 'A token of regard, Victoria I. et R', written by the Queen's own hand. So was the Dean carried for the last time into his cathedral between a double line of at least two hundred clergy in surplices, some of whom were of the diocese, but the majority were men, whom Dr Vaughan had himself trained for Holy Orders. The Master of Trinity, his successor at Harrow, read the lesson, at the Dean's wish as it is said, and the Bishops of Winchester and Bath and Wells dividing the service, the Bishop of Llandaff pronouncing the blessing. The grave was dug on the north side of the cathedral ground in the midst of beautiful trees and calm and dignified surroundings.
>
> Few who were present and turned away as the bells broke out into their muffled peal, could fail to see in the scene of glorious autumnal decay, and in its calmness and peace, a token of the great life of noble purpose which had ended here, amidst all the reverence which men could give. [63]

What this account does not mention is that the entire teaching staff and three hundred students from the university college also attended as did a large number of miners from the district and, as *The Times* reported, 'There was also an exceptionally large attendance of Nonconformist ministers and representatives of Nonconformist bodies.' The writer claimed that there were thousands of spectators and that South Wales had never previously witnessed such a huge demonstration of popular sympathy. Fortunately the weather on the day was exceptionally fine which probably had an effect on bringing so many to attend his burial.

Vaughan was remembered at Evensong that same afternoon in Westminster Abbey and there were packed services in Harrow School Chapel and in Doncaster Parish Church to remember him. Canon Ainger, his successor as Master of the Temple, attended the funeral and officiated and preached at a Memorial Service in the Temple Church a fortnight later on the 28th anniversary of Vaughan's first sermon there.

Like his spiritual mentor long ago at Cambridge, Charles Simeon, he was no party man having abstained from church politics and church conflicts all his life, yet like him he remained at heart an Evangelical to the end. The opening extract from his will makes this very clear: 'In the prospect of death, a little nearer or further off, I wish to state explicitly that I have put my whole trust in the revelation of the Gospel as made in the Gospel of St John and in the Epistles of St John and St Paul. I believe in the forgiveness of sins as the foundation stone of the Gospel and commit myself humbly and hopefully to God in this faith for life, death, and eternity.' The words on his tombstone taken from St John's Gospel which he chose himself echo this same faith: 'Not that we loved God, but that He loved us.'

His will was dated 21 May 1897 and a codicil was added on 22 July. His executors were his widow and his nephew, Edward Vaughan Thompson, a solicitor to whom he bequeathed some of his presentation plate plus £250. His estate was valued at £21,865. 9s. 2d [= £2,406,713]. The main beneficiaries, who received £1,000 each, were his two brothers, Sir John Luther Vaughan and Canon David Vaughan, and the Headmaster of the Cathedral School. He bequeathed to his sister Elizabeth Emma Vaughan a life annuity of £50, and to his elder brother Edward Thomas and his wife Mary a life annuity of £100. His nephews and nieces all received £100 each. The orphaned children of his late sister Sarah Dorothea were also remembered. He bequeathed portraits and books to many different individuals and institutions with which he had been connected, and monetary bequests to former servants. His butler, Albert Hammond, received £200 plus one year's wages; to the other indoor servants a half year's wage, and to outdoor servants a quarter of a year's wage. The Cathedral School also benefited and he begged his successor to endeavour 'in all things to promote the interest of the said Cathedral School'. Catherine was to have the benefit of the residue of his estate during her lifetime and after her death it was to be shared between his brother Edward and his family and his Simpkinson nephews and nieces. He directed that all his letters (of which there must have been very many) should be destroyed, unread. But his manuscript sermons, his medals, souvenirs and robes and *Life of the Prince Consort*, a personal gift from the Queen and signed by her, he bequeathed to his wife. And, for an eminent Victorian, he made one very unusual request: 'And it is my special desire that no memoir or other permanent record of my life be either printed or published. I desire no other memorial than the kind thoughts of my former pupils at Harrow, Doncaster, the Temple and Llandaff.' It appears, however, from a letter written by his widow Catherine to Sir Charles Dalrymple that the Dean had made that request at a time when he was deeply depressed and that it was not included in a new will written shortly before his death. [64]

Albert Hammond penned a touching letter to Dalrymple on 15 November in response to one he had received from his master's friend, and the old butler did it in a far more legible hand than his mistress ever wrote with!

> Dear Sir
> I have ventured to show your kind letter to M[rs] Vaughan because there is an interesting relic of my dear Master which I thought would be just the thing for you, and that is a carved oak arm chair, which the Dean always used in the Lecture Room for writing & for the Readings & Lectures to his men, M[rs] Vaughan was not going to take it, & I was afraid that I should stand a poor chance of buying it at the sale, as I know there are several Gentlemen anxious to get hold of any relics of the Dean's.
> M[rs] Vaughan was quite pleased when I suggested it to her, & I am to send it to you. Will you kindly send me the Address where you would like it sent.
> M[rs] Vaughan is fairly well and she leaves here for good on Saturday, stays in London untill [sic] Monday & then goes to Rome for three weeks. I think the Address at Weybridge will be Llandaff House, Weybridge, Surrey which is close to the Railway Station. M[rs] Vaughan is not parting with me, I am glad to say.
> All the Best of the furniture have (sic) gone to Weybridge, but there will be a sale at the Deanery of what remains "including the Dean's Library" the date of the sale not yet fixed. The Dean's (Prize?) Books M[rs] Vaughan is giving away to friends, so as to prevent them from going into a public sale.
> Thanking you Sir, for your kind interest,
> I am Sir Charles your Humble and Obedient Servant, Albert J. Hammond. [65]

She wrote to him herself that same day. The letter begins: 'Did you really think that I should quit this home – without setting aside some relic for you – the best if not the very oldest of his much loved friends?' And she went on to tell him of her travel plans, 'the dream of my life', to visit Rome, Pompei and the Amalfi coast for three weeks; the family

361

physician, Dr Vachell, and his daughter would be accompanying her. 'After that I take up my abode at Llandaff House, Weybridge [Surrey] for the rest of my remaining life & where I shall hope to see you. It is so very accessible 3/4 of an hour from Waterloo.' [66]

Her first letter to him from her new home, dated 29 December, tells of what had been a memorable holiday – 'Yes I have come back & have brought with me memories w[h] will never fade away.' And again she urged him to visit her – depart Waterloo at 2.15 and be in Weybridge at 3. 'What a joy it will be to me to see you once again.' [67]

The collection of sermons which Alfred Pretor had so much wished to see published appeared in November and included the Preface that Vaughan had described to Macmillan as "pathetic":

> . . . Something still lives, even in the printed page, of the refined and winning earnestness which placed Dean Vaughan among the foremost preachers of the century, and gave him a power, almost unrivalled, of influencing from the pulpit the mind and life of our great Universities.
>
> Even praise itself may be a presumption. Yet I cannot refrain from dwelling upon one other feature of these Sermons, for in it, I think, lies their charm. I refer to the intensely human sympathy which is their great, their essential characteristic. It is no hyperbole to say of the author that he could read the thoughts of his hearers: he has translated them into language.
>
> I heard the first of these Sermons when I was a boy of seventeen: the last, when I was a man of forty; and my opinion throughout has never varied, that we have in them no mere passing reflection of contemporary thought, but models, for all time, of what preaching can be made in attractiveness and power.
>
> Yet it will be for others to judge them critically, and more dispassionately than I can, for my ears are still haunted by the pure articulation and fault-less phrasing which held generation after generation of undergraduates bound as with some spell. [68]

Various former 'doves' immediately wrote to Davidson with suggestions for a permanent Vaughan memorial – one was for some scholarships at Trinity College Cambridge tenable for four years for men intending to take Holy Orders (rather like the Liddon Scholarships at Oxford) but the one which was eventually agreed upon by a 'Representative Committee' chaired by Davidson meeting on 11 November was to build a Vaughan Memorial Church in London, and they resolved unanimously to raise £10,000 [= £1,100,690] to that end. On 16 November the Master of Trinity chaired a meeting in Church House to consider a suitable memorial to him at Harrow.

Her husband's 'request' concerning no *Life* to be written had upset Catherine, so it was a great relief when Bishop Westcott wrote to her the following year with a compromise proposal. A flurry of letters written on black edged paper followed as she shared the news with Dalrymple and sought his aid. The first one is dated 17 October 1898.

Dear Sir Charles
You will be interested in what I am going to tell you.
It is that at the earnest request of the Bishop of Durham we have come to the Determination – to make a judicious Selection of the dear Dean's Letters & let them see the daylight.
I consulted his Executor & ascertained from him that there was no prohibition whatever in the Will. (Only?) a desire expressed that the Letters found at his death might be destroyed.
Not a word concerning the Letters he had written. (?) what he said to me was under the influence of great depression - & we cannot but think that if he could now hear what the Bishop says, he would have relented as I think he must have done since the request is not reiterated in the Will w[h] he drew up very shortly before the end came –
At all events we think that the step we propose to take & David Vaughan feels entirely with us & says it would be a most valuable and (fascinating?) volume if brought forth with no comment - & all names suppressed. The Master of Trinity is to be asked to write – if necessary – a Prefatory (?).
I cannot (fully?) express the joy & the relief w[h] it would be to me – it has been a weight upon my heart and mind that what would be so priceless a (treasure?) to so very many should be allowed to lie (buried?) for ever & for ever unseen & unknown.
It will be – hearing that dear Voice once more - & will speak to all (?) – as it is not in the power of any Sermon to do.
But I shall write to all his later Scholars to say that they (will? ? ?) such extracts as may be suitable for inclusion if they do not wish to expose every word of them to the light of day.
I think I know all that you will say and all that you will feel.
Ever yours affectionately C. Vaughan [69]

Dalrymple, as she expected, replied immediately and affirmatively. On 17 October she told him that both her husband's brothers were 'of the opinion that not being repeated in the Will, there is no lawful necessity for observance of them especially as they were uttered when under the (influence?) of dark depression.' [70] The Bishop's support, it seems, had been decisive in the matter. She asked Sir Charles to send her 'any such letters in your possession, as seem to you to be at all suitable for the public – and not too (sacred?) – or too merely business like . . . ' [71] The
363

Times printed a letter from her on 22 October giving notice of the intended volume and requesting material from correspondents. On the 25th she wrote to Macmillan for help in publishing 'this little volume' but was already suspecting there might be problems in finding quotable letters, 'I fear the greater number must have been on business & cannot have been preserved.'[72]

She was grateful for Dalrymple's support in early November when he wrote to disagree with the plan of publishing the letters without the names of their recipients – the idea had originated with David Vaughan and it was one that Catherine had not liked. She had already discovered by then that many of the letters her husband had written to his young men consisted chiefly of advice on practical arrangements, and so many of them began in the same way expressing 'regrets for not having written sooner. Repeating that would make for wearisome reading.' And the question had been raised in her mind about the propriety of including some of his sharp observations on prominent persons such as the "strutting" of the Archbishop of York in front of the Archbishop of Canterbury or his verbal picture of Lord John Russell 'smiling-capering-toiling'. Catherine regarded it as a 'vivid and graphic' one but which, regretfully, she recognized ought to be blotted out. She admitted 'I should be so fearfully sensitive as to any criticism or <u>sneers</u> & would rather the book was condemned as dull than that it should show this "biting sarcasm" described by G. Russell as "sparing neither sex nor age nor friendship nor affinity!" That would be intolerable!'[73] She knew only too well that sharp even sarcastic personal observations had been characteristic of her late husband though she preferred to describe them as examples of 'his remarkable wit'. She was also facing other editorial difficulties: 'I am rather in despair – for it seems more than half the letters that have been sent to men are of so private & necessarily trivial in character as to make them quite unsuitable for the rude light of day.'[74] By the year's end she must have been wondering whether the volume would ever be printed.

She wrote to Sir Charles on 7 February 1899: 'I conclude you are in London now that Parliament has begun again & I return these precious letters - with infinite sadness & pain. But the decree was not to be withstood. That they were too private and too personal for the world to see.'[75] Who made that decree is not clear – his brothers? The Bishop of Durham? Macmillan? Whoever it was, it was the right decision for his letters lack the social, political and theological content found, for example, in the letters of Arnold, his old master, which had made them of such interest to a much wider readership than the original recipients. Most of Vaughan's would have been of no importance except to the recipient. Two such which have survived are a letter commending a Cambridge student in 1874 as a suitable person to be admitted as a reader in the British Library and a Thank You letter for the gift of some game sent to him at the Temple in 1892 by one Ashley Dodd to whom Vaughan wrote, 'I like to feel that I still live in your remembrance as you in mine.' [76] There must have been thousands of letters like these two but also many more of the private and personal kind he wrote to Halsey and earlier favourites which Catherine would not have felt were suitable for inclusion.

Six months later Catherine was dead. She died at her home in Weybridge aged 77 on 2 August 1899. Four days earlier she had dictated her 'Last farewell Wishes' to Miranda Hall directing that certain items of personal jewellery, books and furniture be given to Stanley relatives and friends. [77] Edward Vaughan Thompson who had been the executor of her husband's estate also acted for her. She had written a will in April 1894 , very soon after it appeared that her husband was terminally ill, and she had added codicils in November 1895 and May 1897. Her estate was valued at £25,375 15s. 2d. [= £2,761,370]. The chief beneficiary was Mary Drummond who had helped to care for her brother Arthur after his wife's death; followed by her sister-in-law, Eliza Stanley, and various offspring of her cousins. William Grey, Earl of Stamford, received her plate, pictures and personal effects.

She was buried in Weybridge on the 4th and not with her late husband in Llandaff. That was not unusual as her own parents lay in separate graves in Norwich and Alderley. The Dean of Westminster, Dr Bradley, assisted by three other clergy, officiated at her funeral which took place just two days after her death. The *Morning* Post reported next day that the mourners had included Dr Butler, Master of Trinity College Cambridge, Sir Luther Vaughan, Mr Vaughan Thompson, Miss Bicker-steth, Dr Vachell of Cardiff, Dr Weatherhead of London and the Rev Ernest Owen from Llandaff. Her friend of 46 years standing, Sir Charles Dalrymple, was not at the funeral but he commented in his diary on the 4th: 'I think much of the departed friend of many years, Mrs Vaughan. I first saw her January 12 1853, & ever since, I may safely say, she has been to me a most inter-esting personality.' [78]

The *Surrey Advertiser* printed a brief obituary:

The deceased had resided at Weybridge since the death of her husband,

and, although her advanced age – 78 – and infirmities lately prevented her exerting herself very much, yet she delighted in good works of every description. It was her especial study to give pleasure to hundreds of poor folk from London, and even on what proved her death-bed she insisted on a large party of women being entertained in her grounds, and actually provided a band of music for the occasion. She has been devotedly attended by Dr Sealy, her local medical man, and other doctors, but her life gradually ebbed away, and she died at 11 o'clock on Wednesday morning. She will be greatly missed particularly at Cardiff and Llandaff, in which localities the course of her illness was watched with much sympathetic interest. The funeral took place at Weybridge Cemetery yesterday. [79]

She was the last of Bishop Stanley's children to die - none of whom had had any children.

In time a life size recumbent effigy of Vaughan, sculpted in white marble, would be placed in the Oudoceus Chapel in the Cathedral with the simple inscription:

CHARLES JOHN VAUGHAN D.D.
DEAN OF LLANDAFF 1879-1897
Honoured in his generation as
Scholar, Master,
Preacher, Counsellor.
A man greatly beloved.
"Ambitious to be quiet." – 1 Thess., iv. 11
Born August 6 1816 Died October 15 1897

Above the tomb are the heraldic arms of the Vaughans and the Stanleys. The whole work was carried out by Sir William Goscombe John RA which was particularly fitting as he was one of Cardiff's most distinguished citizens, having grown up in Canton and had been a boy-chorister at the Cathedral. The inscription was composed by Dr Montagu Butler. The sculpture had been exhibited earlier at the Royal Academy where it had attracted much favourable attention.

"He served his Generation well"

A Sermon preached by the Master of Trinity College Cambridge, the Rev. Dr Montagu Butler, in Llandaff Cathedral on the Sunday after the Funeral of the Very Rev. C. J. Vaughan

"After he had served his own generation by the counsel of God, he fell on sleep." Acts xiii. 36

"St Paul" here "writes a lovely epitaph upon the chivalrous King and sweet Psalmist of Israel. 'He served his own generation, and then fell on sleep.' There may be longer, more detailed, more laudatory epitaphs – the fashion of the last century covered the walls of our churches with elaborate and fulsome panegyrics, amongst which this short sentence of St Paul's might have seemed scanty and grudging in its meed of praise – but the truer taste and more reverent feeling of our own age will appreciate the more expressive and in reality more majestic brevity – 'He served his generation, and fell on sleep.'"

Christian friends, these words are not mine. Even as I read them to you, some of you may have recognized

> the touch of a vanished hand,
> And the sound of a voice that is still.

They were spoken at Cambridge (See *University* Sermons, 1888, Sermon xxix) more than twelve years ago in the University Church by him whose living voice has so often pleaded in these sacred walls of yours for "whatsoever things are pure and lovely and of good report." He gave to that Sermon the title, "Life the Service of a Generation." I put it to those who knew him, revered him, loved him – and they were many – does not that title, which describes every noble life, most truly describe his own?

"The text," he says, in his own pithy incisive manner, which never failed him from early youth till his eightieth year, "the text presents us with two pairs of equivalents. Life is Service. Death is Sleep." Again I put it to you, does not this "pair of equivalents" at this very moment place him again before us, almost speaking? It links his work with his grave. "Life is service." "He served his generation." He served it long. He served it faithfully. He served it very lovingly. He served it, we must believe, "by the counsel of God"; and then, at last, in the fullness of years, more tardily than his wearied spirit could have desired, but still calmly and peacefully, "he fell on sleep." "Death is Sleep."

What can be said of such a life? What can be said here, today – here, where he gave and received so much love; today, when the scene of Wednesday last is still so close to our eyes and ears and hearts? What indeed do we wish for in what is called a "Funeral Sermon" in the House of God? Not surely much of narrative. That we may leave to the journalist and biographer. Not much of criticism or analysis, the precise delineation of mental gifts, or the suggestion of mental limits.

Nor, again, an attempt – probably presumptuous, certainly premature – to fix his exact place among the preachers, the teachers, the religious writers of the last half century.

Rather let us be content with very simple words, words of love and reverence and thankfulness, thankfulness to God Who has granted us so rich a blessing, and granted it so long. Never was the voice of a Church ritual more truly the voice of Christian hearts than when we listened to those words of piety, first spoken by the Priest and then chanted by the Choristers whom the Dean had loved so truly: "The Lord gave, and the Lord hath taken away: blessed be the Name of the Lord."

When men are "so strong that they come to fourscore years," we almost forget that they were once sons. Yet I cannot help reminding you, in almost my first words on this revered Master – *he* certainly would not have blamed me for saying it – that he owed much to his father. Just ninety-nine years have passed this very month since his father was elected a Fellow of our Trinity College. I had always hoped to wish his son joy on the completion of the full century, knowing something of the effect which this early victory of his father had exercised on himself. In truth, it bequeathed to him that ardent love of both his College and his University which was one of the few "passions" of his life,

It was in 1802, whilst still one of our Fellows, that "Vaughan of Leicester" as he came to be known far and wide in Evangelical circles, began that memorable ministry at St Martin's which was afterwards carried on by three of his sons, and only ended in 1893. In that Parish the name of Vaughan is still, and must long continue to be, not a "household word" only, but a name of blessing, a name held in memorial before God. It was of this dear and honoured father that his son was thinking when, just forty-six years ago, preaching in St Paul's Cathedral at the Festival of the Sons of the Clergy (See *Personality of the Tempter, and other Sermons*, 1851. Sermon viii) – how well I remember the crowded scene! – he pronounced, if I may borrow his own phrase, this "lovely epitaph":

"Suffer, my brethren, one who has himself known from his childhood the secrets of a ministerial home, to revive for a moment the indelible impression of that devoted life: the morning hours spent in the self-denying labours of parental education; noon and afternoon in the various toils of parochial visitation; evening, till a late midnight, in the painful researches and deep meditations of a theology fruitful in power and in love and in a sound mind; interruptions, wearisome and exhausting, perpetually delaying business and destroying repose; yet, amidst all, the intellect ever occupied with truth, the heart ever communing with the unseen; life at length sacrificed, in the full vigour of manhood, to exertions unresting yet untiring – indeed, indeed, a labourer like this – there were such then, there are such now – a labourer like this is worthy of his hire!"

The quotation is long, but you will more than forgive it. You will see in it, I think, the basis, in part perhaps the cause, of his life-long reverence for the calling of the faithful Parish Priest.

He lost his father early, but the image of that devoted Gospel life, that true "bishopric of souls," was never blurred or faint. It was before him, I am convinced, when, in 1867, he wrote so like himself from Doncaster: "The backbone of the Church of England is its Presbytery; and the work of the Presbytery lies in its Parishes." And again, when, as late as 1893, he said to his beloved clerical pupils, at a memorable gathering in our College Chapel, the Chapel in which he and his father and his younger brother had all been admitted as Fellows, "One thing let us remember – that the true battle of the Church will be fought out in our Parishes. One devoted Parish Priest, whose people are ready to rise up and call him blessed, will be worth more to the National Church, in its day of rebuke and blasphemy, than a whole library of polemical literature or a locust-swarm of smart and telling leaflets. What we have to prove is not that the Church has an indefeasible right to its property, but that the Church of this moment is worth its salt. Not that the Church of England is ancient – older than her municipalities, older than her Parliaments – not that she is ancient, but that she is modern, alive to the sorrows, awake to the wants, of the English people, wise to know the times and alert to minister to them – this is the thing to be proved, and each one of us, my beloved brethren, has it laid upon him, in his place and in his day, either to prove or to disprove it."

In those fine sentences, my friends, I seem to recognise not only the ring of a Churchman's chivalrous devotion, but the memory of a beloved home and the presence, almost the very presence, of an unforgotten father.

The years which he spent as himself a Parish Priest, first, as a very young man, at Leicester, and then, some sixteen years afterwards, at Doncaster, showed what he might have done in great centres like Sheffield, or Nottingham, or Bristol, or Birmingham. Still it is not as a Parish Priest that he will be chiefly remembered. Rather it will be as the restorer, almost the re-Founder, of one of the greatest of our Public Schools; as the much loved Master of the Temple; as the Dean of your restored Cathedral; as the trainer of several hundreds of young men for the work of the Ministry; and, in all these capacities, during the long round of full fifty years, the searching and stirring and persuasive Preacher.

At Harrow – how can I recall those days which are so dear and so bright to some of us? – we all knew that we had at our head a strong ruler, who could not be trifled with. His softness of voice and manner, at first almost startling, never left any illusion, with boys or Masters, as to either his penetrating insight or his resolute will. But he was very gentle with us, more and more so as his time of office drew to its close.

And first – I speak from clear recollection – his bright wit and sense of the ludicrous were not always untinged with sarcasm. But he soon detected and conquered this temptation. No self-conquest was ever more rapid or more complete. Some, I imagine, who have watched him for as much as fifty years will scarcely believe that such a victory was ever needed. But the battle was fought. I saw it.

As to his teaching, his brilliant scholarship and rare clearness of expression gave to almost every lesson something of the finish of a work of art. I have known many of the finest classical scholars of our day, many with whom in respect of mere learning he would never have thought of comparing himself; but for the sheer scholar's instinct, the thinking and feeling in the great tongues of Greece and Rome, more especially the Greek, the exact perception of the force of words, whether separately or in the junction and their cadences, there are few indeed that could be placed by his side. Never were these gifts of teaching more conspicuous, or, I think, exercised with more satisfaction to himself, than when he took us in the Greek Testament, notably in the Epistles to the Romans and the Hebrews. He did not deal much with the larger questions which cluster, as it were, round these great writings – questions of theology, of philosophy, of history, or of ritual – but he had in the highest degree the gift of linking chapter with chapter and verse

370

with verse, tracking the argument through its windings and seeming disappearances, laying his finger on the sequence of each sentence and paragraph, and the exact mission of each word in its own order.

But no doubt his chief chair of teaching, then as afterwards, was the Pulpit. There, for fifteen years, he spoke to us almost every Sunday evening. He was the same man as on other days and in other places, kind, sympathetic, grave, masterful, but here all that was deepest and tenderest in him was, as it were, focussed. He spoke as a man with a message to deliver, a message partly his own, still more that of a Greater. With a quick eye for what was passing in the little world around him, he strove to bring God and Christ, God in Christ, into the simple yet complicated lives of schoolboys. He spoke very seriously, and pitched his standard high, but we did not think he exaggerated; all seemed so real. He seemed to know us, in our lighter as well as our graver moods. When his appeals were most directly spiritual, this secular knowledge of us was always there in the background. Among the many volumes that he has left, the "Memorials of Harrow Sundays" must always, I think, have a place of its own. It stands out as landmark of what Christian teaching could be at school in the central years of the 19th century.

Of his subsequent life at the Temple, so large a portion of his career, I have no call to speak. I saw him there but seldom, but it was impossible to attend even occasionally those beautiful Services, or to read his sermons when published, without seeing how intimately and from the first he had made himself at home with that exceptional audience. Much was due to the rare beauty of his language, for few in our day have written English so terse, so arresting, and so musical; but I would rather speak of his direct grappling with consciences. He was not afraid or shy of those able, critical, highly-cultivated men who were now his appointed "flock". He took them as men, as friends, as brothers, as Christians by profession – tempted, like others, to be worldly and frivolous; needing, like others, the "word in due season," the word of warning and sympathy in "things pertaining to God."

To such men he could speak of the innermost things of the soul in language always riveting, because always fresh, fresh from the mintage of the heart and the life. He was specially happy, I have always thought, when dealing with those commonplaces of life which in less gifted hands are so dull and insipid – such subjects, I mean, as youth and age, restlessness, impulsiveness, purity, peace, "ever learning, never attaining," and the like. Such topics he would bring into what he called "that privacy of publicity, which is the beauty and the safety of

371

congregational worship," (See *Last Words in the Temple* Church, Sermon xii p. 162, and elsewhere) and there, with a delicate touch granted to few, convert the Pulpit, almost imperceptibly, and without losing any of its authority, into the quiet chair of a private interview. He seemed to see before him not the "all men" only, but the "each man"; the individual in the congregation; the friend, known or unknown, in the silent and listening crowd. Does the spell that he threw over his old pupils mislead me, or is it the simple truth, that no man of our Church in this generation has spoken so much from the Pulpit that slipped, as they say, so "inevitably" into the crevices and lurking-places of conscience? There have been a few greater orators. There have been a few who handled with a familiarity which he never claimed problems of the intellect and problems of Church order, but I venture to think there was no man, certainly no man who spoke so often and so continuously, of whom St Paul's words were so habitually true: "thus are the secrets of the man's heart made manifest; and so falling down on his face he will worship God, and report that God is in you of a truth."

Is it not thus, my brethren, that you have felt when he spoke to you here in these latter years as your Dean? Have you not started and almost quivered at the biting force of his penetrating words, the *clairvoyance* with which he read to you some secret of your heart, some dark passage of your daily life, and showed you some unexpected opening for improvement, reform, repentance? Have you not been surprised to see how much he seemed to know of you – your past, your present, almost your future? And as he spoke, did not veneration and love of the man pass on into that incomparably higher thing, the only thing for which he really cared or laboured, the felt presence, the audible appeal, the renewed trust and charge of the Lord Jesus, saying in one or more of His thousand tones of love and generosity and forgiveness – "Follow me. Feed my lambs. Tend my sheep. Become not faithless, but believing"?

It was yours, dear friends – for when I speak to you of him, we seem all to be friends together – it was yours to have at your service all the beauty and mellowness of his later years, with the least possible admixture of his decline. So far as I can judge, many of those sermons which he gave you even up to a year ago, certainly up to three and a half ago, were not inferior in power or in insight, still less in tenderness, to those of what we might call his prime. You felt, you must have felt, their grip, their grace, sometimes their happy ingenuity, when, for instance, he would take a phrase, a title, or even a single word, and somehow put into it a Gospel, nay, *the* Gospel in its fullness; "The Iron Way"; "The Unrecognised Presence"; "The dark River"; "I praised the Dead" "A Sleepless Night"; "The Two Returns"; "Distraction and Dissipation"; "The Man who has trifled once too often"; "A narrow place and no turning"; "Life's a Dialogue"; "The Treasure twice-hidden"; "When I awake"; "Nevertheless." I take the well-known titles almost by chance, and again I put it to you, did you not feel that, as he dealt with such topics, he turned them in some strange way into instruments, I might almost say magnets, of the Cross? No doubt you had before you the trained master of style, the delicate manipulator of words, the subtle dialectician, the veteran explorer of the recesses of Scripture; but there was behind all and above all the preparer of his Master's Way, the loving disciple and herald and witness of the Crucified, taking his place, very humbly but authoritatively, beneath the Cross, and pleading rather than proclaiming, "Behold the Man."

What, then, was it, do any of us ask today – will men and women ask in days to come – which made his personality so singularly attractive, and gave him an influence, as he "served his generation," so widespread, so subtle, so uninterrupted? Not profound learning; not the gift of interpreting other men, or of mirroring in himself the speculations or the deeper questionings of his day. Few first-rate preachers have ever quoted so little, save from the Scriptures. There is hardly a great writer of our day whose influence accounts in a perceptible degree for what he was and what he did. The poets, the historians, the philosophers, the writers on art, the discoverers in science, even the theologians and great preachers, had strangely little effect in shaping his opinions, his feelings, his style, his interpretations of Scripture. In all that he did, or abstained from doing, there was the stamp of "distinctiveness." It was a word that he liked. He loved to draw the line between "distinctiveness" and "distinction." The last he had schooled himself to despise; the first, "distinctiveness," he prized.

He was seldom more himself in his sermons than when speaking of Ambition. Nature had meant him for an ambitious man. While a brilliant student and speaker at Cambridge he looked forward confidently, I at least cannot doubt it, to the very highest honours of the Law. But along with this current of a natural ambition there was another, a supernatural, current of quite exceptional devoutness, a dread of himself, a profound prostration before God in Christ, an overwhelming sense of the danger of personal sin, and of being led by the tempter to a pinnacle and a pitfall. It is, I believe, in the recognition of these two sweeping currents of temperament, and of the pathetic struggle carried on between them, that we shall best see the beauty of his life, the secret of his influence, the key, it may be, to some unexplained decisions at some critical moments.

This it was which gave such weight and momentum to all he ever said on Ambition, and it was one of his favourite topics. Some here, perhaps – some at least of his many pupils – will remember how he loved to dwell on St Paul's threefold use of that great word – to the Thessalonians, "ambitious to be quiet"; to the Corinthians, "ambitious to be well-pleasing to Christ"; to the Romans "ambitious of distinctiveness," of a separate work and a definite mission.

"I am ambitious," writes the great Apostle, "to preach the Gospel, not where Christ was named, lest I should build upon another man's foundation." ... "He was ambitious," thus comments the Preacher, unconsciously portraying himself, "he was ambitious to have a work peculiar to himself, and a province that should be all his own." ... "There is a divine warrant in Scripture for an ambition of distinctiveness. St Paul's ambition was to preach Christ where He was not yet named. The corresponding ambition in a Christian heart now would be to find some neglected spot, and to give a life to its evangelisation."

So he spoke to our young men at Cambridge many years ago. (See *University Sermons*. Sermon vi, "Oblivions and Ambitions of the Life of Grace.") No one, I venture to think, will get to the heart and core of his singular career who fails to understand that in the earliest part of his prosperous life, even at the close of his brilliant Harrow days, he trod down, by the grace of his Master, many vehement and vaulting ambitions, retaining only thee, the three which he found in his beloved St Paul – the three, perhaps the only three, which are not unworthy of a Minister of the Crucified – the ambition of a quiet life and a quiet spirit; the ambition of a distinctive and separate field of labour; lastly, for I instinctively change the order, and keep the best and purest and richest to the last, the ambition of being well-pleasing to his Master and ours, "in that day."

Ah, my friends, who can doubt that this last, this most sacred, this only sacred, ambition, has even now been fully satisfied?

We must hasten to the close. Time, not matter, fails me. How miserably inadequate are words to bring back the living presence, the winning smile of sympathy, the playful dignity, the irresistible charm! I say to myself, If I had only had before me poor words of this kind, what should I have known of him? How should I have felt towards him as one

374

after another – boys and men and women – did feel towards him? How should I have felt as a Harrow scholar, as a Leicester or Doncaster parishioner, as a member of the illustrious Temple, as a citizen of Llandaff or of Cardiff?

But still more, my friends – it is a relief to me to confess it – still more do I feel the utter failure of these poor words to bring back to his "men," as he called them, to the pupils whom he trained to be Ministers of the Gospel, the infinitely dear Friend, Guide, Teacher – I might well add, to the younger at least, Father – who has wrought so powerfully, so uniquely, on their imagination and their affection.

It was this part of his life's work, if I mistake not, that he specially prized, by this that he would specially wish to be remembered. It was here that he found – and he must have been conscious of it – the peculiarity, the "distinctiveness," the special call, the special response, which appealed at once to his conscience, his intellect, his heart. Other men had been successful as Christian Schoolmasters, Christian Parish Priests, Christian Masters and Preachers and Chaplains of the Inns of Courts, Christian Deans of Cathedral Churches. But in giving some thirty-five years without a break to the training of young men for the Ministry of the Gospel, in becoming their life-long counsellor, in keeping close and reconsecrating at not too long intervals the singular tie which bound him to them – in this he was doing a new thing. Here he struck out – may I dare so to apply the sacred words? – "a new and living way" of pastoral service. Here he was "ambitious of distinctiveness," and gained his ambition. In these young men the childless man found his children, the old man found his sons. They were the renewal and more than the renewal of his Harrow youth, the wings, as it were, of his active intellect, the support and comfort and romance of his age. The short Addresses which he delivered to these much loved friends at his various triennial gatherings are among the very best of all his utterances. There is in them the pith, the salt, the subtle humour that made the charm of his style, but all fused and mellowed by the deepest human affection, such as Paul might have felt for Timothy, together with profound thanks to God for having provided him with this untrodden and now well-furrowed field of gratuitous and delightful labour.

These his disciples know – as indeed we all know, but they know it specially – how wise he was, how sane in his judgements, how abhorrent of party spirit, how "kindly affectioned" to all, howsoever divided – whether seemingly or really divided – "who love our Lord Jesus Christ in sincerity"; how jealous of the simplicity of the Gospel, how suspicious of all shibboleths, how deeply humble, how hard upon himself, how charitable to others, how passionately and pathetically convinced that, however much the great and glorious mystery may defy the shackles of logic and of words, it was in the Atoning Blood of our Lord Jesus Christ, Very God and Very Man, that the Christian Faith first received, and must for all time retain, its originality, its power, its essence, its very warrant and credentials. Shortly before his death, a dear friend spoke to him of the "blood of sprinkling." "Yes," he said, "but I need more than that – not aspersion only but immersion," the old instinct of the scholar and the teacher mingling with the present need of the penitent and the saint.

You may have heard possibly that he left some words behind him expressive of his life-long and final faith. It is hard for me to read them in public, but neither does it seem right to withhold them. I will try to read them, and will then add nothing more. We will take our farewell of him in his own words. None can be so simple, so beautiful, so true, so Christian.

"In the prospect of death" so he writes in his will – "in the prospect of death, a little nearer or further off, I wish to state explicitly that I have put my whole trust in the revelation of the Gospel as made in the Gospel of St John and in the Epistles of St John and St Paul. I believe in the forgiveness of sins as the foundation-stone of the Gospel, and commit myself humbly and hopefully to God in this faith for life, death, and eternity."

An Assessment

Obituaries are inevitably a somewhat subjective assessment of a person's life, achievements and personality but they do have the merit of usually being written by someone who knew the deceased well. Huyshe Wolcott Yeatman-Biggs, the Bishop of Southwark and one of Vaughan's 'doves' from Doncaster days, wrote the one in the *Church Times*. He began by noting that 'the testimony of utterance in press, pulpit, and speech in the last week is clear, as showing that few men in Holy Orders have impressed themselves more sincerely upon the religious thought of men; he has done it quietly, without seeming to wish for it, the influence has come with unusual restraint, but it has touched men of thought and emotion, in the Church and outside, in England, in the Colonies, and in America.' [1] The Bishop then focussed on just one great work: 'his undoubted influence over men preparing for the diaconate and priesthood'. Later in the obituary he gave his own personal assessment of his former mentor:

> "What have I done to Thee?" was the title of the Dean's last address to his men. The answer might be, "You have taught us sincerity; you have bid us look deeper and higher than party; you have shewn us what the demand is, which is made upon men, responsible to God and the nation for England's religious life; you have shewn us by example that it is not everything to arrive at place or power, you have interpreted 'dignity' as applied to the ordinary clerical life, you have done all this, and you have founded it upon the closest examination of Holy Writ. By the Gospels, by the Epistles, read and re-read with the aid of every scholarly light, the standard has been tested. Some men might have given a more determined lead in theology, others might have dwelt on what was to be learned from ecclesiastical history, but what you have done to us is that you have asked us to live in the company of Jesus Christ." [2]

The *Times* published a long, detailed and appreciative account of his life and ministry on Saturday 16 October along with the announcement of his death. Two days later it carried a second and somewhat shorter but much more personal obituary. The writer singled out his ability as a preacher and the priority of this role in his life's work:

> At the Temple Church his preaching attracted a congregation that any preacher might have been proud to address, and though there was nothing showy in his style or delivery, his sermons were models of clear thought,

lucid exposition, and graceful, scholarlike expression, informed throughout by earnest piety. To use his own phrase, quoted in our obituary notice on Saturday, he always "assumed the Gospel." Few divines of equal gifts and reputation have thought less of self-advancement. *Nolo episcopari* was in his mouth no empty phrase . . .

DEAN VAUGHAN was not one of those who "to party give up what was meant for mankind." He placed all the weight of brilliant talents, high character and devoted piety at the service of Church and of religion, rather than at any one party in the Church . . . no-one ever labelled him a "High", or "Low" or "Broad" Churchman. No party looked to him as its protagonist . . . The partisanship of a PUSEY or a STANLEY was equally foreign to his nature. No bigot himself, he neither suspected nor, as a rule, noticed bigotry in others. He was before and above all things a Preacher of the Gospel . . . His business was to preach the Gospel; to promote theological learning and devotional life; and to set to his fellow Churchmen, and especially to those younger clergy who looked back with gratitude to him for much that was best in their life and work, an example of sober Churchmanship and of a Christian life.[3]

The *Guardian* likewise noted that 'he seldom appeared on a public platform, and he had no concern with the strifes and vicissitudes of parties. He was a minister of the Gospel, and not an ecclesiastic.' The *Pall Mall Gazette* headed its obituary: 'A LOSS TO THE RELIGIOUS WORLD' and also chose to comment on his irenic character and orthodox views:

Churchmen who denounced Stanley for his "rationalism" and his defence of the notorious "Essays and Reviews" and of Bishop Colenso had no distrust of Vaughan, whose views were moderate and more cautiously expressed, and who had a more decidedly Evangelical creed, with more purely spiritual fervour. Stanley was not a preacher, Vaughan was. Distinguished as was his career at Harrow, his friends frequently used to say that he was born for a pulpit, and he will certainly be remembered as one of the great preachers of our age. [4]

It singled out two volumes of his published addresses for special praise:

Out of these meetings [i.e. of his 'doves'] grew two beautiful and invaluable volumes, consisting of Dr Vaughan's addresses and readings in the Greek Testament, "Addresses to Clergymen" (1875) and "Rest Awhile" (1880). They are among the finest discourses *ad clerum* in our language, and a mine of pastoral theology. These volumes are fully as popular in Nonconformist circles as among clergy of the National Church.[5]

The one line in that particular writer's article which would have given Vaughan most personal satisfaction relates to his time at Harrow where, he wrote, he 'achieved a success which proved him worthy to rank with Arnold.'[6]

The *Illustrated London News* regarded his death as a loss to all Christian people and not just to the Church of England: 'The religious life of the nation is so scarred and seamed by so many antagonisms and divisions that the removal of one who in so distinct a manner belonged rather to Christendom than merely to the Church of England is a loss not easily to be gauged.'[7] The writer sought to pinpoint the source of his wide influence:

> That he might over and over again, have been a Bishop is well known; that he refused an Archbishopric has been widely believed.
>
> Since, then, Dr Vaughan never attained to the highest honours in the Church, to what was his influence due? It may be ascribed very largely to the wonderful simplicity of his character. He was no controversialist; he never wrote or said a word that could encourage the strife of parties. He was no ecclesiastic; and the seminary spirit never touched him. He was a Churchman and valued its position; but did not attack others, or think little of their services. His attitude towards the Bible seemed always to be that of the simplest reader. He raised no questions, and encouraged no doubts. He was content to press upon his hearers, in pure and lucid English, the simplest lessons of faith and duty. Without eloquence, and certainly without sensationalism, he held a congregation largely composed of men of more than common intellectual acuteness. His sermons, when read, appear simplicity itself; and yet these are the most widely known of modern English homiletics . . . but it is for the sake of his patient unworldliness, his gracious disposition, and his simple fidelity to his faith that he will longest be held in memory. [8]

The *South Wales University College Magazine* in its obituary recorded the College's great debt to him and described the ideal he had set before staff and students.

> A brilliant scholar, a great teacher, a wise ruler, a devoted minister, a preacher whose words went home to the hearts of thousands, Dr Vaughan brought to his work for the College all that such a society stands most in need of at every stage of its life, and never more than in the days when each step creates a precedent, and gives a bias, for the future.
>
> As a scholar, he was resolved that no side issue should prevent the College from securing the best possible teachers for its students. As teacher and

divine, he was determined that, so far as he could help it, the College should never sink in to a lifeless machine, but always remain the training-ground of individual energies, bound together by the sense of a common calling and the pursuit of a common end – "plain living and high thinking." Long may the College continue to follow the ideal which its late President held before it! No perfection of machinery, no increase of members, could be worth a tittle in comparison. [9]

The Cardiff papers naturally focussed on his ministry in Wales and the substantial support he had given to the university college in that town. *The Weekly Mail* gave its assessment of him in four terse sub-headings under the headline 'DEATH OF DEAN VAUGHAN':

SCHOLAR, THEOLOGIAN, AND COURTLY ECCLESIASTIC.
"PRINCE OF TEACHERS" AND THE CHRYSOSTOM OF THE PULPIT.
A WELSHMAN OF STERLING PATRIOTISM.
A BROADMINDED LEADER OF THOUGHT.

Among the several contributors to a full page devoted to the Dean's life and ministry was a local Nonconformist minister who singled out for praise the Dean's understanding of the aspirations of the Welsh people and his sympathy for them. Many years earlier a writer had noted the warm approval that Vaughan's published sermons enjoyed in Non-conformist circles:

One of the very highest of their periodicals, in an estimate of his life and works, says: - "There are no books we could place more willingly in the hands of thoughtful and cultured young men. He is in full sympathy with their difficulties and aspirations and struggles. He sees so clearly their real needs; he knows so well how to appeal to their higher nature; he is so bent on aiding them towards their true ideal. In fact there is no aspect of life which he has overlooked. The young and the old, the rich and the poor, the ignorant and the learned, the doubter and the believer, the prosperous and the tried, all receive from him a word in season, and his volumes cover well nigh the whole sphere of Christian doctrine and ethics." [10]

The Westminster Budget too wrote approvingly on 22 October of his generous ecumenical spirit and actions:

There was nothing of the narrow Church partisan in the late Dean. At the Church Congress in 1889 at Cardiff, he generously praised the good works of the Welsh Nonconformists – a bold thing to do at a Church meeting in

Wales! He was equally tolerant of and friendly towards the Roman Catholics. In February 1893, he permitted the local Catholics to conduct a pilgrimage, accompanied by suitable religious ceremony, in the Cathedral on a Saint's festival, and to offer up the prayers of that Church within the precincts of the Cathedral itself.

Vaughan would not have liked the *Daily Graphic*'s obituary which referred to his 'Men' as 'Vaughan's Lambs' and added insult to injury by stating: 'To be one of "Vaughan's Lambs" has been deemed a safe passport to advancement in the Church.' It came much nearer the truth, however, by its opinion: 'The influence exerted by him from the Pulpit of the Temple was great, and was all the more valuable because it extended over a time during which a good deal of unsettlement as to faith prevailed amongst thoughtful minds.'

One small detail in the accounts of his last illness was that his butler, Mr Hammond, was one of those who read to him each day. A small detail that points to another side to this man. The Cardiff paper recorded how caring and generous Vaughan had always been to his servants – a characteristic that Chancellor Austen noted too:

The domestic servants were regularly sent out for a drive in the modest Deanery carriage every afternoon, and the master was equally careful of the men servants. It is said that the dean took so deep an interest in a former valet of his that he educated him for the Church . . . And not only servants but others were also objects of the dean's or Mrs Vaughan's special care. Even cottages would be taken and the rent paid direct to the landlord from the Deanery. In whatever light we view Dean Vaughan it reveals him as "one among ten thousand and altogether lovely." I believe that his memory will do more to assuage any ill-feeling which may still be entertained towards the Church of which he was such a saintly representative than many will be able to imagine. His solicitude and toleration, his scholastic greatness, his peaceable disposition, and, above all, his charitableness, embodied as it all was in that sublime personality, made him what seemed a beautiful reflection of the Divine Master he served so well.[11]

It is hardly surprising, then, to learn that he left generous monetary bequests to his servants. He had occasionally preached on the relationship between a master and his servants and he clearly regarded them as equals in soul and body and in some cases in intelligence too – a servant might well be superior in 'tenderness of feeling and in the love of God and man.' He stated that no one should require of a domestic servant any more than he could allow a daughter of his own 'to bear or to do at her age and in her condition.' Anecdotes which illustrate how this charitable and kindly trait in his character revealed itself in so many small ways to people in all walks of life, young and old, are remembered in all the places where he lived and worked – impecunious pupils and students quietly given a helping hand, young girls helped to get a proper training for domestic service, his discerning and enabling young people of ability but without the means to get a higher education, always showing respect to people whom most would have regarded as his social inferiors. His frequently expressed wish to see thousands more young people from the emerging middle classes enjoy the benefit of a university education is another expression of it. As was the welcome he gave, in possibly his last written communication to a Cardiff newspaper, to the breaking down of social divisions which he had witnessed during his lifetime. Even allowing for an element of generous exaggeration on the part of the writer of the above extract, the heart of the account rings true – here was a man who had tried in the small things of life as well as in greater and more public ways to follow Christ's example and command: "love one another as I have loved you." Lionel Tollemache, writing a decade after Vaughan's death, noted this trait in his character:

> The praise of Vaughan is in all the churches, but Harrovians in particular will associate his memory in countless ways with
> '. . . that best portion of a good man's life,
> his little nameless unremembered acts
> of kindness and love,'
> including especially bountiful help to needy scholars. [12]

Archbishop Benson said to Charles Dalrymple of him: "No living man has laid the Church of England under greater obligations." [13] As noted earlier the Archbishop had personal reasons to be grateful to Vaughan and had seen him and his ministry at close quarters, so his judgement is not likely to have been exaggerated. He wrote in his diary on 11 March 1894 at the time of the Dean's illness and expected death:

> The Dean's has been the most serviceable life in the Church in my time. His great sense, true Christianity, and wonderful power of expressing both, in the purest and most idiomatic modern English, have held a constant congregation of the ablest men and lawyers at the Temple, and he has trained 350 of the best young clergy, in scholarship, in love of Scripture, in

wisdom and moderation of view, at a time when all those qualities are least valued and most valuable.[14]

Dr Benjamin Jowett, a former Master of Balliol and close friend of Arthur Stanley, said of him "He was the wisest man I ever knew." [15] Of course, not all agreed with either Benson's or Jowett's assessment of him. Cosmo Gordon Lang, who later became Archbishop of Canterbury, occasionally attended the Temple Church in the 1880s, primarily to enjoy the liturgy and the music, was no fan of Vaughan's preaching! He considered his sermons to be 'very much out of touch with modern life and thought.' [16] G.W.E. Russell described him dismissively as 'that least exciting of teachers' [17] That was not the view of Bishop Westcott who told R.L. White when he went to him in 1895 for ordination in the Diocese of Durham, "No Sunday is to me complete without reading a sermon of Dr Vaughan's." He said further "He is the only father I have left living." [18] Montagu Butler was even more appreciative as he read 'some parts at least' of his sermons *every day* – they were a constant component in his daily devotions. He wrote of his old master in 1893:

> Every sentence of Vaughan's shows the great preacher – each thought, whether deep or not, so fresh, so attractive, so engrossing, so self-revealing, that you cannot get away from it. No doubt there is also a supreme felicity of phrase and cadence which might even interfere with the meaning, but it is the *meaning* to which I refer. Every sentence tells, draws, wins. You cannot help it. Hardly anyone writes such English as he does, and hardly anyone so unlocks the secret drawers of consciences. [19]

Canon Ainger who had known him so well both as a colleague at the Temple Church and as a friend preached at the Memorial Service held there on 7 November which was attended by a great crowd of those to whom Vaughan had once ministered. He chose as his text *Philemon* verse 7 using the revised version that Vaughan had worked on: 'For I had much joy and comfort in thy love, because the hearts of the saints have been refreshed through thee, brother.' He had chosen it, he said, because 'it reflected much of the special quality and therefore of the special strength of the beloved teacher whose departure from us we commemorate today.' He went on,

> It might seem the natural course for me to confine myself, speaking from this pulpit, to one aspect or function of the late Master – that of teacher, for it was in that character that he was all but exclusively known to the

thousands who worshipped from time to time in this church. But we cannot thus isolate any one side or faculty of a religious genius. It was the Pauline combination of religious conviction with personal affectionateness, of a deep knowledge of the human heart, its guiles and sophistries and self-deceptions, with the spirit of tenderness that "looking upon" every such heart "loved it" – this combination, I believe, that constituted the main power and attraction of the teacher we have lost. And Dr Vaughan, besides being a preacher, was eminently a letter-writer. Much, I believe, of his most valued, most effective influence was exerted in thus comforting, strengthening, building up the faith of those who came to him for succour: or else, in counselling and guiding them in points of spiritual and moral casuistry. Such letters have done a blessed work.

Dr Vaughan was not universally popular as a preacher, nor was he always a prophet in his own country. Let us proclaim it as his truest glory that he never descended to use the arts which allure. Again, he was not a party man. Only a Christian, only an attached, if old-fashioned Churchman, only probing men's and women's consciences and pointing them to Christ as the one only interpreter of life and death, the one only deliverance from sin and death – this seemed to many but a poor equipment unless recommended by the shibboleths of one school or the rituals of another. But our departed teacher strove to resemble his Master in this, that "the common people heard him gladly" – the common people, meaning by that, not necessarily the poor, the uneducated, or the commonplace, but those who felt the common feelings and the common needs, shared the common temptations and the common frailties of poor human nature. To these he spoke by these he was heard. On this, the first Sunday of Michaelmas Term, 28 years ago, Dr Vaughan preached his first sermon in this church. In that sermon, as we have lately been reminded, he announced that he presented himself before his hearers as one who "assumed the Gospel." He meant by this that he intended to address himself always to those who accepted in its essentials the message of Jesus Christ to the souls of man, and who needed to be edified – that is, "built up" – in their faith – helped, comforted, instructed and encouraged. He did not intend, he said, he did not profess, to deal with the ordinary alleged difficulties of the sceptic. And in making this announcement there is no doubt that he disappointed a certain class. Dr Vaughan knew his own individuality and his own distinction, and the Church of the saints has been the richer and the better for the knowledge.

It may have been the same fine instinct of where the true field and scope of his powers lay that led him to devote much of his life after leaving Harrow to the task of training young men for Holy Orders instead of accepting any of those highest positions in the Church to which he was invited. But who will venture to say that the Church of England was not better served by Dr Vaughan's labours, extending over some 40 years, in thus diffusing some-thing of his own learning, his own methods, his own experience, his own example, through the length and breadth of England? May I not add, diffusing also his own spirit of friendship and true human helpfulness? For I am certain that I am truly interpreting the feelings of those young men before whom he spread, without money and without price, all the riches of his knowledge – that, as they carried away these riches to their London alleys or their country lanes, it was less the book-knowledge and the training in sermon-writing that helped and strengthened them than the sense of his constant sympathy and his constant prayers, blessing and sanctifying their path, the spirit of the Christian brother and the Christian gentleman, the spirit that breathes through the epistle of St Paul to his far-off disciple and friend Philemon . . . [20]

The Revd S.A. Alexander, Reader at the Temple Church, thought the secret of his influence could be summed up in one word: 'reality'. 'He spoke from the fullness of his own rich experience. Behind all the charm of his personality, the smoothness of his manner, and the art more concealed than intruded, yet very apparent on an analysis of his printed addresses – behind all that lay his genuineness, his reality.' [21]

In its obituary, *The Times* noted that his books were an inexhaustible mine for other clergymen who were too hard-worked or too diffident to compose their own. In this way his words and influence reached a far wider audience throughout the land. When White once asked him if he would mind if at times he made a skeleton from one of his sermons and then preach it himself, Vaughan said he would be very glad: 'I should feel that you and I were preaching from the same pulpit.' [22] It was his ability as a preacher that the *New York Times* chose to note in particular in its brief obituary on 16 October 1897 stating that 'By many good judges of preaching he was regarded as one of the most effective preachers in the Church of England.' He was presumably known in the States through the many volumes of his sermons published by Macmillan and Strahan, both of whom had offices in New York.

In a passage about why these sermons still deserved to be read today, Bishop R.R. Williams noted in 1960 how Vaughan 'applied the message of the Bible to the actual moral and spiritual needs of his hearers with a pointed directness almost unknown today. He could enter into St Paul's words, "We *beseech* you in Christ's stead". No sermon ended without an earnest and plain-spoken appeal to the will and to the heart. Terse, short sentences drove home the message.' [23] Here is one such example:

There are many persons willing enough to hear sermons; admirers of eloquent words, forcible arguments or lively illustrations; but, of these, a large proportion wince, and draw off, and go back, when the plain demand of repentance comes home to them, and when the direct test of personal faith in Christ is closely and powerfully applied. Is it so with any who now hear me? Do you repent of your sins as sins against God? And do you believe on the Lord Jesus Christ as your own Saviour and Redeemer and Lord? [24]

Though famed as the Head of Harrow, some have seen his educational work there as though he were simply Arnold writ small. He certainly loved and learnt much from his old Head and at Harrow followed his example of seeking to turn boys into educated Christian gentlemen, and, like him, he used the chapel and the Sunday sermon as the place and means where boys could be most influenced. It is true that he was no educational innovator at Harrow but he did far more practically for improving educational opportunities than Arnold ever did. Whereas Arnold had been charged in court of running down the junior department at Rugby, thereby reducing the chances of local boys getting sufficient instruction in the classics to be able to enter the upper school and have the benefit there of a free education, Vaughan did the opposite. He did it by helping to establish and support primary and secondary schools, to bring into being the University College of South Wales and to reform universities in need of reformation. These were tasks that his great hero-headmaster never attempted. He was progressive too in his desire to enable girls of little education receive some practical training and in his support for the admission of women to the university college he presided over for a while, though he had not always held this view. In a lecture he gave in Nottingham in 1868 when he presented the prizes and certificates for the Oxford Local Examinations, he had said he feared their admission to higher education 'looked like the first step towards woman suffrage', something he did not favour. He had, however, always favoured the admission of Dissenters to the universities.

It would have been good to have known Farrar's assessment of him as an educator as he worked for four years under him at Harrow and then went on to a headship himself. All we have is a second-hand quotation in the *Pall Mall Gazette*, 'Archdeacon Farrar speaks of him as one "whose name will be identified with Harrow for many a generation."' [25] Farrar published a book entitled *Men I have known* in the year Vaughan died. One chapter is devoted to fifteen bishops and deans but he did not

386

include Vaughan among them. That is a strange omission. Was he aware of Vaughan's desire that no memoir of him should be written? Had he, perhaps, written to his old friend asking his permission to include him and been refused? It could hardly have been an oversight on Farrar's part. Vaughan's request for no memoirs, however, was not heeded by F.D. How who included him in his book *Six Great Schoolmasters* published in 1904. His very inclusion along with Hawtrey, Moberly, Kennedy, Temple and Bradley tells how highly other contemporaries rated him as an educationalist of national standing.

There was much speculation about just how many times he was offered bishoprics – those we know for sure are Rochester in 1860, Worcester in '61, Gloucester in '62, and Ely in '64. Durham in 1861 has also been mentioned, Ceylon in '62, Lichfield in '67, St Albans in '89 and even Canterbury itself. Chancellor Austen mentioned this last one in his reminiscences of Vaughan which he shared at the 1925 meeting of 'doves' at Lambeth Palace: 'Perhaps I may venture to mention here and now that when the see of Canterbury was vacant a friend of the then Prime Minister was authorised to sound him as to whether he would accept the offer if made.' [26]

Would he have been a great Bishop and even Archbishop, had he accepted preferment? Possibly. But his track record of avoiding controversial subjects and his silence on such matters as ritual practice, which loomed so large in the minds of bishops and other dignitaries of the period, suggests he may have lacked some decisive leadership capabilities. *The Record*, an ultra-conservative evangelical paper, in its obituary singled this out as his 'flaw':

> If we may venture, in all reverence for his memory and with a lively gratitude for much that he has taught us, to put our finger upon what we believe to be the flaw in his character and his work, there seemed, we should say, to be about him a settled calm that kept him from exhibiting even a suspicion of partisanship, where partisanship would have been a gain. He could not be a leader where there was conflict; he watched the strife from a serener atmosphere. It is doubtful whether he read much, or cared to keep abreast of current thought. The one book from which he quoted was the Bible. Yet he had a quality which is amongst the highest a leader can possess; he could stamp his own individuality of character on others. He founded a school of character, though he led no party in conflict . . .
>
> In an age in which so many have been tempted to think destructive criticism the only proper study of the Biblical scholar, it was no small

advantage to have one who was content to deal with the Bible as he found it, making its message to the souls of men his one care. [27]

The *Telegraph* too thought he lacked the 'toughness' needed to be a bishop:

> It has, indeed, been alleged that his objection to taking his seat in the House of Lords was the cause of his invariable refusal to become a bishop; but it must be added that some of those who knew him best were of the opinion that he lacked the toughness of fibre and the knowledge of human nature, especially in its worst aspects which are necessary for the proper and successful discharge of episcopal functions. [28]

Its speculation about his reason for refusing bishoprics seems to be quite wild - Vaughan valued highly the presence of Bishops in the Lords. His old pupil and friend, Canon Gosling, was surely nearer the mark when he wrote to Mowbray in 1957 'I should say that Vaughan's refusal of a bishopric (perhaps more than one) was possibly due to the fact that he had started on a particular task, which he was unwilling to discontinue for a higher office in the Ministry.' [29] Once his work of assisting men prepare themselves for Ordination was established and proving to be successful – and that was already the case from early on in his Doncaster years – he would have been extremely reluctant to give it up for episcopal power. Part of the attraction of being Master of the Temple was that it allowed him to continue this work. Also one of Canon Coombs' memories of him from 1894 is apposite here: 'When Master of the Temple he would often remark with a twinkle in his eye, "Many Bishops! ONE Master."' [30]

I believe he would have been an exemplary bishop in several respects: as a guardian and expositor of the Faith, as a pastor and counsellor, as a caring father-in-God and a generous friend to his clergy and their families. His letter to Lightfoot urging him to accept the offer of Durham shows that he had a good understanding of the pastoral and leadership qualities needed in a bishop. He would surely have tried to be a focus of unity for the whole diocese and striven for good relationships with Nonconformists. Not all bishops in the Church of England, then or now, have shown these essential episcopal qualities. His ministry was deeply appreciated by scholars and bishops who acknowledged him as their equal – for Bishop Westcott he was 'the last of those whom I looked to as my masters . . . There is no one to do his unique work'. [31] Six years after his death at a reunion of his men held in Doncaster

Archbishop Davidson stated that time after time when perplexities were rife, he kept wondering what Vaughan's shrewd and big-hearted Christian counsel would have been on particular problems. [32] What a tribute and testimony that is to his old friend's wisdom and the value he had placed on it.

A.V. Magee who was also present at that same reunion described Vaughan's ministry to them as unique – there would never again be such a man as him. Another remembered with constant gratitude the time he spent with him preparing for ordination: 'Dr Vaughan was a truly out-standing Christian gentleman, who influenced every one of his pupils and left his mark on them for life.' It was this work which Davidson rated most highly. For a man to gather round him, year after year, a set of pupils who came not because of any official position he had or because of their membership in any college or society was 'to stand absolutely alone, at all events in modern history. In that position Dr Vaughan had no rival in the history of the Church of England, perhaps in the Church at large.' [33]

His reputation in the longer term, however, was not helped by G.W.E. Russell's various negative 'memories' of him and by the muted biographical article he penned for the *Dictionary of English Church History* edited by Ollard & Crosse in 1912.

Vaughan himself desired no written memorial – the life and work of his "men" were, in his judgement, his best memorial. There were, in fact, many other tangible expressions of people's gratitude for his ministry. Among them the Vaughan Memorial Library in Harrow School and a reredos and medallion portrait of him in the school chapel with inscriptions in Latin and English penned by his devoted pupil, successor and friend. In Harrow the primary school still bears his name as does a road; there are windows and memorials in St George's Doncaster as well as a street bearing his name; a brass plaque in the library of Doncaster Grammar School (now Hall Cross Academy) erected after his death by the old boys of the school 'As a token of their affection and regard in recognition of the invaluable services rendered by him in the restoration of this ancient Grammar School'; an ornate lectern in the Temple (destroyed in bombing during the 2nd World War); a life-size effigy in Llandaff Cathedral and a bust in the Cathedral School; and Christ Church Kensal Rise in London; and along with his father and brothers he is remembered in the Vaughan Porch in Leicester Cathedral. And portraits of him are to be found in Leicester, Rugby, Trinity College Cambridge, Harrow School, the Mansion House Doncaster, the Middle Temple, and a miniature in St George's Doncaster, as well as one in Llandaff Cathedral. The sculptor Herbert H. Hampton created a relief portrait of him dating from the Dean's death possibly as a memorial tribute. A number of copies, all similarly finished with a bronze paint surface, have survived – one is in the National Museum of Wales in Cardiff. *Vanity Fair* pictured him in the pulpit of the Temple when they chose him as one of the '*Men of the Day*' series in 1872 and his photograph was included in Cooper's *Men of Mark* (Sixth Series) published in 1882. For a man who never held any great office in the Church of England, all this is striking testimony to a much-loved and mightily effective minister of the Gospel.

The 'doves' who attended his funeral immediately determined that money would be raised for a permanent memorial. What could be better than a parish church in memory of a man who had so exalted parish ministry? The Dean Vaughan Memorial Church at Kensal Rise in north west London was consecrated on 25 July 1900, Princess Henry of Battenburg having laid the foundation stone a year earlier on behalf of Queen Victoria. They also decided to keep the 4th Sunday in Advent as a 'Day of Remembrance and Prayer'. The reasons given for choosing this date were

> a. the collect for that Sunday was invariably used, at least in later days, by Dr Vaughan in the pulpit before a sermon;
> b. their newsletter *The Advent Record* was issued in that season;
> c. that particular Sunday is one associated with the admission to Holy Orders.

Memories of him were revived at reunions of his 'doves' which were re-started in 1903 when they met at Doncaster; they met again in 1908 at Peterborough, St Martin's Kensal Rise in 1913 and 1916, at York in 1919, St Martin's Kensal Rise in 1921, the Temple 1922, Lambeth Palace 1925, at the Temple again in 1826 for the dedication of the memorial lectern there, at Leicester in 1928 and finally at Kensal Rise in 1934. *The Times* carried reports of these 'Memorial Meetings' – its account of the one held in May 1921 mentioned that 290 of the 'doves' were still living and that 60 of them had assembled at St Martin's the previous week. At it the Vicar spoke of the work and progress in the parish which owed so much to the church built mainly by the gifts of Vaughan's men. His memory lived on there in a way that would have given him much joy: in the ordinary round of English parish life and ministry. One student's store of notes on preaching and pastoral work together with some of Vaughan's sermon outlines that he gave them are preserved in the church.

The example he had set in assisting men prepare for parish ministry was followed by a number of other Church leaders, most notably Bishop Lightfoot of Durham starting in 1879 and continued by his successor, Westcott, and then by Bishop Handley Moule. The Auckland Brotherhood or 'Sons of the House', as they were known in Lightfoot's time as they lived with him in the Palace at Bishop Auckland, numbered two hundred and sixteen in the end. The timetable and content of the training was very similar to Vaughan's, and similar in that there was no allegiance to any party and tuition was given without payment, just as Vaughan had done. And, as with his men, many of these too went on to become notable church dignitaries and exemplary parish priests.

Bishop R.R. Williams described him in 1953 as 'A neglected Victorian Divine' and tried to revive interest in him; seven years later he edited a selection of Vaughan's sermons which he called *The Word of Life*. The Bishop assessed his life's work in these terms:

> During fifty-six years he was a faithful and fervent preacher of the Gospel by which he himself lived, and the influence of his sermons, particularly at Cambridge and at the Temple must have been immense . . .
>
> As a scholar . . . his work is a good example of patient study, entirely subordinated to the pastoral and didactic work of the Ministry . . .
>
> He took little part in the administrative developments of Anglican life during a long career, and to this extent his influence on the history of the Church was limited . . .
>
> As a trainer of ordinands . . . he also broke new ground.
>
> His greatest contribution, however, was his own life, utterly dedicated, exemplary in devotion, in freedom from self-seeking and in earnestness . . .
>
> For many years yet to come he will hold his place as a "preacher's preacher" and an example of a quiet and studious Ministry which the 20th century has made all but impossible to achieve today. [34]

D.D.W. Mowbray, having compared his NT commentaries to those of the Cambridge trio, Lightfoot, Westcott and Hort, found less in them to commend to modern readers as they were written in a pre-critical mode and simply ignored the higher criticism of the late 19th century. But he went on:

> And YET, those who did know him, from the Archbishop to the humblest of the Doves, from the Master of Trinity to the Doncaster Gazette reporter, all speak in a tone ranging from admiration to practically hero-worship. We are bound to press our enquiry in search of an explanation.

The reason seems to lie partly in the force of his personality, which no book can mediate in the same way as the living presence. Further he left upon his hearers the impression of a clear, sensitive intellect; and he possessed an unusual power of expression through voice diction and manner. [35]

Mowbray summarised and concluded in these words:

The life of Charles John Vaughan, spanning best part of the century which saw so extensive a revolution in theological thought and critical method, was something of both a paradox and a paragon. In relation to the advanced state of textual criticism, higher criticism and theology towards the end of the century, he was a noble anachronism. But as a teacher and trainer of men, his appeal and his technique were wonderfully effective right through to the last few Doves in his eighty-second year. As a preacher of the Gospel – as God's prophet – his evangelical passion never waned and the prophetic voice never wavered. His last message, penned with much pain and hesitation, still glows with the old fire. [36]

His nephew, Charles Edwyn Vaughan, in a biographical sketch written for the University College's magazine at the time of Vaughan's appointment as President in 1894, identified his most precious gift – 'He has, in an exceptional degree, the rarest gift which a teacher can receive or acquire; the gift of finding his way to the hearts of his pupils. *And he finds his way to their heart, because he has begun by taking them to his own.*' [37] [my italics]

These many and varied assessments touch on what was, in my judgement, his supreme characteristic and the source of his influence on others. To put it in just four words: *he genuinely loved people*. Because he had taken his Lord's words and example to heart, he was ever seeking to love others as he knew himself to be loved by Christ. This is why he prized the pastoral office so highly. Bishop Yeatman-Biggs observed of him: 'There was no higher call than the pastorate of souls in parish life.'[38] To quote his own words again: 'The Pastoral Office is a hand-to-hand, heart-to-heart, soul-to-soul ministration . . . The individual must be first sought and found – then he in turn becomes a new centre of personal light and warmth to other individual lives and souls around him.' That 'light and warmth' and the love which he had himself received from Christ, he wished to share with others. The source and inspiration of his love for others is stated in the Gospel words he chose for his own tombstone: 'Not that we loved God, but that He loved us.'

This love was to be seen in the constant respect, courtesy and real sympathy which Vaughan showed to all. He loved in particular the boys and men he taught, and many of them recognised this and responded in kind. He had a remarkable capacity for faithful, loving, lasting friendship(s) which, combined with his other gifts as a scholar, teacher and preacher, and his deep devotion to Christ and his unshakable faith, made him the attractive and influential priest and role model that he was. Vaughan had rightly judged that his best memorial would be 'his men' - this childless man lived on in them.

A flawed man for sure, as all men are. Yet one who, despite never accepting high office in the Church and possibly because he chose not to, achieved true and lasting greatness.

Appendix 1

"What shall I do, Lord?" Acts 22.10
A sermon preached before the University of Cambridge
on Trinity Sunday 1861

"What shall I do, Lord?" The words are few, but they are significant and they are pregnant words. On St Paul's lips, at that moment, they meant, "I see my past life to have been, with all its propriety of conduct and with all its zeal for God, a folly and a madness; I see my boasted privileges a delusion, my treasured knowledge a lie; I see that what I thought obedience was rebellion, and what I deemed a mortal sin was in truth the very will of God. And now, Lord, in this uprooting of all that was, be Thou my Guide into that which shall be: I know not – teach Thou me – what is truth: I know not – teach Thou me – what is duty: in this hour of confusion and utter darkness, be Thou the lamp of my path, the light of my steps, Lord, what wilt Thou have me do?"

And the same words had for him thenceforward a fresh meaning with every successive circumstance of life from his conversion to his martyrdom. We will not stay to trace it through changes in which St Paul was but the type of all Christians. When the path of duty is beset with unexpected difficulties, or when it seems to branch off, this way and that, in ambiguous directions; then, again and again, has been heard in every generation from a thousand hearts, the cry for guidance and for decision, "What shall I do, Lord?" And when at some new turn in life's journey it has become necessary to choose between conflicting claims, to do this and refuse that; and the voice of conscience is indistinctly heard, and the arguments of the natural judgement evenly balanced, so that we know not how to walk and to please God in a conjuncture felt to be critical and big with consequences; then too has the cry gone up, and never in vain from sincere and trusting hearts, into the ear of One not seen but loved, "What shall I do, Lord? O Lord, I am oppressed: undertake for me!"

My brethren, there is one question which presses heavily, or which ought to do so, at that point of life at which many members of this congregation stand today. There is one question which concerns, not a particular act of life only, but the whole of life; a question upon the answer to which will depend, for each one of you, the occupations in which, and the circumstances amongst which, this brief but momentous being shall be used and spent. You will all perceive that I speak of what is called the choice of a profession. A "profession": that branch of knowledge which you shall profess to have made your own; that department of human affairs which you shall profess to understand; that employment, be it what it may, for which you shall profess yourself to be qualified. And the "choice" of a profession. Considerable latitude is allowed, in these days, to all young men – entire and absolute freedom to most young men – in determining for themselves that line in which they shall serve their generation and exercise the talents with which God has endowed them. It is due to us, it is due to you, that it should be so. It is the right of a responsible being to be left free in this momentous choice. No man may deliver his brother, no father his son, in the day of God's judgement: therefore no man should prescribe to his brother, no father to his son, when childhood and boyhood are ended, in what particular duties, under what particular influences, he shall spend those years of activity for which he solely and singly will have to give account.

For great indeed are the issues of that choice. Not more various are individual gifts, than individual tendencies, liabilities, and temptations. A profession suitable to one may be misery, may be ruin, to another. I speak not here – though the consideration can never be unimportant – of the chances of success or failure in the race of professional distinction. I speak rather of the chances of the soul in this life and for eternity. And I say that there are constitutions of mind and spirit as diverse in their openness to particular influences for good or evil as are bodily constitutions in their proneness to particular forms of disease. As the physician will prescribe for one a warm climate and for another a bracing, sending this man for health to a region of the world which to that man would be death itself; even so there are employments, callings, whole professions, which for one man may be perilous in the extreme, and for another harmless or even salubrious. Woe to him, therefore, who lets himself drift into a profession, without much serious reflection and great searchings of heart. Woe to him who suffers accident, persuasion, inclination alone, to preside over such a choice. Nay, even gifts, even powers, even great and marked capacities for a particular calling, are not of themselves decisive. These things are elements in the question, but they are not the whole of it. They all demand to be taken into account, but they have no right, singly or together, to settle it. I know that natural faults, constitutional tendencies, pronenesses to particular forms of evil, are neither created nor destroyed by circumstances: it is not a profession that makes nor a profession that can eradicate one of them. But one profession may foster, may encourage, may develop a particular evil tendency, and another may check, suppress, counteract it. And, alas, how few think of these things in choosing. How many, for example, have gone to the Bar, not although, but because, they saw in themselves, or friends admired in them, a promptitude of resource or an ingenuity of invention which might successfully distort truth and make the worse appear the better cause. And how many have gone into the Army, not though, but because, they were already too much addicted to a habit of mental indolence and saw before them in that one direction a possibility of passing decently through life without exertion. If the one had foreseen all that was involved in his choice, he would have felt his readiness of speech and his quickness of invention a reason against rather than for the calling to which he was inclined. And if the other had foreseen all that was involved in his choice, he would have felt it his duty rather to force himself into mental exertion at the risk of inferior success, than to supersede that outward necessity for it from which he more than other men would have profited. But who does foresee all that hangs upon this first decision? Or who, almost, regards with due seriousness his inability to foresee? Who, my brethren, amongst you who are now on the threshold of active life, is really pondering as in God's sight the choice of his earthly calling, taking the measure, so far as he is able, of his own gifts and failings, estimating duty in the light not of time only but of eternity, and, under a deep conviction of his own ignorance and blindness, asking, day by day, of One above, the very question of the text, "What shall I do, Lord? Lord, what wilt Thou have me do?"

It is not much, perhaps, that man can do to answer this question for another. And yet it seems as though the ministry of God's Word, in this place at least, ought not always to be silent on a matter so pressing and so momentous. You will not indeed expect a clergyman, and a parochial clergyman, to be a wholly impartial judge of the conflicting claims of English professions. His life is given to one work; and he knows, of course, better than others, how much that one work wants men. It is natural that he should feel, when he visits once again these scenes of his youth; more especially, where he is set to preach where once he listened, to endeavour to do in the humblest degree for others that which was once done for him from the same pulpit by great men numbered now (in many cases) among the dead; what it would be for his beloved Church if the ranks of her ministry could be largely replenished from the very best and most gifted of those to whom he speaks; if such a sense of the capabilities of this service, of its dignity, of its power, and of its happiness too, could be here awakened, as should make it indeed an ambition to embrace it; not a thing to which here and there knowledge and ability may condescend, but rather that which shall be the desire and the aspiration of the very ablest minds and the very noblest spirits, even as he believes it to be the most direct and the most immediate service of Him from whom every gift comes, and to whose glory all should redound.

I speak not to disparage other callings, even in their bearing upon religion. None knows better than a parochial clergyman how feeble, how ineffective, in any place, much more in the world at large, must be that ministry which is not seconded by the zeal and comforted by the sympathy of Christian laymen. But here, and on this day, bear with me if, in the later words of him whom the text recalls to us, I venture to "magnify my own office". Trinity Sunday is a day of Ordinations. Wherever the Church of Christ has spread itself throughout the whole earth, this day is adding to its ranks new soldiers, new officers, of the Cross. It cannot be unseasonable today to speak to you, as time and strength may permit, of the capabilities and of the requirements of this special service. If by God's blessing upon the words spoken but one heart should be stirred to desire this commission, or but one difficulty removed out of the way of him who has been fearing or hesitating to seek it, it will not be for nothing that I have been permitted to visit you, nor will it be without rejoicing that I return to my appointed place of labour.

1. The capabilities, I said of the Christian ministry. Who can overrate them? What is it to have the Word of God, to which others can but occasionally have recourse in brief moments of devotion, given to us for our study, our meditation, and our stewardship, all the day? What is it to have that charity which with others can be but the employment of rare intervals of absorbing and engrossing business, given to us as the very work of life? To have the chosen occupation of our Lord Himself – "who went about doing good" – consigned to us as our office and our profession? What is it to have a recognized position amongst men as their friend, adviser, and helper, in things pertaining to God? To be allowed, and even expected, to fly to "those who in this transitory life are in trouble, sorrow, need, sickness, or any other adversity," with a message of cheering and consolation from God Himself? What a help this should be to ourselves in living a life of faith and hope: what an aid in walking seriously, thoughtfully, consistently: what an assistance in maintaining

always that "conscience void of offence" which, whether as Christ's ministers or as Christ's servants, is essential as much to happiness now as to hope hereafter.

And who shall limit the capabilities of one special office of our ministry – the much despised ordinance of preaching? I know indeed that preaching may be a very poor thing; a form to the speaker, and therefore a weariness to the hearer. With many, sermons are a very by-word of dullness: God forgive those whose carelessness and coldness, far more than any incapacity, have made them so. But I know also – for I have felt it – what a sermon may be. I have heard sermons delivered from this very place which made the heart burn and the ears tingle; sermons of which the lapse of a quarter of a century has failed to dull the recollection either of sense or sound. I speak to some this day who have within them thoughts and ideas, convictions and aspirations too, which they feel that they cannot rest without communicating. They look on already with no indifferent eye upon the cares and woes, the confusions and the perplexities, of human life. They have found for themselves – and they know it – a standing place amidst doubts, and a covert from storms, by which they behold others still vexed and buffeted. They have sought, and at last have found, that in Christ Himself, crucified first, then risen, there is peace and rest and healing. They have found, and others have not found. What will it be to them to be commissioned in due time to preach? To have an audience gathered for them, without obtrusion or presumption of their own, and to be secure of a hearing? O, what will preaching be in such hands? Where will be dullness and tameness, where will be poor thoughts and a languid utterance in the preacher, where will be drowsiness, inattention and weariness in those that hear, when mind and heart and soul are full of their subject, and when a definite and cherished aim gives point and directness to every word spoken? Depend upon it, preaching, however it may fail of its effect, has every possible chance still given to it. The machinery is ready for use: it needs but the hand to move, but the spirit to animate it. There is still, there is patience, there is expectation, in many there is desire too, a hungering and thirsting after edification, to which it ought to be a delight to minister, which it is a sin of sins wilfully to disappoint. Let more men of thought and culture, more men of mark and power, above all, more men of purpose and devotion, give themselves to the work; and one who knows something of our town and something of our country congregations may be listened to when he promises that such preaching shall never lack attention, that such preaching shall never lose its labour.

But I would tell of the capabilities of the Christian ministry in its more private workings. It is a great mistake — I had almost said it is a great impiety — to represent the ministry as needing no gifts, or as needing gifts only for its preaching. In these days, at all events, there is no gift however eminent which needs to be thrown away in a parish however obscure. Wherever the encounter is made hand to hand between the ministry of Christ and the ministry of Satan, between truth and falsehood, between faith and infidelity, between righteousness and sin, there is room, and there is a demand, for all gifts. It is only for vague and general and distant dealing that small powers or small efforts can be deemed sufficient. Let a Christian minister single out his man — and it is only in single combat that some of the greatest victories of the ministry can be won — let him propose to himself as a definite object the turning of some sinner from the error of his ways; the recovery of some drunkard to sobriety, of some adulterer to chastity, of some profane man to reverence, of some infidel to faith and to worship; and assuredly he will find it necessary to try every resource with which skill and persuasiveness can furnish him, as well as that higher and more availing weapon still, which can be taken only by effectual fervent prayer out of the very armoury of God. But with these aids the words will ever and anon be verified, "Resist the devil, and he will flee from you." Again and again will God give the victory, not to human pride or human skill, but to the working of His Holy Spirit in the heart first, and then by the lips, of His commissioned ministering servant. And men are finding out in these days that no mere machinery of evangelization - no mere building of churches, and no mere multiplication of services, - will do Christ's work effectually, without a constant personal search of the lost, and a warm individual sympathy with the struggling. The Church will not reach at all those who most need her, unless she goes after them: it is a later part of the work, one which testifies of its all but accomplishment, when they seek her. Judge ye, my brethren, whether this sort of work can be done without a large expenditure of ministration; whether one man in a parish of five or of ten thousand souls can avail anything in this labour; the toil of battling singly with hearts unwilling to be conquered, or reclaiming one by one lives sunk and lost in sin.

Strange seems it — strange would it seem, knew we not the cause — that to vigorous and enterprising men any calling should be more attractive than one so full of human interest, so imperious to its demand for human energy. A lawyer may be admirably furnished with every gift of knowledge and of eloquence, and yet he may spend some of the best years of manhood in waiting for a client. A physician may possess science which would qualify him for high advancement, and yet linger long without being summoned to the bedside of one patient. A soldier may be shut up for months together in some gloomy barrack, or live through a forty years' peace and die without once seeing service. But a clergyman has from the day of his ordination clients and patients, battles and sieges, enough and to spare. He waits not for the chances of an opening; he needs not, for his high calling, the advantages of a connection or a patron: around his doors are gathered the souls which ask his service, within his parish rages the battle in which he is to win his crown. Happy he who sees these things, and suffers not his ministry to lack its true reward by turning aside to a recompense low and illusory. Let other professions seek their success in comforts, riches, and honours of this life: he misses both worlds, who first enters a calling of which the very title is holy, and then desecrates it by the pursuit of objects as earthly in their nature as they are precarious and almost casual in their attainment.

2. And well may the Apostle's question sound in our ears, "Who is sufficient for these things?" Is it indeed so, that any man of vigorous mind or of ample knowledge may at once transfer himself to that ministry of which we have thus spoken? Is nothing wanted but vigour? Nothing but a humane care for others? Nothing but a disinterested aim and a willingness to forego ease and honour? Must there not be something yet beyond these things, if a man would make full proof of his ministry? Yes, there is one thing, on which if we dwell not it must be because its necessity is obvious; a true faith in God through Christ; a real devotion to Him; and a life cleansed and consecrated by His indwelling Spirit. It would be a disastrous day for the Church of Christ, on which the door of its special service were thrown wide open to all comers who could just profess a desire for the amelioration of the condition of the poor by the elevation of their social position or the rectification of their moral standard. These objects point not to Ordination: they belong rather to lay callings: happy are those times, happy is that country, which, like our own, can point to many honoured persons, in private, professional, or public life, who are diligently pursuing them. For a clergyman's work there is required not only a charitable spirit, not only a humane intention; not faith only, not devotion, not blamelessness of life only; but preparation – yes, my brethren, a special preparation. Narrow as much as you will the compass of theology; cast out of it all that you may have

of collateral and subsidiary information; you must at least leave to it the Bible and its interpretation; you must at least secure your congregation from ignorance and from error as to the subject-matter of our teaching: and who that knows anything of the Bible can be unaware of the amplitude of that field of study which is contained within these closest and narrowest bounds?

But there is much more than this, which ought to fall, and which I am persuaded does fall, within the scope of the theological discipline of this University. In these times there is need that our clergy be not only pious but well-read and (which is sometimes a different thing) well-educated men. It is not right that in our great manufacturing towns of the north it should be in the power of a hired emissary of infidelity, to defy with impunity, Sunday after Sunday, by public placard, the ministers of the Gospel. It is not right that working men, ignorant perhaps but intelligent and honest-hearted, should be left to grapple as they may, unaided by their pastor, with the scoffs and taunts of the infidel. These things are a new sign of the times, and men must be educated in the full view of them. Nor is it right that, apart from the open avowal of an anti-christian purpose, it should be in the power of any writer, unanswered and unexposed, to dress up old objections as if they were new, and to trouble the minds of unlearned believers by assertions which a deeper knowledge would show perhaps to be inaccurate or unfounded. These things make a great demand upon those to whom the charge of clerical education is entrusted. They ought to be intimately and industriously acquainted with the present condition of the minds of thinking men. They ought to have the tenderest sympathy with real difficulties, and to treat with manly respect anxious doubts which they do not share. They must beware above all things of seeming to stifle enquiry or to dread discovery. They must religiously abstain from all half-answers. No man loses the respect of the young by confessing himself unacquainted with a fact at issue, or unable on the instant to repel attack. But every man loses, and deserves to lose, the respect of listeners young or old, if he so far presumes upon the ignorance of his hearer as to put him off with an answer which he himself who speaks does not feel to be conclusive. These things are of the very alphabet of education. And these things, practised by the teacher, will in turn be imitated and handed on by the learner. A clergyman thus trained by example in habits of candour and of truthfulness will go forth to his Parish, when the time comes, to bear and to forbear; in meekness instructing the ignorant, in simplicity reassuring the doubter, in the power of a true faith convincing or else refuting the gainsayer.

And shall I be pardoned if I say here how important I deem it that clerical education, so far as it consists in learning, should be carried on in our Universities rather than in smaller and more special training fields? We do not want – which is the very best that can be hoped from such methods – to see one man's mind stamped whole upon a section of the clergy. The freer intercourse which a University offers of mind with mind, the larger choice and mutual correction of instructors, not to mention the ampler gifts of learning and ability which such a place affords in its teachers, are invaluable aids in the study of a true theology. Other systems may have their advantage – I doubt not that it is so – in peculiar cases: there are men for whom the temptations of college life have been too strong, and who need to be taken aside from it to learn truth and to practise duty in what is for them a safer atmosphere: But the University, in my opinion, would prove herself most unfaithful to the work with which God has entrusted her, if she allowed it to be said that her best students must turn elsewhere for their theology, because she refused to them either opportunities of instruction or a stimulus to their use.

But has not theology its art as well as its science? Does it come naturally to any man, when once he is master of scriptural doctrine, to manage a parochial school, to organize parochial visiting, to catechise the young, to visit the sick, or to prepare and to preach sermons? It may be so with some few men. There may be those who are gifted with these great aptitudes, and whom a special training in these matters would rather cramp than aid. But surely this is not a common, certainly it is not the normal, condition of a candidate for Holy Orders. Certainly it is not the course pursued by a student of law, or tolerated in a student of medicine. To expect it in this one instance is to expect a miracle. To act upon this expectation is to hand over one Parish after another to be experimented on by an untaught empiric, and to prevent one clergyman after another from ever rising out of the awkwardness of a perpetual beginner, or (at best) the eccentricities and mannerisms of a self-instructed genius. Surely these are powers best and most safely acquired in the observation of their exercise. And where is the experienced Pastor who would not gladly take under his general direction, from time to time, three or four candidates for Holy Orders? Great joy would it carry to the heart of one parochial clergyman – for him I can answer – to receive applications of such a nature; to find that there were men of blameless character, of steady purpose, of open mind, and of true devotion, who were willing to take up their abode in his Parish, before Ordination, to see what he could show them, and to render to him such services, in his schools and amongst his poor, as church order may permit and mutual convenience arrange. Then and not till then would he feel that his Parish was efficiently worked, and he would cherish the hope that what was thus given to him would be repaid in some measure by opportunities of widening experience, and growing in the knowledge alike of man and God.

I can make no apology for having used this last opportunity of addressing you, my beloved brethren, in bringing before you a subject which lies very near my heart. I long to see that reproach rolled away, which is said to rest at this time upon the Church of England, that she is not giving in any large proportion her most distinguished sons to the ministry of the Word and Sacraments. I know that in this place she has given many of them: forgive me if in ignorance I seem to disparage their numbers. But how is it with the younger generation here present before me? Are there no stronger inducements drawing a large proportion of you elsewhere? Are there none, whose talents, whose characters, whose antecedent purposes, seem to destine them for the ministry, yet who, for some reason or (might I say) for no reason, are now looking off from it and shaping for themselves a widely different career? Are there none who might almost say, "Thy vows are upon me, O Lord" – so profound was the desire of a mother's heart, so earnest once their own resolution, to seek this and no other calling – yet who now have erased from their brow that sacred mark, and would fain be anything else rather? My brethren, why is this? I ask it of you seriously, anxiously, affectionately, what has influenced, what has changed you? Is it anything in the Articles [i.e. the 39 Articles of Religion of the Church of England] or formularies of the national Church, which suggests to you some scruple? I cannot counsel you to go against your conscience in the smallest matter: but I would ask, what pains have you taken to get satisfaction upon this point? Have you taken counsel with elder men, men of thought, of piety, of experience? Remember, though you must not profess that which you do not think, yet, on the other hand, there is a call on the positive side as well as the negative; a call to adhere to the work which God had seemed to mark out for you, unless the scruple which has occurred to you be as rational as it may be fanciful, as important as it may be trifling, and as permanent as it may be transitory. Or is that you dread to incur that yoke of bondage which is sometimes laid too heavily upon the clerical by the lay members of our common Church? Is it that you dread to be taunted at some future day with insincerity if you should ever dare to think or to speak with freedom; to find yourself made an offender for a word, and called untrue to your profession if you cannot utter every passing Shibboleth of a conventional theology? We cannot, alas, promise you an exemption from the common lot of all men: nor can we indeed encourage you in the flattering notion that subscription binds you to nothing, or that a man may be a clergyman of the Church and yet teach Universalism, Deism, Pantheism, or what he will. But this we will say to you, Act now upon your present honest convictions, and trust God with the opinions as with the fortunes of your future. Dread not the irrevocability of the pastoral vow, if only your conscience now tells you that Jesus Christ is, and is Lord both of the dead and the living. It may be formidable in prospect to undertake a responsibility absolutely life-long: but each day that you live you will less and less wish to evade it, if only God gives you grace so to live as you will wish that you had done when you lie down to die. "No man having put his hand to the plough, and looking back, is fit for the kingdom of God": then look not back. Day by day, if you faint not, you will rejoice more and more in the choice once made: "and when the chief Shepherd shall appear, you shall receive the crown of glory that fadeth not away."

APPENDIX 2

The published works of Charles John Vaughan
with details of publisher and subsequent editions where known

1834-40 At School & University
1834   *An English Essay recited in Rugby School*
1836   *A Translation into Greek iambics from King Richard II Act II*
1836   *A Translation into Greek iambics from King Lear Act III sc. 2*
1837   *An Oration delivered in Trinity College Chapel, at the Commemoration*
1840   *An Earnest Appeal to the Master and Seniors of Trinity College Cambridge on the Revision of the Statutes by Two of the Fellows* [The other was G.E.L. Cotton]   J.W. Parker

1840 – 44 Vicar of St Martin's Leicester
1842   *Like People, Like Priest: A Sermon preached at the Visitation of the Archdeacon of Leicester*   Hatchard
1843   *The Test of Charity: A Sermon preached on behalf of SPG*

1845 – 59 Headmaster of Harrow School
1846   *Sermons*   J. Murray London, Macmillan Cambridge, & J.S. Crossley Leicester
1847   *Sermons preached in the Chapel of Harrow School* J. Murray
1849   *Nine Sermons preached for the most part in Harrow School*   Macmillan
1849   A *Letter on the late Post Office Agitation*
1850   A *Second Letter on the late Post Office Agitation*
1851   *The Personality of the Tempter, and other Sermons*
1851   *Independence and Submission: the Use and Abuse of each: two Addresses*   1858 re-issued by Macmillan
1852   *Sermon at the Festival of the Sons of the Clergy held in St Paul's Cathedral 15 May 1851*
1852   *Deserters from the Congregation: a Sermon preached at the Re-opening of the Parish Church of St Martin's Leicester on 8 February 1852*   J.W. Parker
1852   *Witnesses to the Truth: a Sermon*
1853   *A few Words on the Crystal Palace Question*

1853   *Sermons preached in the Chapel of Harrow School*
                                            2nd Series J.W. Parker

1853   *A Letter to Viscount Palmerston on the monitorial system at Harrow School*

1854   *A Reply to 'One who was once a Monitor'*

1854   *Passages from the Life of Cicero. A Lecture delivered before the Young Men's Christian Association in Exeter Hall*

1854   *A Nation watching for Tidings: A Sermon at Harrow*

1854   *The Outbreak of War: A Sermon at St Martin's Leicester*

1854   *Seedtime and Harvest: A Sermon at Marlborough College*

1854   *A Discourse on Church Discipline and the Burial Service*

1855   *Hymns for the Chapel of Harrow School* (ed. C.J.V)
                                                Crossley & Clarke

1856   *Address on the Occasion of laying the Foundation Stone of The Chapel of Harrow School ... 26th June 1856*

1857   *The Indian Sorrow, and its Lessons for the Young: a Sermon Preached on the day of the National Humiliation October 7, 1857* Rivington

1857   *To what purpose is this waste? A Sermon, preached in the Chapel of Harrow School at a special service for the inhabitants of Harrow* Rivington

1857   *The Vocation of a Public School: A Sermon... Repton School Tercentenary*

1858   *The Work, the Word and the Promise: a Sermon preached in Westminster Abbey, on Ascension Day, at the Consecration of the Bishop of Calcutta*

1858   *Preparation for the Poor: A Sermon preached in the Parish Church of Kilby at its Reopening* Crossley & Clarke

1859   *Power from on High ; A Sermon preached at an Ordination in St Paul's Cathedral on the 4th Sunday in Advent 1858*

1859   *Notes for Lectures on Confirmation with suitable prayers*
          Macmillan Reprinted 16 times and revised twice 1859-97
                                      71,000 copies

1859   *The Last Enemy Destroyed ... a Sermon* (included in *West- Minster Abbey Sermons for the Working Classes. 2nd Series*)

1859   *Rest: A Sermon*

1859   *The Comparative Blessedness of Giving and Receiving.*

1859   *Memorials of Harrow Sundays A Selection of Sermons*
          Macmillan 750, 1860 750, '61 1,000, '64 2,000, '80 2,000

1859   *Last Words in the Chapel of Harrow School*   Macmillan
1859   *St Paul's Epistle to the Romans. Greek Text with English Notes*
          Macmillan 750, 1861 1,500, revised edition '70 1,500,
          '79 2,500, '80 1.500, '85 1,000, '90 1,000, '93, 1,000

1860 At Southborough

1860   *Epiphany, Lent and Easter: A Selection of Sermons* preached
          in *St Michael's Church, Chester Square, London*
          Macmillan 750, 1861 1,250, '68 1,500
1860   *Revision of the Liturgy Five Discourses*   Macmillan 750 + 500
1860   *The Church's Duties and the Church's Opportunities*   Leicester
1860   *Where art Thou? A Sermon preached in St Paul's Cathedral*

1860 – 69 Vicar of Doncaster & Chancellor of York Minster

1860   *Love the Keynote of the Pastoral Message: A Sermon*
1860   *The Call of the Closing Year: a Sermon*   Doncaster Brooke & Co
1861   *The Joy of Success corrected by the Joy of Safety: An
          Ordination Sermon on St Thomas's day 1860*   Macmillan 500
1861   *Mourning of the Land and the Mourning of its Families.
          A Sermon on the Death of the Prince Consort*
          Macmillan 550 + 500 + 500
1861   *The Revised Code of the Committee of the Council on
          Education dispassionately considered. An Address to the Clergy
          of the Deanery of Doncaster*   Macmillan 500 + 500, '62 500
1861   *Four Sermons*   Macmillan 500
1861   *Lessons of Life and Godliness. A Selection of Sermons
          preached in Doncaster Parish Church*   Macmillan 1,500,
                              1863 1,500, '69 3,000, '70 3,000
1862   *Lectures on St Paul's Epistle to the Philippians*   Macmillan 1,250,
                              1869 1,500, '72 1,500, '82 2,000
1862   *The Three Tabernacles: On the Opening of St Peter's School
          Chapel York*   Macmillan 500
1862   *The Book and the Life: Sermons preached at Cambridge
          University*   Macmillan 1,500, '63 1,000, '64 2,500
1863   *Lectures on the Revelation of St John*   Macmillan 2 vols. 1,250,
                              1875 1,500, '82 single volume edition 2,000
1863   *Words from the Gospels. A second Selection of Sermons
          preached in the Parish Church of Doncaster*   Macmillan 2,000,
                              1865 3,000, '75 2,000

1864   *Domestic Service.* SPCK

1864   *A good old Age.* SPCK

1864   *Quietness and Confidence the Strength of the Church. On the Consecration of Trinity Church, Handsworth*   Macmillan 500

1864   *Rubrical Modification not Liturgical Change. A few Words on the Burial Service*

1864   *Son, Thou art ever with me. In the Chapel of the Magdalen Hospital* Macmillan 500

1864   *The Epistles of St Paul for English Readers. Part 1 containing the 1ˢᵗ Epistle to the Thessalonians*   Macmillan 2,500, 1865 1,000

1864/65 *Church of the First Days: Lectures on the Acts of the Apostles 3 volumes*   Macmillan Vol.1 1864 2,000, '65 2,000, '73 2,000; Vol. 2 '65 2,000, '66 1,500, '74 1,500; Vol. 3 '65 2,000, '66 1,500, '75 1,500, 1890 single volume edition 1,250

1865   *Free and Open Worship in the Parish Churches of England*   Macmillan 750 + 250, 1866 500

1865   *Music in Churches. A Sermon preached in St John's Church Leicester at a Festival of the Church Choral Association*   Macmillan 500

1865   *Life's Work and God's Discipline. Three Sermons preached Before the University of Cambridge in April and May 1865*   Macmillan 1,500 + 750, 1873 2,000

1865   *Voices of the Prophets on Faith, Prayer and Human Life*   Strahan & Hutchinson & Co. reprinted 10 times.

1865   *Plain Words on Christian Living*   Strahan

1866   *Christ the Light of the World*   Strahan

1866   *Characteristics of Christ's Teaching, drawn from the Sermon On the Mount*   Strahan   6ᵗʰ edition 1874

1866   *The Wholesome Words of Jesus Christ: Four Sermons preached before the University of Cambridge in November 1866*   Macmillan 2,000, 1868 2,000

1867   *The Hand and the Scroll: On the Sudden Death of the Mayor of Doncaster*

1867   *Twelve Discourses on Subjects connected with the Liturgy & Worship of the Church of England*   Macmillan 1,500, 1873 1,250

1867   Communion leaflet   Macmillan 500

1868   *Foes of Faith: Four Sermons preached before the University of Cambridge in November 1868*   Macmillan 2,500, 1873 2,000

1868   *Prospects of the Church of England: A Sermon preached on The Occasion of the first Offertory in lieu of a Church-rate*

1869   *Lessons of the Cross & Passion: Six Lectures delivered during the week before Easter 1869 in Hereford Cathedral*
        Macmillan 2,500

1869   *Last Words in the Parish Church of Doncaster*   Strahan

Master of the Temple 1869 - 94

1869   *An Inaugural Sermon preached in the Church of the Temple November 7. 1869*   Macmillan 500

1869   *Christ the Precentor of the Congregation: A Sermon.*

1869   *Progress the Condition of Permanence: A Commemoration Sermon*

1870   *St Paul's Epistle to the Ephesians in Greek*

1870   *Christ satisfying the Instincts of Humanity: Eight Lectures delivered in the Temple Church Lent 1870*   Macmillan 2,500, 1873 2,000

1870   *Counsels for Young Students: Three Sermons preached at Cambridge University at the beginning of the academical years 1870-71*   Macmillan 2,500

1870   *Incompleteness a mark of true work: a Commemoration Sermon*

1871   *Family Prayers*   Strahan 8,000 printed by 1872

1871   *Half-hours in the Temple Church*

1871   *Sundays in the Temple*

1872   *The Book of Light in the Hand of Love. A Plea for the British and Foreign Bible Society: A Sermon*   Longmans

1872   *The Two great Temptations – the Temptation of Man and the Temptation of Christ: Lectures delivered in Lent 1872*
        Macmillan 2,500, 1875 2,000

1872   *The Presence of God in his Temple*   Hutchinson & Co

1872   *The Ministerial Victory and its Explanation: a Sermon preached at the General Ordination of the Lord Bishop of Rochester Sept 29 1872*

1872   *The Boy King's Choice of Wisdom : A Sermon preached at St Olave's School on its 301st Anniversary*   Macmillan 500

1872   *Things new and old: a Sermon preached at the re-opening of the Chapel of Rugby School ... July 21, 1872*   Macmillan 250

1872   *Eight Months on Duty: diary of a young officer in Chanzy's army.* From the French of Roger de M with a preface by C.J. Vaughan

1873 *The Young Life equipping itself for God's Service: Four Sermons preached before the University of Cambridge, October and November 1872* re-issued by Macmillan 1876

1873 *The Father of Lights. A Sermon.* Rivington

1873 *Forget thine own People: an Appeal to the Home Church for Foreign Missions. Three lectures delivered in the Temple Church in the season of Advent*

1874 *Thoughts for these Times: University Sermons*

1874 *The Solidity of True Religion; and other Sermons preached in London during the General Election and Mission Week February 1874* re-issued by Macmillan 1876

1874 *Lay Help: a Sermon preached before the Association of Lay Helpers in the Diocese of London*

1874 *Words of Hope from the Pulpit of the Temple Church* re-issued by Macmillan 1876

1875 *Earnest Words for Earnest Men; or, The Gospel and the Pilgrimage*

1875 *The Lord's Prayer* re-issued by Macmillan 1879

1875 *Words from the Cross: Lent Lectures 1875* Macmillan 2,500

1875 *Useful to Christ: a Sermon preached at the re-opening of the Parish Church of Monkwearmouth, May 20 1875*

1875 *Consecration of the Temple Church. Sermons preached at its 700th Anniversary by the Archbishop of Canterbury, Alfred Ainger & C.J. Vaughan*

1875 *Addresses to Young Clergymen delivered at Salisbury* Macmillan 2,500

1876 *Heroes of Faith: Lectures on the 11th Chapter of the Epistle to the Hebrews.* Macmillan 2,500, 1876 2,000

1876 (ed.) *On Some Ministerial Duties: Catechising, Preaching, etc, by the late Archdeacon Bather* Macmillan

1878 *"My Son, give me thine Heart": Sermons preached before the Universities of Oxford and Cambridge 1876-78* Macmillan 2,500

1879 *Counsel & Might: prayers and meditations adapted from sermons by C.J. Vaughan* compiled by R.N.C. L.J. Nisbet & Co

1879 – 1897 Dean of Llandaff

1880 *Rest Awhile: Addresses to Toilers in the Ministry delivered at Charterhouse in Sept 1879* Macmillan 2,000

1880 *The Family Prayer & Sermon Book* 2 vols. Strahan

1881   *A Funeral Sermon for A.P. Stanley preached in Westminster Abbey on Sunday afternoon, July 24, 1881*   Macmillan 600

1881   *Temple Sermons*   Macmillan 2,500

1882   *Records of a Meeting at Cambridge, September, 1882*

1882   *The Lost Coin: A Sermon* in The Clerical Library Vol. *Expository Sermons on the N.T.*

1882   *St Paul's Prayer & the Answer: A Sermon* in The Clerical Library Vol. *Expository Sermons on the N.T.*

1882   *Authorized or Revised? Sermons on some of the text in which The RV differs from the AV*   Macmillan 2,500

1885   *St Paul's Epistle to the Philippians in Greek with translation, paraphrase , and notes*   Macmillan 1,250

1885   *The Idolatry of Tradition: a Sermon*   printed privately

1885   (ed.) *The School of Life: seven addresses delivered during the London Mission 1885 in St Paul's Church Knightsbridge to Public School men by late and present headmasters*   Rivington

1885   *Memorials of a Meeting at Oxford, September 1885*

1886   *Lessons of the Cross & Passion* [composite edition of four Collections of Lenten Addresses published earlier]   Macmillan

1888   *Addresses given in Pembroke College Chapel Cambridge Sept 11-14 1888*   printed privately

1888   *University Sermons new and old: a Selection of Sermons Preached before the Universities of Oxford and Cambridge, 1861-1887*   Macmillan 2,000

1889   *The Perennial Altar Fire: A Sermon*   Spottiswoode

1890   *The Epistle to the Hebrews in Greek with Notes*   Macmillan

1890   *Church of the First Days. Lectures on the Acts*   New Composite Edition Macmillan 2,000

1891   *The Prayers of Jesus Christ: A closing series of Lent Lectures delivered in the Temple Church*   Macmillan 1,500

1891   *Lessons of Life and Godliness, and Words from the Gospels: two Selections of Sermons preached in the Parish Church of Doncaster*   New Edition Macmillan 1,250

1892   *The Faith and the Bible: a Sermon preached in the Temple Church*   Macmillan

1892   *The sympathy of Jesus Christ with sickness and sorrow: a Sermon preached on January 24, 1892, being the Sunday after the funeral of HRH Prince Albert Victor, Duke of Clarence*   Macmillan

1893   *Sermons and Addresses delivered in the Chapel of Trinity College Cambridge at a Gathering of Former Students for Holy Orders August 29-31 1893*   printed privately

1893   *Restful Thoughts in Restless Times: Sermons delivered in Llandaff Cathedral and the Temple Church*   Macmillan 1,500, 1894 1,500

1893   *Substance of a Speech delivered at a Meeting in Cardiff on Tuesday April 4, 1893 on the subject of the Welsh Church Suspensory Bill*

1894   *Last Words in the Temple Church*   Macmillan 2,000

1895   *When I Awake: a Sermon preached in Llandaff Cathedral on 3 March 1895*   William Lewis Cardiff

1895   *The Festival Life: a Sermon preached in Llandaff Cathedral on Easter Day 1895*   William Lewis Cardiff

1897   *University and other Sermons. 2nd Series . With a Preface by an old Friend and Pupil*   Macmillan 1,000

In 1894 SPCK re-published nine of Vaughan's books in a small, cheap 8vo format 'under the direction of the Tract Committee.' These were:

Characteristics of Christ's Teaching
Christ the Light of the World
Earnest Words for earnest Men
Half-hours in the Temple Church
Last Words in the Parish Church of Doncaster
Plain Words on Christian Living
Sundays in the Temple
The Presence of God in His Temple
Voices of the Prophets on Faith, Prayer & Human Life

APPENDIX 3

Vaughan's 'Doves' who became Bishops

With Vaughan	Consecrated Bishop
1868	G.C. Fisher Bp Suffragan of Ipswich 1899
	H.W. Yeatman-Biggs Bp of Southwark 1891, Worcester 1905 & Coventry 1918
	C.H. Turner Bp Suffragan of Islington 1898
	Hon E.C. Glyn Bp of Peterborough 1897
1870	H.H. Montgomery Bp of Tasmania 1889
1872	R.T. Davidson Bp of Winchester 1895, Archbishop of Canterbury 1903
1873	J.N. Quirk Bp Suffragan of Jarrow 1914
	Sir E. Hoskyns Bart. Bp Suffragan of Burnley 1901, Bp of Southwell 1904
1878	A.G. Rawstorne Bp Suffragan of Whalley 1909
1881	A.H. Baynes Assistant Bp of Birmingham
1883	H.E. Jones Bp Suffragan of Lewes 1914
	E.A. Parry Bp of Guyana 1900 & Archbishop of the West Indies 1917
1885	P.H. Eliot Bp Suffragan of Buckingham 1921
1886	C. Wilson Bp of Bunbury (W. Australia) 1904
1887	J.C. Hill Bp Suffragan of Hulme 1924
1888	J.H. Greig Bp of Guildford 1927
1889	L.J. White-Thomson Bp of Ely 1924
1892	H.M. Hordern Bp Suffragan of Lewes 1929

The first 'doves' who received preferment were

1863	G. Austen who became Chancellor of York Minster
	W.J. Lawrence Dean of St Albans
1864	W.R.W. Stephens Dean of Winchester

The last one to become a cathedral dignitary was

1895	R.L. White Dean of Maritzburg (S. Africa)

Other notable 'doves' were

1888	D. Jenks Director of S.S.M. Kelham
1890	H.L. Goudge Regius Professor of Divinity, Oxford

REFERENCES

Childhood in Leicester and a Father's Influence

1. W. Munk — *The Life of Sir Henry Halford, Bart.* p. 4
2. Leicester R.O. — DE1057/5 letter dated 6 Sept 1844
3. quoted in J.C. Hughes — *Walking in an Air of Glory* p. 23f in *Leicester Cathedral Quarterly* Vol. 5 No 7 July 1966
4. J.V. Morgan ed. — *Welsh Politicians & Educators in the Victorian Era p. 409*
5. All Souls College — Vaughan MS D6/1
6. *ibid* — Vaughan MS D6/2
7. *ibid* — Vaughan MS D6/3
8. C.E. Vaughan — *South Wales & Monmouthshire University College Magazine* Vol. 6. No. 3 June 1894
9. *The American Papers of Sir Charles Richard Vaughan* 27 Feb 1826
10. W. White — *History, Gazeteer and Directory of Leicestershire* p. 79
11. *ibid* — p. 88
12. Leic. R.O. — DE1564/1406 St Martin's Vestry Minute Book 1782-1824
13. E. Stock — *History of CMS* Vol. 1 p. 112
14. A.T. Patterson — *Radical Leicester* p. 161
15. *The Baptist Reporter for 1838* p. 10
16. quoted in Hughes — *op. cit.* p. 20f
17. quoted in T.Y. Cocks — *Historical Biographies* p. 60 1976
18. E.T. Vaughan — *God the Doer of all Things* p. 2 2nd ed 1824
19. *ibid* — p. iii
20. F. Merewether — *The rational Creature, the Moral Instrument of His Creator* p. 6
21. J. Owen — *Strictures on the Rev E.T. Vaughan's Sermon entitled God the Doer of all Things* p. 15
22. Hughes — *op. cit.* p. 21
23. *ibid*
24. A.T. Patterson — *op. cit.* p. 161
25. *The Gentleman's Magazine* Vol. 88 ii p. 348
26. Hughes — *op. cit.* p. 22
27. C.J. Vaughan — *Personality of the Tempter & other Sermons* p. 186
28. *Leicester Journal* 2 Oct 1829
29. *ibid*
30. *Leicester Chronicle* 3 Oct 1829
31. *The Gentleman's Magazine* Vol. 99 July-Dec 1829 p. 378
32. *The Leicester Chronicle* 10 Oct 1829
33. Hughes — *op. cit.* p. 26
34. Munk — *op. cit.* p. 15

35. E.T. Vaughan   *Expository Sermons* 1843 p.iii-iv
36. *ibid*   p. 545f
37. Derbyshire R.O.   D5336/31/214/19 undated
38. *ibid*
39. *ibid*   D5336/31/214/54 8 Oct 1830
40. *ibid*   D5336/2/5/6/4 21 Sept 1840

A Pupil at Rugby – the Master's Disciple

1. R.E. Prothero   *Life and Correspondence of A. P. Stanley* Vol. 1 p. 38
2. *Ibid*   pp. 38-42
3. *ibid*   pp. 103-106
4. A.P. Stanley   *Life of Thomas Arnold DD* p. 107 'Popular Ed.' 1904
5. W.H.D. Rouse   *A History of Rugby School* p. 228
6. A.P. Stanley   *op. cit.* p. 143
7. *ibid*   p. 148f
8. T. Hughes   *Tom Brown's Schooldays* (Oxford ed 1921) p. 151f
9. T. Arnold   *Sermons* Vol. 2 p. 124f
10. W.H.D. Rouse   *op. cit.* p. 258
11. G.T. Fox   *Memoir of Henry Watson Fox* p. 14
12. A.P. Stanley   *op. cit.* p. 92
13. A. Whitridge   *Dr Arnold of Rugby* p. 101
14. All Souls MSS   Vaughan MS D6/4
15. T. Hughes   *op. cit.* p. 221
16. An Old Rugbean   *Recollections of Rugby* p. 99
17. F.H. Doyle   *Reminiscences* p. 48
18. A.J.H. Reeve   *Aspects of the Life of Dr Thomas Arnold* p. 276
19. *ibid*   p. 453
20. L.A. Tollemache   *Old and Odd Memories* p. 126
21. J. Chandos   *Boys Together* p. 157-8
22. A.J.H. Reeve   *op. cit.* p. 233
23. W.R. Freemantle   *Memoir of the Rev Spencer Thornton* p. 7
24. *ibid*   p. 10
25. *ibid*   p. 29
26. *ibid*   p. 33f
27. T. Mackay   *The Reminiscences of Albert Pell* p. 39f
28. Derbyshire R.O.   D5336/3/214/52
29. K. Lake ed.   *Memorials of Dean Lake*   p. vi-vii
30. G.G. Bradley   *My Schooldays from 1830 to 1840* in *19th Century*
                          Vol. XV 1884 p. 465
31. K. Lake ed.   *op. cit.* p. 10
32. A.J. Arbuthnot   *Memories of Rugby and India* p. 35
33. quoted in T Copley   *Black Tom* p. 257
34. Bonamy Price in A.P.Stanley *op. cit.* p. 37
35. C.A. Bristed   *5 Years in an English University* Vol. 1 p. 373

36. K. Lake ed.   *op. cit.* p. 12
37. R.E. Prothero   *op. cit.* p. 87
38. *ibid*   p. 88
39. *ibid*   p. 102f
40. K. Lake   *op. cit.* p. 8
41. A.P. Stanley   *op. cit.* p. 369
42. E.M. Goulburn   *The Book of Rugby School* 1856 p. 63
43. A.J. Arbuthnot   *op. cit.* p. 36
44. A.P. Stanley   *op. cit.* p. 125
45. T Copley   *op. cit.* p. 151
46. E.C. Mack   *Public Schools and British Opinion 1780-1860* p. 269
47. G.G. Bradley   *op. cit.* p. 465
48. A.P. Stanley   *op. cit.* p. 133f
49. R.E. Prothero   *op. cit.* p. 69
50. A.J.H. Reeve   *op. cit.* p. 287
51. A.P. Stanley   *op. cit.* p. 110
52. *ibid*   p. 101
53. K. Lake ed.   *op. cit.* p. 18
54. W.H.D. Rouse   *op. cit.* p. 231
55. R.E. Prothero   *op. cit.* p. 76
56. Gloucester R.O.   D1571/X122 Vaughan Testimonials p. 12
57. *The Rugby Magazine*   No 2 Oct 1835 p. 103f
58. A.P. Stanley   *op. cit.* p. 113
59. *ibid*   p. 118
60. *ibid*   p. 123
61. *ibid*   p. 134
62. *ibid*   p. 137
63. *ibid*   p. 151
64 *ibid*   p. 160f
65. A.J.H. Reeve   *op. cit.* p. 300
66. A.P. Stanley   *op. cit.* p. 175
67. Whitridge   *op. cit.* p. 187
68. quoted in N. Wymer   *Dr Arnold of Rugby* p. 189
69. *ibid*   p. 193

Honours at Trinity College Cambridge

1. J. Smith & C. Stray ed. Cambridge in the 1830s: *The Letters of A.C. Gooden 1831-41* p. 115
2. *ibid*   p. 52
3. *ibid*
4. S. Rothblatt   *The Revolution of the Dons* pp. 198-208
5. J.M.F. Wright   *Alma Mater* Vol. 1 p. 171
6. K. Lake ed.   *op. cit.* p. 156

7. F.R. Hall   *A Letter ... on the defective State of Theological Instruction* p. 5f
8. C. Thirlwall   *A letter to the Rev Thomas Turton ...* p. 6
9. *ibid*   p. 26
10. W. Whewell   *Remarks on some parts of Mr Thirlwall's Letter* p. 20
11. D.A. Winstanley   *Early Victorian Cambridge* p. 390
12. *ibid*   p. 73
13. C. Thirlwall   *op. cit.* p. 60
14. J.P.T. Bury ed.   *Romilly's Cambridge Diary 1832-42* p. 58
15. S. Douglas   *Life of William Whewell* p. 169
16. W. Whewell   *On the Principles of English University Education* p. 112
17. C. Kingsley   *His Letters and Memories of his Life* ed. by his wife p. 18 1895 edition
18. G. Pearson   *The danger of abrogating the Religious Tests* p. 17
19. A. W. Brown   *Recollections of ... Charles Simeon* p. xii
20. *ibid*   p. 52f
21. *ibid*   p. 51
22. quoted in H.C.G. Moule *Charles Simeon* p. 275
23. J.C. Pollock   *A Cambridge Movement* p. 9
24. *ibid*   p. 10f
25. T.T. Perowne   *A Memoir of the Rev T.G. Ragland BD* p. 20f
26. H.D. Rawnsley   *Harvey Goodwin* p. 38
27. C.A. Bristed   *op. cit.* Vol. 2 p. 55f
28. Freeman   *op. cit.* p. 59
29. J.P.T. Bury ed.   *op. cit.* p. 48
30. P. Searby   *History of the University of Cambridge* Vol. 3 p. 641
31. T. Mackay ed.   *Reminiscences of Albert Pell* p. 70
32. C.A. Bristed   *op. cit.* Vol. 1 p. 28
33. *ibid*   Vol. 1 p. 29
34. *ibid*   Vol. 1 p. 164f
35. A.J. Butler   *Life & Letters of William John Butler* p. 6
36 quoted in R. Robson   *Ideas and Institutions of Victorian Britain* p. 326
37. quoted in P. Allen   *The Cambridge Apostles The Early Years* p. 8
38. K. Lake ed.   *op. cit.* p. 155
39. Mrs Cotton ed.   *Memoir of G.E.L. Cotton* p. 8
40. *ibid*   p. 9
41. *ibid*   p. 8f
42. K. Lake   *op. cit.* p. 154
43. *The Rugby Magazine* No 8 July 37 p. 323
44. R.E. Prothero   *op. cit.* Vol. 1 p. 135
45. *ibid*   p. 136
46. *ibid*   p. 137
47. *ibid*

417

48. F.L. Mulhouser ed	*The Correspondence of Arthur Hugh Clough* Vol. 1 p. 26
49. R.E. Prothero	*op. cit.* Vol. 1. p. 173f
50. Cheshire R.O.	DSA 80/1 Letter dated 12th March 1836
51. R.E. Prothero	*op. cit.* p. 180
52. Merivale J.A.	*Autobiography and letters of Charles Merivale Dean of Ely* p. 102
53. BL	Add MS 46,137 f. 234
54. C.J. Vaughan	*An Oration delivered in Trinity College Chapel at the Commemoration 1837: A Hearing and a Reading Age* p. 15f
55. NLW	MS 12877C
56. All Souls College	Vaughan MSS D6/6
57. Gloucester R.O.	D1571/X122 Vaughan Testimonials p. 8
58. C. Stray ed.	*An American in Victorian Cambridge* p. 233f
59. A.P. Stanley	*op. cit.* p. 474f
60. All Souls College	Vaughan MSS D6/5
61. NLW	MS 12877C
62. *ibid*	
63. J.P.T. Bury ed.	*op. cit.* p. 179
64. Bodleian Libraries	MS Eng. lett. d.444 f.3
65. Gloucester R.O.	D1571/X122
66. A.J. Butler	*Life & Letters of Dean Butler* p. 5
67. R.E. Prothero	*op. cit.* Vol. 1 p. 197
68. A.P. Stanley	*op. cit.* p. 453
69. T. Mackay	*op. cit.* p. 257
70. J.V. Morgan ed.	*Welsh Political & Educational Leaders in the Victorian Era* p. 410
71. A.P. Stanley	*op. cit.* p. 572
72. *ibid*	p. 574
73. Bodleian Libraries	MS Eng. lett d.386 ff109-110
74. quoted in Winstanley	*op. cit.* p. 404

Return to Leicester

1. C. Perry	*Clerical Education* p. 9
2. *Leicester Chronicle*	2 October 1841
3. W. White	*op. cit.* p. 81
4. Leicester R.O.	245/50 1-9 Archdeacon's Visitation Papers
5. C. Bridges	*The Christian Ministry* 3rd ed. p. 604
6. S. Best	*Parochial Ministrations* p. 95
7. C.J. Vaughan	*Sermons* p. 329
8. Leicester R.O.	1564/1506 St Martin's Charity School Minute Book
9. *ibid*	
10. *ibid*	1564/1507 St Martin's Charity School Minute Book

11. *ibid*
12. C.J. Vaughan   *op. cit.* p. 102f
13. M. Elliott   Victorian Leicester p. 41
14. *ibid*   p. 92
15. M.B. Young   *Richard Wilton – a forgotten Victorian* p. 53
16. J.P.T. Bury   *op. cit.* p. 202
17. C.J. Vaughan   *op. cit.* p. 163
18. C.J. Vaughan   *op. cit.* p. 96
19. C.J. Vaughan   *Epistle to the Romans* p. xxii (3rd ed.)
20. Leicester R.O.   DE1564/1407 St Martin's Vestry Minute Book
       1826-57

21. *ibid*
22. A.T. Patterson   *Radical Leicester* pp. 327-329 *passim*
23. Leicester R.O.   DE1564/1434 St Martin's Parish Officers Minute Book
24. R.E. Prothero   *op. cit.* Vol. 1 p. 316
25. *ibid*   p. 317
26. Gloucester R.O.   D1571/X122
27. *ibid*   2 Dec 1844
28. *ibid*   Vaughan's Testimonials p. 13
29. *ibid*   p. 13f
30. *ibid*   p. 10
31. Trinity Coll. Library   Blakesley MSS Add MS a.243 13 Sept 1836
32. Gloucester R.O.   D1571/X122 Vaughan's Testimonials p. 4
33. Leicester R.O.   DG24 1062/25 Halford MSS
34. C.J. Vaughan   *op. cit.* p. vi
35. quoted in R. Keene   *Restorations of St Martin's Church Leicester* in
       The Leicestershire Archaeological and Historical
       Society Transactions Vol. XXX 1969-70 p. 58

Harrow – "a great Headmaster"

1. F.D. How   *Six Great Schoolmasters* p. 140
2. F.M. Norman   At School and at Sea p.4
3. HSA   Box R2/7 A1845/1 p. 2
4. *ibid*   p. 18
5. *ibid*   Box R2/7
6. Gloucester R.O.   D1571/X122 8 Feb 1845
7. F.L. Mulhauser   *op. cit.* Vol. 1 p. 142
8. *ibid*   p. 148
9. Derbyshire R.O.   D5336/3/214/222
10. A.J.C. Hare   *The Story of my Life* Vol. 1 p. 214
11. J.G.C. Minchin   *Old Harrow Days* p. 14
12. A.J.C. Hare   *op. cit.* p. 236f
13. J.G.C. Minchin   *op. cit.* p. 19
14. A.J.C. Hare   *op. cit.* p. 241f

15. A. Westcott   *Life & Letters of Brooke Foss Westcott* pp. 103-104
16. G.W.E. Russell   *One Look Back* p. 29
17. E.D. Rendall   *Recollections & Impressions of the Rev John Smith* p. 21
18. H.T. Wood   *Harrow in the 50s* in Cornhill Magazine Vol. 50 Ns p. 396
19. quoted in C. Tyerman   *A History of Harrow School* p. 262
20. H.T. Wood   *op. cit.* pp. 399-401 *passim*
21. Howson E.W. & Warner G.T. *Harrow School* p. 107
22. *ibid*
23. How   *op. cit.* p. 146
24. quoted in J. Chandos   *op. cit.* p. 310
25. Howson & Warner   *op. cit.* p. 113
26. How   *op. cit.* p. 153
27. BL   Add MS 77224 letter dated 11 April 1857
28. L.A. Tollemache   *Old and Odd Memories* p. 118
29. *ibid*   p. 123
30. H. Merivale   *Bar, Stage & Platform* p. 186
31. Howson & Warner   *op. cit.* p. 95
32. H.M. Schueller & R.L. Peters eds. *The Letters of J.A. Symonds* Vol. 1. Letter 27
33. BL   Add MS 77224 letter dated 20 April 1857
34. C.J. Vaughan   *Notes for Lectures on Confirmation* pp. 55, 58
35. Morgan   *op. cit.* p. 415
36. Howson & Warner   *op. cit.* p. 111
37. C.J. Vaughan   *The Indian Sorrow* p. 11
38. *ibid*   p. 16
39. How   *op. cit.* p. 163
40. HSA   Box R2/7 letter dated 11.3.1858
41. E. Graham   *The Harrow Life of Henry Montagu Butler* p. xx
42. P.M. Thornton   *Harrow School and its Surroundings* p. 299
43. L.A. Tollemache   *op. cit.* p. 125f
44. H.M. Butler   *Ten Great and Good Men* p. 283 in *Arnold and other Christian Educators*
45. P. Grosskurth   *John Addington Symonds* p. 306
46. E. Graham   *op. cit.* p. 29
47. H. Merivale   *op. cit.* p. 180
48. *ibid*   p. 198
49. F.R. Cowell   *The Athenaeum. Club and Social Life in London 1824-1974* p.4
50. Mrs Cotton ed.   *op. cit.* p. 61
51. Schueller   *op. cit.* Letter 31
52. BL   Add MS c9146
53. Gloucester R.O.   D1571/X124

54. *ibid*   D1571/X125.
55. C.J. Vaughan   *Foes of Faith* p. 44
56. HSA   Governors Minute Book 3 Feb 1854
57. Hare   *op. cit.* Vol. 1 p. 242
58. Thornton   *op. cit.* p. 299
59. Morgan   *op. cit.* p. 413f
60. Howson & Warner   *op. cit.* p. 109
61. L.A. Tollemache   *op. cit.* pp. 105-110
62. Howson & Warner   *op. cit.* p. 109
63. L.A. Tollemache   *op. cit.* p. 112f
64. Minchin   *op. cit.* p. 106
65. Durham Cath. Lib.   Lightfoot Papers 3.15 3 July 1858
66. BL   Add MS 44389 f. 157-158 16 April 1858
67. Durham Cath. Lib.   Lightfoot Papers 3.23 3 Nov 1858
68. *ibid*   Lightfoot Papers 2.512 15 Nov 1858
69. Gloucester R.O.   D1571/X124
70. *The Life and Letters of Benjamin Jowett* Vol. 1 p. 97 & p. 197
71 Cheshire R.O.   DSA 135
72. BL   Add MS 35793 f. 488, 5.6.1852
73. Tyerman   *op. cit.* p. 265
74. Tollemache   *op. cit.* p. 119f
75. Cheshire R.O.   DSA 135
76. N. Mitford ed.   *The Ladies of Alderley* p. 303
77. N. Mitford ed.   *The Stanleys of Alderley* p. 22
78. *ibid*   p. 23
79. *ibid*   p. 25
80. *ibid*   p. 25f
81. Baron Platt   *Correspondence with Dr Vaughan* p. 4
82. *ibid*   p. 9
83. C.J. Vaughan   *A Letter* p. 9
84. *ibid*
85. *ibid*   p. 12f
86. *ibid*   p. 18
87. Anti-Monitor   *Remarks addressed to The Rev. Dr Vaughan* p. 4
88. *The Times*   April 13th 1854
89. *ibid*   April 15th 1854
90. BL   Add MS 44377 f.94 23 January 1854
91. NLS   MS 25638 f. 84-85
92. C.J. Vaughan   *The Vocation of a Public School* pp. 10-11
93. *ibid*   p. 12
94. Gloucester R.O.   D1571/X124
95. *ibid*   D1571/X125
96. *ibid*
97. *ibid*

98. How	*op. cit.* p. 172
99. Gloucester R.O.	D1571/X127
100. Grosskurth	*op. cit.* p. 36
101. Gloucester R.O.	D1571/X127
102. NLS	MS 25554 f.5
103. *ibid*	f. 9-10
104. Gloucester R.O.	D1571/X127
105. Cheshire R.O.	DSA 135 Letter dated Sept 18 1859
106. *ibid*	Letter dated Sept 27 1859
107. Schueller	*op. cit.* Letter 110
108. Cheshire R.O.	DSA 80/9 Letter dated Sept 21 1859
109. *ibid*	Letter dated Sept 22 1859
110. NLS	MS 25553 f. 20-21
111. *ibid*	MS 25554 f.11-12
112. Graham	*op. cit.* p. 121
113. NLS	MS 25553 f. 13-14
114. HSA	Governors Minute Book 17 Nov 1859
115. NLS	MS 25554 f. 15-16
116. HSA	1 Dec 1859
117. *ibid*	
118. Lambeth Pal. Lib.	Tait Papers Vol. 115 f. 155-158
119. C.J. Vaughan	*Last Words in the Chapel of Harrow School* pp. 12-30 *passim*
120. CJ. Vaughan	University & Other Sermons p. 37
121. *ibid*	p. 50
122. *ibid*	p. 51
123. *The Times*	Dec 7 1859 p. 12
124. *ibid*	
125. *ibid*	
126. NLS	MS 25554 f. 18-20
127. R.W. Moore	*Charles John Vaughan* p. 1

An Allegation of gross Misconduct

1. P. Grosskurth	*The Memoirs of John Addington Symonds* p. 112
2. Schueller	*op. cit.* Vol. 1 *passim*
3. Graham	*op. cit.* p. 29
4. *ibid*	p. 41
5. *ibid*	p. 42
6. D. Newsome	*On the Edge of Paradise. A.C. Benson Diarist* p. 39
7. D. Newsome	*Godliness and Good Learning* p. 84
8. D. Newsome	*On the Edge of Paradise. AC Benson Diarist* p. 81
9. A. Kenny	*The Oxford Diaries of A.H. Clough* p. 173 6 Aug 1841
10. *ibid*	p. 196 8 March 1842
11. *ibid*	p.193 18 Feb 1842

12. *ibid*   p. 197 13 March 1842
13. *ibid*   p. lxiii
14. Graham   *op. cit.* p. xxxviii
15. H.C. Merivale   *op. cit.*   p. 178f
16. *ibid*
17. quoted by C. Tyerman in an unpublished lecture ms at HSA Box R2/7
18. quoted in C. Tyerman *A History of Harrow School* p. 281
19. HSA   Jackson Correspondence
20. NLS   MS 25554 f. 4
21. M. Wagland   *A Matter of Justice* p. 51
22. P. Grosskurth ed.   *The Memoirs*   p. 94
23. *ibid*   p. 97
24. *ibid*   p. 98
25. Schueller   *op. cit.* Letter 64
26. *ibid*   Letter 65
27. J. Connington   *Your Schoolboy Friendships* in *The Rugby
                             Miscellany* 1846
28. Schueller   *op. cit.* Vol. 1 p. 196
29. *ibid*   p. 199
30. *ibid*   Letter 106
31. Grosskurth ed.   *op. cit.* p. 111f
32. Schueller   *op. cit.* Letter 110
33. Wagland   *op. cit.* p. 45
34. Grosskurth ed.   *op. cit.* p. 114
35. NLS   MS 25570 1858 Diary *passim*
36. *ibid*   MS 25571 1859 Diary *passim*
37. *ibid*
38. Graham   *The Harrrow Life of Henry Montagu Butler* p. 190
39. Wagland   *op. cit.* p. 56
40. J. Richards   *'Passing the love of women': manly love and Victorian
                             society* p. 93 in J.A. Mangan & J. Walvin eds.
                             Manliness and Morality
41. O.D.N.B.   Vol. 56 p. 161
42. Wagland   *op. cit.* p. 53
43. A. Pretor   *Ronald & I. Scenes from Life* p. viii

A brief Interlude at Southborough

1. NLS   MS 25554 f. 21-24
2. NLS   MS 25572 1860 Diary 23 Jan
3. A.K. Ashwell & R.G. Wilberforce ed. *Life & Letters of the Rt Revd Samuel
                             Wilberforce* Vol. 2 p. 436
4. P.M. Thornton   *op. cit.* p. 300
5. NLS   MS 25572 17 Feb 1860
6. *ibid*   23 Feb 1860

7. *ibid* 29 Feb 1860
8. N. Mitford ed. The Stanleys *op. cit.* p. 237
9. NLS MS 25553 f. 26
10. BL Add MS a.244.143
11. Cheshire R.O. DSA 134/2
12. NLS MS 25572 16 March 1860
13. *ibid* 15 March 1860
14. C.E. Vaughan *South Wales & Monmouthshire University College Magazine* Vol. VI No. 3 June 1894 p. 4

15. *ibid*
16. Morgan *op. cit.* p. 416f
17. NLS MS 25555 f. 25-27
18. *ibid* MS 25572 2 April 1860
19. *ibid* MS 25554 f. 25-27
20. *ibid*
21. C.J. Vaughan *Epiphany, Lent & Easter* p. 4
22. Lambeth Pal. Lib. Temple Papers MS 4514 ff.30-31, 15.9.1857
23. BL Add MS 44394 ff. 21-22, 11.7.1860
24. Lambeth Pal. Lib. Longley Papers
25. *ibid* MS 2172 f. 73
26. BL Houghton Papers 26.110
27. HSA Jackson Letters 11 Sept 1860
28. Durham Cath. Lib Lightfoot Papers 10.68 9 October 1860
29. BL Houghton Papers 26.111

Doncaster - "Vaughan's Doves"

1. Cheshire R.O. DSA 135 10.8.1860
2. *Doncaster Chronicle* 3 Aug 1860
3. *ibid* 17 Aug 1860
4. NLS MS 25554 f. 28-30
5. Cheshire R.O. DSA 135 5.12.1860
6. NLS MS 25555 f.32
7. *ibid* MS 25554 f. 36
8. *ibid*
9. *ibid* f. 37
10. *ibid* MS 25555 f. 35
11. C.J. Vaughan *Addresses to Young Clergymen* p. xi-xii
12. Durham Cath. Lib. Lightfoot Papers 8.18, 28 Oct 1861
13. *ibid*
14. Cheshire R.O. DSA 135 letter dated 16 Jan - no year stated [1861 or 1862]
15. H.R. Wormald *Modern Doncaster* p. 38
16. NLS MS 25554 f.52-53
17. *ibid* f. 54-57

18. *ibid*   f. 59

19. H.R. Wormald   *op cit.* p. 46

20. quoted in W. Sheardown's Pamphlets Vol. 1. p 289

21. *ibid*   Vol. 3. p 19

22. C.W. Hatfield   *Historical Notes of Doncaster* 2nd Series 1868 p. 447

23. C.J. Vaughan   *Lectures on the Epistle to the Philippians*
                     p. 33 (4th ed.)

24. Morgan ed.   *op. cit.* p. 418

25. G. Swann   *The Doncaster Royal Infirmary 1792-1972* p. 41

26. *ibid*   p. 42

27. BL   Houghton Papers 26. 112

28. *ibid*   26. 113

29. *Doncaster, Nottingham & Lincoln Gazette* 8 May 1863

30. quoted in D.D.W. Mowbray pp. 51-53 from *C.J. Vaughan. Biblical Expositor*

31. E. Royle + R.M. Larsen ed. *Archbishop Thomson's Visitation Returns for the
                     Diocese of York 1865. passim*

32. NLS   MS 25555 f. 64

33. *Gazette*   21 Dec 1866

34. *ibid*   20 Dec 1867

35. F. Keighley   *The Centenary of the Church of St Andrew, Marshgate
                     1867-1967*

36. A. Thrall   *The History of Adult Education in 19th Century
                     Doncaster* p. 39

37. *Gazette*   9 June 1865

38. BL   Add MS 55113 f. 1-2, 28 June 1863

39. *ibid*   f. 5-6, 5 Sept 1863

40. *ibid*   f.10 2 Nov 1863

41. *ibid*

42. *ibid*   f. 13-14, 16 Jan 1864

43. *ibid*   f. 22-23, 17 Nov 1868

44. *ibid*   f.24-25, 19 Nov 1868

45. HSA   letter dated 8 Feb 1865

46. Durham Cath. Lib.   Lightfoot Papers 29 March 1865

47. C.J. Vaughan   *A Primitive Sunday* in *Lectures on the
                     Acts of the Apostles* Vol. 3 Lecture 7

48. C.J. Vaughan   *The Church of the First Days* 1890 edition

49. Camb. Univ. Lib.   MS JRMB M3/1/401

50. C.J. Vaughan   *The Mourning of the Land:A Sermon* pp.10-12 *passim*

51. *Gazette*   30.11.1866

52. C.J. Vaughan   *A Pastoral Retrospect* in *Lectures on the Acts of the
                     Apostles* Vol. 3 Lecture 8

53. F.W.B. Bullock   *History of Training for the Ministry of the Church. of
                     England* p. 118

54. F.D. How   *Six great Schoolmasters* p. 176

55. *ibid*
56. M. Butler   *He served his Generation* p. 14f
57. *Church Times*   22 Oct 1897 Obituary of C.J. Vaughan
58. Durham Cath. Lib.   Lightfoot Papers 10.150, 1 Feb 1866
59. Camb. Univ. Lib.   Add MS 6260/5
60. *ibid*   /12
61. *ibid*   /14
62. *ibid*
63. *ibid*   /19
64. *ibid*   /75
65. *ibid*   /77
66. Borthwick Institute   Lic.C.Reg.1 1848-62 & Reg.2 1863-73 passim
67. *ibid*   Ord.P.1866, Russell, Henry Charles (deacon)
68. Camb. Univ. Lib.   Add MSS 6260 / 17
69. Church Congress Report 1879 p. 538
70. Lambeth Pal. Lib.   Tait Papers Vol. 79 f. 319
71. K. Lake ed.   *op.cit.* p. 204
72. Mowbray   *op. cit.* p. 42
73. *ibid*
74. Lake   *op. cit.* p. 205f
75. Durham Cath. Lib.   Lightfoot Papers 17.23x, 12 March 1866
76. NLS   MS 25555 f. 79-80
77. Lambeth Pal. Lib.   Tait Papers Vol. 83 f. 285
78. BL   Althorp Papers Add MS 77224
79. Bodleian Libraries   MS Eng. Hist. c.961
80. C.J. Vaughan   *Last Words at Doncaster* p. 36f
81. G.W.E. Russell   *One Look Back* pp. 54-56
82. Thrall   *op. cit.* p. 48
83. BL   Add MS 44420 f. 191
84. *ibid*   f. 210
85. Cheshire R.O.   DSA 135 30 June 1869
86. *Doncaster Chronicle* 2 July 1869
87. Durham Cath. Lib.   Lightfoot Papers 2.80, 22 July 1869
88. Lambeth Pal. Lib.   MSS 2146 f. 140, 14 Aug 1869
89. Morgan ed.   *op. cit.* p.422
90. *ibid*   p. 423
91. F. Pigou   *Phases of my Life* p. 256
92. *ibid*   p. 255
93. C.J. Vaughan   *op. cit.* pp. 246-248
94. BL   Add MS 55113 f.28, 22 Sept 1869
95. W. Sheardown   in Sheardown Pamphlets Vol. 2 p. 715f

Master of the Temple - a Popular Preacher

1. T.H. Bayliss   *The Temple Church* p. 48

2. D. Lewer & R. Dark   *The Temple Church in London*   p. 62
3. *ibid*   p. 109
4. *ibid*
5. *ibid*   p. 111
6. C.E.A. Bedwell   *The Temple Church* p. 76 in *C.Q.R.* 1912
7. E. Sichel   *Life & Letters of Alfred Ainger* p. 103
8. L.A. Tollemache   *op. cit.* p. 132f
9. C.J. Vaughan   *An inaugural Sermon* p. 11 + p.13
10. D.C. Lathbury ed.   *Correspondence on Church and Religion of W. E. Gladstone* Vol. 1 p. 202
11. Middle Temple MSS   347 1873 *Memorandum . . .*
12. Leicester R.O.   Pamphlet Box 8a p. 121
13. BL   Add MS 55113 ff. 29-30, 30 Dec 1869
14. *ibid*   f. 49, 27 March 1876
15. Roger de M   *Eight Months on Duty* p .ix
16. *Vanity Fair*   24 Aug 1872 p. 63
17. *The Record*   22 Oct 1897 p. 1064
18. Bayliss   *op. cit.* p. 51
19. Camb. Univ. Lib.   Add MS 6581 251
20. S. Newth   *Lectures on Bible Revision* p. 125
21. BL   Add MS 55113 f.78f
22. *ibid*   Add MS b 66.262 4 Aug 1890
23. A.C. Benson   *Life of Edward White Benson* Vol. 1 p. 326
24. *ibid*   Vol. 2 p. 580
25. *Morning Post*   29 Oct 1869
26. Lambeth Pal. Lib.   Davidson Papers   Vol. 2 f. 77, 30 Oct 1871
27. G.K.A. Bell   *Randall Davidson* p. 29 (3rd ed.)
28. *ibid*
29. *ibid*   p. 28f
30. *ibid*   p. 32
31. Lambeth Pal. Lib.   Davidson Papers Vol. 2 f. 84
32. L.E. Elliott-Binns   *Religion in the Victorian Era*   p. 455
33. F.G. Bettany   *Stewart Headlam: A Biography*   p. 25
34. *ibid*   p. 43
35. *ibid*   p. 73
36. *ibid*   p. 30
37. M. Montgomery   *Bishop Montgomery: A Memoir*   p. 5
38. *ibid*   p. 15f
39. Lambeth Pal. Lib.   Benson Papers Vol. 81 ff. 209f
40. M. Montgomery   *op. cit.* p. 28f
41. *ibid*   p. 104
42. C.E. Tyndale-Biscoe   Tyndale-Biscoe of Kashmir: An Autobiography p.37
43. Durham Cath. Lib.   Lightfoot Papers 7.42, 2 June 1875
44. *ibid*   1.314, 2 Oct 1875

45. C.J. Vaughan   *Addresses to Young Clergymen* p. 131f
46. Lambeth Pal. Lib.   Tait Papers Vol. 281 ff. 128f
47. *ibid*   ff. 130f
48. *ibid*   ff. 132f
49. D. Lewer   *A Spiritual Song* p. 179f
50. R. Roxburgh ed.   Black *Books of Lincoln's Inn* Vol. 5 1845-1914 p. 187
51. Lewer   *op. cit.* p 130
52. P. Hammond   *Dean Stanley of Westminster* p. 157
53. NLS   MS 25555 f. 93-94
54. *ibid*   f. 95
55. *ibid*   f. 105
56. *ibid*   f. 102
57. G.G. Coulton   *Fourscore Years* p. 143
58. O. Sitwell   *Two Generations* p. 288f
59. *ibid*   p. 290f
60. A.C. Harman   *Dean Vaughan and his Men* in *Theology*
                           August 1937 p. 110
61. Merivale   *op. cit.* p. 181
62. G.W.E. Russell   *op. cit.* p. 221
63. Durham Cath. Lib.   Lightfoot Papers 15.21, 25 Jan 1879
64. *ibid*   15.24,
65. *ibid*   20.72, 3 Feb 1883
66. Lambeth Pal. Lib.   Davidson Papers Vol. 3 f. 43
67. *ibid*   Vol. 522 f. 61, 11 May 1883
68. R. Farrar   *The Life of Frederick William Farrar* p. 122f
69. *ibid*   p. 202
70. *ibid*   p. 214f
71. *ibid*   p. 220
72. *ibid*   p. 230
73. BL   Add MS 44449 ff. 281-283, 21 April 1876
74. Lambeth Pal. Lib.   Davidson Papers Vol. 522 f. 77, 23 Sept 1889
75. BL   Althorp Papers Add MS 77224 29 Dec 1857
76. *ibid*   5 April 1857
77. *ibid*   8 Jan 1869
78. *ibid*   30 Aug 1871
79. *ibid*   March 1878
80. Bodleian Libraries   MS Eng. lett. d.444 f. 5
81. *ibid*   f. 8
82. Lambeth Pal. Lib.   Davidson Papers Vol. 2 f. 108
83. *ibid*   f. 136
84. *ibid*   Add MS 44450 f. 87, 18 May 1876
85. *ibid*   Add MS 44459 ff. 144-150
86. HSA   Jackson Letters 9 April 1879

Dean of Llandaff – the twilight Years

1. quoted in Llandaff Cathedral 38th Annual Report p. 12
2. *ibid*
3. Lake   *op. cit.* p. 239
4. J.B. Hilling   *Llandaf Past and Present* p. 83
5. *Church of England Magazine* 31 March 1843
6. *ibid*
7. E.J. Newell   *Diocesan Histories: Llandaff* p. 226f
8. *Cardiff Times & South Wales Weekly* 15 April 1879
9. Church Congress Report 1879 pp. 536-537
10. *ibid*   p. 537
11. quoted in the *Western Mail* 16 Oct 1897
12. W.R. Compton-Davies *Historical & Pictorial Glimpses of Llandaff Cathedral* p. 75
13. *ibid*
14. R.E. Prothero   *op. cit.* Vol. 2 p. 569
15. *ibid*
16. Lambeth Pal. Lib.   Davidson Papers Vol. 522 ff. 56f, 23 July 1881
17. Cheshire R.O.   DSA 80/15
18. *ibid*
19. HSA   Jackson Letters
20. *ibid*
21. Bodleian Libraries   Ms Eng. lett. d.444 ff. 18-20
22. J.V. Morgan   *The Church in Wales in the Light of History* p. 82
23. A.H. Trow & D.J.A. Brown *A Short History of the University College of South Wales & Monmouthshire 1883-1933* p. 14
24. K.V. Jones   *Life of John Viriamu Jones* p. 105f
25. *ibid*   p. 125
26. *ibid*   p. 190f
27. *ibid*   p. 191
28. *ibid*   p. 116f
29. NLW   MS 21958D Letter 12
30. *ibid*   Letter 14
31. *Western Mail*   4 Nov 1885
32. J.G. Jones   *Dean Charles Vaughan, A.J. Williams and the Disestablishment Debate* p. 58 in *The Journal of Welsh Religious History* Vol. 8, 2000
33. *South Wales Daily News* 23 June 1892
34. Lambeth Pal. Lib.   Benson Papers Vol. 121 f. 128
35. *ibid*   Vol. 120 f. 125
36. Lambeth Pal. Lib.   Davidson Papers Vol. 522 ff. 70-72, 6 March 1889
37. R. Dudley ed.   *Harrow A Portrait of an English School* p.198
38. G.G. Coulton   *Fourscore Years: An Autobiography* pp. 143-145 *passim*

39. *ibid*	p. 166
40. J.H. Greig	*Dean Vaughan and his "Doves"* in *The Treasury*, Vol. XI p. 301f
41. A.C. Harman	*Dean Vaughan and His Men* in *Theology* August 1937
42. G.G. Coulton	*op. cit.* p. 149
43. A.C. Harman	*op. cit.* pp. 106-109 *passim*
44. *ibid*	p. 110f
45. B. Jones	*Canton* p. 20
46. Bodleian Libraries	MS Eng. lett. 2284 f. 14f
47. *ibid*	f. 20
48. Durham Cath. Lib.	Lightfoot Papers 5.103, 9 Oct 1885
49. Lambeth Pal. Lib.	Davidson Papers Vol. 522 ff. 62f, 9 Feb 1888
50. *ibid*	f. 84, 14 Jan 1890
51. *ibid*	
52. *ibid*	
53. BL	Add MS 44510 f. 108
54. A. Westcott	*Life & Letters of B.F. Westcott* Vol. 2 p. 148
55. *ibid*	p. 149
56. Lambeth Pal. Lib.	Davidson Papers Vol. 522 ff. 105-106, 27 Sept 1890
57. NLW	MS 8543C
58. Lambeth Pal. Lib.	Davidson Papers Vol. 522 ff. 110f, 27 Nov 1890
59. *ibid*	Vol. 4 f. 97
60. Lake	*op. cit.* p. 311
61. R.H. Benson	*Confessions of a Convert* pp. 23-25
62. Lambeth Pal. Lib.	Davidson Papers Vol. 522 f. 65, 18 March 1881
63. Lambeth Pal. Lib.	Benson Papers Vol. 120 f. 390, 1 Jan 1894
64. NLS	MS25555 f. 135-136
65. *ibid*	f. 139
66. *ibid*	f. 140
67. *ibid*	f. 142
68. Lewer	*op. cit.* p. 202

"Going down hill steadily but with pauses"

1. Middle Temple MSS	354 1894/95
2. Lewer	*op. cit.* p. 202
3. BL	Add MS 51279 f. 197
4. *Western Mail*	23 May 1894
5. J.R.M. Butler	*Henry Montagu Butler: A Memoir* p. 145
6. HSA	Box R2/7
7. Lake	*op. cit.* p. 319f
8. NLS	MS 25555 f. 165
9. *ibid*	f. 168
10. *Advent Record*	p. 3
11. Lambeth Pal. Lib.	Davidson Papers Vol. 522 ff. 114f, 9 Nov 1895

12. *The Guardian*   18 Dec 1895
13. Cardiff Town Council Minutes 13/1 and 21/1 *passim*
14. Ll. Cath. Archives   Coombs Letters
15. *ibid*
16. *ibid*
17. quoted in Mowbray   p. 36
18. *ibid*   p. 54
19. Ll. Cath. Archives   Coombs Letters
20. Mowbray   *op. cit.* p. 48
21. *ibid*
22. *ibid*   p. 49
23. Bodleian Libraries   MS Eng. lett. 2284 f. 20
24. *ibid*   f. 24
25. *ibid*   f. 30f
26. *ibid*   f. 32f
27. *ibid*   f. 34
28. *ibid*   f. 36f
29. *ibid*   f. 39f
30. *ibid*   f. 41f
31. NLW   MS 21958D Letter 20
32. Lambeth Pal. Lib.   Davidson Papers Vol. 522 ff. 118-119, 10 June 1896
33. Mowbray   *op. cit.* p. 51
34. Ll. Cath. Archives   Coombs Letters
35. NLW   MS 21958D Letter 24
36. *ibid*   Letter 26
37. NLS   MS 25555 f. 177
38. *ibid*   f. 179
39. *ibid*   f. 181
40. Lambeth Pal. Lib.   Davidson Papers Vol. 522 ff. 120f, 12 Nov 1896
41. *ibid*   f. 123, 29 Nov 1896
42. R.L. White   Centenary Sermon p. 12 in R.W. Mooore
                            Charles John Vaughan
43. NLW   MS 21958D Letter 27
44. Ll. Cath. Archives   Coombs Letters
45. NLS   MS 25630 ff. 20-21 .
46. BL   Add MS 55113, 156-158, 6 Jan 1897
47. *ibid*   ff. 159-160, 8 Jan 1897
48. *ibid*   f. 161, 18 Jan 1897
49. Ll. Cath. Archives   Coombs Letters
50. Lake   *op. cit.* p. 323
51. BL   Add MS 55113 ff. 162-163, 20 May 1897
52. *ibid*   Add MS 55454 f. 731
53. quoted in *The Record* 22 Oct 1897
54. E. Graham   The *Harrow Life of Henry Montagu Butler* p. 394f

55. *The Guardian*   10 Aug 1897
56. BL   Add MS 55113 f.164, 10 Aug 1897
57. *ibid*   ff. 166-167
58. Lake   *op. cit.* p. 324f
59. White   *op. cit.* p. 11f
60. NLS   MS 25555 f. 185
61. Lambeth Pal. Lib.   Davidson Papers Vol. 50 ff.239-240, 15 Oct 1897
62. *ibid*
63. *Church Times*   22 Oct 1897
64. NLS   MS 25555 f. 193
65. *ibid*   f. 189
66. *ibid*   f. 187
67. *ibid*   f. 191-192
68. C.J. Vaughan   *University and other Sermons 2nd Series* p. ix-x
69. NLS   MS 25555 f. 193-195
70. *ibid*   f. 196-197
71. *ibid*
72. BL   Add MS 55113 f. 176
73. NLS   MS 25555 f. 202-203
74. *ibid*
75. *ibid*   f. 204
76. Bodleian Libraries   MS Autogr. b. 8 f. 1565
77. Cheshire R.O.   DSA 135 includes a typed copy
78. NLS   MS 25612 1899 Journal
79. *Surrey Advertiser*   5 Aug 1899

An Assessment

1. *Church Times*   22 Oct 1897
2. *ibid*
3. *The Times*   18 Oct 1897 p. 9
4. *Pall Mall Gazette*   16 Oct 1897
5. *ibid*
6. *ibid*
7. *Illustrated London News* 23 Oct 1897
8. *ibid*
9. C.E. Vaughan   *South Wales & Monmouthshire University College Magazine* Vol. X No.1 Dec 1897 p. 4
10. Leicester R.O.   Pamphlet Box 8a The Rev C.J. Vaughan D.D.
11. *Weekly Mail*   23 Oct 1897 p. 2
12. L.A.Tollemache   *op. cit.* p. 124
13. Howson & Warner   *op. cit.* p. 114
14. A.C. Benson   *op. cit.* Vol. 2 p. 559
15. quoted in J.V. Morgan *A Study in Nationality* p. 506 (2nd ed. 1912)
16. J.G. Lockhart   *Cosmo Gordon Lang* pp. 52, 63

17. G.W.E. Russell   *Dr. Liddon* p. 113
18. White   *op. cit.* p. 11f
19. J.R.M. Butler   *op. cit.* p. 126f
20. *The Times*   8 Nov 1897
21. quoted in *The Record* 22 Oct 1897
22. White   *op. cit.* p 11
23. R.R. Williams   *The Word of Life* p. 5
24. *ibid*   p. 47
25. *Pall Mall Gazette* 16 Oct 1897
26. quoted in Mowbray   *op. cit.* p. 53
27. *The Record*   22 Oct 97 p. 1073
28. quoted in Mowbray   *op. cit.* p.54
29. *ibid*   p. 36
30. *ibid*   p. 54
31. A. Westcott   *op. cit.* Vol. 2 p. 224
32. Records of a Meeting at Doncaster of Dean Vaughan's Men p. 4
33. F. D. How   *op. cit.* p. 177
34. R.R. Williams   *A Neglected Victorian Divine* in the C.Q.R.
                         No 310 Vol. CLIV p. 84f
35. Mowbray   *op. cit.* p. 467
36. *ibid*   p. 475
37. C.E. Vaughan   *South Wales & Monmouthshire University College
                         Magazine* Vol. VI No. 3 June 1894 p. 5
38. *Church Times*   22 Oct 1897

Bibliography

Primary MSS Sources

Bodleian Libraries, University of Oxford: Halford & Halsey Papers
Bristol University Library: MSS DPI 188-189 Letters of J.A. Symonds
British Library: Add MSS Lord Althorp, W.E. Gladstone, 1st Baron
Houghton & Macmillan Papers
Cambridge University Library: Taylor MSS
Cheshire Record Office: Stanley Papers 1828-1861 DSA 80
Derbyshire Record Office: Pares Papers
Durham Cathedral Library: Lightfoot Papers
Gloucester Record Office: Soberon-Estcourt Papers
Harrow School Archives: Governors Minute Books & Jackson Papers
Lambeth Palace Library: Benson, Davidson, Longley, & Tait Papers
Leicestershire, Leicester & Rutland Record Office: Halford & Pares
Papers, Registers of St Martin's Parish & Vestry Minute Books
Llandaff Cathedral Archives: Coombs Papers
London Library: MS *Memoirs* of J.A. Symonds
All Souls College Oxford: Sir Charles Vaughan Papers
Middle Temple Archives MSS 347 1873 & 354 1894/5
National Library of Scotland: New Hailes MSS (Dalrymple Papers)
National Library of Wales: A.P. Stanley Papers; Alfred Thomas Papers
Borthwick Institute York: Archbishop of York's Registers

19th Century Newspapers

Cardiff Times & South Wales Weekly
Doncaster, Nottingham & Lincoln Gazette; and *Doncaster Chronicle*
Leicester Chronicle; and *Leicester Journal*
Western Mail
Obituaries in *The Times, The Telegraph, The Western Mail, The Church Times, The Guardian, The Record, The Illustrated London News, Pall Mall Gazette, South Wales & Monmouthshire University College Magazine, The Westminster Budget* and *New York Times.*

Journals

Church Quarterly Review; Cornhill Magazine; 19th Century; Gentleman's Magazine; Good Words; South Wales & Monmouthshire University College Magazine; Theology; The Treasury; Victorian Studies; Welsh Journal of Religious History

Secondary Published Works

Rugby

Arbuthnot A.J.	Memories of Rugby and India	1910
	An Old RugbeanSchooldays from 1830-1840 in *19th Century* XV pp. 455-474	1884
Bamford T.W.	Thomas Arnold	1960
Bradley G.G.	My Recollections of Rugby	1848
Chandos J.	Boys Together	1984
Clough A.H.	Poems & Prose Remains with selected	
	Letters & a memoir ed. by his wife Vol.1	1869
Copley T.	Black Tom	2002
Evers C.R.	Rugby	1939
Fox G.T.	Memoir of Henry Watson Fox	1850
Freemantle W.R.	Memoir of the Rev Spencer Thornton	1850
Gathorne-Hardy J.	The Old School Tie	1978
Goulburn E.M.	The Book of Rugby School	1856
Hammond P.	Dean Stanley of Westminster	1987
Honey J.R. de S.	Tom Brown's Universe	1977
Hughes T.	Tom Brown's Schooldays	1856
Kenny A	Arthur Hugh Clough A Poet's Life	2005
Lake K. ed.	Memorials of William Charles Lake	1901
Lake W.C.	Rugby & Oxford 1830-1850 in	
	Good Words pp. 666-670	1895
Mackay T.	Reminiscences of Albert Pell: Sometime	
	MP for South Leicestershire	1908
Minchin J.G.C.	Our Public Schools	1901
Mullhauser F.L.	The Correspondence of A.H. Clough	1957
Prothero R.E.	The Life and Correspondence of	
+ G.G. Bradley	Arthur Penrhyn Stanley 2 Volumes	1893
Rouse W.H.D.	A History of Rugby School	1898
Rugby Miscellany		1846
Rugby School Magazine 2 vols.		1835 & 1836
Stanley A.P.	The Life of Thomas Arnold DD	1844
Wait W.O.	Rugby Past and Present	1893
Whitridge A.	Dr Arnold of Rugby	1928
Witheridge J.	Excellent Dr Stanley	2013
Woodward F.J.	The Doctor's Disciples	1954
Wymer N.	Dr Arnold of Rugby	1953

Cambridge

Bristed C.A.	Five Years at an English University	1854
	Reprinted as 'An American in Victorian Cambridge' ed. Stray C.	2009
Brown A.W.	Recollections of the Conversation Parties of the Rev Charles Simeon	1863
Bury J.P.T.	Romilly's Cambridge Diary 1832-42	1967
Butler A.J.	Life & Letters of William John Butler	1898
Cambridge University Calendar for the years 1834 - 40		
Cotton Mrs ed.	Memoirs of G.E.L. Cotton	1872
Douglas S.	The Life & Selections from the Correspondence of William Whewell DD 2nd ed.	1882
Garland M.M.	Cambridge before Darwin	1980
Lubenow W.C.	The Cambridge Apostles 1820-1914	1998
Perowne J.J.S.	Letters, Literary & Theological of Connop Thirlwall	1881
Perry C.	Clerical Education considered with an especial Reference to the Universities	1841
Robson R. ed.	Ideas and Institutions of Victorian Britain Ch. 11 :Trinity College in the Age of Peel	1966
Rothblatt S.	The Revolution of the Dons	1968
Searby P.	A History of the University of Cambridge Vol. 3 1750-1870	1997
Smith J. & Stray C. ed.	Teaching and Learning in 19th Century Cambridge	2001
Smith J. & Stray C. ed.	Cambridge in the 1830s: the Letters of A.C. Gooden 1831-41	2003
Thirlwall C.	A Letter to the Rev Thomas Turton DD	1834
Trevelyan G.M.	Trinity College. An Historical Sketch	1946
Trevelyan G.M.	Trinity College. A History and Guide	1972
Whewell W.	Remarks on some Parts of Mr Thirlwall's Letter on the Admission of Dissenters to Academical Degrees	1834
Whewell W.	On the Principles of English University Education	1837
Winstanley D.A.	Unreformed Cambridge	1935
Winstanley D.A.	Early Victorian Cambridge	1940
Wright J.M.F.	Alma Mater or Seven Years at the University of Cambridge by a Trinity-man	1827

Leicester

Bridges C.	The Christian Ministry	3rd ed.	1830
Elliott M.	Victorian Leicester		2010
Munk W.	Life of Sir Henry Halford Bart		1895
Patterson A.T.	Radical Leicester 1780-1850		1954
Russell A.	The Clerical Profession		1980
Simmons J.	Life in Victorian Leicester		1971
Simmons J.	Leicester. The Ancient Borough to 1860		1974
Vaughan C.J.	Sermons		1846
White W.	History, Gazeteer & Directory of Leicestershire		1846
The Leicester Almanac & Directory			1816
A Guide to Leicester			1843

Harrow

Butler J.R.M.	Henry Montagu Butler: A Memoir	1925
Dudley R.	Harrow. Portrait of an English School	2004
Farrar R.	The Life of Frederick William Farrar	1904
Galloway Earl of	Observations on the Abused Reform of the Monitorial System in Harrow School	1854
Graham E.	The Harrow Life of H. M. Butler	1920
Grosskurth P.	John Addington Symonds	1964
Grosskurth P. ed.	Memoirs of J.A. Symonds	1984
Hare A.J.C.	The Story of my Life Vol. 1	1896
How F.D.	Six Great Schoolmasters	1904
Howson E.W. & Warner G.T. Harrow School		1898
Laborde E.D.	Harrow School: Yesterday and Today	1948
Mangan J.A. & Walvin J. eds. Manliness and Morality		1987
Merivale H.C.	Bar, Stage and Platform	1902
Minchin J.G.C.	Old Harrow Days	1898
Moore R.W.	Charles John Vaughan Centenary	1945
Morgan J.V. ed.	Welsh Political & Educational Leaders in the Victorian Era pp. 407-4281907	
Newsome D.	Godliness and Good Learning	1961
Newsome D.	On the Edge of Paradise	1980
Norman F.M.	At School and at Sea	1899
Platt B.	Correspondence between the Rev Dr C.J. Vaughan & the Hon Baron Platt	1853
Rendall E.D. & Rendall G.H. Recollections and Impressions of the Rev. John Smith		1913

Schueller H.M. & Peters R.L. eds. The Letters of John Addington
                    Symonds 1844-1868   Vol. 1   1967

Simon B. & Bradley I. eds. The Victorian Public School		1975
Thornton P.M.	Harrow School and its Surroundings	1885
Tollemache L.A.	Essays, Mock Essays & Character Sketches	1898
Tollemache L.A.	Old and Odd Memories	1908
Torre H.J.	Recollections of School Days at Harrow	1890
Tyerman C	A History of Harrow School	2000
Vachell H.A.	The Hill	1905
Vaughan C.J.	Harrow Sermons	1853
Vaughan C.J.	Letter to Lord Palmerston on the Monitorial System	1853
Vaughan C.J.	Memorials of Harrow Sundays	1863
Wagland M.	A Matter of Justice in the *Welsh Journal of Religious History* Vol. 3 pp. 40-57	2008
Welch R.C. ed.	The Harrow School Register 1801-93	1894
Westcott A.	The Life and Letters of Brooke Foss Westcott	1903
Witheridge J.	Excellent Dr Stanley	2013
Wood H. Trueman	Harrow in the Fifties in *Cornhill Magazine* Vol. 50 NS pp. 394-401	1921

Doncaster

Armstrong E.A.	An Historical Guide to Doncaster Parish Church	1926
Bales P.G.	600 Years: A History of Doncaster Grammar School	1950
Hatfield C.W.	Historical Notices of Doncaster	1868
Hatfield C.W.	Parish Church Notes	1866
Herklots H.G.G.	A Hundred Years of Doncaster Parish Church	1958
Keighley F.	The Centenary of the Church of St Andrew Marshgate 1867-1967	1967
Kelly E.V.	Doncaster Public Health, Social Welfare & Local Government 1861-71	1973
Morgan C.	The House of Macmillan (1843-1943)	1943
Phillips E. & Hanby G.	The Story of Doncaster	1921
Pigou F.	Phases of my Life	1900

Royle E + Larsen R.M. ed. Archbishop Thomson's Visitation
Returns for the Diocese of York 1865   2006
Russell G.W.E.   One Look Back   1911
Swann G.   Doncaster Royal Infirmary 1792-1972   1973
Thrall A.   History of Adult Education in 19th Century
                          Doncaster   1977
Vaughan C.J.   Epiphany, Lent & Easter   1860
Vaughan C.J.   Last Words in the Parish Church of
                          Doncaster   1869
Williams R.R.   Christianity and Sound Learning: the
                          Educational Work of C.J. Vaughan   1953
Wormald H.R.   Modern Doncaster   1974

The Temple

Bayliss T.H.   The Temple Church and the Chapel of
                         St Ann: An Historical Record and Guide 1893
Bedwell C.E.A.   The Temple Church in *Church Quarterly
                         Review* Vol. lxxiii   pp. 67-88   1912
Bell G.K.A.   Randall Davidson   3rd ed.   1952
Benson A.C.   Life of Edward White Benson   1899
Bettany F.G.   Stewart Headlam. A Biography   1926
Lewer D.   A Spiritual Song   1961
Lewer D. & Dark R.   The Temple Church in London   1997
Montgomery M.   Bishop Montgomery: A Memoir   1933
Newth S.   Lectures on Bible Revision   1881
Roxburgh R. ed.   The Black Books of Lincoln's Inn Vol. V 1968
Russell G.W.E.   Collections & Recollections   1905
Sichel E.   The Life & Letters of Alfred Ainger   1906
Vaughan C.J.   Addresses to young Clergymen   1875
Vaughan C.J.   Authorised or Revised?   1882
Vaughan C.J. ed.   Consecration of the Temple Church:
                         Sermons preached at the Celebration
                         of its 700th Anniversary   1885

Llandaff

Benson R.H.   Confessions of a Convert   1913
Compton-Davies W.R.   Historical & Pictorial Glimpses of
                         Llandaff Cathedral   1895
Coulton G.G.   Fourscore Years: an Autobiography   1944
Harman A.C.   Dean Vaughan & His Men in *Theology* Aug 1937
Hilling J.B.   Llandaf Past & Present   1978

James J.H.	A History & Survey of Llandaff Cathedral 1898
Jones B.	Canton 1995
Jones J.G.	Dean Charles Vaughan, A.J. Williams and the Dis-establishment Debate of November 1885 in the *Welsh Journal of Religious History* Vol. 8 pp. 43-61 2000
Jones K.V.	Life of John Viriamu Jones 2nd ed. 1921
Llandaff Civic Society	Llandaff 2000
Morgan D.	The Illustrated History of Cardiff's Suburbs 2003
Newell E.J.	Diocesan Histories: Llandaff 1902
Tilney C.	Dean Vaughan and the Restored Cathedral 1879-1897 in the 38th Annual Report of the Friends of Llandaff Cathedral pp 11-26 1971
Trow A.H. & Brown D.J.A.	A Short History of the University College of South Wales and Monmouthshire 1933
Tyndale-Biscoe C.E.	Tyndale-Biscoe of Kashmir 1951
Vaughan C.E.	A Sketch of Dean Vaughan in the *Magazine of the University College of South Wales* 1894
Vaughan C.J.	When I Awake: A Sermon preached in Llandaff Cathedral 3 March 1995 1895

An Assessment

Benson A.C.	The Life of Edward White Benson 2 vols. 1899
Butler H.M.	He served his Generation well 1897
Pretor. A	Ronald & I. Studies from Life 1899
Williams R.R.	A Neglected Victorian Divine in *Church Quarterly Review* No 310 Vol. CLIV 1953
Williams R.R. ed.	The Word of Life 1960

Thesis of the University of Hull

| Reeve A.J.H. | Aspects of the Life of Dr Thomas Arnold (1795-1842) in the Light of the Unpublished Correspondence. Ph.D. thesis 1988 |

Theses of the University of Sheffield

| Mowbray D.D.W. | C.J. Vaughan (1816-1897) Biblical Expositor Ph.D. Thesis No 993 1958 |
| Poole M.D.W. | The Educational Work of the Very Rev C.J. Vaughan MA Thesis No 2156 1966 |

Index

This selective index includes only the main persons named in the book

446